CW00385735

From the Vale to the Veldt

The Yorkshire market town of Easingwold and its contribution to the Boer War

By Dr. A. J. Peacock

Edited by Mr. David Crane

Contributions by Mr. Charles Whiting and Mr. Paul M. Chapman

From the Vale
to the Veldt
By Dr. A. J. Peacock

Published and Printed by

The Advertiser Office
Market Place
Easingwold
York, YO61 3AB
United Kingdom of Great Britain

Tel: 01347 821329 Fax: 01347 822576
email: info@ghsmith.com web: www.ghsmith.com

November 2006

ISBN Nº 0 904775 40 2

FOREWORD

I first heard the story of an Easingwold soldier from the Boer war walking in on his own funeral when I was a teenager in the 1950's. By then the facts had become so embroidered that the tale had developed into a local legend, especially when told by one of the town's more colourful storytellers, himself a veteran of World War One. By this time the soldier's actual name had been forgotten and the church wherein his funeral was being held was thought to have been Raskelf. It was nevertheless, a gripping yarn which was filed away in the nether reaches of my mind, not quite forgotten yet never followed up; that is until the mid 1990's when my wife suggested we go to South Africa on holiday and to Cape Town in particular.

A hundred years earlier, in the 1890's my maternal grandfather had left England for Cape Town to work in the grocery and drapery trade, this he did until the commencement of The Boer War in 1899 when he joined The Medical Corps. He subsequently became a sergeant and served in Lord Methuen's command until being taken prisoner by the Boer general Christian de Wet. At this time the Boers were in some disarray, so after being held for a few weeks he and his fellow prisoners were unceremoniously released from the Boer commando and, minus boots, left to make their own way back to British lines.

This kindled my interest in The Boer War, and on returning home, I resolved to research and attempt to discover the true extent of the contribution of Easingwold and district to this forgotten conflict and in the process perhaps shed some light on the saga of the soldier who'd attended his own funeral. Our company G H Smith & Son, being the printer of the *Easingwold Advertiser* since its inception in 1892, possessed the only local archive of the events of those far off days, and it was from its yellowing pages that the story of Mark Knowlson Brown (for that was the soldier's name) was finally revealed.

Fact was indeed vastly different from the legend as his story in Chapter 22 fully illustrates. What amazed me, however, was that Mark Brown's daughter was alive, living in Long Street, and still in her possession was the fateful telegram from The War Office informing of her father's death together with many other of his artefacts. Dora's married name is Bowman, and coincidentally her late husband's uncle, Arthur Bowman, had actually been in the 11th Company Imperial Yeomanry and involved in the action at Middlepost on 5th and 6th of February 1902 at which Mark Brown had supposedly been killed. Mark, it transpired, had been with Colonel Capper's column at Fish River District a hundred miles away. The Easingwold men in the 11th Company of the 3rd Battalion of Imperial Yeomanry with Arthur Bowman were in fact Frank Weighell and Ted Spence. In Arthur's letter on the events at Middlepost nowhere is there a mention of Mark Brown which also supports the fact of his not being there. When Mark eventually returned full of life to Easingwold, he was with George Hargreaves who was a member of the 66th Yorkshire Company of the 16th Battalion and it is more than possible that Mark belonged to this unit.

An interested and knowledgeable observer of my research efforts thus far had been Dr A J Peacock for whom G H Smith & Son were at the time printing and publishing several historical works. "Alf", radio and TV presenter, and author of numerous historical articles and books was recently retired and looking for a new focus for his formidable powers of research into social and political archives. He soon immersed himself in the quest to bring to life Easingwold at the close of the nineteenth century and to resurrect the stories of the young men who had left this small Yorkshire town to fight in a war in South Africa.

What follows therefore is his unique, detailed, and thought provoking rediscovery of this period of Easingwold's history. Here in Chapters 1 to 7 are all the momentous social and political issues, scandals, sports and festivities together with many colourful characters be they stalwart, pompous, shady or tragic who gave life to the town; a town from which the young men of Chapters 7 to 26 left to fight in The Boer War and whose letters home are vivid and often startling in their youthful reflections of courage in the face of great danger.

D. H. Smith

EASINGWOLD - AND THE BOER WAR

	Foreword	3
Chapter 1	'Thirteen from York and Helmsley'	5
Chapter 2	Football, Cricket, Gambling and other things	71
Chapter 3	The Ooperzootic (and Mashed Turnips)	93
Chapter 4	The RDC and trouble at Alne	105
Chapter 5	Sutton on the Forest, Bolshy Village	135
Chapter 6	Rachel Ann Taylor, the Guardians and conscientious objection	153
Chapter 7	The Outbreak of War	175
Chapter 8	Clash in Africa (Outline of the Boer War Battles)	199
Chapter 9	Gatacre and Boocock	219
Chapter 10	Eccles Foster, Raskelfe	231
Chapter 11	George Milnthorpe	239
Chapter 12	Charles Snaith	245
Chapter 13	Easingwold Volunteers	247
Chapter 14	The Wilkinsons	259
Chapter 15	Trooper Walter Dale, killed in action	271
Chapter 16	The Army	285
Chapter 17	Baden-Powell's Own	295
Chapter 18	Yeomen and Militia Men	299
Chapter 19	Stephen Wombwell	311
Chapter 20	Cpl Littlewood and The Posties	327
Chapter 21	The Strangwayes	329
Chapter 22	Cyril Swarbreck et al	331
Chapter 23	Trooper Mark Knowlson Brown KIA	335
Chapter 24	The Relief of Middlepost (Thomas Cook 11th Company Imperial Yeomanry)	353
Chapter 25	Ted Webster and Hilt Carr	355
Chapter 26	Hubert Baines	365
Chapter 27	Until the Bitter End. Great Britain Triumphant?	369
	Biographies	375
	Boer War Photos	377
	Acknowledgements	378

Chapter 1

'THIRTEEN FROM YORK AND HELMSLEY'

In the Market Square at Easingwold there is a memorial carrying the names of those inhabitants of the town who fell in the 1914-18 war. In the parish church they are also remembered on a beautiful stone plaque. Almost immediately opposite that, on the facing wall, three of them are separately commemorated[1] and not far away is a third memorial. It is to Trooper Walter Dale who, the text says, was killed by dynamite explosion (Boers blew up his train) in South Africa. He was one of the town's victims in the Boer War.

IN MEMORY OF
THOMAS WALTER DALE.
9TH QUEEN'S ROYAL LANCERS.
WHO WAS KILLED IN THE SERVICE OF HIS KING AND COUNTRY
BY DYNAMITE EXPLOSION AT VREDEFORT ROAD.
SOUTH AFRICA.
28TH JUNE 1901. AGED 25 YEARS.
THIS TABLET IS ERECTED BY SOLDIERS' FRIENDS OF THIS DISTRICT
AS A RECOGNITION OF HIS PATRIOTISM.

Memorial Plaque to Thomas Walter Dale.
Easingwold Parish Church. The cause of death is somewhat misleading as he was killed in a Boer attack on his train.

Trooper Dale was a regular soldier, killed in 1901 and his story will appear later in this narrative. He was the son of James Dale, the relieving officer of Easingwold, an important local official involved in the administration of the poor law. What was the town[2] he served like? It had seen dramatic changes in the 19th century as a result of the building of the railway - and as a study of Yorkshire made clear before mid century. 'EASINGWOLD' it said[3]

> is a market town and township, in the parish of its name, and Wapentake of Bulmer, 10 miles from Thirsk, 11 from Boroughbridge, 13 from York and Helmsley ... lying on the high road from London and York to Edinburgh. From being thus situated, the inhabitants derived some benefit, and two good inns were supported thereby, of which they have been almost entirely deprived, by the contiguity of a great railway. The trade is *now but inconsiderable*, except in the articles of bacon and butter, of which large quantities are sent from hence to York, and much reaches the London market. ... George Wombwell Esq., of Newborough Park ... is Lord of the manor ... The Country in this part is fertile, and agriculture prevails ... The scenery in the neighbourhood is of a pleasing character particularly that surveyed from the eminence on which the church is seated, which commands an extensive view of the ancient forest of Galtres and the vale of Mowbray.

Easingwold was once an important coaching centre, then was affected by the march of progress, and the quaint phrase 'now but inconsiderable' indicates that it had been severely hit by the railway. Isaac Slater, in 1875, used the same ugly language, in his huge directory.[4]

> EASINGWOLD is a market town and parish, and head of a poor law union ... 208 miles from London, and 13 N. by W. from York, lying on the high road from London and York to Edinburgh; the North Eastern Railway Company has a station about half a mile from Alne, and three and a half miles from Easingwold. The town which is well built is situated in a good grazing district famous also for breeding horses; it is likewise a good corn country; and there are many flour mills in the vicinity of the town. The trade of the place is very inconsiderable, depending almost entirely on the market. ... The parish, with RASKELF chapelry, contained in 1861 2,274 inhabitants; in 1871 2,666 of which last number 2,153 were returned for the township of Easingwold, and 513 for Raskelf.[5]

In the next quarter of a century Easingwold's railway 'network' was completed when a three and a half mile line came into being. This was the Easingwold Railway Company. It was described in a tongue-in-cheek article which appeared in *The Newcastle Chronicle* early in 1899.[6] *The Chronicle's* correspondent was clearly not very impressed with what he saw of Easingwold on his first fleeting visit. Later that year the "E.R.'s" half yearly meeting was held[7] 'in the Easingwold Town Hall, Mr F. J. H. Robinson, in the absence of Sir [sic] George Orby Wombwell, Bart, chairman of the Company presided. There was a better attendance than usual' and those who did attend heard that in the half year ending 31 December 'a profit of £392 7s 1d had been made, making the balance in hand as per net revenue account £1,128 2s 4d.' The directors recommended that there should be no dividend paid for the half year 'the sum of £1,000' being paid off 'the mortgage debt of £4,000'. During the relevant six months there had been '22,579 passengers over the line, realising £362 2s 9d.' In its advertising columns the paper, announced that it would run excursions cooperating with the North Eastern. More of this later, but on 1 April 1899 there was an ad in the *Advertiser* that was typical.

Easingwold Station, early 1900s

NORTH EASTERN RAILWAY

Excursion trains will run as under:-
MONDAY, APRIL 3rd from ALNE at
8-12 a.m., to NEWCASTLE, returns from Newcastle
at 7.35 P.M.,
and from RASKELF at 3-9 p.m., ALNE at 3-16,
to YORK,
returns from York at 10-45 p.m.

THURSDAY, APRIL 6th, from RASKELF at 1-16,
ALNE at 1-22 p.m., to YORK, returns from York
at 9-30 p.m.
See bills for further particulars.
GEO. S. GIBB, General Manager.
York, March 1899

The next half yearly of the Easingwold Railway Company (the 16th) was held in October, once more in the Town Hall, and once more with F.J.H. Robinson presiding.[8] This time he had better news for shareholders and [so] it was resolved to appropriate £170 1s 8d in paying the shareholders a dividend at the rate of three per cent per annum[9]. At the next half yearly it was reported that: a dividend of three per cent would be paid; the balance in the revenue account had been £234 4 10; the number of passengers 21,563; income from season tickets £349 5 11; while the total dividend would 'absorb £170 1s, the balance being carried forward.' Not long after this two notes appeared in the press about the Easingwold, one of which clearly angered a section of the community.[10] The alteration of the 8-10 p.m. train from Easingwold to 7-55 p.m. had 'greatly interfered with Postal facilities' wrote an irate local journalist 'and is not a very welcome change ...' But there was good news as well - something of a face lift for the ER's solitary engine.

> The Easingwold Engine has just returned from the North Eastern Railway shops, after undergoing thorough repairs. The engine has been repainted after the style of the North Eastern engines which certainly is a great improvement.

The newly painted, impressive Easingwold engine could, in July, have been under threat. An incident of profound importance occurred, was reported at some length, and deserves rescuing (as does the star of the story).[11]

> A VENTURESOME BEAST - On Wednesday afternoon a curious spectacle was seen at Easingwold Station. A fat beast, weighing probably up to 60 stone, the property of Mr W Foster, was depasturing in a field near the railway, but being evidently in an inquisitive frame of mind, it launched out on a voyage of discovery towards the station. What would have happened if the train had been running can only be conjectured, but it certainly would have been "bad for the coo." As it was, however, the beast strolled up to the top of the coal shoots. The first shoot it came to was open, and down went the animal to the bottom, where the aperture only allowed the beast's hind legs to protrude through. Then there was such a bellowing and scrambling as could be heard a mile off. A crowd soon gathered together, though all there was to be seen were two legs dangling in the air. Plenty of willing helpers, under the superintendence of Mr Pettinger, soon extricated the animal from its unenviable position, none the worse for its escapade.

EASINGWOLD No 2.

Easingwold Railway 1905 – second from left Jack Morse

Bulmers Directory of 1890 [12], compiled while the E R was in the planning stage is quite flattering on Easingwold.

"Easingwold has a population of 2,044. Its rateable value is £12,185. The soil is fertile and well cultivated, and the scenery of a lovely pastoral character, diversified with patches of sylvan beauty. ... Though much modernised in recent years, there is just a spice of antiquity left in the timber and plaster houses [of Easingwold], with their quaint gables that remain - a relic of the 16th century."

What was life like then, for the inhabitants of Easingwold at the time of the Boer War? What had it to offer young men of the time? High wages? Hardly. Certainly not those who lived in the surrounding areas.

The economy of Easingwold was an agricultural one, and a large proportion of the populace was employed in that industry. The hirings when, after a break from their earlier service, workers met prospective employers and argued over wages, were highlights of the year. Details of what went on were always reported at length. The hiring in Thirsk of 1899, for example, was the subject of a report which said much about the industry and its difficulties at the time.[13] 'On Monday last the principal hiring statutes were held in the market-place' it was recorded

> and there was a very large attendance, more especially of male farm servants, but as usual there was a dearth of female house hands, most of the girls preferring town situations. Although wages for male servants had an upward tendency, ... Good managing hands and those for all-round general work made from £22 10s to £24 for the twelve months. First hand for ploughing purposes obtained from £18 to £20, second ploughmen from £16 to £17, and farm boys from £12 to £14, or £1 for every year of their age. First female house hands readily obtained up to £18, second girls from £14 10s to £16 ... housemaids from £12 10s to £14, [and] general servants from £11 10s to £12 10s ... owing to females preferring town places they were bad to engage, and were readily picked up, more especially for general work.

The hirings are generally reckoned to have been for agricultural workers, and so they were, though it is clear that, at Thirsk,[14] domestic workers were also recruited. In Easingwold the toll proprietors called the hirings.

EASINGWOLD MARTINMAS HIRING will be held
on FRIDAY, NOVR. 24th,1899
By order of the TOLL PROPRIETORS.

The report of the hiring in the local paper was tiny compared with that quoted from Thirsk.[15]

> THE Martinmas hirings were held at Easingwold 'on Friday last. There was a moderate attendance of farmers and servants and little business was done'.

As always, the day was turned into a fair day and this year 'There was a larger attendance of amusements than usual, and the day being fair, they were well patronised.' The hirings were frequently the occasions for drunkenness and violence.

Work in the country was badly paid (the practice of 'living in' prevailed in the North Riding), and frequently lonely, boring and hard, and it is not to be wondered at that workers were anxious to get off the land. Lord Walsingham recognised the foregoing. 'No doubt the labourers would recognise that wages ... in the healthy country are worth more than half as much again in a town slum, but the country is dull, whereas the town is lively, and so the labourer is forsaking the rural district, leaving behind the aged and infirm to be supported by the rates.'[16] A couple of months earlier J. Fairbank of Appleton-le-Street read a paper on 'Economy in Labour' to the Malton Agricultural Club in which he made some of the same points.[17] He seems to have been an incredibly enlightened man. 'He advocated labour saving machinery to relieve the labourers of drudgery, comfortable cottages and gardens, and kindness to the work people. ... '

There was an acute shortage of labour on the land during the years of the Boer War and outside labour was frequently resorted to. The Irish appeared at harvest time, but despite an acute shortage of labour[18] found the farmers unwilling to give much away. At Thirsk harvest hirings were held in the Market Place on 29 July 1901. The harvest had begun and 'There was a large attendance of Irish harvest labourers, more than for some years.' This undoubtedly strengthened the farmers' position and they 'did not' want to 'give the rate of wages asked.' They rarely did, but what they did agree to 'ranged from £4 5s to £4 10s for the harvest month, with milk and potatoes found. Bargains were almost entirely confined to Irish labour, as the majority of English harvest workmen as, with 'but few exceptions, permanently engaged all the year round on the farms where they obtain their harvesting.'[19]

What is always commented on, is the farmers' alleged meanness. Undoubtedly there were generous employers, but the reputation most got was that they were skinflints, bullies who exploited their workers with long hours, low pay, and ghastly food.[20] Writers sympathetic to the labourers wrote books in the inter-war years about what they called 'the tyranny of the countryside.'[21] That description was for many appropriate, with the law backing it up, and frequent prosecutions of labourers might well have had an element of 'teaching the workers a lesson' about them. There was one law for them, one for us Hodge would have thought.[22] Justice was weighted heavily in the farmers' favour it appeared.

For example, at the East Riding sessions held at York Castle, on a Saturday in January 1901, Archer Ripley, a farm servant of Stillington was prosecuted by his employer (R. J. Carr) for breach of contract. Archer had been engaged on 24 November and absconded, on 22 December. The farmer wanted damages of £3 (his ploughing, he said, had been held up) and got them and his erstwhile servant was ordered to pay the court's costs and return to work. But Ripley was a man of spirit and said he should not return, as he had offers of work at five or six other places. He was [then] told that if 'he did not [sic] return to the farm he would be given work - on the treadmill- at another place.' How Archer could have been expected by the court to pay these fines is beyond comprehension - though in reality it probably did not expect that he would or could. The treadmill was the reality. Several similar cases were reported at some length in the local paper, leading, no doubt, to much comment in the local pubs. Whether they were an incentive to the hinds to serve out what could have been an awful year is doubtful.

Only rarely as in the case of Alfred Draper, who sued his employer Francis Dole a Sessay farmer, did the plaintiff win.

To return for a moment to those cases which it has been suggested did not really look to be fair and could not have helped relationships in the countryside. At the Thirsk petty sessions

R. Smithson's noted pork shop, 1890s. Porky Smithson was famous for his pork pies which were the best in the district.
(2005 Thornton's Butchers)

held on 23 September two boozers appeared before their worships charged with being drunk and disorderly, one was Henry Hart, a shoemaker, who got away with costs and the other was John Terrence 'alias Tosh'. Tosh had been in the cooler, from where he was put up, and if this is the case he had had 48 hours to sit, get over a hangover, contemplate, and enjoy prison fare. He was fined ten shillings by a bench presided over by a Major Bell and ordered to pay costs.[23] Tosh's case, and that of Hart, was reported in the Easingwold press in two column inches. Presumably these two (both nicked by PC Welford) pleaded guilty, unlike the star of a case which took up something like 32 inches, and appeared under the heading 'CHARGE AGAINST AN EASINGWOLD FARMER. A PECULIAR CASE.' It was right next to the inevitable advert for Doan's Backache Kidney Pills ('Don't Neglect Your Kidneys They are the Most Important Organs of the Body'), and one for Charles Forde's Bile Beans for Biliousness.[24] Famous pills those.

There was 'a crowded attendance' of the public at the Easingwold Town Hall when J. Swainston Strangewayes sat with seven other magistrates to decide the case against William Barley, 'a well-known farmer of Low Hawkhills, Easingwold.' It was alleged that he had been drunk on the highway at Alne on 24 August whilst in charge of two horses.[25] There was a cross-summons by the defendant against PC Henry Sayer for assault. The two summonses were taken together and Charles Mellor appeared for the defence, while 'Mr Wilkinson (York) appeared to prosecute for the police.' This, in all probability, was the Quaker K.E.T. Wilkinson, a very prominent York politician.

Wilkinson told the court that 'The facts [of the case] were very simple, and the evidence ... extremely strong.' So it was. 'Briefly, the facts were these: About half-past five Police Constable Henry Sayer was on duty in Carr's Lane, which leads from ... Alne into the York Road, when he saw defendant in charge of two horses - riding one and leading the other, ... the constable saw plainly from the manner in which he was riding that he was certainly drunk and not fit to have charge of the horses. He was very far from steady in his seat, and was leaning forward with his head on the horse's neck, holding the mane to keep himself from falling.' PC Sayer stopped him, 'as it was his duty to do so', and told Barley to get down. He refused and at this stage Capt D'Arcy Strangewayes came up on his bike. The constable again asked Barley to get down 'as he was drunk, and advised him to put the horses up at the Alne Railway Hotel and get off home in a trap.' The farmer did get down and said 'he was perfectly sober and could walk alright. Defendant then attempted to walk four or five paces up the road, but staggered about, and said "I can't find the middle of the road."' Strangewayes then took the horses to the hotel stables, and Barley was taken into custody, but 'behaved so violently, the constable had to engage a trap to take him to Easingwold - he would have had difficulty in getting him home by train.'

Numerous witnesses testified that Barley was drunk, including the constable and Capt Strangewayes. Inspector Pickering was on duty and Barley said to him '"Your man says I am drunk what do you say?" Witness replied "You are certainly drunk"' and said he would keep the farmer there until he was sober. 'Defendant then said, "I must have some witnesses then," and ... sent for Dr Buller Hicks, a well-known Easingwold personality. The Doc attended the station 'and asked what was the matter, [and the] defendant replied, "I've broke my nose" which he hadn't.'

Barley, a prominent local councillor, was said by his counsel to have ridden 20 miles (from Starbeck) and was sitting in an extraordinary position because he was saddle sore and the horses were restive. Buller Hicks said that at 7.30 Barley was 'perfectly sober'. Others agreed and Barley gave evidence himself, and said the PC had tripped him up. What happened?

Easingwold - Horse and buggy early 1900s

'The Bench dismissed the case. The cross-summons was also dismissed. The verdict of the Magistrates was received with great applause.'

There can be little doubt but that those of a cynical turn of mind thought that the farmer was very lucky and had been fortunate to be tried by his mates. Their belief, unfair though it might have been, would not have been damaged by another case heard at Thirsk just over three months later, and involving the same William Barley charged with being drunk in charge of a horse in Thirsk Market Place.[26] This time he was defended by Arthur Wood of York.

Dr. Langford of Thirsk deposed that when he examined the accused in his cell he *was* drunk. Wood called the defendant along with Dr Hicks and a number of others including F.J.H. Robinson, the Easingwold solicitor who was prominent (like Hicks) in just about everything that went on in Easingwold. But this time there was medical evidence to say that Barley had indeed been drunk. He was sure to be convicted - or was he? *Without retiring to consider the verdict the Bench dismissed the case* (my italics).

The conduct of the Barley[27] cases would have been taken as yet more evidence (if it were needed) of the 'tyranny of the countryside'. The labourers were naked before the law - shut out from the courts except as defendants. There were a few things they could do to settle scores, but they *were* a few. They could steal, they could slack on occasions - and they could resort to direct action. Arson was common in the English countryside and was not absent in the Easingwold district. This was by no means as bad an area as some, but Hodge resorted to the torch as he did elsewhere. He did so in the summer of 1899, for example, at Thormanby.

At about 10.30 on Sunday 30 July 'an alarm of fire was raised at Thormanby, when it was seen that a large pike of hay belonging to Mr W.F.T. Plummer, of Birdforth, was on fire in a field near the bottom end of the village.'[28] Whilst it was being attended to flames were seen rising from a stackyard belonging to Mrs Knowlson of the Hall. The Easingwold Fire Brigade was sent for, but, because of the shortage of water it was some time before the fire was subdued.' The damage was 'about £50 or £60 ... The general opinion' is, a report said, 'that the stacks were set on fire wilfully.' The next week the Easingwold Fire Brigade was summoned by telegraph to a stack fire of about 30 tons of clover at Sutton on Forest[29] and an arrest was made for incidents at Thormanby. This was a troubled village and on Friday 18 August 1899 at the Town Hall, Easingwold, James Bye was brought up from custody charged with that offence of setting fire to Plummer's hay pike and Knowlson's wheat stack.[30] Bye, who was a servant to J. T. Robinson of Thormanby Hill, a farmer, was investigated and arrested by PC Timms of Thirkleby. Bye denied setting fire to 'the property mentioned', but said he was going from Carlton Husthwaite to Thormanby and 'lighted his pipe near the hay when the match fell down and lighted the hay'. He had been out boozing, of course, and after his accident with the hay pike went and laid down against the wheat stack and did something like an encore. The 'fire fell out of his pipe', he said, 'and set fire to the stack.' A likely story, but he got off. 'The Bench dismissed the case for want of sufficient evidence.'

Arson was ever present in the countryside, and had been for many years[31] and it may well have provided something of a check on the behaviour. It is hoped so, though farmers were now insuring their stacks and making the fact known in the reports of trouble. The spate of arson in 1899 prompted some movement in Easingwold; it was much needed.

John C. Bannister of the Market Place was secretary of the Easingwold Public Hall Company Ltd and appears in the trade directories[32] under 'Grocers, Tea and Provision Dealers' and 'Wine and Spirit Merchants'. Bannister was also captain of the Easingwold Volunteer Fire Brigade and it was in that capacity that he wrote to the press at the turn of the century. There was a need for the brigade to be modernised, he wrote in a letter headed 'THE RECENT FIRES'.[33]

> The recent fires that have taken place in this district should, I think arouse in the mind of each rate payer the advisability of providing a steam fire engine for the Easingwold Brigade. ... The small dog-cart engine we at present have is very good as far as it goes, but all who have attended the fires will bear me out that our power is a small one. There is invariably a dearth of pumpers and we cannot go to a sufficient distance for water. ... Easingwold is now in wire communication with the majority of villages within a radius of six or seven miles [so] it is quite natural that all these places will send for the nearest engine, and were all to combine in the cost the outlay to each individual would be very small indeed.

Speed in getting to an incident was of paramount importance and the Easingwold brigade had a good record in this respect already, he wrote. There had recently been a fire in Long Street and there the engine arrived at the scene 'in less than five minutes after the firing of the maroon' and it had got to Thormanby within half an hour of receiving the alarm. It got to Sutton half an hour before that from York. Nevertheless, a new, better appliance was needed, Bannister concluded his letter by saying that he had ascertained from 'the Parish Fire Engine Act 1898, that it is within the jurisdiction of the Parish Council to provide a Fire Engine.' Not only was a new light appliance needed, but it should be one which could carry more hose.

Bannister went on to say he was extremely proud of his men, they included: Deputy-Captain W. Foster; Engineer T.D. Cariss; F.E. Rookledge, secretary; and 'Firemen Dr Buller Hicks, J. Watmough, G. T. Sturdy, M. Reynard, G. Crosby, J. W. Sturdy, and Inspector Pickering.' Many of these were well-known Easingwold figures: Edward Buller Hicks, who has been mentioned before, was extremely familiar - a medical practitioner, secretary, and some said saviour of the Easingwold railway, a singer, occasional actor and enthusiastic cricketer; Rookledge was a Methodist, the secretary of the Wesleyan Institute and a chemist; Mark Reynard was the waggish cycle agent whose ads were a regular feature of the *Advertiser's* columns; Thomas Cariss was a plumber of Market Place, a member of a well-known Easingwold family; and Sturdy was[34]

G. T. STURDY
Gardener, Florist, Nurseryman,
and Seedsman,
SPRING STREET & CLAYPENNY HILL,
EASINGWOLD

Capt Bannister had other interests, and his wife was also in business as a grocer. John C.had a notice in the *Easingwold* on 30 January 1897 which detailed one of his businesses. *Bulmers* has an entry under Grocers, Tea and Provision Dealers which reads 'Bannister Mrs Annie, (and wholesale) (& cattle cake &c), Market Place' and another as a Wine and Spirit Merchant. (Just below her was G. H. Smith of the same profession - and much else.) Annie's husband, the captain, had an advertisement in the paper of 30 January 1897 which gave details of yet another of his interests.

Adler 1910. Frank Robinson, Galtres, Easingwold

JOHN C. BANNISTER,
YORKSHIRE STEAM FORAGE WORKS,
now prepared to do
GRINDING, ROLLING & CHOPPING,
on reasonable Terms
See the NEW CROP DRESSER, every particle of
dust taken out.

Old properties meant many fire hazards and it must have appeared that calls from the villages were likely to increase.[35] He had been re-elected as captain in January at the annual general meeting, when it was announced that there was something in excess of £11 in the funds.

Kelly's Directory of the North and East Ridings published in 1901 said the brigade then consisted of ten firemen and two officers. The brigade's engine was a horse-drawn Merryweather, manually operated, and worked by long handles pulled up and down 'by men on each side.' It was kept in the Town Hall until 1905 when it was transferred to a special building at the Victoria Institute. Nothing was done to implement Bannister's request for modernisation, so during the early years of the new century the old Merryweather went out as before. In March 1901 there was a serious stack fire at Haddock's Farm, Aldwark, which it was thought was the result of incendiarism.[36] Bannister and his men succeeded in saving the greater portion of the oat stack which was going up.

Things were improved when the telegraph made its appearance, though it had initial teething problems. In February 1900 there was a dreadful spell of bad weather and the press described the chaos that ensued. The report gives a good flavour of that chaos and shows how vulnerable the new communication system could be.[37]

> THE weather during the most part of the week has been very cold. More snow fell during Thursday, and a violent wind got up. The snow drifted so high in many places that it was impossible to travel either one way or another. The mails from Brandsby and Crayke could not be got through and had to be detained while this morning. The Kilburn postman could get no further on his inward journey than Oulston, so he turned back for Coxwold Station and arrived at Easingwold about 10 p.m. The telegraph wires were broken in all directions and communication with all parts of the country interrupted. It was the worst weather that had been experienced for many years.

Despite this, something like the Dunkirk spirit prevailed. For example, a 'Telegraphic communication was not restored at Easingwold until Wednesday last [21 February]. The linemen were busily engaged repairing on Sunday, but the damage done during the recent storm was so extensive that it has taken some rectifying.'[38]

The dreadful weather of February 1900 coincided with an influenza outbeak, and it was incidentally responsible for the poor attendance at the Fire Brigade's annual dinner.[39] Easingwold then was not a very healthy place and infectious diseases were common. Somewhat earlier there had been a serious outbreak of diphtheria, for example[40] and typhoid was frequently reported. In August 1901, for example, Richard Coverdale, aged 41 died of that scourge in St Monica's Hospital.[41] Later that year there was a serious outbreak of scarlet fever.[42] A month later a report from the chairman of the Easingwold Rural District Council's

Sanitary Committee revealed that in the RDC's area there had been '27 cases of scarlet fever and 7 of enteric fever since the 1st October last.' At the meeting at which that was made public it was also recorded that scarlet fever had appeared at Stearsby and Brandsby while Tholthorpe was said to have been a little better than had been reported.[43]

It comes as no surprise to discover that Easingwold was prone to outbreaks of dangerous infectious diseases - most sizeable Victorian towns were - and the reports from the RDC about the state of water supplies in the area and the sewerage 'systems' in existence reinforce the impression that it was indeed a very unhealthy place. Early in 1901 for example, the council heard of the state of cess pools at Crayke. (There was 'no nuisance at Crayke' Cllr Gilleard said - and he should have known as it was his cesspool that was under discussion.)[44] As well as telling councillors about Crayke William Snowdon, the Sanitary Inspector, also reported on six notified cases of infectious diseases there and said that the water reservoir was urgently 'in need of being thoroughly cleaned out.'[45] Snowdon, incidentally, had been in council service for 18 years, and after telling members of the state of Crayke he asked for a rise. He then got '£50 [as] Sanitary Inspector, £12 [as] Collector of Water Rents and £2 [as] Inspector of Waterworks, the latter two items being paid by the parish of Easingwold.' Snowdon asked in vain, and the RDC moved on to reappoint Buller Hicks as Medical Officer of Health.

Hicks was also Medical Officer of Health to the Easingwold Board of Guardians and early in 1902 he submitted a report on infectious diseases which was very similar to those given to the RDC.[46] Since 16 January, he said, schools had had to be closed

> there had been no less than 22 cases of Scarlet Fever in the following places:- Easingwold 9, Brandsby 5, Crayke 3, Alne 2, there being also out-breaks at Sutton-on-Forest and Stearsby ... Councillor Cholmeley said ... an isolation hospital ought to be provided.
>
> Dr. Hicks stated that so far the [current] cases had been in a mild form, but if it [scarlet fever] did come, as no doubt it would some time, in a severer form it would be [very] different. [He agreed with Cholmeley] An outlay of four or five hundred pounds, spread over the Union, would not mean so much as the loss from a serious outbreak.

Buller Hicks had already raised the question of infectious diseases many times (it was one of his jobs). For example at a guardians' meeting in November 1899.

> The above official (Dr. Hicks) reported the notified cases of infectious diseases as follows - Dyphtheria at Raskelfe and Easingwold, and Enteric Fever at Huby. In connection with the latter he had made an inspection of the premises and ... the water supply. He stated that the analysis of the water showed ... it would be slow poison for pigs ... . The owners of the property were ordered to be written to.

Just a month after Dr Buller had berated Huby for its foul drinking water he had a similar account to give about disease in the local area. It was reported in an issue of the local paper of 1899. He was speaking to the RDC.[47]

> Outbreaks of infectious diseases during the past month [were] as follows [he said]:- diphtheria - 3 at Easingwold, 3 at Huby, and 2 at Brandsby and Raskelfe; enteric fever - Easingwold 2 cases; scarlatina and erysipelas at Brafferton.

Hambleton View, Easingwold early 1900s

> Dr Hicks stated the schools had been notified and all possible precautions taken. In connection with the last reported case of enteric fever he had analysed the drinking water of the household [affected], and since then the water supply on the premises of the milk-seller, the only source of the latter being an open well. ... an open well was not a proper supply. The water in one might be fairly good one day, and bad the next, through contamination, or even a defunct cat or dog being introduced.

Statistics about the health of the Easingwold area are liberally spread throughout the columns of the local paper, but one of the most comprehensive health reports ever appeared on 19 February 1898. A flu outbreak was then affecting Easingwold itself ('INFLUENZA has again visited this neighbourhood'), but the report ranged far wider than that, as the following extracts indicate.

> From the annual report of the Medical Officer of Health for the Easingwold Rural Sanitary District, we learn that the birth-rate per 1,000 for the whole district was 22.9, while the death-rate was 15.2 Rate of infant mortality, 120.3, the zymotic death rate, 1.2 ... In the Easingwold Sub-Division, there is also a low birth-rate, a higher death-rate, a still higher rate of infant mortality, and also a moderate zymotic death-rate. In Easingwold itself, the birth-rate is quite up to the average, the death rate high (18.1), the rate of infant mortality moderate, whilst the zymotic death-rate is higher than that of any other locality. In the Easingwold Division the rate of infant mortality was swelled by the death of children prematurely born, who survived for a short time only, or who lived a little longer, being destitute of vitality from birth.
>
> With regard to the zymotic death-rate, we have had in Easingwold itself and the immediate district an outbreak of diphtheria, on which I made a special report early in the year of 1897, and for which the Church and Wesleyan Schools were closed for the purpose of having some insanitary defects remedied and the Schools disinfected, one of the Schools at all events being regarded as a focus of infection ... The record

of sickness is as follows:- In the whole division, notifications of scarlatina, 18; of diphtheria, 23; of enteric fever, 4; of erysipelas, 12; and it is only necessary to give the figures for the Easingwold Division to show where infectious disease for the most part prevailed. These are - Scarlatina, 17; diphtheria, 20; enteric fever, 4; erysipelas, 9. In Easingwold, a large number of cases of diphtheria were notified, there being two deaths from the same.

Just before Christmas 1898 Hicks had 'to report an epidemic of Typhoid at Raskelfe'. What had caused the trouble? Hicks, had no doubts. He had analysed the water and found it was 'very bad', and notices telling people to boil it had been posted. Anyway a writer to the press took up the issue of Raskelfe. The only remedy was drastic. '"Tinkering" won't cure the nuisance, neither will "talking;" and "tackling" it by re-laying the sewers properly, regardless of cost, is the only [sensible] plan ... human life is the highest consideration ... it is pitiful to think' about what has already occurred 'and is likely to happen in the future, if dirastic [sic] steps are not taken, and at once.' The outbreak 'of typhoid fever [had already] sent some to their graves'. One of the victims was Francis Blackburn whose burial at Raskelfe was recorded in the *Advertiser* of 11 June 1898. He had been 51 years of age and left a widow and seven children.

There were also accounts of other problems in the countryside. There were many serious incidents of sheep worrying (by wild dogs), for example, and a great deal of animal disease. In one issue of the local paper sheep scab was reported at Shipton as well as a 'SERIOUS OUTBREAK OF SWINE FEVER AT EASINGWOLD' itself.[48] During the last week, it was noted, the most serious outbreak 'of Swine Fever which has occurred for some time took place on the premises of Mr James Cowling of the "Pig and Whistle" Inn, White Houses'. On the same page it was noted that anthrax had appeared at Brandsby. It also occurred at Welburn, and many other places. There were other diseases, and stringent regulations were aimed at containing the outbreaks. Sometimes, however, they were recklessly ignored and those responsible prosecuted.

The *Advertisers* of 1898 to 1901 give details of prosecutions against farmers for flaunting the laws regarding sheep scab, swine fever and even anthrax with the resulting fines and corrective actions taken by the Veterinary Inspector. The fines levied on farmers who ignored the regulations relating to diseased animals were not of a level to act as a deterrent to people considering an attempted cover up, but fears of one's herd being infected must have been awesome. At any time, it must have seemed, an epidemic could start, with dreadful consequences.

What the epidemics at the turn of the century could mean to the farming industry might be gauged from reports about the necessary slaughtering. None in the period covered in these notes was anywhere like as serious as those of the 1990s, but the industry was also under threat from other things.

In May 1901, for example, when there was that serious outbreak of scarlet fever which led to schools being closed and at least five deaths (*Advertiser* 1 June) the insect, phyllotreta memorum was swarming all over the northern counties 'in consequence of the recent drought' and causing immense damage.

To discuss matters of common concern agricultural clubs were formed all over the country and there was one in Easingwold. John C. Bannister, was secretary and Buller Hicks joined it in January 1899. It had been set up in 1860[49] and at the end of 1899 it had 73 members. Among them were all the prominent agriculturalists of the area (it seems) and present at the annual dinner of 1899 were H.C. Fairfax Cholmeley, S. Wombwell, H. Hawking, J. Rocliffe and many others. Many of them were Justices of the Peace and the guest speaker (for the third time) was 'The Rev W. B. Lowther (Wesleyan Minister).' He spoke of the goodwill which existed in Easingwold between the various religious bodies and selected what he thought was the most significant event in the town's history in the past year. 'During the past year,' he said, 'there had been one event happened in Easingwold of exceptional interest, he referred to the opening of the Victoria Institute ... in celebration of the Queen's Diamond Jubillee [sic], and ... One thing [that] pleased him [about it]' ... was that the young used it - attending to 'read and have social intercourse, and harmless recreation' there. On the actual subject of agriculture, H. Hawking, wanted more state assistance for his industry and said he favoured the new scheme for old age pensions. W. Lyal complained that the piece of 'Beef was low' and so was that of mutton and wool 'while wheat had fluctuated during the year'. He was not 'sanguine about the future'. People in the towns were fully employed, which made getting agricultural labour difficult. He advised farmers to get all the scientific knowledge they could and Cholmeley agreed, and urged 'Lectures by good men on such topics as microbes, &c'. He thought it would be well worth while for the club to start a fund 'for the purpose of organising hedge-cutting and ploughing competitions.' He also spoke, sympathetically, about old age pensions.

An Easingwold Ploughing and Hedge Cutting Association came into existence and at the end of October 1900 it announced a competition 'for the BEST PLOUGHMAN; Any Plough' with three prizes of £3.3.0, £1.11.6 and 15s.[50] A later advertisement said entries for the competition were 'LIMITED TO SIX MILES RADIUS' and F.J.H. Robinson's name was given as the Association's President.[51] (He was also clerk to the Easingwold RDC.) The first competition was held 'on land in the occupation of Mr W Barley, Low Hawkhills' in appalling weather with 'A thick fog which made it impossible to see from one end of the furrow to the other.' Things improved, however, and the competition got under way in the presence of many of the local great and good, J. Grant Lawson, for example.[52] J. J. Penty however, one of the judges, gave a rather critical assessment of some of the work he had

Easingwold Town Band at Easingwold Show - September 18th, 1907

looked at. Excessive dressing of some of the stacks did not meet with his approval, and 'As to ploughing they had good specimens' but there 'was some [sic] with many faults.' Some of the men 'did not set the ridge as carefully as they might have done, and finished badly, going too deep the last time round, and they [sic] having to go too deep again to make it look decent.'[53]

The Easingwold Ploughing Association was not alone in promoting improvement by example. There were others providing lectures, sponsoring annual shows and so on[54] and providing a platform from which political protests and demands could be made. The difficulties of obtaining labour were frequently mentioned and the Ploughing Association rewarded farm servants for staying put, but the 'drift from the land' that was such a feature of British history in these years, continued. The move from the countryside to Easingwold, however, was not very great, and the farmers did not react to labour shortages by putting up wages, as has been seen. Easingwold had little to offer in reality and when he moved Hodge usually went north. Penty, spoke to a toast to 'the Town and Trade of Easingwold in October 1901, and maintained that Easingwold, in fact, was the place to be in . It was a rather painful effort in promoting the town as one of the healthiest places in Yorkshire.[55]

Penty's observations about the health of his town[56] were incredible, and the fact is that Easingwold really had little to entice people there with work opportunities. The chances of employment in retail could not have been great and the much-needed building work that was often spoken of was simply not happening. So what was there for people to work at who found themselves in the town at the turn of the century? Domestic service, of course, was of prime importance, and the directories of the period, once again, provide a useful and accurate summary of the place. They show that Easingwold was dominated by agriculture and had few organisations that would have employed relatively large numbers of workers. The Easingwold Railway Company, had just that one engine and only a very small staff.

The Easingwold Gaslight and Coke Company Ltd., must also have provided work for a large number (by Easingwold's standards). The town had been lit by gas since the mid century and in the early part of 1900 consumers were promised a price reduction. The manager was Mr. Sturdy and his working model of a gasworks was noted by *The Gas World* which requested that he send it to the 'Junior Engineers Conversatzione, London, on the 10th of March.'[57] But what of those reductions? Local people were buying gas cookers and fires in large numbers and sales of gas, of course, had gone up, so they were reducing charges.

Sturdy had arrived in Easingwold in 1891[58] and had developed the rather antiquated company until meters were introduced in 1898 and more price reductions were contemplated. These were held back because of the high price of coal, so 'the company contented themselves [sic] with not raising the price' as undertakings in a large number of other towns had been forced to do. A new meter and meter house had been constructed in the last decade at a cost of about £1,400.' Incandescent burners 'which temporarily arrested the usual rise in consumption' but which provided 'an excellent light' were also introduced in the decade,[59] and meters were installed free of charge. At 'the end of the year' the total was '70 cookers, 30 gas fires, and 5 gas engines, or one cooker to every three consumers.' Easingwold had every reason to be proud of the Gas and Coke Company. It had been responsible for important improvements, in addition it had lately fitted the whole of the street lamps with the Incandescent Burner, a boon greatly appreciated by the people of the town.

Expectations were fulfilled as was seen when F.E. Rookledge, the secretary, presented his report to the 44th annual general meeting of the Gas Light Company in February 1902.[60] The sale of gas had gone up again (by 'nearly $12^{1}/_{2}$') he reported, and £220.6.6d was available for distribution.

F. E. Rookledge

The Gas Company's reports were optimistic (and the work it did was impressive) but there was still plenty of evidence that Easingwold was stagnating. Some has been mentioned. A letter from the very energetic Francis Eyre Rookledge will make the same point.[61] Rookledge, an enthusiastic Wesleyan, took part in a debate that was reported in the same paper that printed his letter on the subject of 'The Nationalisation of the Drink Traffic.' He was clearly in demand as a speaker and was the holder of the post of treasurer of both the Wesleyans' 'Worn Out Ministers Fund',[62] the Local Preacher's Horse Hire Fund, and the Wesleyan Institute, the Easingwold Parish Council and much else. The Worn Out Minister's Fund sounds alarming.

What was it, though, that most concerned Rookledge in March 1901? It was a matter of deep regret, he said, to have to note 'the gradual but sure decay of the town's ancient market'. Steps could - and should - be taken to revive it. 'We wrangle about sewers and elections,' he said, 'whilst our market dies, and the town becomes impoverished through the farmers and their wives going elsewhere'. Rookledge featured heavily in the paper which published his letters, and it reported that at a sale of property at the George Hotel held some time before his letter appeared about the market he had bought four shares (from a batch of six) in the Easingwold Market Tolls for £46 each.[63]

Long Street, Easingwold, 1905, with the Mill on left hand side

Rookledge's letter leaves no doubt that his town was not flourishing - even if the consumption of gas was going up. Another of the enterprises of that time went bust, as if to prove the point. This was the Easingwold Union Steam Flour Mill which was a limited company. In July 1899 a general meeting of investors was held at the Town Hall at which the liquidator, a Mr T. Hodgson, produced accounts 'showing his acts and dealings in the winding up of the company during the preceding year.'[64] It was resolved 'that the liquidator be requested to make a payment of £1 on account in respect of each share.' Naturally the Steam's demise was seized on as a trading opportunity by possible competitors, and one inserted an advertisement in the press - ostensibly to tell readers that it had 'appointed Mr J. P. Jones of Yearsley, as their 'Traveller and Representative' but really to pick up the unfortunate Union's customers,[65] this was the EASINGWOLD ROLLER FLOUR MILL CO., LTD'. In 1905 Henry Cowles was both manager and secretary. It rarely advertised in the local press.[66]

The old Union Flour Mill had come into existence in the 1850s, situated from the start, in Long Street,[67] like the gas works. A year after it made the modest payment on account mentioned earlier it was announced that it was 'now paying a second and final dividend of 5s 6d per share' and that was the end of a once profitable business. One that was still prospering, however, and another that underlined the dominance to Easingwold of agriculture, had its success noted just below the news of the Union Flour's final payout. 'The Balance Sheet of the Easingwold Farmers' Trading and Auction Mart Company has been issued' it was reported, 'and a dividend of ten per cent declared.

Nineteen hundred and one was a census year, the findings of which would have come as a surprise to no-one as far as Easingwold was concerned. The assessment was taken on a Sunday, and preliminary results were published by the end of April. A report about the Thirsk area said that 'The rural districts throughout, with but few exceptions ... experienced a decrease in population,' while there was 'A SMALL INCREASE IN EASINGWOLD'. We understand, that the census returns for the parish of Easingwold show an increase in the population of 13. The population in 1891 was 1,932, and this year the population is 1,945 [68]. So far as the returns have been verified for the surrounding villages, a local commentator wrote

> the result shows a decrease in the majority of them. It is satisfactory to know that Easingwold has not suffered as many small towns and villages have from the depopulation of rural districts. There is no doubt but that if new houses were built there would soon be a considerable increase in the residential population of the town, which is noted for being a *very healthy place.* [My italics.]

The last Penty-like comment seems quite incredible and it would be quite easy to multiply the instances of epidemics of small pox, influenza and the other scourges already mentioned. But Victorian towns and cities were all pretty unhealthy places, and that Easingwold was too should be no cause for surprise. The census revealed that in 1901 there were 441 inhabited dwellings in the town compared with 432 a decade earlier. The number of families in Easingwold was 448. Between 1891 and 1901 the town had seen 631 marriages, 2,318 births and 1,506 deaths.

The census returns underlined again the fact that the Easingwold area was not prospering throughout at the turn of the century and numerous businesses and small farmers went bust. The failure of the Union Steam Flour Mill has been mentioned and just above an account of the hirings at Sheriff Hutton in a paper of November 1900,[69] there appeared a note about the failure of a farmer. 'The first meeting of the creditors of Edward Tyreman

Easingwold Wesleyan Bazaar - June 26, 1908

of Tholthorpe, farmer, was held at the office of the Official Receiver, York, on Thursday', it said. His deficiency was £125 16s 11d. He attributed his failure to 'high rent, bad seasons, and failure of crops.'

Many people in trouble, like Tyreman, would have appeared at the Town Hall. What was it like?

> The Market Place is a spacious square about two acres in extent. The Old *Toll Booth,* with its flight of stone steps, and the base of the ancient *Market Cross* still remain, but a commodious *Public Hall* has taken the place of a double row of shambles which disfigured the square. It was erected in 1863, by a company of shareholders, at a cost of £1,423, and is let for public meetings, entertainments &c. The *County Court* is held here every alternate month, and *Petty Sessions* the second and last Wednesdays in each month. The *Fire Brigade* occupy a portion of the ground floor. The building is of brick, of a neat design, and surmounted by a tower at the West end, in which is a clock, presented by Thomas Rocliffe, Esq., of Sowerby, Thirsk. Near the Market Cross is a circle, formed of large sized paving stones, with a larger one in the centre. This was the bull-ring, when the barbarous sport of bull-baiting was a favourite amusement in many a Yorkshire village. The *Stocks* and *Whipping Post* are gone, and the *Ducking Stool,* for the reformation of scolds, was long since taken down as totally useless and superfluous.
>
> The market is held ... on Fridays, and is well supplied with butter, bacon and eggs, which are chiefly purchased for York Market; a large quantity of corn is also sold by sample.

Bulmers, from which the foregoing was taken, was published in 1890, Francis Rookledge's letter was written in 1901. They paint very different pictures of the state of Easingwold's Market Place.

The Town Hall, market place, Easingwold 1860s before the addition of the clock tower

The Easingwold bench at the beginning of the last decade of the 19th century was of a kind that would have frightened the life out of labourers in trouble.[70] At one stage H. M. Stapylton of Myton Hall was chairman and among his colleagues were the occupants of Beningbrough Hall and Stillington Hall, John S. Strangewayes of Alne Hall, Capt William Waite of Crayke Castle and John Horatio Love of the Hawkhills. (Eventually Rookledge joined the bench.) What kind of business did these worthies have to deal with? Nothing exceptional, it must be admitted, but revealing, again, much about rural life and life in a small market town. The first meeting of 1901, for example, was held on 2 January, before five Justices.[71] There had been (and were) very serious incidents of sheep worrying in the area, and although these attacks were reckoned to be by wild dogs, that was not always the case. William Ditchburn, a farmer of Haxby, was summoned before Strangewayes and his colleagues 'to answer a claim for £1 10s. damages sustained by Richard Wrightson of Sutton-on-Forest, farmer, by reason of two dogs belonging the defendant [sic] worrying a sheep belonging to the plaintiff.' Ditchburn said that was not the case and pleaded not guilty. He was away on the day in question. It was a case of mistaken identity (or he was being stitched up). Strangewayes and the others did not agree and found the case proved. The list - a very light one - was completed that January day when Thomas Gibson, miller of Stillington and James North, labourer, of the same place, were fined for neglecting to send their children to school in accordance with the bye-laws of the local School Attendance Committee.

The equivalent court meeting of February 1901 (to that mentioned above) began with expressions of sympathy and regret for the death of Queen Victoria[72] and then went on to deal with Henry Skingley, 'farmers hind, [who] was charged by Mr James Dale, vaccination officer, with neglecting to have his child vaccinated.' He was a conscientious objector who had been warned several times about his neglect to protect the child (as the bench saw it) and was ordered to do so within a month.

Two more examples from the Easingwold petty sessions will suffice to give a flavour of the work of Strangewayes and his colleagues. First proceedings of 6 March 1901.[73] Then Edward Ingledew of Parliament Street, York was fined 10s (and costs) for assaulting Alfred Harrison of Myton-on-Swale, then John Authberet, 'bricklayer's labourer, was fined 2s 6d and costs for assaulting George Tinsley, of the same place, farm labourer, on the 2nd inst.' Two punch-ups and the sitting was over. There was a little more for the two Strangewayes (J. Swainston and Capt D'Arcy) and Rawdon Thornton to do at a later sitting in July.[74] What occupied them then? First of all the activities of James Linton, Easingwold, 'a decent fellow when he kept off drink' (which was not very often). James was fined 5s and costs for being drunk and disorderly in Long Street. James Rymer, miller of Brandsby was done for being in charge of a horse and trap without lights at Stillington on 30 May. Rymer said he had 'made a mistake as he expected that the lighting order expired on May 30th, whereas it did not expired [sic] until the 31st.' For that understandable mistake he was 'fined 1/- and costs.' Fred Pannett 'of Raskelfe Station, platelayer, was fined 10/- and costs for assaulting George Blackburn, of the same place, also a platelayer in the employ of the N.E.R. Co.' Lastly Vincent Harrison, farm foreman, and Thomas Mattison, farmer, his employer, of Plump House Farm, were charged by Inspector Fair, RSPCA, with cruelty to two horses at Myton. Awful evidence was given by PC Baker of Helperby about the state of the animals he saw ploughing 'while suffering from large wounds on their shoulders.' Mattison was fined 10s 6d and 16s costs, while the case against his foreman was dismissed on payment of costs.

An Easingwold group 1904. Miss Metcalfe, unknown, Mr & Mrs Walter Metcalfe, Mrs Dyson, seated Mrs G H Smith (senior) master G H Smith

Towards the end of 1898[75] there appeared in the paper a long report of an Easingwold Petty Sessions. It showed that disputes over poaching were not unknown – and revealed some of the newer offences JP's had to deal with, of which the following are selected examples.

Annie Fawcett of Tollerton was ordered to pay a fine of 2s 6d and costs for riding a bicycle on the footpath at Tollerton.

Frank T. Bean was every bit as bad as Annie Fawcett, he rode his bike on the footpath in Alne, and was fined 5s and costs.

James Robert Bean was also fined for riding his bike on the path at Alne and James Castell got himself a police record for commiting the same offence at Tollerton.

The Easingwold court then moved on to consider an 'OFFENCE UNDER THE POACHING PREVENTION ACT.' Joseph Gill was the alleged offender and his persecutor (to start with) was PC Eden. He saw Gill at Brandsby around 6.45 am on 14 October and noted that Joe's 'trousers and ... boots were very wet, and one of his pockets was bulging out. Knowing him to be a poacher', the constable stopped Gill and searched him. Fruitlessly? No. Joe had a rabbit and a snare on his person. Was it a fair cop? Not according to the accused. He explained. He was going to work, he said, 'when he saw the rabbit in a snare about three yards off the highway. He took it out, and put it in his pocket, and just after the witnesses [sic] jumped over a wall and stopped him.' The bench did not believe Gill and he was fined half a crown and costs.

'Gentlemen' also appeared before the court and John Rocliffe was prosecuted for trespassing and shooting game on Mr Kidd's farm at Crankley – he was fined 1s with costs.' The files of the local paper contain many more examples of the likes of poacher Joe Gill at work.[76] In August of the year in which he had his spot of trouble, Rocliffe had a letter published, which caused something of a stir. It was about the Market Place and the state it was in. 'I wish public opinion to be called to the matters contained in this letter,' he said to the editor who gave him a spread of something like 12 column inches.[77] He complained about rubbish in the market place, the dangerous state of the footpaths and the fact that the Fountain was in a poor condition owing to vandalism and juveniles urinating in it. The creaking turnstiles were commented upon and the fact that the horse trough had been moved forcing the cottagers to use the water at Spring Head.

Rocliffe ended with a dreadful description of Easingwold. He had

> known [the town] for more than sixty years, [he said and] during that time it has never been in the wretched, dilapidated, God-forsaken state it at present wears, and instead of attracting visitors or residents, positively repulses them.

A response to this letter by someone who signed himself 'A Ratepayer'[78] commented that the Toll-owners had indeed repaired footpaths, but he had other concerns. Particularly worrying was the noise and dust caused by steam roundabouts when they set up on the greens, '... the patience of long-suffering ratepayers is rapidly becoming exhausted.'[79]

There was a particular kind of refuse that angered people who were concerned about the state of the Market Place, and Easingwold over all. Discarded fish and chip papers were being thrown on the ground, this was something new in the late 1890s, and can be traced to the business of one W. Rogers. He advertised that he was starting something new and, into the market place came a chippy, though it will be noticed that chips were not called chips - yet.

THE FRIED FISH SALOON,
Market Place,
EASINGWOLD,
PROPRIETOR: W. ROGERS

Notice! Notice!! Notice!!!
Fried Fish & Potatoes
Every Night After 7 P.M.
Fridays from 12 till 2 p.m.
Fresh Fish and Shell Fish
Arrives Daily.
A TRIAL IS RESPECTFULLY SOLICITED.

A fish and chip shop, of course, could not appear in a place until rapid transport facilities and refrigerated conveyances were available, and Rogers' daily supplies must have arrived by rail. The importance of what people like him sold was immense, enabling the less well-off to obtain nourishing, hot and, one hopes, cheap food over the counter.

Measures were being taken to improve Easingwold, and it was decided that a Lighting rate would be levied for the following year to enable £75 to be spent on the town's illuminations.

The state of Easingwold *was* alarming, as has been said before, with many of the inhabitants having an appalling water supply, and it is surprising, perhaps, that there were not many more complaints about the threat to public health of decaying rubbish in the streets and so on. In an issue of a newspaper which reported that there was an influenza outbreak in Easingwold[80] a comprehensive account of the contents of the annual report of the Medical Officer of Health for the Easingwold Rural Sanitary District was given. Some of the findings duplicate material already quoted from other slightly later sources, but a section of the 1898 report is worth quoting nevertheless. What did it say?

> ... The record of sickness is as follows:- In the whole division, notifications of scarlatina, 18; of diphtheria, 23; of enteric fever, 4; of erysipelas, 12; and it is only necessary to give the figures for the Easingwold Division to show where infectious diseases for the most part prevailed. These are Scarlatina, 17; diphtheria, 20; enteric fever, 4; erysipelas, 9. In Easingwold, a large number of cases of diphtheria were notified, there being two deaths from the same.

The Easingwold Town Hall was run by a limited company which had J. C. Bannister as its secretary. The Easingwold Town Hall Company Ltd's. annual general meeting of shareholders for 1898-99 was held at the HQ in April.[81] F. J. H. Robinson was in the chair, 'the usual dividend for five per cent [was] declared and the 'retiring directors ... were all re-elected'. No surprises here. They were Robinson, J. S. Strangwayes and F. E. Rookledge. The eighth annual meeting was held in April of 1900 when again five percent was declared, and so it went on from year to year.[82] The ninth, however, was reported at a little greater length than usual. 'The annual report of the directors was laid before the meeting,' it was recorded, when 'The profit and loss account showed a balance of £52 7s 6$^1/_2$, which was available for dividend, and a dividend of 5 per cent per annum was declared payable, the balance to be carried forward.'[83]

The 'Commodious *Public Hall* on which there was that clock donated by Thomas Rocliffe (which was not keeping very good time at the end of the century) was the centre of great

Long Street, Easingwold, 1905, 'Shepherd's Garth', long gone, stood next to the Catholic Church

activity, and was unchallenged as such until the Victoria Institute made its appearance.[84] This was a public hall - to which were attached some alms houses (which replaced some others). The Institute was built to commemorate Queen Victoria's Jubilee and it opened for business in 1898.

A scheme for what became the Victoria Buildings was approved by the Charity Commissioners in September 1897,[85] a couple of months after the impressive local celebrations for the jubilee had been held.[86] (For them, 'The Market cross and fountain were ... nicely decorated,' something which might have pleased John Rocliffe.) The state of almshouses, especially those in Chapel Street, had been a source of concern for some time[87] and despite some worries F E Rookledge had reassured the readers of the Advertiser in 1897[88] that schemes to build the Victoria Institute would certainly go ahead.[89]

It had originally been hoped that the Victoria Buildings would be opened on 22 June, but the need to get the consent of the Charity Commissioners had stopped that. Requests for subscriptions had produced promises of £300 by the end of May 1897.[90] The Jubilee scheme, got under way in reality in February and started with a public meeting at which 'two chief schemes' were put forward. The first was for the pulling down and rebuilding of the almshouses in Little Lane, 'and the widening of the road at that point.' The other scheme, however, 'obtained the most favour, [and] was [for] the erection of a Reading Room.'[91]

Another discussion, this time at the Town Hall, took place on the Jubilee Scheme.[92] Snags had been encountered and F. J. H. Robinson revealed that another scheme 'which he should call No. 4' had been brought forward. The cost of building three almshouses in place of those now standing would be £60 each. The reading room would cost £130 without furniture, £200 with. It fell to Rookledge to present current thinking. Critics had said 'nothing succeeded in Easingwold, but that statement could easily be proved to be wrong,' he said. Some said the current plans were too expensive, but they could borrow if need be and they could hold functions to add to the funds. So Rookledge proposed that they go ahead and

The marriage of Hubert Baines (lately back from the Boer War) and Miss Haynes of Long Street, Easingwold at Easingwold Church, 1903

erect buildings at a cost of about £400, one side of which is to be divided into 2 rooms, one to be used as a reading room, and the other as a recreation room, the former to be used when required as a Parish Council room; the other side of the buildings to be divided into 4 cottages, 3 of which are to be utilized as almshouses, in lieu of the existing 3 at Spring Head, and the fourth to be used as a caretaker's cottage ... The whole building to be handed over to the Parish Council for the benefit of the Parish for ever. The buildings to be called "The Victoria Buildings."

Rookledge's No 4 scheme was enthusiastically adopted.

Throughout 1898 progress on the Victoria Buildings went on. The scheme had something of a make-over in April when it was decided to heat the buildings 'by hot water' and tenders from local firms were accepted,[93] and funds were raised at a 'very good Concert' in the Town Hall[94]. With strong public support the Victoria Institute *had* to succeed and it was scheduled to open on 19 November. In the public notices column of the press it was said that subscriptions were to be '4s per annum or 1s per quarter' and that, 'Anyone over 14 desiring to join can do so by applying to Mr Millions, the caretaker, or to Geo. Sandham, Hon. Sec.'[95] Reports were made of an enthusiastic take-up but the parish council worried about what its part of the deal amounted to. In February 1900 the question of who was to pay the insurance on the Victoria was raised. Should it be the parish or the Victoria's committee of management? G. J. Webster then wondered about the sense of the council leaving the schoolroom, for which it paid 30s a year then 'going there and paying £6 and then being asked to pay the insurance' as well.[96] He had a point, and things got rather heated on the Easingwold PC. In March it was reported that the management committee had paid for the present year, but 'The policy of insuring the Alms houses as well as the reading and recreation room, was adversely criticised by a portion of the Council.'[97] What this really means is not clear, but it, no doubt generated much heat.

A balance sheet of the Victoria Institute published in May 1901 suggests that one of the contentious issues with the parish council had been removed, as the income side of it shows 'Parish Council (Rent) ... 4 10 0.'[98] Subscriptions amounted to £20 10 and the biggest earner, not surprisingly perhaps, was 'Billiards'. There was an imbalance, however, and this was highlighted when the accounts were discussed in public. 'The Annual meeting [of the Vic] ... was held in the Reading Room last night, Mr John Hobson, as chairman of the Parish Council, presiding. The accounts, showing an adverse of 1/5, were presented by Dr. Mills, hon. treasurer, and passed.'[99] Despite this Mills was re-elected as was Sandham as hon secretary. Mark Reynard, G. T. Sturdy, H. Cowling and J. W. Sturdy were chosen to be the committee of management. Earlier the council had elected Rookledge as its representative on it. [100]

The Victoria Institute was a modest addition to Easingwold's stock of places where public meetings and entertainments went on. It proved to be extremely popular.

The moves that ended with the setting up of the Easingwold Victoria Institute began in 1897. What kind of entertainment went on in the town then? Most of the fare provided was of an amateur kind, but undoubtedly good and often put on to raise funds for good causes. The very first 1897 Town Hall function of this kind was an 'ENTERTAINMENT In connection with the Annual School Treat' of St Johns Schools, when '"THE MUSICAL ROBINSON CRUSOE" was rendered by the 'Teachers, Friends and Scholars.' In addition there were readings by M. O. Matthews and, just in case the Easingwold lot did not satisfy the expectations of the paying customers, 'The services of MR. BURDEKIN, of

The Vicarage Bible Class, Easingwold, 1907 - second from right (front row) Ernest Ward

York, Elocutionist and Conjurer, were secured for the occasion.' What were the prices of admission? One shilling for seats at the front, 6d for those at the back.[101]

In April the Town Hall provided the venue for the 12th anniversary of the Salvation Army with a musical festival led by the 'YORK 1 BRASS BAND.'[102] In years to come the Easingwold Town Hall held regular Saturday night dances but it functioned as an occasional ballroom before the turn of the century. In February 1899, for example, the Perseverance Lodge of the Ancient Order of Druids organised a 'Grand Fancy Dress Ball' there.[103] The hall was not overwhelmed with bookings,[104] but it also functioned as something more like a theatre or concert hall. Thus by April 1900, when the Walford Family gave a 'Grand Sacred Concert', they were also able to announce that the 'ALL THE ANIMATED PICTURES OF THE BOER WAR will be re-produced with suitable Military Sacred Music.'[105] 'The programme consisted of both vocal and instrumental music', it said, 'and a series of living pictures produced by the latest non-flickering Cinematograph, depicting scenes in the Transvaal War.'[106]

Dennis Gifford's The *British Film Catalogue*[107] shows that R. W. Paul had made and issued numerous Boer War films before the Walfords gave their concert in Easingwold and it is possible that some of these were among those shown at the Town Hall in April 1900 - films like The *Bombardment of Mafeking, Wrecking An Armoured Train* and *Nurses Attending the Wounded.* At least one contained some authentic footage. This was *Britain v. Boer* described as 'WAR Staged war scenes combined with actuality scenes.' Clyde Jeavons has a brief piece on Boer War films in which he mentions the prevalence of fake material.[108] Quite a few of the fakes were made by Mitchell and Kenyon, who used the outskirts of Blackburn as 'a convenient substitute' for the South African veldt.

The movies had also come to at least one of the villages in the parish over 18 months earlier. Alne was a swinging place as befitted a major railway junction and in September 1898 the inhabitants had an opportunity of learning about a science which had captured the imagination. An item in the *Advertiser* explained all, and the fillers for each evening will be noted.[109]

> PHRENOLOGISTIC LECTURES - On the first three nights of this week, Professor Price, M.A. has been giving lectures in the schoolroom, Alne, on character reading. &c. The lectures which were both interesting and instructive, were beautifully illustrated with lime-light views. The entertainment each evening was wound up with a series of cinematograph pictures of a very novel and amusing character.

The Town Hall, then, was an early, if not the earliest place where films were shown in the Easingwold area, but the Walford show was an exception and the Hall, as well as providing a home for the local fire brigade and the magistrates' court, mainly functioned as a venue for lectures, meetings, concerts and dances. One which deserves rescuing from oblivion, took place in 1901, there was to be dancing to a musical ensemble that might, perhaps, have been named, well, just a little differently.[110]

BALL! BALL! BALL!
MR COWPER'S BALL will take place
on FRIDAY, MAY 3rd, in the TOWN HALL
EASINGWOLD
Mr Cowper's Ball Band will be in attendance

Cowper was someone who went round the villages holding dancing classes. Later on he no longer described the orchestra he led or booked for his dances as his Ball Band, which is understandable, and suggests he may have been on the receiving end of a few bawdy remarks. Very understandable, very possible.

Most of the talent on show at the area's dances and concerts was home grown and reminds one that it was an age when entertainment was by and for people in the locality. There were numerous minstrel troupes and glee clubs in the Easingwold area performing at dinners and, sometimes, the more important local venues. At the Victoria Institute, on one occasion there was an entertainment by the Victoria Institute Minstrel Troupe and at the end of 1902 they appeared at the Town Hall.[111] Such groups were extremely popular. The Ohio Minstrels, for example.[112] This gave an American style minstrel show in the Alne schoolroom. Shortly after this the Apollo Glee singers of Thirsk performed in concert,[113] but the most noticed group was one based in Crayke. The Crayke Glee Party performed at the Easingwold Fire Brigade's dinner, for example,[114] and they also appeared on their home ground in an entertainment to raise money for the village's Piano Fund and Reading Room.[115] The show at Crayke concluded with what was described as a 'humorous dialogue entitled "Uncle Benjamin's Legacies" and Mrs Jarley's Waxworks.' Crayke, a reporter said, is fortunate in having a Glee Party who can either sing or act, and who are always ready to do what they can for any good causes.' Well the Crayke Piano Fund *was* a good cause and members of the Glee were whipped in to take part in 'the waxworks'. Mr Matthews' presented it. 'Mr Matthews' talents as a showman are so well known, not only in Crayke, but in all the surrounding district, that it is hardly necessary to say that his share of the performance left nothing to be desired', it was said, 'The acting, the riddles and the witticisms, of both Mr Matthews and his assistant, kept the audience in a continuous roar of laughter. The following were (some of) the figures: Mr Winslow (Miss Matthews) ... Pear's Soap, "You dirty Boy" (Miss Hogg and J. W. Hogg): Nigger Minstrel (Mr E Colling) ... Darby and Joan (Mr C Dennis and Miss H. Roe); Lord Kitchener of Khartoum (Mr Wilfred Roe); and Viscount Hinton (Mr C Johnson).'

The Boer War was now on and, as part of the war effort, a concert was given 'in aid of war funds' in the schoolroom at Crayke. It was in three parts, 'the first beginning with "Rule Britannia," and consisting chiefly of patriotic songs.' The second was 'taken by the ... Glee Party as "Pierrots", and comprised four solos and two glees. This, the first appearance of the ... Party as "Pierrots" was voted a decided success.' Then Miss Bingham and the always willing Mr Edmanson completed the show. A few tear jerkers amongst the patriotic airs were

Song, 'Rule Britannia' (Mr J Gibson)
Song, 'Don't run old England down' (Mr Bannister)
Song, 'Tommy Atkins' (Mr Edmanson)
Song, 'To Arms' (Mr M. O. Matthews)
Recitation, 'By the Waters' (Miss Bingham) Recitation, '"A.M.B."' (collection) (Edmanson)
Song, 'Comrades in Arms' (Pierrots)
Song, 'Soldiers of the Queen' (Mr C. Dennis)
Song, 'I've got the ooperzootic' (Edmandson)
Song, 'The Englishman' (Mr F. Rickaby)

It will be noticed that Mr Edmandson had publicly confessed on several occasions in public to having the ooperzootic. The AMB was the 'Absent Minded Beggar', of which more later.

The villagers of the Easingwold area were remote in a way that is almost incomprehensible today. Remote, that is, from national events. Remote because of the difficulties of travel. Going to Easingwold on foot (as most had to) for a date, a beer, a concert, or a meeting, having to walk back at night then get up for work at dawn was a definite disincentive to go far 'of an evening'. But things were changing, and one of the things that broke down

Punch and Judy, Easingwold style - early 1900s

the village isolation just a little was the further extension in the area of the telegraph. In November 1898 the following press report appeared.[116]

> POSTAL TELEGRAPHS - A telegraph office will shortly be opened in this village [Stillington], to supply a long felt want of the parish and district. The successful result of an appeal made to the Postmaster General is due in great measure to the exertions of Dr F Sidney Gramshaw, who has been most energetic in pushing the matter forward. The other guarantors are also entitled to the gratitude of all who will benefit by this means of communication.

Brandsby was also put on the telegraph system, and here consideration was given to environmental concerns.

> It has been decided not to take the Brandsby telegraph up the town streets any more than necessary. This will certainly be more in accordance with the wish of the public than the former plan to take the line up Uppleby.

The villages, as has been shown, relied on home-produced talent for their entertainments though musicians were brought in for dances and there was something of a 'circuit' for performers in the area. That Prof Price who appeared at Alne, for example, was on a tour, and Harry Liston, no less, did the villages some times. He was a famous performer who usually worked at Easingwold's number one venue. He features in many music hall histories and was a regular visitor to the area.[117] Harry, amongst other things, was a quick-change artist and his show 'entitled "Merry Moments"' was presented at the Town Hall on one of his visits to 'a large and fashionable audience' on a Wednesday night in February 1898.

Travelling shows were also a regular feature of the life of Easingwold. For example, towards the end of 1901, six years after their last visit, Bostock and Wombwell's Royal No 1 Aggregation, 'A Colossal Amalgamation of Zoological Wonders from the uttermost parts of the Earth' was exhibited (for one day only) on the Easingwold Market Place which had hopefully been cleared up beforehand. This was a 'Travelling Zoo' which included tigers, leopards and lions - 'headed by "Wallace," the King of all Lions.'[118] Other attractions were 'White Wings' the 'LONG MANED HORSE, whose beautiful mane and tail reach upwards of 40 feet' and, of course, a boxing kangaroo and another very special, attraction named after a famous Boer soldier.

> "GENERAL SNYMAN,"
>
> The wonderful Mafeking Bell-Ringing Ape.
> Who has not heard of this wonderful creature, which so ably assisted "B.P." and his gallant band whilst besieged in MAFEKING? This intelligent Ape was trained by one of Baden-Powell's troopers to ring the town bell directly the Boers commenced firing, thereby warning the inhabitants to seek the bomb-proof shelters. At the end of the siege he was brought to London by his owner and trainer, Trooper Wynne, belonging to near Darlington, of Colonel Plumer's force, I.Y., and was eventually purchased for this collection at an enormous cost by Mr Bostock. Though only an Ape, he is deserving of your special attention, and commands the admiration of everybody.

Quite clearly it was not practical to tie up the Town Hall for prolonged theatrical runs so there were regular visits to the town of travelling troupes which took up residence for some time and provided the locals with entertainment of a professional nature (if not always of

Easingwold Pierrot Troupe - Fancy Fair, July 17th, 1907

a professional standard). One of these travelling groups was the Pavilion Theatre which appeared in Easingwold in 1896 and returned for a season in July of the following year.[119]

In 1902 'THE Public of Easingwold and District' were 'respectfully informed that' they were to be visited by yet more travelling players. *The Advertiser* told them that the 'BIJOU THEATRE OF VARIETIES ... situate in Mrs Colpitt's Meadow would open on Friday 9 May, with prices of admission ranging from 4d to 1/6d. That seems very reasonable as the Bijou (its publicity said) had been 'Pronounced by the Press and Public to be the best and most Popular Travelling theatre ever seen.'[120] The opening was delayed because of bad weather, but only for a day. The proprietor, J. B. Beckitt, apologised for the hold-up, but used it to his advantage. He did so in an advert which said that two plays would be presented. One had a title which would not pass without ribald comment today, but will not be commented on here (except to say that it might indicate that the Bijou was operating in a much more innocent era than exists now).[121]

BIJOU THEATRE OF VARIETIES

MRS. COLPITT'S FIELD, EASINGWOLD
Sole Proprietor ... MR. J. B. BECKITT
MR. BECKITT regrets that owing to the unsettled state of the weather, the opening of the Bijou Theatre, situate in Mrs. Colpitt's Field, Easingwold, will be postponed until
SATURDAY, MAY 10th,
When will be presented a New Play, entitled:
THE MIDNIGHT EXPRESS
or, AN ENGINE DRIVER'S STORY.
Characters by the entire Company. Followed with a Grand Variety Entertainment and a Screaming Farce
STAND UP DICK.

The Bijou Theatre of Varieties stayed for a prolonged season in Easingwold in 1902, no doubt to the delight of Mrs Colpitt. It still presented a different play each night, many of them of the 'Murder in the Red Barn' variety, mixed in with which were some weightier pieces. Included were what look like some superb melodramas. (Stand Up Dick seems to have been dropped.)

With the numerous concerts and recitals in Easingwold and the villages, with regular visits from the travelling theatres and with recitals in parish halls and schoolrooms everywhere, there was no shortage of entertainment. There was no shortage of pubs either. Easingwold was famous for some inns, but they were but a small proportion of the 'outlets' in the parish. What there was described annually by the police, and the reports to the annual brewster sessions are a valuable source of information for the historian. In 1900 the Easingwold report was presented to a meeting held in the Town Hall on 29 August. Police superintendent George Dove delivered it. What did it say about the availability of booze at that time? 'I have the honour', he said,[122]

> to lay before you the annual Police Report on the state of the licensed houses in this section of the Bulmer Division, and beg to inform you that there are 57 fully licensed

houses, 2 beer-houses to sell both on and off the premises, 2 beer off only, 2 shopkeepers with spirit licenses, 1 wholesale dealer to sell both beer and spirits, being the same as last year. Total 64 to a population of 9,152, being an average of 143 persons to each licensed house. ... During the year one licensed holder has been proceeded against and convicted ... against one proceeded against and one discharged the previous year. With this exception the ... houses have ... been fairly well conducted. ... During the year 18 persons have been proceeded against and convicted under the Licensing Act for being drunk and disorderly, and all convicted. Of this number 10 are residents in the district, and 8 non-residents tramping through the district, compared with 28 persons the corresponding period last year. .....

Next on the court's list that day was a case headed 'EXCISE PROSECUTION' a report told how 'The John Smith's Tadcaster Brewery Company were charged on the information of Jos Lynch of Thirsk Excise office that on the 4th May last they had on their premises at the Market-place Easingwold certain spirits extracted from the wood of certain casks in contravention of Section 4 of the Finance Act 1898.' The premises referred to above were presumably the local branch office (John J. Penty, Brewery House, Easingwold, 'BRANCH MANAGER'). He has been mentioned previously in this narrative, and was an extremely busy member of the local business community. On the same page as one of his advertisements appeared, near the time of the Brewster's report (actually it was a week later)[123] he appeared as John Smiths branch manager, hon secretary of the 40th annual exhibition of the Easingwold Agricultural Society ('Under the Patronage of H.R.H. THE DUKE OF CAMBRIDGE, K.G.') and the hon secretary of the Ploughing and Hedge Cutting Association. But what about the case that took him and others before the magistrates? Francis Pollard, 'supervisor of excise Ripon' stated that on 4 May he visited the John Smith Market Place premises, with Lynch 'and found there six small casks about nine or ten gallons each amongst other casks. He found some liquor in one and five were empty. There was an odour of spirits from [sic] the five empty casks. He had the contents placed in a half-gallon measure. It was whiskey and water.' He took a sample, and a clerk said 'the casks were kept to send out spirits to customers, and the spirits were obtained by rinsing.' Penty 'stated in defence, that the cask in question was a new one, and had not been[sic] used and the liquor had been put into it to season it.' That was two years ago. The Bench dismissed the case.

The deputy Chief Constable presented his licensing report for the Bulmer West division to a small gathering of magistrates on 18 August 1901.[124] The situation as far as outlets was concerned was that all had been 'fairly well conducted'. Only nine people had been prosecuted for being drunk and disorderly, and all were convicted. This time five were tramps compared with 18 in the 'corresponding period of last year.' The numbers of tramps prosecuted may have gone down, but the number of them visiting the town clearly did not, indeed the situation was so bad that the papers regularly wrote of 'THE BEGGING NUISANCE' and the courts began to hand out some hefty sentences. The case (from 1902) that prompted the 'NUISANCE' caption just quoted told what happened to James Glancy 'of no fixed abode, but supposed to be a native of Liverpool'. Jim was picked up and charged with begging 'and sent to Northallerton Gaol for seven days hard labour.'[125] A little earlier three tramps were arrested and taken from custody to face Henry Hawking. The first (Thomas Selby) got 14 days inside; the second, Daniel Feenery, got 7 days 'for begging in High Street, Easingwold. - Edward Feenery for a similar offence, also in High Street, was committed for 14 days.'[126] In late October James Jackson, tramping labourer, was committed for 7 days for begging at Easingwold. P.C. Todd proved the case.'[127] PC Pennock had a rather more painful case to prove at Malton regarding a tramp John Thompson accusing of biting the constable's leg; Thompson was gaoled for 3 months with hard labour.

John Smith's was the pre-eminent beer sold in the pubs of Easingwold. The company had been engaging in an expansionist policy around the turn of the century and taken over additional outlets in Easingwold. Baxters regularly advertised but gave no details of where one could purchase their excellent product, though one of the town's best known pubs features in one of its ads.[128] It adopted a rather modern knocking the opposition approach in its ads.

NO MEDALS AWARDED

THE UNDERMENTIONED DOES NOT EXHIBIT
BAXTERS SPARKLING ALES.

BE SURE IN ORDERING YOU GIVE
THE PRICE LIST NUMBER

BAXTER'S BREWERY
THORNTON-LE-MOOR
NORTHALLERTON

District Agent:-
JAMES HAYNES
GEORGE HOTEL, Market Place, EASINGWOLD

Many towns had breweries of their own but Easingwold at the turn of the century did not and its boozers relied on firms like Baxters and John Smiths. It had been a modest centre of brewing somewhat earlier, however, and the man who dominated it then, as a producer, passed away as the century was nearing its end. This was William Leadley of Uppleby who was 94 and Easingwold's oldest inhabitant.[129] 'Mr Leadley was formerly proprietor of the Easingwold Brewery, when he also carried on the business of a spirit merchant, but retired from business many years ago after a successful career.'[130] The contents of his will were revealed in February 1898, when his personal estate was seen to be valued at £2,271 12s 9d.

The drinks trade has always had its critics and at the turn of the century there were prolonged and noisy protests about the product itself. Usually people who adopted anti-drink attitudes dwelled on the consequence of over-indulgence, but there were some who agitated for a better product. People and organisations in the Easingwold area took part in demands for 'Pure Beer'. The Rural District Council also did so. At their very last meeting of 1900 when Cllr Young (the Rev H. Young represented Alne),[131] proposed

> that the council support the other Unions in encouraging Sir M Quilter to press his "Pure Beer Bill" forward in Parliament. The Bill not only protected the public from arsenic but from other adulteration. It provided for Beer being made only from malt and hops, and the necessary refining materials. It was not a political idea, and as he understood there was no beer in this district brewed solely from malt and hops, he thought it was just the place to begin.

The chairman agreed with Young and the RDC carried his resolution unanimously and decided to ask Grant Lawson MP for his support.

The question of contamination was of paramount importance in the Easingwold area at the time, the lead pipes through which the nectar made its way were the cause of frequent

Farnley House, Easingwold, early 1900s

poisonings.)[132] Arsenic in the nation's beer was the main cause of concern though. Rightly so.

The demands for a Pure Beer Bill grew and Henry Chaplin, once President of the Board of Agriculture and, more recently, of the Local Government Board, reviewed them.[133] He said that 'The recent cases of poisoning by beer in which some arsenic has been found in dangerous quantities have called renewed attention to some necessity for some revision of the law which regulates the manufacture and the sale of beer.' A Treasury Committee had recently issued a majority report claiming that no legislation was necessary. Sir Henry disagreed and wrote a horrifying rebuttal to the majority's findings. A year after they were made public,[134] he said, accounts appeared almost daily, which showed that

> thousands of people in the North of England and elsewhere have been suffering from the effects of drinking poisoned beer; numerous fresh cases are constantly occurring, and a number of the sufferers ... they are said to exceed 100 ... have already lost their lives in consequence. An inquiry ... is being held by the Local Government Board ... The broad facts [of it though not yet published] ... appear to be as follows ... the beer, by which ... people had been poisoned, was beer in the brewing of which substitutes for malt had been freely used. Dangerous quantities of arsenic were found to be contained in it, and great quantities ... have been condemned and .... destroyed.

Chaplin contended that the existing majority report had been shown to be totally false and that a future enquiry 'ought to be undertaken by the Government themselves' and said it was proposed to form 'an association to promote the purity of beer.' He also thought an Act might go some way to stopping rural depopulation. In a speech to his constituents near Lincoln, Chaplin said the Pure Beer Bill had 'afforded ... [the] Government ... a golden opportunity of killing two birds with one stone - by protecting the public on the one hand from poison in their beer by restricting the use of dangerous materials, and ... at the some [sic] time helping the barley grower by encouraging the use of barley.'[135]

A Royal Commission on Poisoned Beer was set up but was criticised as it did not represent the English barley-growing interest, while one of its members was connected with the largest brewing concern in the country.[136] The Easingwold RDC's concern has been mentioned and it was referred to at a dinner at Sutton-on-the-Forest given by Arthur Duncombe to the tradesmen, farmers and tenants of the Sutton estate.[137] In his speech he stated,'The present beer scare should be taken as an opportunity to urge Parliament to promote a Pure Beer Bill'. A local petition, 'should be forwarded to the Minister of Agriculture to support this.'

Shortly after he spoke a widely publicised inquest was reported which would have done nothing to lessen the panic.[138]

> ARSENIC IN BEER - The inquest held at Manchester on the body of a woman alleged to have died from the effects of arsenic in beer was concluded on Monday. The jury returned an open verdict, but added an expression of their opinion that blame for carelessness attached to the brewers, to Messrs. Nicholson, the manufacturers of the sulphuric acid, and to Mr. Cook and Dr. Morris, the chemists employed by Messrs. Bostock, the glucose-makers

The concern about pure beer (or the absence of it) continued and in March 1901 the Easingwold Board of Guardians discussed the matter again - with some controversy which is difficult to understand. Cuthbert Quilter had his bill before Parliament and W.S. Jones proposed the Guardians write to Grant Lawson asking him to support it. The clerk said he would send the letter, but though he (the clerk) was in favour of a Pure Beer Bill 'he was not in favour of Sir M Quilter's, and he did not think he would support it.' Immediately

Long Street, Easingwold, 1905. The man in the doorway was Hubert Baines, a staunch Methodist, who took over the shop from George Haynes whose name still appears there. Boy on the left is an orphan from Dr. Barnardo's.

Jones backed down saying '"Then I'll not support him, and I hope you others won't."' A clear case of the tail wagging the dog, and an extraordinary back down.[139] Jones was clearly a man of straw.[140]

The revelations that came out in the arguments for a Pure Beer Bill must have convinced advocates of temperance or teetotalism of the merits of their beliefs. They concentrated primarily on the consequences of drink rather than its purity, it is true, but the arsenic scares would have done their cause a power of good. (At the same time, more-or-less, the House of Lords, went into committee on the Bishop of Winchester's Habitual Drunkards Bill, which got great publicity in the nation's press.)[141]

In Easingwold a temperance movement came into being at the end of 1901. In December a meeting to be held in the Town Hall was announced when J. J. Hatch of the United Kingdom Alliance was the principal speaker.[142] W. B. Richardson of Burn Hall was in charge of the proceedings and he said the object of those gathered together was 'to form a temperance society for the town of Easingwold.' The principal support for Hatch came from 'Sergt - Instructor Armstrong of Leeds', someone with a formidable reputation among temperance advocates. It was agreed to create a Society.[143] Support for the move had been given by, among others, Henry Hawking and the representatives of various local churches and chapels - Easingwold (Rev N. Jackson), the Revs R. Renton and R. Whitehead (Wesleyans), and the Rev W. Shaw (Primitive Methodist).

The name chosen for the new pressure group was the Easingwold United Temperance Society and it began its campaigning with a meeting at the Town Hall which had 'turns' as well as speeches.[144] Another meeting held in March was of the same nature, though here Dr Mills, who had been present at the inaugural, 'strongly advocated total abstinence'. This draws attention to the fact that within the anti-drink movements there were always disagreements between the people like Mills - teetotallers - and temperance believers. Once again entertainment was provided with the ever-present Miss Bingham singing and Hatch of the UKA (and Hull) was the speaker.[145] The Easingwold Union's campaigning was intense in its early stages and it met again in April. This time it had a speaker from York who did experiments and the Misses Wood of Stillington sang. An advance notice was ambitious. The society would hold its meeting at the Town Hall, it said, 'when Mr Chas. Casson of the York Temperance Society, will give an address on "A Gallon of Beer," with experiments.'[146] A few regulars from the Town Hall would have been willing participants in the experiments.

There were other temperance or teetotal organisations for various age groups in existence apart from the Easingwold. There was a Raskelfe Band of Hope, for example, and on Easter Monday 1902 it held a public meeting at 'the Parish Hall, when recitations and singing was given [sic].'[147] There was also an 'ADULT TEMPERANCE SOCEITY' [sic] at Sutton-on-the-Forest, another at Huby (the Huby Adult Temperance Society) and others at Stillington and Tollerton.

The Easingwold Temperance Society's winter programme came to an end with the lecture meeting at which Charles Casson demonstrated. (Not like W C Fields did in Tales of Manhattan.) The president of Easingwold's group was Watson C. Wilkinson and he spoke of 'the bright prospect there was for the future of the society, and urged all present, who had not done so, to sign the pledge. Having completed its winter session the Temperance Society took to the streets and the fare provided in the Market Place in May suggests that a considerable organisation had been built up already. 'In addition to an address by Mr Houldershaw, F.C.S. of Newcastle' it was said, 'the Temperance Choir and Band of Hope

Bank House, Market Place, Easingwold, dated August 9th, 1902.
Decorated for the Coronation of Edward VII. The bay window on the left reads 'Yorkshire Banking Co. Ltd. Open 10 to 3, Friday 10 to 4, Saturday 10 to 12'. Window on the left reads 'Post Office' and the oblong sign on the left reads 'Parcel Post Office'.

will sing.'[148] On 23 July a demonstration of all the local temperance societies was held at Burn Hall. As always people like provider of the tea for 300 (Fleetwood Broad of Easingwold) and the presence of the York Industrial School band were mentioned and the names of all the speakers were given. But as always nothing of what they said was given.[149]

In November the Town Hall was the venue for a 'Grand Military' anti-drink meeting when 'several friends from the York Military Depot were announced to take part' as entertainers.[150] One was Cpl Cowling,[151] another was Sgt Davis and a third was Bandsman Sutton. Also on this occasion Colour Sergeant Willougby gave a recitation (no concert was complete without a recitation or two)[152]. Cpl Cowling, however, was the star attraction. He had sung 'on nine occasions, before the Prince of Wales on his recent tour round the world.'

An unbelievably embarrassing, unfunny, monologue, in what today would be regarded rightly as appalling bad taste also made its appearance. It was still going the rounds in the Second World War when it made at least one village child cringe[153] and one hopes it also repelled at least one or two of the Easingwold Town Hall temperance devotees. On this occasion the person who inflicted this deadful stuff on his audience was a Mr Dixon - and he gave it as an encore. 'Mr Dixon with "Down the Vale" caught the popular ear, and subsequently gave "Blow the candle out John." '

In 1902[154] The Temperance Society held the first of its current 'Social Evenings' in a lavishly decorated Town Hall and 200 attended. R.E. Smith covered the evening in a column some ten inches long. Those attending enjoyed a concert followed by refreshments of games draughts, dominoes and ludo.

The temperance movement in the Easingwold area had had a tragedy before the turn of the century. A 'Professor Ray' on a Sunday evening, 'gave a lecture on temperance' at the Town Hall 'interspersed with lime-light views, recitations, and singing.'[155] It was the usual stuff, though the magic lantern was new, but on Saturday 13 February a young lady threw herself under the Pickering to York train shortly after it left Kirkbymoorside.[156] Her head was 'completely severed from her body, which was outside the rails.' She was Ellen Dawson, aged 19 of Kirkbymoorside who worked in service for John Mason Hoggard, a tradesman. An inquest was held on Ellen and Hoggard said she had started visiting Ray's performances, 'a phrenologist, who had been lecturing at Kirkbymoorside' and that he 'observed a marked depression in her demeanour since attending the lectures.' She had gone to see Ray privately and had certainly handed over 12s 6d to him. She then began stealing from her employer, to pay her fees. Prior to Ray's appearance, Hoggard said, he had never missed any money 'and had always considered deceased strictly honest.' She admitted her theft and the coroner's jury was highly critical of the lecturer, bringing in 'a verdict that they were of opinion "that the condition of the deceased's mind was attributable to being under the influence of, and having dealings with, a certain person calling himself "Professor Ray." ' Dr Porter, the coroner, and his jury, regarded Ray as a quack and made their opinion quite obvious.

Temperance movements were prominent in thousands of towns and villages and denunciations of the demon drink were commonplace. Always linked with excessive consumption of alcohol these days are warnings about the dangers of smoking. There were such statements around at the time of the Boer War, but little notice was taken of them. The populace was hooked on 'the weed'.

An advocate of the pleasures and the benefits of smoking was a lady whose story appeared in the *Daily Telegraph*. She was Mrs Ormiston Chant who had been nursing wounded soldiers in Crete, and she told a Sunday afternoon meeting at the Whitfield Tabernacle about her experiences.[157] The nurses, she said,

> had to bear all the sufferings which belonged to campaigning, [and] many a time had she and her colleagues to go without food. On one occasion she was so hungry that she smoked a cigarette. Hitherto she had been under the impression that smoking was a mere useless vice, but having experienced the marvellously soothing effects of tobacco, she could now understand why all men smoked. As the cigarette burned away her hunger was appeased, and for a time she forgot her troubles and was happy.

Mrs Ormiston Chant extolled the virtues and positive benefits of tobacco, and so did no less a person than Professor T. H. Huxley.[158] Addressing a meeting he said he had once 'hated tobacco ...' But then he was converted and he now thought that smoking was a 'comfortable and laudable practice' and, like Mrs Chant, considered it 'productive of good.' There 'is no more harm in a pipe than there is in a cup of tea,' he concluded. This was not the opinion of prominent medical men interviewed for an article in the *Young Man*, however.[159] Dr A. T. Schofield, one of them, wrote that 'no poison on earth can be compared to tobacco poison but prussic acid.'

Prof Huxley must have been a valuable ally for the smoker but the opposition could call on some big names too. In January 1901 Major General Baden-Powell was elected patron of the Western Church League of Health and Manliness, 'an Anti-Smoking Society.'[160] He wrote a circular to members in which he said he thought smoking could lead on to drinking and swearing. The *Lancet* warned readers off, [161] and the *Advertiser* poked fun at the 'Anti-Tobacco Society.'[162]

The *Easingwold Advertiser* devoted much space to the activities of 'the Hunt' when it appeared in the area. It gave over a few of its columns on agricultural matters and always reported the dangerous, regular outbreaks of such things as sheep scab, swine fever and anthrax,[163] but its coverage of the York and Ainsty was huge by comparison with that stuff. Some examples. On Monday 15 February 1897 it met at Sutton Hall and went on at a 'clipping pace' to Low Hawkhills then on to Stillington and North Skeugh Whin. 'Ploughed field after ploughed field were crossed, but still hounds rattled away, giving the field plenty to do to keep on terms with them and then near Stillington Grange they checked suddenly, and all Mr. Green's efforts to hit off the line proved unavailing. The run lasted 45 minutes, and though somewhat of a ring, it was a most enjoyable gallop.' The York and Ainsty met at Easingwold shortly afterwards, but 'The Days' sport was only very poor' with the hounds first making for Peep O'Day Whin then going towards Sessay. On this occasion the paper did its thing by naming as many people involved as possible. There was a 'capital muster of followers,' it said, 'amongst whom we noticed the popular master, Mr Lycett Green', F.J.H. Robinson, Sir G.O. Wombwell, Buller Hicks, Grant Lawson, Dr Gramshaw, and many others.[164] In January 1898 the hunt then viewed a fox in High Carr and ran him to ground in Cass Wood. 'The run only lasted thirteen minutes, but it was top race all the way, and there was plenty of dirty coats to boot before the whoo-whoop was heard.' Then off to Hawkhills, Hawkhills Old Wood and Huby Burn which was 'drawn blank. Dodholme Wood and the rest of the New Parks coverts were tenantless, and then the hounds went home.'[165] Quite clearly this report was written by a participant, as were the many more accounts which appeared in the years covered in this work.

In 1901 an article appeared in the *Advertiser* about the 'commencement' of the York and Ainsty Hunt, reprinted from an edition of *Bailey's Magazine*.[166] It was regularly established, the writer said, in 1818 'and they hunted both fox and hare.' The Ainsty's kennels were once at Easingwold but were then moved to 'opposite the Knavesmire Gate at York' then to Acomb - 'a most inconvenient situation ... within two miles of the Bramham Moor [Hunt].' Sir Charles Slingsby (of Scriven Park) was responsible for the move to Acomb and *Bailey's* heaped praise on him as a 'master, a jockey, a breeder and a leader.' During his mastership he brought the Hunt into great notice' and got the support of many influential landowners and politicians. J. S. Strangwayes, hunted regularly with the Y and A and Thomas Clayton 'of Stainley Hall, who always walked a puppy for Sir Charles, to whom Orvis said "We don't want your money, sir, but a few more like you to walk some young hounds for us."'[167] Mr Clayton says 'that all other sports vanish into thin air compared with fox-hunting.'

Eventually tragedy hit the Ainsty and led to a change at the top. In October 1901 *The Candid Friend* published a long poem about 'A MEMORABLE DAY WITH THE YORK AND AINSTY FOXHOUNDS' with a prefatory note.[168] The lines were said to have been found among the papers of G.W. Nelson of the Manor House, York, and the introduction said 'Sir George Wombwell succeeded Sir Charles Slingsby in the Mastership of the York and Ainsty Hounds ... [and] readers may remember how that well-known sportsman met his death, he being drowned, with his huntsman, whip, and several friends by the upsetting of a ferry-boat crossing the Ouse in flood. Sir George ... was one of the very few survivors of this tragic affair.' The poem told the story of the ferry which, a note said, was '9½ yards long by 3½ yards wide,' and had plenty of space. A verse said

> Full soon the wherry-boat contained,
> Within its ample space,

Sir Charles and ten more men,[169] with steeds,
Intent upon the chase.

What caused the accident? Sir Charles Slingsby's 'old and favourite hunter' Saltfish 'Grew restive, kicked and shied', reared, went overboard and then 'madly plunged Beneath the surging tide.' Slingsby was 'dragged into the deep' and 'The boat capsized.'

Four boats were brought, the river searched;
Alas! 'twas all in vain:
Six bodies to the surface came,
That ne'er would breathe again.
Eight horses, too, were drowned that day,
Of purest hunting blood:
Old Saltfish, who had caused the woe,
Was rescued from the flood.

The hunts were a considerable source of employment in many areas and they provided enjoyable, free, colourful spectacles.

A more modern spectacle took place in 1900. The national Auto Mobile Club had organised a '1000 Miles Trial' which would be watched with great interest the readers of the Easingwold paper were told in a column immediately under one headed 'CAPTURE OF BLOEMFONTEIN'. 'The run,' it went on will, 'be from London to Edingburgh [sic] and back.' On Monday 7 May the automobilists were scheduled to start from the High Level Bridge at Newcastle at 7 am and go through Durham, Darlington, York and Tadcaster and end up at 'Leeds (Briggate, Exhibition).'[170] The progress through Easingwold provided a rare spectacle - in the shape of things to come.[171]

Beckwith's shop, Long Street, Easingwold, early 1900s

ON Monday last quite a commotion was caused in Easingwold by the passing through of the Motor Cars taking part in the 1,000 miles test promoted by the Auto-Mobile Club. The first car passed shortly after twelve o'clock, and then continued to arrived [sic] at intervals the whole of the afternoon. Large crowds collected in Long Street, a good many taking a half day holiday.

There could be no better demonstration of the fact that the motor car age was arriving than the trial through Easingwold. Soon motorists, their cars, and their misdemeanours became regular features of the local news. Earlier in January 1897 'THE Mail Cart plying between Huby and Easingwold Post Office, has been overturned in Uppleby' when on a 'very dark morning' frightened by a motor car, 'the horse swerved' and the upset occurred.[172] Whether this accident prompted action to modernise the service or not is not known, maybe the authorities were already considering an alternative to horse drawn methods, but whatever started it, a change was made. It was decided to motorise the deliveries, and readers of the paper were told what with: 'THE Motor to be used for the conveyance of Mails between Easingwold and Huby will be a six horse power Benz make.'[173] This could well have been the first use of a car for commercial purposes in Easingwold - and the very week before the announcement that it was to be a 'Benz' there appeared another story of a mail cart incident.[174]

RUNAWAY HORSE. - On Sunday evening last, the horse attached to the Mail Cart which runs between Easingwold and Alne, being evidently left unfastened, bolted on the approach of the train and coming into collision with a telegraph post on the Easingwold road and [sic] broke both shafts off the cart. Luckily no one was in the vehicle at the time and no serious damage was done.

Who was responsible for the introduction of motorised deliveries in Easingwold? It was announced in November that [175]

Mr Sydney Smith, Post Office, Easingwold has secured the contract for the conveyance of the mails between Easingwold and Huby. The work is to be done by means of a motor-car.

The roads of the Easingwold area were dangerous enough as the drivers of the mail carts would have testified, and the advent of the motor car, for pleasure as well as business, did nothing to improve matters. It was not long before 'Motor Scorching' - speeding - featured on the court lists. In May 1901 someone who should have behaved better got a lot of unwelcome - if justified - publicity for vastly exceeding the speed limit.[176] John Ernest Hutton, a Justice of the Peace, of Northallerton 'was summoned for driving a light locomotive ... at a greater speed than 14 miles an hour on Easter Day last.' It was said Hutton's car reached a speed of 35 miles an hour, and speeding was not all. 'A railway signalman said the defendant scattered a wedding party ... and nearly ran over a child. The Bench imposed a maximum fine of £10, with £3 17s 6d costs, the Chairman remarking that this was one of the worst cases that had been brought before them.' It probably was, but cases like it rapidly became common as drivers ignored the law, put their foot down and scorched. On 28 October 1901 at Thirsk E. R. Turton 'and a full bench' sat in judgement on C. Johnson, 'secretary for the Automobile Company Whitehall Court London.'[177] He was charged 'with driving a light locomotive on Topcliffe-road to the danger of persons travelling thereon' on the 23rd August. He was also charged with refusing to stop his motor car 'when requested.' Johnson was living dangerously as well as driving dangerously and was found guilty 'and ... fined £10 on each of the two charges, and costs', and quite right too. There were several other cases at the Thirsk court before the end of the year.[178]

A fatal accident was bound to happen and on Sunday 13 July 1902 Mr Francis Pulleyn of Carlton Husthwaite, aged 74, a retired farmer, became one of the first victims - if not the first - to be killed in the Easingwold area by a motor car. It happened on the road to Thirkleby from Carlton Husthwaite. Mr Pulleyn had been tending his cattle and had climbed on a gate to help him get on his horse. As he did so a car driven by William Boulton of Leeds appeared. The horse took fright 'and threw Mr Pulleyn to the ground. The result was that the deceased was run over and killed.' The vehicle that killed him was 'a French car, worth £400, made by the Gladiator Company.'[179]

> An inquest at The Black Lion Hotel, Carlton Husthwaite found a verdict of "Accidental death," and added to it the rider that "beyond the evidence of the occupants of the car there is nothing to show what amount of care was used to avoid the accident".

The Carlton Husthwaite inquest jury was clearly unhappy about the Pulleyn case, and members of it would have noticed that the driver whose car killed the old farmer had been charged at Huntingdon magistrates court with a serious motoring offence, *just the day before the tragedy at Carlton Husthwaite.* A report headed 'THE CARLTON HUSTHWAITE MOTOR FATALITY' appeared,[180] which questioned the defendant's honesty about his driving record. At Huntingdon Police Court ... Mr. Wm. Boulton, of Glebe Terrace, Headingley, Leeds was summoned for driving a motor car at a greater speed than twelve miles an hour on the Great North Road near Huntingdon, on July 12th. There was no defence.

Motor scorchers were also dealt with at Easingwold in 1902 and their dreadful behaviour was reported under a sub heading headed 'THE MOTOR CAR CRUSADE.' J. Swainston Strangwayes, Rawdon Thornton and Capt D'Arcy Strangwayes began their day's work on Wednesday 24 September[181] by transferring the licenses of 'The White Dog', Stillington, 'The Green Tree', Easingwold, and 'The Queen of Trumps', Huby. The next cases were those alleging motor scorching. First of all James Broughton Dugdale of Wroxhall Abbey, Warwickshire was dealt with in his absence. Dugdale, a county councillor and a JP, was charged with driving a motor car furiously on the highway between York and Easingwold on 5 September. Evidence was given by PCs Grainger and Richardson who were on duty 'on the highway near Shipton, about 1-30 p.m. They measured a quarter of a mile,' and shortly afterwards the defendant came along in his car. He was stopped and told he had 'covered the quarter mile in time equal to 19 1/2 miles an hour. Defendant ... said he knew he was going a little too fast.' Inspector Pickering used the opportunity of the Dugdale case to tell those present that a blitz on scorchers was under way. He 'stated that these proceedings had been taken by [sic] the instructions of the Chief Constable, who had received many complaints' about the manner 'in which motor cars were being driven on the highways.'

For his offences Dugdale was fined £5 and 15s costs, then Arthur Watson, cycle agent of Stockton, was dealt with.[182] PC Sayer gave evidence that Watson went along the Easingwold to York road at 18 miles an hour; he was fined £5 and 10s costs.

There were several organisations as concerned as the Chief Constable about the motor car, and the Helmsley District Council was among the most reactionary among them. 'A strongly worded resolution' was passed by it and circulated to the County Council, Members of Parliament 'and each District Council'. 'MOTOR CARS. HELMSLEY DISTRICT COUNCIL ON THE "WAR PATH" an *Advertiser* sub heading said. The resolution got some modest support, but the Chairman poured scorn on it. '... to talk of banishing motor-cars off the roads was simply ridiculous', he said, 'They had come to stay, and had a perfect right on the road so long as they were driven reasonably, and did not interfere with the safety of others using the roads.' His right hand man agreed, and so did the Council. 'The Vice-Chairman

York and Ainsty South Hunt, 1884, Market Place, Easingwold.
The house on the right used to be The Vicarage and was demolished when the Galtres was built.

also thought it a ridiculous resolution, and moved that it be laid on the table.'[183] That is what happened to it.

It was just a matter of time before local bus services were established and Easingwold benefitted from one before the end of 1898, the journeys on which would have seemed endless if the drivers kept to the law about speed. An announcement about a new - rather skeletal - service was made in October.

> On Monday afternoon Mr G. Handyside's Newcastle and Sheffield Motor Car passed through Easingwold. From the circular which has been issued we gather that the Motor Car is intended to run every week from Newcastle to Sheffield, and will pass through Easingwold on Wednesdays about noon.

What kind of services were there that would, eventually, be forced out of business by the likes of Handyside? One featured in a case at the York County Court. Then R. H. Vernon Wragge, a prominent York politician, a barrister, a councillor and sometime Lord Mayor, appeared representing Thomas Jarvis of York who brought an action against Henry Slater, a bus owner of Sutton-on-Forest for damages for injuries received by being run over on the road between York and Sutton.

The jury found 'for the plaintiff with damages of £350 and Mr Wragg's application for payment forthwith was allowed.'

The county court case ruined the carrier, and on 21 June the *Advertiser* recorded his downfall.

> FARMER'S FAILURE. - The first meeting of creditors of Henry Slater, of Sutton-on-the-Forest, lately farmer and carrier, but now of no occupation, against whom a receiving order was made on the 30th ult., was held in the offices of the Official Receiver, York, on Monday. The debtor ... returned the amount of his liabilities expected to rate for dividend at £427.19s.9d. He estimated his assets at £8.2s, of which sum £7.1s.9d was due to preferential creditors, leaving a balance of £1.0s.3d. and a deficiency of £426.19s.6d which the debtor explained as follows:- "Judgement for £350 and costs for personal injuries by an accident obtained against me by Mr. Jarvis and by the death of horses." No trustee was appointed and the estate remains in the hands of the Official Receiver for administration.

How many carriers were there in the Easingwold area? *Bulmers of 1890 listed just one and his timetable.*

CARRIER

> Adams (omnibus), to York, on Saturdays, from the York Hotel, at 8 a.m., returning from the White Horse Inn, Bootham, at 4 p.m.; to Thirsk, on Mondays, at 8 a.m., and returning from Mrs. C. Bosomworth's, Market Place, Thirsk at 4 p.m.

The motor car was well established by the turn of the century and the writing was on the wall for the carriers, and there was another form of locomotion which might well make the generalisations about rural isolation less than absolute. This was the bicycle which could extend the horizons of a country boy enormously. No longer was he - if he owned a bike - restricted to his own immediate locality and the distance he was prepared to walk home.

Because of this the cycle is of enormous importance in social history, but how many people owned and used them? There are no statistics, but evidence of the popularity (and use) of the bike is not totally absent. The number of cycle agents in the town of Easingwold must, surely, be some indicator. The best-known, without a doubt, was M. Reynard, the cycle works, the Market Place.

Reynard did a tremendous amount of advertising in the *Easingwold*, sometimes taking up the double column mid page slot which the casual reader might have thought was the sole preserve of that busy member of the Easingwold community Francis E. Rookledge. In April Francis E. was pushing Trents Family Pills and Parkin's Compound Balsam of Linseed ('one of the best Mixtures made for Coughs, Colds, Asthma, Bronchitis, Influenza, Shortness of Breath, Loss of Voice, and all Disease [sic] of the Throat, Chest and Lungs, arising from Cold. GIVE IT A TRIAL')[184] while Reynard had two major sales pitches on the front page. In the first he advertised the 'LUXURIOUS SWIFT', which retailed at various prices from 'TEN GUINEAS', and he illustrated his description with a line drawing of a bike. From it, he said, the 'superiority' of the Swift was 'immediately recognisable.' Reynard's other ad showed him indulging in a 'funny' sales pitch, something he often did. This box advert, however, contained information about Reynard's business, stock, and prices. '"Duke's Son, Cook's Son, Son of a Belted Earl,"' Reynard, said, 'If they are cyclists, cannot but admit that M. REYNARD has the most up-to-date and Best Cycles in Yorkshire'. He did repairs, sold accessories, hired bikes out, and taught people how to ride them. He gave a price list.

Star Cycles,	from £8.10.0
Swift	10.10.0
Triumph	10.10.0
Flying Arrow	9.10.0
Rudge-Whitworth	10.10.0

Another price list from Reynard contained a list of 14 bikes 'NEW AND SECOND HAND to clear off at ... low prices.' They ranged from £4 to ten guineas.

Gents' Syrus, Palmer Tyres, New, B.S.A. Fittings	10.10.0
Gents' Syrus, Warwick Tyres, New, B.S.A. Fittings	9.15.0
Premier, Helical Tubing Dunlop Tyres	5.0.0
Lady's Goodby, Warwick Tyres	4.10.0
Lady's Goodby, Woodley Tyres	5.10.0
Lady's Buckingham & Adams, Nice Machine	4.0.0

It looks as if the Lady's Buckingham & Adams was Reynard's best buy and the impression one gets is that buying a bike was not beyond the means of most people - even those agricultural labourers who lived in and were asked to go and spend their 'Martinmas money' in Easingwold.

Bulmer's guide of 1890 does not contain a mention of the Mark Reynard business and it seems that he might have commenced trading and repairing seven years later. An announcement of March 1897 appeared which suggests the town had been leafleted about some new bikes, then given more information about where they could be bought[185]

Now we *shan't* be long.
THE
WIN CYCLES
HAVE ARRIVED FROM LONDON
MARK REYNARD
MARKET PLACE, EASINGWOLD,
Is the Sole Agent for the district
Machines by several other makers
of the very best.

Reynard's 'Now we shan't be long' advertisement appeared regularly in the *Advertiser*, then it was changed. In July a block said he was a 'CYCLE AGENT' indeed, but that primarily he was an 'IRONMONGER & GENERAL MACHINIST' selling and repairing 'IRONMONGERY of every discription' but singling out Chaff Cutters and 'wringing machines' for special mention.[186] For some reason or other Reynard's cycle advertisements disappeared altogether for a time and what publicity he did concentrated on the general ironmongery and the cartridges he had in stock for the shooting season.[187] Then, in February 1898, he expanded. He explained in an ad. 'TO CYCLISTS, TRIUMPHS, SWIFTS, RUDGE-WHITWORTH'S, BRADBURY'S, WIN-CYCLES &C. MARK REYNARD WISHES to thank his numerous customers for their kind patronage, and begs to inform them that he has been appointed AGENT for the above well-known machines.'

At the time that Reynard was cutting down on his advertising there was great depression in the cycle industry, something highlighted by a deputation to the Coventry Board of Guardians from a local Trades Council. It said that in the manufacturing area there were 'about 2000 unemployed, mostly belonging to the cycle trade.' The average wage of a 'cycle

One of Easingwold's earlier cars ...? one horse power? ... Now the site of G. F. Baker (Electrical) Ltd.

hand' for the past 16 months 'had not exceeded £1 a week.'[188] But if these troubles in some way affected local trade they passed and it was not long before there was an amazing upsurge in the popularity of cycling. The prices of new bikes (or some of them) have been given, but owning one became a matter of prime importance. Reynard never mentioned 'easy terms' in his ads but he almost certainly had arrangements for 'tick' payments on a weekly basis. Whether he did or not people got machines and, as has been said, the bike was a great liberating force and extremely popular.[189]

Reynard diversified just a little (and began to plug other parts of his service) towards the end of 1899. His business was now titled the Easingwold Cycle Works and his adverts had a logo at the top of them with the capital letters CC surrounded by an announcement that Mark's place was now a 'FREE INFLATING STATION'. He also told readers of the paper that he had 'Sewing Machines by good makers, from £2 upwards [and] Guns at all PRICES'. He also plugged the fact that he dealt in second hand machines. On 14 June 1902 he pushed his various skills and products, one of which looks extremely interesting. He said that 'ENAMELLING AND PLATING', could be done 'AT SHORT NOTICE', and not only that. He had a new line. He had

A few Wheeler and Wilson's and Bradbury's
Sewing Machines to clear at low prices
Accessories of all descriptions
Guns, Ammunition, &c
MOTOR CYCLES BUILT TO ORDER.

There is plenty of evidence of the popularity of cycling at the end of the century in the columns of the Easingwold paper used by Reynard. For example in an edition that gave the residents of Easingwold the welcome news that 'The wolf which has caused such consternation in this district during the past week or two, has been captured' there appeared a note that said the Easingwold and District Cycling Club would hold its annual general meeting on 1 April at the Angel Hotel.[190] At this a programme of 'runs' was announced and Mr. A. W. Shaw presented the club with a bugle(!). A little later the paper announced that 'CYCLING in this district seems to be greatly on the increase especially amongst the ladies.'[191] Now the state of the highways led to protests, and the bikers acted as a pressure group. In one of the papers in which Reynard's list of bargains appeared there was a note saying that now that the cycling season was close at hand bikers, more than ever, wished the roads had been properly rolled. The 'long awaited' council steam roller should have been obtained by now and should have been at work on the roads during the winter.[192] The editor agreed and added his voice to the demands for the RDC to get modern. 'The next thing the Easingwold Rural District Council will have to obtain,' he wrote, 'is a steam roller, then there will be no complaints as to the quantity of loose or large stones on the roads.'

Reynard's witty adverts however continued;

I AM NOT INTERESTED IN
TOBACCO TRUSTS,
STEEL TRUSTS, AND THE LIKE
BUT IF YOU
REQUIRE ANYTHING IN THE
CYCLE LINE
I AM INTERESTED
As you will see if you give me a call.

He ended this bout of advertising on a medical tack. 'If your old Machine is a little out of sorts', he said, 'send it round and have it overhauled before the rush comes, as I expect it to be a busy season.'

Reynard's business benefited from new lighting regulations that came in at the end of 1900. Mark rapidly announced he could cater for the new need, and on 5 January 1901, and regularly thereafter, he told readers of Smith's paper he could do so.

NOTICE!
COUNTY COUNCIL LAMP REGULATION.
M. REYNARD
Has the largest Stock of Lamps in Easingwold,
at the best possible prices.
CARRIAGE LAMPS, COMPLETE, FROM
7/- PER PAIR.
CART LAMPS FROM 1/6 EACH
Oil for Cart Lamps, Carriage Candles, &c.,
in Stock
Lamps fitted on Carts and Carriages, at the
Shortest Notice.
My Burning Oil is a Special Preparation,
and will give no trouble,
no smoke, no smell.
CARRIAGE LAMPS WITH PARAFFIN
BURNERS AT LOWEST PRICES.
GIVE ME A TRIAL.
EASINGWOLD CYCLE WORKS,
MARKET PLACE.

At the end of December the police leafleted the North Riding about 'THE NEW BYE-LAW ... in force from and after the 11th day of December 1900.' It provided that 'Every person who shall cause or permit any vehicle to be in any street or highway between one hour after sunset and one hour before sunrise, from' 1 October to 31 May, shall provide the 'same with a lamp or lamps so constructed and capable of being attached as when lighted to show the front a white light visible within a reasonable distance to persons meeting or approaching the vehicle. If only one lamp is so provided, it shall be attached 'to the off or right side of the vehicle.' If a load - like timber - projected more than six feet at the back then a red rear light had to be used. Every driver was responsible for keeping the new lights 'properly trimmed, lighted, and attached.' Any person contravening the new regulations 'shall be liable' to a penalty not exceeding forty shillings.

There is no lack of evidence to substantiate the *Advertiser* editor's complaints about the state of the Easingwold roads. Letters to the press were not regular features in his paper, but in August he printed one from 'A RATEPAYER' from Stillington who said he wanted to draw the attention of the District Councillors to the disgraceful state of the roads about Stillington, especially the back lane and the main road leading to Easingwold. They were he said, literally covered with loose stones as if sown broadcast out of a hopper. There will be an accident, and only then would 'something ... be done not befor'. Ratepayer continued

'Where is the footpath leading from Stillington to Easingwold that was promised some time ago, and, if I mistake not, the money granted to carry it out?' He suggested a public meeting should be called to pressurise the RDC.[193] On 7 December 1901, in response to requests from readers the local paper published a complaint about 'the disgraceful state of the Husthwaite road, from Peep O' Day Whin' to the village of Husthwaite. 'In its present condition it is nearly impossible for cyclists to travel [on it], and traps and other conveyances have a very rough time.' Some opted to ride on the path instead and run the risk of a fine.

The crime of riding a bike on the footpath angered readers of the *Advertiser*, and a writer who signed himself 'A PEDESTRIAN' had his complaints published by Reginald Ernest Smith (12 November 1898). He was surprised at recent decisions by the Justices sitting at Easingwold, he said. He wanted the administration of the law about bikes on footpaths administered with 'discrimination and common-sense'. He wanted the police to recognise that the roads, were a 'public scandal', and to let people who rode on the paths go on doing so. No-one cares about the roads, he said, but ' the cops come down heavily on those who try to avoid them.'

Old Pedestrian's remarks have a very modern ring about them, but that was not all. 'Now that the hunting season' has started, he said, the police should have their attention drawn to the 'troops of horsemen' who trespass on the footpaths, making them 'as bad or worse than ploughed fields, not only to the discomfort of pedestrians, but to the danger to life and limb of women and children who mostly use them.' Prosecute them as well, he said, otherwise it will 'only add to the ridicule which the unequal administration of the law occasions, not always without some justification.' Quite right.

Mr Geo. Weighell - Carter - from Raskelf Station

Old Pedestrian warmed to his subject early on in his letter and seemed to suggest that the authorities went easy on some malefactors. He was not a master of the written word, but asked, rhetorically, 'Will the police show as much haste to report, it may be a Docto:, [sic] a Lawyer or a Country Squire for riding on the footpath, and if so, will the justices as eagerly convict?' Well they did on at least one occasion.

In the column next to Pedestrian's letter in the *Easingwold* was a story about the local personality who was responsible for getting a telegraph office established at Stillington. He appeared before the magistrates and was fined. What for? For riding his bike on the footpath! His court appearance was reported on 7 April 1900, and his case occupied the attention of a very powerful bench.

> Mr J S Strangwayes presided, and the other magistrates present were Messrs H Hawking and H C Fairfax-Cholmeley. Dr Gramshaw of Stillington, was charged by Police-Constable Walker with riding a bicycle on the highway at Sutton-on-the-Forest, on the 9th of last month, at one a.m., without having a light. The defendant stated that he had to leave home in haste to attend a patient, and could not find his lamp. Fined 10s including the costs.

Ratepayer from Stillington (like Pedestrian) urged that public meetings be held to lobby the local highway authority for better roads. In 1899 a pressure group to do so on a national scale was started. 'Bicyclists in particular' and the users of highways in general will be interested in learning that an association bearing the title of the 'Roads Improvement Association has been incorporated', it was reported.[194]

In spite of the dreadful state of the local roads the Easingwold Cycling Club held an impressive programme of 'runs' and it was not long before competitions were organised and records established and challenged. For example[195] from the same column that announced the establishment of Handysides' Newcastle to Sheffield via Easingwold bus service.

> Mr C F Pool, of York, earned one of the Star Cycling Club's medals on Saturday last, riding from York to Boroughbridge, Thirsk and Easingwold, and back to the city, 51 miles, in 3 hours 5 minutes. This is ten minutes within the time allowed, and the second best performance accomplished over the route.

Not all cyclists were as careful (or as fast) as Mr Pool. The local county court, in June 1899, dealt with the results of a two bike head-on crash in the Thirsk Market Place. As a result Arthur E. Barnes, Inspector of Nuisances for the Thirsk Union 'sued T. Lloyd Greame, of Brafferton Hall, Helperby, for £2 15s 0d for damages caused by the defendant wrongfully running into and damaging' his bike. Just opposite the Assembly Rooms, Barnes said, Greame smacked into him. He was on the wrong side of the road, and, a witness said, took the corner 'at something like 14 miles an hour.'[196] The speed merchant was represented by the well-known Norman Crombie of York, whose defence was that the plaintiff 'was [also] riding at a furious rate.' The judge summed up and expedited matters with some comments about biking. 'His Honour', Judge Templer,

> without asking Mr Crombie to address him,[197] after hearing the evidence of the defendant, considered the evidence of the plaintiff himself, and also that of one of his witnesses, the fact of him going at the rate of 14 miles an hour was ... dangerous. He considered eight miles an hour fast enough round such a dangerous turn as the Castlegate corner, and he could not accuse the defendant of negligence therefore he should give a verdict for the defendant with costs.

Easingwold Salvation Army Band, early 1900s. Billy Sweep playing the big drum.

The Barnes/Greame case seems an extraordinary one. The roads were not blamed in it, however, but they were held responsible at an inquest on a distinguished local figure.[198] It was held at Welburn 'on the body of Major Barstow, of Garrow Hill, who was killed whilst cycling at Crambeck Bridge.' The coroner made strong comments on the road and the jury, in returning a verdict of accidental death, said the attention of the authorities should be called to its state. A very short time later another accident occurred at the very place 'where Major Barstow had been killed a few days before.'[199]William Oxley of Leeds was riding down the hill and approaching Crambeck Bridge from the north when he skidded, fell off and broke his arm. He was 'riding without a brake and his feet on the foot rests' when, trying to avoid a 'conveyance', he got 'on the "bevelled" side of the road' and came off. Cycling was frequently presented as good for health - and so it was - but it got some bad publicity when the Rev Alexander Brown collapsed and died at the beginning of a cycle tour.[200]

The examples given of bike accidents due to 'riding furiously', riding with poorly maintained machines or, one suspects, sometimes riding furiously because rather a lot of beer had been consumed by the rider, were all taken from the local Easingwold paper which is still in existence. It was, to give it its full title, *The Easingwold Advertiser and Weekly News* but was, and is, known everywhere as *The Easingwold Advertiser*. What was a typical issue like? It never changed in any fundamental way, and the issue of 9 March 1901, for example, was very much like it was at the commencement of the period being considered. It was 'No. 479', cost one penny, and the front page of the paper was still devoted primarily to advertisements.[201] It was 'Printed and Published by REGINALD ERNEST SMITH, at his Printing Offices, Market Place, Easingwold, in the County of York.'

The front page consisted of five columns with most of the ads covering one, and in the issue chosen here only John Smiths Celebrated Tadcaster Ales and Stouts had a double column spread. Much of the rest was taken up with forthcoming sales of farming stock and there was a 'WANTED, TO LET, FOR SALE &c, &c.' section. There followed a 'Reynard' ad saying[202]

IF YOU'RE IN LOVE -
THAT'S YOUR BUSINESS!
IF YOU'RE GETTING MARRIED -
THAT'S SENSIBLE BUSINESS!
IF YOU WANT A CYCLE -
THAT'S MY BUSINESS

Reynard said the market was then flooded with 'cheap and nasty' cycles and his ad was followed by one from G. T. Sturdy, for plants, and another from a Sturdy competitor, Bell's Nurseries ('Entrance opposite Railway Station'), and several from drapers. There were others, including one from 'G.H. Smith's Wine and Spirit stores, Market Place.' This was fairly typical of the stuff one saw in local papers of the time.

The items on the inside pages of the *Advertiser* appeared under self explanatory headings like 'Farming Notes' and 'Gardening Gossip' and there was always good coverage of the local government bodies in the area - the RDCs, the Boards of Guardians, and so on. Proceedings in the magistrates courts were always dealt with briefly and two pages usually covered political issues and carried a chapter of a serial. On 9 March this was titled 'Edith's Escape' by Louis Sand. Adverts were used on those pages and on the day when chapter seven of 'Edith's' was produced there was a regular which on this occasion warned customers against fakes.

In order to avoid danger of
SUBSTITUTION
take care that the full name,
Dr Williams' Pink Pills
for Pale People
is on the package - the appearance of which is
shown here - Pink wrapper, wording in red.

The advertisement went on in a most encouraging way, saying Dr. Williams' Pink Pills have cured paralysis, locomotor ataxy, rheumatism, and sciatica, rickets, consumption anaemia, weakness, palpitations, nervous exhaustion and hysteria. These pills are a tonic, not a purgative.

The page that contained the modest claims for Dr Williams' Pinks also carried an illustrated item saying that 'The medals for South Africa [were] being manufactured.' The illustration was of both sides of the medal, a line drawing as were all those used in the *Advertiser* then. The bulk of the paper was obviously bought in.

The back page of the *Advertiser* was given over to local news, and reports from the villages, and from them it is possible to know exactly what went on in the Easingwold parish and the neighbouring areas. No concert went unnoticed it seemed, no sporting event was ignored, everyone involved in everything got a mention. Nothing left out; nobody left out. It must have been good for the paper's circulation.

No reader of the press at the turn of the century could have long remained unaware of a series of small ads which always appeared. These were for abortificants, and they might surprise some who have believed stories about Victorian coyness and prudery, but there was a perceived need for the products of people like E. T. Towle. Penny Royal was well-known for its properties and Towle left readers in no doubt what they were. He included the standard warning about other similar products.[203]

The most prolific advertiser among the producers of pills for ladies was one P. Blanchard, On the back page of the same paper appeared two more small ads, one from him. His copy was usually headed 'BLANCHARD'S FEMALE PILLS' but not on this occasion. The maker made bold claims for them being safe and one hundred per cent effective. What more could he claim?

TOWLE'S PENNY ROYAL & STEEL PILLS
FOR FEMALES
QUICKLY CORRECT ALL IRREGULARITIES, REMOVE
ALL OBSTRUCTIONS, and relieve the distressing
symptoms so prevalent with the sex.
Boxes, 1¹/₂ & 2/9 (the latter contains three times
the quantity), [from]
all Chemists, [can] be sent anywhere,
on receipt of 15 or 34 stamps,
by the Maker - E.T. TOWLE,
Chemist, Nottingham.
Beware of Imitations, injurious and worthless.

Easingwold Small Bore Rifle Club - May 25th, 1908 at the Galtres includes Boer War veterans Pte. Wheatley and Sgt. Crosby wearing their South African campaign medals.

EVERY WOMAN

> SHOULD send two stamps for our 32 page Illustrated Book, containing valuable information how all Irregularities and Obstructions may be entirely avaided [sic] or removed by simple means. Recommended by eminent Physicians, as The only Safe, Sure, and Genuine Remedy, Never Fails. Thousands of Testimonials. Mr. P. BLANCHARD, Forest Road, Dalston, London.

Next to Blanchard's ad was one for C. J. D. Richardson's 'Artificial Ear Drums' and next to that was yet another of interest to women, making a total of eight such items in this one issue of the *Easingwold*. The first, on the front page, was for 'SMITH'S STRONGEST FEMALE PILLS [which would] Quickly and Certainly remove all OBSTRUCTIONS and IRREGULARITIES where all others fail. Guaranteed the best on earth. 2/6 and 4/- per case, post free, privately packed.' The last was from Madame Marie - and the prevalence of French names in these things will have been noted. Marie plugged the French Connection for all she was worth.

> LADIES 'Nothing Succeeds Like Success!! At last I have discovered a Remedy for FEMALE AILMENTS, Irregularities, Obstructions, which is Safe, Speedy, Harmless and Sure, and has met with Unbounded Success, in hundreds of cases, when all others have failed. Before sending elsewhere, write me enclosing stamped envelope for full particulars of my famous French Remedy, which will cure the more obstinate obstructions. By doing so you will save worry, trouble and expense. - MADAME MARIE, 12, Evandale Road, London, S.W.

Several examples have been given of frank ads from people like Madame Marie - all for women, of course. But men had their troubles too. Were they neglected by the patent medicine merchants and the advertisers? They were not. There were remedies for male complaints. In the autumn of 1901, an ad for one appeared regularly, headed 'Lost Manhood' with the second word in heavy type an inch high. It could be obtained from a London address and had miraculous powers. Thousands had been cured of 'DREADFUL MALADIES'. Some were named, and they were pretty explicit: 'It cures NERVOUS DEBILITY, Loss of Energy, Melancholy, Lost Manhood, Youthful Imprudence, Exhausted Vitality, Spermatorrhoea, Variocele, Premature Decay, Despondency ... Noises in the Ears ... and all Diseases of the Urinary Organs. It is a guaranteed remedy ... and sufferers are invited to write for ... particulars and judge for themselves.' Similar claims were put forward for similar complaints in another that appeared on 3 July 1897. It was a transatlantic cure and it was free to sufferers, though there was sure to have been a catch somewhere.

GREAT AMERICAN
PRESCRIPTION
TWENTY YEARS' RESEARCH has brought to light
a guaranteed Remedy for NERVOUS DEBILITY,
the Errors of Youth, Lost Manhood, Spermatorrhoea,
Variencele, Weakness, Dimness of Sight, Bladder, Gravel,
Kidney, Liver Complaints, and all Diseases of the Urinary Organs.
This Prescription is in the hands of a Minister, who will befriend anyone
suffering from these enervating diseases. It has

CURED THOUSANDS.
Merely send self addressed stamped envelope to the
Rev DAVID JONES, Ray Villa, Lewes, England, when the
Prescription will be sent FREE OF CHARGE.
Name this Paper.

Towle had many competitors. On 9 April 1898 there were numerous remedies on offer. Towle's was recommended and so was that from Leslie Martyn. In addition to these, there was a long puff for 'THE "LADY MONTROSE" MIRACULOUS FEMALE TABULES' while Madame Frain of Hackney Road, London, touted for something that was 'INDISPENSABLE TO LADIES' particularly those who desire a quick safe and reliable and non-injurious remedy 'for certain obstructions' and irregularities, 'a medicine which cures'. Most of the advertisements for these products, incidentally, were, as one might expect small - the advertisers would say discreet - and they were usually tucked away on a back page, but not always. Those from Madame Frain and the The Lady Montrose cure, for example, were very prominently displayed with the latter having a six inch single column boxed spread with 'LADIES ONLY' printed in heavy type an inch high. Madame Frain's ad was only marginally smaller. No hiding the message here.[204]

R. E. Smith's weekly also carried a large number of advertisements for cures for more respectable complaints than those mentioned above. In those days one treated oneself, and the majority of people - certainly the working class - put their faith in home-made remedies or stuff bought over the counter. It must have been a huge market. George Coverdale of York,[205] for example, spent enormous sums on advertising his products and on more than one occasion warned readers that the 'flu was 'becoming very prevalent again' and that they should protect themselves and avoid 'a violent attack'. How? By simply taking Coverdale's Influenza Mixture. One 'or two Bottles will completely effect a cure' said the blurb for it, which started off by urging CIM as a prevention but was now selling it as a cure. How much would this cost? It was 'sold in Bottles 1s.6d; Double Size 2s.9d each. Postage 4d extra.' Just above this Coverdale sales pitch, there was another for 'Warner's Safe Cure for Kidney and Urinary Diseases' - the 'only remedy which cures BRIGHT'S DISEASE. "Look to your Kidneys and Good Health will be Yours."'

The best known of Easingwold's chemists, was F. E. Rookledge. He advertised even more frequently than did Mark Reynard, and in the issue of the *Advertiser* which pushed the Coverdale influenza cure, Rookledge announced that 'PARKIN'S Compound Balsam of Linseed is the best Mixture made for Coughs, Colds, Asthma, Bronchitis, Influenza, Shortness of Breath, Loss of Voice, and all Diseases of the Throat, Chest and Lungs, arising from Cold.'

Rookledge also sold animal medicines ('Wiley's Chemical Essence will Cure Lameness in Horses') which he seems to have made himself and his business was something of a general store. He was also a newsagent and when there was a bit of competition started a delivery service. He also started selling cartridges, using aggressive advertising which suggests it was directed at a competitor. He sold 'All British-made Goods. No Foreign Rubbish. Quality the first consideration.' Always on the look-out for a new line to advertise and attract attention Rookledge began selling Dr Tibble's Vi-Cocoa, for which the whole of Easingwold was no doubt extremely grateful. Thousands of pounds must have been spent over the years and throughout the country plugging Dr Tibble's Vi. Rookledge seems to have commenced stocking the wonder drink in 1898, and on 5 March of that year readers of the *Easingwold* were told about the product in a long announcement headed

THE THE
PUBLIC TRADE
AND
DR TIBBLES'
VI-COCOA

Then followed a public notice saying that Rookledge and John Earnshaw, Grocer, Market Street, had become Easingwold agents for Dr Tib's product. A little homily said that 'By nourishing the body, the cheeks become rosy and plump, whilst the strength and nervous energy thus gained are the natural outcome of increased vitality.' Dr Tibble's Vi-Cocoa it was claimed was invaluable, 'as a food beverage, it was pleasant and palatable and built up strength.'

A trade list from the first decade of the 20th century said the purveyor in Easingwold of Vi Cocoa was a 'pharmaceutical chemist & stationer, sole maker of Wiley's chemical essence for lameness in horses, & agent to Barclay & Co. Ltd. bankers' and that his father had been tragically killed when the horse in his carriage bolted, throwing him into the road. Despite Drs Hicks and Gramshaw rapidly attending to him he died of his dreadful injuries about a week later. He was 70 years of age and 'a prominent member and class leader of the Wesleyan Methodist Church ... He was for several years Agent to the York Union Banking Company, at Easingwold, and he also held other important offices.' One of these was treasurer to the Board of Guardians, a post to which his son was unanimously elected in 1899.[206]

It was Rookledge who led the protests about the state of the town's market place, and he was active (as was his father) in raising money for the Wesleyan Twentieth Century Fund. He was also prominent in the committee set up to make arrangements to celebrate the Queen's Jubilee. A great collector of offices, he was the first vice chairman of the parish council and secretary, for a time, of the Easingwold Fire Brigade. On 9 September 2000 the *Advertiser* printed a copy of a photograph of members of the 'EASINGWOLD MINATURE

RIFLE CLUB TAKEN EARLY PART OF 20TH CENTURY'. Next to someone who looks as if he might have been the tallest man in Easingwold is the diminutive Rookledge. Also in the picture is F. J. H. Robinson.

Rookledge was one of the busiest of Easingwold's business community and his advertising and his large claims gave every impression that his operation was a very successful one. It clearly was, and of course eventually a competitor appeared who not only competed with the patent medicine part of the Rookledge business, but with every aspect of it. The market for drugs and patent medicines was huge, but the proprietor of a new outlet announced that it would also sell newspapers, groceries, household goods, 'Tobaccos of every description', and stationery, while 'Veterinary Medicines [were] a speciality.' The competition was to be largely based on a price war, though that was not made at all clear in a specimen price list attached to an 'opening announcement'. This contained a nice clanger and read[207]

> To the Inhabitants of Easingwold and District
> The Opening of
> METCALFE'S
> CASH DRUG STORES,
> MARKET STREET, EASINGWOLD,
> (Opposite the Chapel)
> That ALL may enjoy the same privileges as people
> in larger towns.
>
> BOWEL ARE A FEW SPECIMENS OF OUR PRICES

Metcalfe's got their later advertisements right and made a straightforward comparison with prices paid elsewhere.

> STARTLING REVELATIONS!
> SEE WHAT YOU CAN SAVE
> BY GOING TO
> METCALFE'S DRUG STORES
>
> The following items are given to illustrate
> the amount you can save by purchasing
> goods from us.

There then followed a tabulated list, some extracts from which follow. The reductions were indeed substantial, and the Woodcock's product looks a particularly good offer. [208]

USUAL PRICE			OUR PRICE	
s	d		s	d
	11 1/2	Box Beecham's Pill		11
4	6	Scott's Emulsion	3	3
3	6	Bottle Orange Quinine Wine	1	6
1	0	4oz Compound Liquorice Powder		3 1/2
	11 1/2	Box of Woodcock's Wind Pills		9 1/2

Coverdale was prompted to respond to the threat from the likes of Metcalfes and produced a competitive price list saying that the company offered goods 'CHEAPER THAN THE STORES.'[209] Not long after this George Coverdale's Company started

Long Street, Easingwold. 1900. Note the stone footpath and very small "one up one down" house.

a new line called Coverdale's Febrifuge retailing at 9½d a packet. How large was a packet? Well it made a wine bottle full of medicine. What did it do? The ad said it cured boils, ulcers, pimples, lumbago, indigestion, constipation, and pains in the back.[210]

There was, as has been said, a price war in Easingwold, this would have undoubtedly benefited people in the area, in some cases to quite a considerable extent, but mainly, perhaps, in only a minor way. Often in these pages prices of various items have been given, but these only become useful indicators of the standard of living in the area if they can be compared with wage rates, and rents. Figures for these items are difficult to come by, but it is quite obvious that the less fortunate members of society (like the agricultural day labourers) fared poorly, and they were to fare poorly for a long time to come. There was a soup kitchen set up for them in Easingwold. The local paper reported its appearance on 6 February 1897.

> THE SOUP KITCHEN. - The Easingwold Soup Kitchen was opened on Saturday and Wednesday last, when about seventy gallons of soup were disposed of each day.

Easingwold was experiencing a period of extremely bad weather in January 1897 - with snow storms and frosts and at the end of the month the soup kitchen was still dispensing nourishment to the needy (*Advertiser* 30 January). It was still working in mid February.

The poor were helped by generous benefactors at 'special' times of the year, and there were some extraordinarily generous people in the Easingwold area. What they did for the needy at Christmas 1896 was briefly mentioned in R.E. Smith's report on 'CHRISTMASTIDE AT EASINGWOLD' which he published on 2 January. It is interesting in that it says more than just what charity there was. Christmas was celebrated 'in the same old style as in the days of long ago' and families welcomed back members who had gone to live and work elsewhere. 'The "Waits" were out in the streets early on Christmas day' and had been perambulating the streets for a week or so. 'Christmas singing seems to be somewhat on the decline in this town' opined Smith, but 'there were a few bands round on Christmas day, both instrumental and vocal.' The inmates of the Union Workhouse also had their 'annual treat' and the poor of Easingwold, 'Through the hospitality of J. H. Love', were given a 'dinner of prime roast beef and plum pudding.' On Saturday (the day after Christmas) most of the shops were closed and there was a football match against Husthwaite which the Easingwolders won easily (4:1).

The generosity shown in Easingwold was repeated elsewhere. At Alne, for example, a Christmas dinner was given in the school room by the Rev Young and Mr Slingsby Hunter to widows, those out of work and their children. The invitation extended to the villages of Aldwark, Flawith, Tollerton, Tholthorpe and Youlton 'so there was a large attendance, 129 sitting down to a plentiful' meal.

There were many treats of the kind held at Alne, and around Christmas time gifts were given in large quantities to the occupants of the Workhouse. The *Advertiser* reported these efforts at length, and they must have given great enjoyment to those who were unused to luxuries. Of course all the entertainments given at the concerts and treats were amateur and the performers were rewarded by getting some modest local celebrity for their renderings of such things as the 'humorous' monologue about mashed turnips and seeing their performances praised in print. Just occasionally - very occasionally - someone's contribution to an event was overlooked in which case he or she got a public apology and quite right too. For example[211]

In our report of the entertainment given in the Parish Hall, Raskelfe, last week the name of Mr Charles Shepherd was inadvertently missed from the Minstrel troupe.

Reginald Ernest Smith and the *Advertiser* were right to make amends for their oversight, particularly as the singers were making their public debut. History should do so too, so here is a summary of the show in which Charlie Shepherd took part as a member of the Raskelfe Minstrels.[212] It began with 'a dialogue entitled "A Bow with two strings." Miss Darbyshire and Miss E Preston sustaining with great vivacity the characters of Miss Jemima Hardy, and Miss Rosabella Harebell.' Then came, almost inevitably, 'Mr Rutter's old song "Old Simon the Cellarer," [which] was greatly appreciated, as was "The Fairies' Lullaby," which was sung sweetly by Miss Ivy Darbyshire.' The whole of the second part of the programme was given by the minstrels and their 'performance was capital, and much enjoyed by all.' It opened with an overture and [this was] followed by songs and jokes.'

NOTES

1. The three men are W. H. Cowling, W. H. Duck, and Robert Cowling - killed in either 1915 or 1916. There is no Robert Cowling on the large memorial. There is, however, W. H. and John.
2. Strictly speaking the use of the word town here is incorrect. The Victorian Poor Law was a union of parishes or townships and the word union was often used as shorthand for the dreaded workhouse. It remained so in some areas until after the Second World War.
3. *Williams & Co.s Directory of the Towns and Villages within twenty two miles of the City of York* (Hull). On Easingwold as a coaching centre see T. Bradley, *The Old Coaching Days of Yorkshire* Chap. 7.
4. *Slater's Royal National Commercial Directory of the County of Yorkshire* (Manchester 1875)
5. The Victorians were not consistent with their spelling and Raskelf usually appears in the documents used for this study as Raskelfe. The Strangwayes of Alne suffered regularly.
6. Reprinted as 'WHERE EXTREMES MEET', *The Easingwold Advertiser and Weekly News* (hereafter *Advertiser*), 14 January 1899. There was a reply by one who signed himself 'LILLIPUTIAN'. It contains some corrections. *Ibid* 21 January 1899.
7. *Ibid* 1 April 1899. There is an account of the ER (and the NER) and others appealing against their valuations by The Union Assessment Committee in *Ibid* 15 September 1900. Despite protests the NER's assessment went up - from one of long standing (£47,787). It went up by £23,000. The Easingwold had an increase of £30 15 (to £241). This assessment came as the ER faced heavier coal charges and the cost of engine repairs. See the half yearly of October 1900. *Ibid* 6 October 1900.
8. *Ibid* 28 October 1899. The half yearly meetings were always reported in the local paper. See eg issue of 26 October 1891.
9. *Ibid* 31 March 1900
10. *Ibid* 5 May 1900. There is a humorous [sic] article on the Easingwold in *Ibid* 31 May 1902 titled 'ON THE EASINGWOLD RAILWAY [BY ONE WHO HAS TRAVELLED']. See also K.E. Hartley, The *Easingwold Railway*, wherein a description of the line opening is quoted from the *Yorkshire Evening Press* 27 July 1891. There is also a slight note about what things were like before the Easingwold opened. F. Metcalfe, 'Horse 'Bus Days at Easingwold' *Dalesman* 1952. The EWK gets a mention in A. J. Brown, *Fair North Riding* (1952). Also *Railway Magazine* March and April 1949. The article mentioned in this note by 'ONE WHO HAS TRAVELLED' was challenged.
11. *Ibid* 14 July, 1900.
12. *History, Topography, and Directory of North Yorkshire* (Preston 1890). Usually referred to as *Bulmer's History and Directory of North Yorkshire.*
13. *Advertiser* 18 November 1899. A historian of Easingwold has a small piece on the town's hirings. G. C. Cowling, *The History of Easingwold and the Forest of Galtres* (Huddersfield 1957). There were several hirings in some places.
14. *Advertiser* 18 November 1899.
15. *Ibid* 2 December 1899. On other hirings for example *Ibid* 17 May, 1902. (These were 'May Day' events.) On the hirings in general see p 9. J.P.B. Dunbabin, *Rural Discontent in Nineteenth Century Britain* (1974).
16. This is a contention rarely spoken about.
17. Presumably Fairbank meant the great Act of 1870.
18. Eg 20 June 1901. The situation had been made worse by a heat wave.
19. *Advertiser* 3 August 1901.
20. There are some tape recordings made in East and North Yorkshire with agricultural labourers who recalled 'living in'. They were made by A. J. Peacock and support the impression indicated above.
21. People like F. E. Green.
22. Hodge, a name for the labourers, used, for example, in the book title *Hodge and His Masters.*

23. *Advertiser* 28 September 1901. Bell was R. Bell, The Hall, Thirsk.
24. Doan's and Charles Forde's products were regularly advertised, and the latter's claims always appeared in what looked like perfectly ordinary news reports. This is very confusing (and entertaining). This one was headed 'A MALTON MARTYR'S RESCUE. BILE BEANS CURE ANAEMIA AND INDIGESTION' and contained the testimony of Mrs Elizabeth Tyson of Norton. She suffered, poor old thing, before she came across Forde's concoction. Then all was well, and that was only to be expected. The Beans had repeatedly proved themselves 'an undoubted cure for indigestion, anaemia, "summer-end-fag," headache, biliousness, constipation, piles, liver trouble, bad breath, lassitude, indigestion, dizziness, buzzing in the head, face sores, and all blood impurities.'
25. *Advertiser* 28 September 1901.
26. *Ibid* 18 January 1902.
27. It might be of interest to note that just a week later, also at the Thirsk court, William Carver was done for being drunk in charge of a horse on a road from Thirsk to Boltby. He was fined half a crown and costs. *Ibid* 25 January 1902.
28. *Ibid* 5 August, 1899.
29. *Ibid* 12 August, 1899. But the fires were said, later, to have been caused by a child playing with matches.
30. *Ibid* 19 August, 1899.
31. For an earlier period see, eg., R. P. Hastings, *Essays in North Riding History 1780-1850* (1981) Cowling *op cit* has a list of incidents. The literature on rural protest is voluminous and the most valuable and impressive is E. Hobsbawn, *Captain Swing*.
32. Or rather his wife Annie does.
33. *Advertiser* 19 August 1899
34. Sturdy was a regular advertiser in the *Easingwold*, but the ad quoted in the text came from a freebie from the period of the Great War, *G. H. Smith's Easingwold Almanac for 1917*. The 1917 Almanac also carried ads for T. Tyerman Sturdy, chemist, stationer, and newsagent (who also ran Sturdy's circulating library) and J. R. Sturdy's 'DEPOT FOR HIGH-CLASS FOOTWEAR' located in Long Street.
35. Bannister said in his letter that a 'neighbouring Parish Council' had earlier written urging a joint effort to get a modern appliance.
36. *Advertiser* 16 March 1901.
37. *Ibid* 17 February 1900.
38. *Ibid* 24 February 1900.
39. *Ibid* 3 February 1900.
40. This was in 1890.
41. Of whom more later.
42. *Advertiser* 2 November 1901.
43. *Ibid* 28 December 1901.
44. Well he was the farmer whose effluent was the cause of the complaint. He was a tenant of the Crayke Castle Estate.
45. *Advertiser* 23 March 1901.
46. *Ibid* 25 January 1902.
47. See later and the letter in *Ibid* 22 February 1902.
48. *Ibid* 4 February 1902. For an earlier period see the reports of sheep scab at Helperby *Ibid* 8 December 1900 and at Newton Grange Farm, *Ibid* 27 October 1900. The Welbourn anthrax report *Ibid* 2 March 1901. Other reports of anthrax in *Ibid* 28 January 1899, and 5 April 1902. One of these was at Newtongrange Farm. Incidents of sheep worrying can be found, eg. *Ibid* 3 March 1900. It reached epidemic proportions in the Thirsk area.
49. Cowling op cit. p 135.
50. *Advertiser* 13 October 1900, Advertisement signed by JNO. J. PENTY, Hon Secretary, Easingwold.' A balance sheet was published in *Ibid* 15 December 1900.
51. *Ibid* 27 October 1900.
52. *Ibid* 3 November 1900.
53. *Ibid* 2 November 1901, report of the second competition.
54. There was a very active horticultural society for example. See later.
55. *Advertiser* 26 October 1901. The dinner was the Easingwold Cricket Club's annual, spent in a 'convivial manner', naturally.
56. The same paper that reported Penty's speech announced that 'THE York and Ainsty Hounds [would] meet at Hawkhills on Monday next.' There is a long article about it and its history in *Advertiser* 13 April 1901. See 'THE YORK AND AINSTY HUNT. ITS COMMENCEMENT.' The article is reprinted from *'Bailey's Magazine, 1871'*. In *Advertiser* 20 April 1901 there is a long, fairly typical report of a meet. Also, in that same paper, is a letter from John Rocliffe saying the *Bailey's* article was 'only very partially informed,' a polite way of saying it contained errors.
57. *The Gas World* quoted *Advertiser* 3 March 1900.
58. *Ibid* 16 February 1901.
59. In 1896.
60. *Advertiser* 15 February 1902. For many years John Binnington was the manager of the Easingwold Gas Light and Coke. He was a Primitive Methodist who died at the age of 72 in 1900. *Ibid* 25 August 1900.

61. *Ibid* 30 March 1901.
62. Rookledge'sappointmentastreasureroftheWornOutisreportedintheaccountofaquarterlyMethodistmeeting in *Ibid* 23 September 1899. The appointment as Horse Hire treasurer from *Ibid* 22 March 1902.
63. *Ibid* 15 July, 1899, reported sale of property run by F.J.H. Robinson. There was an auction mart in Easingwold (see eg. *Ibid* 25 March 1899 for a typical day's proceedings). There was another at Alne.
64. *Ibid* 15 July 1899.
65. *Ibid* 20 and 27 May 1899.
66. *Kelly's Directories of the North and East Ridings of Yorkshire* 1905 and 1909. There is an advert in *Advertiser* 19 November 1898.
67. Cowling op cit pp 117 and 133. That statement that the Union Company was then paying 5s 6d from *Advertiser* 18 August 1900. The sale of Hodgson's shares from *Ibid* 20 April 1901. The account of the winding up meeting from *Ibid* 11 and 18 June 1898. Also 2 July 1898 and 10 September (the sale). The registering of the new company in *Ibid* 15 October 1898. The important 1897 meeting mentioned later in *Ibid* 20 February 1897.
68. *Census of England and Wales, 1901. County of York* (1902)
69. *Advertiser* 27 October, 17 November 1900.
70. The personnel of the bench had changed since the list given above - naturally. On this occasion 'the following magistrates were present - Messrs Strangewayes (chairman), Coates, Wm Harrison, H. Hawking, and Rawdon Thornton.' Coates was James Coates.
71. *Advertiser* 5 January 1901.
72. *Ibid* 9 February, 1901.
73. *Ibid* 9 March 1901.
74. *Ibid* 6 July 1901.
75. *Ibid* 5 November 1898.
76. For some examples of poachers caught and tried, see, eg., *Ibid* 6 November 1897 (case at or from Helperby), 5 April 1902 (case of William Granger of Stillington who trespassed in pursuit of game at Sutton-on-Forest. He was fined £1 and costs and it served him right).
77. *Ibid* 13 August 1898.
78. *Ibid* 10 September 1898
79. Letter signed 'AN OLD SUBSCRIBER' *Ibid* 24 September 1898. The facts about the Easingwold fish shop from *Ibid* 15 and 22 May 1897 (the advertisements) and 15 June 1897 (the letter).
80. *Ibid* 19 February 1989.
81. *Ibid* 22 April 1899.
82. *Ibid* 28 April 1900.
83. *Ibid* 6 April 1901.
84. See later.
85. *Advertiser* 11 September 1897.
86. See eg. *Ibid* 26 June 1897 and issues around this date. Detailed reports from the area in issue of 26 June.
87. *Ibid* 10 July and 14 August 1897.
88. Letter in *Ibid* 4 September 1897.
89. *Ibid* 11 September 1897.
90. *Ibid* 29 May and 24 April 1897,
91. *Ibid* 27 February 1897.
92. *Ibid* 27 March 1897.
93. *Ibid* 23 April 1898.
94. *Ibid* 17 and 24 February 1900.
95. *Ibid* 19 and 26 November 1898.
96. *Ibid* 10 February 1900.
97. *Ibid* 17 March 1900.
98. *Ibid* 4 May 1901. The balance sheet is printed in the public notices column.
99. *Ibid* 11 May 1901.
100. Along with J. Haithwaite and Cllr Mountain.
101. *Advertiser* 2 January 1897.
102. *Ibid* 24 April 1897.
103. *Ibid* 25 February 1899.
104. That statement is based on the public notices.
105. *Ibid* 21 April 1900, public notice.
106. *Ibid.*
107. D. Gifford, *The British Film Catalogue : 1895 - 1970.* (Newton Abbott 1973).
108. C. Jeavons, *A Pictorial History of War Films* (1974). The Alne/Klawitter ball reported in *Advertiser* 18 February 1899. The Flood-Porter adverts and 'review' in *Ibid* 6 and 12 March 1898.
109. *Advertiser* 1 October 1898.
110. *Ibid* 27 April 1901.
111. *Ibid* 27 December 1902.
112. *Ibid* 30 November 1901. There was also in existence a group known as The Black Star Minstrels. *Ibid* 15 July 1897.

113. *Ibid* 28 December 1901.
114. *Ibid* 21 January 1899.
115. *Ibid* 18 February 1899.
116. *Ibid* 12 November 1898, and issues of 26 March and 7 May 1897, also about Brandsby and Stillington. The first appearance of the Crayke Glee Party is mentioned in *Ibid* 31 March 1900.
117. *Ibid* 12 February 1898.
118. *Ibid* 26 October. Wallace was the lion featured in a Stanley Holloway monologue recorded before the Second World War.
119. *Ibid* 3, 10, 17 and 24 July, 1897.
120. *Ibid* 3 May 1902, public notices column.
121. *Ibid* 10 May 1902. For the rest of Bijou's stay and reviews see *Ibid* 17, 24 and 31 May, 7, 14 and 21 June 1902.
122. *Advertiser* 1 September 1900.
123. *Ibid* 8 September 1900.
124. *Ibid* 31 August 1901.
125. *Ibid* 4 October 1902.
126. *Ibid* 13 September 1902.
127. *Ibid* 1 November 1902. The P.C. Pennock/Malton case reported in *Ibid* 28 December 1901. The treadmill story from *Ibid* 19 October 1901 and the John Smith case from *Ibid* 21 June 1902.
128. See eg. *Ibid* 29 May 1897.
129. *Ibid* 3 July 1897. Also 10 July (funeral)
130. *Ibid* 26 February 1898.
131. *Ibid* 29 December 1900.
132. See eg. a brief note about it in 'Ropy Beer,' in A.J. Peacock (ed), *Essays in York History* (Easingwold nd).
133. 'PURE BEER' in *Ibid* 19 January 1901.
134. January 1899.
135. *Advertiser* 10 August 1901.
136. *Ibid* 19 January 1901.
137. *Ibid.*
138. *Ibid* 26 January 1901. The *Chambers Journal* quote which follows from *Ibid* 25 May 1901.
139. *Ibid* 23 March 1901.
140. W. I. Jones was the representative of Yearsley.
141. *Advertiser* 17 and 26 May 1901.
142. *Ibid* 14 December 1901.
143. *Ibid* 21 December 1901.
144. *Ibid* 8 February 1902.
145. *Ibid* 8 March 1902.
146. *Ibid* 5 and 12 April 1902.
147. *Ibid* For a meeting of the Sutton Society see eg. *Ibid* 18 October 1902. For Huby see eg *Ibid* 25 October and 22 November 1902. Stillington's meeting in *Ibid* 1 November 1902. For a Tollerton meeting see *Ibid* 13 December 1902. See *Ibid* 23 January 1897 for the Easingwold Wesleyans.
148. *Ibid* 31 May 1902.
149. *Ibid* 2 August 1902. The Tollerton meeting from *Ibid* 15 November 1902.
150. *Ibid* 1 and 8 November 1902.
151. Cowling was the name of an Easingwold chronicler and resident. He wrote that Cowlings cropped up frequently in his town's history. He was right. Cowling's work has been quoted earlier and some occasions in which someone with his surname cropped up in Easingwold history occurred were reported as follows: *Ibid* 10 January 1899 (a Cowling a member of the Easingwold Wesleyan Institute) *Ibid* 6 February 1897; James in court for being Brahms and Liszt, something members of the Wesleyan Institute would not have approved of; *Ibid* 19 April 1902, connected with football; *Ibid* 26 February 1898, public announcement saying William C. was starting a 'TAILORING BUSINESS'. No less than four Cowlings were members of the Victoria Institute's Minstrel Troupe and the paper which reported that also recorded the trials and tribulations of one who was a publican and a very unsuccessful pig dealer.
152. In 1902 a famous cleric - Canon Fleming - gave an entire programme of recitations at the Town Hall in aid of the Husthwaite New Vicarage Building Fund. His programme ('interspersed with vocal and instrumental music') consisted of 'A Man's a Man', 'The Raven', 'Lady Clare', 'Crossing the Bar', 'The Dying Christian', 'The Doctor's Fee', 'Give us Men', 'The Bells' and 'The Bootblacks'. *Advertiser* 18 October, 1 November 1902. 'The recitations by Canon Fleming were marvels of elocution in the opinion of the *Advertiser.*
153. The writer. His village was Histon, near Cambridge. The offending piece is about a couple with deformed mouths who cannot, either of them, blow out the bedroom candle. Eventually someone simply nips the wick in his fingers. So the couple were not only malformed, but daft as well.
154. *Advertiser* 6 December 1902.
155. *Ibid* 23 and 30 January 1897.
156. *Ibid* 20 February 1897.
157. *Daily Telegraph* quoted *Ibid* 19 June 1897.
158. *Ibid* 31 July 1897. Huxley died in June 1895.
159. Quoted *Ibid* 2 October 1897.

160. *Ibid* 19 January 1901.
161. *Lancet* quoted *Ibid* 25 May 1901.
162. *Ibid* 6 July 1901. The paragraph from the training manual is one on 'Smoking on the March.'
163. Eg. *Ibid* 13 March 1897 (swine fever), 5 April 1902 (anthrax).
164. *Ibid* 6 March 1897.
165. *Ibid* 29 January 1898. For some more typical reports of hunt meetings see eg. 'Opening Day with the York and Ainsty Hounds', *Ibid* 11 November 1899. Also *Ibid* 2 December 1899, 16 November 1901, 9 March 1901.
166. *Ibid* 15 April 1901.
167. 'W. Orvis, the "whip".'
168. *The Candid Friend* 19 October 1901, reprinted *Advertiser* 1 March 1902.
169. Slingsby; Sir George Wombwell; Maj Mussinden; The Hon and Capt Molyneux; Capt Key, Fulford; Clare Vyner of Newby Hall; E. Lloyd; E. Robinson; Capt White, 15th Hussars; C. Warriner; Warriner's son; W. Orvis. The Warriners were the boatmen - gardeners and ferrymen at Newby Hall.
170. *Advertiser* 17 March 1900.
171. *Ibid* 5 and 12 may 1900.
172. *Ibid* 14 January 1899.
173. *Ibid* 9 December 1899.
174. *Ibid* 2 December 1899.
175. *Ibid* 25 November 1899.
176. *Ibid* 11 May 1901. The offence was committed at Wansford on the Great North Road. Hutton was dealt with by 'the Norman Cross (Peterborough) magistrates.'
177. *Ibid* 2 November 1902.
178. *Ibid* 11 October 1902. The Thirsk marathon reported in *Ibid* 27 September 1902.
179. *Ibid* 19 July 1902.
180. *Ibid* 2 August 1902.
181. *Ibid* 18 October 1902.
182. *Ibid* 6 September 1902.
183. *Ibid* 15 October 1898. The Sutton/York County Court case from *Ibid* 8 March 1902.
184. The Rookledge and Reynard advertisements in *Advertiser* 7 and 14 April 1900. The second price list from *Ibid* 25 February 1899.
185. *Ibid* 6 and 13 March 1897.
186. *Ibid* 3 July 1897.
187. *Ibid* 28 August 1897. Actually Reynard's ads did not completely disappear from the paper. Occasionally he used the column wherein two and three liners appeared.
188. *Ibid* 1 and 29 October 1898.
189. *Ibid* 27 March and 3 April 1897.
190. *Ibid* 1 May 1897.
191. *Ibid* 25 February 1899.
192. *Ibid* 12 March 1898.
193. *Ibid* 14 August 1897.
194. *Ibid* The report about the Roads Improvement Association from *Ibid* 19 August 1899.
195. *Ibid* 15 October 1898. There was a cycle race track at Thirsk. *Ibid* 26 January 1902.
196. *Ibid* 10 June 1899.
197. To sum up presumably.
198. *Advertiser* 12 August 1899.
199. *Ibid* 19 August 1899.
200. *Ibid* 9 September 1899. Brown was vicar of Normanton. The foregoing examples are taken from one year only.
201. Very occasionally news items were included in the contents of page one.
202. 1n this he said he had 'again' been appointed agent for a number of well-known manufacturers.
203. The York papers also carried adverts of the Towle type.
204. That they were abortificants is beyond doubt, and penny royal certainly was.
205. Coverdale had outlets in York, Lincoln, London, Scarborough, Ripon and Rotherham, but he did not have one of his own in Easingwold.
206. *Kelly's Directory of the North and East Ridings of Yorkshire* (1905). The information about Rookledge senior's death from *Advertiser* 6 and 13 May 1899. Also *Ibid* 3 June 1899 (becoming treasurer to the Guardians), 28 January 1898 (long report about the Fund), the comment on him as a possible small holder based on an advertisement that he had fruit for sale in *Ibid* 10 July 1897.
207. *Ibid* 3 June 1899.
208. Eg *Ibid* 17 June 1899
209. *Ibid* 10 June 1899.
210. *Ibid* 22 July 1899.
211. *Ibid* 2 March 1901.
212. *Ibid* 23 February 1901.

Chapter 2

FOOTBALL, CRICKET, GAMBLING, AND OTHER THINGS

The village concerts and the outings organised by the churches and the chapels were occasional enjoyable events, and there were organisations like the Wesleyan Institute where regular 'improving' lectures were given. There were also a number of sporting clubs which got wide notice in the local paper. What were they like? A football club (which attracted quite respectable crowds to its Saturday games in the years covered in these pages) came into existence. Its origins and exact date of creation are not clear, but it played its home games in the Chase Garth, Long Street. It was in existence, however, at the beginning of the period covered in these pages. In February 1897 'The first of what was intended as an annual event was held at the George Hotel' when the Easingwold Football Club dinner was held.[1] Buller Hicks was speaker and gave the assembled a song, and other prominent local personalities lending their support included J.C. Bannister. The hon secretary and treasurer was John Allison and he gave some details of the club's recent form and achievements. It was a report which admitted there was room for considerable improvement. During 'this season', Allison said, the club had played 14 matches, 7 of which were lost, 5 won and 2 drawn ... there remaining three more ... to play, two of which would be on the home ground. They had not won so many matches as they should have done, and for this ... there were two causes, the first was the lack of scoring power, which he had noticed particularly in the Kirkbymoorside and Ebor Wanderers match, [sic] and the other was practice.' What about the club's finances? Up to the present, receipts for the year had been £17 and expenditure had amounted to £12.

Football was increasing in popularity in the Easingwold area and Huby, for example, created a club,[2] which played its first game 'against an Easingwold eleven' a week after Allison gave his report. Easingwold won 4:0. All the usual ingredients of an *Advertiser* report are present in this one; the naming of names, the high flown descriptions and so on. Shame that Huby lost its first game though.[3]

There were, of course, many other village football teams, and their games were noted, sometimes at considerable length. In one issue of the *Advertiser* there were extensive reports of Crayke losing to St Crux, York, and Stillington playing a return with York Medical Staff.

The increasing popularity of Association Football nationally might be gleaned from the appearance of a column in the *Easingwold* titled 'CURRENT SPORT', but much more attention was paid, of course, to the games of Stillington, Crayke, and the other local teams than to, say, Aston Villa. Quite right too. John Allison, it will be recalled had singled out the Ebor Wanderers for special mention. The first game of the season between the 'homesters' and the Wanderers was played on New Year's Day in 1898.[4] The home team played 'with more dash and vigour than [had] characterised their efforts of late.' Holmes and Mangles scored in a 2:0 victory, and Fras Brown (goalie) and the rest of the Easingwold team were all complemented for a fine performance against a regular foe. Admission to games at the Chase Garth, incidentally, was '2d., Ladies and Members Free.'

Towards the end of January 1898 the *Advertiser* noticed a game between Easingwold and Crayke at considerable length. 'Crayke had the assistance of the brothers Stanbrough for the first time this season.' Nevertheless Easingwold went in at half time 2:0 up. Then there was some magnificent play by the Stanbroughs, particularly following a centre 'by the International.' The brothers 'were always in evidence, their fine dribbling and smart passing being a treat to witness,' but their team lost (2:1). (The Rev M. E. Standborough held the living of St Cuthbert, Crayke.)

Easingwold Football Club. 1905.
Ernest Ward is on the right hand side in the middle row.

For some reason no report of an annual meeting of the Easingwold FC appeared in 1899, although an announcement that it was to be held did. A list of the club's fixtures, however, was given. It gives dates in December, though it was published on 14 January. All the dates were Saturdays and the games marked * were League matches.

1898		
17 Dec	Rowntrees Cocoaworks*	Away
24 Dec	York Trinity	Away
1899		
7 Jan	Stillington	Home
21 Jan	St Clements (York)*	Away
28 Jan	Acomb*	Home
4 Feb	Rowntrees Cocoaworks*	Home
11 Feb	Thirsk	Away
18 Feb	Selby*	Away
25 Feb	Ulleskelf*	Home
4 Mar	Ebor Wanderers*	Home
11 Mar	Army Service Corps (York)	Away
18 Mar	York Trinity	Home
25 Mar	Ulleskelf*	Away
1 April	Thirsk	Home

In March 1902 a match of more than usual interest took place against Tollerton.[5] It was played at Tollerton and attracted a very hostile notice in the *Advertiser*. The pitch was small, it said, and 'the particular attention paid' to the visitors led to them playing well below par. Not only that but the referee repeatedly blew up for infringements 'which could not be seen either by the spectators or players.' He blew for a free kick eventually, from it Tollerton scored, and time was then called 'after a very prolonged second half.'[6] The game ended 1:1. At the outset, because of a mix up over kick off time, the visitors had been kept waiting on the field for nearly an hour.

A row started and the Tollerton club secretary (A. Vasey) explained the confusion about kick off time in a letter to the press. He more or less accused the visitors of dirty play and said that Tollerton's victory was not due to the tiny pitch as some had said. What won the game for them was the fact that Tollerton was a 'suppressive team.' Vasey's letter was responded to by T. Cowling in one that took up some 18 inches.[7] He questioned almost everything the reporter and Vasey had said, being particularly angry about the delayed start. '... our team was allowed to stand for half-an-hour [sic] in a cold north wind without a ball to keep warm,' he wrote, 'and when one did come it had to be blown up. Is this hospitality?' Cowling claimed to be very experienced, having played in the Midlands and 'this district.' Never, he wrote,

> have I taken part in any match where the official in charge of the game showed such a lamentable lack of knowledge of the rudiments of Association Football as on this occasion.
>
> Another novel experience was to hear the words of encouragement offered by the referee to the home team. Personally I heard such phrases as these:- "Goa on ma lad," "By gom tha's doin' weel," "Goa for him." These are a sample of the sayings of a gentleman supposed to be an impartial judge ...
>
> Tollerton had had a 'decisive thrashing' at Easingwold (6:0) and 'I was quite prepared to see they had obtained a good deal of outside help in order to retrieve their lost prestige, but I was not prepared for the ungenerous treatment we received. When our team' went to Tollerton we 'expected to be treated as sportsmen but we certainly were not.' Tollerton, it seems, not only got in outside players but planted a sympathetic referee as well.

Easingwold's last game of the 1901-2 season was away against Old Shiptonians (York). They won a 'gentlemanly' game 4:1. T. Cowling was in the team, R. Cowling as usual was Easingwold's 'custodian.'[8]

The new season began with Easingwold beating three teams, then taking part in another sporting row. This time it involved the game with Clifton Parish Church, and was played in the Chase Garth on 8 November.[9] Clifton was one of three unbeaten teams put to the sword by the home team, and they took their humbling with a bad grace. A protest was made against the result and the case was heard by the committee of the York City and District Football Association on 18 November. Clifton's objections 'were:- (1) Incapability of [the ref], (2) playing seven minutes over time, during which Easingwold secured a goal, and (3) crowding of spectators on the field of play.' The home club was represented at the enquiry by Buller Hicks, J. W. Sturdy and T. Cowling, and the result was a unanimous decision that 'the charges brought by Clifton are frivolous, groundless and altogether unsustained. We wish to express our grave displeasure with the Clifton secretary' it concluded, 'in having brought such an unfounded charge before us.'

*Thatched cottages, **Uppleby**, Easingwold early 1900s, demolished early 1950s*

Easingwold ended its 1902 campaign with games against Fulford, the Priory Street Wesleyans (York) and, the last game, the West Yorks, losing 4:1. Nevertheless, despite this, they ended the year at the top of the League.

York and District Association League

	Pld	Won	Lost	Drawn	Points
Easingwold	13	7	3	3	17
West Yorks Depot	8	7	1	0	14
Clifton P.C.	11	5	2	4	14
Sycamore Res	10	5	2	4	14
Fulford	10	4	3	3	11
Priory St Wes	9	3	4	2	8
Civil Service	8	2	4	2	6
Leeman Rd AS	8	1	5	2	4
Rowntrees' Res	10	1	9	0	2

Cricket games do not seem to have had quite the same potential for trouble that football had, but games and clubs attracted loyal support and much interest from the *Advertiser* which did its usual thing of reporting matches at length and speeches attendances and performances at annual general meetings at even greater length.

Raskelfe had a cricket team and some details of what was involved in running a village club were revealed when its annual general meeting was held in the Reading Room on 8 March 1897.[10] The secretary then revealed that £7 17s had been received from subscriptions and that £5 4s 2d had been expended 'leaving a balance in hand of £2 12s 10d, thus showing the club in a very satisfactory condition.' Husthwaite held a meeting to form a cricket club in March 1897 and Crayke already had one. It announced a fund raising event for which 'The services of the well-known Yorkshire Humorist, Mr R. Blakeborough' had been obtained.[11] The Sutton-on-Forest cricket club held its annual general at the Blackwell Ox when the financial statement presented 'shewed a balance in hand of about £3, which was considered very satisfactory.'[12] Alne had a cricket club and in April the Sessay one announced its fixtures for the coming season and the Easingwold club held its annual general at the George Hotel with Buller Hicks in the chair (who else) [13]. Its season of 1897 began with a game against 'the renowned Duncombe Park team.' Despite having a supposedly weak batting side the Easingwolders won, most of the credit for the victory going to W. Holmes and T. Cowling.[14]

A tremendous amount of cricket was played in the Easingwold area and all the details of teams like Stillington, Easingwold itself,[15] Kilburn, Brandsby, Gilling, Tholthorpe and Myton were duly recorded. Cricket matches were frequently put on as part of village celebrations, and in one issue of the *Advertiser* alone details of no less than six games of this time were given.[16]

The 1898 cricket season began in May[17] and the Easingwold Club decided to erect a new pavilion costing £40.[18] A subscription list had been started, 'The Cricket lovers of Easingwold quickly responded ... and in an amazingly short time almost the whole of the required amount had been promised.' A celebratory game between Easingwold and H.C. Fairfax - Cholmley's XI was arranged for the hand-over day, and admission fees were waived.[19] Prominent in the match reports for this game and those against Sessay[20] and York Revellers[21] were the names of Hicks and J H Robinson. At the end of the 1898 season the Easingwold club produced a statistical analysis of batting and bowling averages for the team. They include the following

BATTING

	No of innings	Times not out	Total runs	Most in an innings	Ave.
M. H. Stanborough	7	1	139	87	23.16
E. B. Hicks	8	1	89	16	12.71
J. R. Allison	12	0	105	35	8.75
F. J. H. Robinson	7	3	29	9	7.25
H. C. F. Cholmeley	7	0	30	24	4.28

BOWLING

	Overs	Mds	Runs	Wkts	Ave.
E. B. Hicks	52	14	96	18	5.33
G. T. Sturdy	9	1	27	2	13.5
H. C. F. Cholmeley	9	2	32	1	32
J. R. Allison	68	20	209	19	11

The *Advertiser's* policy of comprehensive coverage persisted, with games like Alne Star (juniors) versus Easingwold Church Choir and Alne Boys versus White Rose (Boys) getting the name-them-all treatment,[22] as indeed had the Easingwold matches against Kirkbymoorside, Huby and Thirsk [23].

The 1898 annual dinner was held at the George Hotel.[24] Diners heard addresses from the likes of J. C. Bannister, Penty, John Rocliffe and team officials. They also got a song from Buller Hicks, who proposed the club's health in a speech in which he extolled the virtues of England's summer game. Then Allison replied, and revealed that it had been a troubled year. There had been a dispute over a matter not connected with the club which 'ought never to have been brought forward in connection with it.' As a result leading players left and the club was 'riven by internal discord'. Some wished them to fail 'but a few enthusiastic sportsmen ... came [forward] with their purses to help a tottering club.'

No details of the cricket club row were revealed then or later. All was well by the end of the season, though. Water had been laid on to the ground and the pavilion was a source of great pride. An appeal appeared in the press for contributors to a club 'Cake, Cushion and Candy Fair' intended to raise funds. An editorial in the *Advertiser* supported it. Cash crises, it said, hit the cricket club with 'painful regularity'. The town was to be appealed to on 6 July, 'Easingwold old fair day.'[25] The date was altered, however, and the Cushion etc went ahead on the 3rd. Fifty pounds were raised.[26]

In the following season feelings again ran high over a game between two of the local villages. In the *Advertiser* in June there appeared a huge amount of cricket news and a letter from Arthur Brain, of Alne Station. He objected to an *Advertiser* statement saying that the game between Alne and Skelton, played at Skelton, 'ended in a draw'. Where this statement is supposed to have appeared is unknown and all that the paper recorded was the details of the two innings - with the home team scoring 107 and Alne getting 15 for two wickets.[27] Anyway, wherever he got his story from Brain was angry and said the elusive report was untrue. The game, he said, 'came to an end' because the umpires could not agree. The Skelton captain took his men off the field.

Village sport could cause trouble but the sportsmen, like the entertainers, reaped the benefits, sometimes, of becoming local celebrities. Sydney Smith was a photographer based in the Market Place, Easingwold, and Albion Street, Leeds.[28] He specialised in 'Views of

1901. Clearing out the 'Mill' pond and preparing it to be used as the Easingwold Swimming Pool

Easingwold and District, measuring 12 inches by 10' which he sold 'unmounted 1/6 each, mounted on best plate sunk, 18 by 14 mounts, 2/- each.' In addition to these Smith had for sale photographs of the 'Easingwold Cricket Team, Season 1902' at 2s each. Another local photographer, incidentally, who did not have a picture of the cricketers in his catalogue, was Arthur Sturdy.[29] He advertised 'PHOTOGRAPHIC VIEWS OF THE DISTRICT' which he sold for 1s or 6d . (Sydney Smith was brother to Easingwold Advertiser editor R. E. Smith).

Towards the end of August 1901 a photograph was taken in Easingwold which achieved some fleeting fame. On Sunday the 25th, early in the evening a violent thunderstorm passed over the town. Lightning struck three new houses and considerable damage was done, and several inhabitants were injured and were reckoned lucky to have escaped with their lives. One of these was Mrs Cowles the wife of the manager of the Flour Mill and the swimming baths, who was knocked down and stunned. She lived not far from the houses that were hit. The damage was photographed by a local enthusiast and his work was reproduced in a journal published nationally.[30]

The *Advertiser* would eventually use photographs, of course, but in the period covered in these pages there were none. The paper, notably its foreign news section, carried line drawings of the likes of Lord Kitchener and Mr Gladstone; advertisers like John Smith (Gentleman's Outfitter of Easingwold) and Mark Reynard used line illustrations.

Some of the national advertisers, however, sometimes used art work of a high order. In most issues of most papers (it seems) there appeared an ad for James Doan's Backache Kidney Pills. In one used in an edition of the *Easingwold* revealed that the formula for them had been given him by an old lady called Aunt Rogers. There was a drawing of the aunt, who looked as if she should have increased her own dosage of Backache Kidneys, and above it a depiction of James Doan himself, heavily moustached and looking like one of those Wild Western outlaws who stare out from wanted posters.

The creation of a town football club and a town cricket club were important attractions for Easingwold, to add to the numerous concerts and institutes like the Victoria Institute. Something else of great value was a swimming bath, the result of private enterprise and sited on property belonging to a business which has been mentioned in these pages. 'It might interest our readers to know there is [now] a swimming bath in Easingwold, which bids fair to supply a long felt need' opined the *Advertiser* in the summer of 1901.[31] Mr. Cowles, the manager 'of the Flour Mill, has had the mill reservoir thoroughly cleaned out, which makes an ideal swimming bath ... the water is beautifully warm, and fresh water is running through all day long.' At the time of this note there were 'some 50 members who [had] already paid the moderate sum of 2/6 for the privilege of enjoying this exhilarating and refreshing pastime.' By the summer of 1902 the new facility had a proper name.[32] The Coronation Baths, Long Street were now open for the season, an advertisement said: 'Season Tickets 5/-. Single Baths 3d. per hour. Good Dressing Room Accommodation, Lessons in Swimming by Practical Men. ... Lads half-price up to 5 o'clock p.m.'

The creation of the swimming baths was, as has been said, the result of private initiative, so was another recreational venture which, by its nature, was short lived. There appeared during the winter of 1897, a notice about[33]

SKATING

GOOD SKATING at WHITE HOUSE,
ALNE STATION, 60 yards square,
well swept. - Admittance 3d. each.
W. CLEVELAND

Swimming and skating were available (in season) for those who could afford them, but there was also illegal activity. Taking the odd hare, fish or bird was a recognised pastime for many, and so was gaming. This went on in the towns, in places like parks, and on derelict land and pursuits like pitch and toss attracted large crowds - and the attention of the law officers. It went on in the rural areas as well, and cases that ended in court can be found in the local paper. For example 'a youth named Stellings' was sent 'to gaol for month [sic] for gamdling [sic] "shake-cap" with three others, in the outskirts of the town on a Sunday afternoon.'[34]

Quite a few of the cricket matches that were so important in the villages were arranged to be a part of the celebrations when the annual feast was held. A report in the *Advertiser* said that they were in decline and becoming much less frequent. That might be so, but there were still many held in the early years of the 20th century. For example at Husthwaite where 'On Tuesday and Wednesday last [18 and 19 October], the village feast was held. There was the usual complement of swings, shooting galleries, &c., present, but on the first day, owing to the stormy weather, they were unable to open out.' On the Wednesday things had improved, but it was very uncomfortable under foot. The Easingwold Brass Band visited the village and at night a hop was held in the schoolroom, 'and dancing was kept up until the early hours of the morning.'[35] The day before the Husthwaite two day feast started the Coxwold one was held. In the afternoon sports were arranged, and there was dancing in the evening. There was no mention of swings and other fairground features, however, as there had been, a week earlier at Alne[36] and, in the following year, at Flawith. Raskelfe's feast of 1899, a two day event, was reckoned to have been a great success. Again no mention was made of fairground amusements, but two cricket matches were played (against Newton-on-Ouse and Kilburn) and a dance was arranged. On Thursday afternoon the Easingwold Band, under the leadership of Mr I. R. Fox, 'discoursed a capital selection of music' on the cricket ground.[37]

Earlier it was said that it was contended that the village feast was rapidly disappearing. The contention was made in a report on Husthwaite of 1902[38] but the main contention of that report was that if the feast *was* disappearing it was not going from Husthwaite. 'Most village feasts in the North Riding are, it must be said, lingering on to painless extinction, when they will be gone but not forgotten,' but Husthwaite's was 'not in this category.'

Why had the feasts declined? They had traditionally been the time when 'wandering natives' returned to 'the homes of their childhood'. Now, presumably because of better transport, this could be done more easily and more often.

If better communications did lead to something of a decline in the popularity of the feasts in many places, it could well have been because people could now go away on cheap excursions. The North Eastern Railway Company began to arrange 'trips' which they advertised in the *Advertiser*. One could easily find any number of attractive offers. An advertisement by the NER in the summer of 1899, for example, said 'Excursion Trains' would run from 'ALNE at 8-15 a.m., RASKELF, etc., to THORNABY, REDCAR and SALTBURN' and from 'ALNE at 1-25 p.m. to LEEMING LANE, BEDALE, LEYBURN, WENSLEY, REDMIRE, AYSGARTH,

ASKRIGG and HAWES.'[39] Throughout the summer the NER ran excursions, and very popular they appear to have been. Also in August trains went: from Alne to Goathland and Whitby: Scorton, Catterick Bridge and Richmond; York: and Scarborough (twice).[40] On one occasion the Easingwold Railway Company and the NER ran special trains to Helmsley 'to witness the historical play' (this was on 13 July 1898) and there was a mid-week visit to York

> A large number of people from Easingwold and district visited York on Thursday last, for the purpose of attending Barnum and Bailey's great show, which was located there for the day. The Easingwold Railway Company ran a late train that night.

The historical play at Helmsley was first put on in August 1897 but the performance was ruined by a deluge, and was repeated on three days twelve months later.[41]

During the early years of the century a number of bizarre characters pitched up in the town doing weird things who look as if they might have been at home in the freak show part of the Barnum and Bailey extravaganza. Not so W. Baldwin, who got a lot of attention.[42] He deserved it, if his publicity is to be believed.

Mr W. Baldwin, who had recently accomplished a journey round the world, and is 'at present engaged in walking from London to Newcastle, arrived in Easingwold on Saturday evening last' the *Advertiser* said. He put up at the George and the paper told its readers that the trip round the world was

Mr Duckworth's Wedding, Easingwold early 1900s

undertaken under somewhat unique circumstances. It was embarked upon for a wager of 20,000 dollars. The stipulations were that he should go on foot or a wheel, and that he was to start with nothing in his possession but a few newspapers - not even a shirt or a vestige of clothing was to be his until he had earned it - he was to complete his journey in three years, and earn during his wanderings the sum of 2,000 dollars. There followed a catalogue of his experiences.

Mr W. Baldwin sounds too good to be true, but he was not averse to a little notice being taken of him, and neither was a married couple who arrived with a child in Easingwold some three and a half years later. They provided a much better spectacle for the crowds than did Baldwin, and were Herr Hauslian and his wife. He had 'undertaken for a wager of 2,000 Austrian dollars (about £400) to wheel his wife and child in a perambulator around Europe!

The *Advertiser's* description of the Hauslian pram was vague, but one hopes that the owner got back to Vienna safely and that his tormentor duly paid up the £400 he had wagered. Members of the public at that time were fascinated by feats of 'pedestrianism' such as 'A Walk Round The World' by George O. Maillat of Montreal.[43] No doubt John Alcock would also have been welcomed in Easingwold as he was reported as having recently, at the age of 62, walked backwards from Macclesfield Market-place to the Crescent, Buxton, a distance of twelve miles, in 3 hours 14 minutes and 45 seconds. Thousands of people lined the roads and awaited the veteran pedestrian's arrival in Buxton. In 1887 Alcock performed the same feat in 2 hours 44 minutes.

When John Alcock was preparing for his epic walk organisations were beginning to discuss how to celebrate the coronation of Edward VII. The King commanded that Thursday and Friday, 26 and 27 June 1902 were 'to be observed as Public Holidays' and for a couple of months how to use those days was a major topic for committees, councils, clubs and other bodies. Things progressed, but then Edward became seriously ill and the coronation was postponed. What should the various organisations now do? Arrangements were at an advanced stage, so most places decided the celebrations should go on. The Easingwold Cricket Club had arranged some fixtures and serious modifications were made when the fancy dress game was played in whites.' The sports events went on for the children and something like 600 people had tea when Mr Barley's team played that of Mr Bannister. This was the second game of the coronation festivities. The authorities at Alne also went ahead and 'festivities of various kinds were indulged in. A public tea was held and a procession was formed headed by I.R. Fox and the Easingwold Brass Band, and 'about 600 were entertained to tea.' Cycle races were held and 'amusements of all kinds provided. Dancing commenced about 9 p.m. and was kept up with spirit until 12 p.m. and the effect of the limelight which illuminated the trees was charming. Japanese lanterns were also suspended from the branches of the great oaks and beeches.' (The celebrations were held in the park 'kindly lent by' Mr J. Swainston Strangewayes). [44]

The Easingwold festivities ended on Saturday 9 August. At 7.30 in the morning that day, 'the bells at the Parish Church rang a merry peal, and at intervals during the day 'peals of "Grandsires" and "feu de joies" were rung', and the ringers were all named by the *Advertiser*.[45] Of course they were.

At eight o'clock the junior members of the choir, the organist and the choir master wended their way up the church tower where 'beneath the waving folds of the Union Jack, they sang the National Anthem and ... delivered themselves of several hearty if not very voluminous cheers for His Majesty and the Queen.' At eleven o'clock a well attended service was held

Outside the York Hotel early 1900s - great and good of Easingwold's Druids along with Town Band, leader Isaac Fox, second from right, middle row, holding cornet.

in the church. Then there was a set-back. The cricket match with Knaresborough was called off when the Easingwold secretary was informed by wire that 'Knaresbro' could not raise a team, presumably in consequence of their own Coronation festivities, an excuse which the players looked upon as worthy to be placed alongside that of members of the team which some weeks ago were all said to be hay-making.' What all that means is unknown, but there had been a lot in the paper about the Easingwold club making 'arrangements to "wipe something off a slate" in their return match with Knaresborough at home.'

At six o'clock the procession led by the inevitable brass band started from the top of Long Street. Decorated drays and bicycles took part as did groups from the Yeomanry, the Fire Brigade, the Volunteers and 'Druids, in their robes of office (under Bro. J. C. Scholefield, P. A., and Bro. G. T. Sturdy, P.A.), and a sundry assortment of decorated vehicles and mounted personages.' The principal houses in the town were decked out and the main buildings festooned with flags. The lamp posts in Uppleby had all been tastefully decorated with foliage by Miss Leckenby and Miss M. Allison, 'the following of which example would have greatly improved the appearance of other parts of the town.' The procession was eventually called to a halt in the Market Place 'and [a] considerable din was caused by the volley firing of the Yeomanry and Volunteers, followed by the maroons of the Fire Brigade ... [which] brought the proceedings to a close.'

The Easingwold parish council had been responsible for organising the celebrations, and in August it met to consider the accounts. Some items are of interest. The children's tea had cost something like £13, and the flags just over £1 13s. The band had still to be paid, as had the Town Hall. It was reckoned that over all the cost of the town's festivities would 'not be far short of £50.'

The band owed £5 by the Easingwold parish council was that led 'by Mr I. Fox' whose brass band was in existence and getting plenty of work in the area. The band got frequent notices in the *Advertiser*, this is not surprising, really, as, according to one source, Reginald Ernest, the printer and publisher, was its 'manager, secretary and drummer.'[46] When the Fox combo was first formed is unclear, but the enterprising leader, like some of his successors, seems to have run a dance band as well - comprised mainly of the brass banders. Anyway, a Fox group appeared at a dance at Raskelfe early in 1897. This was the place where all the dances went on for incredibly long times and Isaac and his men really earned their pay on this occasion : 'BALL. - On Tuesday the annual ball held under the auspices of the Raskelfe Dancing Class was held in the Parish Hall. ... Dancing commenced at 9-30 p.m., and continued with much spirit until about 5 o'clock next morning. The music was supplied by Mr I R Fox's band and was all that could be desired.'[47] At the end of the month they were at Coxwold where things went on until 'early morning'[48] but this was not the limit worked by the local musicians. The Helmsley String Band played for dancing at a function at Newburgh Priory. There dancing went on 'until about six the following morning.'[49]

In February 1897 Fox had appeared with a group of musicians at a musical evening held in the Husthwaite Wesleyan chapel and on this occasion details of his fellow musicians were given. Among them were some well-known Easingwold names.[50] This was clearly a concert performance.

Fox's dance band work fell off towards Easter and then the Easingwold Temperance Brass Band began to appear. They treated towns-people in the Market Place on at least one Saturday,[51] when 'the playing was excellent' according to the *Advertiser*. The change of name, incidentally, and this is important, does not indicate that Isaac Fox and his men had signed the pledge. It seems to have been nothing more than an advertising ploy, maybe to reassure prospective bookers like the Druids. 'THE Druids Club Walk which was arranged for Sunday May 16th has been altered to the Sunday following. The Temperance Brass Band will as usual head the procession.'[52] At about this time in 1897 the papers had an enormous number of reports about committees and councils debating how to celebrate the forthcoming Diamond Jubilee and Isaac Fox clearly anticipated a key role in Easingwold's festivities. It was not to be, however. The job went elsewhere and Fox and his musicians took their talents to Crayke. Between £60 and £70 was raised to 'defray the expenses of a thoroughly enjoyable day at Crayke', it was announced, initial publicity told people, 'A Brass Band will be engaged for the day', a 'substantial tea' would be provided in a marquee, there would be sports, and other amusements and the day 'will be terminated by the Beacon Fire which along with Husthwaite is classified in the official list of Beacons in England.' There were also to be 'permanent celebrations ... The improvement of the School steps the Parish Church Clock, lamps for the village, and seats near the Castle.'[53]

The Easingwold Temperance did not take a leading part in its town's jubilee celebrations and the reason is that the Salvation Army Band was chosen to perform. Fox took his aggregation to Crayke and Sessay instead.

In Easingwold the creation of the Victoria Institute was a prominent part of the jubilee celebrations.

The Board of Guardians decided to give a shilling to each family in receipt of out-door relief and the lady visitors agreed to take, and pay for, the women and children in the Workhouse to go to the seaside (in July) and the Rural District Council agreed to a half day's paid holiday for the road men. There had been that change in the musical arrangements and the Salvation Army led a procession in the morning which ended up in the Market

General Booth addressing the children in Easingwold, July 6, 1908.
Hilda Sturdy giving the flowers to General Booth afterwards

Place 'where the volunteers fired a "feu de joie"'. In the afternoon the 'augmented band of the Salvation Army' took over. Then followed the sports, a tea in the Town Hall, and more sports. It was all remarkably like the later celebrations for Edward VII's coronation.[54]

The Jubilee celebrations frequently took a practical turn. At Brandsby for example people gathered to witness 'the laying of the Foundation-stone of the New Bath House (a memorial to the sixty years reign) by Mr H. C. Fairfax-Cholmeley' who has appeared in these pages as a cricketer.[55] He said the Brandsby building would probably be 'the first village Bath House in Engand [sic]. 'The use of such a building,' he went on, 'was obvious to all who understood cottage limitations, and was the most fitting memorial for a reign that embraced a period remarkable for its progress.' After '"God Save The Queen" ... there was the Annual Feast',[56] a procession, a tea and sports.

The one-off celebrations of the Jubilee and, later, the coronation, meant much work for the brass bands in the area. Many villages had agricultural shows and occasional galas, but the dances more often than not made do with either just a pianist or a pianist and one other, instead of the likes of Isaac Fox's dance band or the Klawitter Brothers String Band.[57] Certain pianists made regular appearances playing for dancing - people like J. Pennock Thompson - but the Easingwold Temperance seems to have gone through a bad patch. Music at the Easingwold coronation dance, was by a duo, not a full band, and among all the tributes to the helpers a note said who they were (and how long they worked).[58] 'Dancing was kept up until after five o'clock on Coronation morning. Miss M. Allison and Mr Geo. Fox supplied the music which was well rendered', and 'Mr. Wm Medd' had been in charge of the decorations 'which were done in his well-known style, the band stand illuminated with fairy lamps being very pretty.'

There was no mention of an Isaac Fox group at what must have been the most prestigious ball of the 1902 Easingwold season. Perhaps a band was simply too expensive. Anyway there was a crisis of some kind in the Fox organisation.[59] The *Advertiser* recorded incidents from June 1901 when a meeting of the committee and members of the Easingwold Temperance Band 'was held in the St John's School ... [and] decided to call the instruments in and have them sold, any surplus after defraying out-standing accounts to be given to the St John's School Fund.' It looks as if the Temperance simply went out of existence. In August 'the Easingwold Brass Band ... gave much satisfaction' at the tenth annual exhibition of produce organised by the Easingwold Floral and Horticultural Society. It was held in a marquee on the Cricket Field and the show was typical of those that were so important in many localities. The Society, however, was somewhat unusual in that its president was Mrs Love of Hawkhills a fact the *Advertiser* thought was worthy of comment.[60] In the afternoon there was a sports meeting, which included cycle races and a competition for the 'Best decorated bike', which was won by Mrs Love, no less.

The Easingwold Agricultural had a longer history than did the Horticultural Society, and in September 1902 it held its 42nd annual show. President of it was Major Coates, JP, DL, and the secretary was that John J. Penty of Avondale House, who had made the speech about Easingwold being a healthy place. Entrance to the show cost 1s. and many places had similar functions - always much looked forward to and a highlight in the year.[61] There was a show at Huby, for example, (the Huby and Sutton-on-the-Forest Agricultural Society's), and another at Ampleforth, both within weeks of that at Easingwold.[62]

The bands, the excursions, the agricultural shows, the parades, the feasts, the cricket matches and the football matches all contributed, to making what must have been a dull existence for the majority somewhat less so, but the fear of disaster in the form of an illness or an accident was ever present. In the last resort this could mean being taken into 'the Union', the Workhouse. This terrified people, not surprisingly, and on one occasion admission ended in tragedy.[63] On 2 August 1902 an inquest was held on the body of John Cook 'who committed suicide by hanging himself on the previous day.' He had been behaving strangely and was visited by Dr Elvins of Tollerton. The deceased was a labourer, aged 62, who lived alone in Newton-on-Ouse and the doctor, 'after some persuasion' got him to 'go into the Union Workhouse on Saturday.' The coroner heard that 'About three weeks ago when a police constable had also 'tried to persuade him to go to the workhouse, he [had] said, "Not while there is breath in me."' Poor man.

An organisation which provided payments for people who became sick was prominent in Easingwold; how many members did it have? This was Perseverance Lodge 745 of the United Ancient Order of Druids. On 5 January 1898 it held its annual general meeting at the York Hotel - Buller Hicks was elected as medical officer, J. W. Sturdy as secretary, J. H. Cleaver as 'Arch Druid' and L. J. Snowdon as 'Vice-Arch'.[64] In the year there had been an increase of 23 benefit members and the total number of members was 128. The total number of members who had received sick pay and the 'Amount of sickness experienced by the whole of the sick members, [was] 80 weeks and 3 days. The amount being paid to the above being £31 15s 0d. Number of members' wives on whose death 'funeral allowances have been paid, [was] 1.' Total funds of the Perseverance for the year was £182 14s 6d, and that represented an increase for the year of over £37.

The Easingwold branch of the United Ancient Order of Druids ran recruitment campaigns and one of them from 1901 gave details of what benefits were paid. The Reginald E. Smith type setter does not seem to have been on absolute top form, but in the *Advertiser's* public notices a 'Splendid opportunity for Young Men' was announced.[65]

A FRIE INITIATION NI HT
Wiil be he'd
On SATURDAY, MAY 11th, 1901,
AT THE LODGE ROOM,
YORK HOTEL, FASINGWOLD,
At 8-30 o'Clock

Young men from 16 to 38 years of age, wishing to become members, should avail themselves of this exception.l opportunity.
The 10 LLOWING ARE THE BINEFITS -

Sick ... 10s. per week for 26 weeks.
" ... 7s 6d per week for 26 weeks
" ... 5s per week for 52 weeks
Funeral Benefits ... Members, £12 at death
" " ... Members wife £10 at death

The Druids' notice appeared a second time, suitably corrected, after J. W. Sturdy had undoubtedly complained to Reginald Smith (who also appeared in the 'corrected' issue of the *Advertiser* as the auditor of the Victoria Institute's balance sheet for 1899).[66] Nothing was said about contributions, but that was remedied in another 'FREE INITIATION NIGHT' invite in 1902.[67] In an impressive spread readers were told that the United Ancient was 'the

Oldest, Largest, and Wealthiest Order of Druids in existence' , that it had 'a Membership of 88,784, and accumulated Funds of £500,000', and that it was 'established in the Eighteenth Century' and had branches 'in nearly every part of, England and Wales, and also in the Colonies'. The 'SCALE OF CONTRIBUTIONS' was given in detail.

In the year that the following table appeared there was a note in the paper about a Lodge meeting when 36 new members were initiated, their average age being 23 years. 'We are informed by the Secretary that this constitutes a record, beating the opening Lodge night (May 12th, 1888) by 2 members' wrote the *Advertiser*.[68]

16 and under		24	years.,	10d.	per fortnight	
24	,,	27	,,	11d.	,,	
27	,,	30	,,	1s.	,,	
30	,,	32	,,	1s.1d.	,,	
32	,,	34	,,	1s.2d.	,,	
34	,,	36	,,	1s.3d.	,,	
36	,,	38	,,	1s.4d.	,,	
38	,,	40	,,	1s.6d.	,,	

The Contributions meet all payments
No levies.

The Perseverance was a part of the Druids' Hull District in which, at the turn of the century, there were 7,558 members. This was revealed at the Easingwold annual dinner held at the Town Hall, presided over by Hicks, the 'Lodge Surgeon'. J. J. Penty praised him for saving the Easingwold Railway Company from the NER and for his work on and with the RDC. At intervals there were 'selections by the Easingwold Brass Band, items from the Gramaphone [sic] and songs' from various people.

The fear of sickness, debt or an inability to pay the bills that followed a bereavement led people to become subscribers to organisations like the Druids, and there is no doubt whatsoever that in the days before the welfare state they were a powerful force for good.

The gramophone which featured in the entertainment at the Perseverance's annual dinner was clearly new to Easingwold and was still regarded as a novelty. At a grand bazaar in Husthwaite, held to raise funds for a new vicarage to be built 'nearly opposite Beacon Banks', there were numerous stalls on one of which Mr J. Thompson and Mr J. T. Goodrick 'exhibited the polyphone, Edison's phonograph, and electric bells.'[69] This was in 1899, but almost a year and a half before this a demonstration of the Edison machine had been held in Easingwold.[70]

> EDISON'S latest Phonograph is being exhibited this, Friday evening, and to-morrow Saturday, at Miss Fawcett's, Market Place, Easingwold. Mr Edison's Agent operates this marvellous machine, which reproduces with great distinctness, the latest songs, bands, and solos. Among the specialities are speeches by Lord Charles Beresford, M.P., for York; and Sir Chris Furness, the unsuccessful candidate; the famous "Cock o' the North", with the firing of rifles at the Charge of Dargai is reproduced. The charge is only one penny each selection, therefore all should hear it.

Miss Fawcett's demonstration was held in 1898, but the gramophone was still regarded as a novelty some two and a half years later - something that could be a major attraction in a show much larger than could be held in Miss Fawcett's shop in the Market Place. The gram recital caught on for a time. In the public notices column of an *Advertiser* of the early summer of 1901 there were four announcements of events. The first simply told readers that the Easingwold Wesleyan Church would be holding a three-day 'GRAND-BAZAAR' at the Town Hall and the second was from the St John's School where, it was announced, Deaconess Jessie Ransome would 'give an account of her experiences in PEKING DURING THE SIEGE OF THE LEGATIONS.' The third notice was from John Allison, the secretary of the local cricket club, who announced a fund-raiser. Allison said that 'A Cushion Cake and Candy Fair' was to be held 'in the grounds of F. J. ROBINSON, ESQ.' and said he hoped 'that the ladies and gentlemen of the Town will contribute something (money or articles) towards the "Fun of the Fair," which is being provided for the funds of the Grand Old Institution: "The Easingwold Cricket Club."'

Following the appeal from John Allison the Salvation Army announced it had arranged a 'GREAT WHITSUNTDE ATTRACTION' for the three days of the holiday.[71] Once again the Smith typesetters were not at their best.

Reginald Smith reported Jessie Ransome's talk, and supported Allison's appeal for contributions to the Cushion, Cake and Candy, but there was no report about the Monster Gramophone and its uses by the Easingwold Salvationists.

SERGEANT MAJOR HALL
AND
BANDSMAN EVANS
From Darlington, with the
MONSTER GRAMOPHONE
Or Loud-VoicedTalking Machine
This is without doubt one of the best Gramophones
in the North of England.
Saturday Night, the Machine will be used
in the Open-air, and inside Barracks.

—

SUNDAY - Meetings all day.
Aft rroon at 2-45, GRAMOPHONE SERVICE.
TOWN HALL, at 6-15,
When in addition to Special Selections by the
Gramophone.
BANDSMAN EVANS will give the Wonderful
story of his Life, and ROBERT HALL will recite

—

MONDAY NIGHT, at 7-30,
ENTERTAINMENT
when amongst others will be given, selections by
the best bands in the country,
Sidewalk Conversations on Law Suits,
Qua re's, &c., Bird's Concert, Whist-
ling, Pussy Cats' Quarrel, French Laughing Song,
&c.
Come in Crowds. Collections at Doors

The Salvation Army held its 15th anniversary celebrations in Easingwold over two days in the spring of 1900. A public notice revealed that on Sunday 29 April Capt Hawcroft of Mexborough would be 'in charge all day', while the planned proceedings for the 28th were

Easingwold Town Band, 1905.
Outside the 'Galtres'. Front row: centre two Isaac Fox and Herbert Cowling.
Standing: 3rd from left Leonard Smith, 5th from left Edwin Cleaver on right Jack Cleaver.

given in some detail.[72] The details began, as was usual, with an assurance that the catering was going to be good

> HAM TEA (in the Barracks) at 5 o'clock; SUPPER at 8-45; TICKETS SIXPENCE. THANKSGIVING MEETING at 7-30 Officers, Soldiers, and Friends from York and Thirsk will take part.

The Salvation Army always celebrated the commencement of its work in Easingwold with celebrations like that of 1900, spread over a weekend with a public meeting on the Monday.[73] 'Fifteen years ago', the *Advertiser* said, 'they secured, as a barracks, the building they now occupy, - the Old Westerman School, - and since that time they have continued to hold services [there] regularly.' As they did everywhere the Salvationists laid great emphasis on music, had, of course, bands of their own, and frequently promoted concerts by visiting groups. In one year, for example, the 24 strong, highly regarded, York No. 1 was the star attraction.

The Salvation Army was prominent as a temperance organisation, as were the Methodist bodies. The Wesleyans had been in the town since the time of their founder. In the words of the *Bulmer's* guide of 1890: 'The Wesleyan Methodists erected their first chapel [in Easingwold] in the time of John Wesley. This was replaced by a more commodious structure in 1815 at a cost of £970. A school was added in 1836.' In the summer of 1901 a three day grand Bazaar was advertised. It was to be held at the Town Hall under the 'Distinguished Patronage of Lady Julia Wombwell, Henry Hawking, J. Grant Lawson MP, and others and was to be opened on the first day by Mrs C. S. Booth of New Zealand, with Varley's Band in attendance, Hawking on the second and Mrs Driffield of Easingwold on the third. Articles were to be sold and there were to be 'ENTERTAINMENTS, WASHING AND HAT-

TRIMMING COMPETITIONS. MUSIC' and admission was to be First Day, one shilling; Second Day, one shilling after 6 o'clock, sixpence; Third Day, Threepence. [74]

The Wesleyan bazaar was organised by the 'joint secretaries, Mr F E Rookledge and Mr J W Smith.' An introductory paragraph to Reg Smith's account of the three day event explained all.[75]

> Methodism was first introduced to Easingwold by a man named John Nelson, in 1744, while passing through the town in the hands of a press gang. Since that date the followers of John Wesley in the district have grown in numbers until at the present time Easingwold is at the head of a large circuit, including some 23 chapels. The first ... was built in 1784, and thirty years afterwards the present [Easingwold] chapel was erected. For some years, the trustees of the property had [have] felt that the edifice greatly needed repairs, and last year the work of restoration was thoroughly carried out, the building being entirely redecorated and fitted with modern heating appliances at a cost of nearly £300. It was in order to wipe out, if possible, this large debt that the three days' grand bazaar in the Town Hall was organised.

Just a few days before the bazaar opened a quarterly meeting of the Easingwold Wesleyan Circuit was held at the local chapel with the Rev R. Renton presiding. He reported that there were then 554 members in the circuit and '12 on trial, also 53 junior members.' Finances were in 'a sound ... condition' and a benevolent fund for the relief of necessitous poor Methodists in the circuit 'had been set up.' Members from Crayke, Easingwold, Raskelfe, Thormanby, Stillington, Sutton, Thornton Hill, Huby, Sheriff Hutton, Tholthorpe and Alne were present.[76]

The Wesleyans campaigned against the demon drink at every opportunity. They were great advocates of Sunday Schools and directed their drink messages to generations of various branches of the Band of Hope. On one Friday in May 1899 at a 'Band' meeting the Rev R. Ainsworth gave 'An excellent and stirring address' to this effect and was backed up by the Rev F. M. Lowry. Then followed a whole string of recitations: 'The Robin's Temperance Song,' 'The Angel's Story,' 'The Gambler's Wife' and 'Stick to your pledge' among them.[77] By Sept 1898 a return showed that in Yorkshire there were 249 Sunday Schools with 3,668 officers and teachers and a total of 18,597 scholars; the Bands of Hope numbered 97 with 8,447 members.

The Wesleyans were strong and active in Easingwold, with many of their members prominent in the business and the government of the town. They were strongly established in the villages as well. At Husthwaite, for example,[78] where the Sunday School anniversary heard Lily Cariss and others, at a recitation evening in 1901.

The Wesleyans, at the turn of the century were expanding in the villages, and reports presented to quarterly circuit meetings mentioned the building that was going on. For example[79]

> It was reported that a new Sunday Schoolroom had been recently erected adjoining the chapel at Huby, and the opening would take place shortly. With reference to the proposed new chapel at Crayke, it was deemed advisable to open a subscription list, and Mr Beckwith was appointed treasurer for the fund, and Mr Todd secretary. It was also stated that there was a growing desire at Newton-upon-Ouse for a new chapel, and it was resolved that inquiries be made as to a suitable site. The treasurer

of the Twentieth Century Fund reported that 594 guineas had been paid in, and it was resolved that the list of contributions be kept open until the end of the year.

The pages of the *Easingwold Advertiser* carry regular accounts of Wesleyan activity at the places mentioned in the quarterly report. A veritable building boom seemed to be underway. At Oulston, for example, and Helperby, where a convention was held to raise funds for the chapel and enlargement of the schools, and at Coxwold where great and successful efforts were made to 'improve and beautify their church' by the Wesleyans. It was reopened on 15 March 1899.

NOTES

1. *Advertiser* 27 February 1897
2. *Ibid* 6 March. It is not clear whether the Easingwold team was from the EFC or a scratch side. Anyway the team names were given.
3. *Ibid* 13 March 1897. Also *ibid* 20 March 1893 (Stillington game), 27 March 1897 (Crayke and St Crux).
4. *Ibid* 8 January 1898.
5. *Ibid* 15 March 1902.
6. *Ibid* 20 March 1902
7. *Ibid* 5 April 1902.
8. Though one Sharpe took over later in the year. The club's fixture list in *Ibid* 22 November 1902.
9. Report *Ibid* 15 November 1902
10. *Ibid* 13 March 1897.
11. *Ibid* 3 April 1897. Crayke started its season against Hawkhills at Crayke *Ibid* 1 and 8 May 1897. For a report of the Crayke/Blakeborough concert see *Ibid* 15 May 1897.
12. *Ibid* 10 April 1897.
13. *Ibid* 17 April 1897. On Alne's opening game *Ibid* 15 May 1897.
14. Report in *Ibid* 22 May 1897.
15. Its fixture list is printed in *Ibid* 10 July 1897.
16. That of 10 July 1897.
17. With games at Crayke (v Husthwaite), Easingwold (who played St John's College) and Great Ouseburn. *Ibid* 14 May 1898.
18. *Ibid* 21 May 1898.
19. *Ibid* 9 July 1898.
20. There was also a J. C. Hicks in the Easingwold team.
21. *Advertiser* 16 July 1898. The averages from *Ibid* 15 October 1898.
22. *Ibid* 13 August and 10 September 1898.
23. *Ibid.*
24. *Ibid* 12 November 1898.
25. *Ibid* 25 May 1901.
26. *Ibid* 6 July 1901.
27. *Ibid* 31 May and 7 June 1902. See also the letters from Christopher Benson in *Ibid* 16 June 1902 and Edward Crosby in 23 June 1902.
28. See his advert on the front page of *Ibid* 2 August 1902.
29. Eg advertisement in *Ibid* 22 March 1902. The storm and the photograph reported in *Ibid* 31 August 1901.
30. What journal the photograph appeared in is unknown.
31. *Advertiser* 24 August 1901.
32. *Ibid* 31 May 1902.
33. *Ibid* 30 January 1897.
34. *Ibid* 8 September 1900. The venue for Stellings dreadful crime was Norton.
35. *Ibid* 22 October 1898.
36. *Ibid* 15 October 1898.
37. *Ibid* 5 August 1899.
38. *Ibid* 25 October 1902. A report of 1901's feast in *Ibid* 18 October 1901. The 'Helperby' reported in *Ibid* 23 July 1898.
39. *Ibid* 12 August 1899 in connection with the NER, to Helmsley.
40. *Ibid* 19 August 1899. The Barnum and Bailey excursion from *Ibid* 12 August 1899.
41. *Ibid* 16 July 1898.
42. *Ibid* 19 January 1901.
43. *Ibid* 5 April 1902, the Maillet visit in *Ibid* 12 October 1898.
44. Descriptions of the celebrations in *Ibid* 5 and 12 July 1902.

45. *Ibid* 16 August 1902.
46. T. L. Cooper, *Brass Bands of Yorkshire* (Clapham via Lancaster 1974) p15.
47. *Advertiser* 9 January 1897.
48. *Ibid* 23 January 1897.
49. *Ibid* 13 February 1897.
50. The musicians were: Mr J. Caisley, clarinet; Mr Banks, first violin; Mr A Cariss, violoncello; Miss Moncaster, harmonium; Mr G. R. Fox, Cornet. *Ibid* 20 February 1897.
51. *Ibid* 1 May 1897.
52. *Ibid* 8 May 1897.
53. *Ibid* 29 May 12 June 1897.
54. *Ibid* 26 June 1897. The 'Programme of Events' is given in *ibid* 19 June 1897. The reader will be delighted to know that the LGB did agree to the Guardians' hand-out.
55. *Ibid* 3 July 1897.
56. The Brandsby Jubilee festivities and the village feast were held at the same time.
57. The Klawitters at Alne reported in *Advertiser* 18 February 1899. Pennock Thompson at Stillington *Ibid*.
58. *Ibid* 16 August 1902.
59. *Ibid* 8 June 1901.
60. *Ibid* 30 August 1902.
61. *Ibid* 30 August and 13 September 1902 (advertisements). Report 20 September.
62. *Ibid* 9 August 1902 (Huby), 13 September 1902 (Ampleforth).
63. *Ibid* 9 August 1902.
64. *Ibid* 15 January 1898.
65. *Ibid* 4. May 1901.
66. The balance sheet showed an income of £54 9s 0d and a balance in hand of £1 11s 11d. Report of annual meeting also in *ibid* 11 May 1901.
67. *Ibid* 22 February 1902.
68. *Ibid* 1 and 8 March 1902.
69. *Ibid* 5 August 1899.
70. *Ibid* 29 January 1898. For typical adverts from Miss Fawcett, see eg. *Ibid* 22 May and 16 October 1897. Her business was taken over by W. Millions. See his ad in *Ibid* 25 June 1898.
71. *Ibid* 1 June 1901 (the Deaconess) and 25 May 1901 (the Cake, Cushion etc.)
72. *Ibid* 28 April 1900. Public notices column.
73. *Ibid* 5 May 1900. For other anniversary celebrations see eg. *Ibid* 1 May 1897, 26 April and 3 May 1902.
74. *Ibid* 23 June 1901, public notice.
75. *Ibid* 29 June 1901.
76. *Ibid* 22 June 1901.
77. *Ibid* 13 May 1899. The following statistics from a report in *Ibid* 3 September 1898.
78. *Ibid* 6 July 1901. Account of the Wesleyan Sunday School anniversary. The Tommy meeting *Ibid* 12 April 1902. The Crayke contract *Ibid* 3 May 1902.
79. *Ibid* 6 August 1898. Principal guest speaker was the Rev Peter Thompson of the East London Mission. The opening at Coxwold in *Ibid* 18 March 1899.

Long Street, Easingwold, 1905

Chapter 3

THE OOPERZOOTIC (AND MASHED TURNIPS)

In Easingwold there existed an organisation called the Wesleyan Institute which has been mentioned before and was one that the town was justifiably proud of, and with which familiar names were associated. F. E. Rookledge was treasurer and secretary and the Rev Lowry was president, John Rookledge (the 'father' of both the Methodist Society circuit and F.E.) was librarian, and 'The Lanternist, [was] Mr E. Smith', and the pianist, Miss Millington, was also asked to continue for another year. This was at the annual general meeting of September 1897 when a programme was arranged that was considered to be the equal of the 'many excellent ones which during the 16 years of the existence of the Institution had been brought before the members.' It was 'entirely free - no charge for admission is made, nor for the use of the library, a valuable collection of books of considerably over 1000 volumes' and it was not sectarian, 'though the title would lead some to suppose that it' was. Attendances were going up.[1] The Institute put on lectures and deserved the success it received, and its 17th session started with a talk in the vestry on 'Excellence of Character', by the president, in which he extolled the virtues of the likes of Brindley, Inigo Jones, Samuel Smiles and others.[2] The autumn programme of 1901 was a good example of W.I. fare, where talks on Rudyard Kipling and Tennyson appeared alongside lighter offerings. On one occasion J. W. Sturdy read a paper on 'Friendly Societies' a report of which took up over 18 inches of column space in the *Advertiser*.[3]

Wesleyan Chapel, Chapel Street, 1905

The *Advertiser* devoted an enormous amount of its local news coverage to the activities of the Methodists in its area, and in early 1899 it had much to report about the raising of the Wesleyan Twentieth Century Fund. The first meeting in connection with it was held in January 1899. John Rookledge was chairman, and he reminisced about the early days of Wesleyanism in the town.' What then was the Twentieth Century Fund? The Rev F. R. Smith of York explained that the Wesleyans had decided to 'try to raise a million pounds from a million Methodists ... something ... totally apart from circuit or other funds. How was the money collected spent? The item most criticised at that time was the proposed building of a Central Hall in London at a cost of £250,000. Money would also go on educational work, grants would be made to replace 'many a rickety old chapel' in the villages, money would be spent on orphaned Methodist children, and £200,000 'in Home and Foreign Missions.'

Another campaign the Wesleyans gave their support to was one to force the nation's pubs to close on Sundays, and a resolution from a temperance meeting at Helperby would, if implemented, have denied the thirsty the right to partake on the Sabbath. Mrs J. Knox-Lyal and Miss Tinling of the British Women's Temperance Association were the star speakers.[4] This resolution would not have been to the liking of Yorkshire's best-known boozer - a character whose exploits would have regularly alarmed the likes of Knox-Lyal.[5] He frequently appeared in the papers. He deserved to.

JANE CAKEBREAD'S RECORD
BEATEN

At Scarborough, on Tuesday Robert Hunter (47), labourer, William - Street, better known as "Daddy-fra-Cayton," made his 108th appearance on a charge of drunkenness and disorderly conduct. He said he knew nothing about the matter, but would take Sergeant Coultas' word for it. He was committed to York for a month.

Wesleyans would have been united in their condemnation of him, though there were disagreements about other things. John Rookledge said that not everyone was completely in favour of the Twentieth Century Fund and the Wesleyan chapel choir supper of 1898 also caused some bother. Rookledge loaned the choristers his bagatelle board, and there were games, songs, recitations and a meal laid on by Mr Haynes of the Trevelyan Hotel[6]. What went on however infuriated a correspondent who wrote to the *Advertiser* in very militant terms.[7] "A Methodist" complained in forceful detail about the singing and dancing, "... such proceedings are in my humble opinion utterly opposed to Methodism ... ." He continued to quote selectively from the scriptures to support his views.

It is to be hoped that the Rev Lowry did not have too many people with attitudes like those of A Methodist in his congregation, but he was duly replied to by one who signed himself 'Yours, &c., DUM VIVIMUS VIVAMUS.'[8]

He began with a quote from Burns saying

> Ye've nought to do but mark and tell
> Your neebour's faults and folly

then went on. 'There are a class of people on God's earth who serve as a "wet blanket" on everything that savours of enjoyment', he wrote, and 'I think your correspondent ... is one of these.' '

Not long after the dispute about what went on at the Easingwold choir supper the annual general meeting of the Wesleyan Institute was held.[9] During the evening it was announced 'that it was' probably the last meeting' which the Rev F. M. Lowry would take part in, as 'the regulations of the ministry' meant he had to move on.

The Revs Lowry and W. B. Lowther both left Easingwold in late August, to be replaced by R. Renton and R. Whitehead. Lowther went to Tarporley, in Cheshire, and Lowry to Tadcaster.

The Primitive Methodists were also well established in Easingwold, and had had a chapel in Spring Street since 1840, built then for £562 to accommodate 300 persons. In 1901 Easingwold was honoured as it never had been before in the '60 years settlement of the Primitive Methodist Connexion in the town.'[10] The annual meeting of the York and Leeds District was held there, and delegates from all over the area attended. On the Saturday an open air meeting was held at the top of Long Street and, later, a 'Holiness Meeting' in the chapel. On the Sunday there were more open air services and a camp meeting in the Chase Garth where upwards of 1,400 attended. In the evening a love feast was held in the chapel and a 'Platform Meeting' in the Town Hall.

Spring Street, Easingwold, Primitive Methodist Chapel and members, early 1900s

The Primitives, like the Wesleyans, were ardent supporters of the temperance campaigns and also, like the Wesleyans, were well established in the villages – at Helperby for example, where an annual camp meeting was held,[11] and at Crayke[12] and Huby, where the chapel had been 'built four years ago' and they were trying to pay the debt off with the proceeds of bazaars and such things.[13] The Primitives played a role in the village communities where they existed, providing lectures and religious services, and adding to the life of some rather remote places., In 1897, for example, at the Huby PM chapel, 'when a very interesting lecture was given ... by Mr Richardson, York, entitled "Heroes of the olden days."'[14]

On one occasion the Easingwold Primitives had the Rev J. Hind of York over to preach on a Sunday. He stayed over and on the following Monday was scheduled to do 'his popular lecture "Savonarola"' in the chapel.[15] As has been indicated talks like that on Savonarola were somewhat unusual, but there was also a sustained and worthy series of lectures given in the villages which had the support of the North Riding County Council and must have been of immense value to the community. In a copy of the *Easingwold,*[16] there appeared announcements that lectures on sick nursing by a Miss Baigent had been given in both Sheriff Hutton and Gilling. Audiences had averaged 80 at the former place where on one occasion 100 were present. This is remarkable as the lectures were not free and in Sheriff Hutton they actually yielded a profit. Miss Baigent's lectures were also given 'to a class of 70' at Husthwaite.[17] Early in 1899 it was reported that Dr Ellis of Tollerton had agreed to take a 'series of classes ... to be held in the first class waiting room at Alne Station',[18] and nursing classes were held at Welburn at the end of 1898 by Dr Dougall of York. People were attracted to them from many places. They sat an examination at the end of the course, and all were successful.[19]

The nursing classes were a pioneering effort to profile a much needed service and cost money. So did other ventures,and to support them dozens and dozens of concerts were put on at to raise money for them. These gave pleasure to the villagers and brought a modest amount of fame to some of the participants. Mr R. Blakeborough for example.

Blakeborough was known as a 'Yorkshire Humourist' and he appeared in the spring of 1897 at a 'HUMOROUS CONCERT' in the National Schoolroom at Crayke 'promoted by the members of the Crayke Cricket Club.'[20] Earlier Blakeborough had topped the bill at Tollerton at a concert put on 'in aid of the Reading Room funds.'[21] It seems that he performed his sketches in drag and also worked as a stand-up comic. Miss Milburn of York had to follow him and did so with a rendering of 'The flight of Ages'. Then another selection was given which included the old standby 'Jack's the Boy', 'The Coster's Serenade' and 'The Darkie's Love.'[22] An interesting feature of the concert at Crayke was the appearance of the Bigotphone Band in which Von Bohr played. The instrumentation is fascinating.[23] Most of the musicians were females and they played cornet a piston, Horn in G and Trumpet, Oboe, two Bass Clarionets, French Horn, Trombone (played by the Rev M.C. Dickenson), Tenor Horn, Bass Ophicleider and Double Bass Ophicleider. Von Bohr played the last named instrument. The only music mentioned from the Bigotphone performance was 'Selection, "The Geisha"' and 'Medley".[24]

There were other artistes who were booked from outside the area and topped the bill at places like the Tollerton School Room. They were semi-professionals like Fred Hall of York. who appeared at Stillington,[25] while another visiting artist who appeared in the villages in the Easingwold area was 'G. W. Nicholson, society humourist, Leeds.' He was booked to appear at Crayke, where hardly a week went by without a concert it seemed, and in his 'hands the comic part of the programme was indefatigable, he being expressed by the *Vide Press* as "The King of the Comedians."'[26]

The most popular music hall performer to visit Easingwold was the aforementioned Harry Liston who, in February 1898, appeared at the town's number one spot. 'MR HARRY LISTON'S NEW "MERRY MOMENTS," 'was put on at the Town Hall. Tickets were 2s. 1s., and 6d. The star was 'a noted ventriloquist and humorist.' Visit the Town Hall, readers were urged, 'and hear his entirely New Programme, which has created for him a 'world-wide reputation. Mr Liston is an artiste of exceptional ability, his singing, both sentimental and comic, being of a high standard.' It is good to be able to record that a 'large and fashionable audience' turned up to see and hear 'Merry Moments' with Liston also demonstrating his ability as a quick-change artist. 'The rapidity with which he could change from one character to another is astonishing', the *Easingwold's* reporter said, 'and his singing, &c., was greatly appreciated.'[27]

Harry Liston (1843 - 1929) was the only nationally known performer to appear at the Town Hall in the period covered in these notes, and he is an important figure in the history of the British Music Hall. A popular history of it called him 'a sort of Fred Astaire, of the period, with top hat, white tie and tails.'[28]

He was willing and able to play at small venues and returned to the Easingwold area early in 1901. By this time he had altered his repertoire which now reflected the fact that the country was at war, as his publicity (which appeared in the *Advertiser* on 13 April) shows.

EASINGWOLD TOWN HALL,
THURSDAY NEXT, APRIL 19th.
POCKLINGTON VICTORIA HALL,
FRIDAY NEXT, APRIL 19th.
NEW PROGRAMME.
War Songs, Military Sketches, Patriotic Music.
MR HARRY LISTON,
Humourist (from Crystal Palace, Sydenham).
MISS LORD LUMLEY,
"Charming Young Actress," vide "Telegraph" (from London.)
MR PERCY WOODROFFE
Pianist (London Concerts)
Mr Liston as "Lord Roberts."
Society Comedy Sketches, "Merry Moments."
Admission 2/-, 1/-, and (limited) 6d.
Overture at 8. Carriages at 10-15.

Considerable space has been devoted to the entertainments that went on in the villages and in Easingwold itself and the quantity was impressive. Three issues of the *Advertiser* were consulted for the brief note about the first visit by Harry Liston, and each of these either advertised or reported on other shows that must have done much to brighten up their area. In the first: a concert at Brandsby was mentioned; on 12 February Blakeborough's show at Tollerton was reviewed; and on the 19th shows at Newton-on-Ouse, Sutton-on-Forest, and Stillington (yet again) were noticed.[29]

Several minstrel groups performed in the area during the Boer War period and were very popular. People like Von Bohr also blacked up and sang what were offensively known as coon songs, and on Shrove Tuesday 1899, at Crayke, in a show to raise funds for the piano fund a Mr Colling appeared as a 'Nigger Minstrel'.[30] This was in an 'entertainment' which was said to consist 'of a humorous dialogue entitled "Uncle Benjamin's Legacies" and Mrs Jarley's Waxworks' into which were interspersed contributions by Mr C. Dennis (songs) and Mr A. Edmandson (more songs including 'I have got the ooperzootic'). Mr E. was clearly the star of the show, the link man par excellence, and he weighed in with a recitation that was often performed. This was 'Mashed Turnips', which was also inflicted on an audience at the Wesleyan Institute by a lady, though she altered the spelling somewhat. Anyway

'A recitation by Miss Fish, "Mashed Tonups," caused much amusement.'[31] (Edmandson appeared in the press as Edmondson on occasion.)

Recitations (always) and minstrel songs (often) were features of the concerts that were put on for worthy causes and needy organisations. Also ever present were dialect songs and sketches.

Many of the wonderful songs from the minstrel shows have survived to become a standard part of the repertoire of jazz bands of a 'traditional' bent, but the way they were put over and rendered when they first appeared was offensive, and should have appeared as offensive at the time. Eugene Stratton also sang about 'The Dandy-coloured coon,' for example, and there were hundreds of similar compositions that influenced the populace, and led to ghastly racial attitudes and assumptions. Children's comics came to exploit the stereotypes of racial types given to the world by the minstrel shows and advertisers were not backward in doing so. For example 'The Amalgamated Tyre Cos., Ltd.,' regularly advertised in the Easingwold paper and on one occasion it had a two column, five inch deep spread extolling the virtues of one of its products.[32] In the top right hand corner was a drawing of a negro lecturer dressed in frock coat and the usual check trousers with a top hat on the table in front of him, and using a rolled umbrella to make his points. The sales pitch went [33]

DERE BRUDDER CYCLISTS.

ASK yo'self de kwestion why shud yo ride dem tyres dat punctures, dat am slow and heaby, and dat want pumpin' up every time yo set out? Why shud yo be behind de times. Yo must not look a gift 'oss in de mouth; but if yo pay for yo cicycle, yo shud hab de best for yo money. Hab dem dat beat de World's Records, and am derefor de fastest, dat am 2lbs. lighter dan any obers, and am guaranteed more fuller dan any ober. Don't yo buy no pig in a poke Tak my advice, send to der makers for a catalog of

A * B * NON-PUNCTURABLE TYRES

and for some copies of testimonials from 'dem dat am riding 'dem. Yo won't buy no old-fashioned and puncturing tyres den.

There was also in existence an Easingwold Philharmonic Society which provided weightier stuff than the likes of Harry Liston. As a part of the diamond jubilee fund raising it gave a concert 'of exceptional length, but unusually excellent' in April 1898. It was the 'finest Concert that' had 'ever been given in Easingwold,' and was put on to raise money for the Victoria Buildings. It began with the society rendering Verdi's part song 'The Storm King comes forth' and progressed to solo performances of the kind that were always interspersed in the concerts. 'Vianka's Song' was rendered 'creditably' by Miss Mangles, for example, and Mr W. P. Wilson 'whispered Hamilton Grey's *"Heavenly Song"* most devoutly.'

The Miss Mangles who appeared at the Philharmonic concert - and many others - was a part of a family which ran an educational venture sited at Mowbray House. Mrs E. Newton Mangles and her daughters were all principals of the Easingwold High School and Ladies' College at which PUPILS [were] prepared for the Senior and Junior, Local and Higher Cambridge Examinations' and other examinations. 'Private Lessons in Music, Singing, Violin, Painting, &c., with a Lady or Master' could be arranged. The E.H.S. claimed, at the beginning of 1897, to have had considerable 'Success in recent Cambridge Local and

Unknown school, Easingwold area, early 1900s

Incorporated Society of Musicians' Examinations' and employed as visiting master for the violin 'MR W. H. GREGORY, Professor at the Leeds College of Music.'[34]

The Easingwold Philharmonic concert was held at the Town Hall, the venue for many exhibitions, religious meetings, bazaars and dances. Hundreds of dances were reported from elsewhere in the area. What were they like at the turn of the century? It is difficult to know exactly as details were rarely given about what people danced to. (Though on a couple of occasions noted a whole programme was given in the press.) They were extremely popular. On 30 January 1897 there was a typical one held for a good cause at Great Ouseburn, but the report about it said nothing more than that the music was supplied by W. and A. D. Dinsdale and that dancing started at 9.30 and was 'kept up with great spirit until 4-30 next morning.' Next to the Ouseburn account, though, was another from Brandsby - the modestly named annual dance of the Brandsby Club and Institute. Dancing on this occasion 'began at 7 p.m., with the old English dance, "The Triumph" sometimes known as "Down the Middle," and was kept up with great spirit until 1 a.m.' (The Great Ouseburn Reading Room, for which dance funds were collected was reported a year later to have been 'in a prosperous condition, and ... patronised and valued by the larger portion of the young men of the village.'[35] (Creating a village reading room was a regular and popular form of community effort.)

It will have been noticed that certain villages in the Easingwold area were particularly active in promoting community activities and entertainments, creating and supporting football and cricket teams, for example, organising concerts and dances. Raskelfe (for a time) was like that, as was Alne, but Crayke was the place where most went on. In September 1899 the village was intrigued and entertained by a controversy involving a local farmer and a local lady. Next to an ad for Dr Tibbles' Vi-Cocoa appeared a public apology from 'CHRISTOPHER DENNIS, of Mosswood Grange, Crayke, in the County of York, Farmer.' This was not the first of such notices.

Dennis, who may have been the vocalist of that name in the Crayke Shrove Tuesday extravaganza who gave the paying customers 'That was enough for me' and 'The days gone by' and appeared with Miss Roe as Darby and Joan, revealed that he was sorry about something he had said early in August. In the public notices he publicly apologised[36]

> for the insulting and personal remarks I made to, and about MISS METCALFE, and I own they are false and untrue.
>
> I also publicly apologise to DAVID SCOBY in conjunction with the above false remarks, for defaming his character, which were invented by myself.

What Dennis's notice was about - what he said to and about Miss Metcalfe and Scoby - is unclear, but he signed it and dated it. Then, the following week, in another paid-for ad, he denied it all.[37] He said he wished 'to contradict the statement' that had appeared in print. 'As for apologising,' he wrote, 'I never had anything to apologise for, and never thought of doing so. The defaming of the characters originated from another person.' Why then, the readers of the *Easingwold* might have asked, did he make his grovelling apology in the first place.

This was not the end of the affair. Some time went by, then Dennis inserted yet another notice in the *Advertiser*. This was dated 26 August and witnessed by K. E. T. Wilkinson.[38] In it, he *went back* to square one and apologised for 'the gross and insulting imputations which [he] ... made upon' the character of Miss Metcalfe of Wyndham Hall, Crayke.[39] He acknowledged they were 'unfounded and untrue' and he promised not to repeat them or 'assert that they were originally made ... by David Scobey.'

Dennis's bad behaviour was, undoubtedly, *the* major topic of conversation in Crayke in the last year of the 19th century, though what was allegedly said never became clear. Some fairly obvious possibilities spring to mind. The villagers of Crayke would have been concerned about a change of control in the area which was certainly of major importance and could have affected the lives of a huge proportion of the local population. ' ... at Harker's Hotel, York, on WEDNESDAY, JULY 26th, 1899, at 1 for 2 o'clock, unless an acceptable offer for the whole is previously made,' it was announced, the Crayke Hall estate would be sold in 26 lots by Messrs Mabbett & Edge.[40]

In lots of from 2 acres to 135 acres with
Homesteads.

YORKSHIRE - NORTH RIDING.

THE CRAYKE HALL ESTATE, 2 miles from Easingwold,
10 from Thirsk, and 13 from York, comprising an
old-fashioned residence in beautiful grounds commanding
grand views, together with about 530 acres of valuable land
for the most part rich feeding pastures
producing about £750 per annum.

The sale went on - there was no grand offer for the lot - and the *Advertiser* reminded its readers of its extent and profitability.[41] 'The residential and agricultural property know [sic] as the Crayke Hall estate ... is situate in the parishes of Crayke and Stillington, and comprises five grazing, dairy and mixed farms, with homesteads, cottages, etc.' Bidding for it was 'brisk' and 'The prices realised were satisfactory, the total being £17,134, which on the annual rental represents about 30 years' purchase. The purchasers were Messrs Stephen Cliff, of Leeds; H E Leetham, of York; D Mellor, of Bradford; and Samuel Johnson, of Crayke.[42] Leetham bought the hall, some cottages, some pasture, including the 17 acres known as Low Pasture, Crab Mill Close and Little Crab Mill Close; Cliff bought 'the mixed farm, known as "Stocking Hall" (52 acres), ... a holding of accommodation land, measuring nearly 16 acres, for £2,700 ... Mount Pleasant Farm ... Low Langwith Close ... pasture known as "Square Croft" (four acres) for £250, and Mosswood Farm, having and [sic] acreage of 134 acres two roods, for £4,000.'[43]

Leetham rapidly got rid of some of his purchases and the *Easingwold* recorded, less than a month after the sale at Harker's, that 'The house, grounds, and cottages belonging to the Crayke Hall Estate, recently ... bought by Mr H. E. Leetham, Aldersyde, Dringhouses, have been purchased from him by Mr M O Matthews, the tenant.'

Property of a more modest kind was also sold at the George Hotel, Easingwold, when some more indication was given of local values.[44] Two houses in Little Lane, Easingwold, for example, went for £150. Nearby, John Flawith, auctioneer held a sale at the Fox and Goose, Alne, and sold '4 dwelling-houses, situate in the centre of the village.' No more details than that were given, but bidding started at £200 and ran up to £360.[45] In March 1898 Flawith sold grass and arable land to F. J. H. Robinson, [46] and also bought - as an agent - 'a valuable freehold at Helperby.[47] In March he was selling property in Tollerton, a dwelling house for £270 and 2 cottages for £176 each.[48] Shortly afterwards F.A. Rickaby of Prospect House, Easingwold purchased grassland on Raskelfe Road.

When some of the land transfers mentioned above took place the country was at war. Did this lead to an upsurge in political activity in the Easingwold area? It did not. Careful reading of the columns of the *Advertiser* shows that little of a public, political nature went on either in the years before the war or during the conflict in South Africa - but there was some, and reports enable some political affiliations to be identified. In August 1898 the Vale of Mowbray Habitation of the Tory Primrose League held a demonstration.[49] Among those present were Mr and Mrs Wilson whose seat, Gilling Castle, was the venue for the gathering (they were the 'Ruling Councillor and Dame-President of the Habitation'), Mrs and Miss Fairfax-Cholmeley of Brandsby, and a number of clerics including Canon Hudson (Gilling) and the Revs Austen and Swann (of Ampleforth and Brandsby). Mr Lane-Fox the Vice chancellor of the Primrose was also present and Sir William Worsley presided. There was a Conservative government in office which Worsley did not rate very highly and he said that if the League 'could do anything to strengthen the weak knees of [it], they would do a very good work.' He claimed the Primrose League 'was not bound up with the politics of any party' but was simply a pressure group. That would have come as a considerable surprise to many.

Lane-Fox at Gilling said he would 'say something in favour of this so-called "weak-kneed Government." He said, 'many of its supporters' considered the administration to be absolutely radical having passed measures of a 'far more advanced Liberal and Radical character than any others which had been passed in the lifetime of any man in the country.'[50]

In the lapse of time between the Gilling Castle meeting in 1898 and the general election in 1900 there had been little Tory campaigning in the area. An exception occurred in July 1899, however, when the York Conservatives met at Newburgh Priory. Ald J. S. Rymer, presided and J. G. Butcher, one of York's MPs, was present, making a very jingoistic speech. He attacked 'friends of President Kruger in this country' and applauded the government for having got concessions from the South African leader that Joseph Chamberlain had declared could form (maybe would form) the basis of a satisfactory settlement of their differences (about 'fair and just treatment' for our 'fellow subjects'). Butcher said he recognised 'Kruger as a hard nut to crack ... not the kind of man for a small tea party' and went on to congratulate the government on some of its legislation. He welcomed the Tithe Rates Act, which would cost York one tenth of a penny in the pound, but would remove an injustice 'which even Mr Gladstone had in former times admitted', and he naturally referred, proudly, to the Workmen's Compensation Act. This had not led to the ruination of employers as critics had forecast. Insurance premiums had gone down and 'the cost of litigation had enormously decreased.'[51]

People like Butcher often used the agricultural shows to deliver political speeches, but by no stretch of the imagination could the Easingwold area be regarded as a hotbed of political activity. However, though, things changed when the election was called. On Monday 17 September John Grant Lawson, the sitting (Tory) MP, was readopted at a meeting at Thirsk[52] and began his campaign for re-election. He appeared at Easingwold and held a public meeting in the Market Place, supported by H. Hawking, Sir George Wombwell, Capt J. Stapylton and J. C. Bannister. No great details of his speech were given, but clearly he spent most of his time dwelling on the government's record, noting particularly what it had done for agriculture and its conduct of the war (now that things were going better for Britain). These were good tactics that looked as if they amounted to a guarantee of success. The *Advertiser* drew some parallels with earlier contests.[53] 'THE General Election fully reflects the popular view of the war', it said, which it did.

There was a somewhat similar issue before the country in 1812, and again in 1859, and on both these occasions the war party triumphed. In 1812 we were in the thick of the struggle with Napoleon, whose name was then a real terror in this country. In 1859 there was another collapse of the peace party, when Cobden and Bright, and several other leaders of the Manchester School of Politics were defeated at the polls.

The *Advertiser's* prophecy of a Tory victory in 1900 turned out to be correct.

The government was greatly helped in what history knows as 'The Khaki Election' by war enthusiasm, by impeccable timing, and by dissensions among the liberals. The *Advertiser's* coverage of the speeches, manifestos and addresses in the couple of weeks before polling demonstrated those dissensions and on 29 September, for example, there appeared in it paragraphs summarising contributions to the campaign from the likes of Lord Salisbury, Sir William Harcourt, Henry Campbell-Bannerman, A.J. Balfour, John Morley, Joe Chamberlain and H. H. Asquith. Balfour boasted of the government's social reforms and Campbell-Bannerman, a future Prime Minister, complained that it had failed to check or guard against South African militarism.

The *Advertiser* continued to notice speeches by the major politicians and it was rumoured that the opposition would put up a candidate to contest Thirsk and Malton against J. G. Lawson. They held a meeting in the Easingwold Town Hall on 'Current Political Questions' addressed by Joseph Hawes of the National Liberal Federation and under the chairmanship of Hugh C. Fairfax-Cholmeley. No details of what went on were ever given, but it is clear that the gathering was not a success.[54] It may have influenced the liberals profoundly. Whether it did or not, they allowed Grant Lawson a walk-over!

The results of the general election overall were more-or-less as predicted, though some commentators accused Salisbury of dirty tricks. When the counting was over the Tories still had a very healthy majority. The *Advertiser's* 'Retrospect of the Year 1900' quantified it - '30 [October]. Close of the General Election : result, Government majority of 134.'

The visit of Joseph Hawes to Easingwold as a delegate from the National Liberal Federation has been mentioned. This was not his first visit and he had appeared at the Town Hall shortly after the 'newly formed Thirsk and Malton Division Liberal Association came into being.[55] This was just after the death of Gladstone and it was stated that when they had got a proper organisation set up 'a change in the political representation of the division might take place.'

The Liberal Association began organising meetings in the Easingwold area - and Fairfax-Cholmeley, Miss Embleton and others appeared as speakers, for example, at Husthwaite.[56] Their enthusiasm seems to have been short-lived, however, and, as has been seen, no attempt was made in the Khaki Election to dethrone the sitting Member. After that initial flurry of activity at Easingwold and Husthwaite nothing happened.

NOTES

1. *Advertiser* 25 September 1897.
2. *ibid* 2 October 1897 and subsequent issues to 14 December.
3. *Ibid* 2 April 1898.
4. *Ibid* 4 February 1899.
5. *Ibid* 25 February 1899.
6. *Ibid* 29 October 1898.
7. *Ibid* 5 November 1898.
8. *Ibid* 19 November 1898.
9. *Ibid* 1 April 1899.

10. *Ibid* 4, 9 and 11 May 1901.
11. *Ibid* 5 August 1899.
12. Eg *Ibid* 16 April 1898.
13. *Ibid*.
14. *Ibid* 3 April 1897.
15. *Ibid* 12 April 1902.
16. These 'remedies' have been mentioned before. It might be interesting to note that in the edition of the paper being quoted from something like two feet of column inches were devoted to them. There were others who have not been mentioned in these pages.
17. *Advertiser* 19 February, 19 and 26 March 1898.
18. *Ibid* 21 January 1899.
19. *Ibid* 21 January 1899.
20. *Ibid* 15 May 1897.
21. *Ibid* 16 January 1897.
22. *Ibid* 22 February 1898.
23. *Ibid* 16 October 1897. The Crayke group had not yet settled on a permanent name.
24. *Ibid* 27 November 1897.
25. *Ibid* 1 May 1897.
26. *Ibid* 27 February 1897.
27. *Ibid* 5, 12 and 14 February 1897.
28. P. Gammond, *Your Own, Your Very Own!* (1971). The Macqueen-Pope/Harry Liston references are from his *The Melodies Linger On. The Story of the Music Hall* (nd).
29. The Smith type-setter headed the back page of one issue 'OCTBOER 16' which suggests he had been thinking of other things.
30. *Advertiser* 18 February 1899.
31. *Ibid* 11 November 1899. The Sutton on Forest concert *Ibid* 6 March 1897. That one at Tollerton, whereat the 'Nigger' sketch was performed, reported in *Ibid* 17 February 1900.
32. *Ibid* 11 June 1898. It must be said that this is a rare type of advert as far as the *Easingwold* is concerned.
33. Advert on front page. *Ibid* 6 February 1897.
34. The full programme of another Philharmonic is given in *Ibid* 16 and 23 January 1897.
35. *Ibid* 29 January 1898. Report of the Room's annual dinner. There was also a Crayke Reading and Recreation Room. The Victoria Institute was one in York, of course, and there was a 'Village Reading Room' at Raskelfe (see the announcement of 'A GRAND BALL' to raise funds for it in *Ibid* 21 October 1899 and a report in *Ibid* 11 November 1899). The *Advertiser* of 28 April 1900 reported a concert and dance organised by 'the friends of the Reading Room ... in Mr Atkinson's granary' on Easter Monday. A Huby Concert in aid of the 'Cricket Club and Reading Room is reported in *Ibid* 15 December 1900. On 4 January 1897 a reading room opened in Alne. *Ibid* 9 January 1897. The opening of the 'Huby' reported in *Ibid* 11 January 1902.
36. *Ibid* 12 August 1899.
37. *Ibid* 19 August 1899. Dennis (if it was he) seems to have taken a very active part in the local community - in sports events, concerts and so on. See eg. *Ibid* 29 January 1898 (Crayke 'Social Evening') and 11 March 1900 (patriotic concert at Crayke).
38. *Ibid* 2 September 1899.
39. *Bulmer's Directory* has Christopher Turner, farmer, as the occupant. Dennis spelled Scobey's name differently here.
40. *Advertiser*, 'Sales by Auction' column, 1 and 22 July 1899.
41. *Ibid* 29 July 1899.
42. On H. E. Leetham see eg. A. J. Peacock, *York 1900 to 1914* (York nd), and *York in the Great War: 1914-1918* (York 1993) *passim*.
43. *Advertiser* 12 August 1899.
44. *Ibid* 18 July 1899. Much of the sale was of shares. This was the sale when Rookledge bought £92 worth in the Easingwold Market Tolls.
45. *Ibid* 22 January 1898.
46. *Ibid* 5 March 1898.
47. *Ibid* 7 April 1900.
48. *Ibid* 21 April 1900. The Whixley sale from *Ibid* 2 June 1900, that of the land *en route* to Raskelfe *Ibid* 24 November 1900.
49. *Ibid* 13 August 1898.
50. Chief among these was probably the Workmen's Compensation Act 1897. The Agricultural Rates Act was welcomed in the Easingwold area as has been shown, and the government looked at (and maybe highlighted the need for) old age pensions. The quotation about the government elevating social reform to a position of top priority is from R. C. K. Ensor, *England 1870 - 1914* (Oxford 1936) p 237.
51. *Advertiser* 29 July 1899.
52. *Ibid* 29 September 1900.
53. *Ibid* 13 October 1900.
54. *Ibid* 3 March 1900.
55. *Ibid* 21 and 28 May 1898.
56. *Ibid* 11 June 1898.

Chapter 4

THE RDC AND TROUBLE AT ALNE

While the general election campaign was going on so was a local scandal - involving a member of the Church of England, and therefore of great interest. It centred on personalities in the village of Alne, a place where an alleged, mean, 'EMPLOYMENT SWINDLE' had recently been perpetrated on Alice Maud Houlden. Ian Charles Taylor appeared in a York court accused of having obtained £15 from Alice by false pretences. The case got good coverage and Houlden was sent to the Assizes. The lady had applied for a post with the Grimsby based British Fish Supply Company, and got it on payment of a deposit. She got the job, then turned up at Grimsby to find no such company existed.[1] Not an unknown situation.

As Taylor had just been released after serving 9 months for a previous offence and because he had conned Miss Alice before beginning this sentence, Justice Grantham took the view that the nine months he proposed to give Taylor for the current offence was enough, so he more-or-less let Taylor off.

The prisoner thanked his lordship for his leniency, and promised to amend his life.

The issue of the *Advertiser* following the one in which the conclusion to the Taylor case was reported contained another Alne feature. It appeared in the first column of the front page under the heading[2]

ACTION FOR LIBEL BY THE
VICAR OF ALNE
VERDICT FOR THE PLAINTIFFS.

The case involving the vicar of Alne was heard before Mr Commissioner Bosanquet and a special jury at the Yorkshire Assizes lasted four days and featured some of the nation's most famous (and expensive) legal luminaries - including Tindal Atkinson.[3] The action was brought by the Rev Hamilton Young against his father-in-law, Richard Kershaw of Halifax, the owner of the advowson of Alne, for damages for libel said to have been contained in a letter written to the Archbishop of York 'accusing plaintiff with [sic] immorality with Miss Burton, of Alne, who also sued for damages.' In their summaries Scott Fox demanded 'that justice which even a maligned clergyman might expect to find at the hands of an English jury', and Bosanquet taxed the jury at considerable length. If they found 'against the defendant, the charge was so grave and so serious that it warranted substantial damages. It was the worst charge that could be brought against a parson, and if he were a credit to his profession, and devoted to his work, no damages would be too great.' Powerful stuff, but 'After considerable deliberation the jury awarded Mr Young £100, and Miss Burton £1,000.' It clearly did not agree with Bosanquet.

Alne was a place where a great deal went on. The roads were bad, the wells were filthy, the health of the locals was ghastly, but it had a good copy writer for the *Advertiser.* He reported on the village concerts and cricket matches, the skating and the feasts. There were a few court cases and scandals too that made news. The gullible Miss Houlden who was taken in by the Grimsby con man, has been mentioned. She was almost certainly the daughter of William Houlden a farmer of Alne, and the brother of the unfortunately named John Thomas who appeared before a jury at Leeds empanelled to assess damages in a breach of promise case. John Thomas had been engaged to marry Eliza Palfreyman in June 1899. She spent £30 to £40 on the wedding arrangements and on the big day her friends turned up at her mother's house, so did she (of course), but there was no John Thomas.' Then a telegram 'arrived stating "Tom unable to come." "Tom didn't come," said Mr Pulleyne [representing Miss Palfreyman], "and he has not come to this day."' John Thomas, a blacksmith who earned 27s a week, had absconded on his wedding day.[4] Not only that but he wrote to Eliza a few days later asking her for some commission allowed by the Coop. 'The jury assessed the damages at £40.'

The libel action involving the vicar of Alne was more prolonged than that concerning young Houlden. On Wednesday 10 August an application was made on behalf of Kershaw, the writer of the defamatory letter about the vicar of Alne. Sir Edward Clarke asked for a stay of execution pending the hearing of an application for a new trial. The Lord Justice and his colleagues dismissed the application with costs.[5]

Kershaw, nevertheless, went ahead with his appeal.[6] Once more Sir Edward Clarke appeared in a two day hearing in November, where he contended that: the verdict in the original case was against the weight of evidence; that Bosanquet had misdirected the jury; and that further evidence had been discovered. What was this? It was 'that of two men, who, while out for a walk, saw Mr Young and Miss Burton in Goose Lane, about two miles from Alne.' However, 'They did not speak of the incident' until after they had seen a report of the trials in the papers. Lord Justice A. L. Smith had said, when dismissing the attempt to get a new trial, that he thought 'Miss Burton's character was unimpeachable' and was of the opinion that the damages she had received were not even 'one farthing too much.' The application by Kershaw was 'refused with costs,' but this was not the last time that the courts had to deal with the case of the vicar of Alne and others. In May 1900 in the Divorce Division 'the case of Young v. Young and Mintoft (Burton intervening) came on for trial.'[7] The Rev Young alleged that his wife, Sarah Elizabeth, had committed adultery with Thomas John Mintoft, a churchwarden, 'from whom petitioner claimed damages.' The charges were denied and Mrs Young repeated that her husband Hamilton had had an adulterous affair with Mary Ann Burton. Once again there was an impressive array of legal talent on show including - Sir Edward Clarke and Tindal Atkinson.[8]

During submissions it was revealed that the Youngs met in 1891 and four years later went to live in Alne. There they met Mintoft, a man 'of about 40 years of age ... [who] had no employment, but ... was married to a lady some years older than himself, who had some fortune.' In December 1895 the Rev Hamilton looked through a keyhole and saw Mintoft kissing his wife. Young was 'exceedingly angry', but the culprits promised the affair would end (actually they said it had not then started). Mintoft seemingly left Alne briefly, but returned and then the pair really did start an affair. Mrs Young was 'entirely infatuated' with her 40 year old, and they were seen together in York, London and elsewhere. All these meetings, Mrs Young said, 'were accidental.' She eventually left Alne, then the Rev Young became aware that 'he was being watched about the village by detectives.' He saw his wife's solicitor and asked why. He replied because '"we think we have a case against you with regard to Miss Burton, who went over to Brussels to have a child, and you are the father of that child. This is what is said."' Young immediately denied the charge, and the libel trial was the result.

The divorce action was proceeding when R. E. Smith completed the *Advertiser* for 29 May, and the next issue consists only (in the files being used for these notes) of simply the front and back page with nothing on the inside of either.[9]

The Alne libel and divorce cases had still some way to run. On 16 July Mintoft, of Low Hall, Alne, filed a petition in the York Bankruptcy Court and, on his own application, was adjudicated bankrupt.[10] He had been ordered to 'pay £4,000 damages, the costs to be paid' by Mrs Young and Mintoft jointly. 'The liabilities', it was said, were 'stated to be about £10,000.' A week or so later the first meeting of Mintoft's creditors was held.[11] He submitted a statement of affairs showing gross liabilities of £8,203 7s 3d. He had obtained loans, mortgaged land and property and was trying to mortgage some more. He had 'no property in revision or expectancy', though, as had been established earlier, his wife had 'a considerable income from property' invested for her by trustees. (Mintoft was eventually kicked off the RDC and the Guardians.)

Hamilton Young's ordeal was not over. In November William Foster, butcher of Easingwold sued him for £10, the balance of an account for £18. Foster had been a witness and, maybe an investigator for the vicar and had gone to London and other towns for Young, running up travel and hotel bills. 'The case ... collapsed ... a verdict for the defendant being given without costs.'[12]

One of the most extraordinary statements in the prolonged Hamilton Young saga came from the vicar himself. He described how he had not cohabited with his wife after the incident in December 1895, when he had taken a look through the keyhole, and said he and his spouse had led 'a most unhappy life.' Mintoft was always hanging around and Young caught him, Mrs Young and a family governess 'together in the lane near their house.' The governess was sacked immediately, which seems a little harsh, and Mintoft very wisely took off on his bike. But this was not all that went on in 1898; not by a long chalk. In that same year a more serious matter occurred.[13] Mr Mintoft was a candidate as a District Councillor, and so was Hamilton Young, but his wife campaigned for Mintoft and the Rev Young was understandably miffed. Relations between the Youngs 'became more and more strained.' That is understandable and has the appearance of being something of an understatement. There can be little doubt that the election would have been discussed at great length in the Fox and Goose (proprietor 'Crosby Wm., vict., ... farmer and thrashing machine proprietor.')

This would not have been the first time that T. J. Mintoft's life and career came under scrutiny in the Fox and Goose. The *Advertiser* of 5 June 1897 reported that he had just been prosecuted by the RSPCA for 'cruelly beating a bay horse at Alne on April 24th.'

After much vigorous airing of local prejudices, the Bench retired and after only 'a minute or two' returned to announce 'that the case would be dismissed, with costs against the society.' During it, it had been revealed that Mintoft was in fact an RSPCA member. He had clearly been fitted up by someone (or some persons) who had reported him, and the RSPCA had been remiss not to notice they were being involved in a vendetta.

Shortly after his court appearance Mintoft took part in an election for the Alne parish council and was returned with a large majority at the top of a poll in which some sitting councillors were unsuccessful.[14] His dalliance with the vicar's wife and his court appearance, did him no harm at all. The council held its first meeting with Mintoft in the chair in April - but with only two others present. Not a good start. Overseers were elected, J. S. Strangwayes was chosen as chairman for the ensuing year (though he was one of those absent) and the intrepid three decided to call a public meeting about celebrating the Diamond Jubilee.[15] A little later the Rev Young held the annual vestry meeting when Mintoft was elected as 'people's warden' for Alne.[16]

The parish councils were all concerned with Jubilee Day celebrations, but Alne had a benefactor. Mintoft announced that he would provide a tea for around 200.[17] The council elections were then held annually and in 1898 'T. J. Mintoft gentleman' was easily re-elected. On this occasion there were eight nominations for five seats and bottom of the poll, and unelected of course, were 'D'Arcy Strangwayes, gentleman, 17; and J. S. Strangwayes, gentleman, 12.'[18] That was not the end of the matter however. The Rev Young had presided over the annual parish meeting and announced the results as given above whereupon one of the Strangwayes had demanded a poll. All very exciting when compared with the unexciting happenings in places like Flawith, Stillington, Brandsby and Crayke. All was duly reported by the *Easingwold.*

On 4 April 'Considerable excitement prevailed at Alne' when a 'double election took place, and this was the one that so angered the Rev Hamilton Young - not surprisingly, as he was a candidate and his wife was an active supporter of one of his opponents, who just happened to be her lover as well. The first part of the election was for five parish councillors.[19] There were seven candidates after D'Arcy Strangwayes withdrew - he who had demanded the poll - and Mintoft topped the poll. The second part of the election was for two seats on the District Council (the RDC) and the result?

> Rev Hamilton Young ... 65
> Thomas John Mintoft ... 55
> John Swainston Strangwayes ... 50
> James Oxtoby ... 30

Alne had a more exciting history at the turn of the century than did any other of the Easingwold villages, and it also contained some adventurous spirits (as well as T. J. Mintoft) who had been attracted by stories of vast wealth to be made in remote places and won over by advertisements of the kind that appeared in the *Advertiser* in late 1897. One invited readers to apply for the prospectus from the Klondyke Gold-Fields, Special Syndicate, which had offices in New Broad Street, London.[20] Six months later arrangements for an expedition had been completed and a sailing date fixed. Among those going (and presumably investing) were two of Hamilton Young's parishioners.[21]

> Two Bradford gentlemen, Mr Arthur Oates (solicitor) and Mr Edgar Croft (electrical engineer), along with Mr Thomas Buck and Mr Padgett (of Menston), and Mr Burton and Mr Seymour (of Alne), are to take part in an expedition to Klondyke. A small syndicate under the title of the Research Company (Limited) has been formed, consisting of about 20 members. A small steel stern-wheel steamer, length 60 feet, 14 feet beam, has been built and launched on the Mersey for the syndicate. Mr Buck, who holds a mate's certificate, is to command the expedition. The vessel has accommodation for 22 persons, and the members of the party are to work on the vessel. The expedition leaves Liverpool on March 19th by the *Garonne.*

The *Garonne* duly left for the Yukon, and a little more information emerged about the syndicate. Subscribed capital in the Klondyke Research Syndicate was £4,000 and each of the participants contributed £200. The boat they had had built in Liverpool - a stern wheeler 'of the type used for navigating shallow rivers' - they were taking with them.[22] (The Klondike [sic] district of the Yukon was the scene of a gold rush in 1896 which took some 30,000 people to the area. By 1910 'most of the gold had been removed,' however, and the population dwindled.)

Alne, early 1900s

At the time the expedition to the Yukon was preparing to leave parish council elections were held throughout the Easingwold area, at Crayke, Brandsby, Raskelfe, Coxwold, Husthwaite, Tollerton and Sutton-on-the-Forest.[23]

The Easingwold parish meeting was attended by 'a large attendance of electors' and was run by Albert Edward Hayden. Nomination papers were handed in and questions to candidates were invited. For the seven places there were ten nominations and the results were as follows. (An asterisk denotes a member of the retiring council.)

John Hobson*, tanner - 86 votes
W. Simpson * - 80
W. Barley *, farmer, Low Hawkhills - 73
Thomas Hodgson, draper - 63
Tom Lonsdale*, bricklayer - 63
George J. Webster *, innkeeper and saddler - 62
F. E. Rookledge *, chemist - 61
William Lawn, gentleman - 51
Alfred Burland Taylor *, hairdresser - 50
Ralph Smithson, pork butcher - 16

Taylor was the only councillor not to be returned.

Footpath disputes for example occupied much of the council's time and in January 1897 it insisted that work on the path from Easingwold to Alne be carried out forthwith. There were impediments on it, and council resolutions instructing removal had been ignored by the owners. When it was eventually done the 'footpath will be open and passable from Easingwold to Alne station,'[24] reported the Smith organ.

The Easingwold parish council was frequently involved in disputes like that about the Alne footpath. Later in 1897 strong opinions in the council over a bill submitted by Mr T. Poppleton[25] regarding the draining of The Kell Boak Ditch led to A. E. Hayden resigning[26] ... 'We understand that as a protest against the action of the majority of the council in the above matter, Mr. Hayden has resigned his seat' the *Advertiser* recorded.[27]

Shortly after he downed tools a new council was elected[28] and he was absent from the list of candidates. The seven were chosen, without a poll, from a list of ten, and councillors agreed that a reporter could attend their deliberations. John Hobson was chosen to be chairman.

The Easingwold Parish Council had a 'Jubilee Committee' and it was intimately concerned with creating the Victoria Buildings that have been mentioned and permission was obtained from the Charity Commissioners allowing the creation of almshouses.[29]

Jubilee year ended with the Easingwold parish council looking for allotments and the next year began with it claiming control of the so-called Dawnay Pieces. They claimed that, as the rents of the property belonged to them, 'the control of them should belong to the Parish Council.' (They were let out in allotments.) A resolution to this effect was passed - to be forwarded to the RDC.[30] This was not the only source of dispute between the Easingwold Parish Council and the RDC. The two were also at loggerheads over a scheme to drain Uppleby. Rookledge claimed the RDC had ignored their views, and said a scheme proposed by the District Council would necessitate 'a rate of 1/- in the £ on houses, and 3d. on land.' Would it not be better to have the town thoroughly sewered 'at a probable cost of £3000 with borrowed money, a rate of perhaps 6d. being entailed in preference' to having the work done 'piece-meal at an annual cost of at least £200 to £300, with a rate of 1/- risen on current rates.'

At the end of the year the Easingwold Council, was asked to comment on the term of office for councillors, and opted for three years.[31] Henceforth the council met at the Victoria buildings.

The last meeting of the year 1899 'altogether lasted barely ten minutes' and there was practically no business to transact.[32] During the 12 months that had just passed, however, it had more than justified itself. When Rookledge was on it, it had taken steps to clear up the town - particularly the Market Place - and it had pressurised the RDC about footpaths and administered what charities were its responsibility. (Rookledge stood down at the end of 1899, making his announcement to do so at the time his father died.)

In March 1901 elections were held throughout the Easingwold area for new parish councils. On the back page of the *Advertiser* of 9 March the contests (or otherwise) at Husthwaite, Brandsby, Crayke, Alne and Stillington were reported, as was the one for Easingwold itself. John Rocliffe was then chairman there and he stated that he regretted the absence of ladies and went on to analyse the composition of the council. 'In the last' one, he said.[33]

> Uppleby was represented by three councillors, Long street had two, Market Place one, and the outsiders one. Easingwold was a very large parish - extending for six miles, and it was worthy of consideration whether Easingwold itself was not over-represented, and the outsiders under represented. Mr Barley represented the outside very well, but taxation and representation should go together.

There were 11 candidates for office, one withdrew and the seven seats were filled by a show of hands. Four electors then demanded a poll, but five were necessary for this to happen. The results were as follows. (* Means a member of the old council.)

J. J. Penty - 95 votes
William Barley* - 88
John Hobson* - 85
John Haithwaite - 74
William Mountain* - 69
John C. Hicks* - 65
John Dale - 62

J. Waddington* - 49
G. J. Webster* - 39
R. Smithson - 9

At the first meeting of the Easingwold parish council in the municipal year 1901-2 Penty was elected chairman - also for three years - and rapidly the councillors got into disputes about land and allotments. The Dawnay allotments again concerned them, not this time because someone had not paid his rent,[34] but because Walter Hall had diverted a ditch in Dawnay Lane. The R. E. Smith typesetter got that part of the business correct but was a little off course when he recorded that a prominent local figure was leaving his post. 'The Chairman read a letter from Mr Wm Barley resinging [sic] the office of Parish Councillor' the *Advertiser* recorded. Barley was replaced by A. Brownlow in an election by the councillors themselves. That out of the way the council went into something like a secret session, and 'The ... proceeded to discuss the Dawnay Lane watercourse difficulty in Committee'.[35] (Shortly after the clanger about William Barley resinging his seat was perpetrated the *Easingwold* had to apologise for another. It was about a report of a horticultural show. 'WE regret that owing to a clerical error', the paper said, the prize for Apricots in the Amateur class was not awarded to Mr Smith, Stillington, but to Mr J Haithwaite, Easingwold.'[36] Justice for Haithwaite was done).

Refuse in the streets also concerned the parish councillors and so did the local charities. What did these amount to? The accounts for the past year were presented in March 1902, and were then to be submitted to the parish meeting.[37]

> The balance sheet showed that the "Apprentice's Charity" amounted to £8 15s 10d., which was given to four lads at £2 2s 11d each, a tithe rent of 2/1 completing the amount. The "Educational Charity" realised £1 18s., which had been equally divided among the Elementary Schools of the town. The "Charity for widows and poor housekeepers," "G. Wilson's Charity" £3 8 8., and "General Dole Charities" £23 6s.3d., had, with the exception of 16/- in hand, been duly distributed.

The parish council was concerned with local issues of great concern to the inhabitants of the town and it showed that it was prepared to flex its muscles in the interests of the community. Its control over the charities and the alms houses[38] gave it a fairly high profile on occasion and it often proved to be a stepping stone to membership of a more powerful body. Access to councillors must have been easy and in Easingwold their decisions were well-publicised by the *Advertiser.*

The 'parish' was the lowest local government body in Easingwold and the villages. Above it was the Rural District Council, more powerful and representing many different places – a body on which sectional rows about one place being favoured over another could easily appear. The material contained in these pages dates from around 1897. What was the Easingwold RDC like at that time? The earliest meeting of the council at which a full list of attendances was given[39] was held in the board room at the Workhouse on 15 January when they discussed: the possibility of hiring a steam roller for work at Helperby; getting and testing a roller; and 'encroachments' at Sutton-on-Forest and Tollerton. The first encroachment was by the John Smith Brewery which, when renovating the Blackwell Ox, had 'inserted bay windows, projecting over the footpath a distance of 26 inches. This had angered the council. The encroachment at Tollerton involved a fence, the owner of which, ignored the council's instructions.[40]

There was a good turn-out at the Workhouse meeting that talked about steam rollers and encroachments.[41] Making up that good turn-out were H. Hawking, chairman, J. T. Robinson of Thormanby and a large collection of councillors, amongst whom Yorke (Stillington) and Ward (Sutton) were most prominent. Also present were J. S. Strangwayes, the naughty Mintoft, representing Alne, and three men sitting for Easingwold itself. The clerk was another of those multiple office holders, F. J. H. Robinson.

The council which sat in January 1897 had some months of life left, and in March it was announced that there would be contests in a number of places for RDC seats at places like Alne, Sutton and Marton-cum-Moxby.[42] A month later the composition of 'THE NEWLY ELECTED EASINGWOLD RURAL DISTRICT COUNCIL' was published. Not all the contests had been as exciting as that at Alne, but the full council was: [43]

Aldwark - William Jefferson
Alne - Thomas John Mintoft and the Rev Hamilton Young
Angram Grange - Francis Gilling
Beningbrough - William Wood
Brafferton - Thomas N. Driffield
Brandsby-cum-Stearsby - Hugh Charles Fairfax-Cholmeley
Carlton-Husthwaite - William Todd
Coxwold - Richard Buckle and George Kendrew
Crayke - John Gilleard and George Knowles
Dalby-cum-Dewsby - Robert Dobson
Easingwold - William Barley, Francis Bell, Albert Edward Hayden
Farlington - George Johnson and William Williamson
Flawith - John Dunnington
Helperby - William Colley and William Lyal
Huby - Thomas Mercer and James Ward
Husthwaite - William Farrer and William Harrison
Linton-upon-Ouse - William Dawson Hawking
Marton-cum-Moxby - William Mattison
Myton-upon-Swale - Miles John Stapylton
Newburgh - Joseph Robinson
Newton-upon-Ouse - Joseph Cowling and Chapman Elgie
Oulston - John Kendrew
Overton - Thomas Harrison
Raskelfe - Henry Hawking and James Shepherd
Shipton - William Michael Dawson and William Henry Shields
Stillington - William Richardson and Robert Souter
Sutton-on-Forest - John Thomas Boggett and William Proude Willis
Tholthorpe - John Edward Sadler

Above:
'Whinny Pasture' - This footpath was a left turn, when facing towards York at the double lay by half a mile out of Easingwold. It was a favourite place for blackberrying.

Right:
The path and stile are just past the bowling green and at the far end of Curry's Orchard on the way to Kell Balk.

Both 1905.

Thormanby - Joseph Thomas Robinson
Thornton-on-the-Hill - Thomas Batty
Tollerton - Philip Braithwaite and John White
Whenby - Charles Nesfield
Wildon Grange - Richard Barley
Yearsley - William Smith Jones
Youlton - Thomas Inchboard

Overwhelmingly the councillors were farmers with people like Young, a vicar, William Williamson, a builder, Hayden, a solicitor and John Thomas Boggett as exceptions. (The latter's parents might have been, should have been, just a little more careful when naming their offspring. Eric Partridge has shown that John Thomas had had a bawdy meaning at least since the 1840s and long before D. H. Lawrence popularised it.)[44] It was not only the parents of future councillors, however, who recklessly ignored history and lumbered their offspring with a couple of names that, well, could have caused mirth at their expense. In a case at the Easingwold magistrates' court, before Strangwayes and three others, a farmer's son John Thomas Ward was fined £1. 11s. for trespass in pursuit of game.[45]

The Rural District Council had come into existence as part of the one 'harvested sheaf' for the Liberals from the 'overgrown' parliamentary session of 1894.[46] The writer of that phrase was referring to the devastation heaped on Mr Gladstone's attempts to reform local government by the House of Lords. 'No other Bill of importance had survived' the attentions of the peers. That it got through as it did was largely the result of the brilliance of the president of the Local Government Board.[47]

> H. H. Fowler introduced in 1893 what became the Local Government Act 1894, and ... [it] was encountered considerable opposition. The commons spent 38 days on the measure before it went to the Lords; it was eventually passed on 1 March 1894.

The parishes created set up by the 1894 Act numbered around 6,800, and Fowler set up side by side with them the rural and urban district councils that were to be a feature of the British system of local government for many years to come. In the elections for the RDCs and the Urban DCs 'two great innovations were made in favour of women.' The 'Fowler Act ... not only removed the ban on marriage; it laid down that women qualified to vote were qualified to be elected as well.' The 'sharpest point in the controversy in the Bill', however, was not about votes for women but about the provisions which said that[48]

> the Rural District Councillor should represent his parish on the Board of Guardians. As the rural district and the [poor law] union were most frequently identical in boundary this meant a popularly elected Board of Guardians, and the electoral qualification was lower than any ever yet known, no property stipulations being attached to it. Hence the strength of that attack upon the Bill which [persisted] in pointing out that the electors of the new Guardians were very largely prospective, or at least possible, candidates for relief.

In 1903 a study was published which described in great detail the system of how the nation's local government was created and organised, and from which the following is extracted.[49] The RDCs set up in 1894, J. Redlich wrote, were new authorities with every councillor henceforth representing his parish on the Board of Guardians. Where a rural council and a union are identical, the RDC consists of the same people as the Board. Meetings of both bodies were usually held one after the other with members of the RDC sitting first as councillors then as guardians.

What were the statutory obligations imposed on bodies like the Easingwold RDC? 'Of the purely sanitary duties ... the principal may be summarised under the four heads of Water, Drainage, Nuisances, and Diseases.' After 'sanitary duties proper', Redlich went on, 'the most important work' carried out by RDCs 'is the maintenance and regulation of highways and footpaths ... every rural district council became in 1894 the highway authority.' The main roads were the responsibility of the county councils but 'there were other roads' and, when Redlich wrote, 'over 95,554 miles' of them were maintained by rural district councils.

The newly elected Easingwold RDC met for the first time on 6 May 1898 when H. Hawking was again chosen as chairman. Business that day included for example:

i) A parish council had asked that a footpath at Tollerton be protected. The RDC agreed to the request. Philip Braithwaite raised the issue.
ii) On the proposition of Cllr Souter permission was 'granted to erect telegraph poles, &c., on the roadside between Stillington and Brandsby.'
iii) The Cyclists Touring Club were concerned about road safety. They wanted 'danger boards' erected at dangerous spots and were prepared to pay for them. The offer was accepted.
iv) Notice was given that a committee would look at the possibility of purchasing a steam roller.
v) 'The Eatage of the lanes.' Readers of the deliberations of the RDC became familiar with this phrase, and this year the grazing rights were let at public auction for £2 16s 6d. This item took up most time on the RDC's first day, and introduced a dispute. Fairfax-Cholmeley went for the surveyor. Why had he not prosecuted people who were illegally grazing the lanes, he was asked. (They seem to have been let quite improperly by 'the adjoining occupiers.') The official said he had not seen an offence being committed, but was ordered 'to find out if anyone was grazing any of the lanes who had not bought them at the sale.'

The RDC completed its three year term, elections were held, and a new body held its first meeting on 3 May 1901. How did its agenda compare with that of three years earlier? To begin with councillors went through the formality of re-electing Hawking as chairman. R. E. Smith reported the resumé of his second term of office in which he mentioned the most notable achievement of the last three years, the council's concern for good housekeeping, and its determination to carry on as before.[50]

> Councillor Hawking ... said the roads in the district were much improved, and that had necessitated expense. It would be their duty not to incur any unnecessary expense.

The chairman then introduced the business of the day. Starting with a report that

i) The county surveyor had surveyed the main roads and spoke 'highly of the Thirsk and York part of it [sic]'.
ii) The main road near Shipton flooded and it was decided to ask the county surveyor 'to sanction the laying of 360 yards of 6 inch pipes.'
iii) A piece of road at Farlington had been repaired. The clerk was ordered to take steps to get back the £5 plus the RDC had spent doing the work. Then
iv) Cllr Elgey (usually rendered Elgie) proposed successfully that the council appoint a foreman stone-layer so that a piece of mechanical equipment the RDC was the proud owner of could be used more efficiently. A wage of 24s a week was suggested and Elgie's proposal went through (31:9).

v) Robert Curry, the contractor for the Easingwold Chapel Street sewer submitted his bill for £108 11s which was authorised. Then Cllr Driffield asked for information 'as to the explosion in Chapel Street.'

vi) The Sutton Parish Council drew attention to the state of the road from Sutton to Tollerton Station. The District Councillors said the lot from Sutton had nothing to complain of. The road was in a 'fair condition' so nothing would be done.

Highway and footpath issues accounted for practically all the business of the RDC on the first day of the session of 1901, but, water was of prime concern for all the councils and had been for years in the Easingwold area. An enquiry into what the Easingwold RDC wanted to do to supply a large part of its area with good quality water and fulfil its statutory obligations was held in the first year of the C20th, in which some amazing descriptions of the area were given.[51]

The Easingwold RDC had massive problems and it applied 'to borrow the sum of £16,000, for the purpose of providing a Water Supply for the villages of Carlton-Husthwaite, Husthwaite, Raskelfe, Alne, Aldwark, Flawith, Tholthorpe, Youlton, Tollerton, Sutton-on-Forest, and Huby.' F. J. H. Robinson, the clerk, gave the enquiry a resumé of the history of the current proposals. There had been a report made in 1890, he said, by a Local Government Board Inspector 'in which the water supply of most of the [local] villages was condemned.' A year later the old sanitary authority had endorsed these findings. At Alne there had been a 'danger of contamination of wells from cess pools, &c., while Husthwaite was returned as having practically no supply.' Carlton Husthwaite was mainly supplied with water primarily from shallow wells, many of which were 'in close proximity to cess pools.' Raskelfe needed urgent attention and the authority tried to obtain a source of supply for it and Husthwaite. Two hundred pounds was spent in a vain attempt to get a source of supply for Sutton and Huby, so they were 'tacked on' to a scheme, the draft of which was laid before the LGB enquiry. By this 'it appeared that from the 11th of October next, for 60 years, [sic] the springs were let at £30 per annum.'

Dr Hicks re-iterated much of what had been said (frequently by him). Aldwark, Hicks said, was 'the filthiest village in the Union.' He had examined all the places in the proposed scheme, taken samples which he had had analysed and checked independently, and he made some general observations about

> the villages named, ... and ... the surroundings of the same. [where] ... the water ... was mainly drawn from shallow wells of varying depth, often surrounded by defective drains, ashpits, dung pits, and various forms of nuisances. ... As to the efficiency of the supply ... generally there was plenty of water, but it was impure, and everyone knew that was capable of producing a large amount of illness, perhaps not among those who lived there, as they could perhaps get used to anything, but rather among visitors. He was there ... to say the proposed supply was necessary, absolutely and indispensable in fact, and in regard to the general scope of the scheme, the Council were exceptionally fortunate in having such a supply within easy reach.

The RDC's engineer (G. Fairbank) gave evidence to the enquiry and said the council would only take underground water from the spring at Kilburn and the nearby reservoir. He had found on 14 August a total flow of 80,259 gallons each 24 hours, 'inclusive of the overflow from Kilburn waterworks. The total population of the area to be served was allowing a 10 per cent. increase, only 3,988, including Thormanby, which at present was not incluned [sic] in the scheme, but might be at some future time. There would be 1,700 gallons surplus after allowing 18 gallons per head.'

The financial arrangements of the new RDCs rapidly led to resentment and accusations of one place being taxed unfairly as against another. Expenses therefore were divided into categories designated general and special, and providing a water supply came into the latter. Payments were arranged by the issuing of precepts to the overseers who raised the necessary funds by a rate.

Resentment should have been allayed by what seems to have been the very reasonable precept arrangement, but bills still had to be paid, and protesters frequently argued that the work involved was not needed in their area. Hamilton Young, who was against the whole district scheme, along with J. S. Strangwayes and R. Menzies, adopted this attitude as far as Alne was concerned. The scheme 'was absolutely unnecessary' he claimed.

The second of the three objectors opposed the water scheme as it regarded Aldwark [sic].' Menzies represented Lord Walsingham, a life tenant at Aldwark, and he contended that the trouble there came from such things as 'defective spouting, ashpits, &c., and not with the water.' Pressed by clerk Robinson, however, he had to admit that 'There were bad wells, although there were some good ones in the village' as well.

The idea for an area water scheme was first presented to the RDC in February 1899, at a meeting at which Hicks played the most prominent part.[52] He had to record outbreaks of diphtheria and scarlatina at Raskelfe, Whenby, Newton and Linton then report on his inspection of the water at Carlton Husthwaite. He had taken 15 samples 'from different pumps and wells, and ... there was not one sample of good water.' One of the representatives present was offended. Why did Hicks take two samples from his well Cllr Todd asked. Because, the doctor replied, the water was so bad it had

> used up all his available stock of chemicals to analyse it, and he had to send for more. Councillor Todd then asked if the officer knew that the last lot was contained in a bottle which had had some cattle medicine in. The Officer replied that for Mr Todd's information, he might say that if it had a fold yard in it the water could not have been any worse.

Buller Hicks was no mean debater. He was followed by engineer Fairbank who presented the plans and estimates for 'the proposed water supply from Kilburn to Husthwaite, Raskelfe, Carlton Husthwaite, Alne and Thormanby. The total estimated cost was £6,946 11s 8d, inclusive of everything in connection therewith except way-leaves.' It was also decided to order inspections of Aldwark and other villages,[53] and the water scheme was approved.

Aldwark often cropped up in RDC discussions. It did so again in the summer of 1898, when attention centred on 'THE VILLAGE WELL.'[54] It has been closed. No wonder. The inspector had found

> the door was off, and the dead bodies of a toad and bird [were] floating in the water. He suggested that it be protected. ... Councillor Bosomworth [agreed] ... though the water was not fit for domestic use. It was used for other purposes, no other supply being available. ... Some one suggested that the well be filled up ... [then] A desultery [sic] discussion took place in which one gentleman said "The well had been built there ever since the world was built, and the water was not fit for a pig to drink."

Reports from Raskelfe were no better than those from Aldwark. Diphtheria broke out there, the *Easingwold* recorded, on 10 September 1898, and Hicks received reports on water samples from the village which were alarming.

Reginald Ernest Smith(on right hand side), Editor of The Easingwold Advertiser with his future wife Annie Elizabeth Coates, on the left her sister 'Bell' and on the right Ellen Coates who played the part of Brittania in the Boer War parades. Photo taken in 1899.

> He ... read several analysises [sic] of water which had been supplied ... from Raskelfe and other villages, and characterised some of them as "filthy stuff," "sewage," &c.

Towards the end of 1898 Buller Hicks reported to the council (again) on Husthwaite and his account was a comprehensive one which contains much information about the village and, by inference, other villages. There were 29 wells and pumps in the village for a population of about 300. Thirty two samples of water from them had been analysed, and all were 'unsatisfactory'. The problem could well be cured however, by using water from the south side of the village. Hicks went on 'there would be at least 3,000 gallons daily, and [that] would probably be a more economical supply than the wells while the supply would equal 10 gallons per head for all inhabitants daily.'[55]

The Husthwaites were rarely out of the columns of the *Advertiser* and in one issue near Christmas 1898[56] in the RDC column, a further indictment of the state of the village was recorded when 'The *ratione tenurae* roads' there were reported 'as being barely satisfactory. It was agreed to give formal notice to the occupiers to put them in repair.' There then followed an announcement about the loss of an official.

> THE TREASURER OF THE COUNCIL
>
> In consequence of the death of Mr G H Smith, for some years treasurer to the Council, a new appointment was necessary.

On the proposition of Councillor Knowles, seconded by Councillor Shepherd, Mr Reginald Ernest Smith was unanimously appointed.

Reginald Smith was the printer and publisher of the *Easingwold Advertiser*, no less, and G. H. stood for George Hudson. F. J. H. Robinson in a formal notice asked people with claims or demands on the deceased's estate to mark them as 'of Easingwold ... Bank Agent and Postmaster.'[57] George passed away on 7 December. Reg was his son.

G. H. Smith was a relative of the real George Hudson the famous 'Railway King,' one-time MP for Sunderland and Lord Mayor of York on three occasions. An obituary said his Easingwold relative had been

> head-post-master of Easingwold for 29 years, an office which has been in the family for three generations, extending over a considerable period of years. He was also manager of the Easingwold Agency of the Yorkshire Banking Company for the last 16 years. Mr Smith was one of the first promoters of the Easingwold Railway, and deposited the money to get the bill through Parliament, when at a critical stage of "to be, or not to be". He was a director of the company and vice-chairman, and was always interested in business connected therewith. Mr Smith was associated with Mr J J Penty, as secretary to the Easingwold Agricultural Society. He was for two-and-twenty years acting in the capacity of Vicar's warden .. He leaves a widow and three sons ...

G. H. Smith appears in other capacities as a businessman in Easingwold. A directory of 1882 records him establishing a printing works in 1866; he was also a wine and spirit merchant and a tea dealer.

> POST OFFICE, EASINGWOLD
>
> G. H. SMITH's
> CAPABILITIES AS A
> TEA DEALER,
> WINE & SPIRIT MERCHANT, &c.,
> Must ever remain unknown to you
> WITHOUT A TRIAL
> POST OFFICE, EASINGWOLD.

The Easingwold RDC began to experience pressure from the Local Government Board on a fairly regular basis, with the LGB urging it to get on with drainage schemes in the town and the villages - while, of course, horrendous stories about the effects of insanitary conditions continued to emerge, as well as arguments that said the speaker or writer agreed things were indeed bad in, say Brandsby, but that the water was sweet and pure where he lived. The council's attitude was that drainage would have to take second place to getting decent water. This seems very reasonable, but the criticisms from the LGB continued (and continued to get the same response). Sutton was a dreadful place where urgent work was needed. It had frequently been the subject of debates in the council and it was again in the summer of 1899.[58]

> SUTTON SEWERAGE
>
> Another letter was read from the Local Government Board in connection with the above. The communication was couched in similar terms to many previous ones

R E Smith sitting at rear of cart, with the same group as on page 118 visiting the Fauconberg Arms, Coxwold, 1899.

> on the same subject and recommended the work to be carried out forthwith. [Coun Hawking] said other people might think what they liked, but not until the village had got a water supply would he have anything to do with the sewerage scheme.

Hawking's bolshy attitude did not prevail, however, and the clerk was instructed to contact 'the engineers for the Water Supply Scheme, asking them to get on with the plans for the carrying out of the work.' A good thing.

The RDC was dragging its feet as far as sewerage was concerned (and what had been done at Raskelfe was proving to be ineffective),[59] but the water scheme was going ahead, and comprehensive plans were laid before the council towards the end of the year. Fairbank described how he proposed to supply ten villages,[60] with supplies 'from two sources, viz the surplus from Kilburn Reservoir and the Cragg Hall springs'. A reservoir to hold 120,000 gallons would have to be constructed and water taken to the villages in cast iron piping laid with 2ft 6ins of cover. The Ecclesiastical Commissioners were the owners of Cragg Hall and other springs, and they supported the scheme to erect a reservoir.[61]

It was inevitable that there would be objections to the Easingwold Water scheme, and there were. The Thirsk RDC registered its opposition. The Cragg Hall springs, it said, were 'situate within [its] jurisdiction [and] ... at some future time the water there might be required to supply' villages in its area,[62] but the objections were regarded as 'frivolous' and Cllr Harrison thought it best to let the warring parties 'fight it out before the Commissioner.'

In the meeting of the RDC that followed that which the 'frivolous' attitude of the Thirsk RDC was discussed two wage items cropped up. First of all the pay of the driver of the steam roller was put up 'from 26 to 28s per week.' He now had celebrity status in the town, but there was no discussion about his extra two shillings.[63] That was not the case with a group of workers, however.

WAGES OF ROAD LABOURERS

> A lengthy discussion took place on the wages paid to the men on the roads, and it was stated that at several of the villages good able-bodied men could not be obtained to work for what the Council usually paid, viz. 15s per week and it was ultimately agreed to give able-bodied men a rise of 1s. per week for the summer months.

On an earlier occasion one of the labourers had applied personally, and got nowhere.[64] 'An application for an increase', it was recorded, 'was made by one of the men employed on the road.' And that was that. Quite clearly the wages paid to such as that brave soul were linked in some way to those of the agricultural labourers. What hours did the roadmen have to put in for their 15s?[65]

THE HOURS OF THE ROADMEN

> An adjourned discussion took place on the above, the point specially considered being whether the men had to cease work at 4 on Saturdays or go on until 5-30. A resolution proposed by Councillor Cholmeley, seconded by Councillor Dunnington that the time be 4 o'clock was lost, it being decided to make the men work the full time.

The road men worked a long time for their 15s, and they worked on occasion in extremely unpleasant and unhealthy situations. It was therefore no wonder Councillor Linfoot informed the RDC that next time the drains and tanks needed cleansing, 'the Council would have to get someone to do it themselves as his roadmen certainly would not.'[66] Good for Linfoot.

The Local Government Board enquiry into the district water scheme was duly held, and as a result of rising costs and 'some remarks made by the Inspector' the application to borrow £16,000 was increased to £17,600.[67] Early in the new year the LGB announced its decision, leaving the way open for the most necessitous work to go ahead.[68]

> The Local Government Board ... approved ... the proposal to borrow £17,600 for the District Waterworks Scheme. The sum to be apportioned as follows - Aldwark - £1,078; Alne - £2,549; Carlton-Husthwaite - £511; Flawith - £300; Huby - £1,610; Husthwaite - £1,254; Raskelfe - £4,001; Sutton - £1,949; Tholthorpe - £797; Tollerton - £3,206; Youlton - £345.

The pure water scheme was the first part of the RDC's plans to make the Easingwold area healthy, and the second was to provide efficient drainage and sewerage disposal. Councillors did not need reminding of the enormity of the area's problems in that respect but they had to consider Coxwold immediately. Once again the sewer there was blocked and, as predicted, the roadman had objected.[69]

> the cess-pools in connection with the sewer at Coxwold were blocked up, [and] some discussion took place as to whose duty it was to clear them out.

Councillor Smith said that he, along with Councillor Linfoot and the Sanitary Inspector, had been to see them. He would like to know whose duty it was to clean them out. Someone had suggested that the road-man should do the work, but he had refused. It was a very nasty job, and the last time the man did it he spoiled a suit of clothes.

In the deliberations over the water scheme no groups formed, no organisation among councillors is discernible, and no bitter contests about elections were held to replace them. Nomination papers for a new RDC had to be in by 7 March for 30 seats and at the last meeting before the elections the council business included: [70]

1) A discussion on a letter from S. Cliffe, the owner of the Crayke Castle estate saying he would agree to the proposed sewerage plan for the village if the site of a cesspool were moved further away from the house lived in by Cllr Gilleard.
2) District Waterworks. Fairbank laid plans before the council showing 29 miles of piping would be needed, and said all pipes would be tested to double pressure 'as a little leakage meant a lot in a length like that.' Work would start at the Cragg Hall Springs and 'arrangements would be made to fix the service pipes in each village as they came to it, so that water would be available at once.' Tenders would be advertised and opened on 5 April.
3) An announcement that there would have to be a $3^{1}/_{4}$d rise in the rates. The clerk said expenses for the next six months would be £5,381, 'necessitating a rate of 1s $0^{1}/_{2}$d in the pound, against £3,226 the last six months, obtained by a rate of $9^{1}/_{4}$d in the pound.
4) A special rate was imposed on Easingwold for sewerage works, cleaning out tanks and other things.
5) A special rate was laid on Coxwold.
6) The Sanitary Officer's report was received - along with a request from him for an increase in his salary. (A proposition that he be given a rise of £10 was defeated. He got £5.)

Polling for four councillors and guardians for Easingwold was held on Monday 25 March in just two parishes. The result was as follows (* is an existing council member.) Hayden and Francis Bell did not seek re-election, and four seats were available.[71]

William Williamson, Oak Tree House*	152
John James Penty	134
John Hobson, chairman of the parish council	116
Joshua Waddington, Easby House, Parish council member	108
William Barley*	106
William Mountain, parish councillor	51

The *Advertiser* contented itself with a comment about William Barley, and seemed to think that the Easingwold voters were an ungrateful lot. 'Mr Barley has sat on the Board for nearly 20 years,' it said, 'part of that time being for Thornton Hill, which parish his father represented before him.' It might be worth reflecting on the fact that some candidates might well have been popular as councillors but extremely unpopular as guardians. Whatever reason for his defeat, however, Barley had the distinction of being the only councillor chucked off in 1901.

The Jolly Farmers Inn, Easingwold, around the turn of the 20th century. The inn was situated next to Avondale at the top end of Spring Street.

Given that no great campaigning was engaged in in Easingwold in 1901 it ought to be noted that there were issued public appeals for support. Joshua Waddington wrote at length. He had looked at relief lists of the poor and said it seemed to him 'that in certain cases the weekly allowances might be increased,' maybe through savings on 'expenditure on mere matters of fancy and sentiment.' Waddington did not elaborate on what he had in mind in that last sentence, but went on in a powerful way.[72]

> Where the rights of the poor are concerned there seemed to be a regrettable tendency on the part of some persons in office to consider themselves rather Guardians of the Rates, than Guardians of the Poor, apparently forgetting the fact that members of the labouring classes, who are the backbone of the country, who pay a large amount in rates, are when [stricken] by age or misfortune entitled to be treated with all possible kindness and consideration.

Waddington concluded by saying 'the colleciion [sic] and removal of house refuse' left much to be desired and thought water charges were too high. W. Williamson pledged himself to 'economy' and asked to be re-elected.

Waddington got in. What happened elsewhere? The results at Easingwold have been given, and in a couple of places no candidates presented themselves. The following is based primarily on a table published on 16 March 1901.

1) Aldwark - Robinson Bosomworth re-elected.
2) Alne - Hamilton Young did not stand (and his rival Mintoft had long gone). J. C. Abell re-elected along with J. S. Strangwayes.
3) Angram Grange - No nomination.
4) Beningbrough - Mr W Almond takes the place of Mr W. Wood.'
5) Brandsby - Hugh Charles Fairfax-Cholmeley re-elected.
6) Brafferton - Thomas Nelson Driffield re-elected.
7) Carlton-Husthwaite - William Todd re-elected.
8) Coxwold - Two sitting/retiring councillors (J. R. Linfoot and Nicholas Smith) were nominated but withdrew. When the *Easingwold* drew up its list their replacements had also withdrawn, but at the first meeting of the new RDC present, representing Coxwold, were Linfoot and J. J. Hutchinson.
9) Crayke - George Knowles and John Gilleard re-elected.
10) Dalton-cum-Skewsby - Robert Dobson re-elected.
11) Farlington - where there had been great controversy because of the RDC boring for water, no nominations.
12) Flawith - John Dunnington re-elected.
13) Helperby - William Colley and Anthony Brabiner re-elected.
14) Huby - Thomas Mercer re-elected. T. Smith elected in place of James Ward 'who has retired.'
15) Husthwaite - William Harrison and William Farrer re-elected.
16) Linton-on-Ouse - W. Kirby elected. Took the place of William Dawson Hawking.
17) Marton-cum-Moxby - William Mattison re-elected.
18) Myton - Miles J. Stapylton re-elected.
19) Newburgh - Thomas Easton re-elected.
20) Newton-on-Ouse - Joseph Cowling and Chapman Elgie, the retiring councillors, nominated. So too William Tenniswood. The latter then withdrew, so no contest.
21) Oulston - John Kendrew re-elected.
22) Overton - Thomas Harrison re-elected.
23) Raskelfe - Henry Hawking and James Shepherd re-elected.
24) Shipton - William Michael Dawson and William Henry Shields re-elected.
25) Sutton - John Thomas Boggett and William P. Willis, retiring councillors, did not seek re-election. William Ward and W. Wilson nominated in their stead.
26) Tholthorpe - 'Mr William Robinson takes the place of Mr John Edward Sadler (deceased).'
27) Thormanby - Joseph Thomas Robinson re-elected.
28) Thornton Hill - Thomas Batty re-elected.
29) Tollerton - Philip Braithwaite and John White re-elected.
30) Whenby - No nomination.

There was considerable experience on the newly elected body with the overwhelming majority already familiar with the increasingly complex problems that would occupy them. Of the few new members J. S. Strangwayes was well-known locally, as was Penty. [73]

Not long into the life of the 1901 RDC there were a series of explosions in the town that caused great alarm and excitement. The development of the water supply went on, the drainage throughout the area was improved, and so too were the highways. Essential to that road programme was the council's recently acquired roller, the driver of which, as mentioned earlier, became a local celebrity and his vehicle the object of great interest with its whereabouts reported week by week in the *Advertiser*. New members of the council would have heard plenty about the roller, and they would rapidly have become aware, too, of the existence of what were known as the *rationae roads*, and the responsibility for maintaining them. Orders were issued by the RDC to: Brogden and Company about insanitary buildings; to farmers about leaving refuse on the roads; and to landowners about access, but many of the orders - as always - were studiously ignored. Sometimes offenders were threatened with legal proceedings; just occasionally action was taken.[74]

As traffic on the roads grew and changed some places which had presented no problems before, became dangerous sites and the RDC spent considerable sums in effecting improvements to them. One dispute in 1901 concerned the status of a section of road between Aldwark and Adwark Bridge, that was *rationae tenure*. Councillor Ward supported by William Mattison[75] maintained that as the road was on Lord Walsingham's property he should pay for improvements. The council however passed the motion to carry out repairs. At around this time the Thirsk RDC decided to try to have the law relating to *rationae* roads amended and the Easingwold council lent Thirsk its support.[76]

If and when the road was repaired the Easingwold steam roller would certainly have been needed. Reginald Smith, it will be recalled, had said one should be purchased - and so had the cyclists. When one was obtained the town received weekly reports of where it was used and where it was going. 'The Steam Road Roller has this week been at work in the Easingwold streets' readers of the *Advertiser* were told in a typical report.[77] This was just after the thing arrived in York, but what it did, and where it did it, continued to be reported. Easingwold was fascinated by its Aveling and Porter.

The RDC had seriously discussed the question of getting a steam roller - either by hiring or purchasing - in the summer of 1898. Cllr Harrison was responsible for a committee being set up to consider the matter. A smaller group was then appointed to examine the question in detail. Hayden played the economiser and asked 'whether the Committee ... was to report on the price, style, &c., of the Roller and was answered in the affirmative.'[78] After considerable debate the committee was instructed 'to purchase one of 12 tons with all accessories to enable it to be used all the year round.'

The 'Roller Committee' reported to the council in August that Aveling and Porter would supply a 12 tonner, a scarrifier and a water cart 'at a cost ... of £475.'[79] There were delays in supplying it, however, as the firm had 'upwards of 30 similar ones on order.'[80] The RDC became more and more exasperated as more and more letters were received apologising for delays, but eventually councillors heard that the machine had been built and was being tested.[81] That information was given to the council's annual meeting held on 5 May, but according to the *Advertiser,* it was already in the town, and, not only that, it was working'.[82]

> COME AT LAST. - THE STEAM ROLLER - The long looked-for steam roller which was ordered by the Easingwold Rural District Council in September last, arrived at Alne Station on Wednesday last, and is at present working on the Raskelfe roads.

The bill was delivered rather more rapidly than the hardware.

> The accounts for the roller were received from Messrs Aveling and Porter, the total price being £578 15s.

Without doubt the man appointed to drive the Easingwold steamer was there when his machine was handed over and taken to start rolling in Raskelfe. He had had a spot of

The Easingwold Advertiser

£100 Insurance. AND WEEKLY NEWS. **£100 Insurance.**

No. 407 [REGISTERED AT THE GENERAL POST OFFICE AS A NEWSPAPER.] SATURDAY, OCTOBER 21, 1899 PRICE ONE PENNY

SALES BY AUCTION.

EASINGWOLD AUCTION MART.

MR. R. BURTON, Auctioneer and Valuer, will hold his next Sale AT THE ABOVE MART, ON MONDAY, OCT. 30, 1899.

R. B. hopes, by Strict Attention and prompt Settlements, to obtain the patronage of Gentlemen, Farmers and Tradesmen in the surrounding District.

ENTRIES CLOSE FRIDAY, OCT. 27, at FIVE o'clock, p.m.

Entries will be taken by Mr. J. HAYNES, George Hotel; and Mr. SCHOLEFIELD, Coal Depôts, Easingwold.

Address: Mr. R. BURTON, Spassy House, Pannal, Leeds.

Important Announcement.

MESSRS. CASSELL & COMPANY have the pleasure to announce that they will publish WEEKLY, price 1d.,

Sunday Chimes.

A NEW MAGAZINE FOR THE DAY OF REST. Profusely Illustrated. *No. 1 ready Oct. 5th.*

SUNDAY CHIMES will be a bright, cheerful, helpful companion for the Day of Rest.

SUNDAY CHIMES will provide the largest, best, and cheapest pennyworth of popular literature for Sunday ever issued.

SUNDAY CHIMES will be so varied in its contents as to meet all tastes, and will provide literature for every member of the family circle.

SUNDAY CHIMES will be prepared on lines differing essentially from any magazine now published.

SUNDAY CHIMES will contain an immense amount of reading—popular, interesting, diversified, and entertaining.

SUNDAY CHIMES will contain a splendid array of beautiful illustrations.

SUNDAY CHIMES will contain matter for Sunday as high in quality and as attractive in character as that provided by the phenomenally successful publication "THE NEW PENNY MAGAZINE" for the weekday.

** *A Prospectus will be sent post free on application.*

CASSELL & COMPANY, LIMITED, *Ludgate Hill, London; and all Booksellers.*

This is the best time in the year to commence taking in

CHUMS,

the Favourite Magazine for Boys, as the October Part, price 6d., commences a New Volume.

Two New Thrilling Serials. A Most Interesting New Series. The Offer of a Cycle and Pocket-Money Prizes, and other Special Attractions, will be found in the October Part.

** *Also published Weekly, 1d.*

CASSELL & COMPANY, LIMITED; and all Booksellers.

AN ENGROSSING NEW SERIAL by FRANK BARRETT, Author of "Was She Justified?" "An Angel in Black," etc., entitled—

"Breaking the Shackles," is now appearing in

Cassell's Saturday Journal,

WEEKLY, price ONE PENNY.

** Also published Monthly, price 6d.

A New Volume of

THE QUIVER

will commence with the November Part, published Oct. 26, price 6d., and this Number will contain a more than usually attractive list of New Features. A Prospectus will be forwarded free upon application.

CASSELL & COMPANY, LIMITED, London; and all Booksellers.

New Issue in Monthly Parts, price 1d.

Tiny Tots.

A MAGAZINE FOR THE NURSERY. Profusely Illustrated. *Part 1 ready OCT. 26.*

CASSELL & COMPANY, LIMITED, London; and all Booksellers.

** A COMPLETE CATALOGUE of CASSELL & COMPANY'S PUBLICATIONS, *containing a list of upwards of 1,000 Volumes, sent post free on application to* CASSELL & COMPANY, Limited, *Ludgate Hill, London, E.C.*

PUBLIC NOTICES.

RICHARD BARLEY, DECEASED.

ALL PERSONS having any CLAIMS or DEMANDS against the Estate of Mr. RICHARD BARLEY, late of Wildon Hill, Coxwold, Farmer, deceased, are requested to forthwith send detailed particulars thereof to the undersigned, to whom all debts due to the deceased must immediately be paid.

Dated this 18th day of October, 1899.

F. J. H. ROBINSON, Easingwold, Solicitor for the Executors.

RASKELFE.

A GRAND BALL in aid of the funds of the Village Reading Room, will be held in the PARISH HALL, on FRIDAY, NOVEMBER 3rd, 1899. Double Tickets, 2/6; Gent's, 1/6; Ladies', 1/-. M.C.—Mr. Chas. Elsworth. Floor in splendid condition. Dancing at 8 p.m. Mr. J. Pennock Thompson's Band. C. Elsworth, Hon. Sec.

The Secretary, Mr. C. Elsworth, would also be pleased to receive any subscription towards the above fund.

WANTED, TO LET, FOR SALE &c., &c.

AGENTS WANTED, by an old established Firm, for the sale of their Blood and Bone Manures, Feeding Cakes, Calf Meals, Lubricating Oils, &c. Good Commission. No Liability. Apply—X, OFFICE OF THIS PAPER.

THE TRUSTEES invite TENDERS for PAINTING, DECORATING, and RENOVATING the PRIMITIVE METHODIST CHAPEL and SCHOOL at Easingwold. Tenders to be sent to the REV. R. AINSWORTH, Easingwold, on or before the 28th October instant, who will shew the premises.

The Trustees do not bind themselves to accept the lowest or any Tender.

BULBS. BULBS.

THE Choicest Selection of Bulbs sent out this season is that presented by the Proprietors of the Popular Monthly Journal:—"SUCCESS WITH FLOWERS, FRUIT, AND VEGETABLES," to their readers. The cost of a year's subscription to the Journal is 2/6 only, and for this sum the monthly copies are forwarded post free each month as published, while the Big Box of Bulbs is sent at once. The Box contains 1 Hyacinth, 6 Scillas, 5 Tulips, 6 Crocuses, 6 Snowdrops, 6 Irises, 3 Ranunculus, 3 Narcissi, 3 Anemones, 5 Stars of Bethlehem; 40 Grand Selected Bulbs in all. Send at once and secure this really wonderful bargain.—THE PUBLISHER, Hatton House, Gt. Queen Street, London, W.C.

HORNER & WHITEOAK,

NURSERYMEN, SEEDSMEN, AND FLORISTS, BELL'S NURSERIES, EASINGWOLD.

(Entrance opposite Railway Station).

BEG to intimate that they have taken over the business of Mr. Francis Bell, and trust by prompt attention to business, to merit a share of your patronage and support.

All kinds of Forest and Fruit Trees, Shrubs, Roses, &c., in varieties most suitable for the district. Vegetable and Flower Seeds; Bedding-out, Table, and Window Plants; Bouquets, Wreaths, Crosses, &c., to order.

INSPECTION INVITED.

G. H. SMITH'S WINE & SPIRIT STORES

ARE STILL CARRIED ON

NEAR THE POST OFFICE.

Good Invalid Port at 1/6 per bottle. (Strongly recommended).

Champagne in quarter bottles at 1/6.

Other Wines and Spirits at usual prices and of the best Quality.

A TRIAL SOLICITED.

STEAM LAUNDRY Co.

30, ALDWARK, . . YORK.

For the convenience of Customers in Easingwold and the district, arrangements have been made for parcels of soiled linen to be left at

THE GEORGE HOTEL.

The clean linen will be returned to the same place regularly each week.

Full particulars, with list of charges, &c., may be had on application to—

THE GEORGE HOTEL, Easingwold.

SP ALL RACES. Highest Limits. Country Commissions 2/- to any amount free of Charge. Accounts by P.O., Stamps, &c., promptly posted same evening. Rules, &c.—J. TOLLERTON, Victoria Club, Leeds.

TAYLOR'S

HAIRDRESSING, SHAVING, AND SHAMPOOING SALOON, MARKET PLACE, EASINGWOLD.

Razors from 1/- each upwards, Buff Strops, Paste, Brushes, &c., &c.

Razors & Scissors ground & reset on the shortest notice. Umbrellas repaired, &c.

UMBRELLAS RE-COVERED WITH—

Dagmar, from	1s. 6d.		
Union Levantine	2s. 0d.	3s. 6d.	
Silk and Wool	2s. 6d.	3s. 0d.	4s. 6d.
Silk	3s. 6d.	4s. 6d.	

TOBACCO AND CIGARS—Assortment of about 30 kinds and Classes, and best Manufactures kept in stock.

Pipes, Briars, Pouches, Cigarettes, &c.

YOUR PATRONAGE GREATLY ESTEEMED

N.B.—Attendance at own residence when required by notice. A. B. TAYLOR.

SAMUEL BELL

LATE J. BELL & SONS.

ESTABLISHED 1847.

MANUFACTURER OF Pianos, Harmoniums, Reed and Pipe Organs, etc.

Tuner and Repairer of Musical Instruments of every description.

Dealer in all kinds of Musical Instruments.

Pianos, Organs, etc., repaired or taken in exchange, Pianos re-pannelled, re-silked, and polished. Piano hammers re-covered and Pianos re-strung. Harmonium and Organ Reeds supplied.

FULL VALUE GIVEN FOR MONEY. COMPETITION DEFIED. ALL INSTRUMENTS WARRANTED FOR TEN YEARS. CATALOGUES FREE ON APPLICATION.

Our Pianos and Organs have been awarded Four Gold Medals during the last three years, which alone speaks for the quality of the instruments.

NOTE OUR ONLY ADDRESS—SHOW ROOM—14, STONEGATE, FACTORY—SWINEGATE, YORK.

TO WEAK MEN. KING'S VITAL RESTORATIVE PILULES. Recommended by Dr. Farr, the well-known Physician, Ex-Medical Officer of Health, Lambeth, for all Nervous Diseases, Failing Memory, Trembling Sensations, Exhausted Vitality, Premature Decline, Feeling of "Worn Out," Palpitation, Skin Eruptions, Piles, Kidney and Bladder Affections, Discharges, and complaints caused through worry or excess. Deficiency of the vital forces restored in a few doses! Hundreds of testimonials ... £100 forfeited if my statements false. No money returned if no cure! Guarantee of cure in every case undertaken! For Consumption and Kindred Wasting Diseases these miraculous Pilules (easy and pleasant to take) are unparalleled. 2/- per case (stamped by Government), post paid under cover, with any special confidential advice needed. Strictest secrecy observed. L. KING & Co., 48, Silver Crescent, Chiswick, London. Beware of plausible imitations, worthless and injurious. *Kindly mention this paper*

JOHN SMITH'S CELEBRATED TADCASTER ALES AND STOUTS.

AWARDED FIVE GOLD MEDALS IN COMPETITION WITH THE WORLD.

LOCAL BRANCH OFFICES AND STORES:—MARKET PLACE, EASINGWOLD. KIRKGATE, THIRSK. THE BREWERY, MARKET WEIGHTON.

BRANCH MANAGER:—JOHN J. PENTY, BREWERY HOUSE, EASINGWOLD.

Special Notice.—On and after May 13th, the Easingwold Office will close on Saturdays at One o'clock p.m., until October 1st.

THE "GAMAGE" CYCLES

Stand Unrivalled for HONEST VALUE.

The "ILIXUM," £8-10 or by Twelve Monthly Payments of 17/9. Guaranteed for Twelve Months. Fitted with any First Class Tyres.

The Ladies' "ILIXUM," Clean, Chic, Light, Easy Running, £9 10s. (or by Twelve Monthly Payments of 19s. 9d.). Illustrated Catalogue Post Free from

A. W. Gamage, Ltd., Holborn, London, E.C.

TOWLE'S PENNYROYAL & STEEL PILLS FOR FEMALES.

QUICKLY CORRECT ALL IRREGULARITIES, REMOVE ALL OBSTRUCTIONS, and relieve the distressing symptoms so prevalent with the sex. Boxes 1/1½ & 2/9 (contains three times the quantity), of all Chemists. Sent anywhere on receipt of 15 or 34 stamps, by E. T. TOWLE & Co., Manufacturers, Dryden St., Nottingham. Beware of Imitations, injurious and worthless.

NOTICE!

CYCLES! CYCLES!! CYCLES!!!

MARK REYNARD has again taken over the Agency for the following leading Cycles—Triumphs, Swifts, Bradbury's, Wincycles, Rudge-Whitworth's, Syrus, and Flying Arrow Cycles.

These Firms are all pioneers in the Cycle trade, with a first-class reputation.

Riding taught free to purchasers.

Cycles for Hire by Hour, Day, or Week.

Enamelling and Plating well and promptly executed.

Tyres re-lined or new ones fit.

All kinds of Accessories at very low prices.

Every Machine guaranteed twelve months.

Come and see the Stock and judge for yourselves.

THE MALTON FARMERS' MANURE AND TRADING COMPANY, LIMITED.

We beg to ask your continued support to our new Agent for Easingwold and District, viz.:—

MR. WILLIAM MATTISON, MARTON ABBEY.

All orders given him shall have our best attention.

WILLIAM HODGSON, Secretary and General Manager.

Manufacturers of Guaranteed Manures to suit all Crops. Bone Crushers and Dealers in all kinds of Manure Materials.

FRUIT TREES, ROSE TREES, &c.

PLEASE NOTE THAT

G. T. STURDY

Is still sending out Rose Trees, Fruit Trees, &c., of the same high quality as has given such satisfaction during the past nine years.

Apple Trees, from 12/- per doz. Rose Trees, from 5/6 per doz. All kinds of New Garden Seeds.

PRICES MODERATE

Orchards renovated or planted per contract.

REFERENCES GIVEN

NOTE THE ADDRESS—SPRING HEAD, EASINGWOLD.

MRS. W. MILLIONS

Tobacconist, Confectioner, &c., MARKET-PLACE, EASINGWOLD.

BREAD AND TEACAKES FRESH DAILY.

INSPECTION INVITED.

FREE INSURANCE AGAINST ACCIDENTS.

COUPON TICKET

specially guaranteed by the OCEAN ACCIDENT AND GUARANTEE CORPORATION, LIMITED, 40, 42 & 44, Moorgate Street, London, E.C., to whom Notice of Claims, under the following conditions, must be sent within seven days to the above address.

£100 will be paid by the above Corporation to the next-of-kin of anyone who is killed by an accident to the

RAILWAY TRAIN,	CARRIER'S VAN,
TRAM CAR,	CART,
OMNIBUS,	CARRIAGE,
	OR WAGGON,

in the United Kingdom (or Channel Islands), in which the deceased was travelling, or who shall have been injured thereby (should death result within three calendar months after such accident). ... £30, or for the loss of one limb, ... £25 will be paid ... to be good for the current week's ... one Coupon for each holder, ... Ocean Accident and Guarantee Corporation, Limited, Act 1890, "Risks Nos. 3, ..." ... admit that the purchase of this ... payment of a premium under Section 34 ... Railway Servants on duty excepted.

Signature.............................

The Easingwold Advertiser & Weekly News - October 21, 1899

bother over driving in 1899, but that was behind him.[83] A report at the time recorded that on 1 March 'Richard Coverdale, of Easingwold, traction engine driver, was charged ... with driving a traction engine through ... Easingwold ... at a greater speed than two miles an hour, in contravention of the Locomotives Act, 1865.' PC Lodge said that he saw Coverdale, 'with thrashing part attached,' pass his house in Tanpit Lane 'at a great speed'. There was a great deal of smoke and steam about at the time, and Lodge estimated Coverdale was doing five or six miles an hour, a speed that Francis Bell, a tanner, said was about right. Coverdale said he did about three and a half miles an hour and only two from the church to Smith's Yard. John Alderson, farmer, the Lund, testified to the fact that Coverdale was a real knight of the road and that when his trap got near the engine Coverdale stopped 'in an instant' and 'the flag-man led his horse by, and ... he had no cause to complain.' The owner of the engine, E. J. Hodgson, said the thing Coverdale was driving was old 'and could not possibly go five miles an hour.' The case brought by Inspector Pickering was dismissed.

By this time Coverdale had been appointed as the Easingwold RDC Roller-man at a wage that was eventually 26s a week[84] and was presumably filling in time while Aveling and Porter kept his new employers waiting.

Towards the end of August Richard Coverdale died.[85] His job was advertised at 26s a week and the ad said that 'Applicants must have had previous experience in the driving and management of Road Locomotives, be capable of doing repairs and such other work as may be required, and be prepared to act under the directions of the District Surveyor.'

Having established himself as a fast driver and a local celebrity, Coverdale died in St Monica's Hospital of typhoid fever on 5 August. He was 41 years of age and a Primitive Methodist. He was replaced as Roller-man by Reuben Phillips, of Oulston, at 26s.[86] The Easingwold public - or the printer/publisher of the *Advertiser* - continued to report the fascinating perambulations of Reuben and his roller. Typical were these from the period near Christmas 1901.[87] (For the record £336 was spent 'on the highways during the past month.')

> The Surveyor ... reported that the road roller had, during the past month, been engaged at Easingwold, Crayke, Linton-on-Ouse, Tholthorpe, Aldwark, and on the York and Northallerton main road.
>
> The Surveyor (Mr Geo. Thompson) stated that during the past month the road roller had been working at Aldwark, Tholthorpe, Myton and Helperby.

The year 1902 began with a minor political sensation in Easingwold when Joshua Waddington, one of those who had got in at the contested RDC election for the town, was kicked off it. Why? He had failed to attend a single meeting for six months, so his seat was declared vacant.[88] A week later appeals for support to fill it appeared in the press from James Haynes and A. E. Hayden, who lived at the Old Vicarage.[89] There were no other nominations and on 1 January Haynes, who ran the George Hotel was successful. (Haynes 152; Hayden 96.)[90]

> Not long after Haynes was returned there were two other changes on the Easingwold RDC. Cllr Dobson, the representative of Dalby-cum-Skewsby retired because of ill health then William Harrison, who represented Husthwaite, died. George H. Till of Witherholme was nominated to fill Dobson's place at Dalby,[91] while Rhodes Hepplethwaite of Highthorne was elected for Husthwaite.[92]

When Hebblethwaite joined the RDC the district waterworks scheme was well under way and in June 1902 Fairbank reported that but for an accident 'at the ironworks the whole of the mains would now have been laid' and but two days work remained to be done. To date 316 'houses had been connected, and about 20 more were about to be done.'[93] Already disputes were taking place about connections,[94] and the different rates being levied at different places. In July the assistant clerk gave a lengthy explanation about why rates varied. The loan which had been raised had been levied on the parishes based on the rateable value as it then was - but in many places the rateable value had gone up. Alne for example, 'had increased £2,647, Raskelfe £4,420, Tollerton £4,763,' but some places had decreased. Huby by just under £7, for example, and Sutton £20.;'[95]

At the end of June 1902 the council's engineer told the RDC that on that day the last water pipe of its scheme would be laid at Alne.[96] The scheme, of course, applied only to the dozen villages mentioned when the loan was applied for, and there were many places outside it, and there were other waterworks than those. Easingwold had its own, for example, and for many years to come some rural communities relied on wells - although the councils now regularly tested the water from them.

Some examples of the water supply systems and problems in the Easingwold RDC[97] area will show that the RDC had a complex and troublesome system on its hands. In the period covered in these pages Farlington was regularly in the news and on many occasions there were demonstrations of what in a later age might be called nimbyism.

Farlington erupted on to the pages of the *Easingwold* when the RDC received a letter from one John Nicholson. The council at the time were looking for water and Nicholson alleged that workmen had been responsible for blocking 'Mester Wyrill's drean.' That drain [drean] was quite adequate until boring stopped, and the 'boord' sent 'a big suppli into' it, 'sixteen or eighteen hundired gallons a day, which was oppen eneuf to tak it then. This omaist corsed a flood at tawd mans bak dear.' Councillors denied there was any connection between the boring and the blocking of tawd man's open drain, and dismissed Nicholson's letter, though it may have contributed to a decision that does not seem to have favoured Wyrill.[98]

Wyrill appeared personally before the RDC. He gave no clues to whoever his champion was, but demanded payment for leading water to his farm for 250 days, a total of £18 15s. He got nowhere. The 'Council was not responsible' it was decided. In June Fairbank was asked to prepare an estimate for carrying out the work at Farlington.[99] This reiterated what he had said some four months earlier when a Mr Noble had written a (literate) letter of complaint.[100] The drain was at fault the RDC said, and there seems to be some suspicions that Wyrill was trying to work it so that his drain was taken up and relayed.

One gets the impression that the RDC's officers and councillors were understandably exasperated by the hostility shown to their improvement schemes. Again and again ghastly reports were made about the quality of water where remedial work was urgently needed,[101] but not according to the locals. Why? because they were unnecessary. The usual reason given for that contention, was that the local water was already pure and beneficial and inevitably an 80 or 90 year old would be trotted out to 'prove' the point. Just like the defenders of smoking did in the 1960s and 70s.

Of course the water schemes would be expensive. In March 1899 the Medical Officer of Health's engineer had given his estimates for carrying out the water scheme for the western parishes of the RDC area.[102]

Black Bull Public House, Easingwold district.

> Collecting water, reservoir, &c, at Kilburn, £966. Four-inch mains from Kilburn to Goose Lane, near Flawith, £5294 17s 0d. Three-inch mains from Goose Lane, £3,143 2s 0d. Pillar foundations, connections, &c., in villages, £729. Crossing streams, railways, &c., £150. A total of £10,282, in which an allowance had been made for Engineer's and law charges, but nothing for way leaves or water-rights.

A correspondent to the *Easingwold* who signed himself 'A VILLAGER' wrote sarcastically about the manifest unwillingness to change things and make the villages cleaner, healthier places.[103] It was a splendid effort.. Is it not really

> 'A scheme to purge our drains of the effluvia and corruptions which have delighted our nostrils and those of our forefathers for centuries and assisted in producing those dear old-fashioned diseases to which they succumbed and which are daily hurrying us to our graves ... Shall we quietly endure this ... shall we sit meekly down and have these things taken from us ... No I say, a thousand times no. Let us as free born Britons resist this infamous infringement of our rights. Let us take a firm stand in defence of our corruption and uncleanliness. Why should we not rot and die of preventable disease in the old sweet way? ... Let us boldly ... oppose these Sanitary tyrants, who would thrust health upon us unsought and filch from us our beloved stinks and impurities.'

Other letter writers maintained, of course, that local schemes would be cheaper than the district one. One person advocated that Raskelfe should go it alone and suggested an 'independent' scheme taking water into the local mill down over an aqueduct to create a head of ten or 12 feet where 'a ram ... would pump the clear top water into an iron tank,' after which it would find itself 'through pipes to say 3 feet above the ground level of every house in the village.'[104] The writer was, quite reasonably, concerned that Raskelfe was well down the line of supply 'and in a droughty time', might only have what some other place, nearer the source of supply, could spare.

There were replies to the letter about Raskelfe. One applauded the RDC and expressed surprise that its water scheme had critics. Not a word of protest, he said, was heard when it spent '£1,500 for the convenience of tramps', but laying out 'a good round sum for the benefit - the everlasting benefit of the rate payers' was attacked.[105] The person who started the correspondence satisfied himself that the person who wrote about Raskelfe was an engineer 'influenced by "red tapeism" ' who knew nothing about what Raskelfe was like before bureaucrats took over.[106] Raskelfe was 'of an exceptionally healthy character previous to the new sewerage scheme being carried out.' Now, despite the fact that they had 'close to their own village, and under their own control, a water supply more economical and permanent, and superior in every way to any they can get from a distant source' the 'professionals' were taking over and were going to force them to drink inferior water at great expense.

Raskelfe's new, clean, healthy water was planned to come from Oulston though Easingwold itself had a waterworks, the creation of which was briefly - very briefly - noticed by the historian Cowling. 'The early work of the District Council included the provision of sewers for the town and waterworks near Hanover House' he wrote.[107] What was the town's water supply like before this? *Bulmer's* contents itself with a comment at the end of a paragraph about the Easingwold Gas and Coke Company – 'Besides the numerous wells that supply the town with water, there are several medicinal springs in the vicinity, but they have not hitherto attracted much notice.' Almost a decade later an abstract of the RDC's accounts for a half year was published and it contained the following note about the financing of Easingwold's (and Coxwold's) works.[108]

LOAN ACCOUNT

Easingwold Waterworks - Amount borrowed £3,000,
balance owing, £2,558 11s. 9d.
Coxwold Waterworks -
Amount borrowed, £800; balance owing
£773 6s. 8d.

F. J. H. ROBINSON,
Easingwold 31st May, 1898. Clerk to the
Rural District Council.

The RDC clearly did not make much money out of the Coxwold enterprise. Under 'RECEIPTS' the accounts carried notes of what had gone into its coffers. The PUBLIC HEALTH AND MISCELLANEOUS section showed

Water Rents - Easingwold	76	16	10
Do. Coxwold	1	1	4

Just a week after the accounts above were published some more information was given to the RDC about Easingwold's water supply. The MOH talked of a possible deficiency of supply and suggested that it might be wise to call at least a temporary halt to new connections.[109] In view 'of a possible deficiency', he said, 'it would be wise to only grant applications for water for drinking purposes. ... The Inspector of Waterworks ... said that it was correct that a short time ago there was only $1^1/_2$ feet of water in the reservoir.' What was the water from the Easingwold reservoir like? The MOH had given it full marks at the start of 1898 and contrasted it with a village that was not far away.[110]

> The Medical Officer ... reported that he had analysed two samples of water from Helperby and found them both of an impure nature and totally unfit for drinking purposes. He had also analysed a sample of water from the Easingwold Waterworks, and the analysis showed that it was never in a purer state than at the present time.

The Easingwold RDC had trouble with numerous of its villages, but no place caused more concern than did Sutton-on-Forest, another place at the end of a long water supply run. In an unusually hard hitting report the *Advertiser* wrote about activists at Sutton who protested about things they knew nothing about.[111] They had been 'bolshy' about everything the RDC had done to improve their lot. They had objected to a sewerage scheme for the village and had 'solemnly averred ... they were not very partial to the water scheme.' Backed up by the parish council they set out 'to hinder it.'

A major problem facing the authorities when the water schemes were completed was wastage. Appeals were made to consumers in Easingwold and some of the villages, to use water discreetly and a leafleting campaign had to be resorted to at least once. Waste, not helped by inefficient valves and joints, led to crisis situations.[112]

NOTES

1. *Advertiser* 22 and 29 July 1899.
2. *Ibid* 29 July 1899.
3. And Scott Fox, Mr Kemp, Sir Edward Clarke and W. Beverley.
4. *Advertiser* 5 August 1899. The participants in the case changed their addresses. John T. lived in York at the time of the hearing. Eliza was at Millington.
5. *Ibid* 12 August 1899.
6. *Ibid* 25 November 1899.
7. *Ibid* 19 May 1900 and 23 December 1899.
8. Some impression of the costs involved might be gleaned from the *Easingwold's* conclusion to the first paragraph of its report on the petition. 'Mr Inderwick, QC., Mr Scott Fox QC, and Mr Pritchard appeared for the petitioner; Sir Edward Clarke, Q.C., Mr Tindall, Q.C., and Mr Newson for the respondent; Mr Bargrave Deane, Q.C., and Mr Priestly for the co respondent; and Mr Barnard and Mr Bayford for the intervener, Miss Burton.'
9. The files are those held by G. H. Smith & Son.
10. *Advertiser* 21 July 1900.
11. *Ibid* 4 August 1900.
12. *Ibid* 10 November 1900.
13. More serious than Mrs Young and Mintoft meeting in London that is.
14. *Advertiser* April 1897. Elected were: E. Leak; J. Oxtoby; J.S. Strangwayes; and D'Arcy Strangwayes.
15. *Ibid* 24 April 1897.
16. *Ibid* 1 May 1897.
17. *Ibid* 29 May 1897.
18. *Ibid* 19 March 1898.
19. *Ibid* 9 April 1898.
20. *Ibid* 4 September 1897.
21. *Ibid* 5 March 1898.
22. *Ibid* 9 April 1898.
23. All the 'elections' noted above reported in *Ibid* 19 March 1898. There is a work on Sutton which, does not really deal with local politics. E. Mennim, *Sutton on the Forest. Two Thousand Years Change.* (York 1995)
24. *Ibid* 16 January 1897.
25. *Ibid* 6 February 1897. Poppleton's total estimate/bill had been for £25 19s 3d.
26. *Ibid* 20 February 1897.
27. *Ibid* 20 March 1897. Results were as follows. An asterisk indicates a member of the old council. John Hobson* 82; William Simpson* 70; F. E. Rookledge* 68; William Barley* 61; Tom Lonsdale* 58; A. J. Webster 51; Alfred B. Taylor 50. The unsuccessful candidates were: William Mountain 43; Frederick Inns 21; and William Hunter 50.
28. *Ibid* 24 April 1897.
29. *Ibid* 17 September 1897.

30. *Ibid* 5 March 1898.
31. *Ibid* 17 December 1898.
32. *Ibid* 16 December 1899.
33. *Ibid* 7 April 1900.
34. The parish was taking one bad payer to court.
35. *Advertiser* 11 May 1901. The resignation of Barley was just before his little local troubles ended with him going to court.
36. *Ibid* 31 August 1901.
37. *Ibid* 15 March 1902.
38. Discussions were going on towards the end of 1902 about demolishing some.
39. Not the first RDC meeting reported. The *Advertiser* only recorded the names of the chairman and vice chairman on 2 January.
40. At least that appears to be the case.
41. *Advertiser* 16 January 1897.
42. *Ibid* 26 March 1898.
43. *Ibid* 30 April 1898.
44. Eg. E. Partridge, *A Dictionary of Slang and Unconventional English* (4th edition 1951)
45. *Advertiser* 5 February 1898.
46. R. H. Gretton, *A Modern History of the English People 1880-1898* Vol 1 (1913)
47. R. C. K. Ensor, England 1870-1914 (Oxford 1936) pp 213-14. The *Local Government Act, 1894* is 56 and 57, vict, chap 73.
48. Gretton op cit p 346.
49. J. Redlich and F. W. Hirst, *Local Government in England* (1903) Two volumes.
50. *Advertiser* 4 May 1901. 'J. T. Robinson was unanimously re-elected to the vice-chair.'
51. The board of enquiry was held at the Town Hall under one W. A. Ducat. *Ibid.*
52. *Ibid* 25 February 1899.
53. Aldwark, Tholthorpe, Tollerton, Youlton and Flawith. Buller Hicks Junior took over from his father as MOH in 1898.
54. *Advertiser* 18 June 1898. Also 16 July 1898.
55. *Ibid* 5 November 1898.
56. *Ibid* 17 December 1898.
57. Public notices column. *Ibid* 31 December 1898. G. H.'s death reported on 10 December; his funeral on the 17th. On George Hudson see eg R. S. Lambert, *The Railway King* (1934), A. J. Peacock, *George Hudson of York* (Clapham 1971), B. Bailey, *George Hudson, The Rise and Fall of the Railway King* (1995), A. J. Peacock, *George Hudson 1800-1871. The Railway King* (two vols. Reprinted G. H. Smith & Son 1988). There is a great deal on Hudson in various issues of the journal *York History*.
58. *Advertiser* 12 August 1899.
59. *Ibid* 9 September 1899.
60. Actually there were eleven: Husthwaite, Carlton Husthwaite, Raskelfe, Flawith, Alne, Aldwark, Tholthorpe, Youlton, Tollerton, Sutton, Huby.
61. Letter to the RDC. They wanted £30 a year, which seems very reasonable. *Ibid* 23 September 1899. Later it was said that the Commissioners, the Archbishop of York and the Bishop of Chester owned the springs. See *Ibid* 30 July 1900.
62. *Ibid* 24 March 1900.
63. *Ibid* 7 April 1900.
64. *Ibid* 26 August 1899.
65. *Ibid.*
66. *Ibid* 2 June 1900.
67. *Ibid* 8 September 1900.
68. *Ibid* 26 January 1901.
69. *Ibid* 26 January 1901.
70. *Ibid* 22 March 1901.
71. *Ibid* 30 March 1901.
72. *Ibid* 23 March 1901, front page.
73. The new councillors were Penty, Strangwayes, Almond, T. Smith, Kirby, William Ward, Wilson, William Robinson.
74. For example the RDC considered prosecuting people for dumping bottles and tins at Stillington. Report of RDC meeting *Advertiser* 16 November 1901. Brogden and Co owned some insanitary property at Newton on Ouse and the cost of putting the three cottages subject to the dispute into a decent state would have been £2 17s 6d. The matter was before the RDC several times, and instructions were given Brogdens, to carry out remedial work. They were ignored and 'after several notices the owners let things go on', in the words of Fairfax-Cholmeley. Eventually proceedings were taken in a magistrates' court and a 'final notice to remedy the defects' was given on 23 August. In the face of this the council determined to do the work itself. *Ibid* 2 November 1901. The most exciting dispute, however, was between the RDC and the Gas Company. The latter applied for a supply of water for use in the retort house at the Gasworks in Long Street, and offered 1s 6d a quarter. This (rightly) was regarded as 'preposterous' and instructions were given to cut the water off the following day. *Ibid* 19 May 1900.
75. Among many other things he was the recently appointed Easingwold and District agent for the Malton Famers' Manure and Trading Company. This was announced in the paper which contained his observations on *rationae tenure* roads.
76. *Advertiser* 16 November 1901. The decision to support the Thirsk RDC's attempt to change the law reported in *Ibid* 14 January 1902.
77. *Ibid* 13 May 1899.

78. *Ibid* 7 May, 4 June 1898.
79. *Ibid* 13 August 1898.
80. *Ibid* 24 September, 17 December 1898, 14 January, 8 and 22 April 1899.
81. *Ibid* 6 May 1899.
82. *Ibid* The paper was a Saturday one and it referred to the RDC meetings being held 'on Friday last.' That would be 5 May 1899. The great arrival was therefore on 3 May. Or was it? Perhaps it depends on how 'arrived' is defined, but on 2 June the surveyor told the RDC 'that the road roller arrived on the 4th of May.' A solution to this important issue in Easingwold's history might be that R. E. Smith got the arrival at Alne correct and that surveyor Thompson was speaking about when the behemoth, tested and roadworthy, was handed over by the railway men to start its career rolling and crushing at Raskelfe.
83. Cowling *op cit* p 147. Cowling chose Coverdale's case to illustrate the leisurely 'pace of traffic' at the end of the century. The case reported in *Advertiser* 4 March 1899.
84. *Advertiser* 19 November 1898.
85. *Ibid* 10 and 24 August 1891. Job advert in *Ibid* 31 August 1901.
86. *Ibid* 5 October 1901.
87. *Ibid* 14 December 1901 and 11 January 1902. How the figures for highway work were compiled was not said, but amongst them, and rounded off downwards were: Easingwold £20; Tholthorpe £11; Crayke road improvement £18; Tollerton £12; Coxwold £7; Raskelfe £5; Alne £4.
88. *Ibid* 11 January 1902.
89. *Ibid* 18 January 1902.
90. *Ibid* 25 January 1902.
91. *Ibid* 3, 17 and 24 May 1902.
92. *Ibid* 7 June 1902. The Stillington election reported in *Ibid* 8 November 1902.
93. *Ibid* 14 June 1902.
94. Eg see *Ibid*, where a dispute at Huby is described. The Bloomfield Bay Lodge of Oddfellows owned some cottages there and wanted water laid on to them. The RDC said this would necessitate 'an extension ... unprovided for in the plans' and refused to take the mains so far. A compromise was agreed, however. The mains would be laid to the 'end of the lane' and the owners had to complete the work. The cost was £15 12s to the ratepayers.
95. *Ibid* 12 July 1902.
96. *Ibid* 28 June 1902.
97. A portion of Marton was added to it in 1887.
98. *Advertiser* 29 January 1898. The section of the RDC's report containing the draft letter was headed 'SUTTON AND HUBY WATER SCHEME. THE DIFFICULTY AT FARLINGTON.' The entry in *Bulmers* for Farlington contains entries for several Wyrills. George was a joiner and carpenter and there was also 'Wyrill Messrs. J., Sons and Co., agricultural engineers, millwrights, and machine makers and agents; makers of prize agricultural implements, and machine proprietors, North Bridge works, Established 1780.' Under 'Farmers' appears 'Wyrill R. (and land agent)'.
99. *Advertiser* 18 June 1898.
100. *Ibid* 26 February 1898.
101. Though some councillors, when their own villages were to be improved, found excuses to object.
102. *Advertiser* 25 March 1899.
103. *Ibid* 11 March 1898. Letter headed 'THE WATER SUPPLY TO THE VILLAGES.'
104. Letter signed 'SPECTATOR'. *Ibid* 25 February 1899.
105. Letter signed '"ANOTHER" SPECTATOR'. *Ibid* 4 March 1899.
106. *Ibid* 11 March 1899. Letter from 'SPECTATOR.'
107. Cowling *op cit* p 145.
108. *Advertiser* 11 June 1898. For similar abstracts from later periods see *Ibid* 14 January 1899 and 1 March 1902.
109. At least this is my reading of the decision. Applications had to be made for exceptional use. For example the contractor for plastering work at the clerk's new house in the Market Place made such an application for water which was heard at a council meeting reported in *Ibid* 1 January 1898. It was granted.
110. *Ibid* 1 January 1898.
111. *Ibid* 8 March 1902.
112. See eg *ibid* 27 January and (regarding Coxwold) 20 June 1902. Proposals were made about cutting off supplies at certain periods.

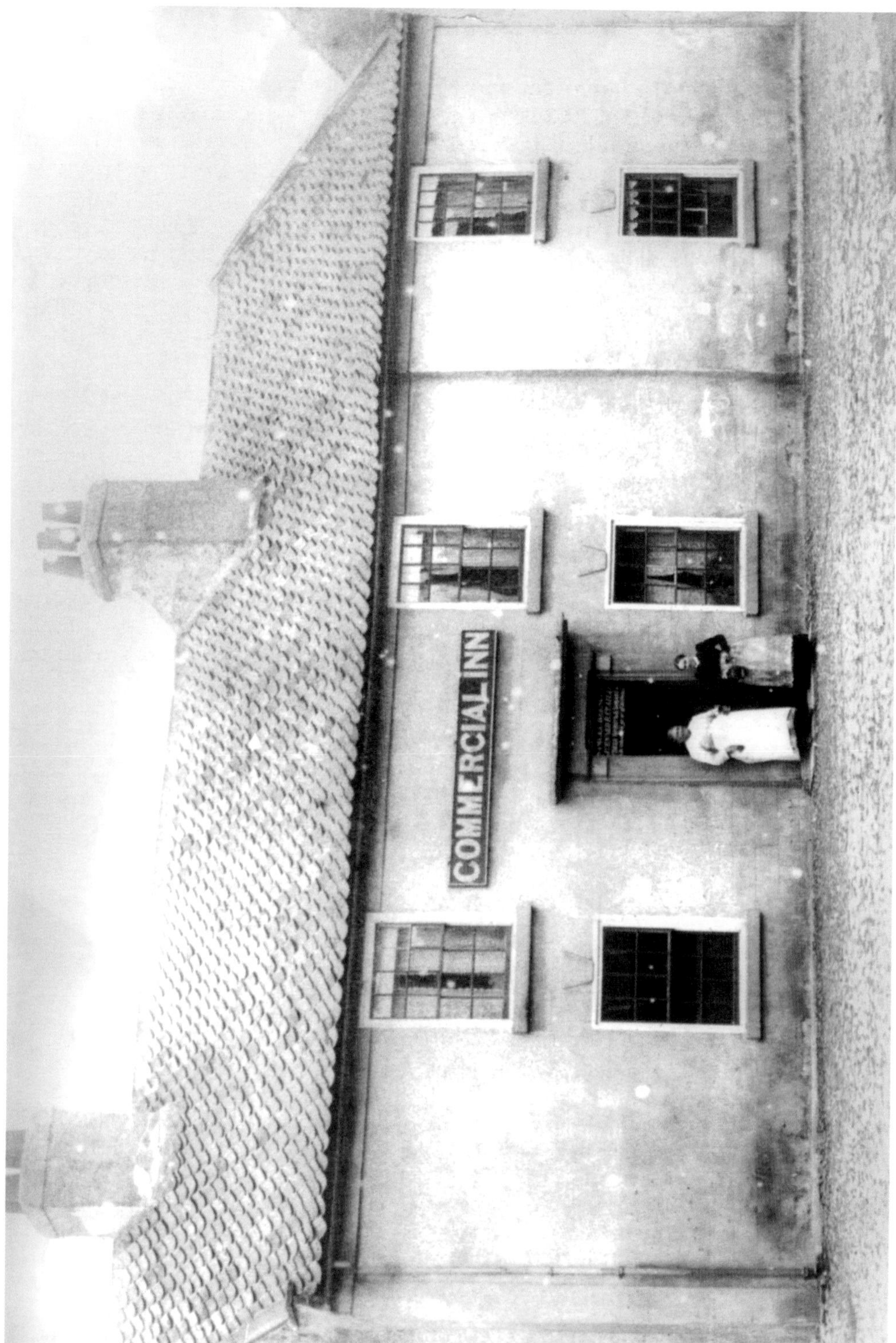

The Commercial Inn, Market Place, Easingwold, 1900

Chapter 5

SUTTON-ON-FOREST. BOLSHY VILLAGE

Sutton's opposition to the improvements of the early years of the century are not well chronicled until the summer of 1902 when the parish council, after having lobbied 'other villages who are to be supplied [sic]' petitioned the Local Government Board 'to have part of the source of supply cut off, owing to the impurity of water.' This is extraordinary, it was based on an analysis of a sample written for by a councillor who was a member of the Water Committee who could indeed have seen the analysis 'any time he liked.' The LGB wrote to the Easingwold council and its reply laid it on heavily, very heavily. It made the point about representatives who sent letters when they could have got what they wanted by simply asking, then said the Parish Council's resolution about the water being impure was 'utterly fallacious.' It was, and a certificate from the county analyst proved the RDC's case.[1]

The Sutton parish council responded and a reading of its proceedings adds to the impression that people in the village were engaged in a thought-out organised campaign against the RDC. Things got very nasty and Arthur Duncombe was the prime defender of the village's council. What could he say? He said it had forced the RDC's hand and highlighted a potential danger. There was now, he said, good reason to believe the analyst. Previously it had been impossible to feel safe when the villagers did not know where the first sample had come from.[2] The first, taken on 23 May 1901, was from the only place then available 'viz., an open water course, hence animacule.' The second, which is the one Sutton people should have concentrated on, was taken nearly a year later from the new collecting chamber. This was on 9 February 1902. The first sample could have been taken to illustrate *why* new work was needed.

Sutton on the Forest early 1900s

A debate ensued about Sutton and it was decided to publish the correspondence that had gone on. After heated discussion it had indeed been resolved to adopt the municipal supply - the 'antiis' had however seized on the bad sample as an example of what would come out of the taps. They had consequently petitioned the LGB and things had got out of hand, naturally they claimed concern over health but were also worried about cost .. Buller Hicks and his father before him had issued countless warnings about the dangers of impure water, so no-one could claim ignorance of them, but when costs were brought up residents often found that their supply was really quite pure. And those deaths? They could be explained away.

Rushing in at the slightest indication of a deficiency was an activity that persisted in Sutton, showing that not much had been learned earlier. It led to a discussion on the RDC which adds to the impression that Cllr Ward might well have been a trouble-maker. It also led to his colleague, Wood, identifying the root cause of dissatisfaction in the village. That was of course money. Mrs Duncombe of Sutton Hall sent a sample of water 'which showed a small deposit at the bottom.' With it was a letter 'conveying a suggestion that the quality of the water supplied from the [district water] works was not as it should be.'[3] Ward supported her vigorously adding that, a basin was kept at the village school, in which the children dipped their mugs when they wanted a drink. The basin was covered 'with a red canker, and the water was not fit to drink.' Not only that. Some cottagers said that potatoes turned black when boiled in it. Cllr Wood was reasonableness itself. He said the reason for the water being rusty was that it had been standing in the pipes. Nothing more, but there was something else. Some people, he said, 'had just had to pay for laying it on, and he believed that stuck worse than the water. (Laughter).' He could have been - was - right.

Sutton eventually did produce a village Hampden willing to engage in a bit of civil disobedience - and he ended up before the magistrates at Easingwold for doing so. Richard Wrightson, a farmer, was summoned by Arthur H. Brown, 'assistant-overseer for Sutton-on-Forest, for the non payment of a special rate laid to meet the expenses in connection with the District Waterworks.' Special rates were a prominent feature of RDC finances but Wrightson objected to paying for something he had yet to benefit from (he said). His comments have a very modern ring about them and no doubt went down well with his mates. They failed to impress J. Swainston Strangwayes, Henry Hawking, M. J. Stapylton and Rawdon Thornton sitting at the Town Hall, though.[4]

> The defendant stated that he objected to pay because he did not owe the money. He had received nothing from Mr. Brown, and did not consider it a just debt. In answer to a question, Mr, [sic] Wrightson said that he lived two miles from Sutton on the York road, and water was not laid on to his farm. In a dry summer he had to carry water three-quarters of a mile, and if they laid water to his farm he would pay. ... An order was made for payment, when Mr Wrightson said he might as well tell the Bench he should not pay, he would rather go to prison.

Supplying clean water was a prime duty of the Rural District Councils and creating decent drainage and sewerage systems were others. Schemes for sewerage systems for the villages were prepared in consultation with the parochial authorities and Sutton's was regularly the subject of discussion by the Easingwold RDC. Sutton certainly had a history of conflict with the RDC; Dr Hicks after reporting on area health matters in 1896[5,] in which he had highlighted cases of Erysipelas at Myton and Scarlatina at Easingwold workhouse, had been critical of the parochial authority's proposed sewerage scheme. Anyway, Hicks was hard on them. While 'giving every credit to those who had been responsible for the drawing up of the scheme', the *Advertiser's* scribe said, he 'appeared to think it inadequate in several

Easingwold Show on the Chase Garth, 1890

particulars to the necessities of the village, and advised the ratepayers to pause a little until the final reports of the Septic Tank Experiments at Exeter were completed.' Another source of friction between the Sutton Parish Council and the RDC had been over The Blackwell Ox's bay windows projecting on to the footpath.[6] The 'Parish' had objected submitting a condemning resolution but the RDC had not supported them, saying that they should deal with the brewery. Cllr Ward had warned the RDC – " ... they would find the Parish Council would not let it drop." [7]

The Blackwell Ox dispute is of no great importance, but it does show that the young parish councils in some places were anxious to make their influence felt. All over the country there would have been parish councils making life difficult for the rural district bodies, and all over the country there would have been people like Ward willing to fire their bullets. They must have been a real check on higher authorities. Going for the Blackwell's overhanging window was one thing,[8] but the vociferous Councillor at work on the water scheme was something else.

From January 1897, at least, Ward objected to mains water being provided for Sutton. He made his views quite clear in a debate on Farlington. There the parish council said it thought the scheme they were presented with was 'very expensive for a village of 70 people as the cost would sum up to £4 a head.' Could not a supply be got cheaper a councillor asked by joining with Sutton and Huby and 'obtaining the water from stand pipes?' Ward pronounced unequivocally that Sutton and Huby did not want a supply.[9]

The water supply and the encroachments of the John Smith company agitated the voluble Ward, and Sutton's sewerage scheme became a pressing concern. In June 1897 the RDC received letters from the Local Government Board 'asking what steps were being taken in connection with the carrying out of Sewerage Works at Sutton-on-Forest and Huby.'[10] Asked about it Hicks said he had no doubt the septic tank process he had mentioned earlier was the best treatment. Why? Its 'main advantage was that it would require less land' than the alternatives 'and in other ways [would] do away with a lot of expense.' (Just before this Fairfax-Cholmeley had initiated a discussion on the progress of the Easingwold scheme. In it Cllr Flawith's contribution sounded like one of Ward's. Nobody in Easingwold wanted the scheme, he said. What would have been nearer the truth, in all probability, was that everybody wanted it, but nobody wanted to pay for it. Flawith excelled himself that day. He was the trustee of property on which there was a well which the Sanitary Inspector said was about six feet deep, three feet across, in a very dangerous state, liable to contamination, and 'greatly in need of protection.' Could this be so Flawith asked? 'From what he had heard the water was of first-class quality.'[11] Denials of this kind were legion - and alarming.

The Gracious Street well at Huby was as bad an example of a polluted water supply as it was possible to find[12] and at the beginning of 1898 a circular letter was received by the RDC linking the epidemics of enteric fever to contaminated supplies. Nothing new in that, but at the same time the Local Government Board again demanded to know what was happening with the scheme for 'sewerage and sewage disposal' for Sutton.[13] The LGB was told that delays were being caused because the RDC was awaiting the outcome of septic tank tests. The Board was clearly becoming exasperated. The RDC was put on a warning that the plans for Sutton would not get a free ride. Cllr Mercer revealed that Mr Ward - who else - 'who was not present, had told him that he should try to hold up the Sutton scheme as long as he was there, 'and after that the others could do as they liked.' Fighting talk. Ward of Sutton v the Local Government Board!

The affairs of Sutton and its neighbouring villages were rarely out of the news; however, the *rationae tenurae* roads in the area were also the cause of continual concern and comment. There had been many complaints about the roads being neglected and instructions ignored. In March 1898 for example a committee was set up to look at and report on the state of the roads in the occupation of Messrs H. Barker and G. Burton. The former of these could well be the farmer whose delightful entry in *Bulmer's* reads 'Barker Arthur, Bohemia' and his colleague might have been George Burton of Alcar Farm. Anyway, the RDC wanted its committee to assess 'the figure at which' the *rationae* roads should be taken over, and this it did. Its report[14] was adopted. It stated that

> the former portion was 880 yards long, and for its being taken over the owner ought to pay £25 down and £7 per year for 12$^1/_2$ years. For the other portion, 1.465 yards [sic] they considered £15 should be paid down and £13 per year for 12$^1/_2$ years. The report ... advised the Council not to take any less than these amounts as they were as low as they possibly could be.

The *rationae tenurae* roads became an issue again towards the end of 1899 and the *Advertiser* of 18 November reported that the RDC considered a report on the state of those on Carolina Farm and the cost of maintaining them if they were taken over 'at the request of the owner, (Mr H. Knowles). The amount estimated was £8 10s per annum.' It was then proposed that the roads be taken over for £106 10s 0d being 12$^1/_2$ years cost of maintenance.' These were the usual terms but some councillors wanted a shorter period.

Spring Street, 1900s

The *rationae* roads were also regularly on the RDC's agendas in the early months of 1900 and, once more it was said that notices ordering the owners to put their roads into 'good repair forthwith' were ignored.

In April 1898 the disputatious Ward lost his seat and Sutton-on-Forest got two new representatives on the RDC. He and A. J. Brown had been the sitting councillors, but Brown withdrew before polling day and the candidates went to a poll with Ward beaten in a tiny turn-out.[15] The result was:

John Thomas Boggett	37
William Proude Willis	29
William Ward	20

Ward was off the RDC for only one term and got back in March 1901. Why he was not elected in 1898 is unknown, and whether he continued agitating against drainage and sewerage schemes for Sutton is unclear, but for some reason plans for the village *were* dropped - at least that is what the RDC said. At the end of the year the Local Government Board once more demanded that it be told what was happening with the 'SUTTON-ON-FOREST SEWERAGE SCHEME.' It got a prompt and unequivocal reply. The 'clerk was instructed to reply that the carrying out of the scheme had been indefinitely postponed' the *Advertiser* recorded.[16]

The RDC meeting which heard that the Sutton sewerage scheme had been shelved was also another of those at which truly alarming statements were given about the state of the area from a health point of view. Buller Hicks had some more dreadful stories. He said that

1) Complaints had been received that the beck which ran through Whinny Pastures was foul. It was, but, significant this, 'it was thought by some, that the condition of the stream was no worse that it had been for years.' Cold comfort for people suffering year in and year out from offensive smells and worse.

2) Providing a clear water supply at the same time as proper drainage systems was desirable and essential. In many places a deplorable lack of interest was shown in the reform proposals being put forward,[17] but not at Husthwaite. There 33 persons met at a parish meeting, but their attitudes were the same as they were elsewhere when cost became an issue. 'A motion advocating that the village be supplied with water by pipes was lost,' it was recorded. Why? The chairman, Cllr Farrer, revealed that occupiers 'were frightened at the expense'. It would be worse if the residents had 'a drainage scheme pushed on them' as well. It would certainly be more expensive.

3) Buller Hicks also reported on an epidemic at Raskelfe. What was the cause of it? The MOH's opinion of the village was well-known and he had no doubts. Insanitary sewers were the cause. Raskelfe, was the worst place in his area and the village should have a supply of decent water for both drinking and draining purposes. The RDC agreed and said the village should/would be supplied from Easingwold.[18] A week before this a letter had appeared in the *Advertiser* headed 'TYPHOID AT RASKELFE' in which the writer described for readers - not for the first time - how its drinking water was obtained.[19] The village stood on 'largish gravel' and through that wells were sunk. This had been done 'for centuries.' But the village's sewerage had been discharged into the gravel which was porous, the wells had become polluted, and 'deleterious matter' had got into them. This meant accumulations of filth that settled at the bottom of the wells but that did not really matter (!) except in a droughty season 'like the last' when the water level was lowered and it became necessary to go into, 'or dangerously near' the filth. Unfortunately, the writer said, 'we know the terrible result.'

It seems incredible that people could resist modern schemes to introduce good water into their villages, but that is what they did.

By early 1899 the RDC reported that the Raskelfe Sewerage Works had been completed at a cost of just over £59. (This had been done rapidly and to Hicks' entire satisfaction.)[20]

The LGB disagreed about the council's contentions,[21] regarding Sutton, though it was frequently pointed out that doing sewerage and water supply work at the same time made a great deal of sense. The supply from Kilburn was then found to be inadequate for the RDC's purposes but Cragg Hall Springs was tested and found to have a flow of 68,611 gallons per 24 hours. This with the overflow from the Kilburn reservoir and collections found in other springs would give more than enough to supply the villages concerned and Sutton and Huby as well.[22] The scheme (for the western parishes) was given the go-ahead in a meeting reported early in June.[23] Hicks said that the samples he had taken showed a high standard of purity, very very soft, 'only ... 12 degrees of hardness, while the Easingwold supply was about 25 degrees.'[24]

The Easingwold RDC persisted in defying the Local Government Board over Sutton and received numerous letters from the LGB asking what was happening. Cllr Hawking, no less, took a very truculent stance. People 'might think what they liked' he said, 'but not until the village had got a water supply would he have anything to do with the sewerage scheme.'[25]

The enquiry into the district waterworks scheme was held and permission to borrow funds for it were given, and the objection that a water supply should be available before work was commenced on sewering and draining the villages would soon be met. Work on the district water scheme was progressing very favourably, the chief engineer reported in August 'and they had [already] got the pipes through the worst portion' of their route.[26] The Local Government Board, at the same time, sent another letter wanting to know 'what steps were being taken towards the drainage of Crayke, Sutton Forest, Huby and Alne.'[27] The LGB, as far as the Easingwold area was concerned, acted in these years as a positive force for reform.

There was still a rearguard action to be fought as far as Sutton was concerned, however, based, believe it or not, on questions of expense and resentment at being ordered to do something. It was early in 1902 and yet another letter was read to the RDC and appeared under business headed 'HUBY AND SUTTON SEWERAGE.'[28] It got short shrift.

> Councillor Ward said he did not think there was anyone at Sutton who wanted to go in for a sewerage scheme. There was a sanitary drain [there] which was good enough if the connections were made.

Interestingly the *Advertiser* always meticulously recorded attendances at the council but there is no Ward among the list of attendances published on 25 January, yet here he was giving one of his reactionary speeches.[29] Very odd.

In May, the RDC's sanitary committee reported on drainage for the village. It recommended that the work be carried out in sections, and of course Ward had some observations to make on that.[30] His mate Cllr Wood said a lot of drainage work had been done at Sutton in the past year 'and it did not want' more than 'a little looking at.' Ward was more forceful and harped on about implied costs. He did not think it necessary to get an engineer to take levels again if the work was to go ahead in sections 'as they had a man at Sutton could do it "as good as any man in Yorkshire."'

> He thought the scheme was a waste of money. The drainage of Sutton had caused a lot of expense, and at the present time there was a drain in the middle as good as could be put in.

Ward continued to fight a prejudiced ill-informed rearguard action against the proposed Sutton improvements.[31] And that was where things stood when 1902 came to an end.

Some of the other parishes in the area also, it was alleged, were reckless and spent too much. In 1901 it became an issue. In June the clerk told the RDC that 'several parishes' had not paid the calls due from them on 24 May.[32] This provoked a heated discussion on the reckless spending in certain parishes and the apparent lack of accountability of coucillors in charge of the various accounts. Consequently Cllr Todd moved 'that no Councillor be allowed to exceed the estimate unless he first obtained the sanction of the Council, as it was not fair for some councillors to try to keep within the estimate, and others be regardless of expense, and the excess to be levied over the whole Union.' Todd's resolution was carried. It will be noted that it was the councillor, not the council, who was held responsible.

Throughout the saga of the attempts to get Sutton-on-Forest modernised, communications to the RDC from the Local Government Board demanding an explanation for the delays continued to arrive. There was one of some significance considered in August 1900.[33] An audit had shown that an increasing proportion of the RDC's expenditure 'appeared to pass

St. Monica's Hospital, Easingwold, 1905

through the Surveyors' book', and that a number of accounts over £2 were paid by him. Not only that. The cash account was made up monthly, but it was not produced before the council or a committee of the council. The vouchers were numerous and contained many errors - an example being when ten days work at two shillings a day 'was settled for £1 2s.' Details of wages 'were often insufficient' and no proper receipts were given. What happened was that councillors brought in bills from the parishes on the day of the RDC meeting and the surveyor paid - seemingly without examining them either then or later. Not a very satisfactory arrangement.

What did the Surveyor say about these criticisms? To begin with he reported that he had stopped paying amounts over £2 when told to. The overpayment of wages singled out for comment was the result of 'the last few lines on the bill' being cramped together and difficult to read, and increasing expenditure going through his hands was the result of the fact that the beloved Easingwold steam roller was being paid for in instalments. Not only that. The roller was in continual use on several road improvements which had been made. Hayden, and others, said the chaos was the result of a 'bad system' - the old and antiquated methods the RDC used in its highway business. Eventually the Surveyor was censured after some 'stormy proceedings' in private, warned about the future and told to 'take care.' Hawking had said the official had been guilty of 'gross carelessness' and he clearly was.

That the steam roller was being paid for on the never never was not the fault of the Surveyor, but the Local Government Board had criticised the council for entering into such an agreement. The Surveyor, C. E. Broad had another brush with the Board, when he was surcharged for 'some accounts paid to a District Councillor instead' of to the men 'who had done the work.'[34] Fairfax-Cholmeley wanted a committee of investigation, but this was defeated as a proposal ('a large number abstained:). It was agreed that the money did eventually get to 'the proper parties', but the Surveyor's reputation was not enhanced.

Uppleby, Easingwold, 1905

The Surveyor had his problems with his employers and some of the councillors were not beyond criticism. Cllr James Ward for example. He came under scrutiny for not carrying out his legal obligations in a report from the much criticised surveyor, and it had to do with the upkeep of the roads.[35] 'The Surveyor had presented his report on the condition of a piece of ratione tenurae road near Huby, in the occupation of Messrs Sturdy and Ward. The [sic] report stated that the road was unfit to drive over on account of its roughness. Ward was not impressed, his road, he said, was not as bad as had been made out. 'They had done a great deal at it, and it was intended to do more. It was now as good as most roads ... he attributed the complaints to the spite of neighbours. ... [He] added that it was impossible to proceed at more than a foot pace on Suet Carr and that was a road belonging to the Council!

Messrs Sturdy and Ward were given notice to repair the road at Huby but the latter was not the only councillor to be criticised for neglecting his obligations. Inchboard, who sat for Youlton, was another. Other places where the *ratione tenurae* roads were allegedly neglected included Farlington, where a threat of legal action was issued, and Raskelfe. The RDC told the Raskelfe owners that it was prepared to 'take the road over for £31 5s, being 12¹/2 years actual cost of maintenance.'

The drainage of Easingwold itself was also, of course, the concern of the RDC, and was another major worry in the years looked at in these pages. The town was as bad as other places in the area and frequent outbreaks of epidemics were reported in it. Some have been referred to. Raskelfe grabbed most of the headlines in this respect, however, and the MOH devoted a huge amount of his time to that place and began, along with the RDC engineer, to look at methods of improving waste disposal. Engineer Fairbank visited Exeter where the experiments on treating sewerage were taking place and came back and reported that the results there were 'simply astonishing'. This was in January 1897[36] and Hicks became an enthusiast for what Fairbank had described and 18 months after first hearing about it the Easingwold RDC adopted it as policy. [37]

The RDC now, it seemed, had a remedy for some of its major problems - and Easingwold itself now became the local matter of great concern, with the Local Government Board, as before, demanding to know what was happening (or not happening). What did happen in Easingwold, however, did so, at least initially, with commendable speed. At the shortest RDC meeting ever held Hayden proposed (in May 1898) that the four Easingwold councillors meet with Fairbank to confer 'as to the means of sewering sundry and certain parts of' the town. They had already met and considered, like good keepers of the public purse, that a scheme could be produced for draining each part of the town separately and by paying for the scheme out of the rates 'it would do away with the necessity for borrowing money and having the expense of a Local Government Board enquiry.'[38] This produced some opposition from Rookledge, who accused the RDC of not giving the ratepayers an opportunity of 'examining and discussing' the proposed 'piecemeal' scheme 'independent of the Local Government Board' which, he said, would be costly. It was a matter of surprise to him, Rookledge said, that the Easingwold councillors had not, to date, thought fit to take the populace into their confidence. This seems reasonable and not a little surprising as the RDC seems to have regularly negotiated with the parish councils in the past. Rookledge wanted 'a complete system' of drainage for his town. He said there was 'uneasiness' about what was being proposed.[39] The RDC agreed to a postponement.[40] After the delay the *Advertiser* said the report on the scheme was considered on a Friday in July 1898.[41] The *Advertiser* said

> four Easingwold Representatives, presented their report on the ... drainage system, which recommended that Uppleby, from the top down to the old culvert in Spring Street, be sewered, such work when completed to form part of a complete system if necessary. ... Councillor Hayden said it was proposed to be paid for in two half-yearly instalments, and could be completed in twelve months, when they could let the other drainage into it. ... It would do away with that nuisance from the open ditch. ... This was unanimously agreed to.

Tenders for the drainage works were asked for and eventually the Council recommended the acceptance of that from T. Bell of Market Weighton for £257 1s.[42] The Easingwold parish council objected again to the RDC scheme, which it said was being rushed through, and once more Rookledge acted as spokesman for them. He reckoned the scheme would necessitate a rate of a shilling in the pound on houses, and 3d on land. He still wanted a comprehensive system which he thought would cost '£3000 with borrowed money, a rate of perhaps 6d.'

The Uppleby part of the Easingwold scheme was completed, then the rows really began, many over technicalities. Hicks claimed householders were reluctant to join into the new sewer and asked whether people could be forced to connect (and forced to pay). He said, in January 1899, that the situation was then very little different from what it had been before the sewer was made. What about connections? Cllr Bell contended they could not force people to use the new facility and the MOH told members that, where more than one house 'was drained into one drain, that drain became a sewer legally and under the control of the Sanitary Authority. Most of the houses in Uppleby were like this.[43]

More details of why it was recommended that Easingwold be drained and sewered in sections appeared in a report from Fairfax-Cholmeley.[44] It complained that in a 'large part of the town there was no sanitary main drain,' and urged that a coordinated approach to improvements be made - that streets should not be repaired only to have them hacked up

1905. On the left of the street a white sign 'Campbell, Dyers, Berth'. On the right 'Tinner Smith's Shop'.

when a drain was put in. That seemed eminently sensible, then Fairfax-Cholmeley reviewed the plans to sewer Easingwold. These had been in existence for some years 'when it was proposed to use the system of land filtration to get rid of the waste.' They had 'allowed for four acres of land for that purpose, but' the Local Government Board[45]

> insisted on ten acres which seemed excessive, and it was decided to carry out the work in sections, thus getting rid of the requirements of the ... Board. Since that time the Septic tank and other bacterial processes had come into use, which would require about two acres of land. What they wanted the Engineer to do was to take the levels, so that if at any future time they would be certain to have the outfall where they could get rid of the sewage. ... the levels taken before were for land filtration, and not for Septic tank or any other process.

The Fairfax-Cholmeley Sanitary Committee report was adapted and Rookledge and the parish council got some (very reasonable) explanations for the policy recommendations about draining Easingwold. The committee in 1901 was a fairly recent creation, but W. Snowden the sanitary inspector revealed that it had not received the support it should have done. Snowden had to give a regular account to the committee which had clearly been set up in response to the amount of work needed to be done in the area, and with a regularly troublesome village.[46]

The first case reported was about some premises at Farlington where the drainage was untrapped, the sewage running into an open ditch. Water there was obtained from a well not more than eight yards from the fold-yard, and within five yards of the defective drain.

This Committee of draining Easingwold looks as if it should have settled the matter, but it had not. Hayden and Barley started the well rehearsed issue again, and once more there were arguments about how sewering the town should be done - and much was was made about the Uppleby drain, done in 1898, not being used.[47] Once more the parish council held a public meeting to discuss the issues. Ratepayers had requisitioned it and it was presided over by John Hobson.[48] It fell to F. J. H. Robinson to explain the history of schemes to improve the town by sewering and properly draining it. He also outlined the cause of the ongoing RDC conflict with the LGB. The LGB had recommended that the Stillington Lane sewerage disposal works be extended from three to ten acres – the RDC not liking the suggestion had simply ignored it.

Robinson next went over the familiar ground about cost and ended his contribution by saying that though there were competing schemes he did not 'see any reasonable doubt as to which was best.' He and those who thought like him wanted 'a modified form' of the septic tank system for the town. He ended by once again telling his hearers of the costs of the competing schemes.[49]

Buller Hicks spoke in favour of a piecemeal approach to Easingwold's sewerage, and said that 'better branch drainage' was 'more imperative than sewering.' He described the various sections of the piecemeal system he favoured,[50] then talked of disposal. Sanitary science, he said, was 'only in its infancy' but he had drawn up a plan to do away with most if not all the 'nuisance in the beck' though that was fouled by drainage from farm houses below where the Easingwold waste went into it. How much would this cost? A thousand pounds Buller thought would cover everything. The RDC's engineer had said the Hicks' ideas were practical.

Quite clearly Hicks had a great deal to do with investing some urgency into the situation as a note in the *Advertiser* confirms.[51]

RURAL DISTRICT COUNCIL

> At the District Council Meeting, this afternoon (Friday), it was decided to proceed with the first section of sewerage from Spring Street to Long Street at once, and to authorise Dr Hicks to try his system for purifying the outfall.

The contract for the Chapel Street sewer was let to Robert Curry of Easingwold,[52] and rapidly accusations about things like bad levels began to be thrown around. J. J. Penty took it upon himself to become the spokesman against the scheme and he did so particularly in an ill informed outburst for which he got strongly corrected by the engineer. He deserved it. *None* of Penty's statements, Fairbank said, was correct.[53]

Penty beat an undignified retreat, but took some part in the discussion about an explosion in Chapel Street which had occurred two months earlier. What was this?[54]

> A REMARKABLE OCCURRENCE - EXPLOSION IN CHAPEL STREET. - On Tuesday morning [the 23rd] a remarkable an [sic] unprecedented occurrence took place in Chapel Street ... by which a considerable portion of the new sewer was wrecked. The laying of the pipes had been finished, and the man-holes were being put in. ... the workmen, before commencing to build, withdrew the plug which was stopping the Market Place end of the drain. Immediately a violent explosion occurred, the sound of which could be heard for a great distance, resembling the booming of a cannon. The workmen were nearly blinded with sand, and the houses near by were shaken to their foundations ... Mortar was blown out of the ... walls ... [and] a rough estimate of

the damage [to] ... the sewer [is] Twenty-five pounds ... about 66 yards of pipes being smashed.

Coal gas was rapidly established as the cause of Easingwold's most exciting event in 1901 and Penty saw an opportunity of getting back at the engineer. It got very nasty.[55] Raskelfe, it will be remembered, had had its problems and Buller Hicks had been encouraged to experiment with purifying the outfalls. There had been problems with ventilators and the man-holes and Penty suggested that the engineer and the council had ignored lessons from there which should have been obvious.[56]

Penty had taken it upon himself to become the arch critic of the Easingwold sewerage scheme and he was responsible not only for the ill informed attacks on Fairbank, but also for attacks on the contractor and indeed on the overall plan. Levels, he said, were different in some places, making connections with the new drains almost impossible. Penty's first major attack was in May and reached that exciting peak in the following month.[57] He was being worsted, but carried on. By June the Uppleby flushing tank had been connected and the consequences, Penty said, were that gases were sent down to the lower end of the system with unpleasant results. Fairbank told Penty he would have another flushing tank put in near Spring Head.[58] Arguments were aired about whether the smells from the ventilators were from sewage or coal gas. Officials and councillors were alarmed at the possibility of another explosion, so much so that the Sanitary Inspector wrote to the RDC. Metal discs, put there to keep the stench down, had been put in the ventilators and this worried Snowden the SI. Understandably. '... if an explosion occurred he should not be held responsible,' he said.[59]

Penty's next move was a drastic one. He moved a resolution saying that all property owners in Chapel Street, 'be compelled to provide efficient drains and make proper connections with the new sewer within one month ... and all ... owners in the other sections up to the top of Uppleby be put under a similar obligation, but have three months in which to do it.' As an 'inducement' Penty proposed that the old sewer be discontinued from the expiry date of the notices.[60] Had the council got the power to force people to connect? Buller Hicks had earlier said he was sure it had.[61] Others differed. A decision on what should happen was made in late October 1901.[62]

Early in 1902 the next stage of the on-going Easingwold sewer scheme was started. John Hobson now proposed that the Engineer be instructed 'to draw up plans for a section from the bottom of Chapel Street.' The 'proposition was carried' with no dissentients.[63] The plans were produced with commendable speed before the end of March. By mid April Penty told the RDC that the Easingwold representatives had met with the MOH and 'had gone through the plans for the sewering of Long Street' and moved 'that tenders be invited for the carrying out of a length from Chapel Street to half-way down Long Street.' This was agreed, and there were no objectors.

Also at this time the RDC, as well as having its ongoing battle with Sutton, had Husthwaite on its agenda in July 1902.[64] What had been happening (or not happening) in Husthwaite to get it there? As a result of some splendid efforts by the local community a new vicarage had been built but 'for some, and no doubt adequate reason' no drain was laid to carry the ecclesiastical 'sewage out of the grounds, tanks near the roadside being made to be emptied as circumstances demanded.' This arrangement had 'not altogether proved successful' and the RDC had received many complaints about the 'overflow from the tanks running on to the highway.' A notice[65] had been served on the vicar ordering him to abate the nuisance but this, like earlier communications, had been ignored. The vicar wrote and said there was

Town Hall and Market Place, 1905 *(Now home to G H Smith & Son, Printers and Publishers)*

no drain in the village for him to drain into. There then followed a predictable contribution from Cllr Farrer, who said, like Ward said for Sutton, there 'was no need of a Sewerage Scheme at Husthwaite,' a remark which people who lived near the Rev Gill's outfall might not have agreed with. At the end of the year the Husthwaite problem still remained and there was yet another warning of the hazards of neglecting filth. It came from a place not a hundred miles from the Rev Gill's parish.[66]

CARLTON-HUSTHWAITE

> It was reported that two cases of scarlatina and five cases of diptheria had been notified from the above village, it being also stated that the conditions were serious, and *there was a probability of a heavy out-break.*

There was an isolation hospital in Easingwold to which, presumably, some of those affected at Carlton-Husthwaite would go, and it had been a cause of concern for all of 1902. In February the chairman of the Sanitary Committee revealed they had 'under consideration figures and details of an 'Isolation Hospital,'[67] and, for the record, and, as a separate item, the MOH reported 'that there had been 22 cases of scarlet fever during the past month, and 3 deaths.'

Bulmer's Directory has a very brief note about the hospital, simply saying in its section about the Poor Law Union that the Workhouse was built in the 1830s and that 'An infirmary for infectious diseases was built in 1869, at a cost of about £700' and that it 'will accommodate 20 patients.' Fairfax-Cholmeley and his colleagues on the Sanitary Committee discussed this and decided to ask for permission to 'transfer the Hospital on the Workhouse premises to' the RDC. Nothing at this stage about moving it. The old one would stay where it was and put 'in good order.' If this happened it could be used for 'Poor Law cases, and fever cases for the district as well.'

The Board of Guardians duly took up the question of a fever hospital with the LGB. They asked the Board to allow them to 'transfer the Union Hospital ... to the Rural District Council, as in its position in the centre of the Workhouse Buildings [sic] it was not in accordance with their requirements for Infectious Diseases Hospitals.' This time the LBG was not cooperative. Henry Hawking who was as familiar as anyone with infectious diseases questioned the logic of the Board's refusal. If it (the existing hospital) was not suitable for the District how could it be suitable for the Workhouse? Quite right. It was indisputedly in a state that was 'very unsatisfactory ... [and] there were always complaints being made about it' and it would 'cost £100 or more to put it right.' So the original proposition was for the RDC to take over the hospital, enlarge it and move infected persons into a place in the middle of the Workhouse. It seems a reckless proposal and Hawking asked his colleagues to consider something more radical. 'Speaking off-hand he did not know whether it would be better to ask the Local Government Board for permission to pull it down altogether, and put one up that would do both for the Union and District.'[68]

Hawking's ideas got support from an LGB inspector. A Mr Lowry visited Easingwold and confirmed that 'The hospital at present was in a very delapidated [sic] condition.' He also suggested they should pull it down, sell the materials 'and ... build one which would be available for all the district.' The present hospital 'was ... nothing but a "white elephant", and ... it would be a waste of money to try and repair it. ... sooner or later, they would have to build an Isolation Hospital for the district, and also a disinfecting chamber, &c. ... only a one storey building would be necessary' so the cost 'need not be large.'[69] M. J. Stapylton added to the picture of a deplorable refuge. How could a place for sick persons, have been allowed to get into what the JP called 'a dirty, filthy condition, [where] the boards were rotting,' which would be inordinately expensive to repair? It was proposed that the building be pulled down and the materials given to the RDC which, it was assumed would be building a new place. This was agreed (33 : 0) by the Guardians. There then followed the inevitable objections to compulsion. A person could only be made to go into the place if the MOH certified they could not be properly isolated at home.

The RDC thus decide and ask for permission 'to pull down the present hospital,'[70] and that was the situation when the year ended to petition the LGB.

NOTES

1. Dated 12 February 1902.
2. *Advertiser* 15 March 1902.
3. *Ibid* 30 August 1902.
4. *Ibid* 6 December 1902.
5. *Ibid* 2 January 1897.
6. *Ibid* 16 January 1897.
7. It is not clear what Ward meant by this.
8. Ward did not let the Blackwell Ox affair drop. See eg *Ibid* 24 April, 8 and 22 May 1897.
9. Farlington eventually went it alone and obtained its water from a spring, the owner of which leased it for 30 years at a rent of £2 2s. *Ibid* 22 May 1897. See also *Ibid* 27 February 1897.
10. *Ibid* 19 June 1897.
11. Really. Hicks analysed the water in the well and said he thought there was a dead cat in it 'or perhaps 5 or 6 dead rats.' It was totally unfit for drinking purposes. (Well it would be.) An attempt to have the well covered and sealed off was not successful. The RDC ordered it to be cleaned out and a water sample taken and analysed. The well was *not* contaminated by drainage. *Ibid* 17 July 1897. What happened? The well 'near Gracious Street, Huby' was duly cleaned out and 'the analysis was worse than the analysis taken before'. *Ibid* 14 August 1897.

12. Though in fairness it should be said it was contended that it was *not* used for drinking supplies. It was also pointed out that the well was not contaminated by seepage from such things as cesspits. (Other places were.) An unsolved mystery then!
13. *Advertiser* 1 January 1898.
14. *Ibid* 9 April 1898. It is not clear what exactly 'former' refers to. A little later a length of *ratione tenurae* road in Carlton Husthwaite was taken over for £100 (payable in four instalments). *Ibid* 22 October 1898.
15. *Ibid* 9 April 1898.
16. *Ibid* 3 December 1898.
17. Eg at Raskelfe where only seven people attended a meeting to consider the village's sewerage - and some of these were interested parties. They decided to support the council's recommendations, however. These were to remove the north end outfall '174 yards further' and that at the south end 127 more yards from the village. Eight ventilating shafts were to be erected and air grates would be closed. This would cost £60, to be added to the original cost of 100 guineas. The RDC decided to levy a special rate of £60 on Raskelfe. *Ibid*, 10 September 1898.
18. This was provisionally decided at the end of 1898. *Ibid* 31 December 1898. But there were second thoughts. See *Ibid* 25 February 1899 for proposals before the RDC to supply Raskelfe, Husthwaite, Carlton Husthwaite, Alne and Thormanby with water from Kilburn. The cost was to be almost £7,000 plus way leaves.
19. Letter signed '"COMMON SENSE."' *Ibid* 24 December 1898.
20. Yet within a year things were as bad as before. See *Ibid* 9 September 1899. An embarrassed Hicks was reminded of his approval. He recommended, now, stopping up the outfall for a few days and supplying each household with permanganate of potash 'to put down their grates.'
21. '... the provision of a water supply was not' absolutely essential before the sewerage scheme 'was proceeded with.' *Advertiser* 25 March 1890.
22. *Ibid* 6 May 1899. the villages to be supplied were Alne, Tholthorpe, Tollerton, Huby, Sutton, Carlton Husthwaite, Husthwaite, Raskelfe, Flawith, Youlton, Aldwark.
23. *Ibid* 3 June 1899.
24. The engineer's report made interesting reading. Population to be supplied was below 3,500. The total flow of water left 'a margin of 46,206 gallons for seasonable variations.'
25. *Advertiser* 12 August 1899.
26. Though the reservoir had yet to be built. When the supply got as far as Husthwaite a temporary one was used. The Cragg Hall structure, the engineer said, could take nine months to build. Tenders for it were asked for in late October.
27. *Advertiser* 10 August 1901.
28. It actually said the Council could keep the deposited plans for the two villages for two more months, and then asked for a progress report. *Ibid* 25 January 1902.
29. *Ibid*. Much time was taken up by complaints about trenches being left open, cobbles not being put back efficiently, mud and so on. All very predictable perhaps. There were also claims for damages against the RDC, and some try-ons.
30. *Ibid* 17 May 1902.
31. Eg *Ibid* 9 August 1902.
32. *Ibid* 29 June 1901. The question about overspending was asked by Cllr Colley. The clerk's reply to him is as given in the *Advertiser.*
33. *Ibid* 11 August 1900.
34. *Ibid* 1 May 1902.
35. *Ibid* 6 April 1901. James Ward did not seek re-election in April 1901. It is easy to confuse him with the much more active William, who has been mentioned before. Concern at the state of the Huby roadside had existed for some considerable time. See eg. *Ibid* 12 February 1898.
36. *Ibid* 30 January 1897.
37. *Ibid* 27 August 1898.
38. *Ibid* 21 May 1898
39. Letter headed 'THE EASINGWOLD DRAINAGE SCHEME'. *Ibid* 28 May 1898. From a later period see eg *ibid* 17 and 24 November 1900.
40. *Ibid* 18 June 1898.
41. ' ... on Friday last.' *Ibid* 16 July 1898.
42. *Ibid* 13 August 1898. It was explained that 'the ... tenders only referred to Uppleby, and did not include the open ditch on the road side leading' to the Workhouse.
43. *Ibid* 28 January 1899.
44. Chairman of the RDC's Sanitary Committee.
45. *Advertiser* 14 July 1900.
46. *Ibid* 11 August 1900.
47. *Ibid* 3 November 1900.
48. *Ibid* 17 and 24 November 1900.
49. To reiterate them, in Robinson's words. If the entire scheme cost £4,000 that would 'necessitate a call for £210 a year for 30 years, which would entail a rate of 8d in the pound on houses and 2d in the pound on land.' The cost of the alternative was estimated at £3,500. If repaid in six years that would need a rate of 2s on houses and 6d on land.

50. Uppleby had been done as far as Spring Street. The next section was 'from the man-hole near the Reading Room [the Victoria Institute] to the bottom of Chapel Street.' The next section 'round the Market Place ... and from the bottom of Chapel Street to the bottom of Long Street.' The other portion of Long Street from the Grammar School to the Bay Horse already had a tunnel - 'as good ... as he had ever seen in his life' Hicks said. That left the part from the Bay Horse to the 'top of Long Street, the Back Lane and Church Street.'
51. The debate which led to the decision to go ahead reported in *Advertiser* 1 December 1900.
52. *Ibid* 26 January, 9 and 23 February 1901.
53. *Ibid* 18 May, 15 June 1901.
54. *Ibid* 27 April 1901.
55. This was in the exchange quoted earlier when Fairbank told Penty he was all wrong.
56. At Raskelfe.
57. *Advertiser* 18 May 1901.
58. *Ibid* 29 June 1901.
59. *Ibid* 7 September 1901.
60. *Ibid* 5 October 1901.
61. Actually the discussion, or the question, was rather narrower than that. What power had the council had in the case of people who had already efficient sanitary drains from their property was the way the question was recorded.
62. *Advertiser* 2 November 1901. A return of owners was called for and made by the Sanitary Committee: 1) Four owners had good drains connected with the new sewer, 2) four had drains connected to the old sewer which would be closed, 3) 13 had drains not made with sanitary pipes which were connected to the old sewer, and 4) as far as one house was concerned it was thought there might not be sufficient fall to joints with the new sewer. It was decided to order all those in category 3) to have proper connections made while the Council would connect those in category 2).
63. *Ibid* 22 February, 22 March, 19 April 1902.
64. *Ibid* 12 July 1902. The 'next stage' was the appointment of a clerk of works. He was a Mr Sharpe.
65. From the RDC's Sanitary Committee. Whether the notice had been sent became a controversial issue for a short time.
66. *Advertiser* 27 December 1902. My Italics.
67. *Ibid* 22 February 1902.
68. *Ibid* 17 May 1902. This is from the report of a Guardians' meeting.
69. It is not clear whether these remarks were from Lowry or Hawkings. They certainly reflected the inspector's ideas.
70. *Advertiser* 30 August, 4 October, 1 November 1902.

Corner of Chapel Street, Easingwold

ALNE STATION & EASINGWOLD

The means of transport between Alne Station and Easingwold before the Easingwold Railway was opened in 1891, was by means of horse buses, of which the proprietor was the late Mr George Hutton, of the Station Hotel, Alne Station, and after his death by his widow.

On ordinary days a single horse bus was used and the fare either way was 1s. On Easingwold market days and York market days (Saturday), the double fare on Saturdays, inclusion of bus and rail was 2s. each.

The photograph we reproduce was taken in 1885, and shows the Martet bus. The names of those appearing in the picture, reading from left to right, are: Mr William Maskew, junr., the late Mr F. J. Haxby Robinson, solicitor, Mr Arthur Swann, who used to deliver parcels; Mr. Harry Harper, the driver, and Mr Sydney Smith, who by the way, drove the first engine up to Easingwold before the Station was completed.

The Station Hotel at Alne, was a busy house in those days before the advent of the Railway to Easingwold, and on a Saturday morning as many as twenty passengers have been taken on the double horse bus. Once when there was a big load on, the back axle broke, near the bridge over the beck nearing Alne Station, and the passengers had to walk for the incoming train.

The horses knew every inch of the road, rough and smooth, in fact they could travel and pass anything without a driver. On occasions the driver would get off at the stile, near Travellers Rest, and meet the bus at Lund corner.

There was quite a useful service, about 5 horses and three drivers were kept for this and other posting work.

Sometimes a little delay would be caused by Willie May, crossing the road at the top of Long Street with Jess his donkey, and cart - neither Jess or Willie were fast movers.

Taken from *Easingwold Advertiser* 1932.

Chapter 6

RACHEL ANN TAYLOR, THE GUARDIANS, AND CONSCIENTIOUS OBJECTION.

When the year 1902 closed much remained to be done before the Easingwold area was anything like a healthy place, but progress over the past few years had been impressive. A clean supply of water had been provided to many places[1] and decent drainage and sewerage schemes were being implemented using up-to-date methods of disposal. At last attempts were to be made to lessen the consequences of the ghastly epidemics which Buller Hicks had had to tell the populace about on a regular basis and the RDC used the courts to punish offenders, for things like selling food deemed unfit for human consumption, before the magistrates.[2] The RDC had become more pro-active as modern jargon might have it, and real attempts were made to improve the roads. The council was then lending its support to attempts to abolish the *ratione tenurae* 'system' and was regulating building for the first time. This was of profound importance, and whether to apply for approval for some draft bye-laws had been under consideration for some time. Once again need was undoubtedly the prime reason for reform, but Cllr Souter made the point that benefits would be widespread, as of course they would be. If adopted he said, 'the Bye-Laws would be a protection to those building as well as those living in the houses when built.'

Application was made to the LGB for sanction for the bye-laws and this was given with commendable speed. In late November 'The Common seal of the council was affixed to the Building bye-laws', and henceforth there were restrictions that took the form of consumer protection.[3]

The RDC, with Buller Hicks' enthusiastic support, also decided to apply for bye-laws to enable them to regulate slaughter houses in the villages. A lot was said about whether a bye-law could be applied to the whole of an area, or whether it had to be implemented village by village. The LGB's opinion was that 'it was not usual to grant powers for a whole rural district.'[4] There were some dissenters, as always, and among them William Ward of Sutton. According to him there had been no complaints about slaughter houses in Sutton. That is probably true as the provisional sanction from the Local Government Board said nothing about his village.[5]

BYE-LAWS

> A letter was read from the Local Government Board provisionally sanctioning a set of Bye-Laws for the regulation of slaughter-houses in the parishes of Easingwold, Tholthorpe, Stillington, Coxwold, Crayke, Huby and Newton-on-Ouse.

The question of provision by The Poor Law Union was also under constant discussion. What existed at the turn of the century was described by *Bulmer's* and mentioned as follows.

> *Easingwold Poor Law Union* comprehends 29 townships, embracing 96 square miles; gross estimated rental, £101,447; and population, 9,533. The Workhouse is a commodious brick building, erected in 1837, at a cost of £2,000, ... capable of accommodating 130.

Claypenny House, Easingwold, originally the Workhouse, 1905

When that description was written Dr E. B. Hicks Snr was medical officer at the Workhouse and the Union was split into a number of districts. All the responsibility of a medical officer.

The 'Union', and, particularly, the Workhouse, was hated by the Victorian poor and the suicide of a man in the Easingwold area who thought he might end up in the Workhouse has been mentioned. Aid to the needy, however, could take the form of outdoor relief. It had been so for a long time.

The Rural District Councillors met as Guardians fortnightly, either just before or just after the RDC deliberations. Their last meeting of 1896 was held two days before Christmas.[6] Business then began with the Workhouse Master's report. He (a Mr Leckenby) told those assembled that since their last meeting two 'persons had been admitted into the house, ... one removed, and one discharged, the number of inmates now in the house being 31 against 40 for the same date last year.' The number of vagrants casually relieved had been 91, compared with 108 for the corresponding fortnight of last year. There was a case of scarlatina in the hospital.[7]

The discussion then went on to the hospital and the comments of Board members showed that the place had been allowed to decay, so badly that urgent work on it was necessary.

The first Guardians' meeting for 1898 indicated a very similar picture to that of a year earlier, with 'the number in the house' being given as 40 and the vagrants casually relieved as 97.[8] A year later the situation was more-or-less the same.[9] The meeting that heard about this was also told of a 'DIFFICULTY' which was to dominate poor law proceedings in 1899. It was about 'A BOARDING OUT DIFFICULTY.' A long discussion, it was said, took place as to the steps to be taken to compel the foster parents of a child who was boarded out with them. [sic] ... the child is now 13 years old, at which age it is usual for them to cease being boarded out, and go to service. The relieving officer had several times applied for the child, but at each time had been flatly refused. [A vote decided] ... that the child be forcibly taken possession of ... [the voting was] for 30, against 4.

The boarding out case was to run and run. At a board meeting which heard that: town water was to be laid on to what was called the 'Public Hall'; that a spot of trouble among top staff had been solved;[10] that tenders from Harry Stephens of Burythorpe had been accepted for improvements at the Workhouse and that an assistant matron had been appointed;[11] it was reported that legal proceedings had been started in the boarding case. '... Legal proceedings had been instituted against the offender, and a writ had been served on him to appear at High Court of Justice.' He appeared before the Board, 'and emphatically declared that he had never signed a paper or agreement of any kind when he took the child.'

The judge wrote asking for details of the child case and rapidly it was realised that it affected 'the whole of the Boarding out system' used by the Guardians. It was summed up by W. Harrison, JP, who took a legalistic view of the situation, and quite properly too.[12] He said

It was either a proper request to have the child delivered up, or it was not. If it was a proper demand the authority of the Board should be upheld, but if it was an improper one, it ought not to have been made. ... he asked the Clerk whether in the case of an adverse decision in this case, the Guardians should not abandon the children at 13 and leave them to the Foster Parents.

Was there an adverse decision? On 14 March Mr Justice Grantham and Mr Justice Kennedy sat as a Divisional Court in the Queen's Bench Division and before them appeared a Mr Dumas, instructed on behalf of the Easingwold Guardians.[13]

to move for an order nisi for a writ of attachment for contempt of court by one Thomas Dunhill, for failing to make any proper return to a writ of "habeas corpus."

Dumas outlined the details of the case. In 1893 'an illegitimate orphan, aged $7^1/_2$ years, named Rachel Ann Taylor' was an inmate of the Easingwold Workhouse and she was boarded out 'under the provisions of the Local Government Board Boarding-out Act, 1889'. She went to Thomas Dunhill who received 4s a week and was responsible for her attending church and school. In November 1898 the Guardians decided it would be 'for her benefit to go out into a domestic situation, and they procured a situation for her.' Dunhill was ordered to give her up by several court orders,[14] but refused to do so or to attend any hearings. One of these was to have been heard by a judge in chambers and a letter was delivered to him. It was

written from Easingwold by Mary Dunhill, and said: "My Lord, - My husband, Thomas Dunhill, is uncle to the child, and is ill, and has been unable to attend. For the last three months he has received nothing, and wishes for nothing. The girl is 13 years of age, is a cripple on one hand, and subject to fits. Both Thomas Dunhill and myself are anxious to keep the child. Praying you will grant my application to retain the custody of the child as she is in good health and wishful to remain with us, - Mary Dunhill."

Thomas, was a labourer of 84 years of age, still working for the princely sum of ten shillings a week.

Mr Justice Grantham pointed out that it was impossible for Dunhill to go to London for a court hearing ('How was it possible for an old man of 84 earning 10s a week, to bring the child to London?'). The girl was well cared for, the Guardians would not have left her with the old couple had she been ill treated. She was attached to them, and wanted to stay with them, 'it was better she should remain as they had been in "loco parentis".' Another enquiry was ordered, meanwhile the case was adjourned. The writ asked for was suspended, 'until after they had learnt the result of the Official Solicitor's inquiries. The question of costs' was also reserved.

The Official Solicitor visited Easingwold and interviewed Guardians and Rachel's foster parents. At a board meeting the clerk said it was rumoured that the judges, on receiving the results of the investigation, 'would refuse to grant the writ of attachment applied for.' These were only rumours, but some members took alarm.[15] Despite that it was decided to fight on and a belief was freely expressed that the Board *would* win.

This was bad publicity and the local Guardians, hated already, might well have suffered also from a much publicised case from Driffield Workhouse where two inmates had died as a result of suffocation from coke fumes – all the workhouse officials had, however, been exonerated.[16]

The troubles over Rachel Taylor continued. In April The case of the Queen v Dunhill came on for hearing in the Queen's Bench. Once again the facts of the case were rehearsed and Justice Kennedy tried to mediate, and Dumas agreed that the Guardians would again consider the case. Rachel had gone to the Dunhills, it was revealed, when her mother - 'a near and close relative' - had died. Before this there were frequent arguments about whether Dunhill had signed a paper saying he would give Rachel up, if asked. He said he had not, but the courts accepted that he had. 'No doubt the old man signed the undertaking to give her up' Kennedy said.

> The Easingwold Board of Guardians considered correspondence about the Dunhill case in which they were told that if they 'held out for their strict rights' the case would have to be argued before them (the judges) by the Attorney General.[17] Despite Cllr Mintoft's protestations on Dunhill's behalf and his stressing that to continue was a waste of ratepayers' money the Guardians pressed on and the Dunhill's case was before the Queen's Bench again in May.[18] A committee was set up to try and reach an agreement with the old boy and gave its report to the Guardians. Dunhill had been seen but resolutely refused to give up the girl and there was bad news for him. To begin with the judge said the Easingwold report was a 'very proper' one and that if Thomas did not give Rachel up the writ would finally be executed. The Official Solicitor agreed. He said he was sorry Dunhill was 'behaving so obstinately' and said he had written to the old lad saying that while his report of a while back 'aimed at keeping him out of prison, he could no longer assist him unless he carried out the suggestion that the girl be hired out; failing that he would go to prison.'[19] Again Cllr Mintoft tried to intervene to help Dunhill even going to see him and subsequently writing to the Official Solicitor but he was severely criticised by fellow Guardians.

Then on 30 May the end for Dunhill seemed to have arrived when Justices Day and Lawrance sat as a divisional court and heard Dumas ask for the rule nisi of 4 March to be made absolute. It was. 'Rule made absolute ... the writ to go.'[20]

Market Place, Easingwold, 1905

Was this the end of the Dunhill matter? It was not. Dunhill wrote to the Official Solicitor saying Rachel was no longer with him. She had been 'sent to a situation with a relative at Smeaton.' A copy was sent to the Easingwold Guardians who dismissed it out of hand. It 'was proved to the satisfaction of the Board that the sending of the child to service was a "sconce,"[21] and she would be brought back as soon as things got settled down a bit.' The Guardians were certainly right - it was a sconce. The place the girl had gone to was a pub half way between Northallerton and Darlington and members of the board had visited it. The mistress there said there had been 'no engagement, the child only receiving its food, there being no arrangement as to clothes.' She said she took Rachel because Tom Dunhill had asked her 'to do so until the job got settled.' Then 'a lengthy discussion' took place when

> It was stated that ... Dunhill had been arrested and lodged in York Castle, previous to being taken to London. ... it was agreed to let the relieving officer proceed with the engaging of the girl to a suitable place.

Tom Dunhill did not remain in the York Castle long.[22] When there he was medically examined, and the examination showed him to be 'bodily in a feeble state of health, while mentally he was childish, and did not appear to know why he was there, and [he] might die at any time.' This was the man presented to the Guardians by one of their members as a troublesome old schemer. He was released 'on the representation of the Board', probably shocked at the state of their adversary. The girl was sent to 'a situation near Easingwold at £6 10s wage, and the only question' outstanding was 'who was to receive the wages - the Board or Dunhill.'

The Easingwold Guardians (on Harrison's suggestion) decided to ask Grant Lawson to question the Home Secretary in Parliament about their case. It had dragged on for six months, 'the Board had the law on their side,' yet found the utmost difficulty in upholding their rights. They wanted the law to be changed.[23]

Mr and Mrs Dunhill and their foster child disappear from the pages of the *Advertiser* with the girl being 'placed' and Thomas being released from prison.

An extract, however, from 30 November 1901, is interesting in that it records yet another Easingwold policy as it related to children of Rachel's age.

HIRING OF CHILDREN

> According to the custom the [Workhouse] children between 13 and 16 years of age, were hired by the Board at wages from £6 to £14 per year.
> It was also stated that R. A. Tate, the subject of [a] boarding-out case in the High Courts, had attained the age of 16 years, and was now out of jurisdiction of the Board.

The busy Guardians also had another court case on their hands when the Dunhill case was going on. The report is self explanatory.[24]

BABY FARMING

> Some discussion took place on the way in which the Infant Life Protection Act was carried out in Easingwold. The clause, which enacts that no person shall keep by hire more than one child under 5 years old, unless registered, was discussed at some length, and as a result it was decided to take proceedings against an Easingwold man, if his house was not registered within 24 hours.

There should have been few objections to the Guardians wanting baby farmers registered and regulated, and the Infant Life Act was a thoroughly worthwhile piece of legislation, but as yet some regarded it as another example of government expansion and interference to put alongside new building regulations, controls over slaughter houses, drains, speed on the roads, the movement and destruction of infected animals and so on. There were endless discussions in the national press and the journals about what rights the individual had, or should have, when faced with compulsion. Never more so than with vaccination.

In the spring of 1898 the British Medical Association produced a pamphlet called *Facts about Small-pox and Vaccination* which was noticed at some length in the *Advertiser.* It gave a large number of statistics and compared countries where vaccination was compulsory (Prussia) and voluntary (Austria and Belgium) and showed quite conclusively that the treatment against smallpox - which periodically appeared in the Easingwold area - was effective. Isolation, it said, was no substitute for vaccination, which was 'very safe, and ... calf lymph is now available to boards of guardians and others for the vaccination of every child in the country.'[25]

Vaccination was compulsory in Britain - but there were vociferous opponents of it. The courts repeatedly saw the appearance of people who were determined to resist the authorities - people who had not got the appropriate legal exemption. These were either simply awkward or 'conscientious objectors'; people like a man from Stillington who was up before an Easingwold bench.[26] The Guardians that day prosecuted several people for not paying maintenance,[27] then

Thomas Hawkeswell, of Stillington, saddler was summoned to show cause why an order should not be made upon him to have his child, two years of age, vaccinated. Mr James Dale, Vaccination Officer, stated the defendant had been served with several notices, but had refused to comply with the law. Defendant stated that he objected to vaccination because the last child of his which was vaccinated had never been well since, and had been medically attended for six years. The Bench made an order for the vaccination of the child, and for the payment of costs, 9s 6d. Defendant said he would not have the child vaccinated.

Not long after the saddler of Stillington made his public declaration of defiance the Vaccination Officer of the Easingwold Union produced his annual report.[28] Dale stated that of the 267 births in the area 242 had been successfully vaccinated. Yet what was the extent nationally of conscientious objection? On 25 August 1900 the *Advertiser* published the following note

CONSCIENTIOUS OBJECTORS

For the first time since the passage of the Vaccination Act, 1898, a full year's figures are to hand on which to base an estimate of its results. The total number of certificates of successful primary inoculation received by the vaccination officers during 1899 was 669,340, showing an increase on the previous year of 169,035, or 33.8 per cent. As 923,265 births were registered in England and Wales, in 1898, and 928,640 in 1899, the respective ratios per cent. of the successful vaccinations to the infants born in these years were 54.2 and 72.1. From the passing of the Act on August 12, 1898, till the end of the same year, certificates of conscientious objection, relating to 230,174 children, were handed to the vaccinatior [sic] officers, and in the ensuing 12 months 32,357 children were exempted in the same manner.

When Mr Dale's report was submitted to his employers a smallpox epidemic was raging and alarming members. They were not that far off Middlesbrough and he feared 'they might get it here', J. T. Robinson, the vice chairman said. Members of the public became alarmed and one wrote to the Board asking them to emulate what the Northallerton guardians had done.[29] They had passed a resolution calling attention 'to the desirability of all persons being vaccinated or re-vaccinated, and recommended that this be done free by the Medical Officer. ... It was also recommended that all vagrants be examined before leaving the Workhouse, by the Medical Officer.' The Workhouse Master produced some statistics regarding vagrants. The 'number now remaining in the house' he wrote, was '37 against 35 for the corresponding period last year. The number of vagrants casually relieved during the past fortnight has been 137 against 118 for the same time last year.'

The Guardians consequently brought in regulations whereby the Medical Officer of Health attended the Workhouse every day and examined each vagrant who passed through the wards,[30] and there was talk everywhere of an epidemic. During discussions about the crisis more alarming facts about the area came out. Not for the first time the Rev J. F. Read of Teasdale House drew attention to the open drain which took sewage from the Workhouse, ran by his house, emitted an 'abominable stench,' and was rarely cleaned out. This was scheduled to be covered in, but in March 1898 it was very unwholesome. Attention was also directed to the Union hospital. Hayden pointed out that the last time there had been an outbreak an Easingwold smallpox case was treated there. Was it in a fit state to be used now? No; it was not kept aired, even though a patient had been housed there a month ago.

There was great concern at a local level about small-pox and the people of the Easingwold area were continually reminded of events in Middlesbrough where it was rampant. The disease also occupied the attention of Parliament.[31]

On 19 April 1898 the second reading of the Vaccination Bill was held - and met with some strong opposition, which, however, got nowhere.[32] The view of Sir W. Foster the President of the Local Government Board was that he wanted to 'abolish compulsion altogether, and ... allow parents who had conscientious scruples to escape from the penalties if they made a formal declaration before a court that they objected to vaccination.' He did not deviate from this belief.

The Vaccination Bill was again debated in the Commons on 23 July and once more speakers dealt at length with the issue of compulsion. Foster moved that if a parent made a statutory declaration before two magistrates of his conscientious objections, no order should be made or proceedings taken with reference to the non-vaccination of the child mentioned in the certificate. Henry Chaplin thought it would lead 'practically to the abandonment of vaccination altogether. Far better was the current system whereby compulsion was backed up by 'substantial' penalties. What was being proposed was a 'very dangerous experiment.'[33]

1897 James Dale, Relieving Officer and his son Septimus

Their Lordships wanted to expunge the 'conscientious objector' clause but the Commons wouldn't accept this and re-presented the Bill.[34] A division was taken, and the Lords backed off. By 55 votes to 45 a 'motion not to insist on the striking out of Clause 2 was carried.'

The Vaccination Act received the Royal Assent on 12 August and the Local Government Board circularized guardians telling them that it would become operative on 1 January 1899, and that until then no parent like the Stillington saddler 'should be liable to any penalty under Section 21 or 31 of the Vaccination Act, 1867 if within four months from the birth of the child' he or she got a justice's certificate saying he genuinely believed the treatment would harm it.[35] The Easingwold board considered the new legislation and decided to 'discontinue vaccination stations ... The children to be vaccinated at their own homes.'[36] They also heard the replies to letters they had sent to their doctors asking what the medics thought they should be paid for vaccinating. Their answers varied.[37] James Dale asked that his fees be fixed 'at 6d and 1/- instead of 3d and 9d respectively, which was the minimum allowed. Two weeks later Dale did get a rise and the fees for people like the accommodating Buller Hicks were fixed (they thought).[38]

VACCINATION FEES

> The following fees ... were agreed to by 20 votes against 6, 1/- being the minimum allowed under the Act for registration with 5/- and 7/6 for each successful domiciliary vaccination, the latter being for cases outside a two mile limit.
> Mr Dale (Vaccination Officer) was allowed 6d instead of 3d, and 1/- instead of 9d an opinion being expressed that the act would make more difference to him than the Medical Officers.

The Easingwold Guardians were a litigious lot on occasion and they were involved in a court case when the above discussions on pay were going on. It reveals a little about what the regime in 'the house' was like.

On 7 December J. S. Strangwayes and others sat in court with a full list before them,[39] not as full however as that before neighbouring Flaxton bench who were dealing wth a mass brawl started by two local men and involving fifty people.[40] Eventually they came to the Guardians' case.

> Frank Thompson, ... of no fixed residence was 'charged with refusing to perform his task of work at the Easingwold Union. The prisoner had slept in the casual wards, and in the morning was required to break two barrow load of stone. He objected to the quantly, [sic] and said the orders of the Local Government Board required that they should be weighed, and after breaking a certain quantity [he] refused to finish the work. He was given into custody, and had been in prison two days. The accused was discharged.

Frank was obviously a cut above your run-of-the-mill casual ward stone breaker. His case and subsequent verdict were discussed at length by the Guardians.[41] Neverthless the fact was the prisoner 'had fully made out his case.' According to law they could not make him 'break more than 4 cwt which was the maximum allowed, and he had been set $4^1/_2$ cwt.' Had the top weight been chosen for the Easingwold vagrants as a matter of policy (and exceeded) in Thompson's case? It had. The Guardians were told why. The clerk

The Convent, Easingwold, 1905

> stated that the minimum weight of stone to be broken was $1^1/_2$ cwt, and the maximum 4 cwt, and as the place was overrun with vagrants they had put the maximum on as a deterrent.
>
> A harsh regime was run at Easingwold!

Frank was not the only militant tramp to be featured in the *Advertiser*. On 26 October 1901, under the eye- catching headline 'MUTINY AT DRIFFIELD WORKHOUSE', the story of three other malcontents was given. Joseph Ratcliffe, Robert Marshall, and Robert Scott had been admitted to the Driffield 'house'. This establishment had a poor reputation among its clients, not surprising, as the following account printed by Reginald Ernest Smith might show.[42]

> The accommodation for tramps at Driffield Workhouse is up-to-date each man having an apartment - by some designated a cell - to himself where he finds a heap of stones with which he can employ himself by breaking them sufficiently small to enable him to pass [them] through a grate at the end of the cell. ... no tramp is accommodated for less than two nights, and as a consequence very few ... patronise Driffield Workhouse. When these particular men were let out of their cells on Sunday morning for a little exercise they refused to go back again, marched about the passages in a defiant manner, and for a time had possession of the place. They came before the Driffield Bench on Monday, when they said that they did not know they would have to remain in the cells from Saturcay [sic] night to Tuesday morning - some thing like sixty hours' confinement. Police cells were much preferable. The Bench committed the men [sic] for a further seven-days experience of police cells at Hull Gaol.

What the three mutinous tramps thought of the Easingwold Union is unknown. Their assessment of it though, might have gone down as a result of alterations to feeding arrangements.[43] A committee drew up a revised draft dietary table to be submitted to

Hicks. They worked with the Workhouse Master and 'carefully estimated' the costs of their proposals. They would mean an increased expenditure of 'about eight pence per inmate per day, though a large proportion of that increase would disappear through bread and other eatables which had not been touched being allowed to be placed on the table a second time. In the past such stuff had been thrown out. The new dietary tables were accepted and sent to the LGB for approval.[44] They were then used at Easingwold and turned out to be more costly than expected. 'Owing to the new dietary table, which provided for the inmates bacon, cheese, &c., the yearly cost of each individual would be increased by about £1.'[45]

Although nothing as violent as the aforementioned brawl appeared before the Easingwold Bench, drunken behaviour was common and on one occasion William Harrison had to deal with one who deserves to be remembered. Reginald Ernest Smith left her story for posterity.[46]

> POLICE. - At the Magistrates' Clerks office, on Sunday last, before Mr W. Harrison, a woman named Nelly Johnson, of no fixed abode, was committed to prison for 14 days, for being drunk and disorderly in Long Street. When arrested, she refused to walk to the Police Station, and had to be conveyed there in a wheelbarrow.

Not long after Nelly Johnson's episode, a conscientious objector appeared in one of the local courts. The Vaccination Act had been in operation since the start of the year when Mr Bacon, the assistant station-master for Northallerton, applied for an exemption certificate. It was granted.[47] Later a minister applied - without success.

> Before the Thirsk Bench ... the Rev J. Rossall, Wesleyan Minister, applied for a certificate regarding his youngest child, but it transpired that the child had passed the age of four months, and the application could not be granted. Mr Rossall said that was rather a pity, as he was determined that the child should not be vaccinated.

Rossall was as good as his word. Tucked away in the columns of the *Easingwold* of 23 February, 1901, the following appeared.

> THIRSK
>
> THE VACCINATION ACT. - The Rev. Richard Rossall, Wesleyan Minister of Sowerby, was at Thirsk Petty Sessions on Monday, fined 20s. and costs for failing to have his child vaccinated.

How many people in the area objected to vaccination? The clerk produced some figures early in 1900.[48] He showed that out of 245 children whose births were registered from the 1st of January to the 31st December, 1898, 206 were successfully vaccinated, one was unsusceptible of vaccination, certificates of conscientious objections had been received in respect of 4; out of 136 children whose births were registered from the 1st January to 30th June, 1899, 125 were successfully vaccinated, 1 was unsusceptiable [sic] to vaccination, a certificate of conscientious objection had been received in respect of one, 7 had died unvaccinated, and 2 had been postponed by medical certificates.

There was some local dissatisfaction about how the Vaccination Act was administered. The Great Ouseburn Guardians, for example, as early as February 1899, followed the lead of the Burslem Union where the Guardians had passed a resolution which they sent to the LGB saying that 'great damage might arise by reason of the conscience clause in the Act of

Uppleby, Easingwold, 1905

1898.' They wanted vaccination to be strictly enforced and the law altered.[49] The Burslem Board not only petitioned the LGB but circularised the petition throughout the country, and later in the year an agitation was 'promoted by the Wycombe Union to secure an alteration of the ... Act, so as to take the power of directing prosecutions out of the hand of the officers solely as it at present stands.'[50]

Wigan campaigned for the penalties imposed to be paid to the boards and Merthyr Tydfil drew attention to the cost of the service. It gave some details of the way fees had gone up on a communication considered by the Easingwold Board in the summer of 1900. In their Union, the Welsh said, fees paid went up from £372 in the year 'previous to the passing of the Act' to £1,084 in 1899.[51] What were the Welsh actually proposing? It is not clear from the published reports, but there was cause for great concern, as was revealed in a truly alarming sentence; '... for the larger sum there were 516 less successfully vacinated [sic] than in 1898.'

The Easingwold Guardians considered the Merthyr circular, though none of them seems to have commented on the fact that the Welsh were reporting about spreading more expense for less efficiency. Souter moved for a return of costs and scales in his area. It was prepared in a commendably short time and, showed a picture that was not to Souter's liking - and nor should it have been. 'Souter ... said that though they had now a system which they could not alter, the cost to the Union was increased, with an efficiency smaller than before.'[52] What had prompted this? Two reports had been considered that day but whether they warranted Souter's harsh condemnation is not clear. The first said that the returns for the last year

> showed that in the Easingwold district (Dr Hicks) there had been 70 births, 50 successful and 20 removed, dead, or unaccounted for. In the Coxwold sub-district (Dr. McCraken) their [sic] had been 12 births, 7 successfully vaccinated, 3 dead, and 2 unaccounted for. In the Stillington district (Dr Gramshaw) there had been 24 births,

15 successfully vaccinated, and 9 unaccounted for. This made a total of 106 births, and 72 successful vaccinations.

THE COST OF VACCINATIONS

> The Clerk (Mr F J H Robinson) presented a return showing the number ... vaccinated under the ... Act ... and the cost, compared with the numbers and cost of vaccinations before the passing of that Act. For the year ending September 28, 1898, the number of vaccinations in the Union were [sic] 168, at an average cost of 5s per head, and the year ending September 29th, 1899, 172 at 6s 11¹/4d per head, the total amount being £59 14s 6d.

Hicks regularly produced statistical returns like that above about the health of his area and these are invaluable as sources of Easingwold history. Less valuable, perhaps, is a long winded controversy that involved the vicar of Raskelfe which occupied many column inches of the *Advertiser* at the end of the century.

In November 1897 the Rev W.E.M. Bull, the vicar of Raskelfe resigned because of failing eyesight,[53] and the new vicar appointed was the Rev Dr Preston.[54] He had been in charge 'of a very large and most trying parish near Liverpool, where he did a good work.' He had hitherto written 'numerous publications of a popular kind which [had] made his name widely known,' had travelled widely and was 'a very keen volunteer, and [had] for many years been Chaplain of the 2nd V.B. Cheshire Regiment. 'Doubtless he will get on in his new parish, as well as he did in his old one' commented the *Advertiser*. Some time later a church parade was held in Raskelfe and Preston joined the march to the venue and preached the sermon. He was in the uniform of the Royal Irish Rifles.

Preston settled into his duties and soon the paper carried a long report of a highly successful 'tea party and entertainment' he put on at the end of February.[55] In the same week the lavish entertainment at Easingwold included a 'ladies washing competition' For the record it should be recorded that Mrs Sarah Cariss and Miss Fish 'were awarded the first and second prizes respectively.' It was the same Miss Fish whose rendering of 'Mashed Tonups' has been mentioned in these pages. Rightly so.[56]

'The Raskelfe entertainment began with a glee, and included a couple of comic songs Not 'Mashed Turnips,' this time, but 'The Idler' and 'The father of a family' from Mr C. Elsworth then numerous contributions from members of the vicar's family. One of them 'sang, with much taste, "Three Fishers"' and a 'pianoforte duet by Mrs and Miss Preston, and a solo on the mandoline from Miss Evelyn Preston, were deservedly appreciated.' A talented lot was the Preston family. But this was not all. The concert over the new vicar addressed his parishioners. He said the choir was 'most excellent' but should 'try for perfection' and members should attend the weekly practices. The day schools, he said, were 'first class' but the church yard was a mess. '"God's Acre"', he said, 'should be as neat and tidy as possible ... could not those who owned graves do something towards keeping them trim and free from disfiguring long grass?'

Preston's contribution at the end of the evening does not read like a study in effective public relations techniques and his mid week sermon to 'a good congregation' at Raskelfe on St Patrick's Day (17 March) suggests he was not the best communicator the church ever produced.[57] He preached about 'ancient Erin' and the career of St Patrick in a talk loaded with references to such as Rapin, Celestius, and Tertullian, but his contentions, and indeed his facts, were rapidly challenged in the columns of the *Advertiser*.[58] The first contributor to what was going to be a long running feature of the Smith paper was John Wright of Husthwaite. Dr Preston had referred to the historian Rapin, quoting his contention that 'it was "strange that the conversion of England should be attributed to Austin rather than to Aidan, Finan, Colman, &c."'[59] Wright questioned the veracity of the contention. 'Query, were Aidan, Finan and Colman evangelists from Ireland?' he asked. No, he went on, all were 'sent in succession ... from the monastery of Hye ... at the request of Oswald, King of Northumbria.'

Immediately below Wright's letter was printed one on the same subject from Father Pearson, OSB. It made Wright of Husthwaite's effort look tame. Preston, really got the treatment. 'Why, in the name of common sense and decency, did Dr Preston bother his head with St Patrick? ... What do the people of Raskelfe care about St Patrick? There are no Irish there save the Vicar's own family.' What was it all about then? 'Dr Preston is an Irishman ... evidently of the orange type. He wants to attack Popery, and does so through St Patrick.' Pearson went on to dissect Preston's arguments, and made the rather good debating point about the contention that 'In the Primitive Irish Church the Bible was read by all.' That was 'clap trap' Pearson said, 'the Bible ... had not at that date been gathered together.' The new vicar of Raskelfe was guilty of misrepresentation, and rendering quotations in an untrustworthy and misleading way.

Preston had been determined to make an immediate impression in his new area - and succeeded. He aggressively ticked off his parishioners, then paraded his views on Irish history from his pulpit and immediately penned a column on thoughts for Good Friday.[60]

Pearson was not the only commentator on the efforts of the scribe from typhoid-ridden Raskelfe. Next to the 'THOUGHTS', and just above a news item saying Florence Maybrick had been left a fortune, [61] a criticism of Preston's contentions appeared from E. H. Lamplugh of Tollerton who corrected Wright of Husthwaite about the use of 'the words "Scotts" and "Scottish"' and told the vicar of Raskelfe to consult his copy of Rapin again, and have a look at 'Cummian's Canons' while he was about it.

Preston's stand paid off (or so it seems) and his Church was crowded at some of the services on Easter Sunday.[62] The choir had improved, no doubt scared to death of the wrath of the new cleric. The singing now was 'remarkably good all through' and a guest organist had been moved in from Runcorn. The choir also looked different. 'For the first time in the history of the Church the choir were robed in surplices, and they looked remarkably well. The uniformity now to be seen in the choir stalls is a great improvement. ...'

The new vicar seemed anxious to smooth any ruffled feathers his aggressive initial speeches and sermons had made, and at the Easter vestry gushed over the choir's 'hearty and valuable services', but his controversy over St Patrick ran on, though he tried to duck out of it. 'I stick to my text, which no avalanche of epistolary rhetoric can overturn, as it is based on the impregnable rock of history and of fact. Briefly, I maintain that the gospel was planted in Ireland in the 2nd century from the East and not from Rome. The Roman Catholic historian, O'Halloran, bears me out in this ...' Preston could not resist calling up other authorities to support his case, and having done so to his own satisfaction said '"Adieu" to good St Patrick whose creed was identical with that now held by the Church of England and by the Church of Ireland.'[63]

It could not have been pleasant for such an arrogant man to have his methodology and his scholarship regularly put under a microscope, so he quoted Germanus, Carew, the Professor

Local wedding party, early 1900s

of Divinity at Maynooth, Lanigan and O'Halloran again[64] then bowed out. His introduction to the Easingwold district should have been a salutary one.

Lamplugh however wouldn't let matters rest. He treated readers of the Smith organ to a long list of quotations and Latin tags from the likes of St Bede, and Fleury and recommended those who read him to write to the Catholic Truth Society and get P. Lynch's pamphlet *The Old Religion in England*.[65] He then again criticised John Wright's letter and this led to further exchanges which featured in the *Advertiser*.[66] 'Wright supported his views with references to T. J. Livesey, *The Primer of English History*.

Father Pearson would not let Preston alone, and his attacks on the Ulster man were savage. Preston 'would have us believe that St. Patrick had nothing to do with Rome.' Preston had made much of his contention that Patrick was not sent to Ireland by the Pope 'but by Germanus, a Gallican bishop.'[67] So what? What could this possibly prove, Pearson asked? Preston was accused of blind prejudice, challenged to produce his sources and 'invited to produce authorities for other statements he had penned.

The readers of the Smith paper undoubtedly waited anxiously for Preston's reply to Father Pearson to appear on 7 May, but all they got was a contribution to the controversy from Lamplugh and another from William Bensley. He was the organist at the Easingwold parish church and he asked Smith for a little space in which to correct a statement going the rounds about an incident that took place at the church 'last Sunday night.'[68] The organ broke down during a service and people were blaming him, Bensley said. They were alleging, that I am 'wanting something doing to the organ, and that it [the breakdown] was a dodge of mine to get it done.' Direct militant action. 'I thought I was better known than to be thought capable of *dodging'*, he wrote. It is true the organ is a bit rough, and should be 'made "up to date",' but I shall get it done, eventually, 'without dodging. ... I shall never stoop to dodging to get it.'

Dr Preston was greatly in demand at this time. In May he preached a sermon to the Perseverance Lodge of the Druids of Easingwold, and got a lengthy report in the press[69] the same issue in which Wright, his tormentor from Husthwaite, asked why he had not taken up the challenge to support his previous assertions. Failure to do so, Wright said, might lead *Advertiser* readers to 'infer that his *impregnable rock of history and fact*, is like a bag of wind, which when punctured, collapses.'

Preston did not attempt to prove his case, and week after week was mocked by one or other of his tormentors. Eventually, the arguments and the letters to the paper stopped.

As has been said, Preston was chaplain to the 2nd V.B. Battalion of the Cheshire Regiment and very early in 1900 a note appeared saying that the Cheshires had all volunteered to go to the front.[70]

THE WAR

> The whole Battalion of the V. B. Cheshire Regiment including their Chaplain Rev Dr Preston Vicar of Raskelfe, has volunteered for active service, or for Garrison duty. The offer is being now considered by the authorities in London.

Not long after Preston and the Cheshires volunteered tragedy hit his family. After an illness of just two days his only son died. He was Dr W. J. D. Preston who had recently 'removed to Cheshire from Masborough, where he had [had] a large medical practice, and was much beloved by all classes and especially the poor.'[71] He was buried in the family vault in Birkenhead cemetery, but this was not the only tragedy that befell the family. In April official confirmation was given of the death of Trooper Trevor Preston at Ladysmith on 6 January.[72] Aged 23 Trevor was the eldest son of the Rev J. E. Preston, Julianstown Rectory, Drogheda. He had gone to South Africa in 1897 and during his stay in East London 'was an enthusiastic member of the Kaffrarian Rifles.' He could 'not resist the call to arms' when the war started and, 'as a true and loyal Britisher gave his life in his Country's cause.' The CO of the Imperial Light Horse gave some details of the action in which Trooper Preston died in a letter to his mother. He was with a small party holding a hill when some Boers attacked. They were driven off, the hill saved, but 'He was shot in the head.'

In 1901 the vicar of Raskelfe said he was offered an important living near Liverpool, which would, have meant a considerable increase in his income, but he chose to stay where he was,[73] to 'the very considerable satisfaction' of his parishioners. He 'alluded to the offer' at his Easter Vestry meeting. It had had 'many advantages', Preston said, 'but tempting as it was he refused it as he was not yet tired of Raskelfe.' Some residents might already have been tired of him though.

That Father Pearson, Preston's opponent, was another difficult customer is beyond doubt. In early 1900 he engaged in a bad tempered spat with the Rural District Council about Crayke, which was in dire need of a 'supply of wholesome drinking water.' The Local Government Board regarded the needs of the village as urgent and pressurised the RDC to attend to them. This was not to Pearson's liking though a recent report of the time revealed 'that of 19 samples of water' taken at Crayke and analysed[74]

Fleece Inn, Long Street, Easingwold (nearly opposite the Fish Shop), early 1900s

> 12 were found to be bad, whilst 17 houses in the village had no supply, the village well being also dry. The quantative analysis made of 3 selected specimens was unsatisfactory in each case, particularly a specimen from the Durham Ox Inn.

Sanitary arrangements in Crayke *were* appalling but Pearson was unmoved by the urgency of the problems facing the village and its population. He refused to cooperate with the Sanitary Inspector and wrote to him and the RDC saying that its actions were 'frivolous', and that 'inspecting a mans property so often was itself a nuisance.' The RDC's officials had wanted to inspect some property owned by Pearson and had been refused access.[75]

Pearson had won his fight with the incumbent of Raskelfe, taking up much space in the *Advertiser* and revealing that he regarded some of Preston's arguments as exposing his anti-catholic prejudices. He was in print once more in autumn 1901 protesting about a petition in circulation which proposed that the clause in the King's Oath branding Roman Catholics as 'idolaters' be retained.. Let them in a straight-forward way publish the petition in your paper adding the names of all those who have signed it.' Pearson ended by using the methods which had paid off so handsomely against Preston. Let us have a guarantee that no names 'have been with-held or with-drawn. Mr Editor I venture to prophecy that such a list will [sic] never be published.'[76]

The *Advertiser* obligingly published the text of the petition which had so angered Pearson. It had been drawn up and was being signed throughout 'England, Ireland, Scotland and the Colonies, [and was] against any alteration in the Law which requires the sovereign of the Realm to make the statutory declaration in force for the last two hundred years.'[77] The petition said that 'the attempt' to 'tamper with the Statutory Declaration required by the Bill of Rights and Act of Settlement. ... is dangerous to the Protestant Succession and the stability of the Throne.' Any attempt to alter the current requirements was 'mischievous and unconstitutional and fraught with great danger to the civil, political, and religious liberties of the people.'

Pearson continued his tirade, 'Let us know what party of the civil or religious community is propagating this petition' he went on, saying it was 'shameless and misleading' in its working anyway.[78] Then Pearson revealed what he thought the petition was really about. It was 'apparently innocent, yet artfully deceptive.' Catholics had no desire to upset the Protestant succession and people who signed it had been misled - and signed a paper which protested against things they knew nothing about. Pearson reckoned 'three hundred and upwards' signed it in the Easingwold area, and once again issued a challenge of the Preston kind. One of the promoters was Buller Hicks.[79] He was challenged to tell readers of the *Advertiser* whether he had ever read a single authoritative Catholic book on the subjects mentioned in the King's Oath. It all had a very familiar ring,

Pearson had said that he knew of one other signatory to the petition and if so this was John Rocliffe who made a nice point when he told the priest that it was not usual to divulge the names on petitions to Parliament. [80] 'Hicks also wrote at length but wisely declined to get into the kind of theological trap Pearson had set for him. He declared himself ignorant of Catholic theology, of no church, yet took some swipes at the beliefs of such as Pearson.[81]

Pearson would not let go and he penned a long reply to Rocliffe and Hicks.[82] It was a savage attack and it clearly rattled the doctor who was told that his quotations (or some of them) were 'beneath the contempt of a Theologian.' Others took part in the controversy. 'BRITON' for example introduced R. E. Smith's readers to a virulently anti-Catholic diatribe warning of the dangers of restoring Papal Supremacy.[83]

Father Pearson of course replied to the last contributors to Easingwold's latest religious controversy and did so in a letter that took up something like 40 inches of page 5 of an edition of Reginald Ernest Smith's organ.[84] Once again he demanded references from his adversaries and started off with a declaration that he could find not a single argument (in "H"s letter') to 'prove any Ruler should be compelled to single out one section of his subjects and grossly insult their religious beliefs.' Pearson's syntax left something to be desired (either that or he had been badly served by that Smith typesetter),[85] but he went on to ask, again, why the Catholics were singled out for special mention in the King's Oath. There were over 700 sects in England alone according to the *Times*, he said.[86] Why were only Catholics chosen for condemnation'. The answer, as Pearson well knew, was in their history - however distorted the facts of that had become.

Pearson declared, as he had done before, that he and those like him accepted the Protestant succession, then went on indulging himself with learned quoting as usual - Lord Macauley,[87] Lecky, Hallam, and several eminent Protestant divines. He then proceeded to ravage Buller Hicks' last effort.[88] By this time the controversy had strayed, somewhat, but Pearson made a superb debating point when he quoted Canon McColl to support him; 'Canon McColl says "the vast majority of those who trouble their heads about it, would gladly see such a relic of senseless bigotry wiped off the Statute Book."' Buller Hicks, however, took the arguments back to the Reformation.[89] You 'employ the language of the historian to condemn Henry VIII as 'the "murderer of his wives,"' he wrote but you must remember, Father, that he had the advantage of your early training, and ... there is reason to fear, that the over indulgence of your Church may have been partly responsible for the defects of his character ...'

Hicks said that Pearson had enveloped him in 'metaphysical dust'; complimented the Rev Father' as a 'gallant and skilful opponent'; but stuck to his guns. Surely someone would write and say that mistakes had been made in the past, but that things were different now. Did Pearson do this? He did not. He simply reiterated what he had said before. It was as if all those long letters had never appeared. Buller Hicks and the others he said, did not know what they were talking about, no sources for their remarks were given.[90] There followed another harsh response from Hicks.

Reg Smith eventually announced that he had received another letter from Pearson. He said he would print it, but that thereafter there would be no more correspondence *'re* the Coronation Oath.' The controversy had gone on from the end of August to the beginning of December, and had taken up a tremendous amount of space in the *Advertiser*- with the letters, moreover, being printed in minute type.

Preston was 'very ill' in 1902, but recovered to take a full part in village church affairs, and in 'defending our Tommies at the front.' He did this in the national press and received a letter about his efforts from a sergeant serving in South Africa. This was printed in the *Easingwold Advertiser*. Writing from Honing Spruit the sergeant said he had read a Preston letter in the *Daily Mail* about 'German slanders.' The British soldier, he wrote, is not indifferent 'to whatever is said of him', but feels 'deeply' in the case that had angered Preston. The Kaiser had done nothing to check the 'vile slanders that were current', even though he held 'high rank' in the British Army. 'Soldiers are not "plaster saints" 'tis true', the writer said, but he had never known a single case when a Boer woman 'has had one word of insult,' yet had seen short rations given to women who had been heaping insults in Dutch on the donors just a short time before.

NOTES

1. Some villages like Stillington were outside the plans for the area at that time, nevertheless.
2. *Advertiser* 29 February 1902.
3. *Ibid* 29 November 1902.
4. *Ibid*.
5. *Ibid* 27 December 1902.
6. *Ibid* 2 January 1897.
7. The Workhouse became Claypenny Hospital. 'Under the Local Government Act, 1929, the poor law functions and premises of the Guardians were transferred to the County Council. It was decided to convert the Union Workhouse into a mental hospital by extensive rebuilding and the addition of new blocks.' Cowling *op cit* p 149.
8. *Advertiser* 1 January 1898.
9. *Ibid* 14 January 1898.
10. Trouble that is between the Master and one of the matrons. The master was reprimanded and told to go to the board and not to a guardian. This was the exact opposite to what a councillor had been told to do on the RDC it will be recalled.
11. A Miss Wilson of Hunslet. She had held the post once before.
12. *Advertiser* 11 and 23 March 1899.
13. *Ibid* 18 March 1899.
14. A notice on Dunhill was served on 10 December, then a summons for *habeas corpus* was issued and served on 3 January. It was returnable on 11 February, then, again, on the 24th.
15. *Advertiser* 8 April 1899.
16. *Ibid* 29 April 1899.
17. *Ibid* 6 May 1899.
18. *Ibid* 13 May 1899.
19. *Ibid* 3 June 1899.
20. *Ibid*
21. *Ibid* 1 July 1899.
22. *Ibid* 29 July 1899.
23. *Ibid* 12 and 26 August, 9 September 1899.

24. *Ibid* 12 August 1899.
25. *Ibid* 30 April 1898.
26. *Ibid* 8 January 1898.
27. One offender was ordered to pay a shilling a week for his father, who lived at Stillington. Two people in Easingwold were ordered to pay a similar amount for their poor old mum.
28. To the Board of Guardians. *Advertiser* 26 February 1898. Buller Hicks senior retired in June to be succeeded by his son as *'Public* Vaccination officer for the district.' *Ibid* 18 June 1898.
29. It is assumed the letter was from a member of the public. It is not absolutely clear.
30. *Advertiser* 26 March 1898 - report of RDC meeting. Hicks applied for a salary increase, of course.
31. *Ibid* 23 April 1898. On the epidemic in Middlesbrough see also *Ibid* 19 January, 8 March 1898. There are many other reports.
32. The debate was adjourned and heard on 9 May when the Bill was carried by 237 to 23.
33. *Advertiser* 23 July 1898. The Vaccination Bill's first hearing in the Lords was on 1 August.
34. *Ibid* 13 August 1898.
35. Report of meeting of the Great Ouseburn Board. *Ibid* 3 September 1898.
36. *Ibid* 8 October 1898.
37. *Ibid* 3 December 1898, For example: Buller Hicks said he would accept whatever the Board offered; McCracken (Coxwold) thought 2s 6d and 10/- (for each birth registered and extra for a domiciliary treatment); Gramshaw thought 2s 6d 'with 5/- under a mile, with 10/- over that distance.'
38. *Ibid* 17 December 1898. The doctors refused the terms. *Ibid* 31 December 1898. The LGB would not accept Dale's rates - even though he had got what he asked for. *Ibid* 28 January 1899.
39. *Ibid* 10 December 1898.
40. They were Henry Clarke and Walter Lane. Their case reported in *Ibid.*
41. *Ibid* 17 December 1898.
42. *Ibid* 26 October 1901.
43. *Ibid* 23 February 1901.
44. *Ibid* 9 March 1901.
45. *Ibid* 13 July 1901.
46. *Ibid* 17 June 1899.
47. This was at the Northallerton Police Court. *Ibid* 14 October 1899. The Rossall case reported in *Ibid* 6 October 1900.
48. *Ibid* 17 February 1900.
49. *Ibid* 4 February 1899.
50. *Ibid* 28 October 1899.
51. *Ibid* 28 July 1900.
52. *Ibid* 25 August 1900. For later statistics of the same kind see eg *Ibid* 23 February 1901. For a typical report during the trouble over building the Easingwold cells see eg *Ibid* 9 March 1901 wherein it is reported that the contractor had not finished his work and that the Board of Guardians would take over and complete the work itself.
53. *Ibid* 20 November 1897.
54. *Ibid* 8 January 1898.
55. *Ibid* 26 February 1898. The church parade reported in *Ibid* 12 July 1902.
56. It is assumed that the Miss Fish of the washing competition and 'Mashed Tonups' are one and the same.
57. *Advertiser* 19 March 1898.
58. *Ibid* 2 April 1898.
59. Paul de Rapin, 1661-1725. Studied at the Protestant College at Saumur. Born in Languedoc. Went to Holland and enlisted in a Huguenot volunteer corps. Followed the Prince of Orange to England in 1688, made ensign the following year. '... distinguished himself at the Boyne and Limerick'. Wrote 'his great *Histoire d'Angleterre* (1724), undoubtedly the best work that had until then appeared.' The work was translated into English by Matthew Tindal.
60. 'THOUGHTS FOR GOOD FRIDAY,' *Advertiser* 9 April 1898.
61. Florence Maybrick, convicted of the murder of her husband James in 1889.
62. *Advertiser* 16 April 1898.
63. *Ibid* 23 April 1989. The Raskelfe Easter vestry meeting is reported in this issue of the *Advertiser.*
64. John Lanigan (1758-1828) born at Cashel wrote a four volume history of the church in Ireland to the 13th century. Took orders in the Roman Catholic church. Taught in Italy, then was a librarian in Dublin.
65. E. H. Lamplugh, 'DR. PRESTON & ST. PATRICK'S DAY,' *Advertiser* 23 April 1898.
66. *Ibid* 30 April 1898. The details of Livesey's book were given in an earlier letter.
67. *Ibid.*
68. 'THE PARISH CHURCH ORGAN'. *Ibid* 7 May 1898.
69. *Ibid* 14 May 1898.
70. *Ibid* 6 January 1900.
71. *Ibid* 10 February 1900.
72. *Ibid* 7 April 1900.
73. *Ibid* 13 April 1901.
74. *Ibid* 31 August 1901.

75. *Ibid* 7 September 1901.
76. *Ibid* 21 September 1901.
77. Actually Pearson's letter was undated, but it appeared on 31 August.
78. In a letter published in the *Advertiser* 28 September 1901.
79. *Ibid* 5 October 1901. It was Buller Hicks the younger who was involved.
80. *Ibid* 26 October 1901. Letters also from 'H' and Nathan Jackson, the vicar of Easingwold.
81. *Ibid* 19 October 1901. Briton gives no indication of where he came from.
82. *Ibid* 26 October 1901.
83. 'The Oath he says is a survival from the time when our fathers not only believed that their "faith" and "liberties"; and fought and bled for that "form of Christian faith" which they prefer, and for which they would die to-morrow.'
84. *Times* 13 January 1885.
85. '... his Essay on Hallam.'
86. *Advertiser* 2 November 1901.
87. *Ibid* 23 November 1901.
88. *Ibid* 30 November 1901.
89. *Ibid* 7 December 1901.
90. *Ibid* 3 January 1903.

Top of Long Street, Easingwold - the surface still "mud-bound" circa 1901

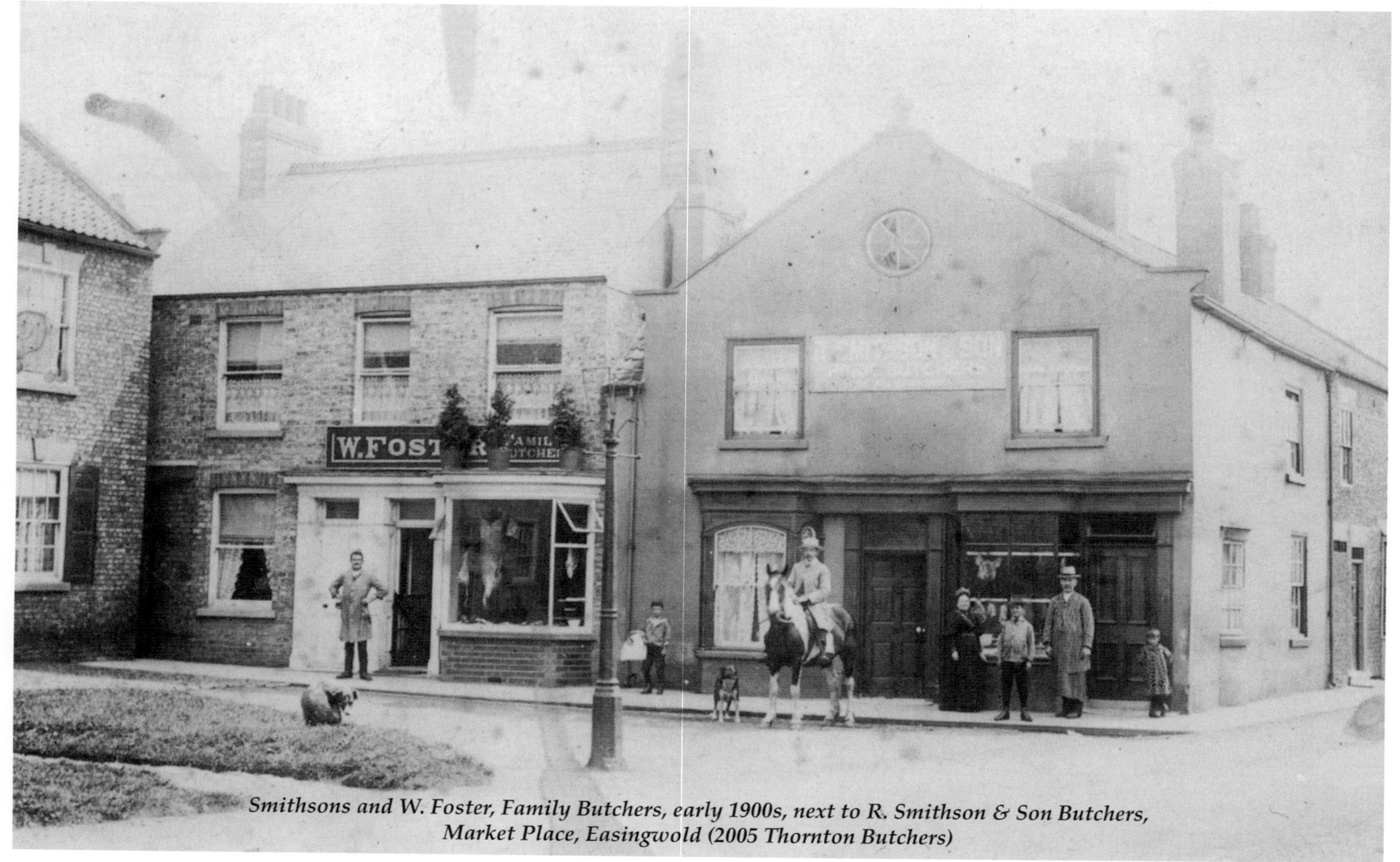

Smithsons and W. Foster, Family Butchers, early 1900s, next to R. Smithson & Son Butchers, Market Place, Easingwold (2005 Thornton Butchers)

Chapter 7

THE OUTBREAK OF WAR

The Boer War started in 1899 and lasted until May 1902. Men from Easingwold, soldiers of various kinds, went to South Africa and some had some hair-raising experiences which, naturally, the R. E. Smith paper publicised – mainly using the letters they wrote home. In the first months of the Great War local newspapers carried numerous 'Letters From the Front' which are a valuable source for the chronicler of the early days of that struggle. It was generally thought then that 'it would all be over by Christmas' so the letters were seized on by editors as human documents in what was to be a short (and of course victorious) conflict. But things changed. The war turned out to be a long one and letters home became commonplace – and censored – though they still appeared at times of particular stress and importance. This also happened, on a smaller scale, of course, in the South African War.

It is quite clear (as it was in 1914) that some soldiers actually wrote for publication, knowing that their parents were waiting to send the correspondence to a local editor. Getting one's 'name in the paper' was as attractive then as it was later. It lifted the writer from obscurity, and bestowed on him the status, for a short time, of a local celebrity, writing about a place thousands of miles away and referring to the dangers he encountered in places with strange-sounding names. Using those names gave an air of authority to what the men wrote. Were they well prepared for what they were in for? It seems that they knew as little about the issues that had led to the Boer War as did their successors in 1914. The men of Easingwold were no different from those of other places, but it is a fact that through the columns of the *Advertiser* they were offered, week by week, a wide ranging and impressive survey of national and international news, though nothing can be inferred from this about who and how many read it.

The Royal Oak (no longer a pub) in the middle distance, Long Street, Easingwold, 1905

Several examples of *Advertiser* ads have been recorded and there were some which should have made people realise war was more than just a remote possibility. The Volunteers, for example, needed recruits and advertised for them. The military ads said that there was

WANTED, for the EASINGWOLD VOLUNTEERS, a few respectable Young Men. Application should be made to the INSTRUCTOR at the "ROYAL OAK," Long Street, every Tuesday from 6 to 7p.m., or to CORPL. J.H. PIPES, UPPLEBY.

Other front page ads were given over to such things as Savonite Auxiliary Gas Burners, Baxter's Beer[1], and the Guarantee Company's Poultry Powders ('The Finest Preparation in the WORLD FOR ALL KINDS OF POULTRY AND PHEASANTS'). The Guarantee Company also marketed a range of 'Pig Powders' in a rather unusual way. The prices of their Two Registered Preparations, SWINE'S FRIEND for thriving and fattening and ... curing diseases... [and] SWINE'S COMPANION [sic] for disinfecting all places where stock is kept' were given, after a reassurance that might have been expected to cost the GC Co a customer or two. It was, P.E. Handson wrote, 'The only Company which subscribes towards the loss of a pig after using the Friend or the Companion.'[2]

Next F.C. Russell[3] announced that he had had "EXTRAORDINARY SUCCESS IN THE TREATMENT OF OBESITY" and advertised his book "Corpulency and the Cure" (256 pages). Another book offered to readers was The Cure of Consumption[4] and a whole series of works from the catalogue of Jarrold and Son were mentioned; the Wife's Guide to Health and Happiness, Sickness or Health? or, The Danger of Trifling Ailments, The Girls' Own Book of Health and Beauty, and *The Boys' Book of Health and Strength.* There was a time when no house was complete without a 'medical book'.

The 'medical book' might have identified an illness – and there were plenty of remedies to resort to. One concoction was fairly typical in that it made over-the-top claims saying that it was sure-fire (while leaving the proprietor a get-out), was perfectly safe, and certainly was expensive.[5]

THE OLD GOUT CURE IN THE WORLD.
MARK'S CURE
FOR
Gout, Rheumatism, Sciatica,
Cramp in the Limbs, &c.
The 4s.6d. Bottle contains 20 Doses,
sufficient for 3 Weeks.
The Proprietors do not claim Infallibility for it; but so far as experience goes,
IT HAS NEVER YET FAILED TO PERMANENTLY CURE.
It is purely Vegetable. No Mineral Drugs, Citrate or Lithia or Colchicum
enter its composition.

It is a "DISEASE CURE", not a "SYMPTOM CURE" only.
In its action it goes direct to the root of the complaint, expelling all excess of
Uric Acid, thus attacking the cause and destroying the effect. Every drop of the
mixture is worth its weight in diamonds. It is marvellous, safe, and effective.
Prices: 2s.9d; and 4s 6d. at all Chemists and Medicine Vendors, or direct from
the Factory (post free) for the same price.
PREPARED ONLY AT THE FACTORY:
6, Artillery Street, Bishopsgate Street.

Just one page in January 1895 was given over to local news. R. Blakeborough gave a humorous entertainment in the village school-room at Raskelfe and Capt Bannister presided over the Easingwold Fire Brigade's annual dinner. An incident at the Hawkhills was reported at length and the regrettable fact that the Easingwold Soup Kitchen had had to be re-opened during a period of very bad weather, was noted.[6]

In the not-too-distant future the *Advertiser* would be devoting much of its space to events in South Africa, but in the spring of 1895[7] other conflicts demanded its attention and readers made their acquaintance with casualty lists of a kind that were to become familiar in the new century. In one issue, next to a report that Oscar Fingall O'Flaherty Wills Wilde had appeared at the Bow Street Police Court, charged with an offence 'of a very grave and shocking description', there was an account of the Chitral expedition[8]. Appended was a casualty list.

PREPAID ADVERTISEMENT

THE ATTENTION OF ADVERTISERS IS
INVITED TO
THE EASINGWOLD ADVERTISER
AND WEEKLY NEWS
AS AN ADVERTISING MEDIUM.

PREPAID SCALE OF CHARGES
for the following Classes of Advertisements only:
SITUATIONS WANTED.
SITUATIONS OFFERED.
APARTMENTS TO LET.
APARTMENTS WANTED.
MISCELLANEOUS WANTS.
MONEY WANTED.
MONEY TO LEND.
PARTNERSHIPS WANTED.
BUSINESSES FOR SALE.
LOST AND FOUND.
Houses, Shops, Offices, Public Houses to Let or Sell, Specific Articles for Sale by Private Contract.

	s.	d.
20 words	1	0
30 "	1	6
40 "	2	0
50 "	2	6
60 "	3	0

N.B. – The above Scale does not apply to Advertisements from Public Bodies. Cash must accompany the order, otherwise an extra charge is made.
While we take great pains to secure the correct printing of Advertisements, we cannot be answerable for inaccuracies or for any consequences arising there from.
*** PERSONS ANSWERING ADVERTISEMENTS addressed by initials, or otherwise, to the *Advertiser Office,* must DO SO BY LETTER, and not by Personal Application to this Office.

The Easingwold Advertiser and Weekly News had first appeared on 2 January 1892. Issue number one consisted of seven pages, only two of which were set up and printed by Reginald Smith at Easingwold.[9] The tops of the pages had the paper's title and the date put on them, and the buying in of the bulk of the copy went on for many, many years. Presumably he paid for the copy then made his money from charging for the paper (one penny) and the advertisements. Details of the charges levied for these were given on 9 January.

By the third week of its existence the proprietor announced that '*The Easingwold Advertiser and Weekly News* circulates largely in the following places weekly, and is, therefore, a valuable advertising medium'. A list of some 40 places was then given.

Reginald Smith, it is clear, relied heavily on local correspondents who sent in accounts of village, church and sporting activities, but occasionally 'special correspondents' were used to report on such things as Guardians and RDC meetings.

COMMERCIAL PRINTING
Of every description, executed with Neatness and Despatch, at
G.H. SMITH'S, POST OFFICE,
EASINGWOLD.

The *Advertiser* gradually took on its familiar appearance and the local news expanded. Methodist activities in the town and the villages received a large amount of space, and market information was given which must have been of great value to the farming community[10]. Sporting events made their appearance, and accounts of cricket matches became very important. The hirings were covered in some depressing detail;[11] the proceedings at the area's courts were covered, and those who read the accounts of them would not have been unaware of the penalties that could be levied for not sending a child to school.[12] James Dale the Schools' Attendance Officer reported statistics which, he said, were 'deplorable'. The average attendance was only 72 per cent of children on the registers. There were 400 children 'away… every time the schools were open and matters had become worse since the advent of free education…' Poor attendances meant less money for them as grants in aid were based on attendance. The loss to Easingwold district ratepayers because of this was £360, but of most concern to the deputation was the employment of children. Lynch and his colleagues said it was a commonly held belief that 'the magistrates would not support the school attendance committees in their work'.

The few local business enterprises of any size got good coverage from the *Advertiser,* the Flour Mill Company, for example, and the Easingwold Railway. Proceedings at the half-yearly shareholders' meeting of the latter in May 1892 were exciting and of unusual interest when G.H. Smith was at the centre of things. The Hon F.H. Dawnay was also present and J. Horatio Love presided. They were all directors.

The railway secretary was J. Hetherton and he presented a report on 'the expenditure account'. He then received some very bad news, delivered by the ubiquitous Dr Hicks, no less.[13] Hetherton must have had some idea of what was going to happen, but Hicks proposed that he be sacked (with three months' notice). Why? Because the railway was not flourishing and should reduce expenditure (without 'endangering the efficiency of the line'). Hetherton had been paid a large salary, but the future was 'different'. Who would conduct negotiations with the NER if the secretary was got rid of, Dawnay asked. A 'secretary at a nominal salary' Hicks said. No more sinecures. Dawnay said that Hicks was organising an anti-directors campaign. 'Not at all,' the doctor replied, 'whenever we feel that we have not confidence in the directors you may rest assured that we shall not lack the courage to show

THE

Easingwold Advertiser.

THE WAR IN SOUTH AFRICA.

The enthusiasm excited on Saturday, both in London and Southampton, by the departure of Sir Redvers Buller was only one of many demonstrations which have been evoked by the drafting of troops to South Africa. The occasion was rendered the more notable by the presence of the Prince of Wales, and the veteran Duke of Cambridge, Lord Wolseley, Lord Lansdowne and a number of other distinguished people being also on the platform. Great as was the cheering, it can hardly be said that it exceeded the ardour of previous manifestations for enthusiasm had already reached the maximum when the New South Wales Lancers and other regiments left London and the force of loyalty and admiration could no further go. It is evident that the heart of the nation is with our gallant troops that the insolent "ultimatum" and confident arrogance of the Boers have put the British upon their mettle, and that by their own acts the Dutch States have forfeited the sympathy which might still have been felt for them by some of our people. On all hands a disposition has been manifested to respond to Lord Roseberry's patriotic suggestion that the nation should close its ranks, and "relegate party controversy to a more convenient season". Mr Asquith for example, in his speech at Newburgh remarked, that without in any way abating the keenness of their political principles or partly enthusiasm, it was the duty of our people to do what they could to present a united front, and other members of the Liberal party have followed these statesmen by tendering similar advice, Mr Rudyard Kipling, it will be noticed takes it for granted that when the war is over we shall re-establish the Dutch Republics upon an improved basis, but as to what our policy will be when the time comes remains to be seen, although it is perhaps a little significant that the foreign press take it for granted that we shall annex both States. The officers whose departure has been delayed, have some apprehension that by the time they get to South Africa the war will be over. Perhaps that is too much to expect for this war is a very different business from the Soudan Campaign, but there appears to be every reason to believe that the British force already in South Africa is quite strong enough to hold its own until further troops arrive. The chief danger in the situation arises from the disaffection of the Dutch in British territory. The Boer agents are naturally doing their utmost to provoke rebellion and on the frontier there is clearly a disposition among the farmers to help the Boers. With the constant arrival of fresh British troops this aspect of the situation will become more reassuring and except for the unfriendly attitude of the Cape Dutch, there would be no serious cause for anxiety. The are more British troops at the seat of war than there were in Natal when the Transvaal was retroceded in 1881 and it was generally agreed at that time that the force would have been sufficient to bring the campaign to a speedy and triumphant conclusion. Whether or not the shooting of the Boers has deteriorated. it is tolerably certain that if our own soldiers has improved, and in a hundred ways our troops—with the experience of the former war to guide them—are in a better position to meet the Boers than they were in 1881. At that time several fatal mistakes were made, the cause of most of them being that we under-estimated the strength of our enemies, and failed to appreciate the fact that their mode of warfare a particularly effective one for the country, placed them at home advantage in comparison with our forces. These mistakes are scarcely likely to be repeated, and while the ultimate triumph of British arms is assured, it is only a question of the time to be occupied, and the loss of life which must unhappily occur.

EASINGWOLD.

DURING this week the weather has been more or less foggy.

IT was decided at the meeting of the District Council on Friday last, to purchase a Mud Cart for Easingwold.

TO-DAY (Friday) the half-yearly meeting of the Shareholders of the Easingwold Railway Company will be held in the Town Hall.

WE are glad to notice that the state of the roadway in Chapel Street is claiming the attention of the District Council, and a committee has been instructed to inspect and make a report.

WESLEYAN INSTITUTE. — The usual weekly meeting of the above Institute was held on Friday evening last, the Rev R Whitehead. presiding, when a lantern lecture on "South Africa," was delivered by Mr F E Rookledge, the lantern being ably manipulated by Mr J W Sturdy. There was a good attendance, and the evening was profitably spent.

AUCTION MART.—Mr Robert Burton's auction mart was held on Monday, when there was a very fair entry of stock. Buyers attended in good numbers. There was not quite such a good supply of beasts, but the quality was good. Best quality of beef sold at 7s 3d to 7s 6d; secondary quality up to 7s per stone; shearling sheep made up to 49s each; choicest mutton made 7½d per lb; lamb 8d per lb. The pig trade was brisk. Porkers made 5s 6d to 6s per stone; store pigs, 9s to 20s each. Altogether there were about 200 entries.

WESLEYAN BAND OF HOPE.—On Monday evening the first meeting for the winter months of the Wesleyan Band of Hope was held in the vestry of the Chapel, which was crowded. Mr J Francis Todd, one of the conductors, presided, and conducted the proceedings in an admirable manner. The programme was a very interesting one, and the two recitations were given in good style. The Rev Robert Renton's address was most instructive and interesting to the children, who appeared to be quite at home with him, and answering questions put to them in an intelligent manner. Mr Watson C Wilkinson also said a few words of encouragement. The following was the programme:—Opening hymn; prayer; hymn; recitation, "Robbing a Methodist," Miss M Pearce; address by the Rev R Renton on "Drink, a Waster"; hymn; recitation, "Support the Bands of Hope," Master Ernest Hunter; Chairman's Speech; concluding hymn.

A FARM SERVANT'S THEFT.—On Friday afternoon last, before Messrs Strangwayes, Hawking, and Fairfax-Cholmeley, at Easingwold, William Kiddle, of Scackleton, farm servant, was brought up in custody on remand charged with stealing three £5 notes from Wm Robson, farm foreman, of Scackleton, who stated that he and the prisoner were both in the service of Mr J Hicks, farmer. Prosecutor said he had the notes in his box which was locked, and the key was in a garment which was hanging in the bedroom. On the 29th ult. the prosecutor missed the key and forced the box open, when he discovered that the notes had been taken. The prisoner having been at York, was suspected by the prosecutor, who, when going to inform the police, met the prisoner and asked him if he knew anything about the key, and prisoner answered in the negative. P.C. Eden apprehended the prisoner, who admitted having stolen the notes. He got them changed at York. He then showed the constable a place in a corner of a field where a purse containing twelve sovereigns was buried. Two sovereigns more were found in prisoner's possession. He now said he was sorry for what he had done, and would repay the one pound he had spent. The Bench committed him to prison for a month, with hard labour.

ALNE.

BIBLE SOCIETY MEETING.—A meeting in connection with the British and Foreign Bible Society was held the Wesleyan Chapel Alne, on Wednesday evening last, when the Rev F D Thompson, deputation, gave a most interesting address on the work of the Society in England, Ireland, Russia, Germany, France, and Africa, dealing chiefly with the Transvaal. The chair was occupied by Mr W C Wilkinson, of Easingwold. There was a good collection taken towards the funds of the Society.

COXWOLD.

FEAST.—The annual village Feast was held on Monday last in very favourable weather. There was, as usual, a capital programme of sports arranged for the afternoon, and in the evening a ball was held which was well attended, dancing being kept up with spirit until the early hours of morning. There was a good attendance of people from Easingwold and the surrounding villages.

HUSTHWAITE.

PARISH CHURCH.—Our Husthwaite correspondent informs us that Sir George Orby Wombwell, Bart, of Newburgh Priory, has presented to Husthwaite Church a Communion Cup and Paten in fine old silver. Both pieces of plate are of beautiful design and are nearly two hundred years old.

MISSIONARY MEETING. — The annual missionary meeting was held in the Wesleyan Chapel on Tuesday evening last, when addresses were given by the Rev R Renton and Rev R Whitehead. The chair was occupied by Mr J F Todd, of Easingwold. There was a good congregation present, and a collection was taken in aid of the funds of the Foreign Missionary Soctety. The services will be continued on Sunday next.

ANNUAL FEAST.—On Tuesday and Wednesday the annual village feast was held. There was the usual complement of attractions present, and although on Tuesday there seemed to be a falling off in the attendance, it was up to the average on Wednesday. The Cricket Club had arranged a match for Tuesday, but through some unforeseen circumstance the visiting team failed to put in an appearance, which was very disappointing. A dance was held in the School-room on Wednesday night, and was well attended, the dancing being kept up until the early hours of morning The music was supplied by Mr Walter Cariss, of Thormanby.

DEATH.

WRIGHT.—On October 13th, 1899, at Pleasley, Notts., Robert Wright, late of Raskelfe, aged 58 years, of heart disease and pneumonia.

THE DEMAND FOR HORSES.

On Wednesday, the Liverpool Municipal Authorities received a notification from the War Office to the effect that the Goverment required 200 of the local tramway horses for purposes of transport to the Transvaal. This is the maximum number of horses which the Government are entitled to take. The Corporation have been receiving a subsidy of £800 a year, or in other words £4 per horse. The Council can claim £50 for each animal which cost the Corporation £30 per head. Horse traction is being replaced by electricity.

SUTTON-ON-FOREST.

On Tuesday last P C Walker stationed at Sutton on Forest, apprehended at Marton Lordship, James Jefferson (14) a native of North Shields and Bertie Gray (12) of Cardiff who had absconded from the York Industrial School about midnight on Monday. The officer captured them aided by his bicycle after an exciting chase.

STILLINGTON.

A meeting of the Stillington Parish Council was held in the National school-room on Wednesday evening, October 11th, at 7-30. Present Rev W H Jemison (chairman), and Messrs T Gibson, Thompson, Lunn, Richardson, and the clerk Wm Gibson. A cheque was issued for cost of cleaning out the ditch in the York lane. It was agreed that Wm Bradley be further engaged to clean out the bridge and ditch as far as necessary; and that Messrs Richardson and Souter be deputed to see the work done. It was also resolved that having reconsidered the subject of the Lucy Balk footpath the repairs be effected with bricks and sand to the extent of ten loads of bricks or not exceeding 20 and that Messrs Richardson, Lunn, and Gibson be deputed to carry out the work.

HARVEST THANKSGIVING.—The Harvest Thanksgiving Services were held in the Parish Church Stillington on Sunday last, the vicar, the Rev W H Jemison, officiating at both the morning and evening service. The musical portions of the services were pleasingly rendered, and the Church was very tastefully decorated, the effect of which was much aided by the cleaning down of the interior of the building during the past summer. The congregations were, perhaps, the largest for some years past, as were also the amounts collected. The latter were in aid of the York County Hospital.

RASKELFE.

THE BIBLE SOCIETY. — The annual meeting of the British and Foreign Bible Society was held in Raskelfe on Tuesday evening. The School-room was crowded, and several could not gain admission. The Rev Dr Preston occupied the chair, and remarked that the Society deserved the support of every true christian. It is the first and most important of all Societies. without it our Missionary Societies could not carry on their operations. Its aim was to place the infallible Word of God in the hands of every man, woman, and child, in all parts of the world. Such an object should be dear to the heart of every professing christian. That Book gives "light to the understanding." It "makes wise the simple." It was given to be a "Lamp to our feet, and a light to our paths," and all are commanded to "Search the Scriptures." To withhold it from any, or to prevent it being read is to oppose the mind of God. Any church which refuses to put the Bible into the hands of her people shows she fears the book, and that her teaching is not in accordance with it. Surely if what a minister teaches he really in harmony with the Gospel he ought to be too glad to invite his people to duly test his doctrine by the inspired Word. The Church which keeps her people in the dark as to its full teaching, and which will not allow them to study it for themselves, and does not aim to circulate it wholesale, proves that she is afraid of the Book, because her doctrines are not in agreement with it. The Raskelfe Branch of the Bible Society was to be congratulated on doing so well, in sending up a very good sum of money to head-quarters. In proportion it was doing much better than in his old parish in Cheshire where there was a population of some 6,000. He hoped they would even improve on what they were doing, and send up a larger amount next year. The Vicar next introduced the deputation, the Rev F Thompson, of Leeds, who gave a most interesting lantern lecture. The various views exhibited were admirable. He began with Wales and went on to Jerusalem and to Rome. He said that the Bibles had no general existence in Rome till the Italian troops, under Victor Emmanuel, took possession of the city. Till then it was a prohibited book. Now it was circulated freely. He stated that thousands of the copies of the Scriptures left London daily for various parts of the world. A hearty vote of thanks to the lecturer was proposed by Mr Henry Hawking, who said he was glad to see Mr Thompson and the Vicar there, and so earnest for the dissemination of the Book of Life. He hoped that all would do their best to support the Bible Society, and augment its funds. Mr Churchwarden Shepherd seconded this. A collection was was made which was in excess of that of last year. The proceedings terminated with the blessing given by the Vicar.

EASINGWOLD BOARD OF GUARDIANS

The usual fortnightly meeting of the above board was held on Friday last, when Mr H Hawking occupied the chair and Mr J T Robinson the vice-chair.

THE WORKHOUSE MASTER'S REPORT was read, which stated that since the last meeting of the Board 1 person had been admitted into the house, 0 discharged, the number of inmates at present in the house being 30 against 30 for the corresponding period of last year. The number of vagrants casually relieved during the same period had been 134 against 163 the corresponding period of last year.

THE CHARGES AGAINST THE MEDICAL OFFICERS.

AN APOLOGY TO DR ELLIS.

The Clerk read a letter from Dr Ellis the Medical Officer for the Tollerton subdistrict in which that gentleman said that there was absolutely no foundation whatever for the statements that had been made at the last meeting of the Board as to his treatment of a patient at Overton. He was at a loss to understand the bringing of such a charge as he had attended to the case the same day as he was called. He also reminded the Board that he had been their Medical Officer for 7 years and not once during that time had there been a complaint against him and he thought an apology was needed from the gentleman who made the statements. Mr T Harrison said that as he was the Guardian who brought the matter forward, it was his duty to say that he had been mis-led. Since the last meeting he had found out that the Dr had been on the day he was called. The person a relative of the patient who reported the matter to him, had acknowledged that she had been mistaken. In conclusion Mr Harrison said that he tendered a sincere apology to Dr Ellis for bringing the matter forward there (hear hear). The Chairman said that all agreed that it was a very proper thing to do, and they would accept Mr Harrison expressions of regret.

A letter was also read from Dr Gramshaw as to the case of a lad at Stillington, which was mentioned at the last meeting. The letter stated that at the last meeting an attempt had been at made mis-representation as he had had the lad under his charge as a private patient for three weeks previous and when he got to know he was worse, he went across to see him at once. The letter also contained sundry observations of a personal nature referring to the Guardian who had brought the matter forward.

Mr Souter on rising said that though the indictment was rather serious he was not going to take up the time of the Board to explain it. As he thought the writer of the letter was sufficiently well known. If the Dr had been attending the lad privately he ought to have known that the lad was in a very dangerous condition. Continuing he said he protested very strongly and was understood to say that there was hardly a case where the poor were attended to as they should be. He (the speaker) would welcome a Local Government Board enquiry and meet any charge that was brought forward.

Mr Cholmeley remarked that the alleged neglect was a very serious matter and should be looked into.

Mr Hayden also spoke and it was decided to let the matter stand over and see if the Local Government Inspector made a report and ordered an inquiry. Mr Souter said that he would like the Board to say that no blame attached to him for bringing the matter forward, it was not a pleasant thing to do, to bring a thing like that out of his own parish.

Several Guardians expressed their approval of Mr Souter's action and the Chairman conveyed to him the Board's expressions to that effect in a few appropriate remarks.

Mr Shields said it was all very well clearing Mr Souter but what about the remarks contained in the letter, and if such remarks were tolerated from one, why not pass them round the table at the Board. It was ultimately decided on the proposition of Mr Stapylton, J.P., to acknowledge the receipt of Dr Gramshaw's letter and inform him that the Board considered the remarks about Mr Souter were uncalled for.

Rev Young proposed that Dr Gramshaw's explanation be accepted, but he was ruled out of order.

RE-ASSESSMENT OF RAILWAY AND PUBLIC HOUSE PROPERTY.

The Chairman proposed that power be granted to the Assessment Committee to appoint a professional valuer to re-value the Railway and Public Houses in the Union. The additional line had been opened by the North Eastern Railway and the committee thought it was time that the property was valued again. As regarded the Public House property it was very desirable to have that re-valued, and if they were tied houses to value them at what they were actually worth if they had not been tied houses.

Councillor Robinson, vice-chairman seconded.

Councillor Hayden proposed that the matter be adjourned for a month to enable the result of valuations by neighbouring Unions to be made known. If people were to judge what they did not see, by what they did see by the valuations on the list, he thought it was time the whole of the property in the Union was re-valued. It was a matter of vital importance that such bodies as the Board should act up to their responsibility in these matters, or some time it might be taken out of their hands.

Councillor Driffield said the last speaker's remarks looked rather like doubting the ability of the Assessment Committee.

Councillor F Bell seconded Councillor Hayden.

Councillor Cholmeley remarked that there was no reason to waste money in valuing the land to which Councillor Bell replied that there would not be any waste by adjourning the matter for a month.

Councillor Dunnington supported Mr Hayden's amendment which on being put to the vote was lost by a large majority only four members holding up their hands in favour of it.

WORKHOUSE IMPROVEMENT.

The architects certificate for the payment of £200 to the contractor for the improvements at the Workhouse was received and a cheque was issued for the amount.

It was decided on the recommendation of the Cells Committee to fix water closets instead of earth closets as specified.

VISITING COMMITTEE.

The Chairman nominated Messrs Gilling, Mercer, and Shields as Visiting Committee of the Workhouse for the ensuing fortnight and the same were appointed.

This concluded the business.

REFERENCE COLUMN.

CHURCH SERVICES.—SUNDAY NEXT.

ST. JOHN'S CHURCH.—Vicar—Rev. N. Jackson M.A.—Holy Communion at 8. Morning Prayer at 10-30.—Hymns—202, 295, 361. Litany or Shortened Evensong at 2-15. Evening Prayer at 6-30.—Hymns—362, 366, 447.

BIBLE CLASS SERVICE for Men held at the Grammar School every Sunday Afternoon at 2 o'Clock, conducted by Mr. Herring.

THE CATHOLIC CHURCH.—Priest—Rev. Father Pearson, O.S.B. Holy Communion at 8-30 a.m. High Mass (with Sermon) at 10-30. Sunday School at 2 p.m. Evening Service at 6-30 p.m. Week-days—Mass (daily) at 8-30 a.m. Church always open for private devotions.

WESLEYAN CHAPEL.—Morning at 10—Rev. R. Renton. Evening at 6—Mr. J. Cowling. Thursday Evening at 7—Mr. Crosby.

PRIMITIVE METHODIST CHAPEL.—Morning at 10-30.—Mr. W. Hebden. Evening at 6—Mr T. J. Holmes. Monday Evening at 7.—Rev. R. Ainsworth.

SALVATION ARMY.—Capt. Hewett, Lieut. Payne Morning, 10-45 a.m., 3 and 6-30 p.m. Week-nights, 8 p.m.

CORN MARKET.

WAKEFIELD MARKET.—This Day (Friday)—Foreign Wheat 3d. to 6d. easier, oats 6d. dearer, others unchanged.

PROVISION MARKET.

EASINGWOLD MARKET—Eggs, 8 and 9 for 1/- Butter, 1/3. to 1/4 per lb.

Printed and Published by REGINALD ERNEST SMITH, at his Printing Offices, Market Place Easingwold, in the County of York, Saturday, October 21, 1899.

The Easingwold Advertiser & Weekly News - October 21, 1899

it. Hicks did not convince another Smith of his intentions. 'Mr W. Smith... regarded the resolution as a mark of want of confidence in the directorate.' it clearly was.

Much was said about costs incurred by the railway company; then G.H. Smith took the floor. F.J.H. Robinson was concerned about the directors who had not paid him,[14] but G.H. revealed that *he* had not sent in a demand for what was due to him. What could this have been for? He could have claimed, for 'services rendered before the opening of the railway', he said, as well as for 'interest on money advanced, rent of offices, travelling and other expenses.' He told those assembled that support for the company had been found wanting when really needed. When a third provisional director had been required to take responsibility for creating the business 'along with Sir G.O. Wombwell and Mr. Love, several of the inhabitants in the town had been asked but all declined except himself to take the risk which would have ended in a very serious loss, if the railway had not been made.' Dawnay only joined the directorate when there was no risk of that sort, and the danger was over. He [G.H. Smith] also advanced the money out of his own pocket to carry the company's bill through the House of Lords, and had to work very hard to keep down parliamentary expenses. He said there was one shareholder in the room who knew what work he had done for the company, and could, if he would, make a statement.

The shareholder G.H. had in mind was Hicks, and he confirmed what the printer/ postmaster had said, and stressed that the town of Easingwold clearly owed a great deal to that energetic businessman.

In the months following, the Easingwold Railway had a dreadful time. Boiler tubes burnt out and the company got some dreadful publicity. It did not get compensation from the manufacturer of their unreliable rolling stock, however.[15]

When G.H. Smith and Buller Hicks were campaigning for a change in the running of the railway company a general election campaign was going on. When it was all over J. Grant Lawson was elected as MP for Thirsk and Malton.[16]

After a year's existence the *Easingwold Advertiser* was well established and more and more local correspondents used it to publicise themselves and the activities they were responsible for. The columns of the paper covered the tentative moves to make Easingwold and the neighbouring villages healthier[17] and the deliberations of such bodies as the Guardians were given considerable coverage, as were the activities of the poachers (of all kinds) who had been caught and taken before the magistrates. There were constant reminders of the harsh life that many led and the need to institute reforms of the kind the sanitary authority had embarked on. Influenza had hit the town when the first issue of the *Advertiser* appeared[18], and animal diseases were common.[19]

The year 1892 ended with Reginald Ernest Smith reporting on a rare show of militancy in Easingwold.[20] The issue seems to have been referred to first, in print, in the *Advertiser* by someone signing himself 'Townsman'. The back page that day had some obvious padding, with extracts from Thomas Gill's *History and Antiquities of Easingwold and its Neighbourhood*[21]. Townsman, however, wrote about 'THE BLUE BELL PASSAGE'. Please allow me to draw attention to the fact that the passage near the house in High Street, formerly the Blue Bell pub, has been barricaded up, he said. It has (the passage) been a public thoroughfare for all the time the town's oldest inhabitant had been around. Surely 'some action' to restore the rights of the public will be taken. A smart alec who signed himself 'INFORMER' thought not. The passage was not a road, he said, it was only a road to a pub.[22] Nonsense, another writer said. He had known it for 70 years.[23]

The perpetrator of this attack on the people's rights, it was revealed, was a Mr Williamson, who had bought the pub and blocked off the passage – used as 'a convenient thoroughfare into the Back-Lane, Market-Place and Long-street.' (And much more one imagines). He rapidly became known as one of Easingwold's major nasties and 'Several of the Inhabtants [sic] of High Street' took the door down.[24] Williamson then put up a completely new one. At about 8.30, 'several stalwart men' demolished it with crow-bars.

A calm descended in the Easingwold 'DISPUTED RIGHT OF WAY' business, but not for long. Almost the last news item of 1892 from R.E. Smith said that another door was put up and once again 'several of the inhabitants' demolished it.[25] The affair of the Blue Bell door generated much interest and excitement, more than had the general election of a while back.

It was some seven years after the trouble over the door to Blue Bell Passage that the South African War started, and by then the town's paper had grown and established itself as an important local advertising and news medium. The format was as before, though there was more local news. Its coverage was no longer confined to the back page only, as was said earlier, but the format of the reports were still the same, with many tiny contributions to Wesleyan concerts, and cricket club smokers, lovingly recorded and every village footballer or cricketer written up as if he were W.G. Grace or Steve Bloomer. The bulk of the paper was still 'bought in' and there, in the bought-in parts, the avid reader of the *Easingwold* was given comment and coverage of events on the dark continent. The first of 1896, for example, devoted much space to recent events in the Transvaal and printed a line drawing of a very young-looking '"OOM PAUL" KRUGER, PRESIDENT OF THE SOUTH AFRICAN REPUBLIC'.

The Transvaal lies between the rivers Limpopo and Vaal and diamonds were discovered near Pretoria and began to be mined in the late 1880s. The area was 'settled from 1836 by Boers from Cape Colony.' They 'subdued' the Zulus, then set up a republic recognised by Britain as independent in 1852. Twenty-five years later it was annexed by Britain, but after a very short time the Transvaal rebelled and a famous, humiliating defeat was inflicted on the British (1881) at Majuba Hill. Eventually peace came, rule was restored, and the area pacified and put under British suzerainty.' The settlement that set up the system, though, led to immense trouble (it and many other things). It was the result (12 April 1877) of extraordinary negotiations between President Burgers and Sir Theophilus Shepstone, Minister for Native Affairs in Natal.[26]

By 1896 Paul Kruger was President of the Transvaal,[27] and the lack of political rights for vocal sections of the populace was causing great concern. Speeches by Gladstone had not helped in the '80s, and the removal of the Zulu threat to the Transvaal at the Battle of Ulundi allowed the Boers of the Republic something like a free hand. Hitherto they had lived in terror of their neighbour who had inflicted the disaster of Isandhlwana.[28] The removal of the menace posed by the Zulu King, Cetshwayo 'bore the same relation to the subsequent successful revolt of the Transvaal, as the expulsion of France from Canada in the eighteenth century bore to the revolt of the thirteen colonies.'

When gold was discovered on the Witwatersrand foreigners flocked to the Transvaal and year after year their numbers grew. The attitude of Kruger's government towards these 'Uitlanders' was uncompromising from the word go, and R.C.K Ensor summarised it.[29]

> 'We will not exclude you,' they said in effect, 'but this is our country and if you come here to seek wealth, it must be entirely on our terms. They are that you shall have no

From Billy Holmes archive, Building a Block House

votes and no rights, and we shall so tax you, both directly on the mine profits and indirectly by enormous duties on imported mine-requisites, that a large part of what you get will pass to us.' The Uitlanders preferred coming even on this footing to not coming at all; and Kruger treated their doing so as justifying any hardship that he might care to put on them. 'They need not have come,' was his refrain, 'but having come they must abide the consequences.' 'You need not have admitted them,' was the British retort later on, 'but having admitted them you must treat them justly.'

The Transvaal flourished and Kruger's ambitions increased, he bought arms and entered into negotiations with Berlin.[30] He breached the '84 convention and made no concessions to the Uitlanders. Joseph Chamberlain fully expected there would be a rising in Johannesburg, eventually, and Kruger spoke of the agitation in the mining capital. A heading about events there in the *Advertiser* was a cryptic 'PANIC IN JOHANNESBURG',[31] and it went on to say that 'leading inhabitants' had sent a letter to a Dr Jameson at Mafeking saying they feared there would be a conflict 'between the Government and the Uitlander population.' Why? Because of 'the internal and external policy of the Boer Government.' They called on Dr Jameson to come to their aid. He did. He 'invaded' the Transvaal and his venture ended in farce. He was captured, and eventually tried in Britain. This was the infamous 'Jameson Raid'.

Jameson was Dr Leander Starr Jameson, born 1859, who studied medicine at London. He began to practice at Kimberley in 1878, then entered into the service of Cecil Rhodes as administrator of the South Africa Company at Fort Salisbury. He was immensely popular, and much of his popularity was based on his military exploits. In late 1893 Mashonaland and Matabeleland were taken under white control, the latter after an armed struggle. Jameson then commanded a small force of mounted police which crushed and subdued the natives. 'The campaign was really little more than an early demonstration of the effect of machine-guns'[32] but the memories of 'Isandhlwana and Rorke's Drift', 14 years earlier 'made it seem an exploit of fantastic brilliance... Jameson's head was turned by it.'

Jameson ignored orders and was denounced by the politicians. Readers of the *Advertiser* of 11 January were given some facts about the Transvaal and the task Jameson had set himself. He'd crossed the border at Mafeking and set off for Johannesburg, a distance of some 160 miles, clearly expecting support from the local 'disaffected British dwellers in the Republic,' but none was forthcoming. At Krugersdorp his force was 'stopped and surrounded by burghers' and he had been 'compelled to surrender'. Not for the first time a liberator had found he was not as popular as he had thought he was.[33]

Following the account of the Jameson fiasco, the *Advertiser* gave details of an interview with Henry Hess, 'the well-known champion of English rights in the Transvaal.' It was typical of the anti-Boer propaganda that was to feature in the press in the years to come and was intended to prepare the nation for war. Hess gave population figures, saying that despite their numbers the Uitlanders were unfairly taxed, as Kruger had promised they would be. Not only that, but the republic itself was corrupt. It was all true and it is worth quoting Hess at some length to show what people were being told.[34]

> The English pay nine-tenths of the taxes. Taxation is so arranged that its incidence falls unfairly on them, and they are denied all the benefits of good government. The public schools ... are carried on in Dutch, and the English have had to start schools of their own besides paying for the Dutch. Johannesburg, which has ... attracted the scum of the world, is absolutely refused adequate police protection. Judges ... have been found guilty of fraud. Every monopoly and privilege goes to the Germans and Boers, and the whole administration is rotten and corrupt from beginning to end. ... Money disappears by wholesale out of the State Treasury.' "Our great grievance is less our exclusion from the franchise than ... corruption ..." Mr. Hess continued.

Hess painted a picture of impending disaster in the Transvaal, the situation there, he said, was 'as grave as it well can be'. Kruger was arming ('A few weeks' ago 'the government' imported 150,000 rifles') and the miners were getting weapons. The English, he concluded, 'have stood all they can of aggression, plundering, and injustice.' *How* they were treated was described at some length in an editorial in the *Advertiser* shortly afterwards. The rulers there, it said, feared that political reform would mean the end of the Transvaal's independence. 'the Boers protest that if the "Outlanders" are given equal citizen rights, the first thing that will happen will be the hauling down of the Transvaal flag.'

The immediate crisis over the inquests on recent events in the Transvaal started and were aired at length in the *Advertiser.* Why did the Johannesburgers fail to help Jameson, for example,[35] and what was the Kaiser up to with his messages of support to Oom Paul?[36] Had the Johannesburg Uitlanders been conned by a fake message from the doctor? The issues of South Africa had become a major concern and events there were reported at length. The attacks of the British government on Cecil Rhodes, the House of Commons' committee's deliberations on the authorship of the raid, the trials of the rebels. All these things were reported at length, and the role actually played in the whole sorry business by Joseph Chamberlain was raised repeatedly. Did Joe know of the proposed raid?[37] It seems not, but he *was* privy to preparations for a rising in Johannesburg, and the suspicions of Britain and Chamberlain poisoned relations between Great Britain and Kruger's state.

Matters worsened with the murder of Tom Edgar an English workman, and when the policeman who killed him was arrested, bailed, tried before a jury consisting entirely of Boers, then acquitted, and their action commended by the judge'. Violence broke out and a huge petition to the Queen was organised by British subjects on the Rand. The British government 'took up the petition (in May) and futile negotiations were engaged in. The franchise question was discussed, and the Orange Free State threw in its lot with the Transvaal, meaning the two states could if they wanted field a combined force of around 50,000 mounted infantry. War was apparently becoming inevitable and on 9 October the Boers issued an ultimatum demanding the withdrawal of British troops and the ending of reinforcements. Readers of the *Advertiser* had for three years been regaled with informative articles about the Jameson trial and its outcome, the tortuous 'negotiations' with Kruger and Joe Chamberlain's attacks on Oom Paul. Now (1899) the reports they read at their breakfast tables seemed to amount to a countdown to conflict. In late August Reginald Ernest Smith deviated from his usual practice and included a note in the *Easingwold Advertiser* about international affairs suggesting if war came it would actually be popular.[38] But he was optimistic.

> LATEST intelligence from the Transvaal... We are led to believe that President Kruger and his advisers have at length grasped the fact that Britain is bent on seeking proper consideration for the claims of the Uitlander, and the Boers will yield with what grace they can command. It will be well, for bloodshed hereanent would indeed be an ever-regrettable happening.

The feeling about the Transvaal that had been built up was one of overwhelming sympathy for the Uitlanders who paid the bulk of the State's taxes, yet had few political rights. In July 1899, the York Conservatives held a rally at Newburgh Priory at which prominent politicians aired their views. J.G. Butcher M.P.[39] ended his speech on the Transvaal by saying (more-or-less) that the British government would use force in the last resort if necessary. The government had the support of a patriotic country in demanding fair and just treatment for our fellow-subjects. He said all this, Butcher concluded, to combat the possibility that Kruger's friends 'in this country might endeavour to persuade him that the British Government were not in earnest.'

Later on, during the war, certain politicians (like Lloyd George) became prominent as 'pro Boers', and were much hated for the anti-war stance they took. A huge demonstration of

From Billy Holmes archive, out on patrol in the Veldt

such people took place in Trafalgar Square on a Sunday afternoon at the end of September, which was well covered in the Easingwold paper.[40] Between 500 and 600 police were on duty to protect the speakers, and their services were needed. Missiles were hurled at the likes of H.M. Hyndman; their utterances were drowned out by repeated cheers for Joseph Chamberlain, and groans for Kruger. What was the message Hyndman and the others were trying to get over? It was that the current government should be condemned and that there was 'no difficulty that could not be settled by arbitration.' The crowd thought otherwise. The prevailing attitude was that Kruger was a selfish dictator who would have to be brought into line by force. In June, Sir Alfred Milner, the High Commissioner, was meeting the President in Bloemfontein about the position of the Uitlanders in the Transvaal, and the *Morning Post* told its readers about Kruger's rule.[41] It had become

> an anomaly and an anachronism. Though nominally a Boer republic, it is virtually an Oligarchy, in which the institutions have survived from a previous cycle in its history. Numerically, socially, economically, and financially, the State has advanced by leaps and bounds, but its political growth has been arrested by the selfishness of the few in power.

Another effect of the prolonged troubles with the Transvaal was that Germany replaced France in popular opinion as Britain's number one adversary on the continent, an attitude strengthened by the arms buying by Kruger, and arms supplying by the Kaiser.

SKETCH MAP OF SOUTH AFRICA.

All line drawings to the end of the book are taken from the Easingwold Advertiser & Weekly News covering the Boer War years.

Paul Kruger was identified as a tyrant. What were people told about his troops? What were the men like who the British would have to fight – should war come? A lot was written and said about them. They were presented as formidable foes, and excellent marksmen.[42]

The Boers' ability as horsemen and marksmen was frequently commented on [43] at the time of the South African War and has been written about in numerous books and articles since. Lord Roberts, the nation's favourite soldier, addressed himself to the question, and his remarks formed the basis of an article in the *Advertiser.*[44] He had been campaigning for some 15 years for better shooting skills in the British forces and, though an artilleryman himself, still reckoned the infantryman could, if he was good enough, sway a battle. And the Boer reputation, he said, had been won when things were different. They got it, Roberts said,

> in circumstances which were exceptionally favourable to them when they were engaged against British forces of inferior strength, fighting for the most part in red coats, and wearing white helmets which made them a conspicuous mark for Boer bullets. Now our men fight in the serviceable khaki (dust coloured uniforms), which are admirably adapted for fighting in South Africa, and it has been evident for some weeks that the Government has no intention of repeating the blunders of 1881 by underestimating the strength of the Boers. ... the battles of the future will be won at the rifle range, and in the exercises of the drill ground.

War with the Transvaal and the Orange Free State started in October 1899. How did the *Advertiser* break the news to its readers? To start with, there was published an illustrated article on Natal and the opinion was vouchsafed that if that colony were to be invaded, the Boers would debouch from the mountainous Orange Free State border, through Muller's Pass. Further north the danger points were Volksrust, where there was an extensive Boer encampment, and Laing's Nek (actually in Natal territory). Not far away was Majuba Hill. Then came the official pronouncements. They began with 'THE QUEEN'S PROCLAMATIONS', and it was announced that 'by "The Reserve Forces, 1882"[45] the Army Reserve had been ordered to be called out on 'Permanent Service'.[46] (Parliament was prorogued to 17 October.)[47] Another proclamation was 'For Continuing Soldiers in Army Service' – by which soldiers 'entitled in pursuance of the terms of their enlistment to be transferred to the Reserve shall continue in Army Service.'[48] This could mean that some men who had been in civilian life for a long time, could get their call-up papers. This happened frequently, and it happened again in 1914. Books about the period are full of the suffering of men who had gone soft in their years out of the services.[49]

After the proclamations the *Advertiser* printed instructions to reservists and a schedule showing the units to which men were to report. Among the huge list were 'All of Section B and C transferred from 10th (Prince of Wales Own Royal) Hussars and sections of the Northumberland Fusiliers and the Prince of Wales Own (West Yorkshire Regiment).[50] Those on the Reserve living in South Africa were specially mentioned, and, readers were told, the 'field force' to be mobilised was to be done 'in accordance with the "Regulations for the mobilisation of a full force for service in South Africa, 1899."' 'The 'ninth day of October' was 'to be considered the first day of mobilisation' and the reservists so ordered were to rejoin on or before 17 October. The proclamation, it was reckoned, would affect between 30,000 and 40,000 men.

The first reservist to get his papers to be mentioned in the *Advertiser* came from some distance away.[51] He was PC Metcalfe of the West Riding Police Force, who had been stationed at South Kirby for the past four years.[52] This means he must have been very close to completing his period as a reservist. He was ordered to report 'on Monday next for

From Billy Holmes archive, unknown Yeomanry soldier

Chelsea Barracks to join his old regiment, the Coldstream Guards.' The following appeared on the back page of the paper, which recorded Metcalfe's call to duty.

> NORTHALLERTON SOLDIERS AT THE FRONT – Lieutenant Ernest Caffin of the 10th Regiment, a battalion of which was stationed in India, has volunteered for active service, and is now attached to the Devonshire Regiment, and has been for the last fortnight in camp at Ladysmith. He writes home to Northallerton to say that the troops are in excellent health and spirits. Another Northallerton soldier is George Albert Baker, who is a bandsman with the Gloucester Regiment. He has written to his parents ... to say that the change from India to the Cape has proved a pleasant one. A third man from Northallerton is a young fellow named Hogg, who is now attached to the Flying Squadron. All the Reservemen at Northallerton have received notice to rejoin their regiments.

Then came news of the first Easingwold man;

> EASINGWOLD is not without its representative on the Transvaal Frontier. Sergeant Crosby, son of Mr George Crosby, Market Place, is with the Leicester Regiment at Glencoe.

Just below the report about Crosby, it was recorded that the Easingwold Wesleyan Institute had arranged for 'To-night a lantern lecture on "South Africa"', which, R.E. thought, 'should prove very interesting.'

Glencoe, where Crosby was stationed, was on the railway that ran from Durban to Pietermaritzburg, Estcourt, Ladysmith, then on to Newcastle and Johannesburg. A major strategic Boer objective in the early days of the war was to cut the five-mile link. They did so for a short time.

When the news about Sgt Crosby, PC Metcalfe and Lt Caffin was given to readers of the *Advertiser,* war had not been declared, and RE Smith's editorial dwelled largely on a recent speech by Sir Henry Campbell-Bannerman. The future Liberal Prime Minister dealt at length with Britain's most recent demands which, he said, were 'reasonable'. They were, but Kruger had had them for two weeks and had not replied. Instead he had massed troops on the frontiers and made 'truculent speeches' in which he declared that the Boers 'would not rest until "entirely free of England."' The Boers were, in reality, spoiling for a fight. By the time the next issue of the *Advertiser* appeared, hostilities *had* started.[53] Henceforth campaign reports would replace stories about futile negotiations centred round Kruger.

The first details about the war given in the *Advertiser* were about the Boers capturing and shelling an armoured train. This was about 40 miles south of Mafeking. The Boers in the east were reported by the *Scotsman* to have 'come down through Van Reenen's Pass, with 11 guns, and a battle now rages'. What was the object of the incursion? It was 'apparently to attack the three towns of Dundee, Glencoe and Ladysmith, which constitute

Sgt. George Crosby wearing his South African medal. Photo taken around 1905 when he was one of the crackshots in the Rifle Club.

the headquarters of the British forces in Natal'. Sgt Crosby, it will be recalled, was stationed at Glencoe. General Sir George White had left Ladysmith to seek a fight with the Boers, but had returned without doing so. The *Daily Telegraph* said he was 'indisposed to remain inactive', and would not be so if he could get the Boers 'obligingly to come into the open'. We 'shall not be drawn in passes in small detachments to be picked off by sharpshooters securely placed behind rocks', a 'source' assured a reporter.

In the *Advertiser* a great deal of space was devoted to the early fighting in Natal where the Boers, it was said, had been 'outfought' and taught that they had consistently underrated 'the British soldier and his leaders'. How had they been taught their lesson? By the defeats that had been inflicted on them in the very 'first great battle of the Transvaal War.' Where? 'At Talana Hill on Friday of last week', for example, 'where the British stormed the Boer position' and routed him 'with heavy loss'.[54] (The Hill is just north of the town of Dundee, which was served by a short railway line to Glencoe.) At Elandslaagte, General French 'issuing from Ladysmith, stormed another Boer position and inflicted a crushing blow, thus restoring the "cut" railway communication between the two British camps [of Glencoe and Dundee].' At the same time General Joubert endeavoured to storm the British camp at Glencoe, with disastrous results.

All the papers of the early days of the Boer War carried line drawings of senior participants and biographical sketches about them, both British and Boers. On the page of the *Advertiser* where the events in Natal were recorded, there were features, for example, on General Symons, killed at Glencoe,[55] and Commandant Cronje, who had defeated Jameson outside Krugersdorp. Cronje, whose name was to become very familiar to British readers, was said to hold 'fire-eating' opinions and had been concerned in 'the attack on the British armoured train ... which formed really the first active incident of the war.' French did not get a line drawing, but got a note – which had clearly been written some time before.

> MAJOR-GENERAL FRENCH ... possesses most of the qualifications of a typical cavalry officer. He is dashing, clear-headed, quick tempered and good looking. Like General Sir Evelyn Wood, he commenced his career in the Navy, but soon discovered a preference for the other arm of the services, and has been identified with two regiments of hussars.

French was Commander in Chief of the British Army in the early part of the Great War.[56]

To the *Advertiser,* the events of the first days of the war indicated there would be a certain rapid British victory, but its editorial of 28 October had some misgivings. There is some reason to believe

> that the lives of some of the officers were sacrificed needlessly, either through their reckless courage, or else through the Boers being able to distinguish them as officers. The number of casualties in the commissioned ranks is so much out of proportion with that among the non-commissioned officers and men, that it is obvious there must be some explanation. [Some thought it was because] the officers neglected to seek shelter in the way they urged upon the men. ...It is a theory of the War Office... that the enemy cannot distinguish the officers from the men. All ranks are now dressed very much alike, except that the officers carry a sword instead of a rifle.

Newspaper readers rapidly became familiar with casualty lists, and those for Glencoe and other places were published in the *Advertiser* of 28 October. Sir George White telegraphed to the War Office a list of 'casualties sustained in the action on Friday of last week.' It reported

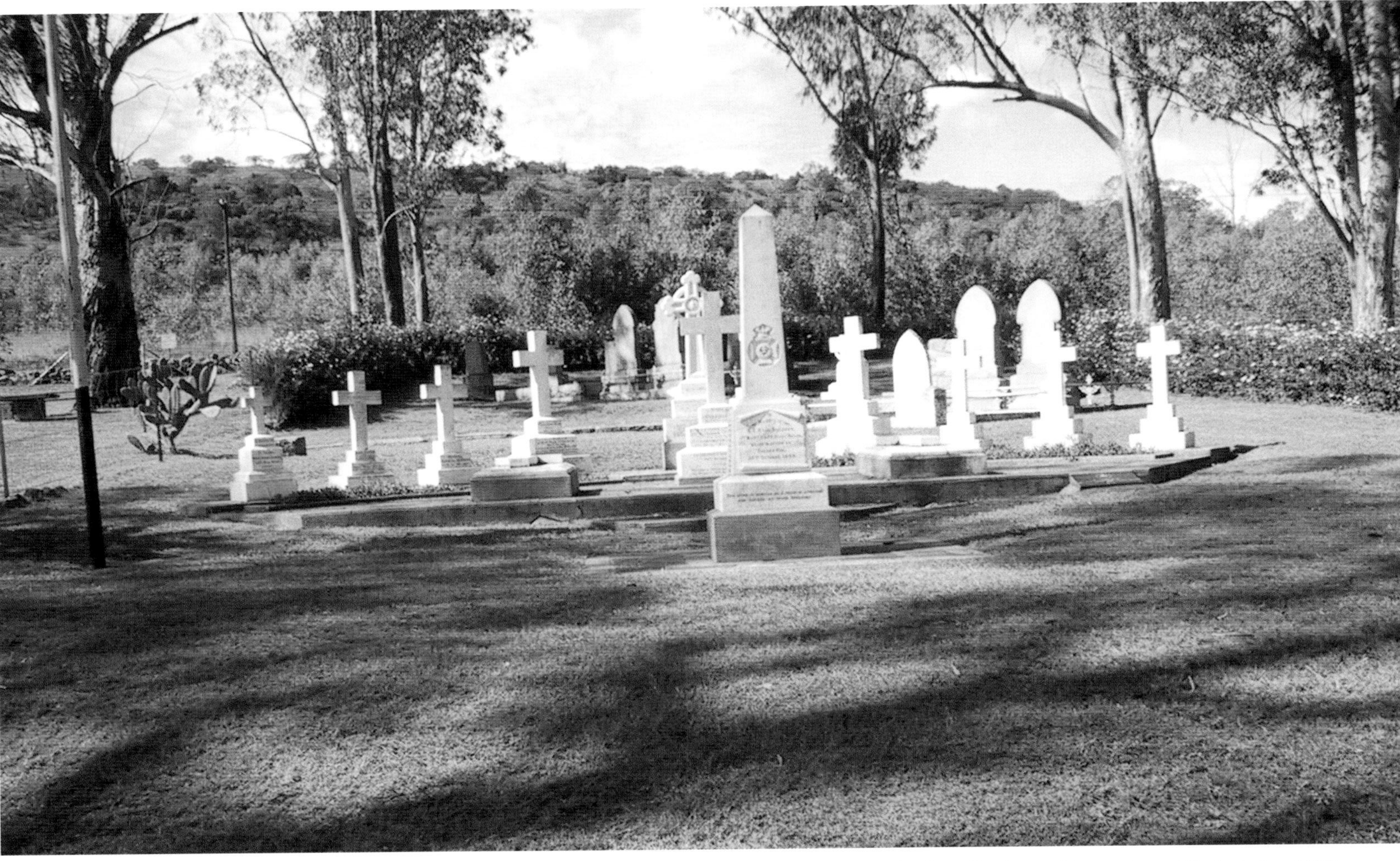

Memorial to British dead at Talana, Dundee, Natal. Talana Hill in background. Sgt. Crosby from Easingwold was here. Photo taken 2000.

From Billy Holmes archive, unknown Yeomanry soldier

'a total of 224 killed and wounded in the British force'. Later, in the same column, it was recorded that 'the main northern column of the Boers, under General Joubert, 'renewed the attack on Glencoe. An 'OFFICIAL ANALYSIS OF BRITISH LOSSES IN THE FIGHT AT GLENCOE' was published and some were from Sgt Crosby's regiment.

The incidents of 20 October 1899 came to be known officially as the Battle of Dundee, and it was at Dundee that the ill-fated General Symons concentrated his forces.[57] Natal went up in a wedge between the Orange Free State and the Transvaal,[58] and Symons had decided to 'abandon the extreme north of' that part 'where lie the ill-omened battlefields of Laing's Nek, Majuba and the Ingogo.' When reinforcements arrived, the force equalled 4,600, with 18 guns. The British did not expect the Boers to move south fast, but they did. They seized Laing's Nek, crossed the Drakensburg hills, then invested Symons' force.

Glencoe and Dundee, as has been said, were a few miles apart, and just to the north of the connecting railway between the two lies a place which rapidly became famous for a number of reasons. This was Talana Hill, which was stormed and taken by the British. H.W. Wilson recorded the events in his usual breathless style. 'Here fell Colonel Gunning and Captain Pechell,' he wrote, 'in front of their men, as soldiers and Englishmen should fall.'[59] Talana Hill also saw an example of Boer 'treachery'. They began to retreat, and the British should have opened up on them, 'But the guns did not open; the enemy had hoisted the white flag, and by this shameful ruse covered the retreat.' Many Boer atrocities and dirty tricks were recorded at this time, no doubt giving cause for alarm among families of the soldiers at the front. A despatch of 26 October said that the Boers, on arriving in Dundee and finding arms in the hands of some of the Town Guard, pistolled several of them in cold blood. At Rowan's Farm (two miles from Dundee) 20 Town Guardsmen were forced out of a house by shell fire, and they ran on to the neighbouring hill. 'They were chased and surrounded by 300 of the enemy 'and shot down'. A few got away and made off towards Dundee. The Boers 'following them up, dragged some civilians out of their houses and shot them in the streets.' All this contrasted dramatically with stories of the treatment (on both sides) of (important) prisoners,[60] but clearly the message was that the men at the sharp end were not to be trusted. 'It is becoming generally recognised, after recent experience, that the hoisting of the white flag by the Boers is merely a subterfuge to assist a retreat or to draw our men under fire.' There was another example of what would be called Hunnish behaviour later on. The 'Dublin Fusiliers and the Rifles' fought their way to the summit

> of the Kopje at Glencoe, [when] the Boers showed a white flag, and asked for a truce to bury their dead. Our artillery were at once ordered to cease firing, and the cavalry reined in. The enemy took immediate advantage of the position to continue their retreat, hurrying away safely in dense masses, which otherwise would have been decimated in the fire of our guns.

Some 30 miles to the south of Glencoe, is another place, which became famous as a war centre in the early days of the South African War. This was Ladysmith, where the first soldier mentioned in these pages was stationed. It was on the railway line that ran south through the Biggarsberg hills to Elandslaagte, then Reitfontein. Elandslaagte, which has been mentioned before, was the scene of an action involving British cavalry of 'the Imperial Light Horse, raised from the British Outlanders, six guns of the Natal Artillery, and 400 of the Manchester regiment in a train.' The commander of the cavalry was French and H.W. Wilson could not refrain from moralising. 'Our weapons,' he wrote, 'were old and feeble 7-pounders, the Boer guns long-range quick-firing 14 pounders – the weapons lost in the shameful Raid, and now by strange retribution, pointed against the brave men who had to pay for the deplorable mistakes of the past.'[61]

French sent for reinforcements, and they arrived under Col Ian Hamilton, a veteran of earlier South African wars.[62] The British then attacked the Boers whose 'main position was on a long, rocky ridge which dropped at the northern end to a "nek" or pass.' Twelve hundred men from the Devonshire regiment had been among the relief force, and they took part in the ensuing advance – 'the Devons were as steady as on parade, firing volleys from time to time and always slowly gaining ground.' The Boer positions were reached, the men at the field guns were bayonetted and those running down the other side of the hill were fired on. Then the British behaved in a way that might go some way to explaining some of the South African atrocities. The war was not a month old, and[63]

> as the enemy fled in the falling darkness, the Lancers and Light Horse rode at them. From the nature of things they could give no mercy. The terrible steel spears did their work amongst the yelling, panic-stricken fugitives; the Light Horse, too, had much to avenge - the murder of Edgar and innumerable shameful outrages in the past - and they avenged it. It was a complete and decisive victory, the first that had been gained in the war.

The Devonshires were prominent at Elandslaagte, and Lt. Ernest G. Caffin may have taken part in the fight. References to him are few in the local paper, but a year earlier news had been received from India (in March 1898) saying he had been 'severely wounded while fighting with the 2nd Princess of Wales's Own Yorkshire Regiment on the Indian Frontier', but had 'nicely recovered'.[64] He then volunteered for South Africa, and might have been amongst those who fought at Elandslaagte. If he was there he got through the day safely, but was severely wounded a second time and sent home. His return was a very sad and subdued affair.[65]

When General Symons was killed his command was taken over by General James Herbert Yule. He led a famous, exhausting march to Ladysmith, which attracted a great deal of justified press attention. Caffin might well have been on it.[66] The march (or retreat) was undertaken because Dundee was practically surrounded and, as the column neared Ladysmith, the weather broke. Yule's health was shattered and he was invalided home. His column had consisted of some 4,500 men.[67]

The Devons' introduction to war in South Africa was described in a letter published by R.E. Smith early in December.[68] The writer was 'A colour-sergeant of the 1st Devons' who played 'such a splendid part in the charge at Elandslaagte'. His letter, the *Advertiser* said,[69] was one of several containing dramatic descriptions of the conflict.

VIVID EXTRACTS FROM PRIVATE LETTERS

The letters home of our soldiers at the front form most interesting reading, as the following extracts will show: A colour-sergeant of the 1st Devons, who played a splendid part in the charge at Elandslaagte, writing home, incidentally gives some details throwing a light upon the serious side of the soldier's character, so singularly free from cant: "It simply hailed bullets when we got to within 600 yards of the enemy's position. But on we went with fixed bayonets, charged the position, and won; but at what a cost! The sights would turn you cold – headless bodies, limbs lying about everywhere, for our artillery made grand work

From Billy Holmes archive, horse of the Yeomanry.

on the enemy. I found one young fellow badly wounded, talking about his mother and his home, and it touched me, for the enemy are white people like ourselves. We had to remain on the battlefield all night collecting the dead and wounded of both sides. What with the continuous rain and the groans of the wounded, it was a sight I will never forget. I offered a small prayer up, thanking God for my safety. It is rough work, sometimes no food all day. But we are soldiers doing soldiers' duty."

General White decided to hold on to Ladysmith, and eventually the town was cut off. There was a disastrous sortie which ended in humiliation for the Brits on a day known subsequently as 'Mournful Monday',[70] but the place 'was besieged. There were 5,500 white civilians, 2,500 Africans and Indians and 13,500 officers and men' there. Amongst them, of course, was Lt Caffin. His injury was reported in the Easingwold paper of 6 January 1900.

SHELL IN A MESS TENT

> During an active bombardment of Ladysmith, one of the enemy's shells struck the mess tent of the Devonshire Regiment, killing Captain Dalzel and wounding Lieutenants Price-Dent, Twiss, Tringham and Caffyn [sic] slightly.

The siege of Ladysmith went on and a couple of extraordinary incidents occurred there. In the first a group of Boers led by Commandant De Villiers, rushed a party at Wagon Point, that included Ian Hamilton, and a fight with pistols at point blank range ensued, which ended with De Villiers and others being killed. Personal combat involving the commanders of both sides! Then the Devonshires were called from the north and charged the enemy. They fled to the next hill and[71]

> Here they attempted to stand until dusk, determined not to be hunted down the hill in daylight, but by dusk they had all retired and the Devons had won the day. This charge was an outstanding achievement. In a few seconds the Devons… lost all their company officers and a third of their men.
> The remainder of the siege was a matter of endurance against disease and starvation, rather than action. The Boers never attacked again. Rations were progressively reduced, and the state of the men steadily deteriorated. The supply officer… made horse-flesh sausages palatable, and the men used dubbin for frying… all this under a tropical heat.

The siege of Ladysmith lasted 122 days.

NOTES

1. *Advertiser* 12 January 1895.
2. Baxters brewed at Thornton-le-Moor.
3. Handson was the manager of the Guarantee, which was based at Kirton, Lincolnshire. He signed the advertisement.
4. F.C. Russell, Woburn House, Bedford Square, London.
5. Author of one was J.F. Churchill
6. The weather was bad, many places were snowed-in, and much damage was done by gales. The Yearsley Wesleyan Chapel had its roof 'nearly stripped'. The bad spell was a prolonged one. See eg *Advertiser* 9 February 1895 and the front-page article in there. Influenza was rife.
7. *Ibid* 9 March 1895.

8. *Ibid* 13 April 1895. Also 20 and 27 April 1895.
9. It would be more correct to say that most of the two pages were set at Easingwold. The amount set locally varied as time went on.
10. The information was received 'by Electric Telegraph', and on 7 May consisted of details of: prices from corn markets at Wakefield, Thirsk, Darlington and London; cattle markets at Thirsk, Darlington and London; pig markets at Selby and Thirsk; provisions markets at Easingwold 'This Day (Friday)', Selby, Pickering and Darlington; potato markets at Thirsk, Selby and London; and the hay and straw market at Thirsk.
11. *Advertiser*, 7 May 1892, for the Thirsk hirings. (Depressing because of the level of wages offered.)
12. The Easingwold bench of 4 May heard six cases. There was a case of drunkenness and a denizen of Raskelfe was done for not having a license for his dog. The last four cases were brought by James Dale, the school attendance officer. All the offenders – parents – were fined 5s 6d.
13. *Ibid*.
14. Hicks successfully proposed that the disputed, unpaid bills, be put before an independent committee of shareholders.
15. See eg the report on the troubles with the engines *Advertiser*.
4 June 1892.
16. List of results in *Ibid* 23 July 1892.
17. A waterworks had recently been constructed and the *Advertiser* recommended all householders to get on the mains. See eg *Ibid* 2 April 1892.
18. *Ibid* 2 January 1892. Albeit of a 'mild type' this time.
19. *Ibid* 18 June, 2 July 1892. See the article on foot and mouth in 5 March 1892.
20. *Ibid* 22 October 1892.
21. Reginald Ernest Smith frequently had to resort to fillers in this first year, and Gill came in very handy.
22. 'THE BLUE BELL PASSAGE', *Advertiser*, 29 October 1892.
23. Letter from 'Corrector' *Ibid* 5 November 1892.
24. *Ibid* 12 November 1892.
25. *Ibid* 31 December 1892.
26. eg G.M. Theal, *History of South Africa from 1873 to 1884* (1919).
27. He became president in 1883 at the age of 58.
28. Where over 1,300 men of the British invasion force were killed by the Zulu army. Cetshwayo was the Zulu king. Usually called Cetewayo in Britain.
29. R.C.K. Ensor, *England, 1870-1914* (Oxford 1936) p.226.
30. Illegally in contravention of the terms of the 1884, a convention that forbade the Transvaal from dealing with foreign governments (other than that of the Orange Free State) except through Great Britain.
31. *Advertiser*, 4 January 1896. There is a biographical article reprinted from the Morning *Advertiser* in *Ibid* 11 January 1896. E. Pakenham, *Jameson's Raid* (1960).
32. 'The… Maxim gun began to appear on colonial battlefields in the 1890s, to be used to best effect in the Matabele war of 1893, when armed police of the chartered company and volunteers simply laargared their wagons and mowed down the Africans, who charged with reckless courage.' D. Porch, 'Imperial Wars from the Seven Years War to the First World War', in C. Townshend, *The Illustrated History of Modern Warfare* (Oxford 1997).
33. On the raid see 'The Transvaal Trouble', *Ibid*.
34. A very popular two-volume book, which could not be accused of being pro-Boer, is H.W. Wilson, *With The Flag to Pretoria. A History of the Boer War of 1899-1900* (1900 and 1901). In the years following the end of the war, as Thomas Pakenham said, there was a torrent of books on the conflict, including a seven-volume *Times History*, and an official history. T. Pakenham, *The Boer War* (1979), Introduction.
35. *Advertiser*, 1 February 1896.
36. Notably the famous Kruger Telegram, which congratulated the President on his recent victory over the 'armed hordes' that were Jameson's raiders.
37. For a typical example of the South African coverage shortly after the raid see, eg 'THE JAMESON TRIAL. SCENE AT BOW STREET', *Advertiser*, 14 March 1896. This issue also contained a report from the *African Critic* about the surrender of Jameson. The request for help to Jameson from the Uitlanders of Johannesburg, dated 20 December 1895, is published *in extenso* in *Ibid* 21 March 1896.
38. *Ibid* 26 August 1899.
39. *Ibid* 29 July 1899.
40. *Ibid* 30 September 1899.
41. Quoted *Ibid* 10 June 1899. It might be noted that in all the commenting and reporting on the Transvaal in which the Boers and the Uitlanders featured, very little, if anything, was said about the coloured population. There was an exception, however. In September 1899. The *Advertiser* then reported that a Green Book had been issued at Pretoria. In the correspondence with it was a letter 'intimating strong disapproval of the way these people were treated'. The reply was a denial of the charges. *Ibid* 2 September 1899.
42. *Ibid* 12 August 1899.
43. Eg the short piece in S. Simmons (ed), *The Military Horse – a Story of Equestrian Warriors* (1984) p55.
44. *Advertiser* 30 September. Roberts had just published a book of essays.
45. The proclamation was published in the *London Gazette*, 7 October.
46. *Advertiser*, 14 October 1899.

47. This is important. The procedure was used when Parliament was not sitting.
48. There were three proclamations in all.
49. A very famous reservist from a town not far from Easingwold who was called up was Harry Blanshard Wood. He became time expired during his service and left it – as he had every right to do. He was then called up in his forties, went to France, and won the MM and the VC. A remarkable story. On him see A.J. Peacock, 'Reluctant Hero. Harry Blanshard Wood of York (and Bristol). A Great War VC', *Gun Fire* No 28.
50. There were several sections of the Reserve. Men of Section D were not liable.
51. First that is in the paper. Some others from Northallerton appear in the text.
52. *Advertiser*, 14 October 1899.
53. *Ibid* 21 October 1899.
54. *Ibid* 28 October 1899.
55. He subsequently died of his wounds.
56. He wrote a highly contentious book about the period before he was replaced.
57. The contemporary accounts of events at Glencoe and Dundee are extremely confusing.
58. 'The whole of the frontier between Natal and the Orange Free State... runs along the top of the Drakensburg hills.'
59. Wilson op cit p35. Gunning was the Lt Col mentioned in the text. He was the eldest son of Sir G.W. Gunning of Little Horton House, Northampton. Pechell was Mark Horace Kerr Pechell of the 1st KRR. He was the eldest son of an admiral, who joined the Army in 1888. He served in the Hazara and Isazai expeditions and was with the Chitral Relief Force under Sir Robert Low. Pechell's name was sometimes rendered Perchell.
60. See eg the case of Capt Nisbett, captured and taken to Lichtenburg and thence to Pretoria. Cronje gave permission for a native to deliver a letter from Nisbett saying he was being well treated.
61. Wilson op cit p27. L.S. Amery, *Times History of the War in South Africa* (1905) Vol 2.
62. I. Hamilton, *The Happy Warrior* (1966). This is a biography of Hamilton by his nephew. Chapter 11 is 'Elandslaagte, 1899'.
63. Wilson op cit p29. A telegram from a special correspondent giving an account of 'THE BATTLE OF ELANDSLAAGTE' is reproduced (from the *Times*) in *Advertiser*, 28 October 1899. There is a brief description of 'Elandslaagte' (and some splendid photographs) in M.M. Evans, *The Boer War South Africa 1899-1902* (1999) pp21-23. The author quotes an American serving with the Irish Brigade alongside the Boers who said 'the Lancers acted as if [they were] fighting Indians, and gave no quarter, stabbing and murdering ... That lot ... are down in our black book... if the opportunity presents itself ... we will wipe them off the rolls.'
64. *Advertiser*, 19 March 1989.
65. *Ibid* 28 April 1900.
66. And General Sir George White, the GOC Natal, who went as a spectator. The press made much of his presence and his refusal to take over from French. It also made much of French giving Hamilton a free hand (more-or-less).
67. There is a biographical sketch and a drawing of Yule in *Advertiser*, 4 November 1899.
68. The sergeant's letter was in the 'bought in' part of the paper of course. R. Holmes, *The Little Field-Marshal. Sir John French* (1981).
69. *Advertiser* 9 December 1899.
70. This was the affair at Nicholson's Nek when 'Thirty-seven officers and 917 men were taken prisoner while 69 lay dead and 249 were wounded.' Evans op cit p27.
71. Hamilton op cit p149.

Chapel Street, Easingwold, 1903

Chapter 8

CLASH IN AFRICA

Outline of the Boer War Battles

1899

The Battle of Dundee

On the morning of 11 October 1899, the head of the small South African Republic of Transvaal declared war. Grossly overweight and sombre in the fashion of the Dutch Reformed Church, President Paul Kruger was about to fight the greatest empire that the world had seen since the days of the Romans. Not that he feared the clash this hot Thursday. At the moment he had more men under arms than his opponents in South Africa did. Indeed his force of armed militia groups, formed into 'commandos' under leaders which they elected themselves from their neighbours, outnumbered the British they would attack that very night by five to four fighting men. In addition they were better armed and better mounted, brought up since childhood using weapons to shoot game, natives and now and again pesky British uitlanders (foreigners). Besides their only permanent military force, the 800 strong, grey-uniformed artillery corps, was equipped with the latest French and German cannon, which had the advantage of 1,000 yards on any gun currently in use in the British Army in Africa.

BOER BIG GUN.

Now, after a day of palaver, drinking and boasting, a force of 25,000 horsemen, commanded by hardened Boer veterans and young hot-heads who hated the British (who they thought were out to destroy their pious, Calvinist Dutch world), swept out in clouds of dust to the cheers and cries of the women and old men they were leaving behind to fight and beat the British.

Their plan was simple, as befitted a force that was not a trained army. They would attack and beat the British before the greatest empire of the time could supply reinforcements from faraway England. With a bit of luck, they could capture the key towns they had already

selected and then make the British sue for peace. That was the plan. But it wouldn't turn out that way. There would be some swift and painless victories. But the quick war the Boer command envisaged would last three bloody years. It would cost Britain alone 22,000 dead and would have, as writer and war correspondent Rudyard Kipling wrote after it was all over, "taught the 'redcoats' who thought they were going to fight natives, armed with shields and spears," no end of a lesson.

For, as Lt.Reggie Kentish of the Royal Irish Fusiliers wrote to his parents one day after the Boers declared war, "I don't think the Boers will have a chance, although I expect there will be one or two stiff little shows here and there…I think they are awful idiots to fight, although we are, of course, very keen that they should."

But eager young Kentish who like most of his brother officers proclaimed in the Fusiliers' mess in the frontier town of Dundee "I know chaps, it's a little war, but it is the only war we have, what" was in for a great surprise. Then the first of those fierce Boer commandos was already riding over the frontier of British-held Natal state, its objective, Dundee.

Dundee, named by earlier Scottish settlers to the area, overshadowed by Mount Impati was normally a sleepy provincial town with little to distinguish it from such places in Southern Africa at the turn of the $19^{th}/20^{th}$ century. Now with the crisis threatening, it had been transformed. Now it was packed with 4,000 British infantry, including Lt Kentish's 2nd Dublin Fusiliers and a regiment of cavalry. Since Kruger had declared war on Britain the men of General Symons's infantry brigade had been expecting some sort of trouble. Clad in their drab khaki, passing their time with parades and drinking – naturally, tea, for the rank-and-file, the troops knew there might be a fight. Now and then some wag would point to the usually fog-shrouded Mountain and cry "there they are" in order to raise a laugh. But, in fact, the Boer attackers did not materialise and the troops and the local civilians were getting bored with waiting, exclaiming, "if only the Boers would buck up and do something."

At dawn on Friday 20th October the Boers arrived. Having a breakfast cup of tea inside his tent, Lt Maurice Crum of the 60th Rifles was disturbed by someone outside crying, "What's them blokes on that blooming hill, mates?" Suffering from a slight fever as he was, Crum was intrigued enough to reach for his sword and glasses and go outside. He gasped with shock at what he saw. Some two miles away there were hoards of horsemen, clad for the most part in what looked like civilian clothes, milling around as if they were wondering what they should do next. But the sick young officer didn't need to possess a crystal ball to guess what it would be. For with the horsemen, he could make out three field guns. The Boers had crossed the border of Natal to fight. It was six o' clock that morning and first real battle of the terrible, blood-soaked war to come was about to commence.

As the alarm sounded, the buglers blasting out the urgent notes over the sleepy little frontier town, with the infantrymen running hither and thither, tumbling into their fighting equipment, NCOs red-faced and seemingly angry, as they formed them into company files, the French guns bought by the Boers, opened up. The first real shell that screeched across the valley landed harmlessly in some marsh ground. The second hit the earth just behind the Dublin Fusiliers. That shell seemed to make the British officers aware that the Boers were really attacking. Swiftly the brigade's two batteries of 15 pounders were brought into action and the counter fire was started. But while the Boers' 75mm cannon could hit targets in Dundee, the British fire fell short of Lucas Meyer's Boer commando. It was going to be the same tale throughout the first stages of the new war.

Now General Symons in command of the British infantry, who had just studied the Boers though his telescope, gave out his orders. It was going to be an Aldershot set-piece, the kind of thing the regulars had carried out often enough in training back in the UK. Once the British artillery had ceased firing, the infantry would advance at a steady pace, company after company. On the order to do so, they would charge the mass of the Boers, while the cavalry wheeled round behind the enemy and tried to cut off any attempt to retreat. They had done it often enough on manoeuvres and when it was called for in reality against 'natives' armed with spears and shields, throughout the Empire. There was no reason, it seemed, why the same tactic should not succeed against the Boers, although they were white and carried modern Mauser rifles.

GENERAL SYMONS.

So the infantry marched to war. The Dublin Fusiliers first, the Rifles after them, with the Irish Fusiliers bringing up the rear. Civilians cheered them. Women threw hysterical fits. Kids called, "Good Luck, lads." Most of the men were short-term, green recruits, but they belonged to regiments that had faced the Boers before, some 20 years ago and had suffered defeat. Now they were going to avenge that defeat at the Battle of Majuba. As one infantry colonel called out to his soldiers about to begin the battle, "Remember Majuba, God and our Country. Forward Men, Over the top."

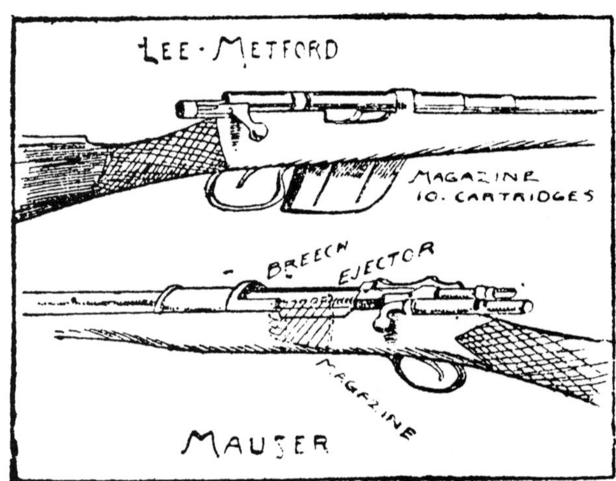

And over the top they went, straight into a hail of very accurate Boer fire. The attack started to bog down at once. NCOs swore, Officers waved their bright, flashing swords; Symons personally rode up, his adjutant carrying a clear target for Boers, a scarlet pennant. He rallied the men. Moments later he was hit. He didn't let his men see that he had been. Instead he got his ADC to put him on his horse. Bleeding heavily, he hung onto the saddle pommel, his ADC still carrying that damned scarlet pennant, which now seemed as if it had been dipped in blood. When he was out of sight down the hill, he collapsed and the Indian stretcher bearers carried him away to the hard-pressed doctors, now with their hands full with badly wounded and dying soldiers.

Now the infantry, a lot of them Irish, had their blood up. They were taking too many casualties and the Boers, on the high ground above them, had every advantage on their side. Still they climbed the hill, head down against the bullets as if fighting their way against violent and terrible wind. Captain Nugent told *The Times* correspondent what it was like for him. He had just climbed a wall when "I was hit for the first time…through the knee. The shock was as if someone had hit me full strength with a club. I spun round, my helmet flung one way, my pistol the other." He was hit again "by a bullet above my right leg and came out of my thigh." Still he continued to pull himself up by grass sods inch by inch. He was hit yet again in the spine, but finally managed to reach the top and found it deserted. The Boers had fled. The British had won. Then the brave, thrice-wounded captain collapsed....

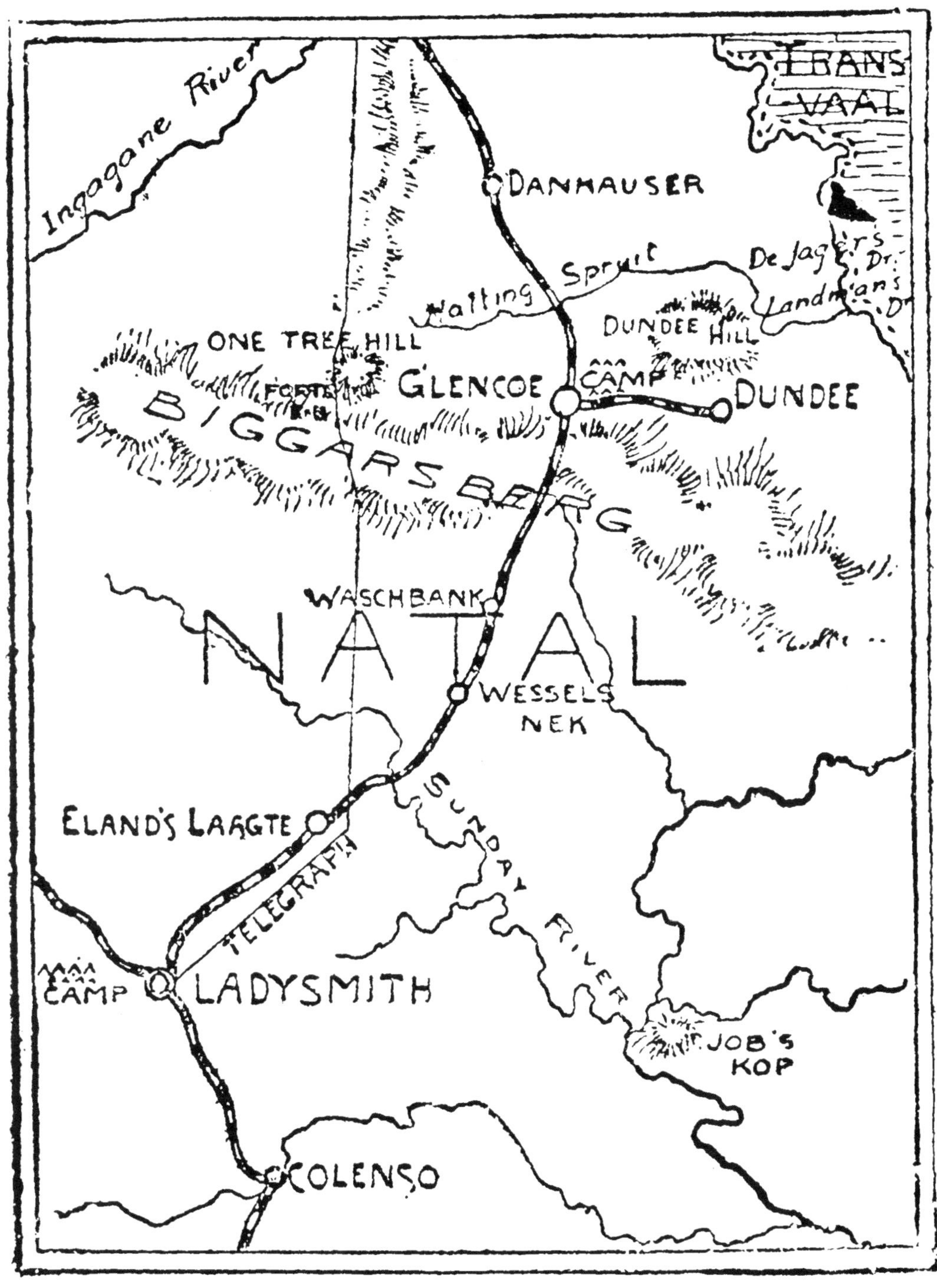

Yes, the Boers had gone and the field of blood remained in the hands of the victorious British infantry. But the price they had paid for the victory had been high. Two generals had been so badly wounded that they would die before the week was out. Each infantry battalion had had officers killed or wounded and there had been nearly 250 other casualties. As for the cavalry, sent to cut off any Boer retreat, they had vanished totally until it was announced several days later by the Boers that they had suffered disaster and had been forced to surrender to the Boers.

It was a bitter victory for the British. Now the Boer artillery had returned and was pounding the British infantry who lay huddled in their greatcoats on the freezing hillside waiting for the order to march again. But while the infantry on the hillside were relatively safe, their wounded comrades massed together in tents below were savagely shelled by the Boer 'Long Toms' as their heavy long-range French cannons were nicknamed. This, despite the fact that the field hospital, commanded by two exhausted Irish doctors, were clearly designated by the Red Cross flag.

But soon both the infantry and the wounded were going to gain some respite from that merciless pounding. For the new commander of the infantry brigade, a General Yule had decided to pull out, leaving the wounded to fend for themselves protected solely by the two brave Irish MOs. His infantry were to march back through the night and the following day to the nearest large-scale British outpost, another obscure provincial township like Dundee, but whose name would soon be famous throughout the British Empire. It was called Ladysmith.

Thus as the Boers started to enter an abandoned Dundee, their sole victory of any importance so far, Yule's men marched south-westwards. They were hungry, cold and footsore. Not the new Boer victors. They seized Dundee with glee, looting the abandoned British camp, the stores and naturally supplies of hard liquor they could find. For pious as they were supposed to be, they were very fond of the genever, that strong clear gin which they had brought with them from their native land of origin, Holland.

Yet, while the Boers celebrated, the retreating British infantry found few to welcome their arrival in Ladysmith. Indeed many were ashamed of them, as if they had personally let down "our dear old Queen." As war correspondent Nevison recorded, "They came back slowly, tired and disheartened and sick with useless losses...as soon as they were out of range, they wandered away in groups to town, sick and angry, but longing above all things for water and sleep." Sleep they would find easily. Water was a different matter. For Ladysmith was already under siege and water as well as every other supply would soon be rationed and men who stole essential foodstuffs etc would be shot or flogged to within an inch of their lives for doing so. It was as if the survivors of the debacle at Dundee had fallen out of the frying pan into the fire.

But although the Boers had won the initial battle for Ladysmith and now had some twenty camps of commandos surrounding the place, Joubert, the 68 year old overall Transvaal commander was hesitant to commit himself to an all-out attack on the besieged town. His spies told him that the British were suffering shortages and were apprehensive, yet their fighting morale was still high. That of his own troops was not. They had their victories but they had had their losses too and some of his civilians masquerading as soldiers were getting bored with the whole war. They wanted to go home to their families and farms and more and more of them were doing so without permission. Indeed he was losing men, who were going on leave and not returning, so rapidly that he cabled President Kruger for help.

Kruger, known as 'uncle' to his people in the Transvaal 'Afrikaans' language acted. Stubborn and dour as he was, he wanted to continue the fight come what may and thrash the British. He ordered that anyone found returned home without permission should be sent back to the front immediately – or imprisoned. Railways were ordered not to sell tickets to members of the commandos unless they had a bonafide leave pass from an officer. That didn't work well because the officers themselves were slipping away back to their farms without passes too.

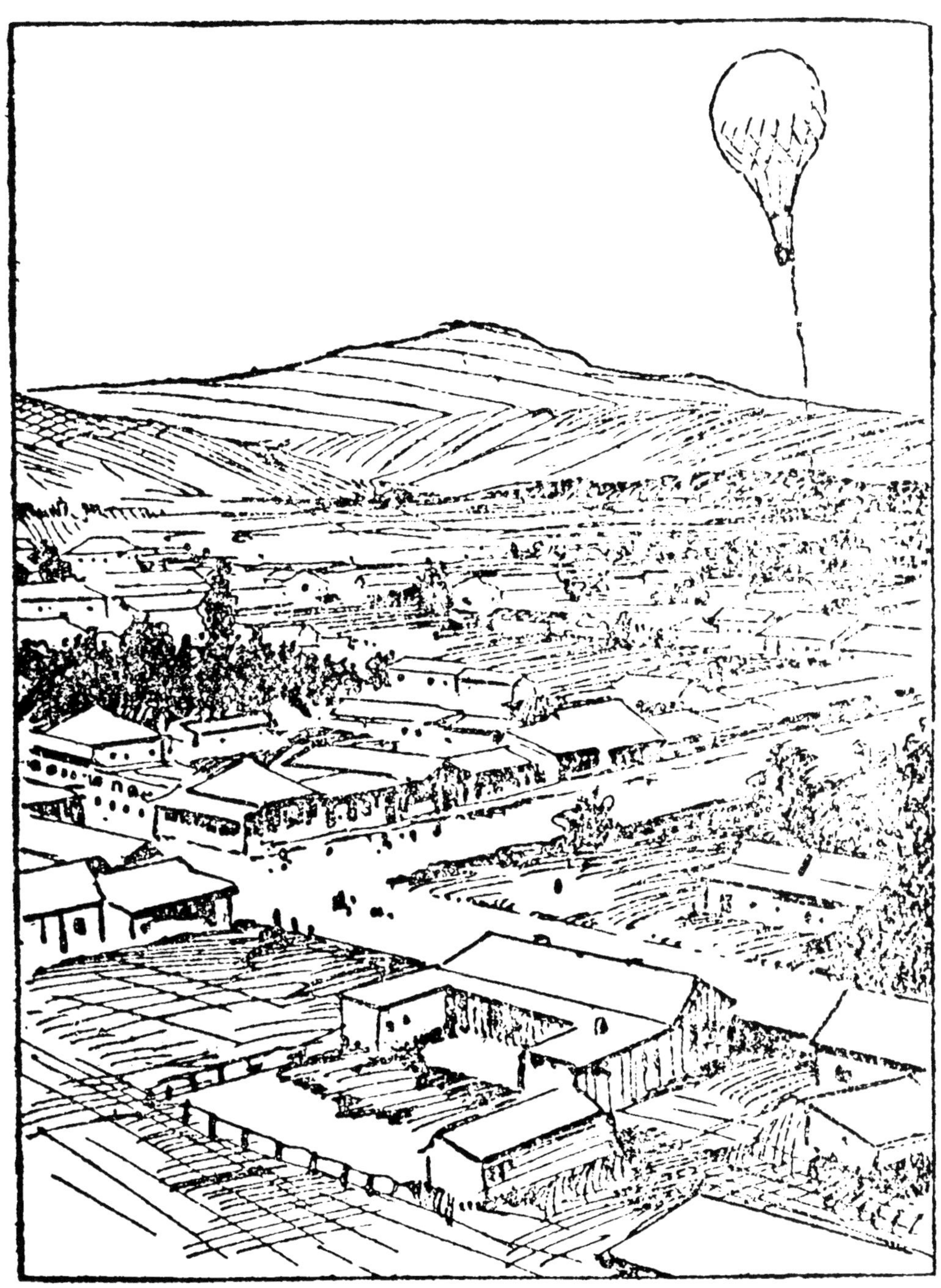

LADYSMITH.—GENERAL VIEW.

But it was not only the Transvaalers who were causing Joubert problems; their neighbours and allies, the men of the Orange Free State, were as well. They frankly refused to join in any out-and-out attack on the British in Ladysmith. Instead they wanted to sap the garrison's strength by depriving them of food, military supplies and reinforcements. They wanted to cut any remaining supply lines to Ladysmith and let the 'redcoats' wither on the vine.

PRESIDENT KRUGER.

At first the plan seemed to be succeeding when a worried Joubert gave in and let his troops divert their attentions to the surrounds of Ladysmith instead of the key township itself. In one spectacular coup they ambushed the armoured train which maintained the supply route into Ladysmith and indeed captured the whole length of the strategic railway. It was a coup that went round the world, especially as one of their prisoners was a young war correspondent and former officer of the British 4th Hussars of aristocratic lineage. His name was Winston Churchill!

But despite this success Joubert at 68, a worn and anxious commander at the best of times, was losing his nerve. He suffered a bad accident and seemed to have panicked. By now the British had two brigades of Sir Redvers Buller's Army Corps in the general area of that part of Natal and it was clear that the heavy-set British general, newly arrived in South Africa, was spoiling for a fight. Joubert made his decision. It was time to pull back, especially from the Ladysmith area as spies had reported that Buller intended a two-pronged attack to relieve the besieged township.

MR. WINSTON SPENCER CHURCHILL.

So the decision was made. Many of the hot-headed younger commandos were against it. All the same as irregular troops used to swift movement they didn't particularly like sitting in their trenches and 'dog holes' besieging towns like Ladysmith and the diamond centre of Kimberley. They pulled back and once they had reached the frontier of Natal with their own states prepared to meet the 'redcoats' once again (which they would). One of the newer commanders, who was taking over from a broken Joubert, Louis Botha, with a plentiful supply of forced black labour (one might even say slaves) at his disposal started building a massive defensive line along the Tugela River. Another who had opposed the war at first, de la Rey, also started building another defensive position along the line of the Moffer River. But de la Rey disdained the standard Boer tactic of digging in on the top of hillsides, the 'kopjes'. He believed that although these positions gave a good overview of the surrounding plains, they were easily isolated and open to enemy artillery fire.

GENERAL SIR REDVERS BULLER, V.C.

The Battle of the Modder River

So de la Rey formed his defensive line along the mud banks of the Modder, so close that his men in their trenches and 'dog holes' would not be visible till the enemy stumbled upon them. They then could slaughter the attackers at point blank range. But both these positions along the border rivers, the one on the heights and the other in the mud, were formidable. All the same Buller was determined to attack them. Thus, as the first year of the conflict started to come to an end, with the Boers defending the rivers waiting for the first cry of alarm, 'daar kom de Britische'*, Buller's force marched on the Modder commanded by General Lord Methuen.

*There come the British

Buller's men arrived along the river lines earlier than de la Rey had anticipated. But as soon as his mounted scouts informed them that the 'khakis' were on their way, he was confident that he could thrash them. Buller's men would walk straight into the trap and would be slaughtered by the hidden defenders of the Modder River. De la Rey however, was going to be let down by his own people. For the smaller and adjoining river, the Riet, was defended by a commando the British called 'a little black man', Andries Cronje, a hot-headed, general who hated the British and felt little better about his fellow Boer, de la Rey.

COMMANDANT CRONJE.

Now as the men of Britain's most elite regiment 1st Battalion Grenadier Guards of Buller's Guards Brigade came level with the hidden Boers, Cronje couldn't contain himself. With or without de la Rey's permission he was going to tackle this tempting target. For the British didn't seem to have a care in the world, it was as if the Boers were miles away. Indeed as the divisional commander Methuen wrote to his wife after the 'bloody slaughter', "I thought the enemy had cleared off, as did everyone else, whereas Kronje, de la Rey and 9,000 men were waiting for me in an awful position. I never saw a Boer but even at 2,000 yards, when I rode

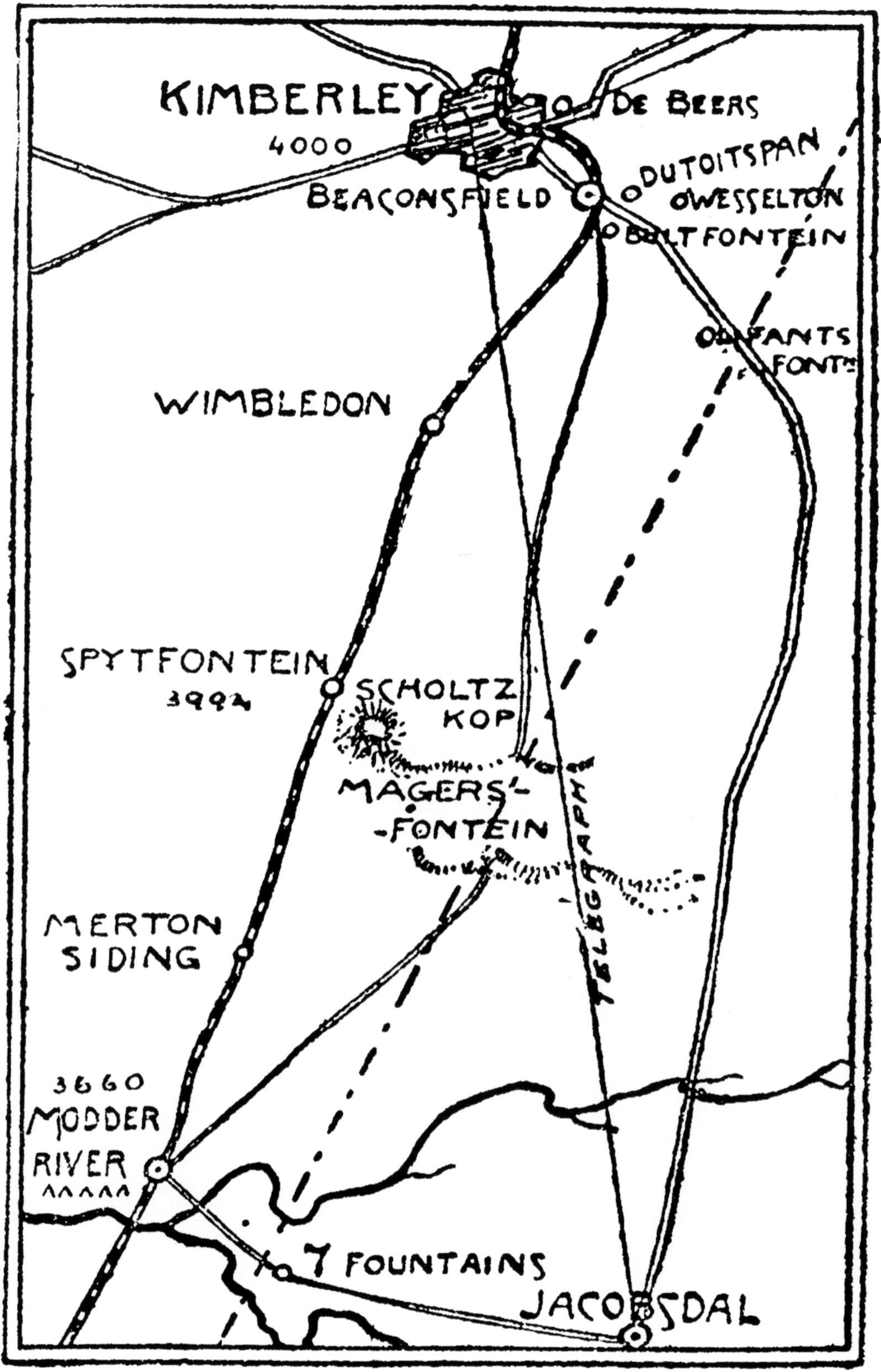
KIMBERLEY
4000
DE BEERS
DUTOITSPAN
BEACONSFIELD
WESSELTON
BULTFONTEIN
OLIFANTS FONTN
WIMBLEDON
SPYTFONTEIN
3992
SCHOLTZ KOP
MAGERS'-FONTEIN
TELEGRAPH
MERTON SIDING
3660
MODDER RIVER
7 FOUNTAINS
JACOBSDAL

a horse, I had a hail of bullets surround me. It seems like Dante's Inferno out of which we hope some day to emerge."

If it was 'Dante's Inferno, it wasn't that total one that an enraged de la Rey had envisaged for that December day. For contrary to their agreement, Cronje on seeing the Guards approach, had not been patient enough to allow them to march into the real trap, but had opened fire of his own accord and on the limited front of the River Riet.

The Guards went to ground immediately all the same. The Boers had more machine guns than they did. The Scots Guards had a single one for instance and it was knocked out almost at once. For hours most of the Guards lay on their bellies. Under intense fire, they dare not even move to take a sip from their water bottles. Parched with thirst, head tucked close to the earth as the bullets zipped over them in a lethal morse, they stuck it out taking casualties all the time. It looked even after Cronje had spoiled the grand surprise ambush, as if de la Rey was going to beat the 'khakis' after all.

THE BRITISH NAVAL GUN.

But the Boers had not reckoned with the well-trained British gunners. Now they took up the challenge. Twelve 15 pounders and four 12 pounders of the Naval artillery started firing over the prostrate infantry's heads. In essence they were trying to knock out the Boer artillery under Major Albrecht, a former sergeant in the Prussian Artillery. While the cannon roared and belched fire, on the right flank Cronje's men were being engaged by another British Brigade commanded by General Pole-Carew. The men of this brigade were darting forward in small rushes in small numbers, the best tactic for tackling dug-in positions. And they were pushing Cronje's Free Staters back. Soon they'd be fleeing for their lives and de la Rey started to fear that his flank would be turned and he'd have to order a general withdrawal or a fight to the death.

De la Rey's difficulties mounted. His son Adriaan was gravely wounded. Cronje's men were retreating, even fleeing everywhere. That night the two generals met on a road. Cronje asked, "How did the battle go?" Bitterly de la Rey asked his own question, "Why did you leave us in the lurch? We saw nothing of you all day." Cronje had no answer for that overwhelming question. One hour later Adriaan died in his father's arms and de la Rey knew that on the river line at least he had failed. If they were still going to win the Boers would have to develop new tactics.

On Sunday 9 December, General Andrew Wauchope, Commander of the Highland Brigade strode into General Methuen's HQ located in the Crown and Anchor Hotel on the Modder River. Two weeks before de la Rey and Cronje had frequented what was really a common pub themselves. Now the tall spare highland general of whom it was said he had been wounded in every battle in which he had participated, was there to receive orders from Methuen (he was just recovering from his wound at the Modder River). The Scots' orders were simple and not one bit to his liking. He was to take his Highlanders on a long night march and when they reached their objective (it was the Kopje at Magersfonein, to which the Boers had retreated from the Modder) they'd attack immediately. Still he returned to his Brigade. Here the men were busy concealing their tell-tale kilts with khaki aprons and covering their brass buttons and badges with mud.

LIEUT.-GENERAL LORD METHUEN.

At three that Sunday afternoon 3,500 Highlanders and five artillery batteries set off for the new battle in sleety rain. Their mood was sombre. At dusk they reached their target. Here despite the icy rain, they were told there'd be no fires and no smoking. It was cold beef sandwiches and water; not the ideal diet for a red-blooded Highlander preparing for combat.

Nine hours later at midnight they set off. It was a rough night. A thunderstorm raged and the files of wet infantry in their bedraggled kilts had difficulty keeping in touch. In the end the Black Watch, the Argylls, the Highland Light Infantry, kept together by means of ten foot long ropes, held by the left hand man of each file. So they went into battle like a lot of black slaves chained together by African slave dealers.

Not for long. The Black Watch were within 400 yards away from the hidden Boers when a single shot rang out. The Boers opened fire the very next instant. As one sergeant of the Argylls recorded later after the debacle, "It was as if someone had pressed a button and turned on a million electric lights."

Most of the Boer bullets went high. But that first intense volley caused nightmarish paralysis in the Black Watch. Someone ordered retirement. The withdrawal turned into a stampede. The officers tried to restore order but they were being shot down mercilessly by the Boers. Two infantry colonels were killed that night or stamped to the ground by their own men.

Order was soon restored but the damage was done. The Highlanders were definitely shaky now. The Scots were failing to push home their attack. Indeed some of them were hiding beneath bushes or actually raising their hands in surrender. More and more officers trying to restore order were wounded or killed. Britain's premier marquis Major Lord Winchester was only one of the men who succumbed that grim night and morning. Now Methuen could only hope that the Boers would retreat again. Next morning, however, as the British observers balloon rose to survey the battlefield, strewn with the bodies of the Highlanders in their grey-green kilts, thrown up obscenely to reveal their naked loins, it was clear the Boers were still in position. The British had lost yet another battle...

1900

The Battle of Spion Kop

In London they shivered in the first January snow. The mood of the Londoners was equally subdued and cold. For the last days of December 1899 were being called the 'black week'. For the invincible British Army had been defeated time and time again by a handful of farmers on horseback, the Boers, in far-off South Africa.

In South Africa it was mid-summer and the country, torn by war, was sweltering in a heat wave. Men were collapsing, even the Boers, in such temperatures as they campaigned in the parched, open veldt. The Boers were used to it, but the 'khakis' rushed out to fight them from England, who had little time to acclimatise, weren't. And water was in short supply. But regulars, many of whom, especially the Irish among them, had volunteered for the Army in order to escape poverty and be assured of three square meals a day, were accustomed to hardship. They fought on.

For General Buller, well admired among his men for being a fighting soldier, who tried to lead from the front, was determined to defeat the Boer whatever the weather and avenge the recent defeats of 'black week'. Thus it was that he now set about attacking Louis Botha's 'Tugela Position' and especially the height at Spion Kop (Spy Head) to the rear of Botha's defences. He was confident he could do it because the Boers were thin on the ground at certain key spots where he would break through and they had not fortified all the kopjes with their deadly cannons, as they usually did.

So on the morning of 24th January 1900 he sent in his infantry, most from the 'Diehards', the Middlesex Regiment (and they were going to live up to that traditional nickname this day, especially the dying part of it). Thus it was after some initial confusion with some of the British infantry about to surrender, their commander, big red-faced General Thorneycroft, ran up and shouted at the victorious Boers, "Tell your men to go to hell....I allow no surrender". Tamely enough the Boers did so and the British started to win. Now it was the Boers' turn to surrender or flee.

Just in sight of the twin peaks of Spion Kop the Middlesex charged. The Boer defenders were flung back and the key height was in British hands as Buller had planned. But the Boers reacted quickly as they usually did. They started to pour down a merciless fire in the 'Diehards'. Thorneycroft signalled back to his superior, "What reinforcements can you send to hold the hill tonight? We are badly in need of water. There are many killed and wounded."

The staff reacted immediately. The Scottish Rifles and the King's Royal Rifles were alerted to move up immediately. A diversion was planned to take the pressure off a hard-pressed Thorneycroft. More importantly the defending general needed heavy guns brought up to ward off the Boer counter-attack which would probably come on the dawn of the 25th.

Nothing seemed to work of the hastily drawn up relief plan save for one surprise. Former POW and war correspondent Winston Churchill* had now become a soldier once more. Against orders he led a troop of the South African Light Horse to the beleaguered twin peaks. Winston Churchill had fought at the great Battle of Omdurman but what he saw now shocked him more than the slaughter of the 'Fuzzy Wuzzies' in the Sudan. As he wrote later, "Men were staggering along alone, or supported by comrades or crawling on hands and knees...corpses lay here and there...the splinters and fragments (of the Boer artillery) had torn and mutilated them in the most ghastly manner. I passed about two hundred when I was climbing up...(but) the fighting was proceeding."

In reality it wasn't fighting, it was sheer bloody slaughter. Later when the Boers photographed the British trenches, the pictures showed packed dead, slaughtered in lines in their rocky scoops with hardly a space to fall down. To some observers it didn't look like the results of a battle but more like those of a cold-blooded massacre.

In the meantime Churchill made a second appearance in the firing line. He found Thorneycroft sitting on the ground among the dead of the regiment he had raised personally. He brought with him good news. The Navy with their heavy guns were on their way. But it was too late. After twelve hours under intense fire Thorneycroft seemed at the end of his tether, his nerve gone. He wanted to retreat. He told Churchill, "Better six good battalions down the hill than a bloody mop-up in the morning."

Some of his COs were shocked. They wanted to stay and fight. Thorneycroft was adamant. He overruled them. So the survivors started to pull back. As the moon rose they crept away leaving their seriously wounded behind them and 263 dead bodies of their comrades piled three deep. The Boers had won yet again. But they too were exhausted and although General Buller wouldn't survive this final defeat, he had gained the key to Ladysmith. From now onwards, the British would suffer minor defeats but the Boers' run of successes was over. Soon they'd be defeated and the 'khakis' would take a terrible revenge on them.

Now the new men took over in South Africa, both were Irishmen and both knew little about the modern British Army. Then the one Lord Roberts, known as 'Bobs' had served most of his military career in India, the other Field Marshal Kitchener had passed years in Egypt. Still both possessed an iron will, determined to make success out of failure in South Africa.

*The Boers accused Churchill of breaking his parole in order to escape.

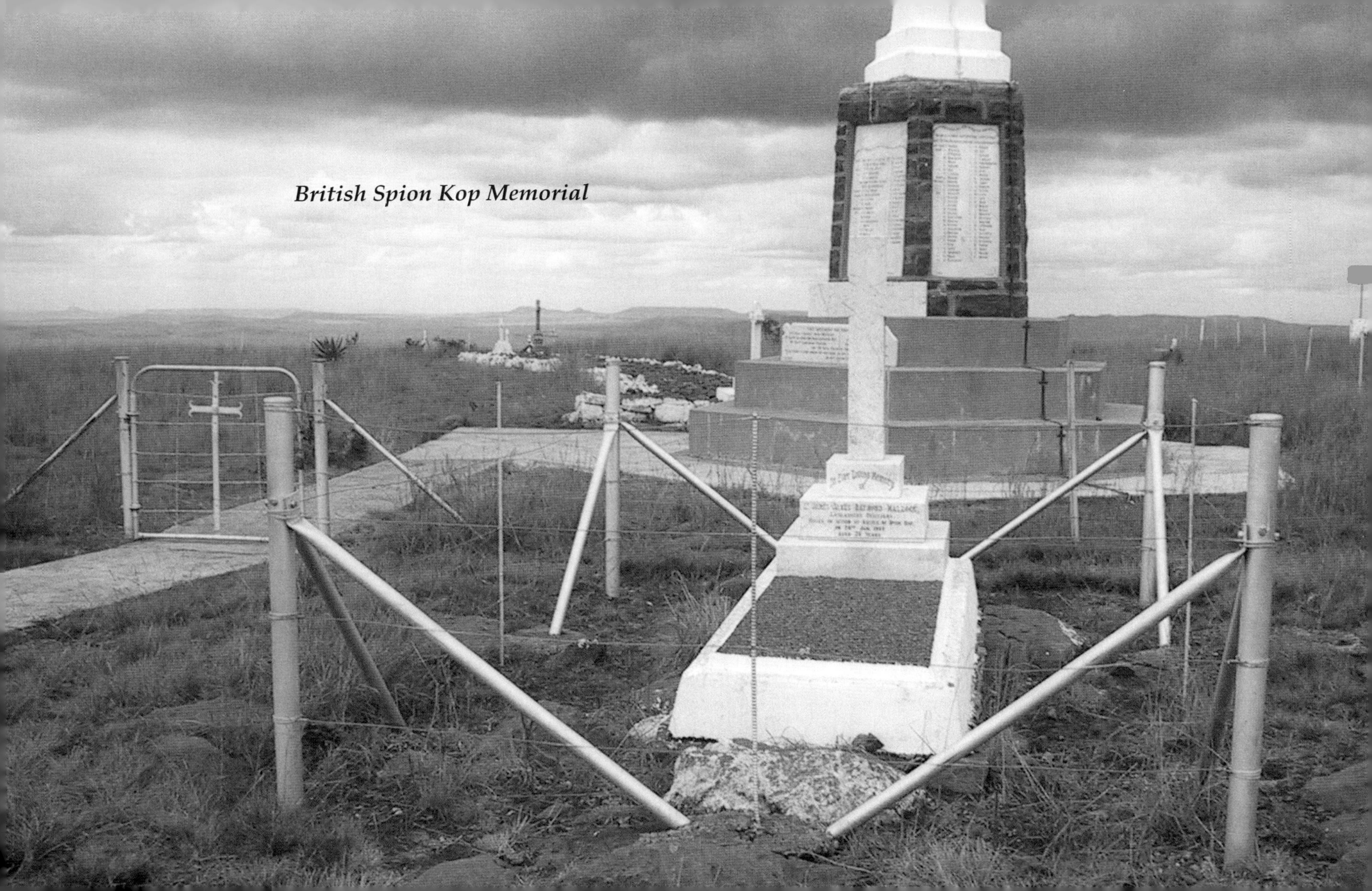

British Spion Kop Memorial

The Battle of Paardeberg

The British had their first success in the relief of Kimberley after a siege of 124 days. In the meanwhile 'Sepoy General' or 'Bobs' had journeyed personally to the front facing Cronje and his 5,000 Boers. He set up his HQ on the Riet River. Cronje pulled back. The Free Stater was losing his nerve. He was losing horses rapidly and running out of supplies. His nervousness spread to some of his men who knew the 'Khakis' had an army of 40,000 men in the field now. But some of his subordinates, in particular, curly-haired, heavily built de Wet were still determined to fight on.

On 15 February, the 'hawks' were still powerful enough to teach the British one final great lesson. Believing they were fighting some kind of 'native' troops with primitive weapons, Roberts and Kitchener pushed ahead vigorously at Paardeberg. They were going to use steam-roller tactics, lots of infantry and heavy artillery bombardments, not realising that Boer tactics were superior, relying very much on mobility. The 'rebels' would fight from cover, inflicting heavy casualties as long as they could on the attackers and then when their defensive positions became untenable, they'd mount their ponies and be off ready to fight another day.

Now Cronje retreated with some 4,000 of his Boers and then he turned and dug in, while the British waded the Modder at a place called Paardeberg. Here Cronje was waiting for the full British brigade which was going to attack. The men of the brigade, who had promised their commander they wouldn't shave off their beards until they had beaten the Boers, were hungry, worn and cut off from their supplies, but they attacked bravely enough all the same.

But they failed. They didn't manage to get closer than 300 yards from the Boer trenches. Instead they were cut down by rifle and artillery fire mercilessly. Indeed at the Battle of Paardeberg, the British in South Africa suffered their greatest losses of any day of the war; a total of 1,270, the equivalent of half a brigade. But it turned out to be a pyrrhic victory for Cronje. He and his men had been retreating under constant pressure from the 'khakis' for three days and although their losses had been low (de Wet had even been able to counter attack with 300 men), they were exhausted and totally dispirited.

The Battle of Bloemfontein

Now even de Wet decided he'd had enough. He left his position and some of his men surrendered as did Cronje with some 4,000 men and 50 women. It was the greatest victory for the British of the campaign. The Boers' luck was running out fast. Now it was the turn of the British. That 27th February 1900 when Cronje surrendered could be said to be the turning point of the war. One month after the surrender of Cronje and his men, the Free Staters secretly fled their own capital, Bloemfontein, a pretty place the British thought, which it should be with a name like 'Fountain of Flowers' (ie Bloemfontein in Afrikaans). The men who had once fought so stubbornly around Kimberley and Ladysmith, abandoned their own capital without even an apology for a fight. Their president Steyn just managed to escape by train

COLONEL BADEN-POWELL.

before Roberts' 'khakis' blew up the line.

De Wet still fought on. He had lost his homeland but not his courage and boldness. He besieged 1,900 fellow Afrikaner from Cape Colony at Wepener who had volunteered to serve against their fellow countrymen for five shillings a day in Brabant's Horse. But they proved a tough nut to crack even for de Wet. He abandoned the siege. Soon he would be a hunted man even in his own homeland.

In April, Mafaking, under siege for nearly a year and commanded by the strange soldier, Col Baden-Powell, who became famous after the war for his foundation of the Boy Scouts (some said much later that his youth movement was the role model in part for the Nazis' Hitler Youth), followed. The siege was finally lifted and the news flashed throughout the world. In London the aptly named 'Mafeking Night' was celebrated wildly. It was said that many of the children created that night, in and out of wedlock, lived to fight in another war some 40 years later, though most of them had long forgotten that 'little war' that had been instrumental in creating them.

The Battle of Diamond Hill

FIELD-MARSHAL LORD ROBERTS.

Diamond Hill followed in June. Called Donkerhoek by the Boers, it was just a modest success for the British. It succeeded for Roberts in that it drove off Botha's thrust to his flanks but it cost the lives of 180 British. It showed the Boers were not yet finished and gave Botha, De Wet and the other commando leaders who had the 8,000 Boers left fighting with them, new hope and breathing space. For now as guerrilla leaders from the states the Transvaal and the Free States (now annexed by the British) they were fighting a different war than before; they were virtual outlaws, whose own people, in the main part, wanted them to surrender so that peace could return.

As de Wet, who had been on the run for two months, expressed it, "Ah, many a time when I was forced to yield to the enemy, I felt so degraded that I could scarcely look a child in the face…Why did I run away? No one can guess the horror which overcame me when I had to retreat…But how could they make it again, outnumbered by twelve to one?"

The Battle of the Guerrillas

But victory on the battlefield didn't mean the end of the war. It would go on for another year. Many Boers fought on as feared guerrillas. In an attempt to cut the guerrillas and their leaders, such as de Wet from supplies, support and intelligence, the British burned farms, cordoned off the land and drove many families away from it to be interned in what became known as 'concentration camps' (a word which as we know became infamous in years to come). But in the end Kitchener's policy, for he in the main was responsible for the harsh treatment of the Boer civilians, proved to be counterproductive. The Boers fought in increased savagery and in some cases just as brutally as the British. Relieved of the necessity of being responsible for their families, they became a kind of outlaw, who concentrated solely on fighting, looting and destruction.

1902

Peace at Pretoria

On 31 May 1902 the Treaty of Vereeniging was signed. The Boers agreed at last to accept British Sovereignty. That Sunday night the Boer representatives who were rushed to Pretoria to sign what some declared was their 'death warrants' were met by Field Marshal Kitchener personally, who had fourteen years to live before he too was killed at sea in World War One. "We are good friends now" he declared to the dazed Boers upon whom he had inflicted so much suffering – and he really meant it.

As for the 'Tommies', those who had survived, some of them declared in old age, long after all the key British and Boer leaders were long dead, "It was a cruel war..we were half starved…never saw the point of it…Johnny Boer, he used to shoot blacks like you'd shoot a dog…it was all for the gold mines."

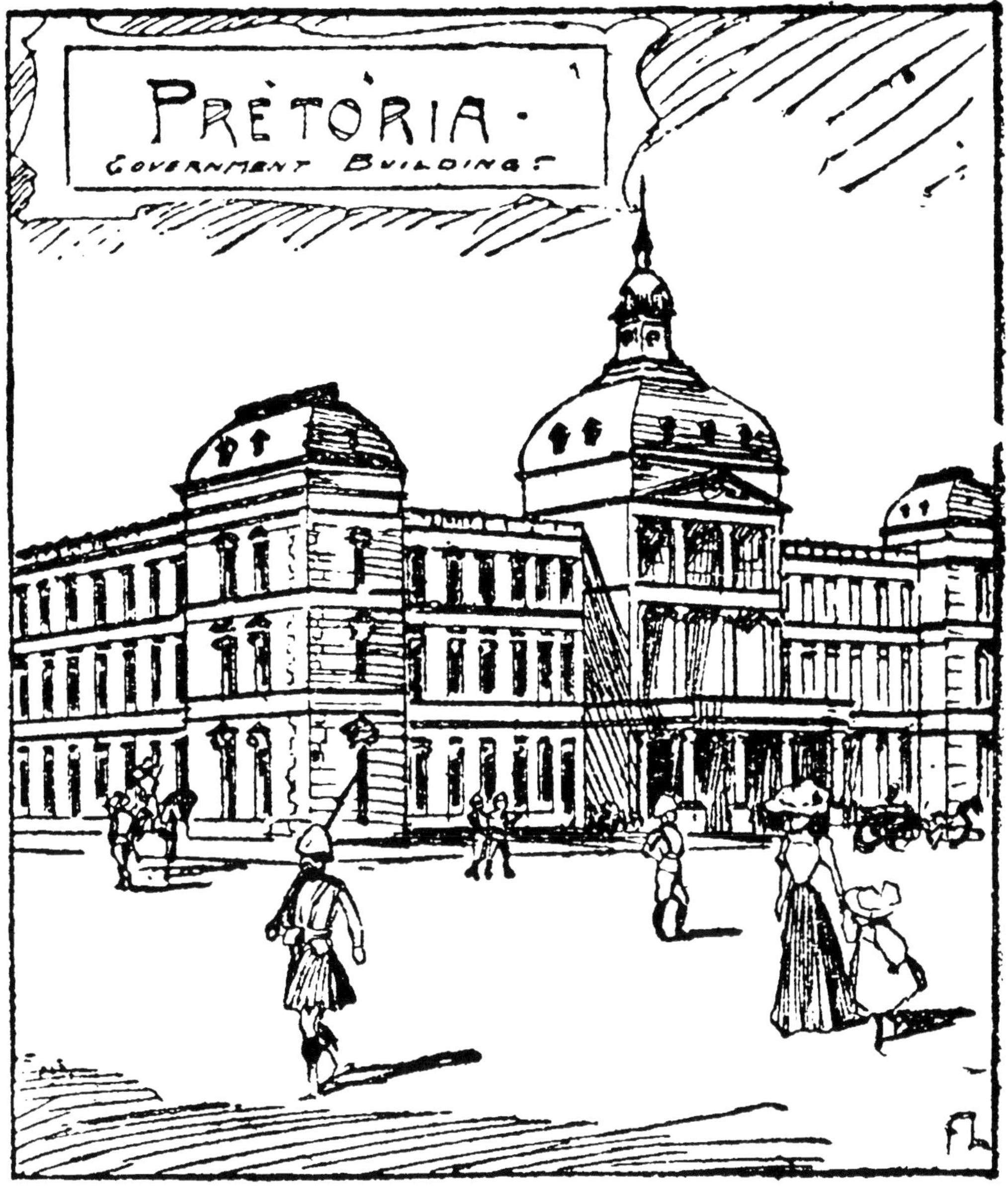

So the 'Tommies' returned home, some to their native North Yorkshire. They had marched away to the strains of 'Goodbye Dolly Gray' played by military bands, cheered by the 'civvies' they were leaving behind, filled with a sense of adventure and a feeling of patriotism. They came back, older and wiser men, still proud of themselves for having gone but perhaps a little cynical. Some would fight and not survive the 'Great War' to come. The survivors would live through the 20s and 30s proudly wearing their fancy uniforms, with great broad brimmed cowboy hats and leather jack boots, clinking with chain epaulettes and medals on 'Empire Sundays' and when the next war came they'd join the Home Guard. In due course the media would make fun of them as 'Colonel Blimps' fighting the war before last. Then they would be dead **And** forgotten....

Charles Whiting

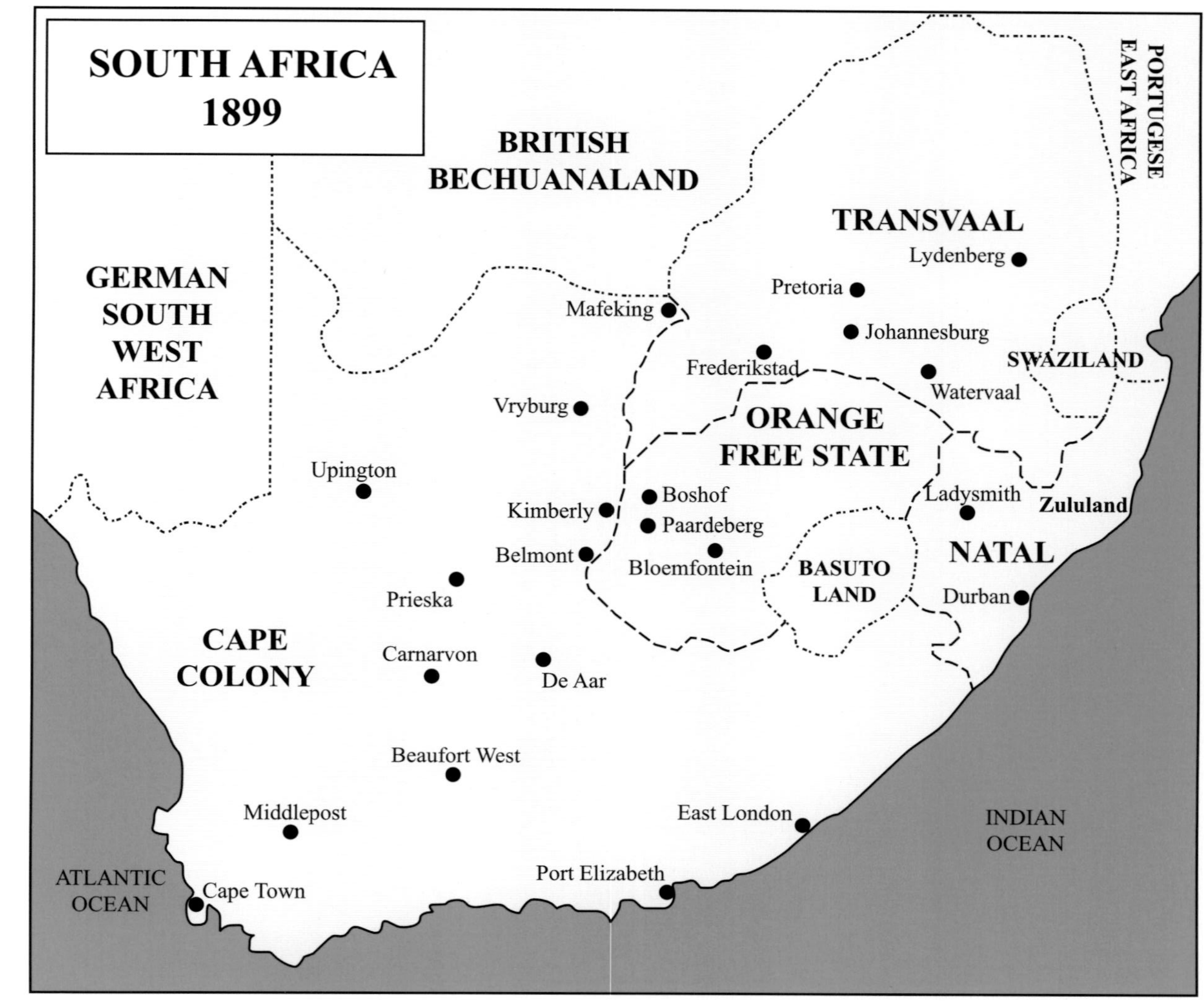
SOUTH AFRICA
1899
BRITISH
BECHUANALAND
GERMAN
SOUTH
WEST
AFRICA
PORTUGESE
EAST AFRICA
TRANSVAAL
Lydenberg
Pretoria
Mafeking
Johannesburg
Frederikstad
SWAZILAND
Watervaal
Vryburg
ORANGE
FREE STATE
Upington
Boshof
Kimberly
Paardeberg
Ladysmith
Zululand
Belmont
Bloemfontein
BASUTO
LAND
NATAL
Prieska
Durban
CAPE
COLONY
Carnarvon
De Aar
Beaufort West
Middlepost
East London
INDIAN
OCEAN
ATLANTIC
OCEAN
Port Elizabeth
Cape Town

Chapter 9

GATACRE AND BOOCOCK

The sending of family letters to the press, was a common practice in the Boer War, and some editors asked families to send in their correspondence as space was devoted to them. There is no record of Reginald Ernest Smith doing so, but early in 1900 a soldier from Brandsby got some wide coverage in the *Advertiser.* His first appearance took up over eight column inches.[1]

FROM THE FRONT

The following is a letter received from the son of Mr J. S. Boocock, Brandsby, who is a trooper in the C.M.R. [Cape Mounted Rifles] Artillery now stationed at the Pen Hock, Sterkstroom:–

Pen Hock, Sterkstroom
January 8th, 1900

"We are all in the best of health. We have just come back from a five days patrol to Dordrecht. We left here with 4 guns (two being left behind to guard the Hock), and an escort of C.M.R. and Brabant's Horse. We arrived in Dordrecht the same night. By the way we had an awful hailstorm that day; the hailstones being quite as large are pigeon's eggs. The horses nearly went mad with fright and pain combined. Luckily we were near a farm house at the time, and got behind some trees, but they did hurt. I never saw anything like it before. It rained the first night we reached Dordrecht, and all the following day. The next day Montmorency went out with a patrol to try and locate the Boers. He found them in laager about 5 miles from Dordrecht, and after skirmishing, for some time 25 of our men were surrounded by the enemy in a donga (ravine). Montmorency went into camp for reinforcements, and every man was sent out except us (Artillery), but it grew dark and they had to retire to camp, the Boers firing at them with a 12 pounder, That night we hardly slept a wink. They woke us at 1 a.m. and we ran the guns forward into position. Everyone expected they would try and attack us for we were only 250 strong, and they were anything from 800 upwards. They did not come through and we left camp at daybreak, and went in the direction of the laager. We got there and shelled the side of the hill while the mounted infantry skirmished up and rescued the men in the donga. They were all right except two men who were wounded in the thigh and the hand. They were in the donga from 1 p.m. one day until 5 a.m. the following day. The Boers were on three sides of them, and though they were only 25 they kept them at bay. All their horses were simply riddled with bullets and they in turn shot several of the Boer horses and several Boers. When we retired the Boers opened fire on us with their 12 pounders, but luckily their shells did not burst and no one was hurt. We met General Gatacre at a place called Bird's River, and he spoke to us and said that he was very pleased with us. Colonel Dalgettey with about 400 C.M.R. is at Bird's River guarding the road from Dordrecht. You asked in your last letter how to pronounce Mafeking. It is Maf-e-king with the accent on the last syllable. There are no trees in this part of the country, and so we have nothing but cow dung for fuel. All the farmers who live in this part of the country use nothing else, they cut it out of the cattle kraals (a cattle kraal is the enclosure where the cattle are penned up at night) in square blocks and stack it up as we do peat at home, it makes splendid fuel. I saw a covey of 6 partridges this morning. We have had very showery weather lately with a good deal of thunder. Five of us are sleeping under a waggon, our tent having gone astray somewhere. We have pulled the waggon sail over and made a fine house – I prefer it to a tent as you have more room. The Boers shelled

Memorial to the Colonial Division at Wepener.
Gunner Boocock from Brandsby served here with the Cape Mounted Rifles (Artillery)

Cyphergatt and Molteno the day before yesterday. We heard the firing from here (about 12 noon, I would say across country). Our troops went out with field batteries and drove them back. There were no casualties.

Another letter appeared from Boocock towards the end of June, about six weeks after it had been written.[2]

Boocock's letters are crammed full of information, which give a vivid impression of some aspects of the fighting in South Africa in the first half of 1900. There are some references in the first, however, which, perhaps, ought to be explained (soldiers always seemed to delight in using local expressions and place-names that could have caused problems in places like Brandsby. CMR, was an abbreviation for Cape Mounted Rifles, and Sterkstroom can be found on modern maps to the west of the national road running from East London to Bloemfontein in the Eastern cape – then Basutoland. It is north of Queenstown, and on the eastern side of the N6 is Dordrecht. Molteno lies not far away to the west. Dordrecht, like Dundee further north, was on a short branch line, which connected with the main railway, which ran from East London north to Bloemfontein). The Trooper explained some of the Boer names like donga for his parents. *The Easingwold Advertiser* did more. It produced A PHONETIC SUMMARY OF SOUTH AFRICAN NAMES AND PLACES for its readers.[3]

AFRIKANDER (Aff-ry-Kaner). – A white man born in South Africa of European stock.
BERG. – A hill.
BILTONG. – Strips of dried meat, used by Boers as provender on the veldt.
COMMANDO (Com-man-do). – An irregular regiment of Boers.
COMMANDANT (Com-man-dant) – The chief officer of a commando.
DONGA (Dong-gah). – A deep ditch or waterhole with steep sides, a gaping crack in the ground.
DORP. – A village.
DRIFT. – A ford through a river.
KLOOF. – A declivity or ravine on a mountain.
KOPJES (Koppies). – Small hills or boulders, or any rising ground of small dimensions.
KRANTZ (Krants). – A valley, or cleft between two hills.
LAAGER (Larger). – Boer method of forming a camp; waggons placed end to end, forming an oblong enclosure.
NEK (Neck). – The saddle connecting two hills.
ROOINEK (Roynek). – Red neck. Boer nickname for Englishman.
SPRUIT (Sproot). – A small river or stream.

Trooper Boocock's first published letter mentions a famous British general who had only recently arrived in South Africa, and whose first foray was disastrous. Sir William Forbes Gatacre was born in 1843 and entered the Army in 1862. Between 1875 and '79 he was Instructor of Military Surveying at the Royal Military College, then was 'Deputy Adjutant and Q.M.G. with the Hazara Expedition, 1888; served in Burma, 1889, Chitral, 1895, Soudan, 1898, and commanded the British Division at the battle of Khartoum; in command of South-Eastern District, 1898; appointed to command the 3rd Division South Africa, with rank of Lieut-General, October 1899.' He had a well deserved reputation for being a difficult customer, and on 8 November arrived in Cape Town to be told of the British reverses in Natal, and the retreat into Ladysmith.[4] He was regarded as sure to make his mark on the

From Billy Holmes archive, encampment on the Veldt

South African campaign, and he did – but not quite in the way Leo Amery had had in mind.[5]

The British were about to go on the offensive, and Gatacre was in command of what came to be called the 'Central Front', the area where Trooper Boocock was. The Free Staters had stormed across the border and taken Stormberg Junction on the East London railway. Gatacre was seriously undermanned, but got some reinforcements by the beginning of December, and decided to retake it.[6]

> From Queenstown it is reported that the enemy re-occupied Stormberg on Sunday morning, and that General Gatacre was to begin his advance to the front on Monday. Meantime reinforcements were reaching him.

The week after that report was issued, a brief note appeared in the communiqués saying that Gatacre's progress was delayed, the reason being that a 'far larger force' opposed him than the British had been aware of,[7] and the following week the news was really grim. There had been a disaster. The steam roller, which Amery had said was to roll over South Africa, had been well and truly halted. *The Morning Post,* using the first despatch from the area, said what had happened. Gatacre and his troops left Putters Kraal by train, and detrained at Molteno. They then made a forced march of a dozen miles against the Boer positions above Stormberg. The Boers allowed the British to advance unmolested, then 'The engagement began at 4.15 a.m. on Sunday,[8] and lasted till seven, when, after an artillery duel, our men withdrew and marched back to Molteno.' The official announcements made dismal reading. Gatacre had to make what amounted to a public confession. Not only had he underestimated the strength if the enemy, but he was let down as well.

OFFICIAL ANNOUNCEMENT

The following telegrams from the General, Cape Town, dated December 10, have been received at the War Office.

(1) Following from Gateacre this morning:

Deeply regret to inform you that I have met with serious reverse in attack this morning on Stormberg.

I was misled to enemy's position by guides, and found impracticable ground.

Later, among the same day's reports from South Africa, some further information appeared:

THE STORMBERG REBUFF

The *Times* special correspondent at Molteno, sent under Sunday's date, some further details with respect to General Gatacre's forces which attacked the Boer position at Stormberg. He says that the total number of men engaged on our side was about 2500. Owing to errors by the guides and other accidents, the attack was delivered against the wrong part of the position, where the hill was quite impregnable. The troops were obliged to retire, which they did in admirable order, but, being fatigued by a long night march and subjected to a constant shell fire from the heights, they got into disorder. The artillery occupied successive positions throughout the retirement, averting a disaster. A Pretoria telegram stated that 672 prisoners were taken at Stormberg.

A modern writer has stated that the figure for men missing and captured in the Stormberg fighting was actually 696,[9] and a contemporary report said that the whole ghastly business was made worse by friendly fire – the British artillery shelling its own troops. A letter published in the *Advertiser* on 20 January described it.

GENERAL GATACRE'S DISTRESS

Writing from Queenstown, Cape Colony, a former member of the staff of a Scarborough newspaper says:

"When the wounded arrived at night we learnt something of what had happened. The guide had misled the troops right into the jaws of death. Then another mistake was made. When he saw the hot corner they were in, the General ... ordered a retreat, and they were doing so in good order when a terrible mishap occurred. Our artillery mistook the columns for the enemy and commenced a disastrous sheet-fire, and between that and the Boer rifles our men lost heavily. One shell is said to have killed and wounded the Colonel and two Majors of the Royal Irish. After being extricated from this position the retreat was carried out, the enemy following for seven miles. Every man one speaks to cannot explain why they were not all shot. It is a horrible muddle and yet one cannot help pitying Gatacre's distress of mind. A gentleman told me he was to be seen lying with his head in his hands on the table at Molteno Station. The last artillery we had here belonged to His Majesty's ship, Powerful, but they were suddenly ordered to join Methuen's column. A day or two before they went I witnessed a cricket match between the officers and the local club and had the pleasure of seeing Commander Ethelston and Major Plumber make the two highest scores, and then a day or two afterwards both these gallant fellows were killed. The Dutch parson here has been saying that the Boers want as many prisoners as possible so that they may place them in the centre of Pretoria, in order to prevent the British shelling of the town. Not a bad idea, is it? What about the siege train in that case?"

Gatacre was eventually replaced as commander of the 3rd division by Lt General H.C. Chermside, and a report of his arrival back in England appeared in the *Advertiser* of 19 May 1900. Surprisingly, he was dealt with at the start with great leniency by the British press, with the papers tending to run stories about his eccentric behaviour. For example, there was what was called an 'extremely good story' about him foxhunting in the *Daily News,* on 10 May 1900. It seems to have been frequently reported.

When details of Gatacre's South African engagement appeared a catalogue of ghastly series of mistakes was revealed. The train journey to Molteno took two hours longer than planned and there was a delay at Bushman's Hoek, which should have been avoided. As a result the three-hour rest the men were promised before they set off on their night march was cut down to one. A telegram telling a force of Brabant's Horse at Penhoek to arrange a meeting with Gatacre was not sent, and a wrong turning was taken just north of Molteno. Near Stormberg Junction, guides mistook the route and caused Gatacre's men to march 18 instead of nine miles, and end up on the Boer right rear instead of his right front. Then suddenly a ferocious fire was opened on them. Some artillery pieces were lost, and then the order to retreat was given, with the two remaining gun batteries covering the retreat. Almost 30 hours after they set out the survivors got back to Molteno. Gatacre decided not to stay there and fell back to Bushman's Hoek, where he established his headquarters.

When the stories of the Stormberg disaster became known to the public, there was a change of attitude towards the commander. The sympathy shown to him when he first returned went, to be replaced by severe condemnation. One of his critics was Lord Durham, who made a vitriolic speech reported as follows. He was quick off the mark. 'Stormberg' took place on 9/10 December, and his Lordship spoke on the 11.[10]

From Billy Holmes archive, target practice

CONDEMNING GENERAL GATEACRE

Lord Durham, speaking at his Christmas fat stock sale at Bowes House on Monday, said the news that had been received about the reverse to General Gateacre was, to his mind, about the most grievous event in the whole history of the war. He was not one to kick those in misfortune, but he must say, and he said it deliberately, that he did not think General Gateacre should have had a command in South Africa.

Certainly Gateacre was a brave man but Lord Durham then outlined his views on the General's lack of ability and wished to state that the War Office had been to blame for appointing him. General Gateacre blamed the guides, but would a boy of 13 or 14 have been so foolish as to trust in guides who had proved themselves lying and deceitful men? He was sorry to make that attack, but the country had shown such patience and such calmness during the war that it was right that they should express their opinion to those who were responsible for its conduct. The War Office should give them a proper explanation.

His lordship's remarks were loudly cheered.

It is generally said that the troops did not condemn Gatacre for the Stormberg disaster, and there was no criticism of him from Trooper Boocock. It is by no means clear that he was in that awful battle, but it is more than likely that he was. He was certainly involved in actions thereafter, as he described in his letter of 5 January. What did the published dispatches say about the period? Very little, it must be said.[11]

> A Reuter dispatch... December 25, says a quiet Christmas was spent in General Gatacre's camp. At Molteno, which was visited by the armoured train, there were no signs of the enemy, but they were understood to have been greatly reinforced at Stormberg, where they continue to strengthen their intrenchments.

There was nothing in the dispatches about the expedition described by Boocock, but there was something about some summary justice said to have been meted out by Gatacre on his incompetent guide.[12]

HOW GATEACRE SHOT THE GUIDE

The statement that General Gateacre shot the treacherous guide who led him into a Boer ambush at Stormberg is confirmed in a letter received at Coventry from a gunner of the 77th Battery. He says: "When the General saw the trap we were in, he ordered us to retire, and take a different position. Then he went straight up to the guide, and shot him on the spot. Our battery got out of their deadly fire with the loss of one man and the major wounded. One of our lieutenants had a bullet pass through his water bottle without injuring him."

Another soldier in the 4th Royal Irish Rifles writing to his wife in Belfast, says that when General Gateacre saw what the guide had done, he shot him on the spot with his revolver.

Gatacre endured some enforced idleness, then undertook a 'reconnaissance' in force towards Stormberg. During this 'De Montmorency's Scouts' were severely mauled and de Montmorency himself – mentioned by Trooper Boocock – was killed.[13] The reporter of the incident revealed alarm about Gatacre. 'It is to be hoped,' he said, 'that the British General... is not going to take his forces once more against a stone wall.' A little later Gatacre's forces became very active, and he advanced towards and took Springfontein, in the Free State.[14] He also made for Stormberg and he and Brabant poised to take it.

Where exactly Trooper Boocock was on the Gatacre central front is not absolutely clear, but in his second letter home he mentioned the town of Wepener. This is to the east of the railway line to Bloemfontein, near the Basutoland border. The Boers had invested the place, but on 16 April the siege was lifted and they went into a full retreat in a north-north-easterly direction.[15]

> In their anxiety to escape, they are hugging the Basutoland border as closely as possible, and will probably pass east of Ladybrand.
> The Basutos are marching parallel with them along the frontier, and watching eagerly for even the slightest encroachment.

The place most frequently talked about, as a major objective for those engaged on the central front was Bloemfontein the capital city of the Orange Free State. It fell on 13 March to forces controlled by Lord Roberts, when the Boers simply fled in an extraordinary – and unexpected – episode. 'Those men who had fought so stubbornly to hold their trenches in British territory around Kimberley, abandoned [them] without even an apology for a fight. The result was something of an anticlimax.'[16]

Readers of the Easingwold paper might have read a tiny note saying that General French had reached the outskirts of Bloemfontein, and that Roberts had ordered him to seize the railway station, but had been told that French had met with 'considerable opposition'.[17] It looked as if there might be a serious fight, then in the next issue came news of that extraordinary Boer collapse. Major Aylmer Gould Hunter-Weston[18] had seized the Bloemfontein rolling stock after French had occupied the complex south of the town, and contributed greatly to the Boers' problems, inhibiting a relief expedition alleged to be on its way.

While Roberts and French were taking the Free State capital, Gatacre was going north and receiving plaudits. 'General Gatacre is conducting his operations with great energy, and does not let the grass grow under his feet,' a communiqué said, adding that his scouts had taken the railway junction of Springfontein.'[19] It looked as if he was about to rehabilitate himself, but it was not to be. His next venture was to be his last, and was much like a re-run of Stormberg.

A small British force was falling back from Dewetsdorp to Reddersburg, two places south of Bloemfontein. The Boers (under General Christian De Wet) shadowed them, then surrounded them. Appeals for help (which was available) yielded nothing. Eventually the British showed the white flag, and Gatacre was sacked. The *Dictionary of National Biography* summarised the events that led to what some might regard as Gatacre's delayed departure for home: 'Known as "General Backaches" [he] … occupied Dewetsdorp and sent detachment on to Reddersburg; detachment surrounded and surrendered owing to Gatacre's failure to relieve it (April); relieved from command.'[20]

The second Gatacre disaster took place on 4 April, and it introduced more names and personalities to the British newspaper reader. Many of them are mentioned in Boocock's letter – Thaba N'chu, the Jummersberg Drift, Mozar's Hoek and Bethanie, for example. And Wepener.

The Boers were expected to attack the railway line ('the all-important line of communication upon which the very existence of the Army at Bloemfontein depended') but they confused the British by demonstrating what Wilson called a lamentable 'want of strategic insight' and went for Wepener instead. This place lies some 80 miles north of Aliwal on the eastern confine of the Free State and close to the Johannesburg Drift, where there was an important bridge over the river Caledon. Wepener was occupied from 29 March by a British force, some 1600 strong, under Col Dalgety.[21] It consisted of detachments of the 1st and 2nd Brabants, the Cape Mounted Rifles, Kafrarian Rifles and Driscoll's Scouts. There were also engineers and artillery forces.

A siege began on 9 April. An attack of that day was repulsed and the area settled down to something like trench fighting, with the beseigers sapping towards Dalgety's lines. Food began to run out, and dysentery affected the garrison. Then news of a relief was received by heliograph. The enemy was said to be 7,000 strong, and on 21 April the Dalgety forces were shelled by ten 'Boer guns and "Pom-Poms",' then attacked. But the attack fizzled out ('Never was there a more complete and miserable fiasco') and three days later the Boers retreated. 'Thus ended a memorable defence.' Trooper Boocock described it in a long letter.[22]

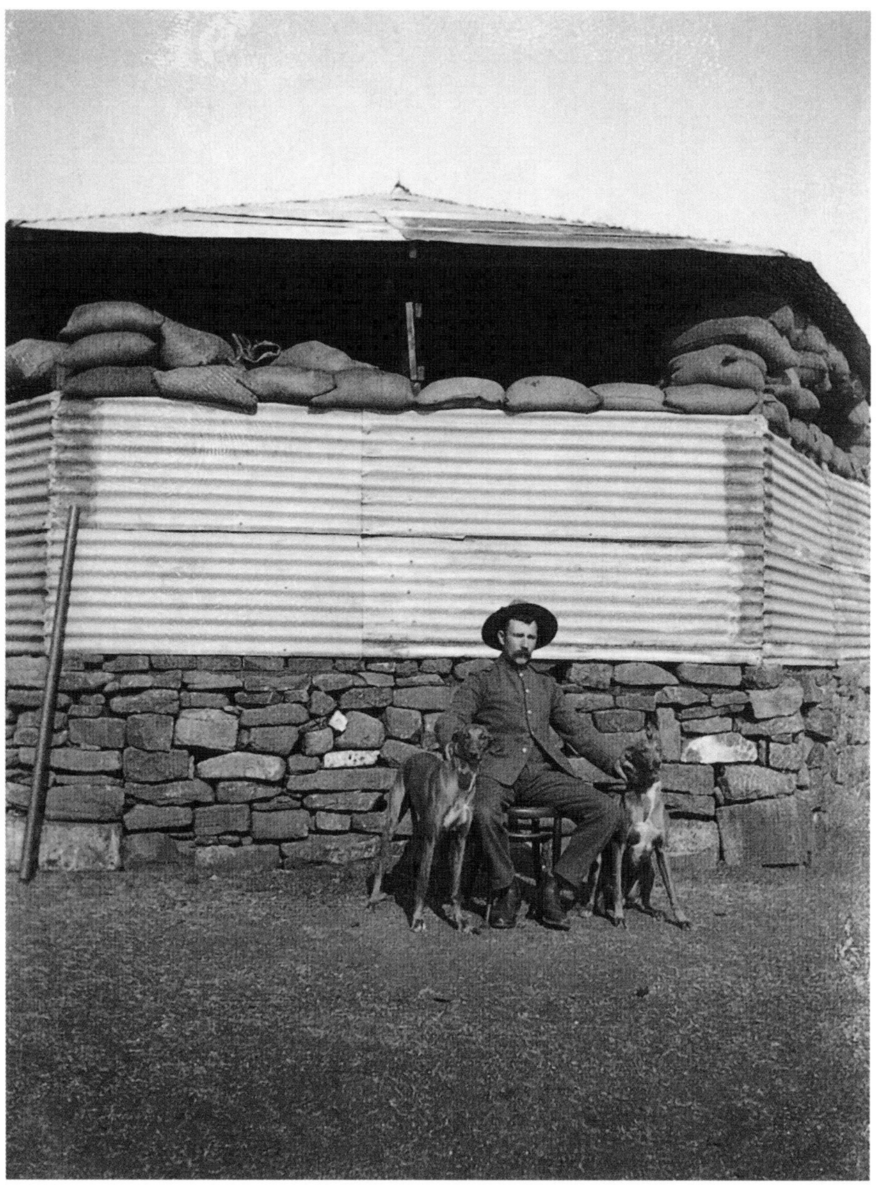

From Billy Holmes archive, block house

FROM THE FRONT

The following is a letter received from the son of Mr J S Boocock, Brandsby, who is a trooper in the C.M.R. Artillery.

General Brabant's Camp
About 20 miles to the East of Thaba Nchu.
May 12th, 1900

We are having a day's rest and I hear that a post is going out to-night so I will try and send you an account of the fight at Wepener. We left Aliwal on the 1st of April, and went through Rouxville to Bushman's Kop to Wepener. The last 32 miles we did in one day, leaving the waggons behind for we heard that the Boers were surrounding that portion of our Division that went on before us. When we got there on Friday the 6th, we found that the Boers had not attacked them but had sent in a messenger telling them to surrender. We took up our position on the Saturday and put the guns into pits. Our position was like an arc of a circle, the chord of the arc being the Caledon River. We had 2 fifteen pounders, 2 sevens, 2 naval 1 pounders, and one Hotchkiss (12 pounder quick firer). We were about 2,000 strong all told. The attack began on Monday morning (the 9th) about 6 o'clock. We had expected the attack, and everybody stood to the trenches two hours before day-break. The Boers began shelling us from a flat topped kopje on our left front and then from our right front and then the pom-pom began on the left. The main attack was on the Cape Mounted Rifle's trenches and raged throughout the day but our fellows held their own although we lost heavily. You see the Cape Mounted Rifles' side was the weakest part of the position. The Boers had guns all round us. The first day they brought eight guns into action and after that they kept putting them into new positions and bringing fresh ones up. After the first day they put two guns on top of the Jammersburg, a big mountain on the Basutoland border from where they could command the whole position. Day after day it was the same, our guns keeping down the fire of the enemy's guns as much as possible and yet husbanding the ammunition for we had but little. The enemy made three separate night attacks, and were beaten off each time. The first one was the worst which happened on the second night. It was on the Cape Mounted Rifles' trenches and began about 9 p.m. and lasted till nearly three in the morning. We were up all day and then at night perhaps at work building up the gun-pits where they had been knocked down by the enemy's shells during the day, or building new ones, and shifting the guns into them. The worst part of the whole affair was the rain. For five days it rained intermittently and the trenches and gun-pits were knee deep in water. You see there was no leaving the trenches or gun-pits either day or night. All day you dare not lift your head and in the night you dare not stand up for the sniping was something frightful. You see it was as light as day during the first 10 nights or so, and they used to snipe the whole night through. The moment you showed yourself against the skyline you would get a shower of bullets. The sentries had to lie down behind schanzes of stone. The Boers never shelled us on a Sunday, but the sniping went on just the same. We expected reinforcements after the first week but none came. About the 13th day of the siege we heard firing at Bushman's Kop and again on the 15th day. On the 25th day of April the Boers cleared and we fired at them as they were retreating northward. They had sent a commando to oppose Gen Hart who came up from Aliwal but he drove them before him and when he was about 8 miles from Wepener they cleared. You can imagine how relieved we were for our ammunition was nearly spent. The Hotchkiss ammunition was finished about four days before they retreated. Our total casualties were 140 wounded and 19 killed, but some have since died from their wounds. We (the Cape Mounted Rifles) lost the heaviest having 80 wounded and 14 killed outright and 11 have since died from their wounds. The Artillery (Cape Mounted Rifles) were the only Artillery, we had lost 1 man killed and 6 wounded. Our Sergeant Major was the man killed. He was one of the smartest men and one of the bravest that ever breathed. I assure you that every man of us felt as if we had lost a near relation when he was killed. The Boers were very sick, I believe, about failing to capture us. They were about 9,000 strong. I believe they lost very heavily. They were using two of our guns against us which they [had] captured at Thaba Nchu. The pom-pom is a very demoralising thing and makes an awful noise. They must have thrown some thousands of shells at us. I know where one man built a little schanze for himself with shrapnel cases. When we left Wepener we went up the Ladybrand road until we came in touch with the Boers and then retired and went to Dewetsdorp and from there to Thaba Nchu and then on here. I don't know what they call this place, I suppose it has no name for there are no houses or anything only a few Basuto huts. We were about 20 miles N.E. of Thaba Nchu (pronounced Taban Choo). We were out reconnoitring yesterday but did not meet the enemy. They were somewhere about for our fellows collared two Boer pickets this morning, I think 16 men. We have had no news of the outside world since we left Aliwal. One of the worst things that happened during the siege was the failure of the tobacco supply. There was none in the camp and of course it was impossible to get any, some of us tried tea leaves and some, straw. We are a little better off now but not much for we have nowhere to buy it except a little Basuto tobacco, from the natives. However a lot of our waggons went into Bloemfontein for supplies and they are sure to bring a lot of Government tobacco with them. They should be here in a couple of days. I have only had one letter since I left Aliwal and that was addressed to Sterksroom, so there must be a lot for me somewhere, I think they will come with the waggons from Bloemfontein. By jove I would like to see today's Post, to see how the war is going on in other parts. Talk about dirty faces, our riflemen did not get a wash for 17 days at Wepener, I was pretty lucky and managed to get one on the sixth night. I don't know where we are going I believe we are attached to General Rundle's Division, I could not tell you where he is but sometimes some of the Imperial Yeomanry come in with despatches so he can't be far away.

Only two of Trooper Boocock's letters were printed in the *Advertiser,* though he appeared in a list of the town's soldiers serving in South Africa, published in the week when Easingwold celebrated the relief of Mafeking. He was among the town's regulars:

> Gunner Boocock, Brandsby, Artillery, supposed to be with Sir Leslie Rundle.

NOTES

1. *Advertiser,* 3 February 1900.
2. *Ibid* 23 June 1900. Printed in full later.
3. *Ibid* 11 November 1899. There is another in, eg R. Kruger, *Good-Bye Dolly Gray* (1959). There are more.
4. S.M. Miller, *Lord Methuen and the British Army* (1999).
5. In the *Official History,* quoted *ibid* p82, fn47. The 3rd Division was composed mainly of the 6th (Fusiliers) Brigade and the 5th (Irish) Brigade.
6. *Advertiser,* 2 December 1899.
7. *Ibid* 9 December 1899.
8. Quoted *Ibid* 16 December 1899.
9. T. Pakenham, *The Boer War* (1979) p24.
10. *Advertiser,* December 1899.
11. *Ibid* 6 January 1900.
12. *Ibid* 20 January 1900.
13. *Ibid* 3 March 1900. De Montmorency was the holder of a VC which he won at Omdurman.
14. 24 March 1900. Also 10 and 17 March.
15. *Advertiser* 21 April 1900.
16. Pakenham, op cit p372.
17. *Advertiser,* 17 March 1900.

18. There is a biographical note and a sketch of him in *Ibid* 24 March 1900. The stock consisted of '23 locomotives, including 17 of large class, 13 carriages, eight brake vans, and 124 short wagons.'
19. *Ibid* 24 March 1900.
20. *The Concise Dictionary of National Biography* Vol 2. 470 prisoners were taken by De Wet, he said. Wilson op cit Vol 2, p573 has different figures.
21. Picture of Dalgety in Wilson op cit p577.
22. *Advertiser,* 23 June 1900.

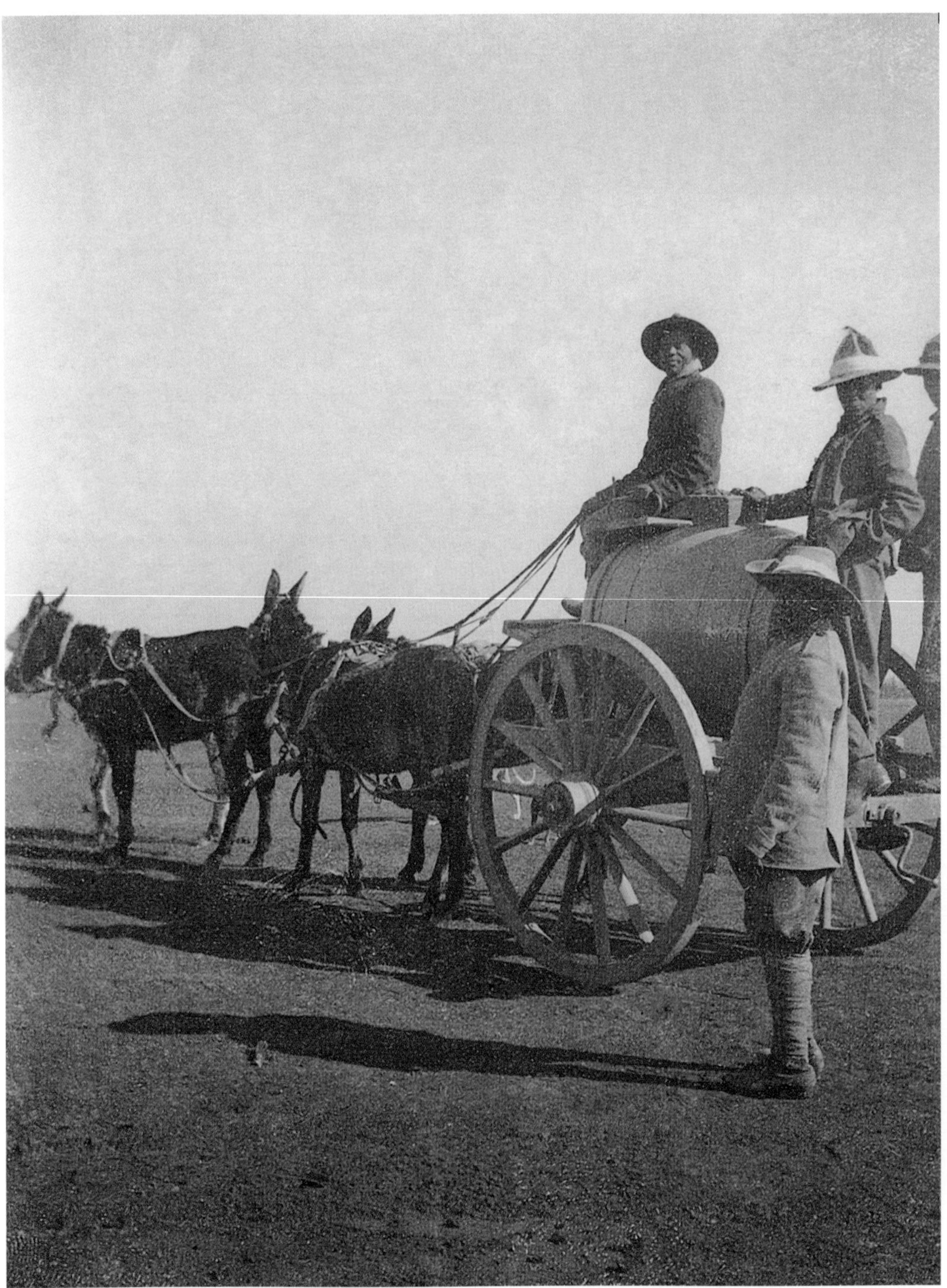

From Billy Holmes archive, Africans moving water

Chapter 10

ECCLES FOSTER, RASKELFE

The village of Raskelfe has featured regularly in these pages, and was dominated by the Rev Preston. In April 1900, his nephew, who had gone to South Africa before the war, was killed at Ladysmith. The account of his death said that he had joined a local force, a unit of which was present at Wepener.[1]

REV. DR. PRESTON'S NEPHEW KILLED AT LADYSMITH

We are informed that official confirmation has been received in the traffic manager's office of the death of Trooper Trevor Preston, of the Imperial Light Horse, who was reported killed in the engagement at Ladysmith on 8th January. Mr Preston, 23 years old, was the eldest son of the Rev. J. E. Preston, Julianstown Rectory, Drogheda, Ireland, and nephew of the Rev. Dr. Preston, Raskelfe, and came to South Africa in 1897. Mr Preston was an enthusiastic member of the Kaffrarian Rifles during his stay in East London. [He] could not resist the call to arms, and as a true and loyal Britisher he gave his life in his country's cause.

Confirming the above report, a letter received on 26th March from the colonel commanding the Imperial Light Horse says:–

Dear Sir:- I deeply regret to announce the death of your son. He was killed on the 6th January whilst gallantly holding a position with a few comrades against a strong force of Boers who were attacking Ladysmith, but I am pleased to say that by the gallant conduct of himself and others the enemy were driven off and the hill was saved. He was shot in the head. – With all deep sympathy, &c. I remain, &c.

Not long before this sad news, and just under a note saying that the proprietors of Beecham's Pills would send 'a gratis box' of their product to 'any individual now on active service in South Africa', a notice appeared about Dr Preston (*Advertiser* on 6 January). It has been mentioned before.

THE WAR

> The whole battalion of the 2nd V.B. Cheshire Regiment including their Chaplain, Rev Dr Preston, Vicar of Raskelfe has volunteered for active service, or for Garrison duty. The offer is now being considered by the authorities in London.

The list of soldiers produced at the time of the Mafeking celebrations contained the name of a regular who came from Alne, and one of his brothers. He was captured by the Boers at certainly the most famous of all South African battle sites.[2]

> Private Eccles Foster, 2nd Lancashire Fusiliers, taken prisoner at Spion Kop; and his brother Gunner A. Foster, H.M.S. Monarch, wounded in two places at Belmont, and now returned to duty.

Eccles did not make his entrance into 'Easingwold' history because he was at Spion Kop, but because, earlier, he had been involved in a spot of bother that landed him before the beaks sitting at the Town Hall. He got considerable coverage.[3]

From Billy Holmes archive, brewing up

Sandwiched between an account of the deliberations of the Easingwold Parish Council and an account of a meeting of the Board of Guardians, the spot of bother that the Foster brothers found themselves in, and was reported. The Parish Council had talked about the need to remove a dangerous corner on the York road near the Whinny Pastures[4] and the Guardians heard from Dr Hicks about 'Dyptheria at Raskelfe and Easingwold, and Enteric Fever at Huby.' The Board also set up a committee of enquiry to look at complaints about another of its medical officers who had been with them for 26 years.[5] This was exciting stuff, but nothing like what Messrs J.S. Strangwayes, S. Wombwell and others had to deal with.[6]

After several judgements on drunken behaviour, the bench dealt with cases headed 'REFUSING TO QUIT AND ASSAULT AT ALNE. A BATCH OF CASES.' K.E.T. Wilkinson, mentioned in these pages before, appeared representing Thomas and Eccles. He said that the brothers had gone into the Railway Inn, Alne, and there assaulted Samuel Hindle, a slater of Leeds. Hindle was taken to Buller Hicks' surgery, where it was found 'that at least one rib was broken, and there were bruises more or less all over his body.' Eccles was fined '£2 and costs was inflicted, £3 6s.6d in all.' [sic]

The day at the Town Hall ended, as far as the Fosters were concerned, when Thomas was charged with assaulting Alfred Pickersgill, Sam Hindle's mate. Alfred said Tom 'set about him with a stick, and "brayed" him through the door with it.' The defendant 'stoutly denied ever using a stick', but the bench did not believe him and fined him '2s 6d and costs, amounting to 10s altogether.'

LADYSMITH: THE HIGH STREET.

About three weeks after the Fosters' case was reported in the *Advertiser,* another news item appeared in the section devoted to Alne.[7] Eccles had got his calling-up papers.

> ARMY RESERVE – Mr Eccles Foster, of Alne, an Army Reserve man, left to rejoin the colours on Monday last. He has served for about 8 years in the Lancashire Fusiliers and had been at home only 2 months.

Eccles might have been back in Alne for only a short time, but he had done his level best to liven the place up! In the editorial column where his departure was announced, readers were told that there were 4000 total abstainers in the forces now engaged in South Africa' and that many were members 'of the Gleaners' Union, an organisation of helpers of the Church Missionary Society.'[8] Eccles was certainly not a gleaner. That same editorial also, incidentally, contained the following report about some soldiers on the Reserve who were not too keen on going to South Africa.

> The war has resulted in the discovery of two very different types of British soldiers. One is that of the comparatively very few, who, having drawn their pay in time of peace, hasten to desert as soon as their regiments are ordered to South Africa. According to the strict letter of the law, these men who desert in time of war are liable to be sentenced to death ... The other type ... are soldiers who have deserted and escaped detection, but upon hearing that their regiments have been ordered to the seat of war, have given themselves up, in the hope of sharing in the fighting.

Eccles Foster left Alne to rejoin his regiment on 27 November 1899. Just over two months later the following item appeared about him.[9]

> In the list of casualties at Spion Kop we see that Private Eccles Foster, 2nd Lancashire Fusiliers, was returned as missing, and as no further particulars are to hand concerning him, the chances are that by this time he will be taking part in the involuntary occupation of Pretoria.

The *Advertiser's* optimism was justified, and in April brother Tom, who had taken part in the punch-up at the Railway got some good news. R.E. Smith's report said:[10]

> ALNE
>
> A PRETORIA PRISONER. – Mr Thomas Foster, of Alne, has received information from official sources that his brother, 3861 Private J E Banks, (Eccles Foster), 2nd Battalion Lancashire Fusiliers, who has been missing since the battle of Spion Kop, is now a prisoner in Pretoria.

A couple of months after the news that Eccles had become a prisoner a letter appeared from him in the *Advertiser.* It was undated.[11]

AN ALNE MAN AT THE FRONT

Private John Eccles Banks, No. 3861, 2nd Battalion Lancashire Fusiliers, writing to his friends at Alne, says:–

Just a few lines to let you know how I am. We are on the line of communication at Homing Spruit, and we are having a very bad time of it, for there are about two hundred Boers in the hills here, and they are blowing the line up every night. De Wet is surrounded here, we were shelling him and his two hundred yesterday. He will be caught before you get my letter, and then the war will soon be over, and we sha'nt be sorry. You would see it in the papers about Spion Kop. It was really rough; we lost forty per cent of our men. We had over ten thousand Boers around us. I can tell you it was a bit hot – what with the heat of the day and the firing. I call it grand. The wounded moaning was awful. I fired six hundred rounds of ammunition at the Boers that day, but we had to give in at the finish. But I cannot say that the Boers behaved badly to us. They gave us nearly all they had. But of course it

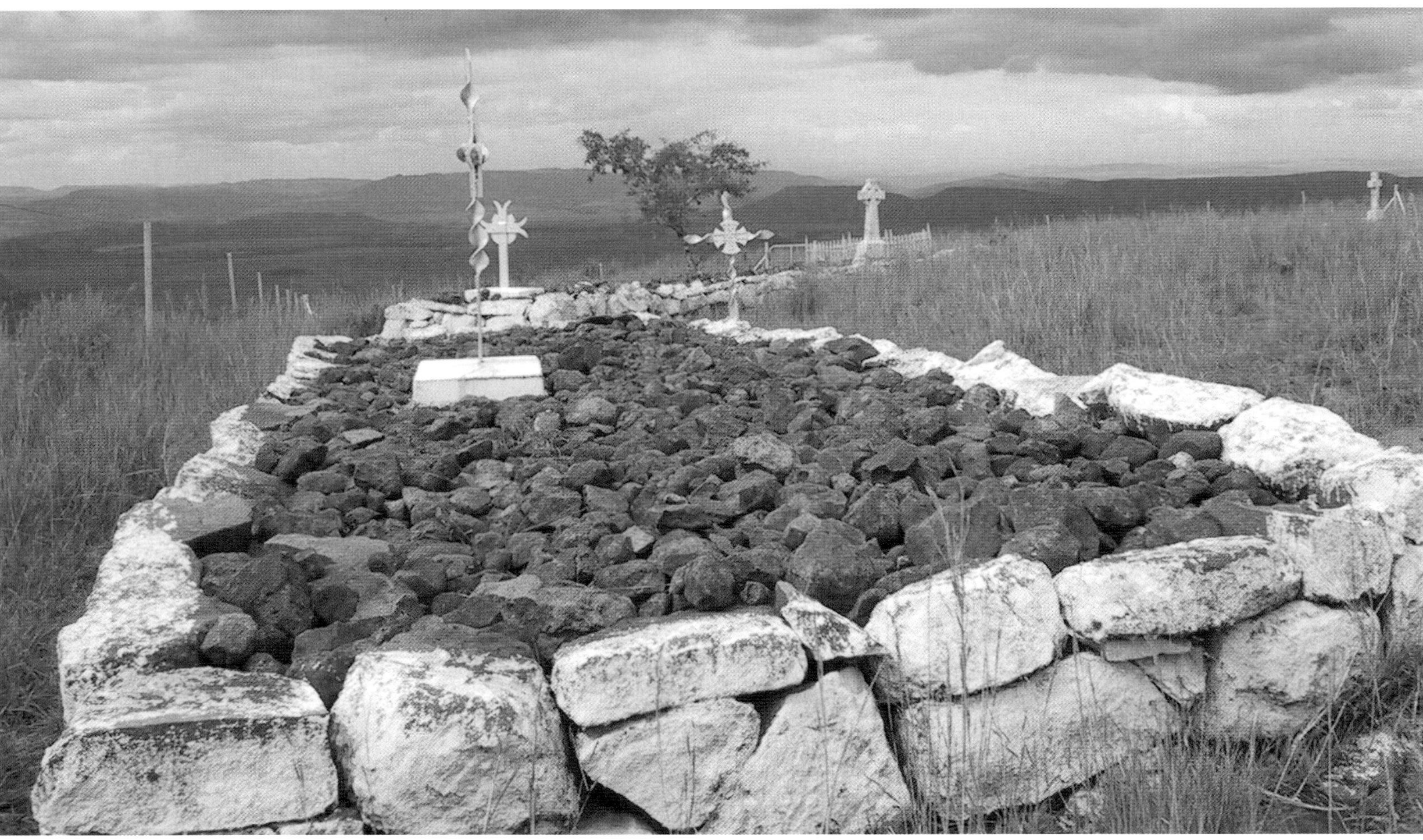

View from the British position on Spion Kop - The extended grave was the site of a British Trench where the casualties were so heavy that the trench was filled in as a grave. Metrick Till was fatally wounded here, Eccles Foster captured. Photo taken 2000.

was worse for us the day we made our escape, they gave us a good shelling, but I don't think that they hurt any of us. Our duty here is very heavy – we are guarding the line and bridges five nights out of seven. I have only seen one man that I know, and that was Sydney Smith, from the Hanover, Easingwold, and he was a prisoner with me at Watervaal. I think the Reserve men will come home the first, I have been all over Pretoria. I saw old Kruger's house. They are going to fetch him soon. The Boers turned a train only four miles from here. De Wet is seven miles from here. We don't often get any money out here, but I always have a "quid" in my pocket. I think I have told you all. Give my best respects to all. You need not write back, as we never know where we are going. We might be a hundred miles away to-morrow.

Good bye.

From Eccles Banks.

Eccles Foster went into captivity, and into very unpleasant surroundings. Lord Roberts complained to Kruger about POW conditions, and in doing so mentioned one of the places known to Eccles Foster. He said that prisoners in the Transvaal capital were badly fed. 'I also learn that at Waterval there are 90 cases of enteric fever and dysentery among the prisoners,' he said, 'and that the doctor [there] resigned because he found it impossible to get proper medicines or medical comforts for them.[12] Not only that, but the POWs had to bivouac in the open veldt, with no shelter and only straw to lie on, while the sick were kept in 'an unroofed shed.'[13]

Spion Kop, where Eccles fought, lies to the south of Ladysmith, above the Tugela River. It was to be taken by the British troops *en route* to relieve Ladysmith and the ground over which they had to advance was described as 'a succession of ridges, intersected at right angles by water courses, cutting deep gorges in the mountain side… thus sundering and separating the attacking force.' Changes were made in the original plan of attack. The Boers, not for the first time, lured the British on, then shelled them unmercifully. Losses on 20 January were considerable, and the troops had to bivouac that night on the mountain. Next day the fight was renewed, with the British artillery hopelessly ineffective because of the Boer positions and because it was outranged.

On 21 January Bastion Hill had to be given up. The advanced Boer line was taken, but behind it was a second line of earth redoubts, breastworks and trenches, and there could have been a third and fourth line as well. Sir Charles Warren's army 'was assaulting a fortress of immense strength held by splendid soldiers' – without adequate artillery support. Once more the troops spent the night on the mountainside, having suffered severe losses. Winston Churchill reported the events of the day.[14] What should the British do? On 22 January no progress was made, then it was decided to storm Spion Kop, but General Buller prevaricated. He still wanted to try 'a turning movement on the left' – which was the original plan – but eventually assented to the storming of Spion. The attacking force paraded at six o'clock in the evening, and amongst them were eight companies of Eccles Foster's regiment.[15] The attack was to be made at night and orders were given that there was to be no firing. The bayonet was to be used. The men were led by Major General E.R.P. Woodgate and Col Bloomfield.

After seven hours climbing there was a skirmish in which the Lancashire Fusiliers took the most prominent part. The British went up and on until they reached a plateau where there were some poor Boer entrenchments. They then made a terrible mistake. Spion Kop was the key position in the area and its possession would unlock the door to Ladysmith.

From Billy Holmes archive, impressive Church on the Veldt

The Boers sent in reinforcements from far away; the British were exposed to converging and enfilading fire from all sides, and had neglected to provide a decent communications system for themselves. Once more the British artillery fired on British troops. General Woodgate was killed.

There followed a dreadful British defeat, another in a lengthening list. How did the despatches published in the *Advertiser* report the events that Eccles Foster was involved in? Buller's move north to relieve Ladysmith was underway and on 20 January a cable from him said his troops had reached the flooded Tugela and had 'seized the ... ferry.' In the issue of 3 February there was a rough map of the Tugela country and a description of it. From the north bank of the river the land rose 'to a rough table land up to the Kopje round Brakfontein.' This extended to the 'east and west between Brakfontein and Spion Kop or Hills, and is the position which has been chosen by the Boers to stop Lytellton's brigade in their advance from Potgeiter's Drift, and Warren's Brigade, which is working along the Acton Homes road to Ladysmith.' The report ended with a comment that confirms the oft repeated statement that the British had no adequate maps to work from.

> Spion Kop has hitherto been shown on all published maps, west of Venter's Spruit, but it has become evident that the correspondents have confused this name with Spoen Kop, which is the name of a farm lying on the north bank of the Tugela between Potgeiter's and Triechardt's Drifts... Spion Kop... is situate as shown in our sketch map...

On Saturday 3 February the *Easingwold* carried headlines about the real Spion Kop and casualty lists for the officers killed and wounded there. From Eccles Foster's battalion Capt G.M. Stewart and two Lieutenants were killed and Maj W.F. Walter and four others wounded. The despatches included one from Buller who described Warren taking the Kop and holding it, but having to abandon it on Buller's instructions. He singled out for special mention 'the 2nd Lancashire Fusiliers, and 2nd Middlesex, who magnificently maintained the best traditions of the British Army throughout the trying day of the 24th.' Buller praised the troops on the retreat beyond the Tugela.

> that the force could withdraw from actual touch... with the enemy, in the perfect manner it did is... evidence of the *moral* of the troops... we... [withdrew] our cumbrous ox and mule transport, across a river 85 yards broad with 20ft. banks and a very swift stream, unmolested...

Almost immediately stories of heroism were told and published that have been repeated many times since. The *Advertiser* used one of them about the 2nd Lancashire Fusiliers.[16]

> In one of the numerous desperate melées at the top of Spion Kop... a Lancashire Fusilier was impaled upon a Boer bayonet. Nevertheless... the lad grappled with his enemy, thrust him inch by inch to the edge of a precipice, and finally hurled him bodily, bayonet and all, into a chasm hundreds of feet deep.

NOTES

1. *Advertiser,* 7 April 1900.
2. *Ibid* 26 May 1900.
3. *Ibid* 4 November 1899.
4. This was actually an RDC responsibility. The Parish 'called its attention... to the matter'.
5. This was Dr Gramshaw who was accused of neglect.
6. Strangwayes (chair), Coates, Wombwell, H. Hawking, R. Thornton and J. Rocliffe.
7. *Advertiser,* 25 November 1899.
8. The Gleaners published a journal titled, predictably, the *Church Missionary Gleaner.*
9. *Advertiser,* 10 February 1900.
10. *Ibid* 21 April 1900. Presumably the E in this version of his name is Eccles.
11. *Ibid* 1 September 1900.
12. This seems to have been a Dr Vangreldt. Perhaps threatened to resign would be correct. The next paragraph says that.
13. *Advertiser,* 21 April 1900. A famous World War One soldier was also captured (along with Winston Churchill) at about this time and imprisoned in Pretoria. This was Aylmer Haldane – who escaped. See A. Haldane, *A Soldier's Saga* (1948) particularly Chapter 21. He was locked up in the Staats Model School, where conditions were tolerable. Also *Advertiser* 14 April 1900.
14. He was reporting for a national newspaper and had been involved in a celebrated incident involving an armoured train (with Haldane).
15. And, 17th Company of Royal Engineers – in all about 1,500 men.'
16. *Advertiser,* 10 February 1900.

Chapter 11

GEORGE MILNTHORPE

In the list of Easingwold soldiers produced at the time of the relief of Mafeking, and entered with the regulars, appeared simply 'Milnthorpe, Helperby, 10th Hussars.' He was George C. Milnthorpe, another of the soldiers who had a long letter published by Reginald Ernest Smith.

The twin villages of Helperby and Brafferton recently (2000) produced a booklet on those places, but though space is devoted to soldiers who served from there in 1914-18, nothing is said about the South African War because the authors concentrated on those who did not return.[1]

Bulmer's History, Topography and Directory of North Yorkshire of 1900, used before in these pages, shows two people named Milnthorpe in Helperby township. These were 'Milnthorp Edwin, managing maltster' and 'Milnthorp William K., maltster, Hornby Close.' It will be noticed that *Bulmer's* spells the surname without an E at the end; it might also be noticed that Reginald Ernest Smith in the letter from George he published in the *Advertiser,* gives him as Milnthorp, while George himself has Milnthorpe. The Helperby and Brafferton booklet has the following entries in its pubs and inns section.[2]

> *The Brewery in Back Lane*
> In 1872, Henry Rich was operating as a brewer from Back Lane Brewery, which we must assume was connected with the Star Inn, for by 1879 he had sold out to Milnthorpe & Sessions, who were brewing and malting to the rear of the Star Inn and had re-named the [business the] Star Brewery. They were no longer brewing by 1893, and the pub had passed into the hands of Ramsden, and was subsequently de-licensed.
> *The Maltings*
> ...remembered now by the road called The Maltings. A Thomas Buttery was a maltster [there] in the first half of the 19th century, but by 1872 the dominant name as maltsters was Milnthorp. The business passed from Milnthorp to the Robinson family at the end of the 19th century...

A member of the Milnthorpe family was a doctor and an entry in the *Medical Register* shows him living in Leeds, having qualified in May 1900.[3] The *Advertiser* reported his success.[4]

> HELPERBY
>
> Amongst the candidates who were successful at the examinations for the Diploma of Members of the Royal College of Surgeons and Licentiate of the Royal College of Physicians, London, was Mr R Milnthorpe, son of the late Mr W.K. Milnthorpe, of Helperby. Mr Milnthorpe has been appointed a Resident Medical Officer at the Leeds Dispensary.

At the end of the year Dr Milnthorpe decided to go to South Africa where his brother was.[5]

Thomas Whorley joined up on 16th January, 1900 and it is very likely that he was one of the two Helperby men mentioned in the send off of the Easingwold Volunteers (page 247) on 5th February, 1900 with the Volunteer Company of the Yorkshire Regiment.

Rebecca Whaley
given to Thomas
Whorley
by his loving
mother
on going to the War
January 16, 1900

Thomas Whorley, 1940's

Helperby & Brafferton Militia (1899) in front of Oak Tree Inn with Thomas Whorley 5th from right.

From Billy Holmes archive, taking a break, outside a blockhouse

Important Announcement
FOR A HELPERBY DOCTOR

We learn that Mr R. Milnthorpe, of Helperby, has received the appointment of civil surgeon to Her Majesty's Forces in South Africa. Until lately he has been a resident house surgeon at the Leeds Public Dispensary.

George Milnthorp's letter was sent to his aunt.[6]

TOLLERTON

The following is a letter received by Mrs J. Snowdon, Tollerton, from her Nephew George C. Milnthorpe, of the 10th Hussars who is [a] dispatch rider for the Essex Regiment.

I am dropping you a line or two to let you know how things are going on in this part of the world. I suppose you will have heard of the adventure we had on sea. The S.S. Ismore getting on the rocks and having to take to the boats at once. We lost all horses, but the troops and crew were saved. After arriving at Cape Town we had to get horses etc, and joined the regiment just before Christmas and we arrived here on New Year's Day. We are just outside Colesburg near the Free State and expect to be in in a day or two. The battle commenced about 8.45a.m. on New Year's Day, and still continues. At present we are holding a position we drove the enemy from, and we have had some narrow escapes, but up to now I am all complete and in the best of health. A week ago our camp was shelled out by the enemy but nobody was injured and our Artillery silenced the Boer's big guns as soon as they opened fire. I saw father in camp near Cape Town, he came over for the afternoon he seemed very well. It is a most dreary country. I should think we are pretty near the first human beings in this part. I have not managed to undress this year yet, but occasionally manage a wash and boots off. We have been sleeping out in the open until two nights ago, under a wall and a few sacks, but we have a tent now. A few men in my Squadron have been killed and several wounded, one Major killed and one wounded. Generals French and Brabazon are our Commanders, the former a very good man and has had a lot to do with the 10th. It is awfully hot during the day but the nights are bitterly cold almost like winter. I am attached to the Essex Regiment as dispatch carrier and I do get some hot rides. I was with the Suffolks first, but last Saturday they got cut up and the Essex relieved them. I ride over to our camp (10th Hussars) occasionally for letters etc. They are about five miles away, but all belong to the same Brigade. They have just been mounting a gun onto a kopje about 400 yards high and are going to shell Colesburg tomorrow. We live very well here on Boer cattle about three beasts a day but the general ration is tinned beef and biscuits, so we think it a great treat. I must conclude now with love and best wishes, hoping you had a Merry Christmas and will have a prosperous New Year.

I remain
Your affectionate Nephew,
GEORGE C. MILNTHORPE

George's letter contains that rather puzzling remark about his father meeting him at the Cape. His father, according to the note about his son's success in his medical exams, was dead. The aunt was probably the wife of James Snowdon, corn factor's agent, and three Milnthorps were recorded as living in Tollerton. These were Alfred, maltster; Mrs Eliz. Greenfield house, and Thomas, a cowkeeper.

George Milnthorp's voyage to South Africa was more exciting than most. What happened? Among the communiqués and reports that appeared was the following which revealed more exactly what George Milnthorp's unit was,[7]

BRITISH TRANSPORT ASHORE - TROOPS LANDED

From General at Cape Town to Secretary of State for War

Cape Town
December 3, 8 p.m.

Officers commanding the troops on board the hired transport Ismore telegraphs from Vredenburg, December 3: Gone ashore this morning on the rocks in St. Helens Bay. All the troops safely conveyed from the ship to the shore, but horses still on board, and difficult to land them. Her Majesty's ships Doris and Niobe and hired transport Columbian, with three lighters, proceed at once to render every assistance. Weather to all appearances calm.

[The Ismore had on board the 63rd Battery Royal Field Artillery, the A Squadron and one troop of B Squadron 10th Hussars, and No. 9 Company of the Royal Army Medical Corps.]

That rather curt report of what happened to Milnthorp might be put alongside an account sent to a member of the aristocracy. A famous British soldier, in an unbelievably trite book,[8] experienced some of the problems mentioned by Lord Frederick Blackwood to his father.[9]

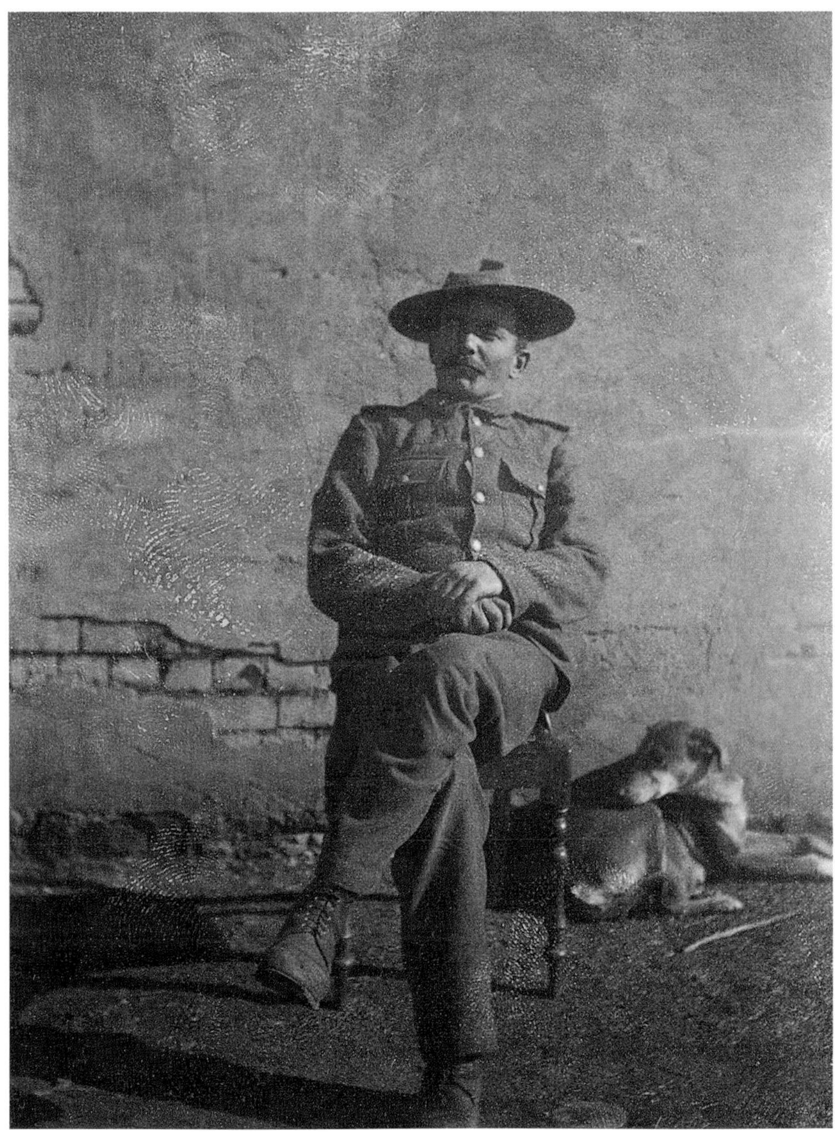

From Billy Holmes archive, still accompanied by the dog

A TRANSPORT IN A STORM

The following extracts are from an interesting letter written by Lord Frederick Blackwood to his father, Lord Dufferin, giving an account of the terrible storm encountered by Squadron C of the 9th Lancers whilst in transport off the East Coast of Africa, and published by the *Northern Whig:*

"We got to Durban all safe and happy as larks on October 9th, expecting to disembark, and go up to the front immediately. To our disgust, however, we were told not to land, but to go off at once to the Cape. Accordingly, at five that night, we started off again. Next morning the sea seemed fairly calm, and we were all laughing and joking at the way we were rolling about. You must understand that our troop of horses were in wooden stalls on the upper deck. This was my troop, consisting of 38 troop horses, together with my own chargers, and 12 mules. All the other troops and their horses were down below between decks. "Stables" were at eleven p.m., when it had begun to get rather rough. However, we still sailed, but the rolling got worse and worse. [Eventually] ... the rolling became terrific and the seas enormous. All my troop were drenched over and over again; one man, a corporal, got washed off his feet, and was thrown four times with great force up and down the deck. The extraordinary thing was he did not break anything. At last the wooden framework of the stabling began to creak, and I expected every minute to see the whole thing collapse and all my men killed. I then went to Lund (a captain in the 9th Lancers), and told him I thought it was getting dangerous for my men to stay on any longer, and he gave the order for No. 1 troop horses to be abandoned. Five minutes after that one entire side of the woodwork gave way. Two of my chargers and four others were immediately washed overboard. Now came the most horrible scene I have ever witnessed. The deck was covered with one mass of struggling horses and mules, mixed up with the broken woodwork of the stables, the whole being hurled first to one side of the deck and then to the other – all horribly wounded, most with broken legs and some with eyes torn out. My first charger – the one you gave me, and the nicest horse I am ever likely to have – was amongst them, but I managed from a hatchway to get a shot at her with my revolver. To make a long story short, out of 50 horses and mules on my deck, only three were saved, two horses, whose stalls had remained intact, and one mule, which had a most miraculous escape, having been washed down the hatchway into the hold below, and being absolutely unhurt. Things were hardly better between decks below. On one deck a huge water tank broke loose, went hurling about, killing two horses. On this account this deck had to be abandoned by the men. It was a horrible thing having to jump this way and that to avoid horses that kept hurling up and down kicking and screaming. The arms racks gave way, and I was sent to try and collect the carbines. We had managed to stack most of them when an enormous roll came, and down they went, rushing from one side to the other. Luckily, we were all able to jump on tables, except one man, who fell among the wreckage cutting his head and laying him out. All the men below remained with the horses till 6 p.m., when they were ordered up, and they all huddled in the passages and on the top of the engine-room, shivering and chattering all night with cold. All my own men had been long since drenched to the skin, and not a man got a bite of food except what we could give them in the way of a few biscuits. I wish you could have seen the way the men behaved. It was really magnificent. They never thought of letting go of their horses until they were absolutely ordered to, though they did not know when the wooden frame might give way. All this time, as the captain told us, the ship was not under control, and would not steer."

NOTES

1. Brafferton Parish Council, *Brafferton & Helperby. A Millennium Miscellany* (Easingwold 2000). Readers of the 1914-18 section will have noticed a rather basic error which should be corrected. There is a story there 'of five young men, "The Gallant Band of Five" who all went to France with the 4th Batallion [sic] of the Yorkshire Regiment. They were all killed by a shell on 2nd May 1915 while suffering 'from sickness and giddiness after an earlier mustard gas attack'. Mustard was not then in use. See, for its introduction etc. R Parkinson, *Encyclopaedia of Modern War* (1977) entry on p 38.
2. *Ibid* pp 30 and 32.
3. *The Medical Register* for 1910 p1080.
4. *Advertiser* 19 May 1900.
5. *Ibid* 22 December 1900.
6. *Ibid* 10 February 1900.
7. *Ibid* 9 December 1899.
8. C. Harington, *Tim Harington Looks Back* (1940) chapter 3.
9. *Advertiser,* 18 November 1899.

Chapter 12

CHARLES SNAITH

George Milnthorp wrote one long published letter and was mentioned in passing in the press a couple of times during the war, but that was all. There were others who flitted in and out of the paper's columns. People like Charles Snaith, of Northallerton. He was killed early in the war and a note appeared about him in March 1902.[1]

NORTHALLERTON

Mrs D. Snaith, of South Parade, Northallerton, has received from the War Office a silver medal, clasp and ribbon, which were won by her late son, Chas. F. Snaith, who was a private in the Imperial Light Infantry, and was killed in action at Spion Kop, on January 24th, 1900. The medal bears on one side an excellent likeness of her late Majesty the Queen, and on the reverse a figure of Brittania holding a laurel wreath, with the words "South Africa." On the silver clasp [is] embossed ... "The Relief of Ladysmith." On the edge of the medal the name of Private Snaith is engraved. Private Snaith was the daring cyclist who rode through three Boer camps at the commencement of the war.

NOTES

1. *Advertiser*, 1 March 1902.

From Billy Holmes archive, two unknown women

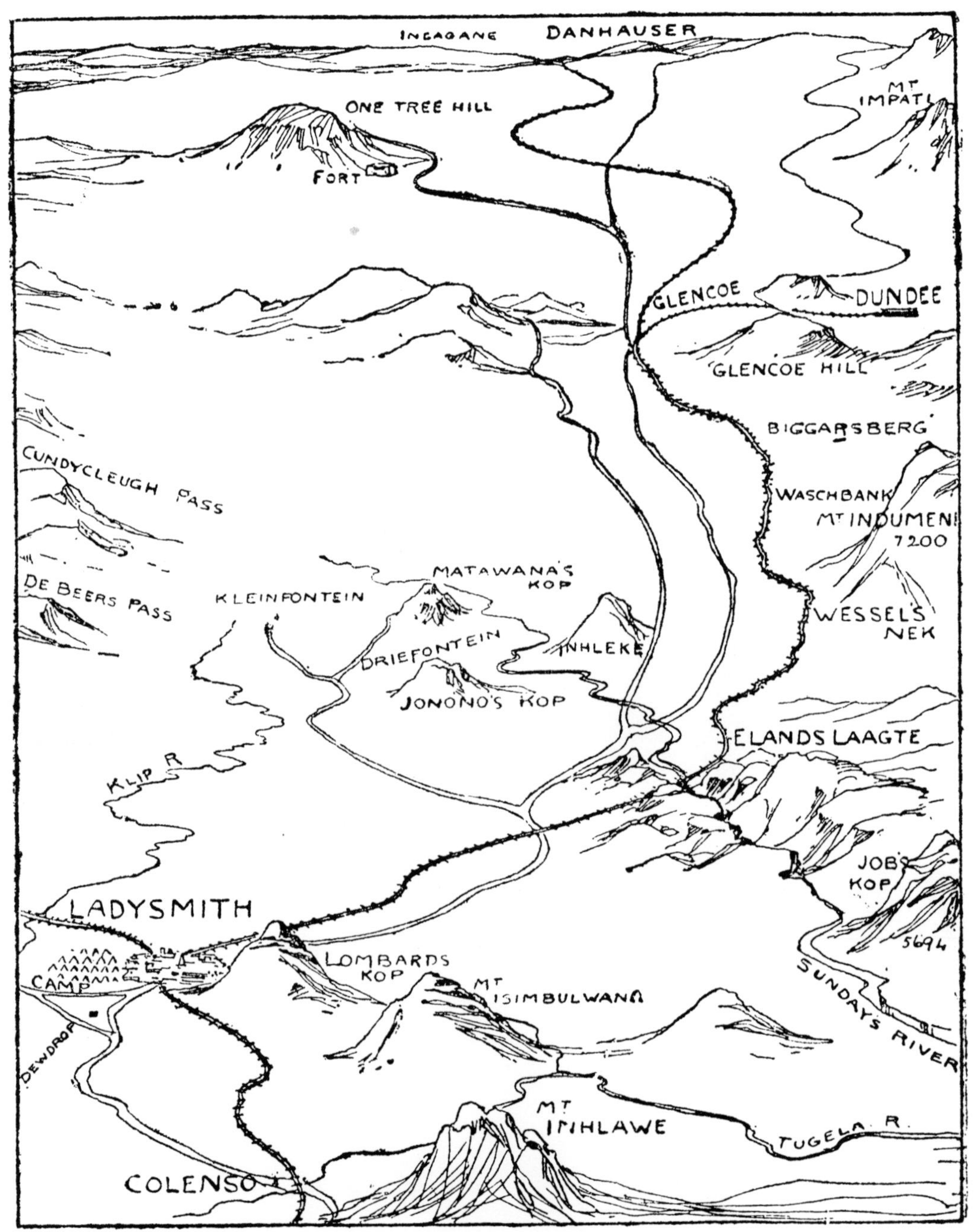

BIRD'S-EYE VIEW OF NORTH NATAL

Chapter 13

EASINGWOLD VOLUNTEERS

On Monday 5 February 1900 'a hearty "send off" was given' in Easingwold to a party of [1]

> four volunteers who were leaving to join the Line Battalion in South Africa. There [sic] names are T Cariss, T Russell, E Wheatley and F Rhodes, and with two from Helperby and six from Thirsk, made up the twelve which "I" Company of the Princess of Wales' Own Yorkshire Regiment Volunteers are sending.

Edward Wheatley was the 'son of Mr S. Wheatly, [sic] Long Street, Easingwold' and 'the doings' of the Easingwold volunteers was told at some length after their return to Britain in the summer of 1901. Tom Cariss provided the details for the *Advertiser*.[2]

THE EASINGWOLD VOLUNTEERS AT THE FRONT
THE VOLUNTEER COMPANY OF FIRST YORKSHIRE REGIMENT

In accordance with an intimation in our last issue, we are pleased to be able to give our readers a brief account of the doings of the Easingwold Volunteers during their 16 months' campaigning in South Africa, in which each did his part to uphold the fame of his country, and the honour and prestige of the Empire.

The names of the Easingwold members were Tom Cariss, Uppleby (who has favoured us with this account); F Rhodes, Oulston Lane; E Wheatley, Long Street; and T Russell, Ninevah; attached to the 1st Yorkshire Regiment. The company also included 7 men from Thirsk and Sowerby, and 2 from Helperby.

The company embarked ... on the 17th February of last year, at Southampton. The Gloucester, Lincoln, York and Lancaster, and other Volunteers also sailed in the same vessel. Rough weather was experienced in the Bay of Biscay, otherwise the voyage was an uneventful one. The men were well fed on board, and well accommodated.

Touching at St Helena, the news of Cronje's surrender was received with cheers. The most optimistic said it would be only a picnic, as the war would be all over when Capetown was reached. When that town was reached however, on the 14th March, it was soon found that there was some fighting left in the Boers yet, as after one clear day at Capetown, the company were sent to Naawepoort, where they stayed two or three days, occupying their time in route-marching, preparatory to joining their regiment. From there, by rail, they went to Norval's Pont where a bridge over the Orange River had been destroyed by the Boers. There the Gordon Highlander Volunteers along with the Yorkshires were employed in making a deviation for the railway.

Then the march was begun to Bloemfontein in easy stages to get the men accustomed to it.

The regiment was joined at a place called Springfield, about four miles east of the capital city. After a stay of about 10 days, the 11th Division, under General Pole-Carew, was formed, and in reviewing them, that General said that Lord Roberts had spoken highly of the Yorkshire Regiment, and he hoped the Volunteer Company would do as well, and he

From Billy Holmes archive - a formal pose

assured them that before Pretoria was reached, they would have plenty of opportunities of showing what they could do.

The following day, the Division set off for the relief of Wepener, but only got as far as Thabachu, when word was received that the relief had already been effected. On that march, the Boers were first encountered 8 miles from Springfield. The Artillery shelled them about $2^1/_2$ miles off, and the Essex Regiment advanced under cover of the fire. The Boers turned a pom-pom on them, but did no damage, and they retreated at night-fall, not caring to come to close quarters. Bloemfontein was ... reached on Sunday, April 29th. After one day's rest, the Regiment received a new rig out of clothes, and on the 1st May, the forward march to Pretoria was begun. The men were all in good heart, and anxious to get at the enemy. The Artillery got into action at Brandfort, but as soon as the Boers saw the men advancing over the burnt veldt (they had burnt the grass to better observe the force), they again retreated.

The Yorkshires were the Advance Guard and Escort to the 84 and 85 Battery when the Volunteers first experienced Boer shell fire, being laid under it about 5 hours. Thanks to the bad shells, not much damage was done, but if one half of them had exploded, there would not have been many men left to tell the tale.

When Kroonstad was reached it was expected there would be a big fight, but when the Boers saw French getting round their flank, they deemed it prudent to retire. It was afterwards found that before leaving, they had burned a large store in the town, and most of them had got well drunk on the rum they found there. They (the British) stayed at Kroonstad a week, waiting for rations to come up, having been on half rations two days then. The time was occupied in making a deviation railway.

Boer War Blockhouse in the Western Cape (2002).
Guarding the railway from Cape Town to Kimberley. The roof is of corrugated iron and the entrance is over 2 metres high.

Resuming the march, the Boers gave way every time they saw the British, until Germiston was reached, where the Boers were looting the houses which was quickly put a stop to by the arrival of the British, the Boers evacuating the town in double quick time, with the Guards close at their heels. At Elands-fontein they were again caught, but after some fighting fled to Johannesburg. Outside that town, word was received that the town would be surrendered the next day, and a halt was called. The following day, when preparations were being made to occupy the town, word came that [the Boers] would not surrender, and that the British would have to fight for it. That was a ruse to get their convoy safely away. The Volunteer Company and 20 men out of H Company (Yorkshires) were then told off to guard one of the Gold Mines belonging to the well-known Simmer and Jack Company, as an attack was apprehended, which however did not come off. A march past was held after the town had been cleared of the enemy. There were a lot of English residents in Johannesburg, and their countrymen were received with great rejoicing, bunting being everywhere displayed.

Another camp was formed 4 or 5 miles out, where another stay of a week was made, to allow rations to be brought up, as for two days the force had been subsisting on half rations, which means two biscuits and half-a-pound of meat a day.

On the resumption of the march, everyone was fit and well, and the only talk was of Pretoria. There was no fighting on the way save a few skirmishes.

On the morning of June 4th, the troops were served with half a pound of flour each, and at night, after fighting from 10.30 to about 5, received a quarter-of-a-pound of tinned meat. That was the roughest fight so far as the Boers were together, and evidently intending turning the British back. The Boers were posted in Sangars (rough stone walls with loop-holes for rifle barrels) on the hills under the cover of the guns in the Pretoria forts. Lyddite was tried on them, and appeared to have a disastrous effect, as their fire slackened, and at dusk they cleared off.

The next morning, Pretoria was occupied, a lot of Boers surrendering in the town. The H Company and the Volunteer Company (Yorkshire), Colonel Bowes leading, were first of the 11th Division in the town, but were called back, to allow the Guards the honour. Another march past was held, and the force proceeded to the west side of the town, when a camp was pitched near the race course, where they stayed two days.

The camp was then shifted to the east side on the Delagoa Bay Railway, where the Langham Hospital for sick and wounded now stands. A stay of a week was made there. The Division was then reformed and proceeded to Sylverton Drift, where a week was put in doing outpost duty and watching the Boers, to keep them from occupying a range of hills. They next went as escort for two Naval guns to Diamond Hill, where a three days' battle took place. The Boers were posted in the hills. An Armistice was granted Botha, and during it the Boers sneaked off. At Eden-Dale close under Diamond Hill, the regiment stayed a month, where they received another suit of clothes, the old ones being in rags. A camp was then made on Bronkhurst Spruit, where the Connaught Rangers were cut up in 1881.

A march was then made to the Wilge River, in getting across which the wagons broke down in mid-stream. The blankets were afterwards retrieved, but the men had to sleep in the rain without covering. That was the most miserable night they spent during the war. The pouring rain, thunder and lightning, black, dark and wet completely through, made them pitiable objects. The next stop was Balmoral, then to Brug Spruit, from which place to Middleburg, a distance of 26½ miles was made in a little over 9 hours on two biscuits and half-a-pound of corned beef. From Middleburg the regiment acted as escort to a convoy for

From Billy Holmes archive - two of his comrades

General Buller to Wonderfontein. Then they came across the Boers again, and were fighting more or less to Belfast, where there was a three day's fight. The Yorkshire Regiment were very lucky, but the King's Rifles lost heavy in storming a kopje, which they carried at the point of the bayonet. The force then marched to Helvetia to keep Buller's lines open until he went to Lydenburg. When Buller returned the Division had to march to a piece of very rough country called the Devil's Kantor, where the waggons had to be unloaded and all the stuff carried up, the men then returning to help to drag the empty waggons.

At Nel Spruit the Boers had considerably damaged the rolling stock, burning the waggons. From there the regiment had the pleasure of a 30 miles ride to Kaap Muiden, one-and-a-half-day's march from Komati Poort in the Portuguese territory. Here a deviation was made for the railway, and the Infantry had to carry goods over for French's force operating in Barberton District. When their orders came in October to mobilise at Pretoria, with a view to being sent home, but instead the Volunteers were sent to Bethulie Bridge, on the line of communication, where they stayed until May, when they left for home, sailing from Capetown on board the "Avondale Castle".

A week before Cariss's account of the Easingwold men's contribution to the South African war appeared – among the accounts of their homecoming – was some more information about the experiences of the town's soldiers.

THE YEOMANRY

Yorkshire Hussars Yeomanry, part of 3rd Battalion Imperial Yeomanry formed at Sheffield, left for Liverpool end of Jan. 1900.

In Easingwold probably the first civilian to volunteer to fight for his Queen and Country, over the seas, was Mr Sydney Smith, son of Mr Thos Smith, Hanover Farm. True it is that Mr Stephen Wombwell, and Mr Thos Wilkinson, (Cold Harbour), volunteered at the same time, but they were old Yeomanry efficients, and 'knew the ropes'. A good shot and a fearless horseman, plenty of pluck, as indeed all four of them had, (Mr Thomas Alfred Wilkinson, son of Mr Watson C. Wilkinson, joined and went out with a second draft) – no wonder that with men like these the Yorkshire Yeomanry should have earned from the Generals at the front an honourable name, and fortunate indeed is England, who numbers among her sons so many who have proved their willingness to risk everything for their country's cause.

After they had got fairly to work at the front, they soon found out that they had other enemies besides the Boers, for enteric fever, which had laid low so many of England's bravest, proved too much for Captain Wombwell who, amid the regrets of all, was laid to rest. Thos Wilkinson was invalided home, and Alfred Wilkinson was for weeks hovering, as it were, between life and death, but happily overcame [his illness] and was able to take his place again in the ranks.

On April 5th, 1900, the Yorkshire Yeomanry received their baptism of fire, serving under Lord Methuen near Boshof, when Villebois-Mareul, the French soldier of fortune, was killed, and 54 Boers surrendered.

Since that time the history of the war is a record of their services everywhere. By the fortune of war, Trooper Smith was for some weeks an unwilling guest of the Boers, having been taken prisoner along with a few others in a Boer attack on a convoy. Ever since they landed in South Africa great interest had been taken in their doings, and the papers eagerly scanned for any news of them.

Edward Wheatley was not among the group of volunteers who returned to Easingwold in the early summer of 1901, but was back in July.[3] Wheatley had been left behind when his mates departed Durban and 'since then' had been 'to the Bermudas, escorting a cargo of Boer prisoners.' On 22 July, however, a telegram was received at the *Advertiser* offices, saying Edward would arrive home that night.[4] (At first it had been reported that he had been left behind – hospitalised – at Springfontein.)

BACK FROM THE FRONT
RETURN OF PRIVATE WHEATLEY

On Monday evening last, Private E Wheatley, son of Mr S Wheatley, Long Street, returned home after a prolonged sojourn at the front. He went out with the volunteers of the Yorkshire Regiment a year ago last February, and on that force leaving Durban for home he was left ill at that place. Since then he has been to the Bermudas, escorting a cargo of Boer prisoners. On Monday afternoon a telegram was received at the *Advertiser* office stating that Wheatley would arrive home that night. The approach of the train conveying him home was heralded by a plentiful supply of fog signals, while at the station were assembled a large crowd of people to give the soldier a hearty welcome home. On the arrival of the train the Band struck up the National Anthem, and enthusiastic [scenes were] witnessed.

Pte. E. Wheatley with S.A. Medal

A procession was then formed and after the town had been paraded it drew up in the Market Place, and Mr A E Hayden said a few words of welcome to Private Wheatley.

Edward Wheatley's homecoming was impressive, but he had missed out on what R.E. Smith thought was a welcome such as 'had not been seen in Easingwold before.' Information had been arriving in the town that such as Trooper Sydney Smith of Hanover House was on his way back,[5] and the landlord of the Station Hotel applied for an extension for a dinner for the men. He could not give an exact date, Mr Bowman told the beaks, but in all probability, [it] would be 'next week'.[6]

On Tuesday evening 11 June, 1901 Troopers Smith and Wilkinson arrived by train to find the station yard packed, as it had been when the volunteers returned. A band was there and two which were 'gaily decorated waggons'. One was loaned by the Flour Mill Company, on which was Miss N. Coates doing her "Britannia" performance aided by a Blue Jacket (Mr Pallister) who had lately 'returned from the front'.[7] There were others in fancy dress and a procession started with Miss Coates and others perambulating the town. The Easingwold Volunteers were there, along with 40 men on horseback representing 'almost every nation under the sun' – though it was sometimes difficult to work out which country was being portrayed (it was said). The procession was completed with the town's school children accommodated on ten wagons and the rear of it was brought up by a traction engine driven by Mr Hebdon 'all spick and span, and decorated with bunting and drawing [yet another]… waggon load of youngsters.' The parade ended in front of the house of John Rocliffe 'who addressed a few words of welcome' to the returned Yeomen. Undoubtedly the pubs thereafter, did better than usual business for a Tuesday. (Closing time was then eleven o'clock.)

About a month before the Easingwold homecoming, the *Advertiser* had reported that 18 squadrons of the Yeomanry in South Africa had embarked for home on the *Mongolian*, probably as a result of questions in the Commons, the editorial said.[8] Anyway the force was to be broken up. The mails from South Africa 'delivered throughout the country on Saturday, brought interesting particulars as to the break-up of Lord Methuen's Brigade of Imperial Yeomanry'[9] the *Easingwold* said. [The brigade consisted of the companies of Yeomanry furnished at the commencement of the war by Yorkshire, Nottingham, Northumberland, Shropshire, Worcestershire, Bucks, Berks, and Oxfordshire.]

There were other receptions at nearby places for troops returning from South Africa. The paper which reported the Easingwold homecomings, recorded the return of men to Thirsk. 'Never within the memory of the oldest inhabitant has the Market Square at Thirsk and the streets leading to the railway station been so crowded as they were on Monday night', when the eight members of the "I" Company (Thirsk) Volunteers [returned] from South Africa,' it was recorded. Two had been left invalided in De Aar Hospital, namely L Cpl Jeffreys and Private Neesam. The usual procession took place and hardly a house was without bunting. At Boroughbridge, at the Drill Hall, ten marble timepieces were presented to the local volunteers,[10] and at Alne a popular officer was welcomed back.[11] At Bedale plans were announced for a parade, a thanksgiving service and presentations at the Hall in honour of the Bedale Volunteers.[12]

In Easingwold, it was decided to present its returned soldiers with a 'good watch', suitably inscribed, and money left over from a Mafeking Day collection started a fund which was topped up by a house-to-house collection. Then the Station Hotel dinner was held.[13] Hicks was the main speaker and, proposing a toast to 'The Army, Navy and Auxiliary Forces' he reminded guests of when, he said, there was 'a disturbed and saddened expression on the

From Billy Holmes archive. On guard

face of every man they met in the street.' News from South Africa had been bad, 'a British reverse had been sustained, and such a reverse as was unknown to any living man of to-day.' Ten guns had been taken by the Boers, and it was obvious that more men were needed. Volunteers were asked for, old men like their guests volunteered. The guests responded, then J.J. Penty spoke, and during his remarks said it had been said 'many times' that our Volunteers were wasters ... no ... good whatever, and would never be deserving ... support from the British public. Penty denied this calumny vehemently. Well, he would.

As has been said it was decided to present the Easingwold soldiers with a gift paid for by public subscription organised by John Hobson, and the Easingwold Imperial Yeomanry and Volunteers Presentation Fund got under way in July.[14] It kept the names of the men well to the fore.

> The following are names of the Volunteers and Yeomen to whom presentations will be made. Imperial Yeomen – Messrs S Smith, S Frank, TA Wilkinson and T Williamson. Volunteers – Messrs Cariss, Russell, F Rhodes and E Wheatley.

Before the presentation was made two other yeomen received some fleeting publicity. The following appeared in the *Advertiser.* [15]

Two York Yeomen, Troopers W Hood and Cadman, received the South African war medal from the King on Friday last, when three thousand men were massed on the Horse Guard's Parade for that purpose. They served with the 66th Company, and were amongst the thirty selected by ballot to represent their company on this important occasion. The medals have the late Queen's head on one side, and a battle scene on the other, with a figure of Victory holding a laurel wreath towards the troops.

The medals were to be awarded to all forces and nurses who had served in South Africa from October 11, 1899.[16] Clasps inscribed with place names (Belmont, Wittebergen, Relief of Mafeking, Transvaal and Wepener for example) were to be issued.[17]

By the end of September the Easingwold fund-raisers had completed their work and in an 'incessant downpour of rain' another celebration the like of which had 'never been seen in Easingwold before' was held. Forty pounds had been collected and spent on silver, keyless, half-hunter English lever watches, suitably inscribed. Once again Britannia and a band led the parade, though whether Miss Coates was Britannia this time was not recorded. The druids, the fire brigade and (wet) children on waggons were much in evidence. The march ended at the Town Hall where the presentations were made by Mrs Katharine Love of Hawkhills.[18]

The six men, who were honoured in September 1901, became local celebrities and must have enjoyed their status. Had they featured as letter writers and correspondents in the *Advertiser?* Some had. Smith for example.

Sid (or Syd) appeared in an *Advertiser* column about the town's 'Absent Minded Beggars' who were in South Africa. Readers of the papers then were never very far away from the soldiers being referred to as absent minded beggars, the phrase being called up when a hack's inspiration flagged, or when he felt like being a wag. Kipling had created the AMB.

He's an absent-minded beggar, and his
weaknesses are great –
But we and Paul must take him as we find him –
He is out on active service, wiping something
off a slate –
And he's left a lot of Little things behind him.

The Absent Minded Beggar was sung and recited endlessly, and for a time it must have seemed that no concert could go on without Kipling's work being given an airing. At Raskelfe in January 1900, for example, a show ended with the musical version by 'youthful performers' who had been specially trained by the vicar's daughters. 'At the close of the evening', it was recorded, '"The Absent Minded Beggar", was sung by the kind permission of the "Daily Mail" and the tambourine collection' of £1 0s 7d, was sent 'to the A.M.B. fund.'[19] Just a week later Dr Gramshaw, then in trouble with the guardians and the police (for riding his bike illegally) recited "The Absent Minded Beggar" in good style just before the collection for the War Relief Fund.[20] It comes as something of a surprise to find that at Husthwaite, the recitations at a Wesleyan prize giving did not contain the AMB – though the patriotic theme was present when E. Fox gave them 'The fight for the armoured train'.[21] This serious omission by the Wesleyans was not repeated by their fellow religionists at Tollerton when, though wintery conditions and a flu outbreak kept attendances down, a 'pleasant evening was spent.' On this occasion, the Kipling lines were sung by a Mr W. Holmes and it looks as if his rendition caused people to dig into their pockets a second time – the proceeds included another 30s. after the recitation and amounted to over £8.[22] This was another crowded programme, and the offerings included minstrel, temperance and patriotic songs. A last example of the patriotic concert and the kind of thing performed there might be taken from Crayke.[23] A concert there was divided into three sections and part was run on the lines of a minstrel show – with Mr M.O. Matthews as Interlocuter, and Messrs Gibson and Watson as corner men. The first part was devoted largely to patriotic songs. The second featured the Crayke Glee Party as pierrots and the third was 'comic'. In that Mr. Edmanson rendered 'song, "I've got the ooperzootic",' but earlier had done some more serious stuff. Mr Edmanson, the Advertiser report said, 'recited the "A.M.B." with telling pathos,' and topped the bill and closed the show with a rendition of "A little thing like that is very handy".

The *Advertiser* on 23 December 1899 reported a concert at Birdforth 'in aid of the War Fund' in which the vicar was the star. He began the proceedings 'with a song (with violin obligato) "Awake"' then duetted with a Mr Cooper on "Could a man be Secure?" A Mr Hale gave an 'amusing reading … in the Yorkshire dialect' then

> The last item on the programme was the song,"The Absent-minded Beggar," by the Rev G M Hutton, who announced that it was sung by special permission of the proprietors of the "Daily Mail", and that the words were by Mr Rudyard Kipling, and the music by Sir Arthur Sullivan. The audience joined heartily in the chorus, and afterwards a collection was taken in the room for the Patriotic Fund, which amounted to over 17s.

What of those absent minded beggars from Easingwold who were presented with timepieces? Are there letters from them or notes about them like those quoted from Trooper Boocock and George Milnthorpe? There are and one of the most noted during his army service was Sid Smith. He left Britain a little earlier than the Volunteers and went with the 'Yorks and Notts' contigents [sic] of the Imperial Yeomanry on the *Winnefredian* and was expected to reach the Cape 'about the 20th inst'.[24] Not long afterwards he appeared in the missing section of a list of losses suffered by the Yorkshire Hussars.[25]

> Private S. Smith, Hanover House, Easingwold.
>
> Private Sidney Smith, second son of Mr Thomas Smith Hanover Farm, Easingwold, who formerly lived some years in New Zealand, a fine plucky lad of 22, a good shot and rider with no previous military experience, is one of three old Easingwold Grammar School lads who are all at the front, having joined the Imperial Yeomanry.

A month after the Hussars 'casualty list' was published, Sidney Smith was thought to be in Pretoria,[26] and Eccles Foster, as has been noted, said that the two had been in prison together in Waterval and, when he wrote, Eccles was in Pretoria.[27] Sid was, in the opinion of the editor of the *Easingwold Advertiser,* probably the first civilian to volunteer to fight for his Queen and Country over the seas. He was promoted to corporal in 1900.

NOTES

1. *Advertiser,* 10 February 1900.
2. *Ibid* 22 June 1901.
3. *Ibid* 15 July 1901.
4. *Ibid* 27 July 1901.
5. *Ibid* 1 June 1901. As in so many other cases the spelling of names was not consistent. Smith was both Sydney and Sidney. But in a letter thanking the people of Easingwold, Sid signed himself – Sid Smith.
6. *Ibid* 8 June 1901.
7. Nothing is known about Blue Jacket.
8. *Ibid* 18 May 1901.
9. *Ibid.*
10. *Ibid* 22 June 1901. The men were: Lt Collier, Sgt J.H. Bruce, LCpl Lindsey, and Privates C.W. Bryan, T. West, T. Langley, - Hall, F. Watson, - Spence and C. Sutcliffe.
11. This was Capt Darcy Strangwayes, see later. *Advertiser,* 8 June 1901.
12. *Ibid* 25 May 1901.
13. *Ibid* 22 June 1901.
14. *Ibid* 6 July 1901.
15. *Ibid* 3 August 1901.
16. *Ibid* 13 April 1901.
17. For example the clasp 'inscribed "Wepener" will be granted to all troops engaged in the defence of that place between April 9, 1900, and April 25, 1900, both days inclusive.'
18. *Advertiser* 28 September 1901. The inscriptions on the watches are given in this account.
19. *Ibid* 6 January 1900.
20. *Ibid* 20 January 1900.
21. *Ibid* 10 February 1900.
22. *Ibid* 17 February 1900. The report said that Holmes recited the AMB and that it was a performed as a song.
23. *Ibid* 31 March 1900.
24. *Ibid* 10 February 1900.
25. *Ibid* 28 April 1900.
26. Report in the account of the Easingwold Mafeking celebrations. *Ibid* 26 May 1906.
27. *Ibid* 1 September 1900.

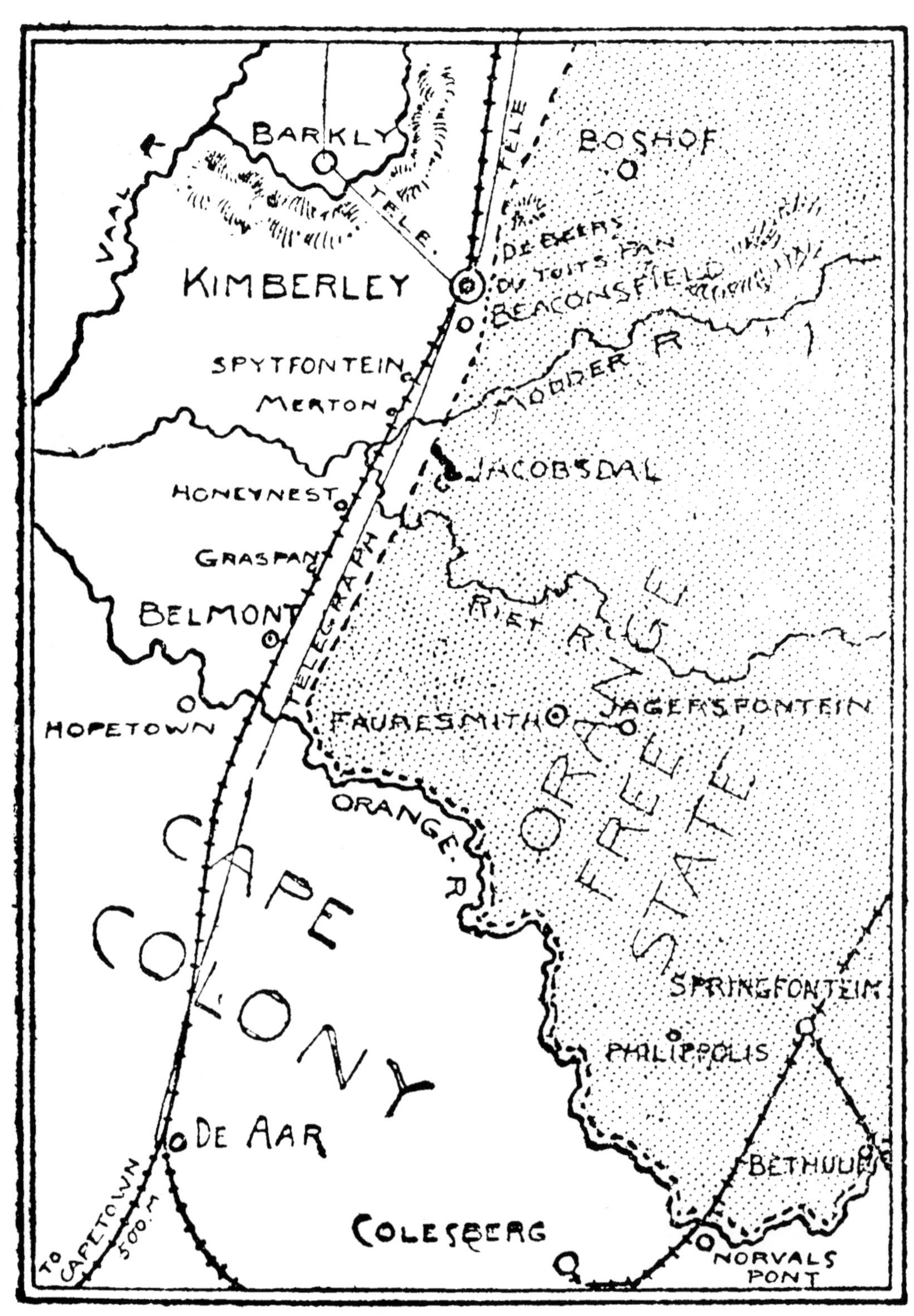

SKETCH MAP OF THE KIMBERLEY DISTRICT.

Chapter 14

THE WILKINSONS

A colleague of Sid Smith's at the presentation of watches in front of the Town Hall at Easingwold, another yeoman, was one of two local men who served in South Africa named Wilkinson. The beginning of his career in the Boer War was mentioned in the Easingwold local news section of the *Advertiser* immediately under a similar note about someone who did not return. Here are the two notes.[1]

> MR WOMBWELL, only son of Sir George Orby Wombwell, Bart., of Newburgh Priory, Easingwold, who [went] through the Crimean War and, [was] in the Balaclava charge has volunteered for service in South Africa and hopes to be appointed to the Imperial Yeomanry commanded by Lord Chesham.
>
> We understand that Mr. Thos. Wilkinson, Cold Harbour, Easingwold has volunteered for active service in South Africa. For some years Mr. Wilkinson was a trooper in the Yorkshire Hussars. He is a capital shot, and a good horseman, having been a keen follower of the York and Ainsty fox-hounds since his boyhood.

Below this were two other items of interest – the first was an announcement about the following Thursday's 'Patriotic Concert ... in aid of the Funds for the Widows and Orphans of the Transvaal War', when 'A programme of an entirely patriotic nature' would be rendered by the Crayke Glee Party and the likes of T. Cariss, F. J.H. Robinson and J.J. Penty.[2]

The second point of interest in the Easingwold local news contained a contention about the flocking to the colours that was going on. The volunteering was an unalloyed good thing, the *Easingwold* said. Why? It said why in rather flamboyant language.[3]

The Empire is ringing from end to end with patriotism; the [people] everywhere are bubbling over with warrior enthusiasm, and yeomen and citizens at home [are] eagerly volunteering for the front. The War Office people now are actually civil to the components of the Reserve forces. This is well, for if we are to escape the curse of conscription it will not pay to snub the volunteer at all. And the volunteer has in the past suffered many snubs from the superfine military redtapists of Pall Mall.

The idea of a conscription was anathema to British people and when Tom Wilkinson volunteered the war was going badly for Britain. There had been serious reverses in several places and at Colenso 'Sir Redvers Buller ... had over 1,000 casualties in his ineffective attempt to cross the Tugela' and Lord Roberts and Kitchener had been ordered to take over from him.

The second of the Easingwold men named Wilkinson to be honoured in the rain on that day in the Market Place was T.A. – Thomas Alfred Wilkinson also of the Imperial Yeomanry. He wrote a long letter after he had been in South Africa some four months.

LETTER FROM TROOPER ALF WILKINSON

The following letter has been received by Mr W.C. Wilkinson, Long Street, Easingwold, from his son:

CapeTown
April 10th, 1900

My dear Father and Mother

We arrived here this morning at 3 o'clock in very calm weather. The captain says it is one of the calmest journeys he has ever travelled so you see we have been favoured especially in March which is generally rough at sea. After leaving Maderia we were a bit unfortunate with our horses, the heat seemed really too much for them they used to lay down in their stalls and put their tongues out like dogs and gasp for breath. We had to kill one it seemed in agonies and when we throw them overboard they swim for about 100 yards and then we could see the sharks come and devour them and then they would follow us all day expecting another we lost five in all. We all have to do stable guard in our turns, and when the ship rolls it is a fearful job. Some of the fellows get frightened. The horses seem as if they cannot stand, and the men roll and sometimes are all laid in a heap. We have them to clean out and groom every other day and have drill and target practice every day and have a deal more work to do than we had at first. We float a target behind the boat and everybody shoots in his turn the first day we fired we shot the target away and had to make another, I am getting quite a crack shot. It has been a lot longer journey than we expected, it has taken us 28 days, and I have never been sick or felt bad at all since the first night so you see I am a good sailor. I have been innoculated against enteric fever it is a fearful sensation about two hours after it has been done but I got over it very well, some of the chaps faint and look very bad and they are the most likely to get it. We have got a splendid doctor. We never got any war news after leaving Liverpool only vessels that pass by and that was very little so when we arrived here the first thing we did was to buy a newspaper which cost 3d so that gives a bit of an idea of the price of things here.

We have not disembarked yet we have been lying in harbour all day, but shall be off tomorrow and are going to Maitland camp for a week and then are going straight up country. The harbour is full of vessels of all descriptions, there was a boat load of Canadian Volunteers followed us in and another boat load of Boer prisoners going out bound for St Helena. The latter part of the voyage we lived like gentlemen, I weigh ten pounds more than what I did when we left but I think that is with not having quite so much exercise. We have not much news on board a ship so you must not think I am writing very short letters considering the distance we are apart because ship life is the same day after day so I hope the next will be a very long one. You must write as often as you can as letters will be very acceptable out here, I expect when we get on the march we shall not have a minute to call our own. I forgot to give you my address in last letter but I put in on the envelope it is 12333, Trooper T.A. Wilkinson, 66th Company, 16th Battalion, Imperial Yeomanry, Field Force, South Africa. We are at the head of the Battalion and there are other 5 companies to join us so I think we shall never see Thomas unless we happen to meet and I hope we shall. We have got some splendid officers they get up obstacle races and boxing contests every day or two and give a £1 for the first prize and 5s for the second I go in for them all but have not won the lucky quid yet. We have a dog on board that came with us from Doncaster when we were there it followed us all over so we had no difficulty getting it in the train but had to put it in a box and call it luggage or they would not let us take it and we shall have to smuggle it off it is a fox terrier, well I must conclude now with love to all at home and all at the shop.[4]

I remain
Your Affectionate Son
T.A. Wilkinson

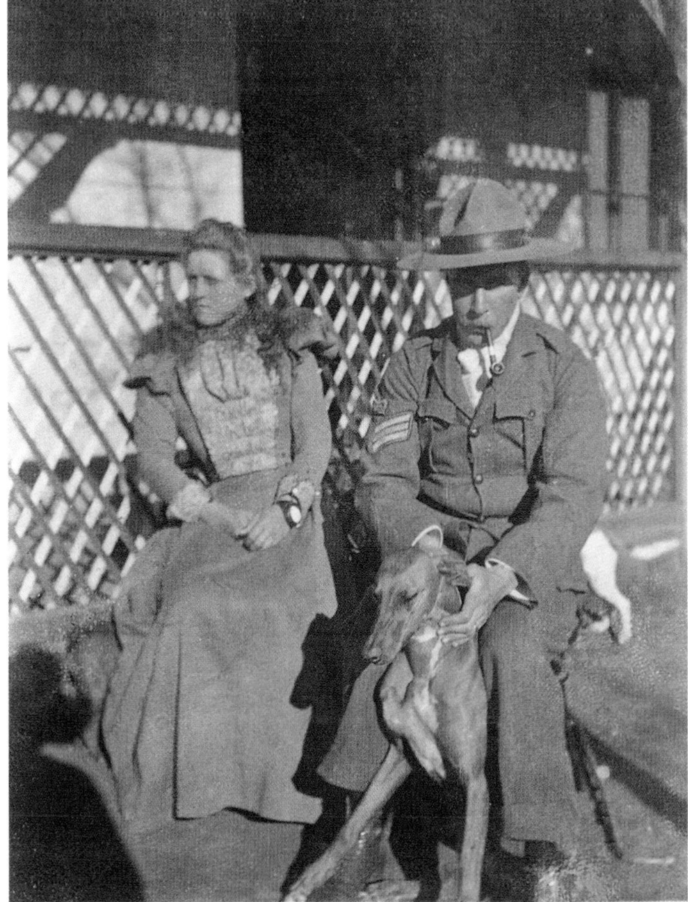

From Billy Holmes archive. A domestic scene

News of Thomas Alfred's departure for the war zone had been given in the local paper, which also recorded the arrival at the Cape of the Yorkshire Volunteers, and Lord Roberts' announcement that Bloemfontein had been captured. The volunteers arrived at Cape Town on the transport 'Guelph' on which were the four Easingwold Volunteers[sic] and just below this readers of the *Advertiser* were told that[5]

> in the list of those men who comprise the third Yorkshire Company of Imperial Yeomanry, who left Doncaster on Tuesday for Liverpool to embark on the S.S. Hilarious, for South Africa, we notice the names of T.A. Wilkinson, Easingwold, and S.M. Frank of Marton Lordship, Easingwold.

T.A. Wilkinson was the son of Watson C. Wilkinson and found out rapidly, at the front;

> They had other enemies beside the Boers, for enteric fever, which had laid low so many of England's bravest, proved too much for Captain Wombwell ... Thos Wilkinson was invalided home and Alfred ... was for weeks hovering between life and death, but happily overcame [sic] and was able to take his place again in the ranks.

T.A. Wilkinson received more mentions in the press than most of his contemporaries. His return was noted in July 1901,[6] and he was a good correspondent. He wrote to his parents from the Orange River Colony in July 1900. His letter was published.[7]

A LETTER FROM TROOPER T.A. WILKINSON

The following letter has been received by Mr W.C. Wilkinson from his son who is a trooper in the Imperial Yeomanry, South Africa.

Wymberg,
Orange River Colony
July 1900

My dear father and mother,

You will think it a long time since you had a letter from me, I suppose you will know the reason why. Well we got properly baptised I can tell you. We started on June 21st to guard a convoy to Senekal, we went about 9 miles the first day we started. Next day we had just got nicely out of the laager when in came a shell and half a dozen came in quick succession, before we knew what we were doing. We galloped on the left to take a position, when bullets began to fly past. We were in the open at the time, so we took the horses behind a small kopje and dismounted, and advanced on foot. We were not many minutes before we caught sight of the Boers. They were about 800 yards away, so we laid down and had a pop. We were firing for about an hour, and then we advanced and got about five hundred yards off. We had not put many volleys in before we saw them flying on all sides. When we got up to the place where they had been, we found 20 dead and a lot wounded. We only lost 3 wounded. In our company we had a horse or two killed in the laager with the shells. We were in the saddle from 4am until 10pm. When we got back, each man was served with a quarter of a gill of rum and a pint of coffee, and we were fit for it I can tell you. We did not take much rocking to sleep, but had to turn out again at 3 next morning. This was my first experience of fire, and felt awfully queer till we started firing, and then my senses came to me and I never held a rifle steadier. We then marched on to Senekal without any more opposition. From there we were sent to Bethlehem, and had 18 days fighting out of 21. We are under General Clements, and we had some marvellous escapes. We only lost 2 killed and about 12 wounded. We had more horses killed than men, I had mine shot. I was not mounted at the time, I was stood with my arms through the reigns looking through my field glasses, so I rode back in the guns. We have no clothing now only what we stand up in, and I went as long as 8 days without a wash, and we never shave now, we do look a black lot. We were on three-quarter rations every bit of the time - three biscuits per day, but I feel as fit as ever. Our company is only about 90 strong out of 140. Every place we go to we leave someone behind. I think this march knocked a lot of them up, but take it on the whole, our fellows have stood it well. The day we took Bethlehem we captured one of their guns, it was one Gatacre lost at Stormberg. The loyal people in Bethlehem seemed very pleased to see British troops march in. They did cheer. They said they had had a rough time for the last 6 months. The Boers had turned them out of their homes, and taken everything they had. You will think this a short letter, but I will write a longer one in a day or two.

Your affectionate son,
T.A. Wilkinson.

Few of the Easingwold 'South African' soldiers left recorded marks on their town's history, apart from their war service, and it is difficult to find out much about them. This is not surprising. Unless a parent sent a letter to R.E. Smith who recognised its worth, nothing of their stories would be known. Most confined themselves to curt notes of the hope you are well as it leaves me variety, though there were exceptions as some of the extracts published in these pages show. Most of the soldiers, however, are simply names which appear briefly in the *Advertiser* columns and disappear. Thomas Henry Russell, for example. He is on the list of those honoured by Katharine Love (and the town) and is one who was given neither

From Billy Holmes archive, Africans attached to the British Forces

a Christian name or initial. He set off for South Africa for a *second time* late in the war and the townspeople turned out to wish him and his mates, *bon voyage*. The paper named them and said something about his earlier service with the colours.[8]

OFF TO THE WAR - DEPARTURE OF EASINGWOLD YEOMEN

On Tuesday night an enthusiastic crowd gathered at the station to witness the departure of another batch of Yeomen for the front. The names of the young men are: William Smith, son of Mr Thos. Smith, Hanover House; Thos. Henry Russell, son of Mrs Kirbyson, Thirsk Road; Hilton Carr, son of Mr W. Carr, Long Street; Wm. Armstrong, late with Mr Mark Reynard, blacksmith; Frank Bean, son of Mr James Bean, Long Street; and George Clark. T.H. Russell went through the early part of the war with the Volunteer Company P.W.O. Regiment, and returned home last June. Wm. Smith is brother to Mr S. Smith, who served in the late Capt. Stephen Wombwell's Company Imperial Yeomanry, under Lord Methuen. As the train steamed out of the station hearty cheers were given, and fog signals placed on the line were exploded.

In January 1901 the Easingwold Volunteers had their annual dinner at the Station Hotel, but Tom Russell, of course, was not there. A letter from him and another from a colleague, however, was printed in the paper that contained details of the dinner and the death of the Queen. Here are the two letters with R.E. Smith's introduction.[9]

NEWS FROM THE FRONT

The following letters are perhaps more interesting from the fact that a fortnight ago Lord Kitchener gave orders that no more letters were to be sent from the seat of war.

The first one is from Mr Ted Webster, son of Mr J G Webster, the Jolly Farmer, who was called up as a reservist to join his comrades of the Yorkshire Light Infantry at the front last May. Going out at a time when most people at home thought the war practically at an end, he has had many exciting experiences in the fighting line. Previous to being called up he had seen active service in India.

The second letter is from Private Tom Russell, who was one of the four Easingwold Volunteers who went out to fight the country's battles in January last year. They have been practically in the front line ever since landing, and have had a good share of the strange vicissitudes of life on the veldt. The letters received from them, despite the hardships endured, have all been marked by cheery good humour and contentment.

Pretoria
19th December 1900

Dear Parents

A few lines to tell you I am still living and in good health, and hope this will find you all the same. You will have seen the account of the terrible slaughter we have had up here. I am thankful to say I am all right. It was simply murder. The Boers were mad with the liquor they found on the convoy. They took a couple of days before the fight, and it gave them a bit of pluck, but they will not forget it of a sudden. They were cut down like a field of hay. I do not know the proper number of casualties yet, you will be able to get a better account in the papers than I can get here. I told you when I wrote you a couple of months ago the war was not nearly finished. You see now that I am right. Some of the Yeomanry have got themselves into a nice mess. They galloped for their lives, and about 50 of them are to be tried for cowardice. I am glad to say they are not the Yorkshire Companies. You will see by the papers that my regiment has had heavy losses. There were only 8 sound men left in the "A" Company when the role was called, and several casualties in all the Companies. The Boers were using explosive bullets. I am down in Pretoria. I came in here the night before last with a convoy of 82 wounded belonging to different regiments. I am going in again today. There are a lot more wounded to come down yet. It is a long way to bring the poor fellows in ox transports. It shakes them terribly, and some of them have fearful wounds, but there is no railway out that way. I cannot understand not getting any letters from you. I have only had one letter since I have been out here. I am wondering if you are all well. I had a good look around Pretoria yesterday. It is a grand place. I had a look at old Kruger's house, his wife still living in it. Everything is scandlously dear here. I should have bought you some Christmas present, but it is simply throwing money away buying anything but what is necessary. I am sending you some Kruger coins. I am sending you them to divide among you as you think fit. I think I have no more to say this time. Wishing you all a merry Christmas and a happy New Year. Love to you all.

Ted.

P.S. This is the first time I have been in a civilized place since last July.

FRANK RHODES

Above: with parents, brothers and sisters. House (no longer there) was between Crayke and Oulston Crossroads.

Right: in dress uniform of Volunteer Company of 1st Yorkshire Regiment (now Green Howards).

Below: with friend in fatigue drill in Volunteer Company, Yorkshire Regiment

The Boers Orange River, Cape Colony.
December 14th, 1900

Dear Friend

Just a few lines to you hoping to find you all well, as it leaves me at present. We have had it very rough up the country - heavy marches and short rations. We started marching from Noval's Pont, which is the border of the Cape Colony, and joined our regiment at Bloemfontein, and then went out for eight days, when we first saw the Boers. Then we came back to Bloemfontein ready for the general advance to Pretoria. We met the enemy several times, but they always had to retire; they made a bit of a stand at Pretoria on the 4th of June. It was a bit lively all day; bullets and shells came in all directions, but our company has been very lucky. I think we were firing until dark, and then had to retire for the night. We all expected another go the next morning, but they came out with the white flag and said that the town had surrendered. But the Boers had gone so we marched through the town and camped for a few days. Then we went to Diamond Hill, where there was three days heavy fighting. Our casualties were heavy, but the Boers were much worse. Belfast was another big fight, and our men got at short range with their big guns, and cut them down with case shot. They lost very heavy there. Then we went on to Kapmaden, and stayed there a fortnight, and then left the regiment thinking we were going home, but they have stopped us here to guard the bridge which crosses the Orange River. De Wet is still at large, so I don't think we shall get away yet.

All the Easingwold lads are in good health, and wish to be remembered to all. We have not seen Ted yet, nor Sid Smith.

Yours truly,
Tom Russell

Wilkinson came home and went back to South Africa, as has been said. In January 1902 he was again at home and attended yet another dinner at Bowman's Station Hotel. He responded to a toast to the Imperial Yeomanry.[10]

Another of the Yeomen present along with the Wilkinsons at the ceremonies connected with their presentations has been mentioned in passing. He was Sam W. Frank of Marton Lordship, in the electoral division of Stillington a place which in 1890 was 2,379 acres in extent, had a rateable value of £2,058 and a population of 144. There is no 'village' recorded *Bulmers* 'the houses lie scattered, chiefly' on the east side of the Foss, the work said.

The second Wilkinson to receive a token of Easingwold's gratitude in the Boer War, was Tom but the first of the Volunteers to be mentioned in the *Advertiser* was Thomas Cariss. He was one of numerous people in the town with that surname as even a cursory glance at the directories immediately shows. That of 1890 had a William Cariss, Market Place for example. Miss Ellen was a dressmaker in Long Street and Miss Annie traded as a 'Grocer, Tea and Provision Dealer' (and Draper). Thomas Douglas was a plumber, and members of the clan regularly performed in concerts and shows in the area and gave them a song after a dinner with all the confidence of a Buller Hicks.

Tom Cariss wrote a letter home in April 1900 that gave some details about where he was and had been. He comes over as a bit of a wag (with a rather macabre sense of humour).[11]

A LETTER FROM TOM CARISS
"BISCUITS AS HARD AS BRICKS"

The following has been received by Mr G.J. Webster, the "Jolly Farmer" Inn, from Private Tom Cariss, one of the Easingwold Volunteers, who volunteered for the front in March, and is now in General Pole-Carew's Division.

Bloemfontein
April 18th, 1900

Dear Friend
Just a line or two to say that we are all getting on well. It is raining every day, and we get wet through, and have to stand in the sun until we dry. Just tell Harry S....n to come out this way, as he would do a good trade, for when we are on the march, we see scores of horses and bullocks laying dead and not buried, and if Jane B.... was here she could get heaps of bones.

We have marched here from Norval's Point, a distance of 140 miles in 8 days, on a pound of corned beef and a pound of bread a day, and when we had no bread we had two dog biscuits as hard as bricks.

Just remember us to all our friends as we are going to make for Pretoria in a week or so. It was reported here yesterday that Mafeking had been relieved, and 8,000 prisoners taken. No more at present with love to all.

Yours, &c.,
Private Tom Cariss, SS Company,
1st P.W.O. Yorkshire Regiment,
Field Force, South Africa.

Earlier in the paper Tom Cariss's account of the Easingwold Volunteers campaigning during their 16 month stay in South Africa was printed in full.

Tom Cariss shared the platform to receive his presentation from Katharine Love with three other volunteers, one of whom was Frank Rhodes. He left for the war with Cariss, Russell and Wheatley, as has been noted. [12]

Frank Rhodes entered the ranks of Easingwold's published letter writers and in February 1901 one to his sister was used by Reg Smith.[13]

LETTER FROM THE FRONT

The following letter has been received by Mrs Slater, Crayke Road, from her brother Private Frank Rhodes, who went out with the Easingwold Volunteers last year.

Bethulie Bridge
January 20th, 1901

Dear Sister
I just write a few lines to you hoping to find you well, as it leaves me at present in the best of health. We are still here at this God-forsaken place and likely to be here for a long time yet. We never hear anything about moving, and as for coming home we have given up all thoughts of that. We are sick of this. We are only allowed to go for a wash twice a week and

that is a good mile. I would rather be after the Boers than stuck here, because we are on guard every other night, and we are up every morning at three o'clock, so you may guess we have an awful time of it. There are no Boers about here now, and we have not heard anything of De Wet for a fortnight. He was round this way but we were too strong for him. We drove him off and killed four of his men, and a lot of his horses, but they did us no harm. We have been in nineteen battles, and never had a man killed, we have lost five men, but they have all died of fever, and one died on the ship as we came out. We have had a lot gone sick since we came here and no wonder for we have no tents, and we have had some heavy rains, and our blankets are getting very thin. As for clothes, we have none. We got a new suit at Pretoria but they are done now. We got a new shirt in June, and we have not had one since, and when we want it washing we have to go without one till it drys, so if you don't hear anything about us coming home you must send me one and a pair of socks. I should not like to come home until the war is over. I should like to join the mounted, but we cannot get our discharge from this company. When you write back I wish you would send me a bit of reading of some kind, as it is worse than been lost being stuck up here.

From your loving brother,
Private F.E. Rhodes

Frank was the son of John Rhodes of Crayke Lane, Easingwold and there is a photograph of him, in a group, taken outside a 'stone cottage' between Crayke and Oulston in 1902.

The last of the men sharing in the Easingwold celebrations was that Edward Wheatley whose return had been delayed when he had to be part of an escort taking Boer prisoners to Bermuda.

Above, it has been mentioned that many men who went to the South African war got only the briefest of mentions in the *Advertiser.* There clearly were others – though these would not have been the volunteers who R.E. Smith (and the town) were so extraordinarily proud of. They would have made up a large group. How large that was it is impossible to say with certainty, but, added to the likes of Edward Wheatley and Arthur Bowman, would have been the regulars from the area, and the reservists who got their papers after hostilities started. Many of these were noted as they left. Few of the regulars were.

In March 2000 a letter appeared in the *Easingwold Advertiser* about Thomas Whorley of Helperby.[14] It was written by Mavis Hartley, his granddaughter, who said that her ancestor was born in 1865, and was 'one of the two Helperby men who went to serve in the Boer War'. Accompanying two photographs was an illustration of a page from a 'New Testament' ... given to hm [sic] by his mother, Rebecca Whorley, on going to war Jan. 16th, 1900. An inscription gave a date. Rebecca Whorley given to Thomass [sic] Whorley by his loving mother on going to the War, Janary [sic] 16, 1900. Mrs Hartley said that her mother, Thomas's daughter, was born in August 1900 and 'baptised Alice Pretoria, my grand-father having taken part in the relief of Pretoria in June 1900'. A second photograph, is of eleven men in uniform, standing outside a village pub. The caption says 'Helperby & Brafferton Militia (1899) in front of Oak Tree Inn with Thomas Whorley 5th from right'.

Thomas Whorley might have been one of two Helperby men who R.E. Smith, in a rare lapse did not name in a report of February 1900, when a 'hearty "send off"' was given to Edward Wheatley and three other Easingwolders who were off to South Africa with two from Helperby and six from Thirsk, as part of a contingent that the Princess of Wales Yorkshire Regiment of Volunteers were sending to the front.[15] Whorley must have changed from being a militiaman.

The Helperby militia was not a group which was noted frequently – if ever – in the *Easingwold Advertiser.* Not until 2000 did that happen, it seems.[16]

NOTES

1. *Advertiser* 23 December 1899
2. *Ibid* 30 December 1899
3. *Ibid* 23 December 1899
4. *Ibid* 12 May 1900
5. *Ibid* 17 March 1900
6. *Ibid* 14 July 1901
7. *Ibid* 18 August 1900
8. *Ibid* 15 March 1902
9. *Ibid* 26 January 1901
10. *Ibid* 25 January 1902
11. *Ibid* 19 May 1900
12. *Ibid* 10 February 1900
13. *Ibid* 16 February 1901
14. *Ibid* 11 March 2000
15. This report has also been used elsewhere in these pages.
16. A close perusal of the files for the half year before the war broke out, for example.

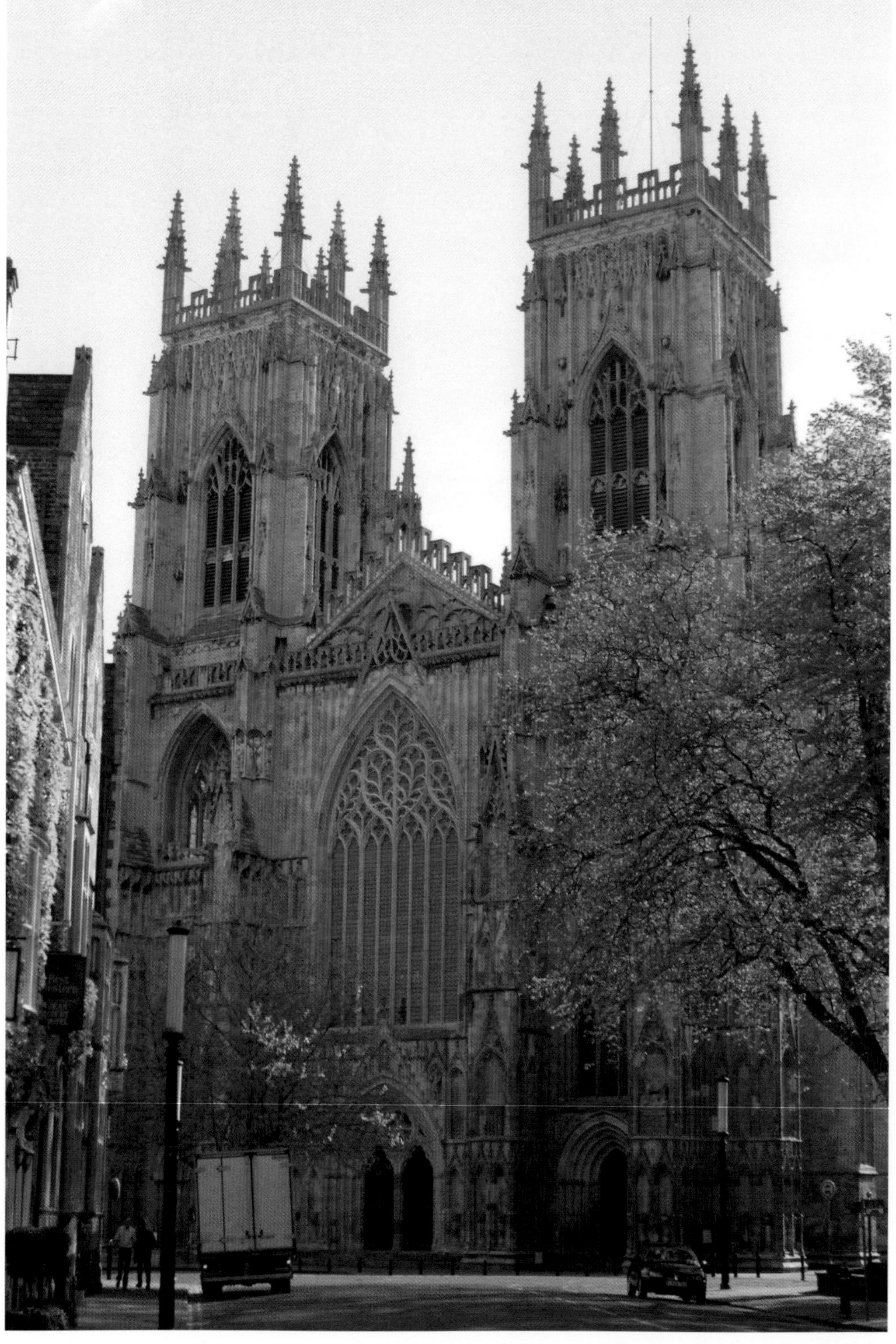

York Minster in all its splendour on a sunny spring morning.
The Boer War Memorial to the fallen of Yorkshire is within a couple of hundred yards.

Chapter 15

TROOPER WALTER DALE. KILLED IN ACTION

Without any doubt the best known Easingwold 'South African' soldier was Trooper Walter Dale, the son of the relieving officer for the local Poor Law Union (and he held other posts of a similar nature).[1] He , it is, who is commemorated in the Parish Church.

Trooper Dale was a regular soldier and a note about him appeared in the local paper in March 1900, in a column devoted to the local '"Absent Minded Beggars," at the front, who are so nobly fighting the nation's battles in South Africa'. Three men were singled out – Sidney Ellis, of Crayke, Metrick Till and Walter Dale, who was stationed in India when the war started.[2]

THE WAR
ITEMS OF LOCAL INTEREST

IN MEMORY OF
THOMAS WALTER DALE,
9TH QUEEN'S ROYAL LANCERS,
WHO WAS KILLED IN THE SERVICE OF HIS KING AND COUNTRY
BY DYNAMITE EXPLOSION AT VREDEFORT ROAD,
SOUTH AFRICA.
28TH JUNE 1901, AGED 25 YEARS.
THIS TABLET IS ERECTED BY SOLDIERS' FRIENDS OF THIS DISTRICT
AS A RECOGNITION OF HIS PATRIOTISM.

Memorial in Easingwold Church

Among the "Absent-minded Beggars" at the front, who are so nobly fighting the nation's battles in South Africa, are many from the immediate neighbourhood. Some of them we appear to lose sight of for a time, until the casualty list appears, when first one and then another well-known name we come across, which brings home the reality of the struggle.

In General Buller's advance to Ladysmith we notice that another local man has been wounded - Lance-Corporal Metrick Till, of the 2nd West Yorks Regiment. He comes of a well-known Carlton Husthwaite family, of which place he is a native.

Another, who has so far fortunately escaped injury, must have had some exciting experiences. We refer to Walter Dale, son of Mr James Dale, relieving officer. When the 9th Lancers, in which he is a trooper, left India at the beginning of the war, he had to be left behind, having been suffering from fever, but it was not long before he was well enough to follow his comrades, and since then they have been with General French, getting to the front when that General was holding the Boers in check at Rensburg. Since then, the cavalry brigade, under their clever leader, have done grand work, and we do not believe but that Trooper Dale has done his share.

In consequence of the "entanglement" of Ladysmith the 1st Royal Rifles have been shut up for some weeks, and the reservists of that regiment found they were unable to get through, and have had to take part in Buller's advance for its relief. One of the reserves called out was Sidney Ellis, son of Mrs Richard Ellis, Mount Pleasant, Crayke. The last letter received from him was sent from Chiveley about a month ago, and though the forces were fighting an uphill battle, they were not in the least disheartened, but appeared always ready to have another dig at the enemy, and confident of ultimate success.

Since then, the tide of war has turned in our favour, and we are confident that the men who fought their way to Ladysmith, and manoeuvred with French, and the Yeomanry and Volunteers we sent out, will do whatever mortal man can do, and it is pleasant to think that Easingwold is represented among them.

In midsummer two letters from Walter Dale were published. They were dated a week apart and are self-explanatory.[3]

The following letters have been received by Mr James Dale, Long Street, Easingwold, from his son Walter, serving with the 9th Lancers in South Africa:-

9th Lancers,
Bloemfontein.
May 7th, 1900.

Dearest Mother and All,

Since I wrote you the last letter we have been on another fortnight's stiff fighting, and lost thirty-six in killed and wounded, and nearly everyone of the wounded are dying through poisoned bullets, but thank God I have got through it all right, and returned to Bloemfontein for two days, then we are going on to Brandfort to rejoin Lord Roberts. On Monday, 8th May, you will see in the papers where we have been fighting, about 30 miles from Bloemfontein, and it has been the hardest bit of fighting we have had, all the men and horses alike on half rations. Other regiments in our brigade are working with us, but they cannot hold a candle to the old 9th. General Gordon is in charge of our brigade, and French of our division. General French gave a splendid speech when we were on parade with all of the brigade, upon the gallant way in which we did our work and how we were the means of saving the position time after time, and that we should get our reward after the war was over, and that he should never forget the regiment whilst it was a regiment. It seems to be very probable that we shall return to England after the war, and we think that is what General French means about being rewarded. He did not say anything about the other regiments. The 17th rather disgraced themselves, they ran away from a position that commanded the day, then we were sent and had to fly to regain the position, and only just got in by the skin of our teeth, that is where we lost so many men, including two officers killed and one wounded. We are very busy indeed now, so I have not time to write a long

The Dale Family, 1897
Back row: Reg., Frank, Edith, Clarence, Albert, Jenny, Walter, Everard.
Front row: Mable, Father, Septimus, Mother, Ivy.

Thomas Walter Dale in his 9th Lancers Uniform with his family in Easingwold (1897). He has his arm around his brother Everard who died in WW1. The young man in the sailor suit is Sepp Dale, badly wounded in the Somme and for many years landlord of The George.

letter, as we only arrived in Bloemfontein on Friday, and leaving early on Monday. We have got a new regiment of horses today, and have all the new saddlery to fit. I am in the best of health, hoping you are all the same. With love to all, and double to little Ivy. I have sent the chocolate box home, so hope you will have got it before this letter arrives. I think this is the general advance with Lord Roberts this time.

From your loving Son,
Walter Dale

May 12th, 1900

Dearest Mother and All,

I know you will be getting very anxious about me not writing before, but it is impossible to write when we are out. You will see that I wrote a letter to you in Bloemfontein, but could not get a chance to post it, so I had to carry it in my pocket to Kronstad, where we are now.

We have had very little fighting, but have been driving the Boers back all the way. If they come across a good position then they make a bit of a stand, but not for long. They have been doing more damage to the railway than anything else. We have not had any casualties in our regiment since we left Bloemfontein. We are staying in Kronstad for one day's rest, then are off again. I think it is about half way, so shall not be long before we are at Pretoria. I think they expect to be there by the 24th. We expect a big fight on the Vaal River, but I suppose it will be something like Kronstad. I don't think it will be very long before it is all over. I have not time to write any adventures, but am in the best of health and spirits. Hoping you are all same.

So no more at present, from your loving Son.
Walter Dale

The issue of the *Advertiser* in which Walter Dale's letters appeared carried the following editorial note on "conscription".

> IT has been said that no other than a voluntary system of soldiering would put up with the blundering of the military authorities. If "Tommy Atkins" was a conscript and forced to, under [endure] such treatment, as he was thoughtlessly subjected to last week, he would not put up with it ... the British people would not stand such aggravations, and, after a few examples such as the Aldershot affair,[4] the whole Army would be in rebellion. [But] ... "Tommy Atkins" ... is there [in South Africa] of his own free will, and he takes the [bungling and the blunders as being] ... all in the day's work ... in the same spirit, he views his generally bad conditions. ... In South Africa. Under a conscript system it would be very different. The soldier then [would] be a much keener critic, and ... mistakes ... such as characterised the early conduct of the war, would ... have ruined the morale of a conscript army.

Powerful stuff, but what was the Aldershot Affair? It had been raised in the Commons and Major Gen Brook, commanding the Aldershot District said that parts of the press had reported it in a very unfair and un-British spirit, and wrongly condemned those responsible. What had happened?[5] Thirty thousand 'Regulars, Militia, and Volunteers' took part in field operations 'several hundred' were prostrated and there were four deaths. It was evidence of downright, tragic incompetence, Smith contended.

> Many of the soldiers had to fall out on the plains, where the heat was 110 deg. It was just like our War Office intelligence to let this occur. With the glass jumping up as it did in the beginning of the week there should have been someone with authority at Aldershot to postpone the manoeuvres to a more suitable day.

On 13 July 1901, Trooper Dale's parents heard that Walter had been killed.[6] The press notice said

DEATH OF AN EASINGWOLD SOLDIER
IN SOUTH AFRICA

Our readers will be sorry to hear of the death in active service in South Africa, of Trooper Walter T Dale, son of Mr James Dale, relieving officer, Easingwold. On the 13th first word was received, in reply to enquiries from his father, that he had been killed by an explosion of a mine on the railway near Vredefort Road in the Transvaal.

From Billy Holmes archive

The dead soldier joined the 9th Lancers seven years ago, and [went] through the Matabele War. From there he went to India, and then back to South Africa at the commencement of the present war where he joined General French's Division. He had his horse shot under him during the operations for the relief of Kimberley. After the defeat of Cronje, he formed one of Lord Roberts' body guard on his entry into Bloemfontein. He also served under Generals Methuen, Ian Hamilton and Broadwood, and was one of General Knox's force in the memorable hunt after De Wet.

Last Christmas he volunteered to drive a train on the Military Imperial Railway from Bloemfontein to Kronstad and Elandsfontein. Soon after he commmenced his duties he wrote home saying that the work was very hard, and they had many steep hills to climb, but he was glad to say he was strong and healthy, and equal to it. When on the railway he had a severe attack of enteric fever, and recovered, only to be killed as stated above. No particulars are on hand [to] say how he met his death ...

In his last letter home, received on the 18th of June, he said he was glad the Boers had not thrown him off the line yet, though they had several times fired upon him, and obliged him to run back as soon as possible. He also mentioned the fact that his mate, a driver named Gough, had been killed by the Boers at Klip River. He also said he hoped to be back in England in a few months. Deceased was 25 years of age.

Great sympathy is felt for Mr and Mrs Dale and family in their sad bereavement.

Kroonstad
O.R.C.
Loco. Dept. I. M. R.
28/6/01

Dear Mr Dale

I sincerely regret to inform you that your poor boy was killed by the explosion of dynamite placed on the line by Boers this morning at 7 a.m.
He was fireman on No. 65 engine working the up passenger train, & although I haven't been to the scene of the accident it is reported that his end was instantaneous, poor lad, he was one of my dearest friends, & thought the world of, by those who knew him. —
I left him last night at 8 p.m. & we were chatting about old friends; little did I think of having to inform you of this sad loss on the morrow. —
I am trying to get him brought into this Station, to give him the least he deserves, a decent burial, & if I can manage it, I will have a photo taken of the spot. — I am too cut up to write more, & may God give you all strength to bide over so great a loss. —

With deepest sympathy, & regards
I am yours sincerely
Gordon Bland
"Late of Scarboro"

Later. 29/6/01
P.S. We are burying him to-day at Kroonstad, with full military honours.

A well attended memorial service was held in the Easingwold Parish Church on Sunday afternoon last, conducted by the Vicar, the Rev. N. Jackson M.A. who made touching reference to the sad event which had brought them together. The hymns "O God our help in ages past" and "On the resurrection morning", were impressively sung by the choir, and at the conclusion of the service "O rest in the Lord" was played on the organ by Mrs R E Smith, in the absence of the organist.

Towards the end of the year it was decided to erect a memorial to Walter Dale, and an appeal was made for funds and an announcement [was] made about what form the memorial was to take. (Jackson was the Rev Nathan Jackson, Vicar of St. John the Baptist, the Parish church).[7]

EASINGWOLD NOTICE

It is the intention of the inhabitants of Easingwold to perpetuate the memory of Thomas Walter Dale, private in the 9th Queen's Royal Lancers; the only one whose life has been sacrificed in his service of the country from the town, in the South African campaign; by the erection of a tablet in the church. Anyone wishing to contribute one shilling or more to the fund, on paying the sum to any member of the undersigned committee, will have their names enrolled on the list of subscribers to be presented to his mourning parents and family.

Members of the Committee –

REV. N JACKSON
JOHN ROCLIFFE
F. J. H. ROBINSON
JOHN HOBSON

The subscription for a tablet went ahead and in March 1902, Walter's parents publicly thanked contributors.[8]

THANKS.

Mr. and Mrs. Dale and Family wish to thank one and all who have contributed to the beautiful tablet, which has been erected in Easingwold Church, to perpetuate the memory of their dear son, who was killed in South Africa.

The tablet is an impressive one – it reads:-

IN MEMORY OF
THOMAS WALTER DALE
9TH QUEEN'S ROYAL LANCERS,
KILLED IN THE SERVICE OF HIS KING AND COUNTRY
BY DYNAMITE EXPLOSION AT VREDEFORT ROAD,
SOUTH AFRICA.
JUNE 1901, AGED 25 YEARS
ERECTED BY SOLDIER FRIENDS OF THIS DISTRICT
AS A RECOGNITION OF HIS PATRIOTISM.

Kroonstad Military Cemetery where Walter Dale is buried. Over half of the circular metal plaques have been stolen for scrap, including Walter Dale's. He is commemorated on a memorial in the Entrance Gate, but his initials are incorrect, although his number and date of death are accurate. Photo taken 2000.

Walter Dale had had some narrow escapes and was an accomplished letter writer. The following had appeared in the *Advertiser* next to an account of Lt Caffin's return to Northallerton.[9]

AN EASINGWOLD MAN AT THE FRONT
HIS HORSE SHOT UNDER HIM

The following letter has been received by Mrs Wm Tebb of York, from her brother Private Walter Dale, of the 9th Lancers, son of Mr James Dale, relieving officer, Easingwold, and dated "Bloemfontein, March 21st", 1900.

I received your very welcome letter on the 19th. You say you wonder if I have been under fire yet; when I tell you that I have had my horse shot from under me you will see that I have been among the rifle-fire, and those pom-poms. Kindersburg Drift was the first big battle I was in; that was when we were stationed on the Modder, where we seem to have got so much praise. Then we left the Modder River, and went to the relief of Kimberley. We had another big fight at Rill Drift, where I got my horse shot. I had just been signalling to a young officer of ours, and had just mounted my horse again, and just got into a gallop down the opposite side of the hill, when my horse stumbled and fell, and I flew over his head into the rocks, and lay there stunned for about four hours, when I was found by an Infantry man, of the Grenadier Guards. I was then sent back to Modder River, and from there to De Aar. I had not hurt my head so much in falling, but through my hat falling off, and my head being exposed to the sun, it took hold of me, and I caught a little fever. I was down at De Aar a fortnight, and left there on the 3rd of March to rejoin the regiment, just past where old Cronje was captured, and where we had another big fight. We lost nearly all our horses there, and more men than we had lost all the time.

From Orange River we had to do Infantry work. Our regiment itself drove the Boers back off two kopjes, and captured two guns. I think our regiment did their best work there as Lord Roberts mentioned us specially in dispatches.

Then we marched on Bloemfontein - four days march - where we expected another big battle, but when we got there we found the enemy had flown. The whole division formed up about four miles out of the town, and Lord Roberts sent a galloper to say that it was his special request that the 9th Queen's Royal Lancers should form his bodyguard through Bloemfontein. I can tell you, that made the Life Guards, and all the other Cavalry corps look down their noses, so we were the only regiment that marched through the town. We did feel big guns I can assure you. Some with proper helmets, some with Boer caps, some with civilian clothes, and others with handkerchiefs tied on their heads for helmets, and all with big long beards, and we had not had a wash for over a week. Oh! It was lovely.

Now we are all stationed at Bloemfontein, and we don't like it at all. We would sooner ten times be on the move. The fighting is champion, we do not seem to have the least fear, but when we come to be in a standing camp with no tents, and the sun burning all day, then perhaps it will come on rain and we get wet through, then it is when we get sick of the war.

I don't think our regiment will go any further than Bloemfontein, as everybody seems to think we have done enough fighting but I hope not, as I want to go on to Pretoria.

Walter Dale (3769) 9th Lancers.

Walter Dale's letter did not contain any criticisms of the conduct of the war, but the editorial in the *Easingwold*, carried more comments of a kind that were becoming familiar. Lord Roberts had taken over as supremo in South Africa and he issued despatches, which were highly critical of what had gone on there so far. What he said was 'the common talk of the Army for weeks; and would have been viewed with mixed feelings by Tommy Atkins, though their publication did indicate a healthy unwillingness to shield officers in high places. The men in the ranks however were lauded to the skies, and compliments to them frequently published. The captured Boer Col Allbrecht, for example, 'said of our troops that not only were they "better than our German infantry", but that "they will advance when no one else in the world will advance".' Mr Treves, an eminent surgeon who went out to Natal, 'had the highest opinion' of them.[10]

> Whoever else has blundered all have spoken well of Tommy Atkins, and it would be fatal to the Army if he loses all confidence in his leaders ...

When Trooper Dale died regular Boer attacks on British trains were being made. For example, towards the end of April 1901 one was captured near Molteno. The front engine escaped and got to Stormberg. It returned and it was discovered that the driver and stoker of the other train had been captured and the train set on fire.[11] There were other incidents of wrecking reported from the early months of 1901.[12] and in June an exciting account of a hold-up appeared which introduced a swashbuckling figure into the narrative of what was now largely a guerrilla war.[13]

HOW A SUPPLY TRAIN WAS "HELD UP"

The special correspondent of the Standard at Kaapmuiden, writing on the 30th ult, says: The Boers are fleeing in considerable numbers before the advance of General Sir Bindon Blood. It is believed they are seeking a means of escape round the Kaap Hills, and thence across to the North by Hectorspruit. Others are reported to be trekking into Gazaland.

Later details of the recent holding up of a supply train between Alkmaar and Elandshoek have now been received. The dynamited train consisted of two engines and several trucks. A Boer leader, named Hindon, a notorious train wrecker, stationed himself with 50 men, close to the line, at a sharp curve on the top of a steep gradient. He himself wore the uniform of a captain in the British army, and the majority of his band were dressed in khaki.

As the second engine, which was placed at about the middle of the train, reached the place of observation Hindon exploded a mine composed of 60 dynamite cartridges. The engine and trucks were thrown over, and the train brought to a standstill.

Behind the trucks were a van and carriage containing some fever-stricken men of the Welsh Regiment and other details, behind that another van, and lastly, an armoured truck manned by a lieutenant and four men. The Boers, thinking the carriage contained officers, riddled it with bullets, killing two men and wounding another two.

The fireman on the first engine jumped off and escaped, but the driver stuck to his post, and was shot dead with his hand on the lever. The stoker on the second engine was wounded in the thigh.

The instant the explosion occurred the small escort in the armoured truck opened fire. The Boers for the most part kept carefully out of the way of the bullets and Hindon sent a party of them up the hill to fire down on the truck. The British, however, kept well under the shelter of its sides, and the Boers, seeing that [their] manoeuvre was a failure, climbed the dismantled trucks, got on top of the van, and attempted to pot their enemy from that position.

This attempt was also fruitless and the Boers, hearing the command to fix bayonets, fell off the van on both sides and ran back to cover. As a last resource, Hindon sent a Boer, covered by a British prisoner, up the track to demand the surrender of the escort, whom he threatened otherwise, to dynamite. The little band of British, however, stood firm, and the Boers, seeing that the case was hopeless, and hearing the approach of an armoured train, decamped.

Before they left they robbed everybody on board the train and took away with them one wounded man, a civilian passenger, and the driver of the second engine. These, after stripping them, they abandoned in the bush on being shelled by the armoured train. They would have undoubtedly looted the whole of the valuable stores and supplies had it not been for the gallant defence offered by the small armed escort.

The main South African campaign news published on the day that the story of Hindon's exploits appeared; referred to an attack on a convoy at Ventersdorp (due west of Johannesburg); the losses sustained by Gen Dixon's forces near Vlakfontein; and the advance being made by Gen Bindon Blood.[14] It is more than just a remote possibility that Hindon was in charge of the raid that ended with Walter Dale's death.

Although Hindon does not feature prominently in British Boer war studies, there is a lot about him in South African sources. There is an article published by Herman Labuschagne, for example, in which it is said that 'The greatest train-wrecker of all ... was ... Captain Oliver Jack Hindon, a Scot by birth,' who 'once took three trains in spectacular fashion within twenty minutes'. The British, the author went on, gave orders that 'Hindon and his men were to be pursued specially and that no prisoners were to be taken'. The wrecker became the subject of correspondence between Kitchener and Louis Botha. It accused Hindon and his men of attacking women on the trains 'they targeted. This was nonsense, Botha replied and said he and his men had every right to attack the lines of communication and supply of [their] enemies'.[15]

An account of the attack which killed Walter Dale, has already been given and several of the features described look very similar to the Hindon attack, and several place names given by the *Advertiser* are on the line running from Bloemfontein to Johannesburg. Kronstadt (Kroonstad) is about half way between these two places and Vredefort is practically on the border of the Orange Free State and Transvaal. On the day that Walter Dale was killed, a friend wrote to his father with the terrible news. A copy of this letter still exists.[16] It is not, this time, from the *Advertiser.*

The railway on which Trooper Dale worked had a number of small branches, one below Kroonstad going off to the east and terminating at Winburg a few miles away. Further north, a branch went from the main track (at Wolverhoek Siding) to the town of Heilbron. Walter Dale might well have worked on that branch as well as on the main line. Not far from the terminus at Heilbron is the Klip River where his friend was killed. (It is crossed by the road that runs from Heilbron to Frankfort.)

The description of where the Dale tragedy occurred might be misleading. The stations on the main line are frequently named after a nearby road – Heilbron Road and Winburg Road for example – and reports of Dale's death, and the tablet in Easingwold church, read as if there is one called Vredefort Road.

From Billy Holmes archive. Rough country

Walter Dale did not survive the war. What happened to the notorious Hindon? He eventually surrendered and the *Advertiser* reported the event in its issue of 24 May 1902.

SURRENDER OF HINDON - A NOTORIOUS TRAINWRECKER

Reuter's Pretoria correspondent states that C.J. Hindon, known as Jack Hindon, who has been associated with various exploits as an officer under the Boers, has surrendered at Balmoral. The Central News adds that the notorious trainwrecker was despatched at once to Pretoria, where he arrived on Friday night of last week. For nearly two years (says the "Daily Telegraph") Hindon has had the reputation of being the most expert among the gang of wreckers who rendered the railway lines on the Transvaal and Orange River Colonies so insecure that it was never certain, when a train started on its journey, whether it would ever reach its destination. These men cared nothing whether the coaches blown up or derailed contained combatants or merely women and children and invalids. Loot was generally the object, though "patriotism" was the excuse, and their victims were generally robbed of everything on them, in many cases even their clothing being stolen. Much of this dastardly work was carried out on the Pretoria-Delagoa line, notably at Naboomspruit and near Waterval, the latter being the occasion when Col. Vandelour was killed and a score of men also lost their lives, while a nurse who was attending the invalids whom the train carried, was wounded. According to the "Daily Express" Hindon is credited with having boasted that he was the only man who succeeded in stealing anything from ex-president Kruger. He stole two of Kruger's horses.

Walter Dale is buried in Kroonstad Military Cemetery, which is in a very sorry state.

Inside of Easingwold Church with Walter Dale Memorial

NOTES

1. The Dale family lived in Long Street. One of the father's other duties was to administer the Vaccination Acts. The regulating legislation established that there was an obligation to have this done, but there was a right of objection. Many exercised this right, and became the nations first conscientious objectors. This has been dealt with.
2. *Advertiser* 10 March 1900
3. *Ibid* 23 June 1900
4. The 'ALDERSHOT SCANDAL' *Ibid*. 23 June 1900. Brook was addressing the West Yorkshire Volunteer Brigade. Also *Ibid* 16 June 1900.
5. *Ibid* 16 June 1900
6. *Ibid* 20 July 1901
7. *Ibid* 5 October 1901
8. *Ibid* 1 March 1902. List of subscribers in *Ibid* 16 February 1901
9. *Ibid* 28 April 1900
10. Sir Frederick Treves (1853-1923). Famous for his skills in abdominal surgery and his accuracy of 'operative treatment of appendicitisi'. Acquired world-wide fame when he operated on Edward VII. Sir Frederick went to South Africa during the Boer War. On his appointment (and career) and that of Sir William MacCormac see *Ibid* 4 November 1899. MacCormac also performed 'a daring operation' on Private O'Leary of the West Surreys at Maritzburg. The private had been shot in the head and the bullet had lodged in his brain. He was recovering when the story broke. *Ibid* 10 March 1900. There is an article on, and a drawing of, O'Leary in *Ibid* 31 March 1900. He died in December 1901.
11. The driver and stoker were released. 'A native had been killed, and another wounded' *Ibid* 22 April 1901.
12. *Ibid* 30 March 1901
13. *Ibid* 8 June 1901
14. With the Boers 'fleeing in considerable numbers and seeking a means of escape round the Kaap Hills.'
15. H. Labuschagne, *'The Train Wreckers. The Men who Battled Against Her Majesty's Iron Horses'*, based on a 1916 Johannesburg work titled *Kaptein Hindon; Oorlogsa venture van 'n Baas Verkener.*
16. Copy sent to the author.

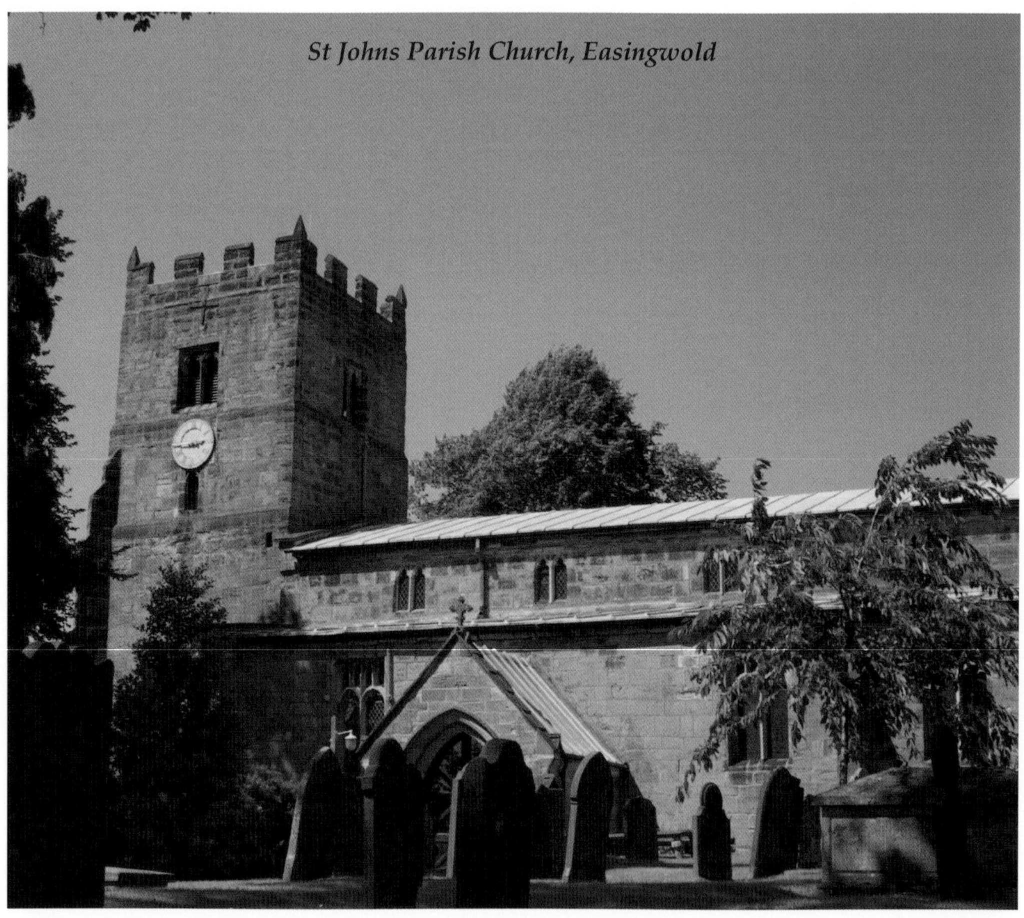
St Johns Parish Church, Easingwold

Chapter 16

THE ARMY

The British Army in 1899 was the product of reforms of the mid 19th century, but they were, in the words of Corelli Barnett, one of Britain's most famous military historians, half-baked.[1] War had been expected for some five years, but no preparations for campaigning that made sense had been made. No part of the army structure, with a notable exception, escaped criticism in the *Report of His Majesty's Commissioners on the War in South Africa,* published in 1903, and this from the 'then Commander-in-Chief, down to the private soldier'. The exception to the blanket condemnations was the Director of Military Intelligence whose advice was ignored.[2]

> as early as 1896, the D.M.I. had warned that the Boer plan would probably be to invade Natal. In 1897 [he] ... warned in the event of war, two months would elapse before British reinforcements could reach South Africa; that in the meantime a Boer offensive would fall on the troops already there; and that the British ought to be raising their strength [there] ... In 1898 the D.M.I. repeated his warnings ... [Given that] it was not altogether remarkable that no plan of campaign ever existed for operations in South Africa.

Almost 'all aspects of the British military system' were found 'wanting in a war against 50,000 farmers' Barnett concluded when dealing with the inquests into the Boer War.[3]

The most recent biographer of one of the major participants in the Boer War devoted a whole section of his work to 'THE GOVERNMENT'S FAILURE TO PREPARE FOR WAR'.[4] The maps the army was supplied with were 'worse than useless…', a positive danger and delusion the author said (quoting General Hunter) and, for the Transvaal, the British had to make do largely with Jeppe's farm survey made in the 1850s. In addition there were serious equipment problems. It was a terrible story of incompetence and Lt Gen Goodenough's warnings about equipment (he was on the spot)[5] were ignored,[6] in the way that Gen Ardagh's observations on the course a war in South Africa would take were also ignored.[7]

The exposés and the criticisms of the government after the end of the Boer War were sensational and (one suspects) not entirely unexpected. The death rate amongst soldiers in barracks was higher than in the nearby civilian populations. TB was rife and E.L. Woodward's summary of conditions in the army, on the eve of the Crimean War fifty years earlier, read very much like those of Gen Goodenough, quoted above. [8]

The politician responsible for beginning army reforms in the late 19th century, this as a result of the Franco-Prussian War of 1870, was Edward Cardwell. Viscount Edward Cardwell, who had been Secretary for War for several years, began the moves which established him as 'the greatest British Army reformer during the nineteenth century'. He had already abolished flogging,[9] and troops were taken from the self-governing colonies and the colonies and they were encouraged to raise local forces. Then the purchasing of commissions was abolished and short service was instituted with engagements of six years with the colours followed by six in the reserves replacing the 21 years men had had to serve hitherto – it had been flogging and long service which, R.C.K. Ensor said, had given 'army service its penal servitude character'. Lastly Cardwell 'territorialised' the army, creating 69 county regiments of at least two regular battalions with one normally serving at home while the other was on foreign duty. This was Cardwell's famous 'linked battalion' arrangement.

This was the system that was in existence when the South African war started, but there were ancillary – part time – forces as well, and at least one of the groups of this kind had a very high profile in Easingwold. Cardwell's 69 new regiments took over the old units and they included the local militia and volunteer infantry, membership of which had for years given prestige to members, none more so than the commanding officers. This not-very-original insight might be gathered or supported by an Army Order of the period 1896-97. Its reception was noted by the *Easingwold Advertiser*.[10] Tenure was quite long.

> In volunteer circles the new order as to four years in command of regiments has … been much discussed, and … [its contents] have given rise to controversy … as to how many times an extension of time may be given to any individual officer. The general opinion seems to be that it is intended that no officer shall hold command after he has been accorded one extension of four years ...

Shortly after this, an Army Order clarified the situation. All appointments to the command of militia or yeomanry units, it said, made on or after 1 April 1890, were to be 'for terms not exceeding five years' and 'Any extensions were to be' for terms not exceeding five years. No officer would be allowed to retain his command beyond the age 'fixed in the Militia and Yeomanry Regulations respectively'. [11]

Local yeomanry units in the North Riding were very much social organisations, and the highlight of their year was always the annual dinner. Proceedings there often revealed not only the names of participants, but sometimes a little about how the yeomen were regarded. The Thirsk group met in January 1897 and after meeting, eating and speechifying, held another of those dances which went on well into the following day.[12]

The Easingwold Volunteers were as keen on socialising as those at Thirsk, and there is a long report of their "beano" of 1895.[13] Three years later 'The Annual Dinner of the 1st Vol. Bn. P.W.O. Yorks. Regt. (Easingwold Detachment)' was held at the Station Hotel, Sgt Instructor Walker was chairman and Major Reginald Bell, sent his apologies. His task of responding to a toast to 'The Army, Navy and Auxilliary [sic]' fell by default to Cpl Lowry. He acquitted himself well in a 'short and pointed' speech, in which he said he hoped the young men of Easingwold 'would always remember their duty as Englishmen? Lowry ended by enthusing about his mates.[14]

> The shooting of the detachment, general efficiency, in comparison to other outlying sections is excellent, there not being a single third-class shot. The full number of men enrolled attended the annual camp training, this itself is very creditable.

Sgt Pipes thanked the rest of Easingwold for the way they 'had supported the Volunteer movement'. Pipes was the oldest Volunteer.

The last Volunteer annual dinner before the war broke out was held at Bowman's hotel. Once more the chair was occupied by Walker, now described as 'The late Sergeant Instructor'. He had completed his term of service and had been obliged to 'return to civil life'. His successor was named later.[15]

Every year, in Easingwold, an appeal for funds for the Fire Brigade's annual dinner appeared over the signature of Capt J.C. Bannister,[16] and clearly the Volunteers solicited

From Billy Holmes archive, beached boats

funds in the same way. Cpl Lowry said so. In a response he 'expressed his appreciation of the manner in which the people of Easingwold and District, had so handsomely contributed towards the annual dinner'. He said 'it plainly showed' that they 'recognised the value of the volunteer force'. That is typically not the impression the late Sgt Instructor gave, he had told his charges that the annual training was more like a holiday than spring military training. It probably was, and in 1899 the Easingwold men went to the coast.[17] 'The Easingwold Volunteers Corps went to Redcar on Saturday last for a week's training,' the *Advertiser* recorded in June.

When the Easingwold detachment was at Redcar the political crisis in South Africa was coming to a head and much publicity was given to the Volunteers and their training. Massive coverage was given to the Easter Musters at Colchester, Canterbury, Winchester and Aldershot, for example, where Redvers Buller was 'in the field during the manoeuvres'.[18] Tremendous coverage was given to the exercises involving not only the infantry, but the medical services and the artillery as well.[19] A notable feature of them was the use to which cyclists were put.

All over the country volunteers trained at Easter and during the summer of 1899. The Easingwold men were at Redcar and that great self-publicist the Vicar of Raskelf was at Blackpool with the Cheshire Regiment.[20] In July a huge review was held in London, when men representing the Metropolitan Volunteer Corps was held to commemorate the centenary of a review by George III.[21] 'Close on 27,000 men ... defiled in an hour and three-quarters, and the impression left on all beholders was that our volunteers are, after all, a force and a real force.' Parades were held in small places throughout the country. Reginald

Ernest Smith described one and did some calculations for his readers.[22] (Once more the typesetter was below par.)

> CHURCH PARADE. – On Sunday the members of the Thirsk company of the P.W.O., Yorkshire Volunteers held a church parade at Easingwold. The Thirsk detachment numbered 32 and the Easingwold 10, which brought the total number of men up to 42. Sergeant Cotton was in command and ... the band played up and down the Market Place while the men were falling in. The whole company afterwards counter-marched at each end of the square and produced a military effect that was highly appreciated by the large number of spectators who had assembled. Led by the band, the company then marched to the Parish church …

At the end of September the papers reported troop movements to and in South Africa. Buller, and Gen Sir George White went over and the 1st Royal Irish Fusiliers sailed from Alexandria for Durban. War, the continental papers opined, was 'almost inevitable' and the *Advertiser* of 14 October carried details about mobilisation. ('The ninth day of October, 1899, is to be considered the first day of mobilisation.') What sections of the Reserve had to report immediately were detailed, but what of the part-timers? The first of their number to elect to go to South Africa might have been from Kent .[23]

> EAST KENT YEOMEN TO GO
>
> The offer of some 50 members of the Royal East Kent Yeomanry to volunteer for service in South Africa has been accepted, and they have been instructed to hold themselves ready for embarkation at an early date.

On Sunday 17 December the War Office announced that the remaining sections of the Reserve were to be called up; that volunteering to serve in South Africa would be made easier; that 'A strong force of volunteers' was to be formed to go to the front; and that members of the militia could also volunteer. Things were going very badly for the British and, according to the *Advertiser,* the WO's announcements were welcomed.[24]

> VOLUNTEER ENTHUSIASM
>
> The intimations [about raising the above-mentioned force] … for services in South Africa … are meeting with a most patriotic and gratifying response. In … all parts … members of volunteer corps are eagerly offering their services, and in many cases their commanders have already been able to intimate that almost the whole strength of their battalions will be at the disposal of the War Office.

The *Advertiser* reported in February that Tom Cariss and others had decided to go to South Africa. A few weeks later it told its readers that no less a person than The Duke of Norfolk had also volunteered for the front. He had been Postmaster General since 1895 and a very popular one ('… as near the ideal Postmaster General, as anybody who has occupied the position'). He resigned and left for the front on 31 March. He had long been known as an enthusiastic supporter 'of the Volunteer movement' but held a commission in the 2nd Royal Sussex Volunteers and had been honorary colonel of the 4th Yorkshires since 1864. Many members of the Royal Sussex were already in South Africa.

The *Advertiser* commented on 'the readiness of our volunteers, whether' at home or elsewhere to 'offer their services at the front' and said it afforded 'a splendid spectacle to the world, [that] no one can say … is a mere spasmodic exhibition of Jingoism'. They offered themselves, too, at a time of full employment. Enlisted for home service only they were showing a willingness to give their services in a war 6,000 miles away in such large numbers that the Army could not take all who offered themselves.[25]

In Easingwold there was an enthusiastic farewell to the half a dozen men who had decided to go abroad. The *Advertiser's* report of their enthusiastic send-off has been referred to earlier.[26]

On 12 February Lord Lansdowne told the House of Lords of the needs of the government to conduct the South African war properly. He dealt at length with the volunteers. They had 'an establishment of 265,000 but their present strength was only 221,000', he said. The War Office would encourage all volunteer battalions to recruit up to their full strength of 1,000, and 'when that target was reached' encourage the formation of a second battalion of a more moderate size.'[27] It was hoped that men who had completed their terms of service in the Reserve would enlist for one year. The Volunteers' artillery would be re-equipped[28] and new officers found from the colonies, universities and public schools. Lansdowne hoped for 100,000 more men – but would not consider conscription.

> Men were now coming forward spontaneously and with great enthusiasm throughout the Empire, and in his view the present was not the moment for adopting the ballot or conscription. What was wanted was not compulsion, but only encouragement. That encouragement the War Office intended to give....

The initial response to Lansdowne's appeal for men to enlist was disappointing, and this became the major concern of an *Advertiser* editorial in March.[29] The response to the appeals from Lansdowne and others had 'not been satisfactory'. This was in marked contrast to what was being said only a short time before. Some men had had second thoughts and many had failed their medical. (Rather 'a severe one'.) Not only that, but 'A very large number had failed to pass the shooting test and many who could have passed that ... have failed to get accepted because they could not ride'. Easingwold's proud boast about the skills of its shooters was clearly not the norm. Recognising that some men *were* probably poor shots 'owing to the absence of' places to learn at, the government allocated £100,000 to construct and improve local ranges. But, the *Advertiser* continued, it is not good enough just to 'encourage short-range shooting, there should also be facilities for practising firing at long ranges, to a much greater extent than is now possible'.

There was great criticism being voiced about medical examinations and requirements when the calls went out for volunteers for overseas service. An article in *Sandow's Magazine* criticised them severely, for example.[30] It mocked the way measurements were taken, and said 'the height standard' was a useless measurement, and an 'exploded idea'. An absurdity of the height regulations? If Lord Roberts went for his commission now he would be refused it.

A year passed, the length of service contracted for was up in what must have seemed no time at all and the Volunteers who had elected to go to South Africa were back – to enthusiastic welcomes in Easingwold and elsewhere. There had been trouble with their service arrangements. Lord Roberts had promised that men who had left good jobs would be the first to be sent back, and things went wrong with the London Scottish Volunteer Detachment of the 2nd Gordon Highlanders, for example.[31] They had been 'out' for a year on active service and were entitled to return home, but instead had been 'sent up country to act as convoy escort in the passes' of a 'wild hill district'. Roberts, replying to his critics, said that the relief 'of the Volunteer Companies in South Africa, is now practically settled',

Opening of Miniature Rifle Range in Easingwold Town Hall 1906. Yorkshire Regiment Volunteers - note the two soldiers in centre and one behind wearing their South African medals.

and that the time-expired men would 'soon' be returned – though this did not mean that volunteers would no longer be at the front. The report giving Roberts' reply to a questioner about the Gordons, for example, recorded that men specially enrolled to relieve their comrades had sailed for Cape Town on the *Montrose.* (A War Office return issued on 20 May 1901, gave the strength of forces in South Africa. Five categories were given for officers and men and two of them were: Regulars .... 138,002; Volunteers 9,385.[32]

> By the end of the year a general election had been held, and the Hon St John Brodrick had replaced Lansdowne as Secretary of State for War, and some alterations in the terms and conditions under which the Volunteers served were contemplated. The *Advertiser* had mentioned them in an editorial of March 1901.[33]

The ambitious plans of St John Brodrick however were not heeded and Britain had to wait for fundamental army reforms, but in the time left that the South African war had to run there were some changes as far as the Volunteers were concerned. The *Advertiser* noted them at length. On 30 March it carried a long article about the 'NEW ARMY RIFLE' about to be produced and tested – a weapon of 'somewhat gouty appearance' that was 'really a compromise between the rifle and the carbine'. The paper also carried details of peace proposals being offered to Louis Botha and a note of the War Office regulations on the 'TRAINING OF VOLUNTEERS'. This showed that, at last, the government and the Army had realised that perhaps taking men to an annual camp where they engaged in 'worthless' exercises was a waste of time and effort. 'Close order drill, ceremonial parades, and rifle or physical exercises will not [henceforth] be practised while Corps are in camp', a document said. Some improvements in pay were made and the length of training increased for some.[34] The duration of the annual camps was henceforth to be 13 days.

From Billy Holmes archive

On 13 May Brodrick formally moved a resolution embodying the new scheme of army reform which was immediately attacked by, among others, Sir Charles Dilke, Sir Henry Campbell-Bannerman and Winston Churchill, who said 'We [are] spending too much on our army'.[35] The same day that Churchill's remarks were reported, it was announced that one group of Volunteers had suffered extreme deprivation in South Africa.

HARD ON THE VOLUNTEERS.

> For three whole days the Welsh Volunteers were without food altogether, while on the march across the veldt, and for three weeks had only a quarter of a pound of flour each. This, by mixing with water, they made into chupatties, and cooked them in their mess tins over the fire. These hardships were endured on account of the transport waggons not arriving.

Early in 1902 the Army estimates were published and it was seen that there were increases for 'volunteer capitation grants for an additional number of efficients'.[36] Then 'details of the men under arms on 1 January 1902' were given. The Volunteers were a formidable force.

Regular force	322,263
Army reserve	23,980
Militia	109,853
Yeomanry	17,407
Volunteers	277,396

Some men however left something to be desired. Three appeared in court in March 1902[37] at Thornaby and were fined for being non-efficient, missing drills, and being absent from the annual inspection.

The improvements in pay and maybe the reverses of the war at that time – led to a move in Easingwold to get a Volunteer organisation of its own (it will be recalled that the local volunteers until then had been part of a Thirsk unit). On 25 March 1902, largely through the efforts of J.W. Sturdy and John Rocliffe 'A very successful and patriotic meeting' was held in the Town Hall. Present were a large number of 'leading Gentlemen of the Town and District' – people like Dr Preston, F.J.H. Robinson and Buller Hicks. A Col Mott 'FROM HEADQUARTERS,' said that he hoped large numbers of men would come forth from Easingwold as 'the battalion numbered about 800, … 300 less than they were granted for'. Sgt. Instructor Colton was in the town looking for recruits. Drills for the new men were to be held on evening at the Station Hotel.[38] (At the George men could join the Yorkshire Hussars Imperial Yeomanry.)

The Easingwold Volunteers were duly formed and in the summer took part in a church parade at Raskelfe.[39] Some of them were wearing the South African medal, the *Advertiser* reported, and were met outside the village by Preston, in uniform, who preached to them a sermon from John xiv 6, 'I am the way' and made special reference 'to the late Captain Hedley Vicars, of the 97th,' as an example which every soldier might follow, 'a brave, fearless soldier of the Sovereign, and a noble and dedicated Christian'.

Preston was never far from a controversy of some kind or another and took part in one about 'our Tommies' in 1902[40] in which he'd written to the *Daily Mail* supporting them against "German Slanders". A grateful 'Tommy' had replied to thank him, "... it is good to know that there are true hearts at home to champion our cause."

When Preston held his church parade the war had just a short time to run. The news that peace had come was greeted with a decided lack of enthusiasm according to R.E. Smith.[41]

> THE long looked for news of Peace was made known in Easingwold early on Monday morning [2 June 1902]. There was not the demonstration of joy which might be expected on this all important occasion. In the evening the bells of the Parish Church sounded the glad tidings, while flags were displayed by the inhabitants of the town.

The annual camp for 1902 was arranged for June and on Saturday the 14th 'THE EASINGWOLD DETACHMENT of the 1st Battalion P.W.O. Yorkshire Regiment left' by special train for Duncombe Park. They were in the charge of Cpl J.W. Sturdy and numbered 'about 30'.[42]

NOTES

1. Corelli Barnett, *Britain and Her Army* 1509-1970 (1974)
2. *Ibid* p 341
3. There was another enquiry into how men of 'moderate means' could be enabled to obtain commissions. This was Lord Stanley's Committee.
4. S.M. Miller, *Lord Methuen and the British Army* (1999)
5. He was GOC in South Africa
6. What were Goodenough's observations? 'The helmets, for example, were too heavy and offered no protection from the sun. The khaki trousers and jacket were too restricting. The water bottles were unreliable and waterproof sheets were not thick enough to protect the men from the damp ground'. It was also impossible to get supplies from local farms. Miller op cit pp73-74.
7. Maj Gen John Ardagh was the DMI.
8. E.L. Woodward, *The Age of Reform 1815-1870* (Oxford 1938) pp 256-67
9. In peace time. It was not abolished for men on active service until 1880.
10. 'THE NEW VOLUNTEER OFFICER' *Advertiser* 2 January 1897
11. *Ibid* 9 January 1897
12. *Ibid*
13. *Ibid* 26 January 1895
14. *Ibid* 1 and 22 January 1898
15. *Ibid* 14 January 1899
16. One appeared in *Ibid* 7 January 1899
17. *Ibid* 17 June 1899
18. 'EASTERTIDE VOLUNTEERING', *Ibid* 8 April 1899. Buller was present at the muster of the London Volunteer Brigade.
19. Eg the 3rd Middlesex Artillery detachment and the 2nd Kent Volunteer Artillery who were at Lydd.
20. As chaplain. *Advertiser* 6 June 1899
21. *Ibid* 15 July 1899
22. *Ibid* 22 July 1899
23. *Ibid* 21 October 1899
24. *Ibid* 30 December 1899
25. *Ibid* 10 February 1900
26. *Ibid* 20 January 1900 (and editorial)
27. *Ibid* 17 February 1900. Parliamentary reports. On the Secretary for War see, eg Lord Newton, *Lord Lansdowne A Biography* (1929). Mr Wyndham made a similar report to the Commons. (as did Lansdowne) on 12 March. *Advertiser* 17 March 1900.
28. they had 98 batteries ... all armed with guns of an obsolete type.
29. *Advertiser* 10 March 1900
30. Reprinted. *Ibid* 9 June 1900. The examinations, it should be said, were for commissions.
31. See the letter from James Keir, a civil engineer 'of London and Arbroath' and Roberts' reply. *Ibid* 16 March 1901
32. *Ibid* 25 May 1901
33. *Ibid* 16 March 1901
34. For example hours for artillery engineers were increased from 72 to 144.
35. Report in *Advertiser* 18 May 1901
36. *Ibid* 22 February 1902
37. *Ibid* 29 March 1902
38. *Ibid*
39. *Ibid* 12 July 1900. Much earlier the inconsistent spelling of the name of this place was commented on. In this issue of the *Advertiser,* the village news takes up about six inches of space. It is headed 'RASKELFE' then carries, immediately, a story about a 'RASKELF POTATO MERCHANT' in a spot of bother at Thirsk County Court. Then follows the church parade story with the village's name given, this time, an e.
40. *Ibid* 26 April 1902
41. *Ibid* 7 June 1902
42. *Ibid* 21 June 1902

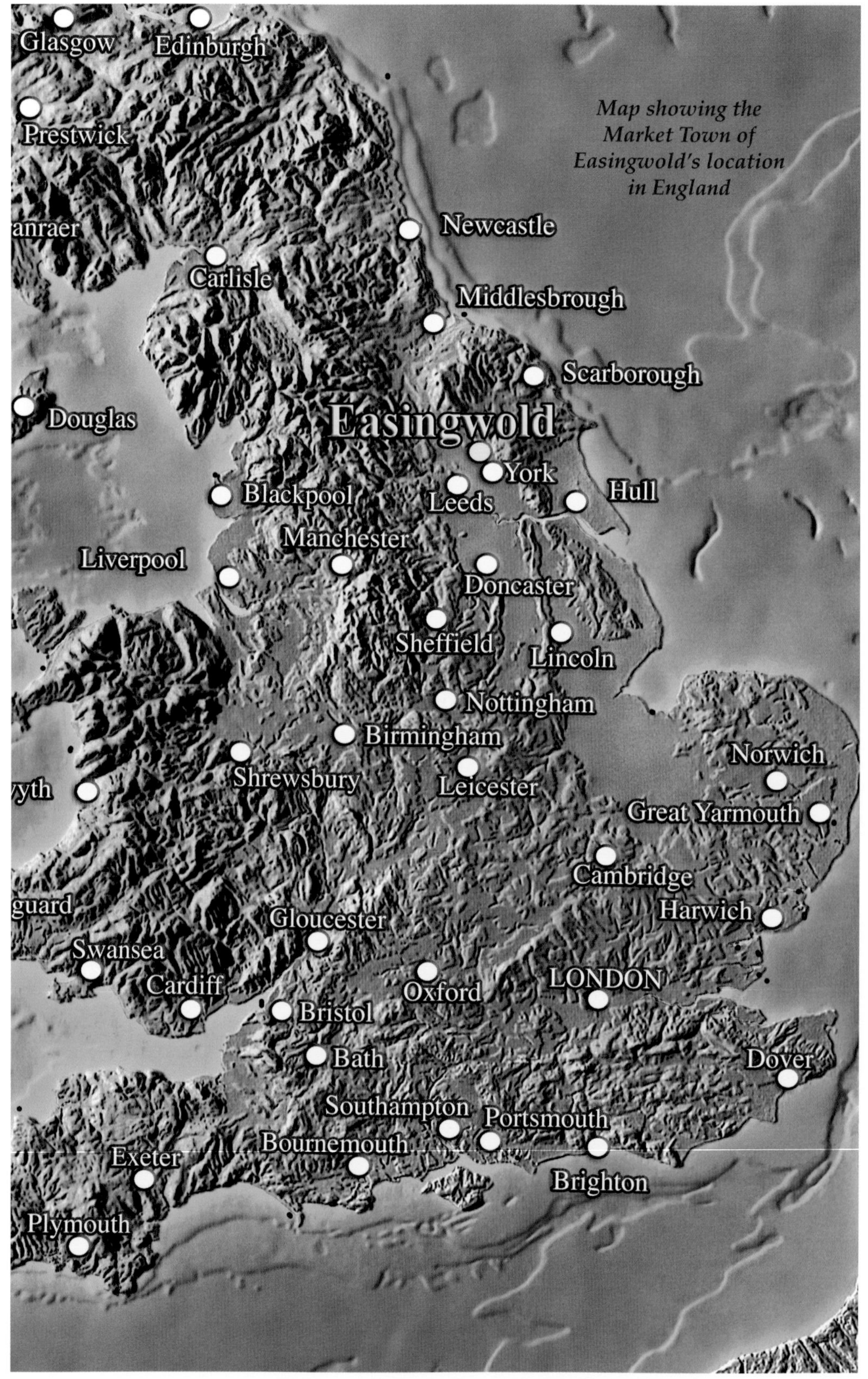
Glasgow
Edinburgh
Prestwick
Map showing the
Market Town of
Easingwold's location
in England
anraer
Newcastle
Carlisle
Middlesbrough
Scarborough
Douglas
Easingwold
York
Blackpool
Leeds
Hull
Manchester
Liverpool
Doncaster
Sheffield
Lincoln
Nottingham
Birmingham
Norwich
Shrewsbury
Leicester
ywth
Great Yarmouth
Cambridge
guard
Harwich
Gloucester
Swansea
LONDON
Cardiff
Oxford
Bristol
Bath
Dover
Southampton
Portsmouth
Bournemouth
Exeter
Brighton
Plymouth

Chapter 17

BADEN-POWELL'S OWN

There were dozens of volunteer groups, raised in Britain, the colonies and South Africa itself during the Boer War. A random selection of the official war reports from almost any time would have made the point, to even the most casual contemporary newspaper reader. An organisation that also recruited at this time – and to which the Easingwold area contributed modestly – was associated with Col R.S.S. Baden-Powell, the soldier Thomas Pakenham referred to as 'the hero of the war' and Lansdowne's and Joseph Chamberlain's 'secret weapon' in the summer of 1899. They had[1]

> hoped to force Kruger to a 'climb-down' simply by the 'moral effect' of B-P and a thousand men threatening the northern borders of the Transvaal. Failing the climb-down, B-P's secret instructions ... were to *raid* the Transvaal; the moment that war broke out ... a plan to attack ... 'a la Jameson' as B-P rightly described it.

Baden-Powell's raid was called off and he took charge of forces besieged at Mafeking where his plan 'was to provoke the Boers without exposing himself to the risks of a raid'. The siege went on until May 1900 then things started to get better for the British. Lord Roberts sent Baden-Powell, who had been chasing De Wet, the elusive Boer leader, a telegram.[2]

> Major-General Baden-Powell I want you to see me without delay regarding the formation of Police Force for Transvaal, Orange River Colony, and Swaziland.

Baden-Powell set about organising the police force, and what was officially known as the South African Constabulary came into existence on 22 October 1900. It was to have a military role as well as responsibility for 'preserving the peace and preventing crimes' throughout the now subdued (and annexed) Transvaal and Orange River Colony, and before the war ended the SAC functioned as an army unit. Indeed, it saw no police duty while the war lasted.

'As quickly as Baden-Powell could get his men trained and equipped, they were sent into active duty, some ... to man blockhouses, some ... to take part in ... cross country drives'.[3] And there was a desperate need for recruits, and Baden-Powell had to resort to drastic measures. Many men came forward from South Africa, but not nearly enough. (The government had agreed in December to increase the size of the SAC to 10,000.) So B-P

> Foiled in his attempts to get the officers he needed from the Army ... turned to an army camp near Cape Town that had recently added a word to the English language: to be 'stellenboschbed', to be relegated to a position in which little harm could be done. With Milner's blessing[4] he went to secure some of his officer material at Stellenbosch – 'a sort of purgatory in which officers were placed who had been responsible for any "regrettable" incident in the campaign'. He took the view that 'these men had made their mistakes and were therefore all the more likely not do so in the future'. His faith proved justified.

It was decided to recruit for the South African police in the United Kingdom and at the end of 1900 an announcement appeared saying that large number of men would be taken – if possible.[5]

THE SOUTH AFRICAN CONSTABULARY

It has been decided to recruit up to 5000 men for this force in the United Kingdom, but only single men between the ages of 20 and 35 who can ride and shoot can be accepted.

One of the first men from the Easingwold area to join the B-P police enlisted at York in the early days of 1901 and was enroute to South Africa before the end of the first week of January.[6]

FOR THE FRONT.–Last Sunday Mr Geo Williamson, second son of Mr. Wm Williamson, of Oak Tree House, left Easingwold for Southampton, en-route for Pretoria, to join the newly formed Baden-Powell's Police, into which he had been enrolled at York a few days ago.

A week after Williamson left Britain a statement of overall recruiting appeared. It was an impressive account, in which the figure for the needs of B-P was lower than that given earlier.[7]

BADEN POWELL'S POLICE

A large number of men are still required to complete the 5000 which are being enrolled in this country for Baden Powell's Police. Applications for enlistment are, however, being made in thousands and it requires a very considerable staff at the recruiting office in Delahay Street, Westminster, to deal with them. Altogether, about 30,000 applications have been received and more than 3,000 men are still required to supplement this number which has already been passed. The riding and shooting tests are now being conducted at Aldershot, and the medical examination of candidates is being made at the recruiting office at Westminster on Thursdays only. About 270 men have already been sent to South Africa and a second contingent of 500 or 600 will leave Southampton by the Canada on the 14th June.

COLONEL BADEN-POWELL.

Baden-Powell was an able publicist, and notably in the *Natal Witness* he sold his new organisation effectively. It resembled in some ways, he said, the force which had been set up 'in the early days of Rhodesia'. Then, in a scheme which worked 'remarkably well', men in the enlisted police force used their spare time on house building, irrigation works and other pursuits which gave them 'some start' after their discharge. Getting out to take up well-paid work was made easy. The men of the new force being raised, however, would not be permitted to take part-time work, but simply encouraged to 'look around' with an eye to the future. As with the Rhodesian force, discharges would be easy to obtain with the men going on to the reserve. The reason for making leaving comparatively easy rested in the fact that.[8]

the authorities are desious of creating … a strong reserve force of Constabulary which can be mobilised, if necessary, with the rapidity of a Boer commando. Membership of

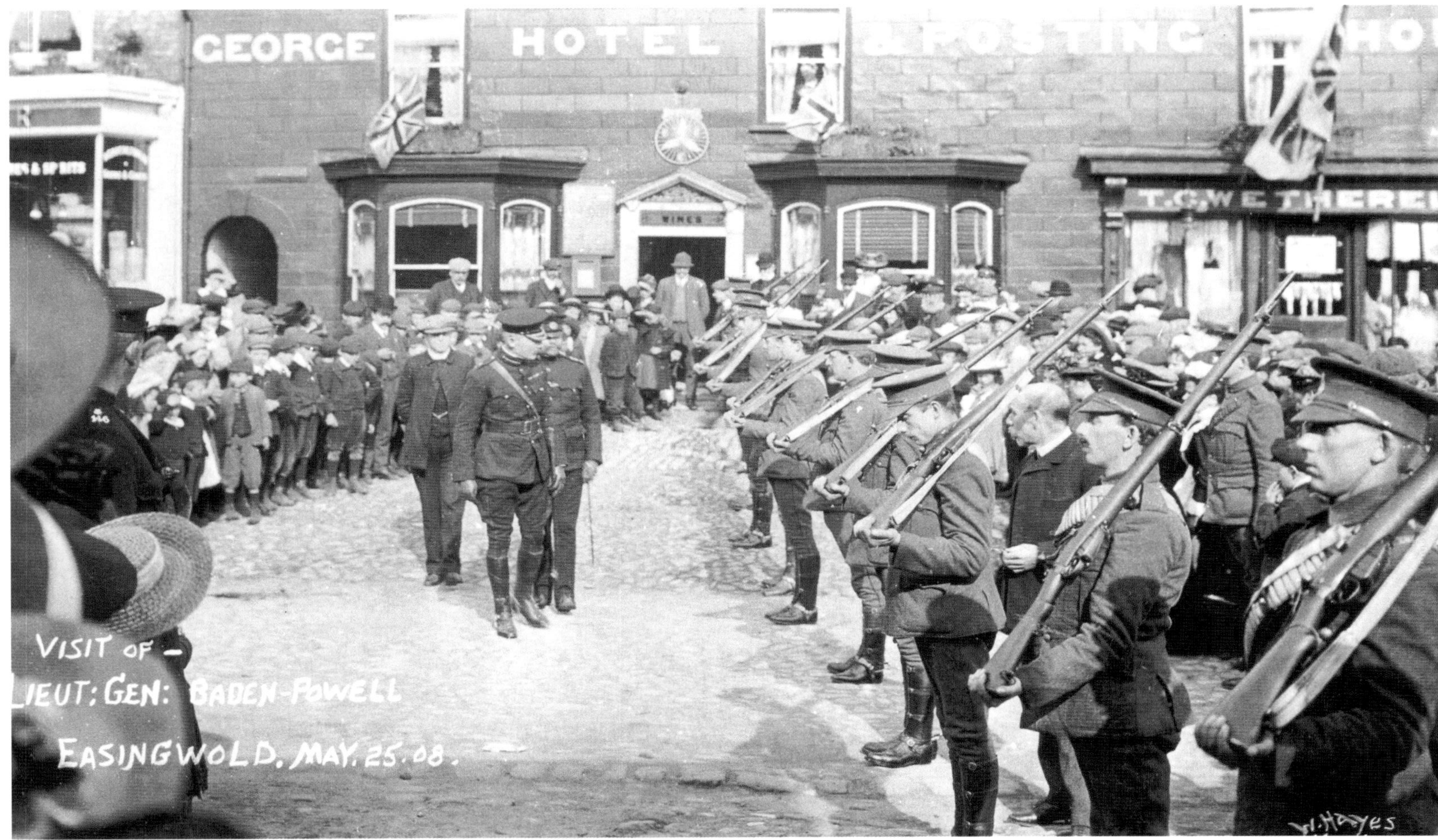

B-P inspecting the Yorkshire Hussars Imperial Yeomanry outside The George Hotel, Market Place, Easingwold

> this reserve will entail very little or no military work, unless there be treasons, plots, and strategems, revolutions, or rebellions.

The terms being offered by B-P were attractive and another Easingwold man signed up. He was already a policeman.[9]

> PC EDEN who has for some time been stationed at Brandsby, has been accepted for Baden-Powell's Police, and will proceed to South Africa shortly.

Eden would have been rapidly set to work if his experience was the same as that of earlier recruits. Baden-Powell wrote in February or March to say a third batch of police had arrived at Bloemfontein. He described how old soldiers were picked out and given the task of passing on their knowledge to groups of five or six men. Three of the five divisions the force was to be divided into had been 'nearly completed' and the men went in at the deep end. Clearly they were being used to support the army. 'No time is lost in drill or theoretical training' Baden-Powell wrote, 'the men are put to work almost as soon as they arrive at their station'. How many had gone over so far?

> Five thousand [sic] is the number of men to be raised in this country, and of this number 3900 have already been accepted; 2680 have been sent to South Africa, 850 will sail in the Canada on March 12, and 450 will embark a week or so later.[10]

The *Pall Mall Gazette* referred to the SAC as 'Baden-Powell's Own'.

NOTES

1. Pakenham op cit pp 398-99.
2. W. Hillcourt and Lady Baden-Powell, *Baden-Powell. The Two Lives of a Hero* (1964). p. 46. B-P had been promoted after the relief of Mafeking and became the youngest Major-General in the British Army. The creation of the police force gets only scant attention in D. James, *Lord Roberts* (1954). Later the report will be quoted in which B-P stated that the South African force had been based on the Rhodesian model. James said that Lord Roberts wanted a constabulary 'on the lines by which he had solved the Burmese problem fifteen years before'.
3. *Ibid* p. 233
4. Sir Alfred, the High Commissioner, had started the moves to create the SAC.
5. *Advertiser* 22 December 1900
6. *Ibid* 5 January 1901
7. *Ibid* 12 January 1901
8. Quoted *Ibid* 9 March 1901. Enlistment was for three years. The *Pall Mall Gazette* thought the SAC was 'perhaps, the best paid and most comfortably kitted corps ever raised in any country.' Quoted *Ibid* 23 November 1901.
9. *Ibid* 9 March 1901
10. *Ibid 16 March 1901.* A few married men had been accepted. This recruiting had now been stopped as the quota had been filled.

Chapter 18

YEOMEN AND MILITIA MEN

J.K. Dunlop produced a comprehensive study of the British Army from the turn of the century to the eve of the Great War, and it carried a foreword by Gen Sir Frederick Maurice.[1] This period, Maurice wrote, saw the reforms that led to the regular British Army being organised into the formations familiar from the 1914-18 war and a 'complete change in our attitude towards the auxiliary forces of the crown'. The reorganisation 'involved many enquiries and much controversy. The greatest of them was the reorganisation of the inchoate mass of Yeomanry, Militia and Volunteers'.[2]

> The Auxiliary Forces in 1899 consisted of: The Militia (including the Militia Reserve), The Yeomanry, and the Volunteers. The duties and liabilities of these three organisations differed in important particulars; they had varying terms of training and of enlistment. In short, the whole organisation of the Auxiliary Forces ... was in a highly confused condition. [This] state of affairs bore eloquent testimony to the fact ... that [they] ... had evolved in a haphazard way and had never been properly coordinated.

The Militia was poorly officered, poorly trained, was for home duties only, and was often regarded frequently as a simple 'stepping stone to the Regular army', and by far the greatest occupational group in it were agricultural workers. The Militia Reserve consisted of men who, for an additional bounty of £1 a year, accepted an obligation to serve overseas if in time of war they were called upon to do so. They clearly, most of them,

> thought they were on a fairly safe thing when they took an extra sovereign per annum for a remote contingency, and their arrival at camps in South Africa was regarded as something of 'a jest'.

The Militia does not feature prominently in the history of the Easingwold area, and whether many of the regular soldiers of the area had used it as a 'stepping stone' to the regular army is not clear from reports published locally, though Dunlop gave some interesting figures about the extent of the overall moves from the Militia to the regulars. 'It has been said that many ... young recruits were bound for the Regular Army;' he wrote. In the year under review [1898] 15,167 Militiamen joined the Regulars. '[Though] In the same period, 8,716 deserted or were struck off the roll as absentees.'

Two months before the South African War started the War Office 'decided to proceed with their policy of' recruiting for the militia.[3] There had been a continuous falling off in enlistments, and when the recruiting campaign of 1899 started, the force needed 21,000 men 'to bring it up to standard'. What the standards of the militia frequently were was a constant source of music hall jokes and comic writing, but a week after war was declared they were 'called up'.

THE MILITIA
MEANING AND EFFECT OF THE PROCLAMATION

The calling out of the Militia by Proclamation under her Majesty's Sign Manual will undoubtedly (says the *Daily Mail*) cause great satisfaction, especially among its officers, whose complaint of recent years has been that their force is neglected by the Government.

The Militia of the United Kingdom is maintained for the purposes of augmenting the military strength of the country in case of imminent national danger or great emergency. By Royal proclamation the whole or part of the force is liable to be embodied, and placed on active military service within the confines of the United Kingdom, but men may volunteer to serve in the Channel Islands, Isle of Man, Malta and Gibraltar.

Recruits, who are drawn from practically the same classes as the regular Army, undergo preliminary training of not more than six months, and an annual training usually lasting 23 days for the six years of their service, and at the end of each training are given a bounty of £1. At the close of their first period of service the men can re-enlist for another six years, during which time the annual bounty is increased by one-half.

Attached to and forming part of their territorial battalions, the officers and men when called out are liable for duty with the regulars, and are, to all intents and purposes, regular troops, and this also applies to the Militia artillery, engineers, and marine miners.

The system of recruiting is practically the same as for the regulars - voluntary enlistment - but, in the event of any county or place not providing sufficient men the ballot may be resorted to. Each Militia regiment has a permanent staff consisting of an adjutant, a small body of non-commissioned officers and drummers to conduct recruiting, drills, and the ordinary business of the corps.

The Militia Reserve is formed of men who, belonging to the Militia, voluntarily undertake the liability to join the regular forces and serve in any place to which they may be ordered in case of necessity. These men receive a double bounty of £2 at each training and are on the same footing as the Army Reserve. The returns for the last year give the strength of this force as 27,761.

The effective strength of the entire Militia force, according to the latest returns, is about 135,000, consisting of 125 infantry battalions, thirty-two corps of artillery, two fortress corps of engineers, ten divisions of submarine miners, and two companies of the Medical Staff Corps.

There is nothing particularly extraordinary in the procedure ordered by the Queen's proclamation, as during the Crimea, the Indian Mutiny, and the Soudan war of 1885 the Militia were embodied ... as they will [be] now, to undertake garrison service to replace regiments ordered abroad. There is no suggestion that events in the Transvaal will need the despatch of any of the Militia Reserve, and the embodiment is simply what has been for some days considered certain by military authorities.[4]

Early in 1902 proceedings at the Town Hall, Easingwold were enlivened when two of the kind of men Col Dunlop described appeared before the local magistrates. Once again Reginald Ernest Smith's typesetter was not on absolutely top form[5]

MILITIA ABSENTEES. – On the 4th inst., Arthur James Warren and John Coleman, both absentees from the 4th Batt. West Yorkshire Malitia. were apprehended by P.C. Scaife in Long Street. They were brought before the Magistrates on the following morning, and were remanded until a military escort should be sent.

The Militia was not prominent in the life of Easingwold, much more high profile were the Yeomen and photographs of them frequently appear in local collections,[6] and the *Advertiser* always reported their activities and devoted considerable space to the force in general. For example, its last issue of 1899 published a piece on 'THE ORIGIN OF YEOMANRY CAVALRY',[7] in which the story of Arthur Young's inspired idea of 'forming a "militia of property"', was given, and Young claimed responsibility for a movement which spread like wildfire. (He served as a private in a corps raised in the vicinity of Bury St Edmunds.)

Yeomen from Easingwold went to South Africa, as has been mentioned, and early in March 1902 some of them were in an accident that was the subject of a reprint in Smith's journal.[8]

John Thomas Ward of Laund House, Shipton was born on 20th April, 1872 and then educated at Laund House and Easingwold Grammar School.

At 27 years of age at the outbreak of the war and as an accomplished horseman, good shot, he joined the Yorkshire Hussars who became part of the Imperial Yeomanry raised after 'Black Week' in December 1899.

Taking his own horse to war along with the likes of Lt. Stephen Wombwell, Sid Smith and Thomas Wilkinson, they mustered at Sheffield and left there on 20th January, 1900 to embark at Liverpool on the transport Winnefordian wich reached the Cape about 20th February, 1900. They were all in the 9th Company 3rd Imperial Yeomanry, and in due course joined the Yeomanry Brigade commanded by Lord Chesham which was part of Lord Methuen's 1st Division and they were based at Kimberley. Their first action was the defence of a convoy in April 1900 as described in a letter by Stephen Wombwell. There is an excellent photo of J. T. Ward's 'Mafeking' pipe and he probably purchased this when Lord Chesham's Yeomanry Brigade spent a week of rest there in September 1900.

We know that Sid Smith and Thomas Wilkinson returned to Easingwold on 11th June, 1901, it is most likely that J. T. Ward returned at the same time, where he was carried shoulder high by his friends, back to Laund House. During his time in South Africa he contracted a severe malaria attack and was not expected to survive (but he did.)

NARROW ESCAPE OF YEOMANRY

From a copy of the 'Graaf Reinet Advertiser', which has been handed to us, there is an account of the wreck of a horse train and narrow escape of Yeomanry, amongst whom were those who went from Easingwold a little over a year ago.

The accident happened within half-a-mile of the local Station. From the paper mentioned it appears that the first of a series of trains conveying Colonel Doran's column, arrived at the top of Semel's Poort Hoogte at about 6.45a.m. The distance from there to the bridge over Sunday River is roughly given as a mile, and the gradient is one in forty.

The train which ran to destruction on this occasion was made up of several carriages, some open trucks, and eighteen horse-boxes filled with horses, the carriages and trucks

John Thomas Ward, Laund House, Shipton by Beningbrough, York

J. T. Ward (20th April 1872 - 31st January 1962) in the uniform of Yorkshire Hussars Imperial Yeomanry prior to departure for South Africa in January ***1900. On the right his dress uniform still in the possession of his family.***

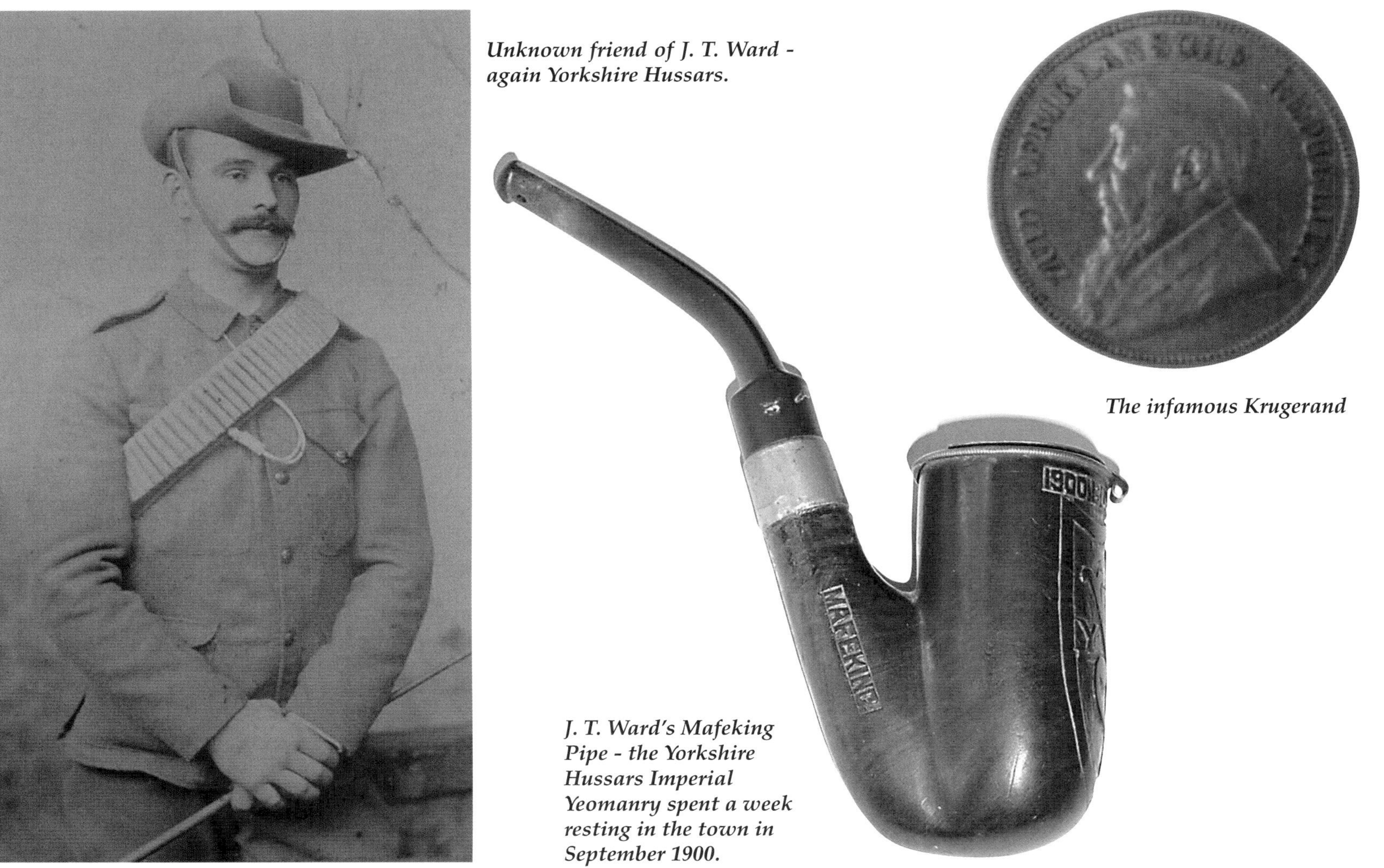

Unknown friend of J. T. Ward - again Yorkshire Hussars.

J. T. Ward's Mafeking Pipe - the Yorkshire Hussars Imperial Yeomanry spent a week resting in the town in September 1900.

The infamous Krugerand

containing the Yeomanry officers and men. In going down the incline the driver could not apply the brakes, and so the engine was reversed, but the weight of the train and the impetus already gained, prevented that having any result. It was then apparent that nothing could stop it until it had completed the descent, and a quarter of a mile from the bridge the speed was terrific. In its rush down, the back part of the train, which was made up of horse boxes, began to oscillate, and as the speed quickened, the swaying motion increased, doubtless by the horses being thrown from one side to the other. The last one eventually pitched off the line, and the slight check had the effect of breaking the coupling of the 15 trucks ahead. The leading truck of the detached part also left the rails, and struck the parapet of the bridge and was smashed up.

When the train reached the station it was got in hand, but the trucks behind each of them smashed into one another which made a complete wreck of ten of the eighteen trucks and boxes. A number of horses, of which the train carried 200 were thrown clear of the wreck, and escaped with slight damage, but many others were dead, and others had to be shot. Amongst the debris lay a number of dead and mutilated animals with limbs contorted in all shapes, and mangled into shapeless masses.

After considerable time it was found that 54 horses had been killed, and about 50 made unfit for work.

The Easingwold men were in an open truck which took second place in the wrecked portion of the train, and when the leading truck struck the parapet the truck in which they were was flung off the line. From the parapet to the edge of the river bank, which at that place is 25 feet deep, was a sandbag breast-work erected for military purposes. Against this the Yeoman truck was hurled, and the men pitched out close to the river's edge. Not one of them was hurt. The breast-work broke the force of the truck's impetus, and held it hanging over a 25 feet drop, and but for that protection, nothing could have saved the truck with its contents from being dashed into the river, when a great loss of life must have taken place. It took half a day to clear the line for traffic again.

Britain was ill prepared for the Boer War, and the early defeats in what became known as Black Week necessitated some drastic action and 'One of the immediate consequences of the news of the week's dreadful set-backs, was 'the formation of the Imperial Yeomanry.' It was a desperate measure to meet a desperate situation – and it was by no means an unqualified success.[9] Men from Easingwold served with the IY and were ready to go overseas in mid March 1900. The paper that noted their imminent departure, incidentally, also recorded that the four Easingwold Volunteers had got to South Africa. The report about the IY men was printed next to one announcing the 'CAPTURE OF BLOEMFONTEIN' and read.[10]

> IN the list of men who compose the third Yorkshire Company of Imperial Yeomanry, who left Doncaster on Tuesday for Liverpool to embark on the S.S. Hilarious for South Africa, we notice the names of T.A. Wilkinson, Easingwold, and S.M. Frank of Marton Lordship, Easingwold.

A much longer report had already appeared about the departure of men of the Yorkshire contingent of Imperial Yeomen from Sheffield. The authorities had arranged for this to take place at five o'clock in the morning to discourage crowds of well wishers and the men breakfasted at midnight.[11] They had been quartered at barracks in Sheffield for several weeks and they marched to Wadsley Bridge station from whence they were conveyed in three trains to Liverpool. They were said – all of them – to be 'good shots, good riders, and speaking generally, smart men in every way.'

From Billy Holmes archive. By the river

One of the major problems with the IY had been officering it, and officers had had to be taken to it from regular Yeomanry regiments. Mentioned in the Sheffield departure report were Major Gascoigne, Capt C.W.E. Duncombe, Capt J Mackillop and Lts Stephen Wombwell, Beresford-Pierce and R.B. Wilson. All were Hussars.

The lack of training of the Imperial Yeomanry has frequently been noticed by historians and how brief and inadequate it usually was might be gleaned from a note about mobilisation.[12]

IMPERIAL YEOMANRY MOBILISATION

The larger portion of the 5000 Imperial Yeomanry called for service in South Africa will be mobilised at Aldershot. Instructions have been given to prepare the East Cavalry Barracks for the reception and requirements of the Yeomanry, who will be drafted out to the front in companies as soon as mobilised and equipped. A short course of instruction, lasting 10 days or so, will be given before embarkation, and the men will also be furnished with horses and tried in the riding school before leaving. Major H. D. Fanshaw, second in command of the 2nd Dragoon Guards, has been appointed Commandant of the Yeomanry depot.

The first 'contingent' of Imperial Yeomanry was duly raised and men were sent to South Africa. The IY rapidly proved to be extremely costly, however, and, as the war seemed to be rapidly approaching a successful conclusion, recruiting was wound up. There was dissatisfaction in the ranks in South Africa and many of the commanders became openly critical – harshly and unfairly on occasion – of the prowess and record of the Imperials. Kitchener did so, for example, in a despatch dated 8 July which, however, did not go unchallenged.[13]

THE NEW YEOMANRY

AN OFFICER'S TRIBUTE TO A CRITICISED FORCE

An Officer who has commanded a force of the New Yeomanry in South Africa sends an interesting statement of his experiences with these troops, some of whom came in for adverse criticism from Lord Kitchener in his despatch of July 8, on account of their inability to shoot and ride and their physical defects.

"Neither Lord Kitchener nor the public would expect men suddenly released fom civil employment to be trained men in the strictest sense of the term," says this officer, "but after commanding a body of these troops in course of transit from Cape Town to their base at Elandsfontein, near Johannesburg, and afterwards accompanying them 'on trek', I venture to say that the strong point in favour of the new Yeomanry is their medical fitness to bear the privations required of seasoned troops in the field. Afterwards I had some opportunity of testing their skill in the use of the rifle and the horse, as well as their medical fitness. The horses served out were in so poor a condition that ... they constantly died on the 'lines' during the night. It must not be forgotten that within a month or six weeks the men were thrown into action half a dozen times on convoy duty between Pretoria and Rustenburg, the Boers opening fire on the scouts on one occasion at 80 yards, and that by dysentery, by enteric, by bullets and by capture, they had at least 40 per cent of their number placed hors de combat, and lost 60 per cent of their horses within a couple of months of their leaving their base at Elandsfontein. My admiration for them dates from our first night out from Elandsfontein, when they bore the hardships inseparable from camping on the frosty veldt without complaint."

Expectations of an early end to the war were not fulfilled and a rapid change of plans had to be made. A second contingent of Yeomanry was called for by the War Office (this was on 14 January 1901) and rates of pay were increased. New arrangements for recruiting were made and tests on riding and shooting (frequently ignored) were improved. Kitchener decided that what came to be known as the 'New Yeomanry' would be trained in South Africa.

There was also to be a third contingent. This was to be raised by an order dated 19 December 1901 and eventually, 'A force of 7,221 men was ... raised', which came to be known as 'the 1902 Yeomanry'. This time training was given at camps at Aldershot, the Curragh and Edinburgh, sometimes for as long as five months.[14] But by the time they got to the front the war was over.

Early in 1902 there was a surge of patriotism in Easingwold as the local Volunteers mounted a recruiting campaign – led by the enthusiastic John Rocliffe. Several recruits were obtained and the *Advertiser* said it was confident that the group would grow, and that their force would eventually 'occupy a position more in accord with the go-ahead patriotism of the town', than presumably it currently occupied.[15] At the same time, more or less, a last batch of Easingwold Yeomen left for the front. They were not to know that their services would not be needed when they got there.[16] Details of them – indeed the whole of the *Advertiser's* report of their departure – will be given later.

Shortly after the moves to strengthen the Easingwold Volunteers occurred, it was announced that there would also be attempts to create a local Yeomanry troop.[17]

FORMATION OF A YEOMANRY TROOP
AT EASINGWOLD

The martial spirit now appears to have been thoroughly aroused in Easingwold as, in addition to the Volunteer revival, when over 30 recruits were enrolled, steps are being taken to form a troop of Yeomanry, to be, when raised, under the command of Captain Miles J. Stapylton, who we are given to understand, has received permission to transfer from the Bedale troop. The Sergeant-Instructor attended at the George Hotel on Wednesday evening last, when several eligible young men were enrolled. A drill will be held on Wednesday evening, when any young men wishing to join are invited to attend.

In the public notices column of the *Advertiser* issued after the report just quoted there appeared a notice over the signature of a very well-known local personality.[18]

In May 1902 the *Advertiser's* editorial expressed the nation's hope that the Conference of Boer delegates which is to take place next week, would result in peace,[19] and gave readers figures of the casualties of two and a half years of incessant campaigning – saying they compared very favourably with earlier campaigns,[20] which they certainly did. A few days later another public announcement was printed with instructions for the 'Easingwold Detachment'.[21]

"C" SQUADRON
YORKSHIRE (P.W.O.) HUSSARS, I.Y.

Detachment Orders by Captain Miles J. Stapylton

The Easingwold Detachment will parade in Drill Order at 10.15 a.m., on Wednesday, 21st inst., in front of the George Hotel, Easingwold.

They will march off at 11.30 a.m. sharp, marching via Myton, Boro'bridge, and Knaresbro', to Harrogate, picking up the detachments as they march through these places.

All baggage to be sent so as to be in Camp on arrival of men and horses. It must be clearly addressed with man's name followed by
"C Squadron.
Yorkshire Hussars
Camp, Harrogate."
By Order,
(Sd.)
MILES J. STAPYLTON, Capt.
Commanding Detachment.
Easingwold, 13th May 1902.

The paper reported arrangements for a march to Harrogate for 'the annual training'. The troops leaving Easingwold were 11 in number and in charge was to be Cpl Sidney Smith (Hanover). More men were to be picked up *en route*.[22] At Harrogate Pte Bannister was awarded the prize 'for best recruit and turnout' and Pte Dixon was highly commended. That information comes from a report of the Easingwolders' performance at the musketry course.[23] Lord Roberts and others, it will be recalled, had been appalled at the dreadful shooting standards shown by Volunteers and had laid down regulations for recruits and encouraged the building of ranges. The *Advertiser* gave details of the rules of the shoot and the names of the participants (and their scores).[24]

At last Easingwold had two military organisations and the first ceremonial duty of the youngest of them must have been in the coronation parade of August. After the 'Parade of Decorated Horses and Drays and decorated bikes there was to be a procession. Heading it was a 'Band' and the next three groups were 'Children in wagons', Yeomanry' and 'Volunteers'.[25]

The men who joined up in these last months of the Boer War had been part of a huge expansion that St John Brodrick spoke about in November.[26]

WE ARE READY FOR WAR

Mr. Brodrick, speaking at Dewsbury, the other night, said our army was never so strong as at the present time. The cavalry were 6000 men above strength, and the artillery, of which at the beginning of war there was only enough for three army corps, was now full to the whole extent of five army corps. In sixteen months the Yeomanry had been raised from 9000 to 26,000. The Reserve had, of course, fallen off, but under the new system that would repair itself rapidly. They could mobilise again to a much larger extent in the way of stores tomorrow than they could at the beginning of the Boer War.

YORKSHIRE HUSSARS
IMPERIAL YEOMANRY

Lord Bolton, Colonel Commanding the Yorkshire Hussars Imperial Yeomanry, having sanctioned the formation of a Troop with Headquarters at Easingwold, to form part of the "C" Squadron Yorkshire Hussars, under the command of Major Stainforth. I hereby invite any Young Man who can ride well and who is desirous of joining the Easingwold Troop to give in his name to MR. HAYNES, of the George Hotel, Easingwold.

All information with regard to the conditions of enlistment and service in the Yorkshire Hussars Imperial Yeomanry can be had on application to SERGEANT MAJOR STEDMAN, Yorkshire Hussars, Fisher Gate, Knaresborough.

All men will be required to be passed by the Medical Officer before they can be properly attested.

MILES J. STAPYLON,
Captain, Yorkshire Hussars.

NOTES

1. J.K. Dunlop *The Development of the British Army 1899-1914* (1938)
2. *Ibid* p 42. The quote is from Col Dunlop's text, not Maurice's foreword
3. *Advertiser* 19 August 1899
4. Quoted *Ibid* 28 October 1899
5. *Ibid* 8 February 1902
6. Eg *Easingwold Memories*, Easingwold (nd)
7. *Advertiser* 8 March 1902
8. *Ibid* 9 March 1900
9. Marquess of Anglesey, *A History of the British Cavalry 1816-1919*. Vol 4 (1986) chap 7 passim.
10. *Advertiser* 17 March 1900
11. *Ibid* 3 February 1900
12. *Ibid* 2 February 1901
13. *Ibid* 7 September 1901
14. Anglesey op cit p 100
15. *Advertiser* 1 and 29 March 1902
16. *Ibid* 15 March 1902
17. *Ibid* 5 April 1902
18. *Ibid* 12 April 1902. Miles Staplyton got a considerable amount of publicity from his campaign for taxing bicycles. *Ibid* 11 October 1902
19. *Ibid* 10 May 1902. The same comparisons (more or less) were made in the note 'THEY DIED FOR ENGLAND' in *Ibid* 5 July 1902. *Ibid* 12 April 1902.
20. The figures it gave were the loss of 22,000 lives from all causes since October 1899. A comparison was made with Waterloo 'when the Duke of Wellington had 15,000 killed and wounded, and the Prussians 7,000.' A more comprehensive list of figures based on a return from the Adjutant General was reported on 13 September 1902
21. *Advertiser* 17 May 1902
22. *Ibid* 24 May 1902
23. *Ibid* 12 July 1902
24. A maximum of 196 points could be obtained from firing: 21 rounds at 200 yards, 7 at 300, 7 at 400, 7 at 500 and 7 at 600. The highest scores were by Cpl Smith (154) and the lowest 84. The participants (no initials or christian names were given) were all privates, except Smith and were Coates, Bannister, Batty, Smith, Cowling, Dixon, Stephenson, Brogan and Shaw. Pte Smith was the exception to the rule of no initials. He was P.
25. *Advertiser* 2 and 16 August 1902
26. 'WE ARE READY FOR WAR', *Ibid* 22 November 1902

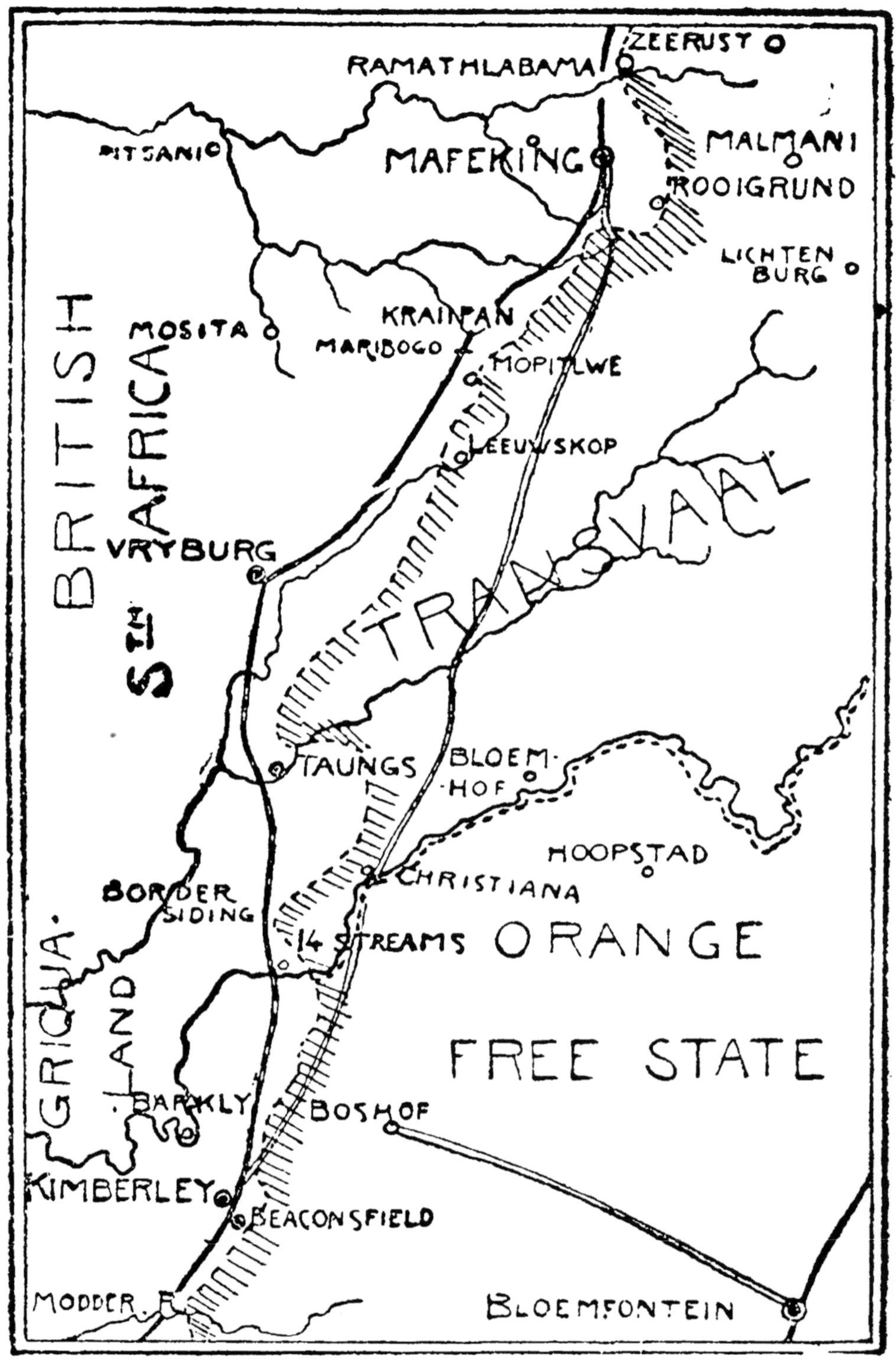

SKETCH MAP, SHOWING THE RHODESIAN BORDER.

Vryburg where Stephen Wombwell died, and Boshof where he was stationed

Chapter 19

STEPHEN WOMBWELL

On 23 December 1899 the following note appeared in the *Advertiser* about a young man whose life was to end tragically in the not-very-distant future. It has been quoted earlier. He was Stephen Wombwell who 'joined the Yorkshire Hussars (or Duke of Yorks Own) a yeomanry regiment, one of the first to be sent out' to South Africa, and he wrote home from Wettenburg in November wishing his family 'a merry christmas and a Happy New Year'.[1] This is according to a writer about the Wombwell family, but the *Advertiser,* in a report which has also been referred to before said he was in Sheffield on 21 January and left there in 'the early hours for Liverpool and South Africa' in the company of, Major Gascoigne and Capt C.W.E. Duncombe.[2] The departure, it will be recalled, was staged at an early hour because the authorities wanted to avoid the scenes 'which characterised the sending off of the C.I.V. in London.'

In the second week of February a note was published about the progress of the troopship which Stephen Wombwell was almost certainly on.[3] (He was definitely with Sidney Smith.)

> THE YEOMANRY
>
> The transport, "Winnefredian", which carries the Yorks and Notts contingents of the Imperial Yeomanry, is reported as having passed St Vincent, and is expected to reach the Cape about the 20th inst. Troopers Sidney Smith and Thomas Wilkinson, from Easingwold, are included in the above.

The official war news (or at least the parts published locally) do not seem to have carried any reports about what happened to Stephen Wombwell's unit for about six weeks after he docked. Then there appeared an account of an action he was involved in. It contained yet another example of the Boers allegedly abusing the white flag – there were dozens of these – [4] and mentioned a famous French soldier called Villebois Mareuil who was fighting with the Boers. The following is from the *Advertiser* of 14 April, 1900.

LORD METHUEN'S SUCCESS

The War Office announces that the following is the list of casualties reported by Lord Roberts as having occurred among non-commissioned officers and men in the encounter at Tweifontein, near Boshof, on the 5th inst.

IMPERIAL YEOMANRY

KILLED – 4810 Sergeant Patrick Campbell. This officer was the husband of the well-known actress, and only went out, with other gentlemen, as a trooper in the Yeomanry some two months ago.

SEVERELY WOUNDED – 7967 Sergeant J. Gibbard, 768 Sergeant D. Turner, 4992 Corporal A Little, 744 Privates C. Fisher and and 8023 G. Strutt.

SLIGHTLY WOUNDED – 1234 Colour-Sergeant Cole, 8025 Privates B. Throckmorton , and 7454 E. Christian.

KIMBERLEY MOUNTED CORPS

SLIGHTLY WOUNDED – Privates C. N. Judd and D. Hurst.

The War Office announced at 11.5 on Sunday night in a further telegram from Lord Roberts that the officer from the Imperial Yeomanry previously reported killed in the encounter near Boshof is Lieutenant A.C. Williams.

Later there was a supplementary report about the above action.

Who was General Villebois-Mareuil? He was known as the Boer Von Moltke who acted as Chief of the General Staff of the Transvaal forces. He was a retired French Colonel who had left the St Cyr academy in 1868 and was a veteran of the Franco-German war. He served in Cochin China, and Algeria, and for a time commanded a regiment of the Foreign Legion. A writer in the April issue of the *Temple Magazine* attributed purely mercenary motives to his service with the Boers. He was 53 years of age when he died,[5] and the deal with him to help the Boers was negotiated by a Dr Leyds. The *Advertiser* in an editorial, commented on his death.[6]

> Poor Villebois de Mareuil is buried in the Transvaal under a French tricolour, amid the respectful regrets of those who have fought against him. It is one of the [customs] of war, as waged by the Briton, that the recently fallen foe is respected. We can hardly exhibit emotions other than those born of satisfaction, however, at contemplation of the fact that three such competent soldier-experts as Villebois, Schiel, and Albrecht can help the Boers no more.

The fight in which Villebois was killed, described at length in a letter to be quoted, was of no great significance in the history of the South African war, and Thomas Pakenham's index contains no reference to the principal place in the story. This was Boshof, which lies above the Modder river and due east of the railway and Kimberley. The Boers were being pushed back, and Kimberley was taken in an extraordinary episode when, effectively, no resistance was offered. Kimberley had been 'besieged by Boer forces for four memorable months,' a South African source recorded.[7]

> From 14 October 1899 when the rail and telephone lines were cut, isolating the town, until General French's exhausted cavalry clattered in on 15 February 1900.

Lord Methuen was in command of the forces[8] in the Kimberley District and his most pressing duties were to repair the railways and pacify the 'area north and north east of Kimberley and … control the North West section of the Orange Free State. He began these operations in earnest on 21 February.'[9]

On 5 April there occurred the little-known Battle of Boshof. Villebois de Mareuil had mistakenly believed Methuen's force to be near Barkly West and Methuen ordered his Imperial Yeomanry to saddle up and go for the Frenchman and his forces. They did and there ensued a bayonet charge. The importance of the battle? Had it any? It had. First of all it restored Methuen's self confidence and came at a time when 'a success was very welcome'.[10] It was also the first time the Imperial Yeomanry 'had engaged the enemy, and they acquitted themselves well' – acting 'like veteran troops'. They lost an officer (Lt A.C. Williams) who was shot after a white flag had been raised. His assassin was immediately executed on Methuen's order.

By kind permission of the present Sir George Wombwell

Sir George Orby Wombwell
who survived the Charge of the Light Brigade at Balaclava in the Crimean War.

By kind permission of Sir George Wombwell

Stephen Wombwell's grave near Vryburg, South Africa

Memorial Gate at Coxwold Church

By kind permission of Sir George Wombwell

Stephen Wombwell in Officers Dress Uniform Yorkshire Hussars

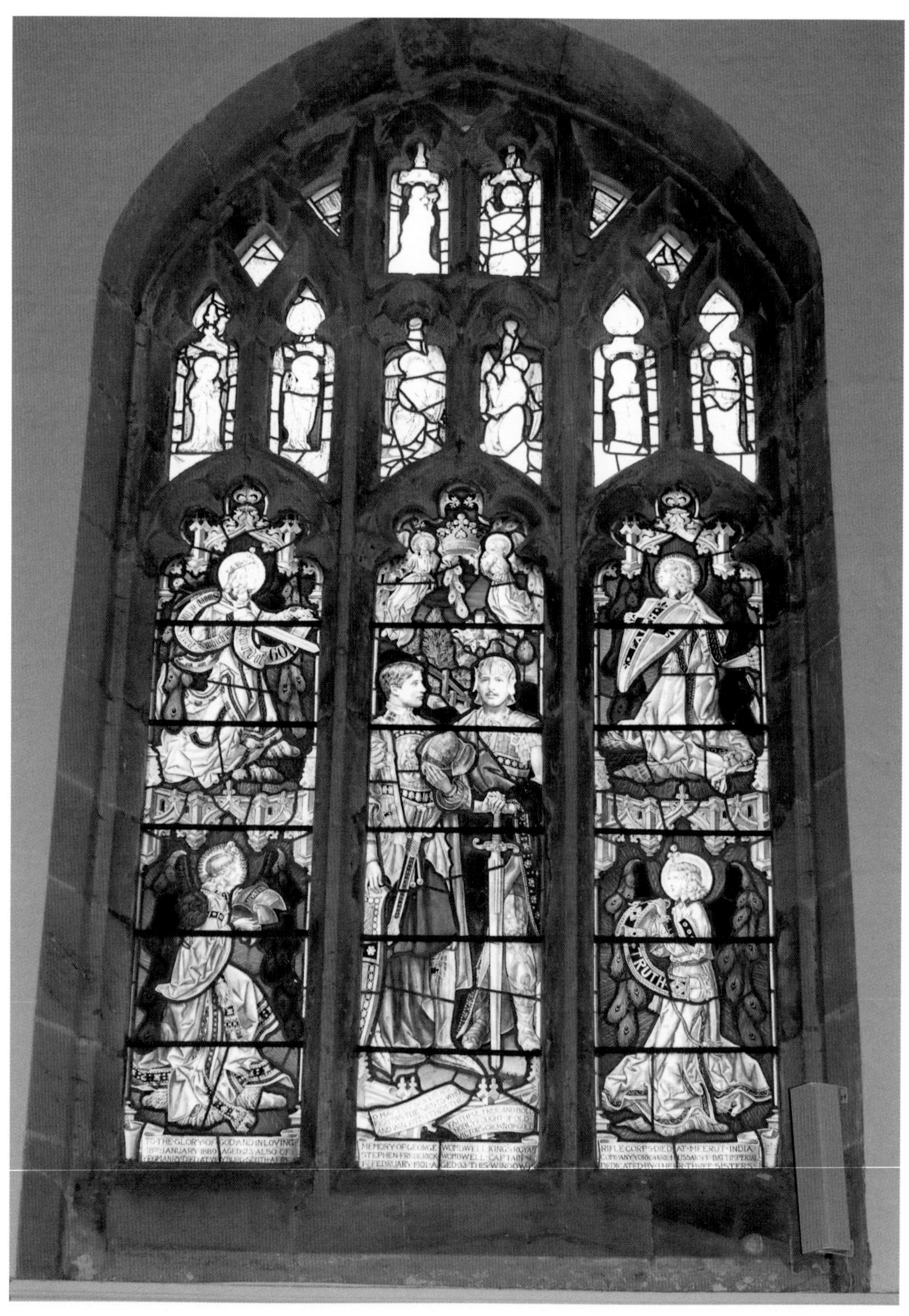

Stained glass window in Coxwold Church in memory of Captain Stephen Wombwell

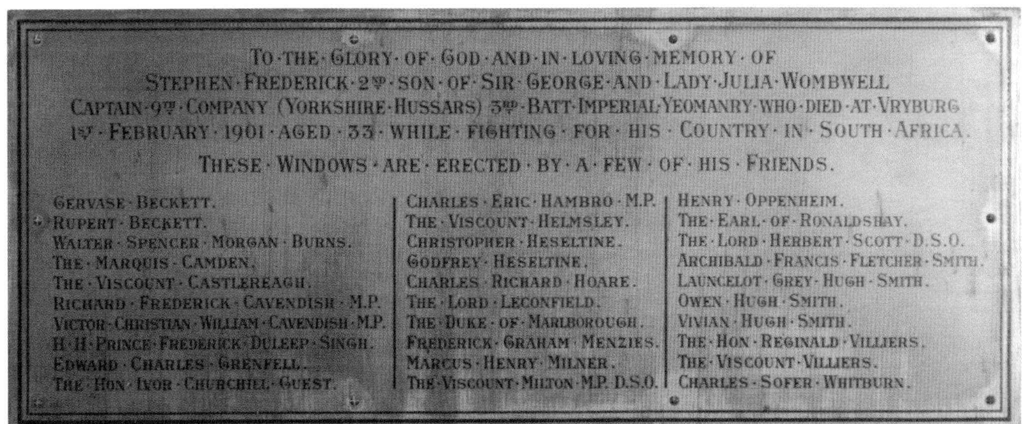

TO·THE·GLORY·OF·GOD·AND·IN·LOVING·MEMORY·OF
STEPHEN·FREDERICK·2ND·SON·OF·SIR·GEORGE·AND·LADY·JULIA·WOMBWELL
CAPTAIN·9TH·COMPANY (YORKSHIRE·HUSSARS) 3RD·BATT·IMPERIAL·YEOMANRY·WHO·DIED·AT·VRYBURG
1ST·FEBRUARY·1901·AGED·33·WHILE·FIGHTING·FOR·HIS·COUNTRY·IN·SOUTH·AFRICA.
THESE·WINDOWS·ARE·ERECTED·BY·A·FEW·OF·HIS·FRIENDS.
GERVASE·BECKETT.
RUPERT·BECKETT.
WALTER·SPENCER·MORGAN·BURNS.
THE·MARQUIS·CAMDEN.
THE·VISCOUNT·CASTLEREAGH.
RICHARD·FREDERICK·CAVENDISH·M.P.
VICTOR·CHRISTIAN·WILLIAM·CAVENDISH·M.P.
H·H·PRINCE·FREDERICK·DULEEP·SINGH.
EDWARD·CHARLES·GRENFELL.
THE·HON·IVOR·CHURCHILL·GUEST.
CHARLES·ERIC·HAMBRO·M.P.
THE·VISCOUNT·HELMSLEY.
CHRISTOPHER·HESELTINE.
GODFREY·HESELTINE.
CHARLES·RICHARD·HOARE.
THE·LORD·LECONFIELD.
THE·DUKE·OF·MARLBOROUGH.
FREDERICK·GRAHAM·MENZIES.
MARCUS·HENRY·MILNER.
THE·VISCOUNT·MILTON·M.P. D.S.O.
HENRY·OPPENHEIM.
THE·EARL·OF·RONALDSHAY.
THE·LORD·HERBERT·SCOTT·D.S.O.
ARCHIBALD·FRANCIS·FLETCHER·SMITH.
LAUNCELOT·GREY·HUGH·SMITH.
OWEN·HUGH·SMITH.
VIVIAN·HUGH·SMITH.
THE·HON·REGINALD·VILLIERS.
THE·VISCOUNT·VILLIERS.
CHARLES·SOFER·WHITBURN.

Plaque in Coxwold Church

Coxwold. Photo 2002

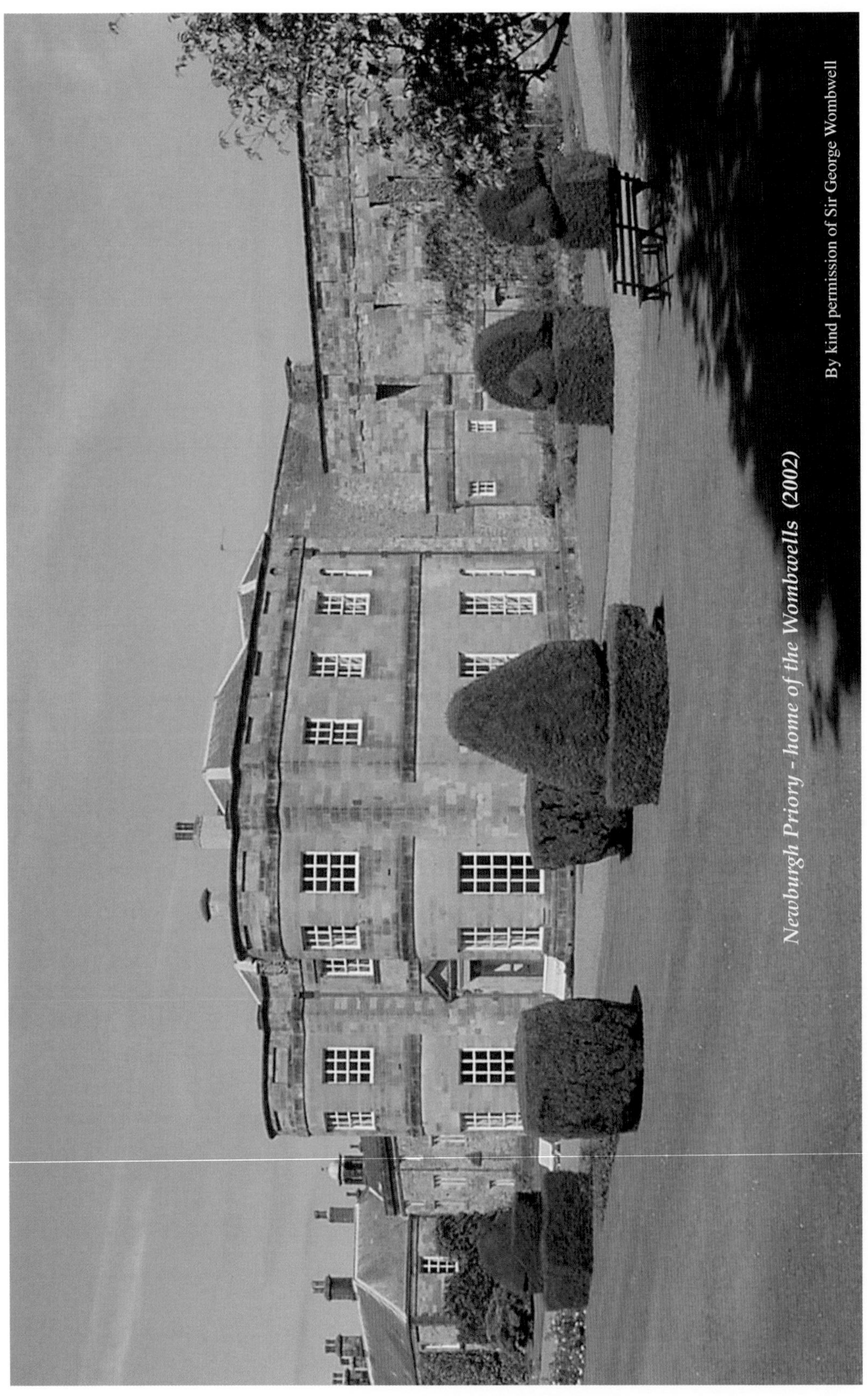

Newburgh Priory - home of the Wombwells (2002)

By kind permission of Sir George Wombwell

Family Coat of Arms

METHUEN'S SUCCESS – GENERAL VILLEBOIS SLAIN

Lord Roberts has forwarded to the War Office a telegram from Lord Methuen, reporting that on Thursday of last week a body of Boers, under the command of General Villebois, was surrounded near Boshof. None of them escaped. Villebois and seven Boers were killed, about eight wounded, and 54 were made prisioners. Our loss was Captain Boyle of the Oxfordshire Yeomanry, Mr Williams, of the Lincolnshire Yeomanry and two other Yeomen killed, and about seven wounded. The Times special correspondent states that Captain Boyle was deliberately shot by one of the enemy after they had shown the white flag, and that this man who perpetated the act was himself shot.

Stephen Wombwell wrote an account of the events of early April in a letter which was published in the *Advertiser.* Here it is in full.[11]

A LETTER FROM MR STEPHEN WOMBWELL

The following is the copy of a letter received by Sir George O. Wombwell, Bart, Newburgh Priory, from his son, who is now serving with the Imperial Yeomanry in South Africa.

April 6th
Boshof

Mr Dearest Father,

Yesterday we had our first engagement with the Boers, and I will tell you all about it. It was about 11 a.m. when all the horses were out grazing and most of us in the town when the order came for our Battalion and the 10th Batt. (Lord Chesham's) and the Kimberley Light Horse and one Battery of Artillery to turn out at once. Unfortunately for this Company the Yorkshire Hussars we were providing the captain of the day and, orderly officers, and had to remain behind, but I was lucky and got a job. One section of this company had to go as guard to the ammunition cart and water cart, and luckily I just happened to be standing next to Lord Scarborough, and I asked him to let me take my section, and he said I might as the other officers were not on the spot. The first and second sections ought to have gone before me. Needless to say I rushed out and collected my lot and in 10 minutes was following on behind as quick as possible, which was not fast, only walking pace. We flogged the wretched mules along, the whole country being honeycombed with holes. After going 12 or 15 miles out, I came up to a kopje where the dismounted horses were left and the artillery, just as the first shot was fired, so there I halted my waggons and mounted the kopje to have a look round. The Bucks Yeomanry were on it blazing away at the enemy who occupied a kopje 1200 yards off. You could see the Boers easily, crawling about though not many of them. There was another kopje about 200 yards further on, where they were going more heavily, so I got on my horse (I was riding Thormanby) and casually walked across. When half way I heard a thud, and a bullet hit the ground at about 20 yards from me, then came another about 5 yards off, so I stuck my spurs in and galloped as hard as I could go. Then I dismounted, and climbed up to the top of the kopje, got behind a big rock, and sat there the rest of the day watching the fight, and in comparative safety, except when I put my head out to have a look. The Kimberley men were on this kopje and the gunners, and the former were blazing away in grand style, and the bullets came over our heads with such a whiz. We kept ducking our heads every time we heard them, not that it would be any use if the bullet was coming your way, but you can't help it, and we all laughed. We had fairly got the Boers like rats in a trap. They never expected us, and all their ponies were grazing half a mile from the kopje, which was only a small one about a mile square, so they could not get at them, and in the meanwhile our men were surrounding them. When we had them completely surrounded firing got brisk and the bullets came whizzing over, a good many of them from our own men on the other side. This went on till 5 o'clock, and I was afraid they would hold out till dark and escape, when suddenly we saw the Boers rushing along our side of the hill. Then the gunners opened fire with their 15 pounders. It really was splendid. I might have been sitting in a stall at Drury Lane. Had a good bird's eye view at everything. Then I saw our men attacking the hill on all sides and they gradually swarmed the kopje and fixed bayonets and charged. Suddenly up goes the white flag, and somebody shouts out "Put your heads down" and lucky it was we did so, as they were up to their old tricks, and the moment after a shower of bullets came over our kopje. Then a splendidly directed shell from our guns burst right amongst them and they threw down their arms and surrendered. Lord Chesham and his staff came galloping up to our kopje, and then on to the one the Boers were on, and I joined in and went on with him, and left my lot to look after themselves. When we got there they were bringing down the prisoners, such a mixed crew, French, Germans, Polish Jews and bringing in the dead and wounded. There were not many casualties. We had two officers, Williams and Boyle, and two or three killed and ten wounded. The Boers lost about ten killed and several wounded. I am so sorry about poor Williams, he was such a nice fellow - in the Sherwood Rangers, - I brought all his things back with me. I did not know Boyle, he was with the Oxford Yeomanry. They are to be buried this afternoon. We killed General Villebois, one of the Boers best Generals a Frenchman. I went to look at him, and recognised him easily from his picture in the English papers. He was shot in the forehead. Poor Williams was killed just at the last rush. The Boers hoisted two white flags, and up he jumped, and they shot him through the heart. As in everything there was the comic side in the fight, though it seems rather heartless to say so. Just at the end one Boer for some reason took to the open. I suppose he wanted to catch a pony and escape, but he ran like a rabbit amidst a storm of bullets, you can see them strike on the veldt, after going 200 yards he was bowled over like a rabbit, had five bullets in him. Then again when anybody tried to cross between the two kopjes I mentioned before, the one I was on and the first one, they always had to run the gauntlet. They only hit one man though. Then after everybody had been brought in, we started home again, and I had the most awful time of it I ever had in my life. It was just getting dark, and I galloped off to collect my waggons and my section and the water cart, but the ammunition and store carts were nowhere to be found, which was rather serious. However I had to give them up, and we started home at a very slow walk the whole way. It soon got pitch dark, you could not see the man in front of you, and the most terrific thunderstorm I ever saw, and a perfect deluge of rain broke overhead, and this continued the whole way. The lightning was something wonderful. It absolutely blinded you. I had to wait for the next flash to see if I was blinded or not. It really was rather a good thing in a way, as it lighted up our track. I don't know how we should have got on without it, as I did not know the way. We presently came across a track which I stuck to, and fortunately it led straight into Boshof. We got back about 10.30 without any casualty, and glad I was to get back. Never had such a time in my life as that journey home. We kept getting into holes, and running against dead horses left in the road and all sorts of things. We were precious hungry too, only had one biscuit all day. Our food was in the lost forage cart. Thank goodness both waggons turned up all right. We had not got our tents up, and the ground was inches under water, but I slept like a pig on my valise, till I woke up early in the morning with two loose horses sniffing about my head. They have just brought the prisoners in, they look the most horrid scoundrels. A lot of them are wounded. One of them is an Englishman. I expect they will shoot some of those that fired after the white flag was hoisted. My horse behaved too wonderfully, he did not take the slightest notice of the firing, not even of the big guns, when they went off at 10 yards from him. Both my horses are doing splendidly. I hear we start off tomorrow with two day's rations after more Boers, Lord Methuen was in command. I hope we shall march to

Pretoria in time. There are all sorts of reports about what the Boers are going to do. This is the latest, and I should think, the truest and most likely. They are all going to assemble at Cronstad and make a determined stand there. Old Kruger has commandeered every man between 20 and 70 years of age to go there, under penalty of death. Others say they will split up in small parties and go plundering the country. That would be awful, as the war would go on for an indefinite time. I forgot to say that the reason we caught so few Boers yesterday was that the Boer force, 600 strong, left that very morning, and what we caught was more or less a rear-guard. I can't understand a man like Villebois being caught napping so easily. They had no idea we were about. I must say they fought heroically, and only gave in when we were 30 yards off them. There was a lot of Boers about, I believe, so we are likely to see a bit of fighting. I have just discovered the post went last night, so worse luck, I have missed next week's mail. I have been waiting till we got here to send you a wire as to my whereabouts, and now we have got here, I can't send one, as the Military authorities have seized it. So I am sending it to a man at Kimberley to forward on.

I hope Mamma got my letter I wrote last week from Kimberley a long one, but I am rather frightened about it, as I gave it to a man to post in the town, and he got very drunk and may have lost it, or forgotten about it. I also gave him one for Julia. This camp is crammed with troops, thousands of them. I hear Arthur Paget has arrived here to command an Infantry Brigade. I wonder what he has done with his guardsmen. I was very glad to get your letter the other day, and to hear all is well at Newburgh. What wretched weather you have had. Another thunderstorm is raging now. This occurs every day. I keep very well indeed, never was better. My heel keeps the same no better and no worse, but I regret to say my one and only pair of boots won't last much longer. I bought a pair of Cape shoes, but can't wear them on account of my heel. Please give my best love to all, and remember me to all at Newburgh.

Yours etc.,

STEPHEN WOMBWELL

Patrick Campbell husband to Mrs P.C. was killed yesterday.

Shortly after, he wrote another letter:

My dearest Mamma, I wrote a very hurried line this morning to tell you we had had a sharp fight and that I was alright. I just chanced to hear as I was dressing at 5 a.m. that a man was going to Kimberley and that a letter posted tonight would catch next Wednesday's mail, so down I flopped and scribbled off the letter, and then had to gallop two miles after him to catch him too as he had already started. I had little more than a shirt and a pair of socks on! I only hope he won't be captured by the Boers. They are all over the place and it is just an even chance if he reaches Kimberley or not. I must now thank you so much for sending me the silk handkerchiefs, meat lozenges and chocolate… They are most welcome, and it is too good of you sending them and all your letters I revel in.

And now I will tell you about the fight…as it is the first in which our Company, the Yorkshire Hussars, were engaged in and we bore the brunt of the whole fight. From the patrols we had been sending out every day we discovered the Boers were collecting in force and had a big laager about 6 or 8 miles from our camp, Zwartkoppenfontein. On Friday 20th at midday we suddenly got orders to pack up and return to Boshof in two hours time. All the convoy was loaded and a precious big one it is. It extends five good miles. We were told off to act as rearguard. I expected the Boers would trouble us a bit, but little expected what we were in for. We waited till the convoy started and just as the last few waggons were passing by we heard firing. The Bucks Yeomanry were sent to occupy one kopje, and presently we were despatched to another close by.

On arriving there we dismounted and took up our position and every man got behind the biggest rock he could find...We had no sooner settled when I saw a pack of Boers advancing in line. They then began shelling the kopje the Bucks were on, and it was not long before it got too hot for them, and they began to retire. This looked rather serious for us, as their kopje was higher than ours and also commanded ours altogether – it was about 800 yards off – and their original orders were to hold it as long as possible. Major Gascoigne then sent me with a message to ask them what they were doing and to stay there; but before I could get to my horse they were already mounted and halfway to ours. I gave them my message but they said they could hold it no longer and rode off to another kopje some way off to our left. The Boers then occupied the kopje vacated by the Bucks and opened fire on the Yorkshiremen – and such a fire too! They had our range to an inch, and the bullets fairly whizzed about us. We returned the fire for about an hour, when we were ordered to cease fire as we could not discover where they were. There is absolutely no smoke with these modern rifles and cartridges. Boer reinforcements came up and the firing got so hot, it was not safe to move your little finger out of the shelter of your rock. The two men next to me got hit early on, one in the back, the other in the arm, but there was nothing I could do for them as it was certain death to move.

Well, we laid here for about an hour and the convoy, having got well ahead we were ordered to retire; at the same time the Boers had got round to another kopje on our right and we were receiving a terrible cross-fire – at one time I thought we were going to be surrounded and that it was to be our first and last engagement! When we were told to retire I did not think a single man could possibly get across the top of our kopje, 200 yards long, without being either killed or wounded, and then the difficulty was to get the men to retire from their shelter.

However, they soon had to make up their minds as the Boers, seeing us turning back, immediately jumped on their horses and galloped over to our kopje. So off they went, some crawling, others running. I began by crawling, but it was too slow a progress, so I ran 20 yards, then dropped, and so on...We reached the horses presently and found them under heavy fire from the Boers on our right, and the horses floundering all over the place. I found my mare after a time, simply terrified – she had knocked the man holding her down three times – and tried to get my section together but only five turning up, and seeing everybody galloping to the next hill about a mile and a quarter away, I told them to go too. It was the hottest ride I ever was in...

The Boers had ascended our kopje and we had to gallop over the plain under this cross-fire and the ground was a mass of holes, some broken wire and a ditch halfway. I had taken the curb off my mare on starting, and she immediately took the bit between her teeth, and away she went, like a mad horse. She was so terrified twenty men could not have stopped her. I can't think how she escaped coming down in the holes. Horses were tumbling in all directions, either shot or getting into holes, but we (most of us) reached the kopje... The Boers were still pelting us but at long range and pretty harmless...Next morning, on calling the roll, there were 19 men missing all of which were accounted for later on in the day, as we sent out a burying party and the Boers told them there were two dead on the kopje, which we buried; they had eleven prisoners, three of them wounded but doing well, and we brought six wounded with us...We also lost 21 horses. Alas! Among the prisoners is poor Smith of Hanover Farm...His parents will be in a state. If you get a chance you might let them know he will be alright, sure to go to Pretoria, and that he fought splendidly...You will think by this account we got a severe hiding and beat an ignominious retreat, but such is not the case. We did what we were ordered, that was to hold the kopje which commanded the high road so as to keep the Boers off the convoy, and this we did. As a matter of fact we ought to have retired earlier. We were fighting against enormous odds. It was only our seventy men and some Kimberley mounted Corps against 1500 to 2000 Boers...The other regiments say we did extremely well, and they all thought we were going to be cut to pieces when the Boers got in their crossfire...We shall not be long before we have another fight, as the Boers have been considerably reinforced these last two days. Very likely about 5000 of them now. Cronje's nephew and son are with them, the former in command. We hear they intend to make a dash on this place Boshof in a day or two, but if they do they will have their work cut out...At the same time the natives say they are not likely to do this, as though they are mostly Transvaalers, there are a great many with them who come from Boshof, and it would be like shelling their own homes. Of course what they want is our convoy, which we do not intend them to have. Failing their attacking us here, what they may do is to slip past us and get between us and Kimberley and cut off our supplies which could be awkward, though we have 15 days rations with us, and that is equal to 30 days rations. And now I hear Sir Archibald Turner is at Kimberley and his division coming in, in which case we should sandwich them and nothing the wily Boer dislikes so much as having his retreat cut off. I rather hope Sir A. Hunter will come up here and we shall join his column and very likely go to relieve [Mafeking], which must be in a bad way now...The marvellous rapidity in which the Boers get about, and the way they conceal themselves is almost incredible, and from the little I have seen it is easy to understand how difficult it is to defeat them.

In the summer of 1900, it was rumoured that Stephen was about to be promoted.[12]

MR STEPHEN WOMBWELL, it is said, will shortly succeed Major Gascoigne in the command of the Yorkshire Hussars, Major Gascoigne taking the command of the 3rd battalion.

Vryburg Hospital, reproduced by kind permission of Vryburg Town Council

Shortly after eight o'clock on Tuesday 29 January 1901, the news of the death of Queen Victoria reached Easingwold and the papers became filled with tributes to her, details of memorial services, stories about her successor and arrangements for her funeral on 2 February. The day before that Stephen Wombwell had passed away.

Stephen Frederick Wombwell died from enteric fever in the hospital at Vryburg, it was reported.[13] His father, Sir George Orby Wombwell, had held a commission in the 17th Lancers and was a Balaclava survivor and his eldest son succumbed to typhoid fever in Meerut whilst serving there as lieutenant in the 4th Battalion of the 60th Rifles. Stephen then became the family heir – at the age of 34, 'having been born on the 19th February, 1867. ... [he] was attached to the third battalion of the Imperial Yeomanry'. He was a North Riding Justice of the Peace.

At about the time Stephen died figures about one of the recruiting campaigns for the Imperial Yeomanry were given and new rates of pay were brought in and publicised. They might be of interest, though they have been referred to earlier. The war had been going on since October 1899 readers were reminded yet 'The returns of the Imperial Yeomanry up to Monday evening [25 February, 1901 showed] that 11,000 men [had] been obtained and 200 officers nominated.' These were impressive totals.[14] The publicity involved in the recruiting was certainly of a kind to appeal to the adventurous, with exotic names abounding throughout it.[15] Lord Chesham, who Stephen Wombwell hoped to serve with, was in charge of training, which went on at a reorganised camp at Germiston.

What of those increased rates of pay (which must have had something to do with the spectacular recruiting figures?) A Royal Warrant had announced that daily rates for NCOs and men in the Imperial Yeomanry were henceforth to be 'as follows: Regimental Sergeant-Major, 9s.; quartermaster sergeant, farrier-sergeant, farrier staff-sergeant, 8s.6d.; company sergeant major, company quartermaster-sergeant 8s., sergeant 7s.; corporal and paid lance-corporal, 6s.; private, 5s'.[16]

On the first anniversary of Stephen Wombwell's death two windows were 'put up' in the church at Coxwold to his memory and that of his brother.[17] A memorial from the Wombwell tenants ('Two busts in white marble') was the work of Herr Fuchs, a famous sculptor 'whose name has recently been brought prominently before the public in connection with the new issue of stamps'. The dedication service was held on 1 February.

Stephen Wombwell had clearly been a very popular officer, as a private letter from a Trooper Roundell demonstrated. It was handed over to the paper and showed, the *Advertiser* said, how 'deeply lamented his death was by his old comrades' 3rd Battalion of Imperial Yeomanry. The introduction to Roundell's letter looks as if the word 'well' might have been 'unwell' in the original and the word has might be a mistake for 'had'.[18] But here is how it appeared towards the end of March.

> Captain Wombwell has been well [had been unwell?] all through [the] campaign until he went into hospital with enteric fever[19] at Vryburg in January. Trooper Roundell says of him:-
>
> We have lost our best friend and a fine leader. We don't care how soon we come home : we seem to have lost all interest since he died. He was awfully kind to us; without doubt he was the most thought about of any officer in the battalion. When we had our concert at Ottoschoop on Christmas Eve he told us we should always have a friend in him; if we would stick to him he would stick to us. He has taken us into some hard fights, but he never took us where he could not bring us out again.

A week after the Roundell letter was published there was an account of 'MORE TRAIN WRECKING'. The Boers had mined a supply train three miles north of Vlarlaagte and the report described how Gen Campbell was delayed at the Klip River and had had to float his waggons across and get their loads over on a raft. 'His men have suffered much from enteric fever' it was said.[20] A little later figures were given for one month.[21] The British casualties ... during April totalled 112 officers and 2851 men. Eighty-six were killed in action, 44 died of wounds and 388 *of disease* ...' (my italics). Losses from the start of the war to the end of April contained Died of disease 232 officers, 8,949 men. H.W. Wilson gave some tables from official sources containing similar categories to the foregoing. They had included figures from the outbreak of hostilities up to and including October 1900. Died of disease were 155 officers and 6,115 men.

At the memorial service to Stephen Wombwell at Coxwold 9 February[22] there were present

> half a dozen of the Yeomanry in Khaki, recently returned from the front, ... who had served under Capt Wombwell ... and seemed to be the link between South Africa and home. One was a trooper whose life the dead officer had saved in the unfortunate affair at Lindley. The sight of these visibly affected a few, and one in particular, a farmer whose son went out with Captain Wombwell, and went with him through many a stiff encounter.

The 'affair at Lindley' occurred on 31 May 1900.

NOTES

1. G. Ridsill Smith, *In Well Beware* (Kineton 1978) pp 203-4
2. *Advertiser* 3 February 1900
3. *Ibid* 10 February 1900
4. See e.g. *Ibid* 17 March 1900
5. *Temple Magazine* quoted *Ibid* 14 April 1900
6. *Ibid* 14 April 1900. Schiel was Lt Col Schiel, taken prisoner at Elandslaagte, and Albrecht was Major Albrecht. Schiel was 'in the Transvaal service'; Albrecht 'in that of the Free State'. Both, captured 1902, were sent to St Helena. Dr Leyds was waging a campaign to try to get European intervention in South Africa. He had little success. See the *Morning Post* quoted *Ibid* 24 March 1900
7. *Diamond Fields N12 Battlefields Route. 1899 – 1902;*
   Copy in the collection of David Smith.
8. It was at this stage that the first Boer War films were shown in Easingwold. See earlier.
9. Miller op cit pp 182-3
10. A Conan Doyle, *The Great Boer War* (1900) p 213
11. *Advertiser* 5 May 1900
12. *Ibid* 11 August 1900
13. *Ibid* 9 February 1901
14. *Ibid* 2 March 1901
15. There were Roughriders and Sharpshooters Corps – both of which were forming second battalions.
16. *Advertiser* 2 March 1901
17. *Ibid* 8 February 1902
18. *Ibid* 23 March 1901
19. 'ENTERIC – A general name for infective fevers of the intestine, especially typhoid and paratyphoid'.
20. *Advertiser* 30 March 1901
21. *Ibid* 11 May 1901
22. *Ibid* 16 February 1901

Chapter 20

CPL LITTLEWOOD AND THE POSTIES

In the summer of 1900 a letter appeared in the *Easingwold Advertiser* from a soldier about whom very few details were given. He wrote from Lichtenburg, a town in the Transvaal lying due west of Johannesburg, and his letter contains no description of any fighting. It does, however, give an idea of the distances men had to travel, and the hours they had to spend in the saddle. Here it is in full.[1]

NEWS FROM THE FRONT

Corporal T Littlewood, of the Medical Staff, in writing home (June 2nd) says "You would have laughed if you had seen me posting your last letter, the post office was a sack fastened to a post, against a railway station, and no one looking after it. Well we are still on the march, we have had a long one to-day. We had to be up by half-past two, breakfast at three, and off at four o'clock; it was quite dark until nearly six o'clock, and we got to camp about half-past two p.m. I wrote the above two days ago. We got into camp to-day about half-past eleven, we only came twelve miles. I expect in two days we come to a town (Lichtenburg). It is very monotonous marching here the country is very flat, a farm house or mud hut here and there. We are the third lot of troops this way, and there are two more columns following us, we have to come in small parties on account of the scarcity of water. We often pass a dead horse or mule or ox, which the troops in front have left, we left a mule behind this morning, and yesterday two dropped. It is just three weeks to-day since we started on this march, and they say we have another fortnight of it. We don't know a bit of news. I hope the war will be over by we reach our destination, we don't know yet whether it is Johannesburg or Pretoria. It was fearfully cold this morning, and now it is just as hot. As soon as the sun goes down it comes in very cold, and it is quite dark at six. I expect to-day is Whit-Monday. I did not expect to be here, I don't know the name of this place, there are such comical names. We marched from Warrenton to Fourteen Streams, then to Plockwani, Pudimoe, White Hart, Taugns, Brussells Drift, Wryburg, Devondale, Doorubult, Mapopo, Graspan, Baterpan, Klipadrift and here, and then when we get through I hope to be taking a train for home. I am just going to do a bit of sewing for myself, and my whiskers are growers, I have lost my razor, so I look alright.

I am just going to post the letter now, we got here (Lichtenberg) yesterday. The troops which came in front of us are camped here, it is only like a village, but is pleasant; most of the people can talk English. I expect we move off again in a couple of days, so we shall get a nice rest. I hear we are for Potchefstrom, about 80 miles that is the nearest railway in the Transvaal. There was a mail in yesterday but no letters for our company, but a convoy is expected in from Mafeking, and they may bring some, I hope they will. I am fairly well off for clothing, I've a good jersey and a Tamo Shanter, which I pull over my ears. I sleep in an ambulance wagon, it is alright, only a bit draughty.

Before the end of 1899 a number of reservists were recalled to the colours and got honourable mentions in the *Advertiser.* In the Northallerton local news section in late November 1899, for example, it was noted that George Doherty, 'an ex-postman' left Northallerton to rejoin the 5th Dragoon Guards at Colchester and on the same day William Appleton, 'a postman' was recalled to Richmond 'to rejoin the 19th (Green Howards) Regiment'.[2] In the same paper, two other reservists, who were also posties, were reported to have been recalled. A large number of Post Office employees gathered to wish G. Gill bon voyage. Gill was described as a 'Post-office official' while B. Ramsden was simply 'Another Harrogate Postman'.

NOTES

1. *Advertiser* 21 July 1900
2. *Ibid* 25 November 1899.

UNIFORMS OF THE C.L.I.V.

City of London Imperial Volunteers

Chapter 21

THE STRANGWAYES

On 4 August 1900, a note appeared in the *Advertiser* saying that a well-known local personality had three sons serving with the forces.

YORKSHIRE OFFICERS AT THE FRONT

Lieutenant Norman Strangwayes, fourth son of Mr John Swainston Strangwayes, Alne Hall, Easingwold, sailed with his regiment, the 4th West Durham Militia, for South Africa on Wednesday last. For the last few months the regiment has been stationed at Bury St Edmunds. The Squire of Alne will now have three of his sons on active service. Captain D'Arcy Strangwayes in the 14th West Yorks, and Lieutenant James Strangwayes with Mr Paget's Imperial Yeomanry.

James Strangwayes had been promoted a short time before the above announcement appeared.[1]

> IMPERIAL YEOMANRY. – Sergeant J De La S Strangwayes has been granted the temporary rank of Lieutenant in the Army

Yet another Strangwayes son also eventually joined up.[2]

FOUR SONS AT THE FRONT

The Squire of Alne sends another son.

Mr Giles S. Strangwayes, second son of Mr John Swainston Strangwayes, J.P., of Alne Hall, has left for Aldershot, previous to his departure for the seat of war, having joined the Imperial Yeomanry. On the arrival of this young gentleman the popular Squire of Alne will have four sons in South Africa fighting their country's battles.

Members of the Imperial Yeomanry were on short term engagements and Lt James Strangwayes returned home in July 1901. He arrived at Alne Station where he was met by a large crowd led by his brother D'Arcy. The village was decorated with flags and banners, 'and a right hearty welcome from all was recorded'.[3]

On reaching the Hall 'a company of men sang "when the war is over", and other patriotic airs' and the young officer made a short speech. Their reception, he told the crowd, compensated for all the hardships of active service abroad. The *Advertiser* reminded readers that James had served at the front in South Africa with Pagets' Horse.

Capt D'Arcy had returned to a similar reception some six weeks earlier. The *Advertiser* said he had served in the Baden-Powell police.[4]

WELCOME HOME TO CAPTAIN STRANGWAYES OF ALNE

On Saturday evening last, the village of Alne was aroused to a state of turbulence in consequence of the return of Captain d'Arcy Strangwayes, the eldest son of the popular squire of Alne, and of Baden Powell's police, from the front.

The inhabitants made hasty preparations to give the gallant officer a very hearty welcome and on the 7.10 train steaming into Alne, the tenants living on the Alne Hall estate, all mounted, and numerous friends were awaiting his arrival. The horses were taken from the carriage, which was drawn by hand from the station to the lawn in front of the hall, amid loud cheering. At the hall, Captain Strangwayes expressed his appreciation of the welcome given him, and said that it was almost more than he could realise to be at home to meet his much beloved relatives and friends again. Afterwards, all were entertained to a sumptuous repast in the hall, and the crowd sang many patriotic songs, ending with the National Anthem.

D'Arcy was given a double celebration in Alne,[5] and the following report gives an indication of the generosity of members of the Strangwayes family.

DOUBLE CELEBRATION AT ALNE

On Saturday last the village of Alne was en fete in celebration of the marriage of Miss Strangwayes to Lieutenant H Oxley, 4th Battalion 5th Northumberland Fusiliers, and to welcome Captain D'Arcy Strangwayes, who has recently returned from the front. Mr and Mrs Strangwayes entertained upwards of 500 villagers and friends to tea. This was given in the school-room. Sports were afterwards indulged in, and a cricket match was played in the park between the Alne eleven and the Fusiliers. The band of the Fusiliers was in attendance and played on the lawn and in the park at intervals. The Rev J Williams proposed the health of Mr and Mrs Oxley, Captain Strangwayes and Mr and Mrs Strangwayes, and all those present responded with cheers. In the evening dancing was indulged in, and the "National Anthem" brought an enjoyable gathering to a close.

NOTES

1. *Advertiser* 30 June 1900
2. *Ibid* 16 February 1901
3. *Ibid* 27 July 1901
4. *Ibid* 8 June 1901
5. *Ibid* 22 June 1901

Chapter 22

CYRIL SWARBRECK ET AL

Several soldiers from Easingwold were regularly featured in the press, when their parents allowed the *Advertiser* to use their letters. Others got only the briefest mention, maybe when they first joined up. (If they were wounded they would certainly be noticed.) Here, to begin with are some names from the very early days of the war.

Cyril Swarbreck was the son of a solicitor from Thirsk.[1] Cyril was 22 years of age when he sailed for the Cape, having received an appointment in the Cape Mounted Rifles. His father was a 'Superintendent Registrar' and much more. *Bulmer's* directory has this about him:-

> Swarbeck Charles McCartney (Swarbreck & Rhodes), solicitor, clerk to Guardians and Assessment Com., Rural Sanitary Authority and School Attendance com., registrar of County Courts for Thirsk district; Sowerby, Thirsk.

This was still not all. Under 'Fire & Life Insurance Offices &c' appears *Yorkshire* (Fire and Life); C. Mc C. Swarbreck, Market pl.[2]

Also appearing in the Easingwold paper in November 1899 was the following.[3] The subject was either a regular or a reservist

> Lieutenant E W Appleby, of the Durham Light Infantry, who sailed aboard the Servia to join his Regiment in South Africa, is well known in Easingwold

Sometimes soldiers got even less coverage than did Appleby. Take a Mr Pallister for example, no christian name or initial, or address was given for him. When the welcome home celebrations were held, there was a procession, Pallister was there and it was said that he had been in South Africa.[4]

Earlier the return from the wars of the son of a Thirsk solicitor was mentioned. Another son of a member of the legal profession from there also got back in May 1901.[5] The *Advertiser* noted his return.

THIRSK

> HOME FROM THE FRONT – On Monday night Private Frederic Smith, the only son of the late Henry Smith, solicitor, and for many years Clerk for the Thirsk Spring and Autumn Race Meetings, arrived at his home Sowerby, Thirsk, being invalided from South Africa.

Fred's father had operated from offices in the Market Place, Thirsk. Like Swarbreck he had also been involved in the insurance business. ('*Phoenix* (Fire); Henry Smith, solicitor, Market place'). He had also been clerk to the Thirsk Burial Board, a commissioner for oaths and an estate agent.

The papers had many reports of celebrations for returning soldiers at this time (of course) and there was one at Boroughbridge reported in full by the *Advertiser* in June 1901.[6]

There were many others, who also got only fleeting mentions in their local paper. Men like George Albert Barker who appeared in a paragraph giving the news about Lt Caffin. Barker was referred to as[7]

> a bandsman with the Gloucester Regiment. He has written to say that the change from India to the Cape has proved a pleasant one. A third man from Northallerton is a young-fellow named Hogg, who is now attached to the Flying Squadron.

Yet another young man who got only the briefest of mentions in his local paper was Trooper Edgar Buck. He left for the war on 12 March 1901.[8]

WELBURN TROOPER
LEAVING FOR THE FRONT

On Tuesday, Trooper Edgar Buck, youngest son of Mr Thomas Buck, Welburn left home for the front, having joined the Durham Imperial Yeomanry. Before leaving Durham, where he has been an assistant master in the Blue Coat School, he was the recipient of several interesting presents from his pupils and colleagues, and also of a handsome silver watch from the members of the Durham Conservative Club. He left Welburn with a hearty send-off.

There is rather more information about Edgar Buck than almost any of the other 'Easingwold' Boer War soldiers. The *Advertiser's* note of his leaving, gave details of his unit, his political beliefs and his profession. Those details can be supplemented from material in a family archive.[9]

Edgar was the second son of Thomas and Mary Buck. He was born on 15 July 1879 and went to the village school at Welburn. His sister, Florence Selina, had also attended the Wellburn school and when she left went to the Ripon Training College for teachers. (From January 1899 to December 1900.) Later she obtained BA and MA degrees from Durham University and held appointments at the Holy Trinity Practising School at Ripon (at a salary of £45 per annum) and Trimdon Grange, County Durham, where she became head.[10]

Edgar Buck's father had also attended Welburn village school and worked as a gardener at Castle Howard. He and Mary Kirby were married at Welburn on 3 February 1869. His son Edgar left school, then, like his sister, went into the teaching profession. He never became certificated, however, but worked at Norton as a pupil teacher. Later, according to his son, he went to York, maybe in the same capacity, then to the Durham Blue Coat School, as the *Advertiser* recorded. A letter from the headmaster there said (this was May 1898) that Edgar was a strict disciplinarian, 'and a capital teacher of drill'. He was a very capable Ex P.T. (pupil teacher).[11]

When exactly, did Edgar Buck enlist? A document (Army Form B128) among his papers gives details. His number was 29496; he was born in Wellbourne [sic]; and attested at Newcastle on Tyne on 14 February 1901 for the Imperial Yeomanry. Form B128 was in fact his discharge certificate and it revealed that he was dispensed with 'having been found medically unfit for further Service'. There was a summary of his service career and a description of him. He had a total Army service behind him of one year and 67 days and the length of his service abroad was one year and four days. The discharge form was dated Shorncliffe 21 April 1902 and Edgar's age was 22 years and eight months, He had served all the time with the 14th I.Y.

Edgar Buck went back to the Durham Blue Coat School (and built on his reputation as a strict disciplinarian) but did not stay in the teaching profession. He left and his son described a variety of occupations he had later – including farmer, publican and auctioneer. He joined the Army again during the Great War, but did not go abroad. For a time he was a member of the RDC. He married (April 1908) a lady named Alice who also became a schoolteacher. She was a pupil teacher at Terrington for a time, studied for two years at Durham, then qualified in 1902. She taught for a time at Woodbourn School, Sheffield and there is in existence a letter from her head which suggests that the post was not a sinecure. She 'taught a large class (80) of Standard IV. girls', he wrote, 'and a backward class of Standard III', with equal success. Alice also worked for a time at the Thirsk Interdenominational School. In the early 1920s she applied for promotion, and eventually became head of the village school at Skirpenbeck. Her husband passed away in 1955 and there was an inquest. His death certificate recorded a verdict of accidental death.

NOTES

1. *Advertiser* 18 November 1899
2. *Ibid* 11 November 1899
3. *Ibid* 15 June 1901
4. There was one on a Monday, then another the next day, when Troopers Smith and Wilkinson returned.
5. *Advertiser* 25 May 1901.
6. *Ibid* 22 June 1901
7. *Ibid* 14 October 1899
8. *Ibid* 16 March 1901
9. The following is based on those family documents and a lengthy interview with Edgar's son in 2000. Copies in the possession of A.J. Peacock filed, predictably, as 'Easingwold Letters'.
10. She retired in 1935
11. The letter was written on 21 October 1904

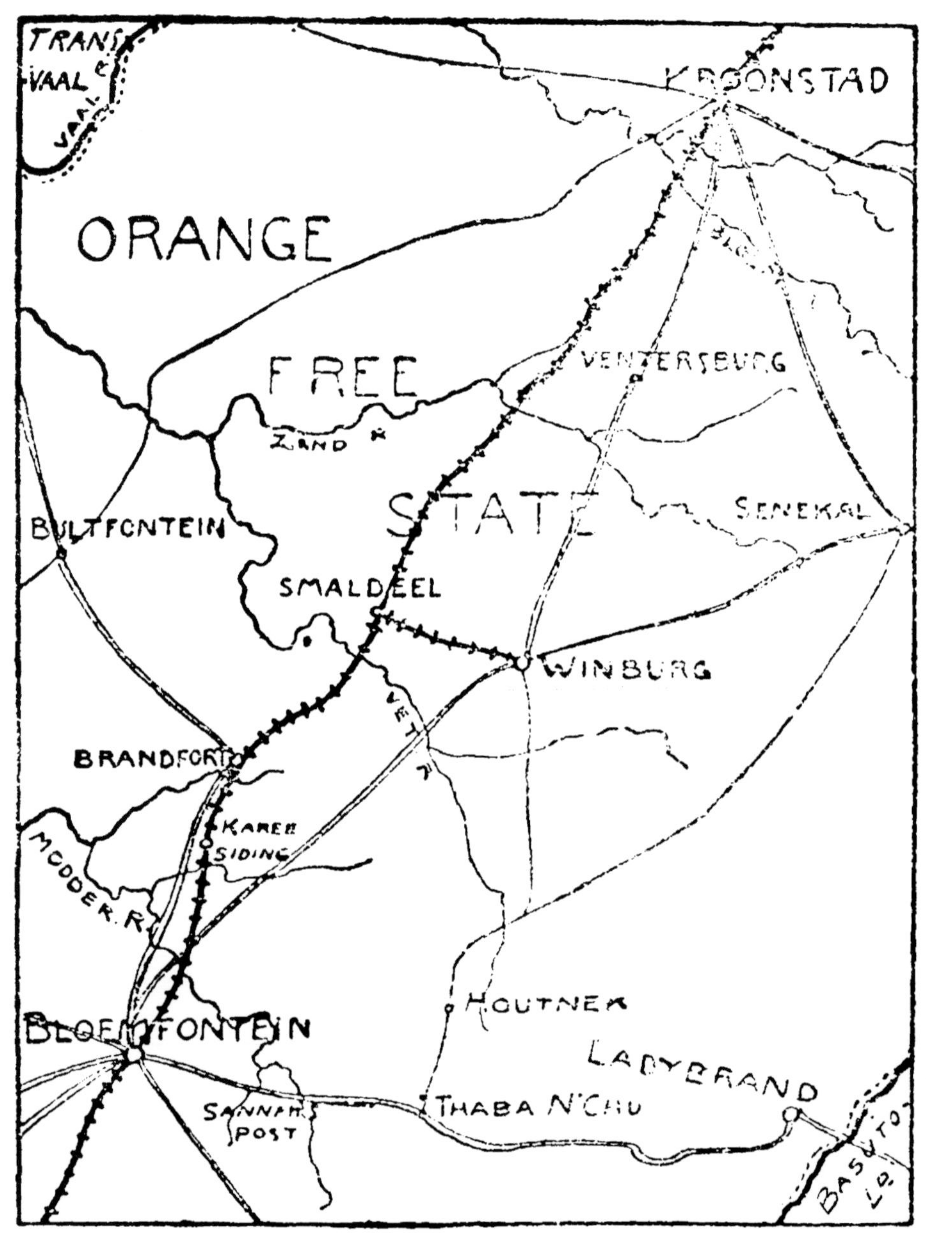

SKETCH MAP OF THE COUNTRY BETWEEN BLOEMFONTEIN AND KROONSTAD.

Chapter 23

TROOPER MARK KNOWLSON BROWN KIA

Mark Brown was an Easingwold sportsman who was one of that party of four who had volunteered for service in the Imperial Yeomanry in one of its later recruiting campaigns. Their leaving was sensational. Here is how Reg Smith reported it, again.[1]

> THE most enthusiastic send off which has been given to Easingwold men took place on Monday evening last, when four young men – Frank Weighell, Arthur Bowman, James Spence, and Mark Brown – left by the 7-55 train for Aldershot to join the Imperial Yeomanry, previous to going to the front. A large crowd assembled at the station, giving them loud cheers as the train steamed out.

Frank Weighell was not one of those soldiers whose letters were regularly sent to the press by his family – and he did not become involved in anything which made him newsworthy. However, the contents of one was made known which showed that he had been in action – and wounded.[2]

> ON Sunday last a letter was received from Trooper Frank Weighell which gives a full description of the fight at Middlepost on February 6th and says that one officer, one sergeant, and four men were killed, but makes no mention of further casualties excepting a slight wound himself, and a narrow escape of Trooper Arthur Bowman.

Bowman was the son of a well-known and popular publican, at whose establishment the Easingwold Volunteers held their meetings and their dinners. Arthur had been in action and wrote to mine host at the Station Hotel on 1 March giving 'full particulars' of the affair he, Weighell and others had been involved in.[3]

Station Hotel, 1905 - the venue for many celebrations

Arthur Bowman

INTERESTING LETTER FROM TROOPER ARTHUR BOWMAN

FULL PARTICULARS OF THE MIDDLEPOST AFFAIR

Frank Weighell

The following letter was received on Sunday morning last, by Mr Bowman, Station Hotel, from his son, who is serving with the Imperial Yeomanry in South Africa.

March 1st, 1902

Dear Father and Mother

Just a few lines to let you know I am still living, as I thought you must think I was dead, as I have not received any letters for eight weeks. We had an awful fight on the 5th and 6th of February, at a place called Middlepost. I should think you have seen the report in the papers before now. We got it pretty hot.

On the night of the 4th, the Colonel took out a patrol of 150 men, and I, with 22 more and 2 officers of the 11th squadron were left behind. There were 30 of the C.M.R's and about 40 men out of each of the 13 and 14 I.Y. started with the convoy at 5 o'clock the next morning, and we stopped at 11 o'clock at Middlepost. We had just got our dinner, and were getting laid down to have a sleep, when a party of Boers were reported coming towards us. We got our horses saddled and we rushed up with the big guns on to a kopje we had just left when the Boers sent in a volley into the camp, and then the guns started popping shells among them. We got laid down on the kopje and then started sending them in. We kept up the firing all the afternoon, but we could not shift them. As soon as it got dark our lot had to go and take up a position on a kopje at the back of a farm close at hand. We had to lay on the kopje all night; about 10 o'clock the Boers started firing again, and we rushed in among our waggons. There were two or three artillerymen who had gone for their blankets, and the Boers captured them. We saw a light against a waggon, and we had not long to wait and see what was happening. All our convoy was soon ablaze, but we were sending volley after volley into the waggons; but we could not save a single biscuit - every mortal thing we had was burnt; we did not save a single blanket.

The Boers tried to rush our kopje but we managed to keep them back. We had a very lively night, I can tell you. The Boers retired just before daybreak, and we thought they had gone, but as soon as it was light they came back (about 800 of them). They came in different directions and we were surrounded on three sides. We saw about 20 Boers galloping for a kopje on our left, and our officer told me and three men to gallop for this kopje and try to get there before the Boers. We went for all we were worth, but they managed to get on to the top before we were half way up. We laid all our long length on the ground, and the bullets flew over our heads. We returned their fire, and knocked one or two of them over. They just grazed our officer in the neck, and shot his horse. Then we retired, and the shot dropped round us like hail, but we got safely back to the other kopje. We had not long been on the kopje before about 20 Boers rushed up the kopje, and only 4 reached the top. There were only eight of us unscratched and 2 or 3 of us were about blinded with the stones the Boers threw at us. As they were coming up they rushed us off the kopje and fired as we were going down, but lucky enough they missed us all. At about 7 o'clock the Colonel came to our relief, and we all retired, but we had 13 men, including two officers, killed and 29 wounded, but the Boers had about 100 casualties. Our own doctor dressed 40 of them. We had to make the best of our way to Ceres, a distance of 150 miles, which we did in 5 days. We had nothing but half a pint of mealie meal and water, and our horses had nothing but what they could pick up. I lost all my saddlery, and had to ride to Ceres bareback, with nothing but the headrope in the animal's mouth, but thank God I have got over it. We are now getting rigged out for another go at them, which I hope will not be long, so as we can get a bit of our own back. Both Jim and Frank are all right.

I think I have told you all. Hoping I shall get a letter soon, remember me to Robert, and tell him I hope to be back soon.

From your loving son,
Arthur.

Arthur Bowman got back to Britain safely and on 25 September 1902 he and others were honoured at a dinner at the Station Hotel (where else).[4] The chairman was J.J. Penty (who congratulated 'Host Bowman' for putting on the celebration) and then came the songs. J.W. Sturdy gave them 'The Horse the Missus drys the clothes on' then another vocalist took the musical contributions on to a slightly higher plane by giving them 'The Death of Nelson' and 'Queen of the Earth'. There were other songs from other singers – and then a funny from that star of the board room, the cricket field and much more. Buller Hicks created 'roars of laughter' the *Advertiser* said, with his rendition of the 'comic song "Morrison's Vegetable Pills". Penty, who was suffering from a sore throat, and unable to sing, 'recited the tale of "The Major and the Boy", in the tip top style' instead. No-one gave out with the Absent Minded Beggar. An odd omission.

Some brief notes exist on the Bowmans.[5] The family went to Easingwold sometime after the Station Hotel was opened, and Frederick ran it, until he retired around 1920. He passed away in 1924 aged 64. His wife died in 1940, aged 84.

The last of that quartet of budding Imperial Yeomen who left Easingwold became the object of much speculation. He was Mark K. Brown and he returned home in August 1902 to one of those enthusiastic welcomes which had become a familiar feature of the town's life. The *Advertiser* carried a substantial report about it.[6]

THE RETURN OF YEOMANRY
TROOPER M BROWN ARRIVES HOME

On Wednesday evening last Troopers Mark K. Brown and Geo. H. Hargreaves, Yorkshire Imperial Yeomanry, arrived at Easingwold from South Africa, where they had served since February, 1901. Much interest was evidenced in the return of the former, and he will have the pleasure attained by very few, of living to read his own death notices, the War Office for some months holding the opinion that he was killed.

The arrival of the train was heralded by fog signals, and cheers were heartily given as the train came into the station. On the men alighting from the train the National Anthem was played by an augmented band. A procession was then formed in the following order: band, returned Yeomanry, local detachment of Yorkshire Hussars under Corporal Sidney Smith (Hanover), local Volunteers under Sergeants J.H. Pipes and J.W. Sturdy, decorated waggons, mounted men, &c. A march was made in that order through the town, large crowds lining the streets, but the falling darkness and the pouring rain partly spoiled the spectacular effect of the whole affair.

At the close the National Anthem was played, and the returned Yeomen carried shoulder-high to their homes.

Main Street, Middlepost - little changed in 100 years (except for petrol pumps). No footpaths, dirt roads and 85 km from the nearest hard road; but plenty of sun: Middlepost is midway between the towns of Sutherland and Calvinia in the Northern Cape.

Site of the Ambush of the British Convoy at Middlepost, February 5/6, 1902. Relics can still be found here today. Situated in the semi desert of the Great Karoo - the average annual rainfall is only 28mm (just over 1 inch).

The Imperial Yeomanry Memorial at Middlepost with Trooper Brown's name heading the other ranks tablet. Situated on the side of the Middlepost Hotel, the local community have caringly looked after it for over 100 years. Photo: 2000

News of Mark Knowlson Brown's 'death' had appeared in a report of February 1902 which gave some details about him and his parents.[7]

AN EASINGWOLD YEOMAN KILLED AT THE WAR

Since the commencement of the war the Yeomen and Volunteers, to the number of 20 from Easingwold, have been very fortunate, amid all the slaughter, to avoid paying the greatest sacrifice for their country. True, some among them have undergone terms of enforced idleness, and have been near death's door in the hospitals. They have been sniped at, and wounded, been prisoners with the enemy for months, but remarkable to relate, despite the frequency with which they have been in action, none of them, until now, have been laid to rest in that far country - victims to their country's cause.

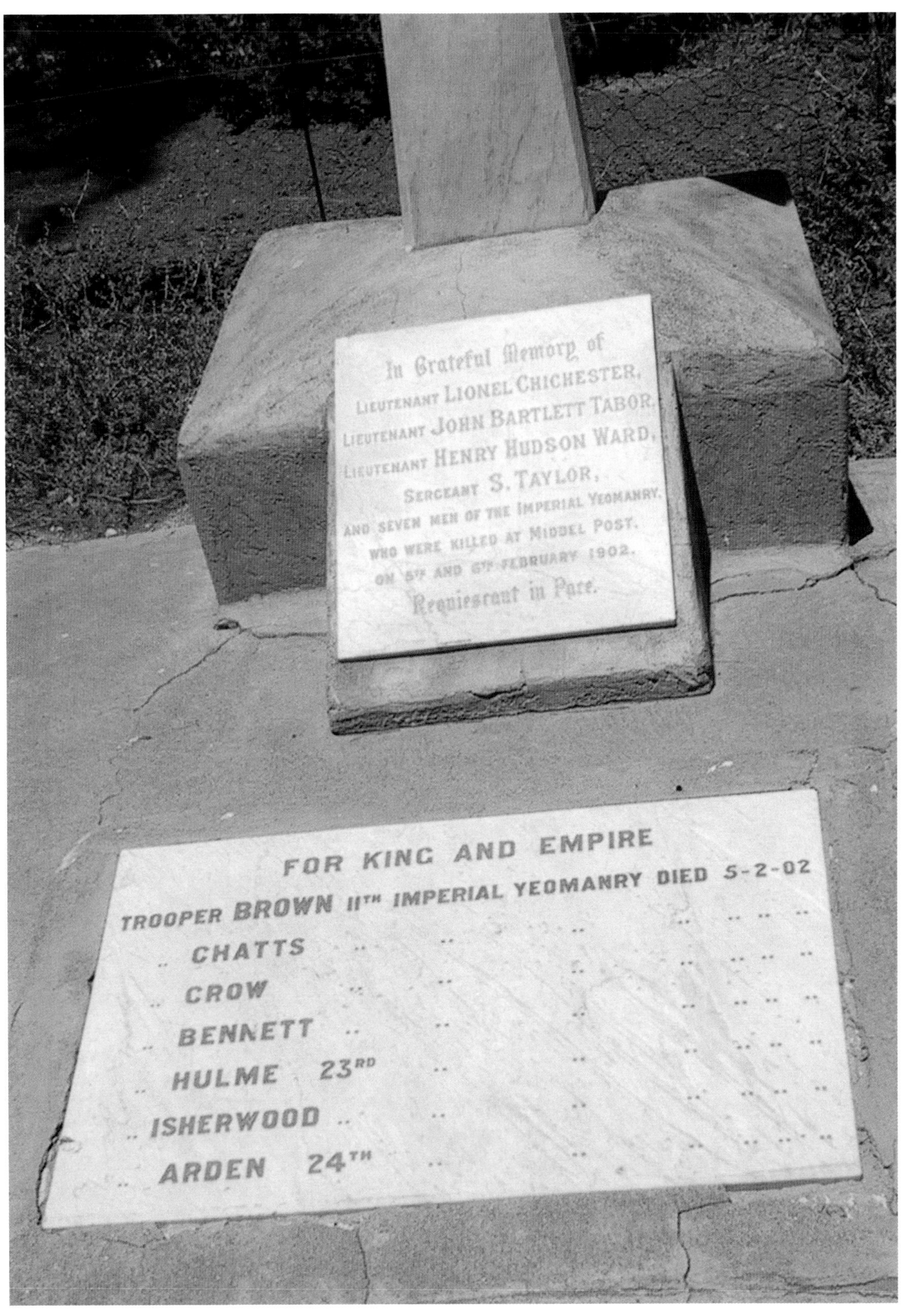
In Grateful Memory of
Lieutenant LIONEL CHICHESTER,
Lieutenant JOHN BARTLETT TABOR,
Lieutenant HENRY HUDSON WARD,
Sergeant S. TAYLOR,
and seven men of the Imperial Yeomanry,
who were killed at Middel Post,
on 5th and 6th February 1902.
Requiescant in Pace.
FOR KING AND EMPIRE
TROOPER BROWN 11TH IMPERIAL YEOMANRY DIED 5-2-02
CHATTS
CROW
BENNETT
HULME 23RD
ISHERWOOD
ARDEN 24TH

Trooper Mark Knowlson Brown, son of Mr. Wm. Brown, farmer, Long Street, was 19 years old when he volunteered just a year ago. A fine strapping young fellow, the very picture of health, he was selected, and with three others from Easingwold, passed on to the front.

Since then he has kept up a regular correspondence with his relatives and friends in Easingwold, and the last letter from him came from Dordrecht, stating that his company had been chasing the Boers, and were preparing for another movement against Flouche and Myrburg.

On Tuesday evening last a telegram from the War Office was handed to his parents, conveying the sad information that he had been killed at Middlepost, Cape Colony on February 6th. No further particulars were obtainable.

Great sympathy is felt for Mr and Mrs Brown and family in their sad bereavement.

We understand that a Memorial Service will be held in the Parish Church on Sunday afternoon, and as the young soldier was a member of the local lodge of Druids, that body will attend.

A memorial service was held for Mark Brown on Sunday 23 February 1902 and the account of the sad event revealed that Mark had been a Volunteer before joining the IY.[8] Much was made in the account in R.E.Smith's paper about young Mark joining the Druids – and what a force they were might be gauged from their representatives present at the service.

MEMORIAL SERVICE TO TROOPER MARK K BROWN

As befitting the memory of the first Easingwold volunteer who has laid down his life for his country's cause, the Memorial Service which was held at the Parish Church on Sunday afternoon last, was the largest gathering which has been seen for some time within its hallowed walls. The service for the late Queen a year ago was attended by all - some as from duty bound, and others from nobler motives. Since then, the deaths of the lamented Captain Wombwell, and Trooper Walter Dale (9th Lancers) at the front, have been the cause of similar expressions of sympathy.

But perhaps never was there a more direct appeal to the hearts of the people than in the death of Trooper Brown, in fact the whole circumstances tend to lend a glow to the life so ruthlessly cut short. He was young and strong, and the picture of health, and with a foresight to be commended had, some years ago, by joining the Local Lodge of Druids, made provision for misfortune which an all seeing Providence had decreed he should never live to see. Nor was the act of his volunteering for the front a year ago, the result of some whim, or outburst of patriotic fervour. By previously joining the local Volunteers he had shown that he was willing to do his share in the defence of his country, and though the fortunes of war have laid him low in a far off land, his memory will be ever dear to all who admire pluck and courage.

At half past two on Sunday afternoon the ringing of a muffled peal announced that some event of more than usual sadness had occurred in the old town; and soon after the church began to fill with people desirous of showing their last mark of respect, not only to the young man but the cause he represented. The Volunteers marched to the church, followed by the Ancient Druids to the number of over one hundred, headed by Bro. F.J.H. Robinson, Bro. J.J. Penty, Bro. J.C. Scholefield, P.A., Bro. J.W. Sturdy, (secretary); Bro. Geo Taylor, P.A., Bro. C.R. Sharpe, A.D. and others.

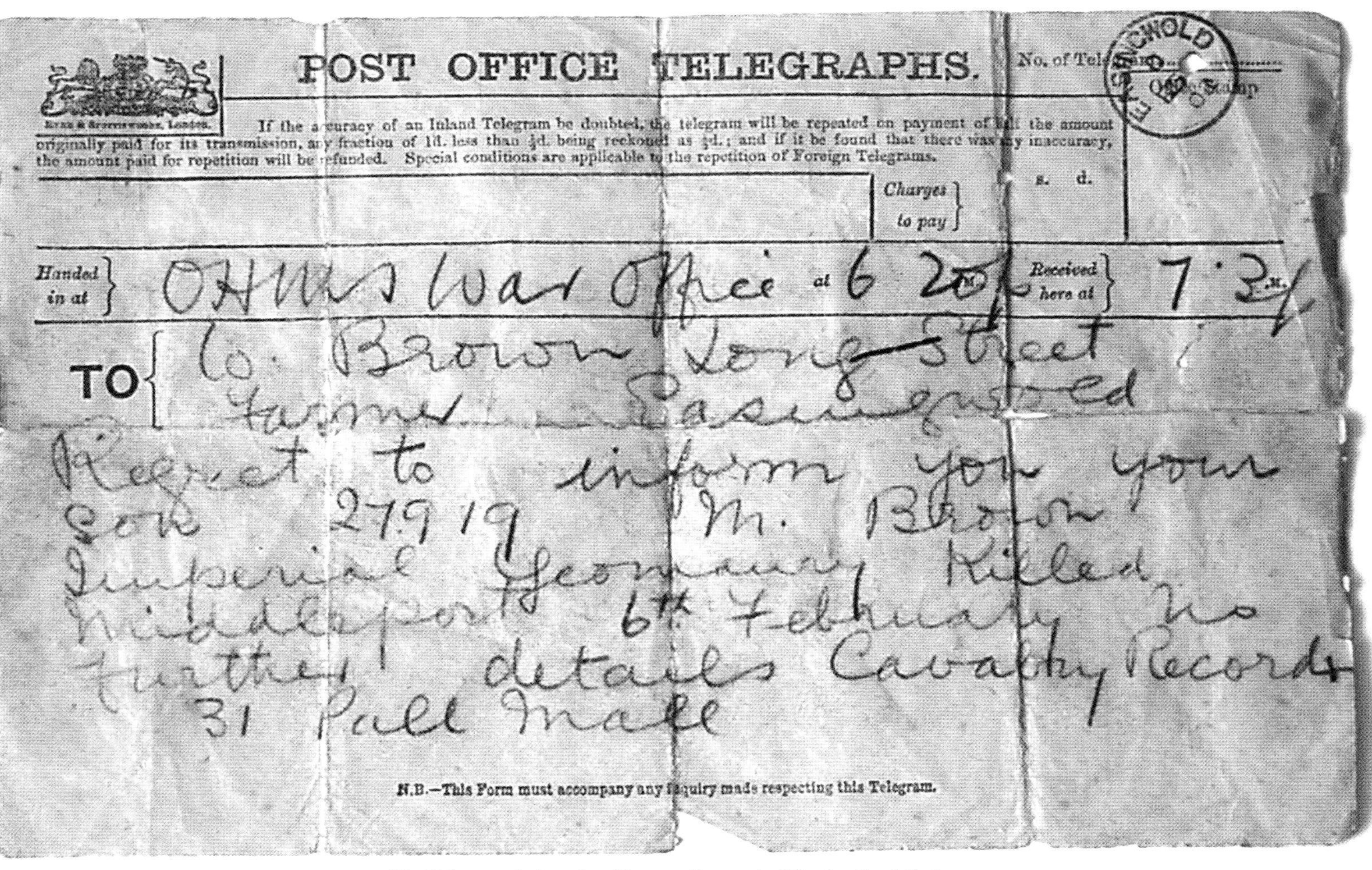

POST OFFICE TELEGRAPHS.

No. of Telegram ....

Office Stamp: EASINGWOLD

If the accuracy of an Inland Telegram be doubted, the telegram will be repeated on payment of half the amount originally paid for its transmission, any fraction of 1d. less than ½d. being reckoned as ½d.; and if it be found that there was any inaccuracy, the amount paid for repetition will be refunded. Special conditions are applicable to the repetition of Foreign Telegrams.

Charges to pay   s. d.

Handed in at OHMS War Office at 6 20 p.m. Received here at 7·3 p.m.

TO W. Brown Long Street
Farmer Easingwold

Regret to inform you your son 27919 M. Brown Imperial Yeomanry killed Middlepost 6th February no further details Cavalry Records 31 Pall Mall

N.B.—This Form must accompany any Inquiry made respecting this Telegram.

The Telegram informing 'Brown, Farmer' of the death of their son.

Mark Brown's South Africa Medal with Five Clasps

ALEXANDRA
PRINCESS OF WALES OWN
YORKSHIRE HUSSARS.
PRESENTED TO
PRIVATE M. BROWN
BY HIS OFFICERS

Mark Brown - cup for the Best Recruit 1903

Above:
Mark Brown in 1911 (4th from left) at Hawkhills

Mark Brown in the
Yeomanry Uniform of 1914

By a quarter to three the church was pretty well filled, when the mother and father, brothers and sisters of the dead man walked to the reserved pews near the lectern, - a touching sight to see them there, lamenting over one dear to them, whom Providence had decreed to die - if not among strangers - in a strange land, in a noble cause. By the time the service was to commence the church was literally packed, and several were unable to gain admission.

The service was commenced by the robed choir singing a processional hymn. The lesson was read by Mr Herring, the remainder of the service being taken by the Rev. Nathan Jackson, the vicar, who delivered an impressive and touching discourse on the words 'I am the Resurrection and the Life'.

At the close, Mr Bensley, the organist, played the Dead March *in Saul*, the congregation standing.

Two weeks after the memorial service, a rather strange note was published in the *Advertiser.*[9]

TROOPER MARK BROWN - Certain rumours, perhaps not altogether unfounded, are in the air about Trooper Brown, who was reported by the War Office as killed on February 6th last, and whose death we noticed in our issue a fortnight ago. Avoiding undue haste in the matter, we expect to publish in our next issue, what we hope to be reliable information.

Just below the report of rumours about Mark Knowlson's demise the last of the great send offs was reported. The men who went were those who found they were not required as fighters when they got there. Here is the *Advertiser's* reported of their departure.[10]

OFF TO THE WAR – DEPARTURE OF
EASINGWOLD YEOMEN

On Tuesday night an enthusiastic crowd gathered at the station to witness the departure of another batch of Yeomen for the front. The names of the young men are: William Smith, son of Mr Thos. Smith, Hanover House; Thos. Henry Russell, son of Mrs Kirbyson, Thirsk Road; Hilton Carr, son of Mr W. Carr, Long Street; Wm. Armstrong, late with Mr Mark Reynard, blacksmith; Frank Bean, son of Mr James Bean, Long Street; and George Clark. T.H. Russell went through the early part of the war with the Volunteer Company P.W.O. Regiment, and returned home last June. Wm. Smith is brother to Mr S. Smith, who served in the late Capt. Stephen Wombwell's Company Imperial Yeomanry, under Lord Methuen. As the train steamed out of the station hearty cheers were given, and fog signals placed on the line were exploded.

There was good news from R.E. Smith and Mark Brown. He had been reported killed then wrote home eight days later.[11]

TROOPER M BROWN
"IS HE DEAD?"

Never was the saying "Truth is stranger than fiction" better exemplified than in the case of the reported death, at the front, of Trooper Mark Knowlson Brown, in whose memory a memorial service was held at the Parish Church three weeks ago, amid every sign of sorrow and sadness. The cause of it was a telegram received on the 18th of February by his parents from the War Office, as follows: "Regret to inform you that your son, 27919 M. Brown, Imperial Yeomanry, killed Middlepost 6th February. No further details." In reply to a request for further information, the War Office wrote to his parents: "In reply to your enquiry regarding 27919 M. Brown, Imperial Yeomanry, I beg to inform you that you should receive by an early mail from South Africa full particulars of your son's death."

On the 8th of March further particulars were received, but of a kind certainly not expected. They took the form of a letter from Trooper Brown, dated February 14th, eight days after his reported death. In it he referred, among other matters, to the attack on Crabbe's column on January 29th, he being present.

The War Office were again written to and told of the letter. Their reply was contained in a telegram of March 10th - "27919 M. Brown, Imperial Yeomanry, was reported killed at Middlepost on 6th February. This is your son's regimental number. If you will forward letter received by you from Mark Knowlson Brown, enquiries will at once be made." Since then nothing further has been heard either from the Central Authority or Trooper Brown.

On Sunday last a letter was received from Trooper Frank Weighell which gives a full description of the fight at Middlepost on February 6th, and says that one officer, one sergeant, and four men were killed, but makes no mention of further casualties excepting a slight wound of himself, and a narrow escape of Trooper Arthur Bowman.

Further particulars will be published as soon as received.

The issue of the *Advertiser* which contained the above also carried a note about another personality who deserves to be rescued from oblivion. She was one of Dr Preston's parishioners named Minnie Blackburn,who was leaving for South Africa.

RASKELFE

Teachers for South Africa. - Miss Minnie Blackburn, formerly a pupil teacher in the Raskelfe School, has been chosen by His Majesty's Government as one of those teachers required to go out to South Africa to teach Boer children in the Concentration Camps. Miss Blackburn leaves Raskelfe on March 21st, and will sail in the "Scott" from Southampton on the 22nd. She carries with her the hearty good wishes of all her many friends in Raskelfe.

It was still some time before details of the M.K. Brown story was cleared up, but readers of the *Advertiser* were told how and what had actually happened in May.[12] A letter from Mark himself said something about where he (they) had been.

There exists a collection of photographs and memorabilia of Mark Knowlson Brown, amongst it is a telegram (see page 343). It was 'Handed in at OHMS War Office' and received at Easingwold.

Mark Brown's South African medal ribbon has five clasps on it: South Africa 1902; South Africa 1901; Transvaal, Orange Free State; and Cape Colony. Also among his effects is a cup inscribed 'ALEXANDRA PRINCESS OF WALES OWN YORKSHIRE HUSSARS. PRESENTED TO PRIVATE M. BROWN BY HIS OFFICERS. AS BEST RECRUIT. 1903'. Mark had clearly not had enough of the Army and he died in the Great War, while still very young, on 5 November 1918, just a few days before the armistice. A card records that he was born on 13 May 1882 and buried 'in Easingwold Churchyard'.

Two months after the Brown mystery was solved it was announced that he, along with 'the 2nd batch of Imperial Yeomen, who went to the front' were on their way home and were expected to receive 'a suitable reception' in Easingwold.[13] 'Particularly should this be in the case of Trooper Mark Brown, whom the War Office for so long persisted in regarding as dead'. The townspeople agreed. The weather spoiled things somewhat, though, and why Trooper Mark's mate Hargreaves was not there was not revealed.[14]

George H. Hargreaves made only a very occasional appearance in the prime source for Easingwold history, but there is information about him from Mr Tony Bolton.[15] He owns Harry Hargreaves' South African War Medal and the details on that refer to George as private 23103 in the 66th Company of the IY and the clasps he was awarded were: Cape Colony; Orange Free State; Transvaal; South Africa 1901; and South Africa 1902. For some time, Mr Bolton wrote, Harry 'worked at or next door to the York Hotel in Easingwold, Market Place, when it was a distribution depot for John Smith's Brewery.

One of the few occasions when George Hargreaves *did* get a mention in the paper is of minor interest. Yet another volunteer dinner was held at the Station Hotel, and present and giving out with a song, were those who went off to the Imperial Yeomanry later on. Their names, and the titles of their contributions were given in full, as always.[16] Frank Weighell gave the assembled 'Soldiers of the Queen', and later rendered 'Hearts of Oak' for them. Mr Armstrong sang twice. First of all giving his fellow diners 'I'll be your Sweetheart' then followed it with 'Sunshine of Paradise Alley'. Mr. J Spence rendered 'When Jack comes home again' and 'Slap-Dab'. Mark Knowlson Brown's contribution was 'Kitty Wells' and Arthur Bowman as mentioned before gave them that Betty Grable favourite 'Sweet Rosy O'Grady. But what about George Hargreaves? His contribution that old tear-jerker 'Break the News to Mother'. All good stuff.

George Hargreaves' medals kindly lent by Mr. Tony Bolton

TROOPER M.K. BROWN
THE MYSTERY CLEARED UP

A native of the Sister Isle once said that "it was worth a man's while to die once in a life-time to hear the many nice things said about him." Trooper Mark Knowlson Brown would be certainly excused if he was tempted to produce a similar opinion, for on the official notification of his death, the expressions of sympathy with his parents and kindly regard for his memory were spontaneous from all classes of the community. Not till then did some of the townspeople realise the quality and grit of the men who had boldly volunteered to fight the nation's battles in South Africa. Then many nice things were said, and his memory honoured as befitted one whose life had been sacrificed for his country. Not but that the expressions were thoroughly honest and sincere, the result of allowing the wave of patriotic feeling to run away with the calmer reflections of their peaceful moments. Nor would there be the least wish to retract one word or one action from what was done at the time - in the firm unquestioned belief that Trooper Brown was no more.

It is not given to many men to read accounts of their own death and funeral, and Trooper Brown, one of those privileged few, will have a noble estimate of his character ready made to live up to, should the fortune of war still continue to favour him with her smile, and allow him to return to his native place.

It will be remembered with what sorrow the War Office communication was received on February 18th that Trooper Brown, 11th Company Imperial Yeomanry, had been killed in action at Middlepost, in Cape Colony, on February 6th. On the following Sunday, muffled peals were rung on the church bells and a largely attended memorial service held amid every expression of sorrow and regret. Requests by his parents to the War Office for further particulars were answered by the statement that they would be forwarded as soon as received but holding out no hope that the dead Yeoman was any other than their son. Letters were also posted to Trooper Brown at the same time by his parents and friends at Easingwold.

A letter was afterwards received in Easingwold from him, dated February 16th, which was forwarded to the War Office, who promised to make enquiries, and on April 25th the following was received:

Cavalry Record Office
42 Pall Mall, SW
25/4/1902

Sir,
In reply to your enquiry dated 20/4/02 regarding your son M.K. Brown, Imperial Yeomanry, I beg to inform you that a reply has been received from South Africa which states next-of-kin of No 27919, M. Brown, is Father, 125 Cleveland Road, Doncaster. As this does not agree with the recorded next-of-kin on the attestation of your son whose number is given, we have referred the question back again to South Africa.

I may point out there is Number 22911, Matthew Brown, serving in South Africa whose father formerly lived at 52, Cleveland Road, Doncaster, and it is possible he is the man who has been killed. I will let you know the result of the enquiry immediately it comes from South Africa.

I am, Sir,
Your obedient servant,
ENOTT, Colone
A.A.G for Cavalry.

Mr W. Brown,
Farmer,
Long Street,
Easingwold.

On Sunday morning last three letters were received from him, one to his mother was dated Williston, April 10th, and ran as follows:

"Just a line to let you know I am in good health, and hoping this will find you the same. I have heard that you got some news in mistake of a Doncaster lad, but you must cheer up. I am worth a lot of dead ones yet. We have not heard anything about coming home yet, but I think we shall not be long, as we expect that there are some new drafts of Yeomanry coming out to relieve us. There are a lot of Boers in the country around us, but there is not much fighting in them. We engaged 300 of them last Saturday. We only just got the 15 pounders into action, and then they galloped off leaving a few horses."

After referring to the blockhouse system, the writer stated that he was in Colonel Cappers column, operating in the Fish River district. In concluding his letter he wished to be remembered to all his friends.

The following is an extract from a letter to Mr A.B. Taylor, dated Williston, April 11th.

"Dear Mr and Mrs Taylor, - Just a few lines hoping to find you all in the best of health and spirits, as it leaves me at present. I was very sorry that my mother got such sad news in mistake. But I think all will be right now they get my letter. I saw the list of killed and wounded in the "York Herald" the night before I received your letter, and then I said to some of my chums, that they must have got word at home about it, which must have upset them very much. I should have liked to have walked into the town when the funeral procession was going. It is not much use telling you any war news as you get it as soon, or sooner, than we do."

Concluding, he wished Mr Taylor to excuse the paper "as we are without envelopes, and you can see what sort of state we are in."

Your Sincere Friend,
Mark.

Druids Committee, Back row: J. A. Sykes, A. Bowman (served at Middlepost), G. T Sturdy, T. Snowball, F. Weighell (served at Middlepost), J. H. Cleaver Front row: J. N. Passman, T. Cowling, T. C. Wetherell, J. W. Sturdy

NOTES

1. *Advertiser* 2 March 1901
2. *Ibid* 22 March 1902
3. *Ibid* 29 March 1902. The units involved were the 11th, 23rd and 24th Imperial Yeomanry. The G. H. Smith typesetter was probably having another bad day.
4. *Ibid* 11 October 1902
5. 'NOTES ON ARTHUR BOWMAN RELATIVES' sent to David Smith by Geoff Bowman.
6. *Advertiser* 30 August 1902
7. *Ibid* 22 February 1902
8. *Ibid* 1 March 1902
9. *Ibid* 15 March 1902
10. *Ibid*
11. *Ibid* 22 March 1902
12. *Ibid* 17 May 1902
13. *Ibid* 16 August 1902
14. *Ibid* 30 August 1902
15. Tony Bolton to A.J. Peacock, 20 July 2000
16. *Advertiser* 26 January 1901. It is assumed Frank Weighell was the one who went abroad.

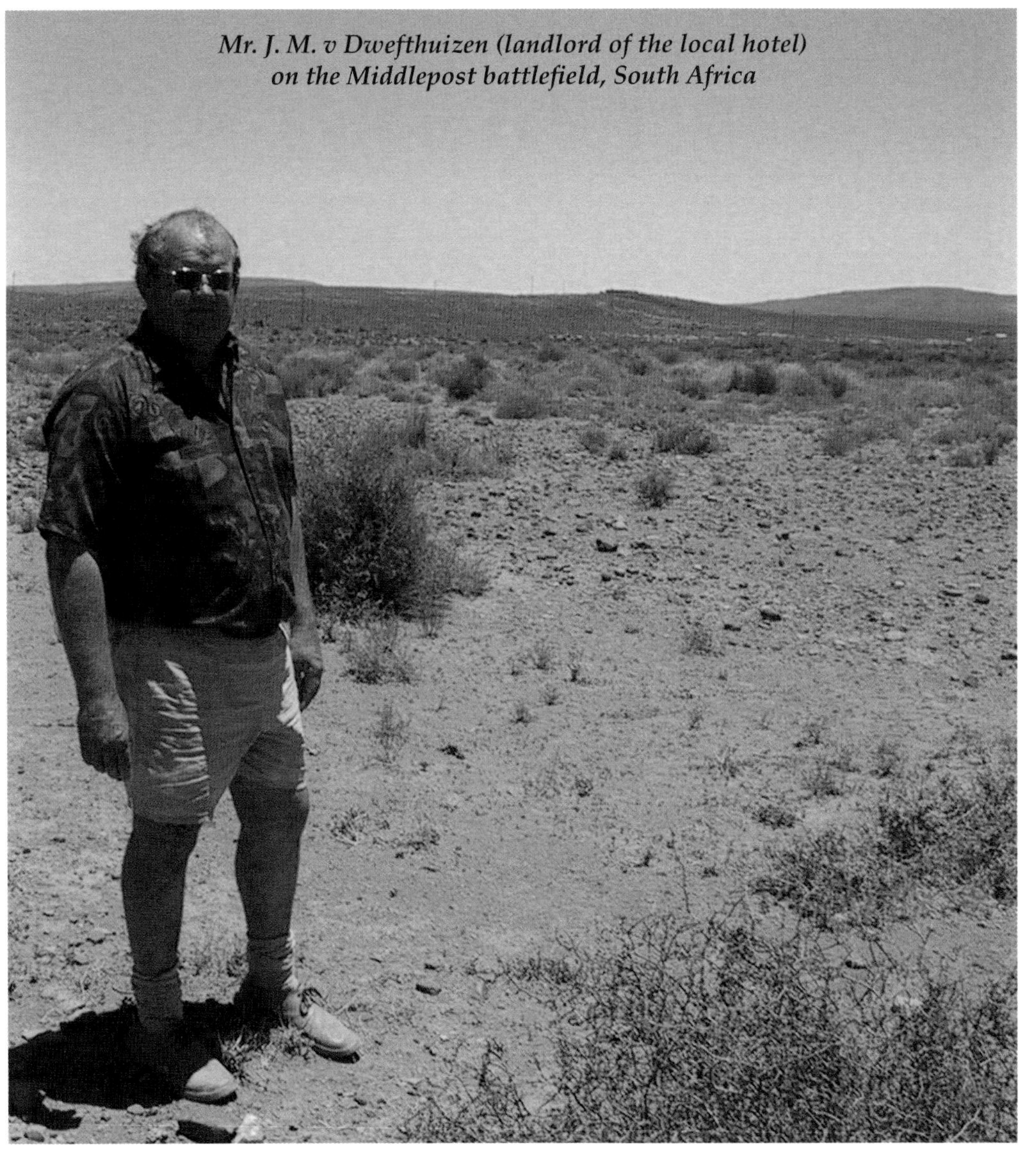

Mr. J. M. v Dwefthuizen (landlord of the local hotel) on the Middlepost battlefield, South Africa

Poppies and Wreath Card which was sent for the 100th Anniversary of the Battle of Middlepost

100th Anniversary 5th & 6th February 1902

THE BATTLE AT MIDDLEPOST

In memory of the brave British and Boer soldiers who were killed in action here. Also to the four soldiers of the Imperial Yeomanry who took part in the battle and came from the small market town of Easingwold in North Yorkshire:-

MARK KNOWLSON BROWN
ARTHUR BOWMAN
TED SPENCE
FRANK WEIGHELL

In Remembrance

Donated by the people of Easingwold

Chapter 24

THE RELIEF OF MIDDLEPOST

THOMAS COOK - 11TH COMPANY IMPERIAL YEOMANRY

Thomas Cook enlisted for the Imperial Yeomanry on the 15th of February 1901 at Doncaster. On enlistment he was described as a 20 year old, born in Osgodby near Selby, Yorkshire and a postman by trade – at the time he was serving with the Yorkshire Hussars. After receiving his notice from a man by the name of Latham Huckle and having been sworn in by Captain W.G. Eley he is given a medical which finds him to be 5ft 9in tall, 11 stone 2lbs, 34 inch chest, fresh complexion, blue eyes and brown hair – his religious denomination was Church of England. The surgeon finds him fit for service and his service is approved on the 19th of February, at which point he is numbered as No.27941 and sent to Aldershot for training. He embarked for South Africa on the 14th of March 1901 as a member of the 11th Company, 3rd Battalion Imperial Yeomanry (Yorkshire Dragoons) and returned to England on the 24th of August 1902, a period of 1 year and 163 days overseas service. For service in the Boer War he is granted the Queen's South Africa Medal with clasps for Cape Colony, Orange Free State, Transvaal, South Africa 1901 & South Africa 1902. He is discharged at Aldershot on the 30th of August 1902 at the termination of his engagement, giving his place of residence as his father's house (18 Providence Terrace, Harrogate). Thomas Cook wrote an account of his period in South Africa, and this was kindly sent to me by Natalie Cook, a descendent of his.

The Battle of Middlepost

We reached Actor Kop on 4th February and, learning that the Boers were in the vicinity, a patrol composed of 100 men was at once picked out to follow and engage them. On these patrols our cloak and one blanket were strapped on the saddle and rations for three or four days taken in the wallets. We always carried 200 rounds of ammunition, 150 in bandoliers and 50 rounds in wallets. Leaving the Kop at midnight we found Johnny Boer about dawn and commenced a race from ridge to ridge till the middle of the afternoon when, our horses being done up, we had to camp.

Meanwhile, those left behind with the convoy trekked after us camping at noon at Middlepost Farm, Dchoop District, some 20 miles distance from us. At about 1 o'clock clouds of dust were reported on their right flank, but expecting it was the patrol returning not much notice was taken until the quantity of dust convinced the officer in charge that it was some larger party. The scouts were sent out but soon returned reporting from 500-800 Boers rapidly approaching. Preparations were at once made for the attack but our position as well as numbers were alike inferior to the Boers who were the joined Commandos of Smuts, Van de Venter, Fouchee and, I think, Malan. Fighting went on till late at night, then the Boers seized the wagons and set fire to them. Our party were again at a disadvantage, the blaze giving away their position completely. They therefore shifted some small distance and took the kraals and some ridges as their position. A successful attempt was made to send a despatch rider to the patrol whose picquets he surprised about 4 in the morning. We saddled at once and arrived at Middlepost just before noon. We acted in reserve until 5 o'clock when a retirement was made. The guns with only three rounds left came first then the men, who after fighting 27 hours were faded out, filed through our line. We closed in and the march to Ceres commenced.

That the Boers had had enough was proved by their not attempting to follow us. Their casualties numbered over 100 and an armistice for the purpose of removing the dead and wounded was arranged early in the morning and 42 Boers were removed from one ridge, our ambulance wagon being used. About 45 of our chaps fell. Our kits containing what few curios we had collected were burnt along with all the rations. A wagon with some shells packed on it was also among the captured lot and blew up while we were there, bursting the wagon and scattering the rest which kept going off as long as the fire lasted. We left our wounded in charge of a doctor and orderlies, who also buried our dead. None of those left behind, except the doctors and orderlies, ever joined us again but were invalided home, most of them from Wynberg Hospital.

We trekked on that night to the farm where the patrol had been camped. Next morning we were served out with a cup of porridge made of mealy flour and water, prepared for us by the wife of the farmer. For seven days after this we existed on a small cup of flour per day and fresh meat when we could get it. The flour we commandeered from the few farms we passed on our way, but as they were so far out we could not take much, they having much difficulty getting it for themselves. At Waggon Drift we had the run of some goats that were half wild, and these appeased our hunger a little.

Thomas Cook of the 11th Company Imperial Yeomanry in South Africa 1901-02

Kindly reproduced by Kevin J Asplin, archive of the Imperial Yeomanry in the Boer War.

Chapter 25

TED WEBSTER AND HILT CARR

Among the men who went over to South Africa in March 1902 with T.H. Russell, making his second visit to the front, was one who was the subject of some notes from his grandson.[1] He was,

William Wilkinson Hilton Carr who was born at Melbourne, in 1882, 'the eldest son of William Carr, corn miller and farmer.' In 1892 the family moved to Uppleby and later took up residence in Long Street. 'Hilt' was employed as an errand boy when he left school, then, at the age of 16, went to work at the Flour Mill. He volunteered for the IY, was accepted, and duly went off to Aldershot. He became a close friend of William Armstrong from Thirkleby, who had been an apprentice with Mark Reynard.

When he returned to Easingwold, Hilt was employed again at the Flour Mill and finished his apprenticeship. He then took on various haulage jobs, mostly on a steam waggon. He eventually moved to Hull and served with the West Yorkshires in France in the Great War as a Lewis gunner. In 1927 he moved to Farlington and started 'a coal & haulage business'. He ground corn which he sold in Leeds for cattle feed, and he sold coal in the villages around Easingwold.

Hilton Carr's mate, the singer Bill Armstrong, lived to be a great age. He died on 15 March 1983 aged 99.

Carr and Armstrong were volunteers; Ted Webster was a reservist and the son of a local publican. The *Advertiser* which reported the relief of Mafeking listed those in the regular army already in South Africa, and Ted Webster was due to join them. For the record – though they have been mentioned before – R.E. Smith's list consisted of

Walter Dale, 9th Lancers
Gunner Boocock, Brandsby, Artillery
– Milnthorpe, Helperby, 10th Hussars
Pte Eccles Foster, 2nd Lancashire Fusiliers
Gunner A Foster, HMS Monarch

The news about Webster was given in a short paragraph.[2]

> We understand that Mr Ted Webster, son of Mr G J Webster, Jolly Farmer, one of the King's Own Yorkshire Light Infantry, has received notice to prepare for departure to the front on June 1st. Mr Webster was a reservist and was called to garrison duty in March.

Ted had a long letter published by the *Advertiser* on 6 October 1900. It follows in full.[3]

AN EASINGWOLD MAN'S LETTER FROM THE FRONT

The following letter has been received from Mr Ted Webster, son of Mr G J Webster, Jolly Farmers' Inn, Easingwold, who is a reservist in the Yorkshire Regiment, and who was called out in May last. The letter is dated Warm Baths, 27th August 1900.

Dear Parents

A few lines hoping to find you in good health as the same leaves me at present. We have done a good deal of moving about since I wrote you from Bloemfontein. We left there on the 20th of last month, and went to a place called Vet River, where we stayed 18 days, and from there to Holfontein for a night attack, which did not come off. The Boers wrecked and fired a provision train there. From there to Kronstad, but our stay there was short, and we went from there to a place called Krugersdorp, where Jameson's raid came to an end, it is about 40 miles past Johannesburg. We stayed in Johannesburg one night. It is a grand place but we had no chance to look around. There are scores of gold mines standing idle all around there. We went from Krugersdorp to a place called Bauk about 40 miles further on. We had to get out of bed in the middle of the night, we were sleeping in some miners' huts. We have had no tents since we left Bloemfontein, and things have been a bit rough. It is hot in the day and fearfully cold in the night. We have been all through the Orange Free State and we crossed the Val River on the 8th of this month. There are about 60 railway bridges between Bloemfontein and here, all of which have been blown up by the Boers. The lines have been torn up for miles in some places. We got into Pretoria on the 18th of this month. I was just going to write from there, when we got orders to pack up and go with Paget's Brigade at two in the afternoon. We have been marching every day since. We had to turn out twice in the middle of the night to go to Baden-Powell's aid. We passed through Water-Val, 6 miles north of Pretoria, where all the English prisoners were. It is a large stockade where they were confined, all fenced off with barbed wire and lit up by electric light. The engine and everything are still there. Pretoria is a fine place, but it looks deserted. We were fighting before we left Water-Val three miles. We had two killed and ten wounded. Baden-Powell's lot went on in front from there, and was attacked from some farm houses. They killed a Colonel and six of his men. We fired the houses the next day, and took about 400 head of cattle, some horses and pigs. We marched in here on the 25th. We had a bit of a fight, but they got wind of us coming in. We are the first troops that have been here. We got one shell in that made havoc among them. It killed and wounded over 40 Boers. We got a lot of cattle and arms, and waggons here besides releasing a lot of English prisoners. This is a summer resort, there is a fine hotel and 150 baths. All the water comes out of hot springs. We are having a rest for a bit. I have not seen our regiment yet. I have no ink to write with. I addressed a few envelopes at Bloemfontein. I don't think there will be any more big fights. They soon clear away now. I don't know how the Boers manage for horses, as ours are soon played out. There are any amount lying about dead. There were a lot of letters came to Pretoria for the Regiment. We opened the bags when we were there, but there was none for us. Never attempt to send me anything but letters. I saw a lot of things that had been sent to people, and the wrappings and addresses had all got torn off. I have had good health all the time I have been here. The worst of it is things are so very dear. We do not get any news of the war or anything else, and do not know where we are going to be for an hour together. I shall be pleased to have a letter from home. It seems a long time since I left. We are all as brown as berries with the sun and wind. I don't think I have anything more to tell you this time. Remember me to all our friends. Hoping to be with you soon. Love to all.

Ted.

A second letter from Webster was published a month after the above.[4]

AN INTERESTING LETTER FROM THE FRONT

The following letter has been received by Mr G J Webster the "Jolly Farmer" Inn, Easingwold, from his son who is now serving in South Africa.

Reitfontein
24th September, 1900

Dear Parents

Received your letter on the 14th. I was glad to hear you are all in good health, as the same leaves me at present. The letter has been a long time reaching here; I see it was posted on July 28th, but we are a long way up country. We came here ten days after I wrote you from Warm-bath, and have been moving around here ever since. We were in Nitral's Nek a week, the place where the Lincoln regiment was cut up not long since. We have had a few smart skirmishes since we came here; over 40 of the Munster Fusilers wounded in one day, but only two killed. There is a strong Boer commando 15 miles from here, and a lot of snipers all round. They fired at four of us coming off pickets yesterday morning. There is a Cavalry Brigade going out there now. We are out on picket every other night; we do not get much rest, but it is better than trekking every day. Bread is very scarce here, but we can have plenty of fresh mutton and beef. We captured a lot of provisions, cattle and ammunition here. Matches and soap are very hard to get. We are only eighteen miles from Pretoria. Everything is very dear there. You will have seen General Schoeman's name in the papers - a Boer General. We are staying at his farm. It has been a grand house but everything is in ruins now. He has his own private grave-yard: there is a marble monument in it that cost him £500. The house is about 400 yards from the Crocodile River. It cost him hundreds of pounds to get a cutting for the water to run into his compound. He had some splendid gardens when he was in full swing. We keep getting prisoners here every day. I expect there will be a big smash here in a few days now. All the cavalry is up here, it is about time they did something. The Boers seem to be well equipped with provisions. All the cattle and horses we take from them seem to be in better condition than ours are. There is some sorry sights among some of our cavalry horses and trek bullocks. The country is stinking with dead animals lying about in the veldt. Every place where we camp we have to bury some or else burn them. The whole place is infested with flies now the hot season has commenced. There is one blessing, there is plenty of water handy, but it has to be boiled before we can drink it. I don't know how long we are staying here; when we move I hope it will be back to Pretoria and the Cape. All the prisoners we get say they are fed up with the war. Three hundred of Botha's men refused to fight last week. Have you heard anything about any reservists being discharged from the regimental depots in England. Most of the reservists out here are married; all their talk is about their wives. They give one the "hump". I think there is no more to say this time. Remember me to all friends. Love to you all.

Ted.

At the beginning of 1901 Ted Webster had a third letter published – this time coupled with one from Tom Russell. Ted wanted to know why he got so few letters from home – a constantly reiterated question in Boer War soldiers' letters, as it always was in 1914-18.[5]

Another reservist who went to South Africa was L Cpl Metrick Till who was on a different part of the front from most of the Easingwold men. The plans for those early days of the war (after they had had to be changed) was that there would be a three-pronged British advance. Lord Methuen would (and did) advance along the western railway to Kimberley; and on the right Buller would relieve Ladysmith. Till was with the latter.[6]

In General Buller's advance to Ladysmith we notice that another local man has been wounded, - Lance Corporal Metrick Till, of the 2nd West Yorkshire Regiment. He comes of a well-known Carlton-Husthwaite family, of which place he is a native.

The editor of *Bulmers'* from 1890, records several people with the surname Till in Carlton Husthwaite. They are: Mrs Ann, grocer and farmer; George 'shoemaker and Church Warden', The Laurels; James, farmer; and James and John, farmers. Also among the residents was William Mettrick Relton of Poplar House. He was a farmer and cattle dealer.

Metrick Till fought at Spion Kop where he was severely wounded.[7] He 'received a gunshot wound in the head ... from the effects of which he died at Mooi River Hospital ... a youthful victim of the war at the early age of 23.'

Another Easingwold soldier – another reservist – was, like Till, involved in the fighting in the Ladysmith area. R.E. Smith summarised his career in the first months of the war. He ended on a splendid patriotic note.[8]

In consequence of the "entanglement" of Ladysmith with 1st Royal Rifles have been shut up for some weeks, and the reservists of that regiment found they were unable to get through, and have had to take part in Buller's advance for its relief. One of the reserves call out was Sidney Ellis, son of Mrs Richard Ellis, Mount Pleasant, Crayke. The last letter received from him was sent from Chieveley about a month ago, and though the forces were fighting a very uphill battle, they were not in the least disheartened, but appeared always ready to have another dig at the enemy and confident of ultimate success.

Since then the tide of war has turned in our favour, and we are confident that the men who fought their way to Ladysmith, and manoeuvred with French, and the Yeomanry and Volunteers we sent out, will do whatever mortal man can do, and it is pleasant to think that Easingwold is represented amongst them.

Sidney Ellis did not feature much in the Easingwold news. He got a little note when the *Advertiser* mentioned that he had sent his box of the Queen's chocolate to his mother, and nothing more.[9] This was a gift sent to the soldiers, to become in this case, no doubt, a valuable memento of the war. It was also reported that Mrs Rogers of the Market Place, Easingwold had received a similar item from her son 'who is serving under General Buller.'[10] There has been no soldier called Rogers discovered in the work for these notes, incidentally, but there are many possible explanations for this.

At the beginning of 1902 the death of another Easingwold soldier was announced. The report mentions a brother about whom no other information has been found.[11]

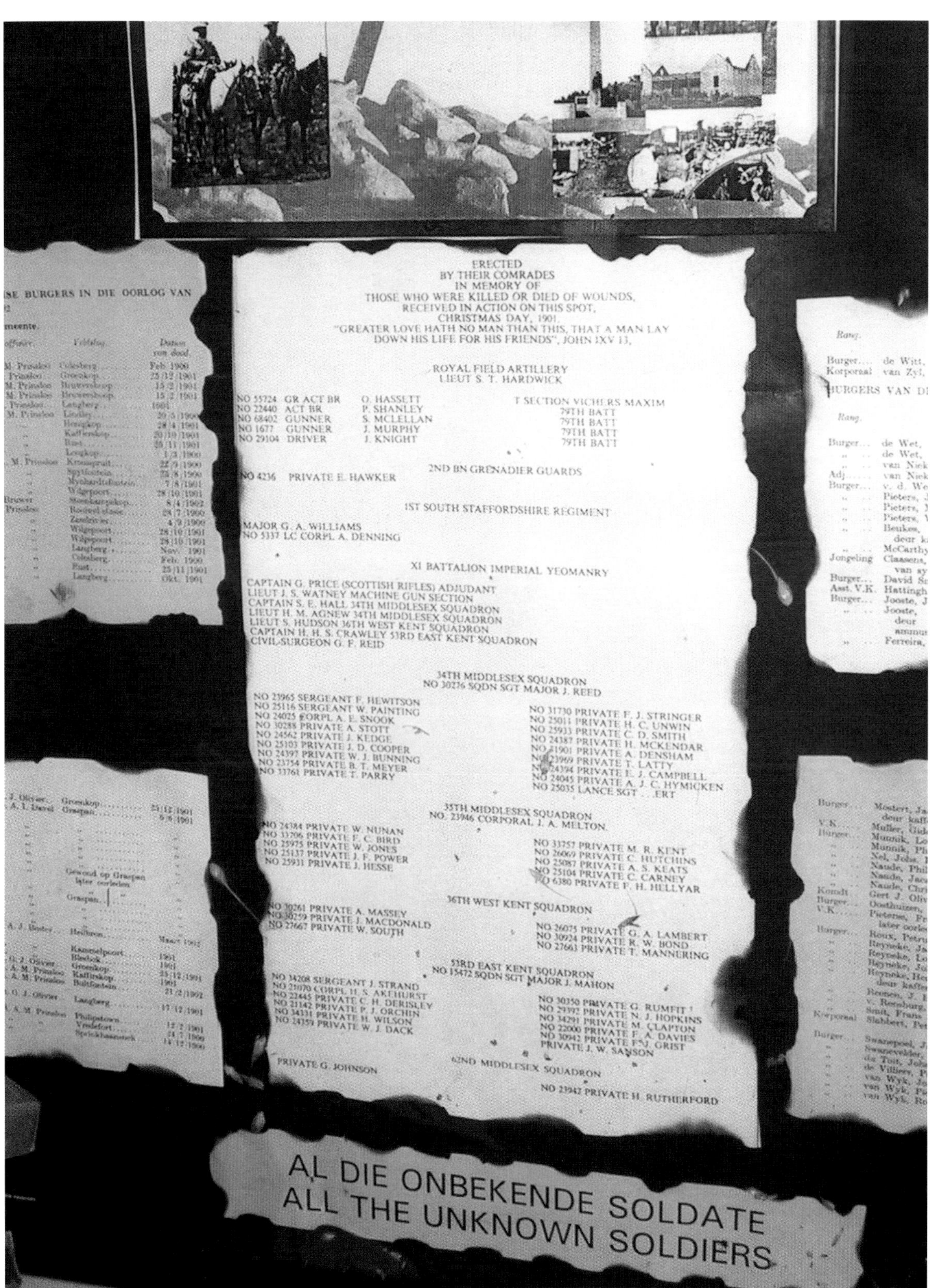

Memorial to British casualties at Groenkop 25-12-01
in Information Centre at Kestel

From summit of Groenkop, showing direction from which De Wet attacked.
The Boers called the Battle 'Tweefontein' after the nearby farm, the British named it 'Groenkop' after the hill. Alphonso Stott was killed near the summit.

DEATH OF AN ALNE PRIVATE

> Among the list of killed at Tweefontein is Private Alphonso Stott, aged 19 years (34th Company Imperial Yeomanry), the youngest son of Mr. John Stott, Station Hotel, Alne near Easingwold, County Court Bailiff. Another son, Henry, is in the same Company, and much anxiety is felt about him. Great sympathy is felt for Mr. and Mrs. Stott and family in their sad bereavement.

ALNE

> A Memorial Service in memory of the late Private Alphonso Stott, son of Mr. and Mrs. Stott, Station Hotel, Alne, who was killed in action on Christmas morning in the conflict with De Wet, will be held in the Alne Parish Church on Sunday morning next, at half-past ten.

There was no report of Alphonso Stott's memorial service, but there is a letter from a soldier who was in the Christmas Day fighting in which he was shot.[12] It was published in the *Advertiser.*

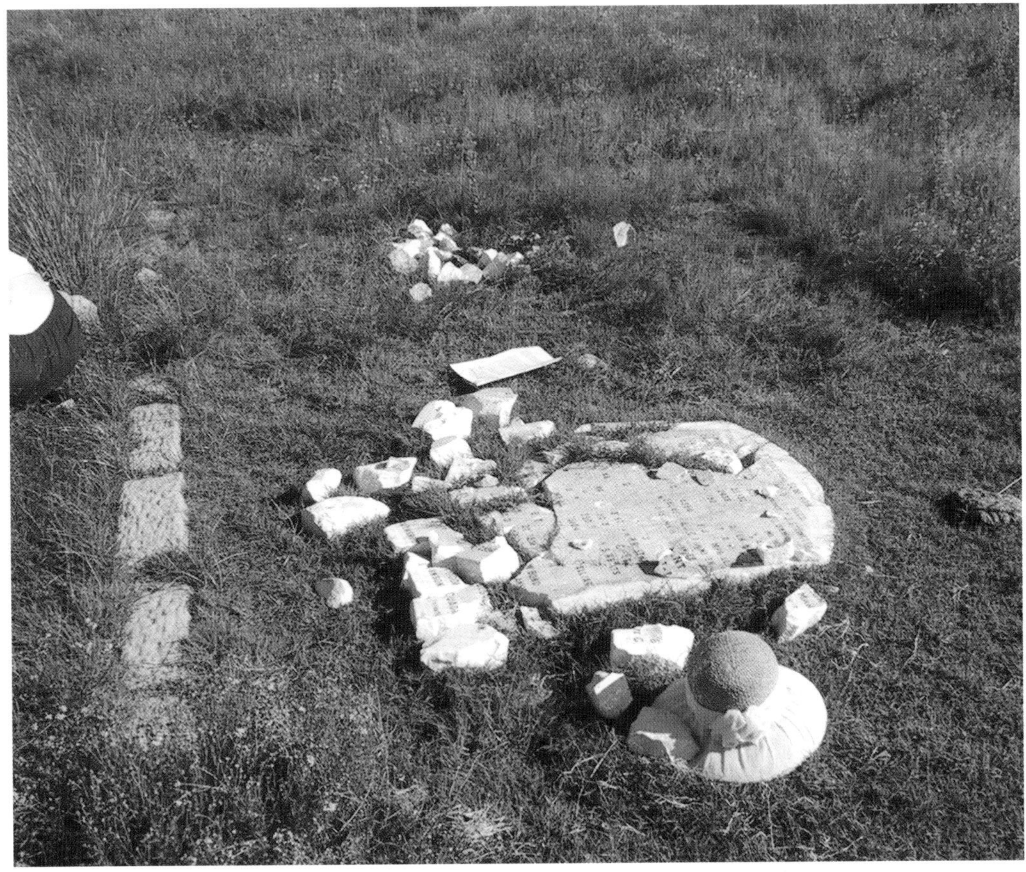

The vandalised memorial tablets on Groenkop (Green Hill) containing Alphonso Stott's name.

A SOLDIER'S CHRISTMAS AT TWEEFONTEIN

> Writing from Tweefontein on December 26th, a Leeds man, Private Clark of the 2nd East Yorkshire Regiment, describes his Christmas Day:-
>
> "We were surprised," he writes "on Christmas morning, and a good number of us put out of mess. We buried 52 non-commissioned officers and men, six officers and 15 natives. We expected all handing in our checks, every minute, though we should have made a good stand first. The Boers came from what is called the Lion's Den, and it is a proper den too. It has been another sad mistake on the part of the Yeomanry not having outposts enough out.

Early on in these notes the name of the belligerent Eccles Foster appeared. Eccles, like several more, had a brother also serving at the front. He was an early casualty.[13]

WOUNDED AT BELMONT

> In the "Cape Argus" of January 3rd, now to hand, we find the photo of Gunner Albert Foster, of H.M.S. "Monarch", who, while operating in the Naval Brigade at Belmont, had the misfortune to be wounded severely in the left leg and arm. Gunner Foster is a native of Easingwold.

Clearly Albert Foster's injuries were not as serious as they first appeared and in May 1900 the *Advertiser* said he had recovered. In an introductory paragraph to his account of Easingwold's Mafeking celebrations R.E. Smith did not say he was again at the front, but that he had recovered.[14] He spoke of 'Gunner Foster … wounded in two places at Belmont, and now returned to duty'.

Gunner Foster made only a brief appearance on the pages of the *Easingwold*. Cpl Littlewood made but one brief entry into the pages of the R.E. Smith journal with a letter he sent home. There was no address for him and only the briefest note about his unit. However, his letter showed how isolated the men often were and another indication of the long marches they had to undertake.[15]

Over 30 men served in the Boer War who came from what has liberally been described as the Easingwold area. The last soldier's letter to be quoted, from one of them is J.G. Lawn from Northallerton. He was a married man, a volunteer, and his short service was almost up, though he did not know when he would return.

A NORTHALLERTON HERO

A letter received from Corporal J G Lawn, of the Yorkshire Volunteer Service Corps. has proved very welcome to his friends and well-wishers in Northallerton and district. It was rumoured that Corporal Lawn had been missing for close upon two months, and colour was lent to this statement by letters which were received from other Northallerton Volunteers at the front. But the letter which Corporal Lawn wrote home to his wife, dated Christmas Day, explains how he has been absent from his company on special service. Sergeant Lawn - for he was promoted to the rank of sergeant on the 10th of December last - gives a graphic description of a battle where a small party of English soldiers held some 500 Boers at bay. They were summoned to surrender under a flag of truce, and were given twenty minutes in which to make up their minds. But the officer in charge sent an answer that he certainly could not give in, and they gallantly held their position until they were reinforced. Sergeant Lawn does not know when he is likely to return home. It is to be hoped that he, along with seven other Northallerton men, will be able to share the enthusiastic welcome which the Reception Committee formed at a meeting held a week or two ago.

NOTES

1. D.A. Carr to A.J. Peacock. Undated.
2. *Advertiser* 26 May 1900
3. *Ibid* 6 October 1900
4. *Ibid* 10 November 1900
5. *Ibid* 26 January 1901
6. *Ibid* 10 March 1900
7. *Ibid* 26 May 1900
8. *Ibid* 10 March 1900
9. *Ibid* 14 April 1900
10. *Ibid*
11. *Ibid* 1 February 1902
12. *Ibid* 10 February 1900
13. *Ibid* 26 May 1900
14. *Ibid* 21 July 1900
15. *Ibid* 19 January 1901

Charging the heights under Lord Roberts.

Chapter 26

HUBERT BAINES

The last Easingwold Boer War soldier to be noted in these pages was in the war, but did not go to the front from the town. Information about him is difficult to come by, and what follows is based on family stories about him and notes from David Smith, the publisher of this work.

Hubert Baines was born at Metheringham in 1875 and apprenticed as a draper and grocer. In 1894 he completed his apprenticeship then went to South Africa where he lived and worked in Cape Town. He was there when the war started and 'became a Sgt in the Medical Corps'. What Hubert joined is not clear, but it was probably a South African unit and he must have enlisted very early on in the war. Serving in Lord Methuen's command, he 'was taken prisoner by Gen C.R. de Wet'. Where this happened is not recorded in the family's story, Then, 'after a few weeks [he] with other prisoners were turned loose ... *without their boots* and' began a painful march towards the British lines.[1] They reached safety eventually, but Hubert was 'in a very bad state'. He was hospitalised then 'sent back to England to recover'.

Hubert Baines may or may not have gone first to Lincolnshire, but sometime in 1901 he made his way to Easingwold to work for George Haynes, at the Trevelyan Temperance Hotel in Long Street. He married Mr Haynes' daughter and eventually took over the Trevelyan himself. By then he had branched out into business on his own and there is a splendid photograph of him in 1905, standing outside business premises of the Trevelyan Hotel complex. Was he a draper? He was not. The shop's signs announce that he was a 'CONFECTIONER' and 'GROCER'. Two large windows are inscribed GEORGE HAYNES' and 'REFRESHMENTS' and nearby there is a splendidly turned out delivery boy with a bike and a trailer – the latter in all probability made by Mark Reynard. A file copy of this photograph says 'The boy in pic is probably Frank Weighell.'

Hubert Baines became an enthusiastic member of the Easingwold Volunteers, and, like so many in the town, was an active Methodist. He could not have been resident in the town very long before he appeared as guest speaker at a flourishing organisation which has been referred to in these pages before. At the end of January 1902 he told members of the Wesleyan Institute about the experiences he had marching in the Boer War. It is a shame that all that was recorded was the following.[2]

> WESLEYAN INSTITUTE. - At the weekly meeting of the above, on Friday evening last, a very interesting paper was given by Mr. Baines on his experiences in South Africa, where he served for some time in Lord Methuen's force. There was a large attendance.

NOTES

1. My italics
2. *Advertiser* 1 February 1902

Above:
Opening of VTC Rifle Range, Windmill Field, Crayke Road, Easingwold, September 22, 1900s. Easingwold Volunteers on Parade. Hubert Baines 2nd from left.

Right:
Hubert Baines 1902 after returning from South Africa.

GRANDAD BAINES.

Hubert Baines in Service Uniform, 1914

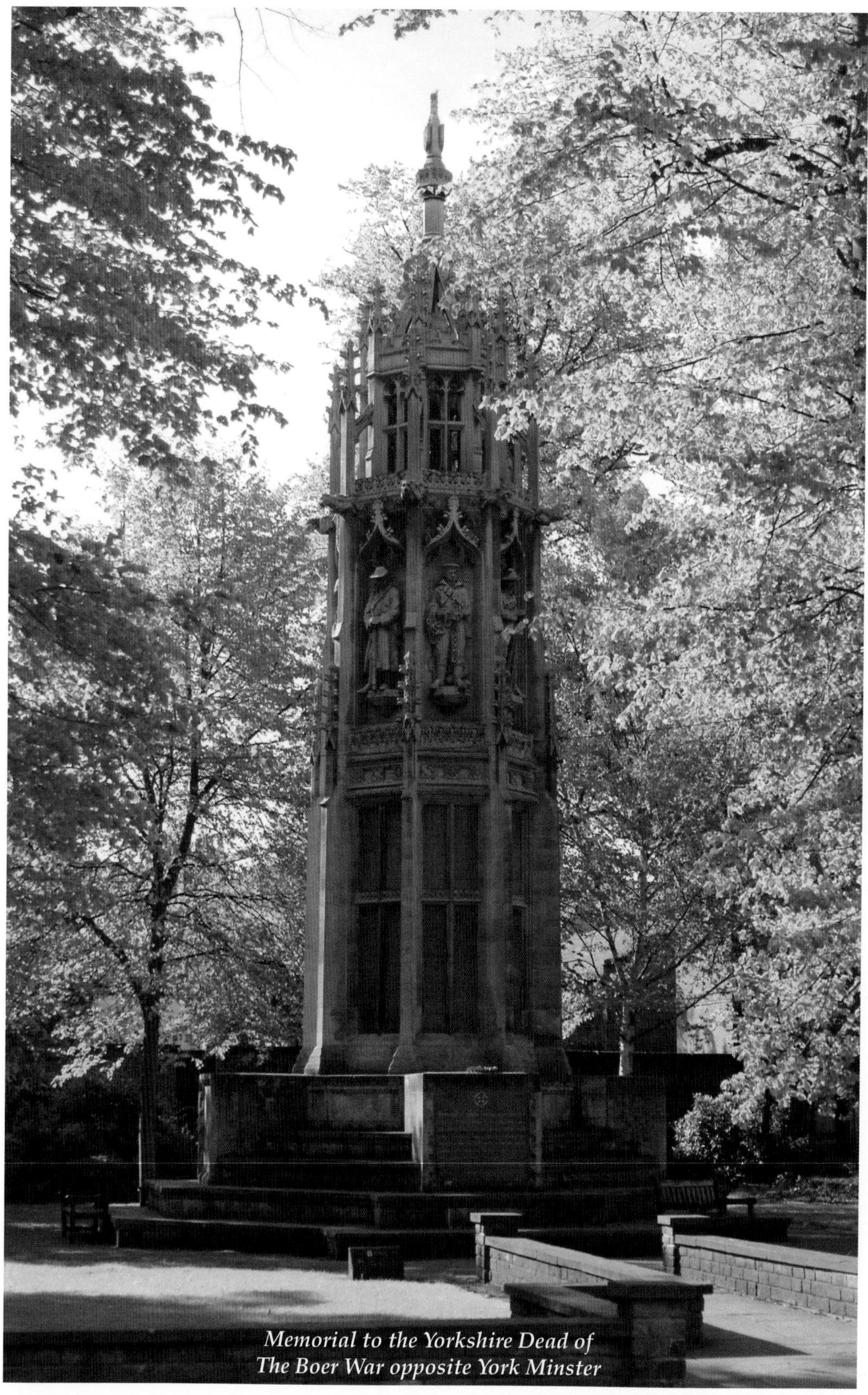

Memorial to the Yorkshire Dead of The Boer War opposite York Minster

Chapter 27

Until the Bitter End

Great Britain Triumphant?

Paul M. Chapman

In October 1900 Smith, Elder & Co. published Arthur Conan Doyle's *The Great Boer War*, a military history of that conflict's regular phase which was, at the time of publication, giving way to a guerrilla war. Doyle, even then best known as the creator of Sherlock Holmes, had spent a number of months near the seat of battle serving as a doctor and therefore, unlike many other commentators, could discuss this most controversial of wars from firsthand experience.

Believing his practical contribution to be over by June 1900, following Lord Roberts' capture of Pretoria, Doyle sailed for home to begin his work as an advocate and apologist for the war and Britain's conduct therein, which would include not only *The Great Boer War*, but also contributions to the press and a 'pamphlet' of some 60,000 words entitled *The War in South Africa: its Cause and Conduct*, all of which would play a part in his being awarded a knighthood in 1902.

However, although he was a skilled propagandist and could be very shrewd and perspicacious in his observations Doyle was not clearsighted enough in 1900 to fully understand the continuing Boer will to resist even after the fall of Bloemfontein, Johannesburg and Pretoria:

> 'Small bands had slipped away to the north and the south, but they were insignificant in numbers and depressed in spirit. The hunting of them down becomes a matter for the mounted policeman rather than part of an organised campaign ... There is still to be told the story of the suppression of the scattered bands of Boer warriors, of the fate of De Wet, of the clearing of the north-eastern part of the Orange River Colony, and of the final suppression of a form of warfare which was approaching every week more closely to brigandage and murder.'

Christiaan De Wet was not the only outstanding problem facing the British Army (and it would be them, rather than Doyle's optimistically mooted mounted policemen, who would bear the brunt of defeating the remaining Boers, who were not in fact 'insignificant in numbers and depressed in spirit'). There remained in the field a number of talented commanders and figureheads, including Marthinus Steyn, Louis Botha, Jacobus De la Rey and Jan Smuts. These men and their followers simply refused to accept British Annexation of the Boer Republics, whose governments - and therefore armies - no longer retained any degree of legitimacy in British eyes, and transformed the nature of the war into one of irregular guerrilla operations, many of which were concentrated in the British-controlled Cape Colony whose considerable Afrikaner population the Boer commandos still hoped to turn against their colonial masters.

Despite this ongoing situation Lord Roberts, who had overseen the most successful phase of the regular war, returned to Britain in January 1901 to take up the post of commander-

LORD KITCHENER.

in-chief, in which he succeeded his great rival Lord Wolseley. In South Africa Roberts was replaced by his chief of staff, Lord Kitchener, a man of a very different stamp, and one in many ways well-suited to conduct the next phase of the war.

Most of Kitchener's service had been in the middle east and he had achieved prominence during his two year campaign against the Mahdists in the Sudan in which a combination of meticulous planning and preparation and sheer ruthlessness had culminated in their total defeat at the decisive Battle of Omdurman in 1898. Although in private Kitchener could be subject to bouts of emotionalism, and even sentimentality, his public and professional face was that of an efficient iron-willed character who inspired fear and respect rather than love, as the Boers were to discover.

However, before Kitchener could fully implement the policies which would make him a figure of hate amongst many Afrikaners, even to this day, there came a brief moment when peace might have been achieved. On 28th February 1901 Kitchener met Louis Botha at Middelburg in order to discuss possible peace terms. A mutual respect existed between the two men and they genuinely felt that they could do business. But the stubborn attitude of certain individuals; Sir Alfred Milner for the British and Steyn and De Wet for the Boers, and specific vexed issues, notably those of Boer independence - to exist as British dependents was unacceptable - and the harsh treatment of Cape Colony Afrikaners who had supported their northern bretheren, proved too divisive and the talks foundered amidst intransigence.

Following the failure of the Middelburg negotiations Kitchener, recognising that this was a war unlikely to be won by any one great knockout battle, began to unveil the strategies which he believed would decisively defeat the Boers. The first was to continue the policy of farm burning which had reluctantly been launched by Lord Roberts. The ostensible aim of this course of action, which entailed not only the destruction of farm buildings and homesteads but also crops and livestock, was to cut off the source of supplies to the roving Boer commandos, whilst also sapping their morale. Roberts was human, and realistic, enough to recognise that wholesale farm burning would ultimately prove counter-productive, and merely serve to strengthen hatred and anti-British resolve. The Boer could stomach the loss of his urban centres, but his farm was something sacred and inviolate. The more ruthless Kitchener, however, increased the level of destruction (around 30,000 farms were torched) believing that the purely military value of these operations outweighed the resultant outrage.

With farm burning came the problem of dispossessed inhabitants, mainly women and children, wandering the veldt or being forced to join the commandos. The British solution was to round up these refugees and place them in specifically designated concentration camps. The idea was first seriously forwarded in a memorandum from Kitchener in December 1900, but became official policy in April 1901 following the failure of the Middelburg talks. As Kitchener wrote to Botha on 16th April:

'As I informed your honour at Middelburg, Owing to the irregular manner in which you have conducted and continue to conduct hostilities, by forcing unwilling and peaceful inhabitants to join your Commandos, a proceeding totally unauthorized by the recognized customs of war, I have no other course open to me, and am forced to take the very unpleasant and repugnant steps of bringing in the women and children.'

The reasoning behind the establishment of these camps was essentially sound. It was for their inhabitants' own well-being and safety, but the reality proved otherwise. Frequently the camps were not particularly well-planned and managed and their organisers often unthinkingly mixed mutually antipathetic groups, because by this point in the war Boer society was dividing between those known as the 'bitter-enders' (bittereinders), who refused to countenance capitulation to the British, and the 'hands-uppers' (hensoppers), who saw continuing the struggle as little more than a futile gesture. This latter group were often burnt out of their farms by the commandos, hence their need for shelter and protection, something that the British, more through oversight than spite, did not always provide.

Of course, with some fifty camps in operation conditions varied considerably between each. But, as is usually the case, it was the poor examples; those which were badly managed, poorly sited or particularly insanitary which attracted the most unwelcome attention. And that attention could be well-deserved. It has been estimated that up to 20,000, including a disproportionate number of children, may have died in the camps, most of which fatalities were due to insanitary conditions and poor personal hygiene. Matters improved considerably when Emily Hobhouse, one of those energetic British women on a mission with which the Victorian era abounded, arrived in South Africa after having been stirred into action by all she had heard of the horror of the camps. Although her presence and influence were undoubtedly positive in her own sphere Kitchener found her to be an irritating distraction, eventually referring to her as 'that bloody woman'. He was not really interested in the fate of the camp inmates; that was somebody else's concern. He had a war to win.

Faced with the problem of a highly mobile enemy fighting on familiar and open ground Kitchener fully understood that the formal doctrines of nineteenth century warfare were singularly inapposite. He needed to rewrite the rules. The result was the adoption of what became known as the blockhouse system, which originated with the necessity to defend the railway network, which was a natural target for Boer saboteurs. What began with a relatively modest number of stone blockhouses was eventually augmented to become a major system of some 8,000 cylindrical blockhouses, principally constructed of corrugated iron, each of which was connected by telegraph and barbed wire (of which there was around 4,000 miles in all). Not only did this provide some degree of protection to the vulnerable rail lines, but also went some way towards taming the wild veldt and the actions of the Boer commandos thereon.

The blockhouse system, which was somewhat unfairly referred to as the blockhead system by an understandably ungracious De Wet, certainly had its drawbacks. It tied a large number of troops to garrison duty and for those involved this life could easily become stultifying and monotonous, leading to a self-defeating laxity. There were some attempts to free British troops from this irksome duty by employing native guards, but their higher level of indiscipline and inattention made this a poor solution. The military historian and tactical thinker General J.F.C. Fuller, then a subaltern, recalled one incident in which startled native garrisons simply blazed away at one another.

In addition to protecting the railways the blockhouses also came to act as a wall against which to push the enemy following the newly adopted tactic of the columnar drive. Just as the formalised tactics of European warfare proved ill-suited to the South African guerrilla war, so the standard military formations proved unwieldy and impractical. Thus battalions, brigades and divisions were replaced by columns, which typically comprised mounted infantry and cavalry with mobile artillery support, and could number from 200 to 1,500 men, although the usual total was around 600. These columns would usually fan out across the veldt on large drives whose primary purpose was to flush out, engage and incapacitate enemy commandos, although farm burning could also form part of their remit.

The earliest drives were often haphazard and ineffective affairs, which led to the development of the more structured and co-ordinated 'new model' drives which began in February 1902 with a drive which utilised 9,000 men across a 54-mile front. Although initial results were less than could have been hoped for Kitchener continued the 'new model' programme for the remainder of the war. If nothing else it demonstrated the reality of British military might and Kitchener's determination to prevail.

Not all columns, however, were used in drives. A number existed as more mobile search and destroy formations. The most successful and celebrated of these was that commanded by Lieutenant Colonel George Elliot Benson, a hard-riding unit of 1,400 men whose effectiveness owed much to the intelligence gathering of Aubrey Woolls-Sampson, who ran a highly efficient network of native agents. Such was Benson's success that Louis Botha set himself the task of destroying his column which was finally accomplished at Bakenlaagte on 30th October 1901, following a savage battle in which Benson was killed.

Kitchener took the news very badly, but an even greater humiliation occurred in March 1902 when a column led by Lord Methuen, one of the most senior British officers in South Africa, and who had been involved (not entirely successfully) in the war since its earliest stages, was defeated at Tweebosch by the troops of Jacobus De la Rey. Methuen himself was wounded and captured, together with around 600 of his command. De la Rey, in a chivalric gesture which was not entirely popular with his men, released his noble captive for hospital treatment. With Methuen went a personal letter of consolation for his wife written by De la Rey.

Kitchener was prostrated by this defeat so late in the war. But it was really a last gasp. Circumstances were against the remaining commandos. The drive system, as refined by Kitchener's chief of staff, Ian Hamilton, was beginning to show results. The concentration camp policy had been reversed, so that the effectiveness of Boer units in the field was once more hampered by the presence of non-combatants. Worse still, there was restlessness amongst the natives, a situation tacitly supported by the British (at least in the short term; Kitchener had no real wish to disturb what he termed 'the just predominance of the white race'), although even they would have had certain reservations about a Zulu attack on a Boer unit at Holkrantz on 6th May 1902.

Most disturbing to the bitter-enders, however, was the growing tide of Afrikaner war-weariness. Numbers of men were now even supporting British forces in their operations against the commandos, and their leaders were not to be ignored. Prominent amongst them were Christiaan De Wet's brother Piet and A.P. Cronje, both former Boer generals. Unless the leaders in the field showed a willingness to negotiate it was evident that in a post-war South Africa the hands-uppers could well become the upper-handers.

Accordingly, in April 1902 British and Boer representatives met for preliminary talks in Pretoria. The following month the proceedings, now transferred to Vereeniging and become more formal, resumed and continued to exhibit some of the intransigence which had characterised the Middelburg negotiations in February 1901. This time, however, there was a recognition that there must be an agreement. In the closing hour of 31st May it came when the Boer delegates signed peace terms in Melrose House, Pretoria. The war which had cost around 21,000 British and Colonial and 24,000 Boer lives (up to 20,000 of those in concentration camps) was finally over.

There was little triumphalism and no unconditional surrender. The terms of the treaty demanded that all Boer combatants were to surrender themselves and their arms. None would be imprisoned or have their property confiscated, nor would they be punished for legitimate acts of war. The Dutch language would be permitted in schools and courts of law, whilst military government would be replaced by civil authority at the earliest opportunity. Former rebels who took the oath of allegiance would be repatriated, and those from the Cape would be disenfranchised rather than imprisoned. No property would be taxed to pay for the war and the British government would pay £3 million to compensate for war damage. A decision on the rights of native Africans was, ominously, postponed.

Of course these terms did not receive universal approval, but the peace held. In 1906, when the Liberals were returned to power in Britain, the former Boer Republics were granted the status of self-governing colonies. Four years later the four South African colonies gained full independence within the British Empire as the Union of South Africa, whose first Prime Minister was Louis Botha. The new country would remain staunchly loyal to Britain throughout both World Wars. At least for the first half of the twentieth century Lord Kitchener's optimistic words spoken in 1902 rang true; 'We are good friends now.'

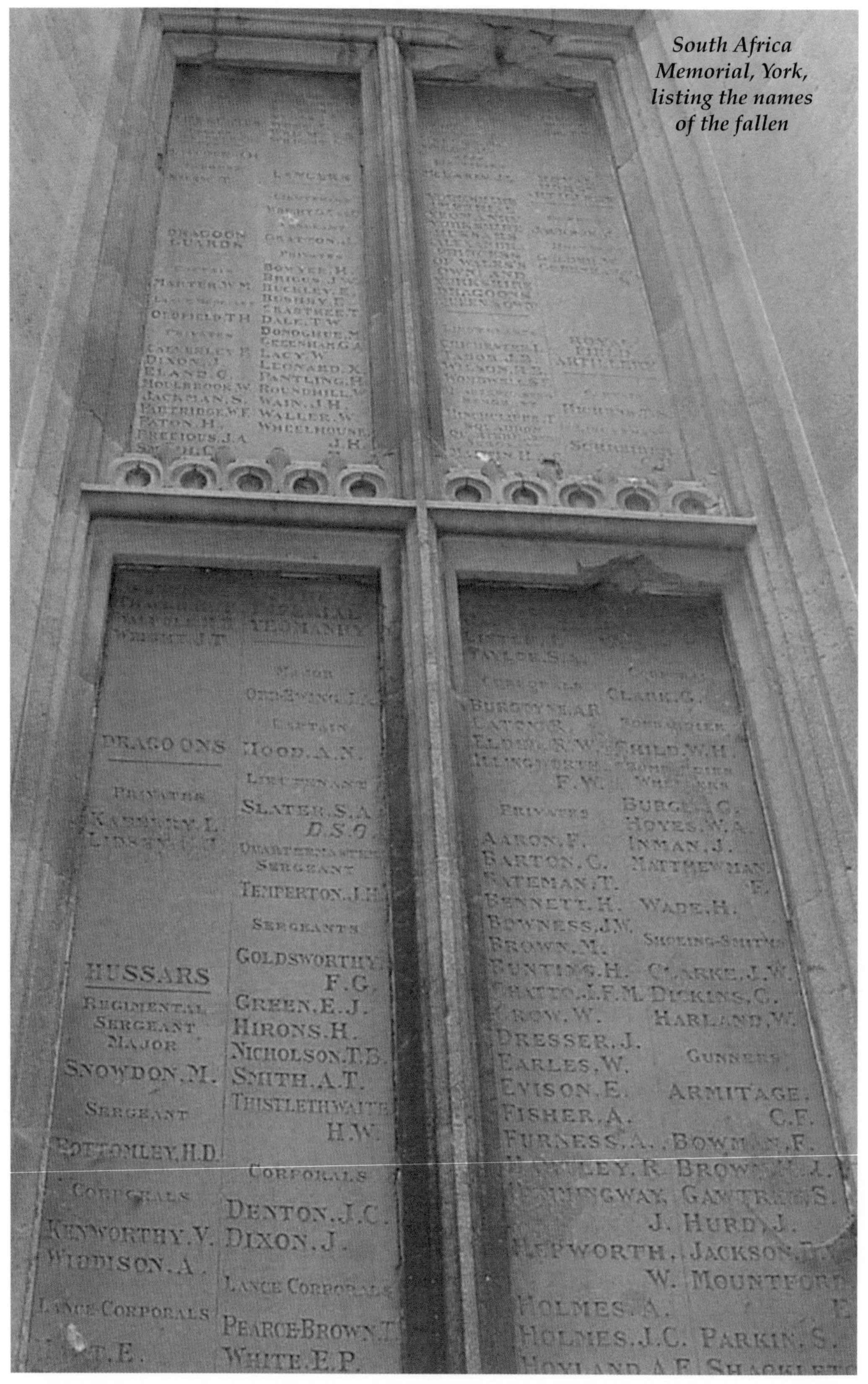

South Africa Memorial, York, listing the names of the fallen

Biographies

DR ALF PEACOCK

Alf Peacock, or to give him his full title, Dr Alfred James Peacock of Holgate Road, York died in January 2004. Perhaps not too well known in the Easingwold area, his legacy for us was to write a History of Easingwold and District at the end of the nineteenth and beginning of the 20th century, and as an add on, the story of the men and women from around the area who served in South Africa in the Boer War. At the time of his death, aged 74 he had also been writing a book on the contribution of Easingwold and District in World War 1 and the large number of men who served. It is hoped to recruit another historian to complete his endeavour.

Born at Histon in Cambridgeshire, Alf trained as an electrician before being awarded a scholarship to Ruskin College, Oxford in his early twenties. He also studied at Southampton and the London School of Economics. From 1960 he was warden of the York Educational Settlement until its closure in 1987. Living next door to his work and only 250 yards from his favourite pub 'The Fox' in Holgate Road, he spent his retirement years researching and writing numerous works, notably a study of the life of the 'notorious' George Hudson the Railway King. Passionately interested in WW1 he was for many years the Chairman of the York Branch of the Western Front Association and editor of the occasional magazine 'Gun Fire'.

Despite a busy professional life he was also an experienced magistrate and chairman of the Licensing Bench, in contrast a lifelong jazz enthusiast who often entertained jazz musicians at his home when they played in York. At his funeral, the music was by Bob Crosby and his Bobcats.

Alf will be long remembered both as a warm personality and man of letters.

DAVID CRANE

Born in Easingwold in 1939. David was educated at the C. of E. Primary before progressing to the old Grammar School and the present Easingwold School. After three years at Loughborough where he specialised in Physical Education and English his teaching career had taken him via Harrogate Grammar School, De La Salle College, Salford, to Richmond where he taught from 1972 to 1999.

A keen sportsman and former English Schools AAA silver medalist and English Universities Athlete, David, in his youth played both football and cricket for the Easingwold clubs. Since moving to Richmond he played for Richmondshire CC where he is now President.

His retirement is never dull and any spare time is taken up delving into history or cycling in the Dales.

CHARLES WHITING

Born in York in 1926, Charles Whiting maintains he has always been embroiled in war even before he was born. His great uncle Mick was wounded at Spion Kop in 1900 in the Boer War; his grandfather Charles Kerrigan after whom he was named was killed in France in 1915 when he was with the West Yorkshire Regiment; his father fought with the Irish Hussars on the North West Frontier and Iraq in the early 1920s and he himself volunteered for the British Army in 1943 at the tender age of 16 and fought with the 52nd Reconnaissance Regiment in Holland and Germany.

Since then he has led a more tranquil life. After studying at the Universities of Leeds, London, Kiel and Cologne he became a university teacher at the Universities of Bradford, Maryland (USA) and Trier (Germany); a journalist with *The Times, Playboy* etc. and finally a full time writer since 1973.

Under his own name and the noms de plume of Leo Kessler, Duncan Harding and John Kerrigan, he has published some 300 books and has been translated into most European languages. He was awarded the Sir George Dowty prize for Literature (Cheltenham Festival). He is a member of the British Society of Authors and the US Guild of American Writers. His two most recent books are *Yorkshire Fights Back* (GH Smith) and *Target Eisenhower: Political/Military Assassination in World War II* (Spellmount).

PAUL M. CHAPMAN

Paul M. Chapman, who studied History at Lancaster University, is the author of 'Birth of a Legend', a monograph tracing Whitby's connection to Bram Stoker and the Dracula phenomenon.

He has also edited 'The Ritual', a study journal devoted to Sherlock Holmes and Sir Arthur Conan Doyle, and written on Holmes, Doyle, crime fiction and criminal history for various publications.

He is chief proof reader for G. H. Smith & Son, printers.

BOER WAR PHOTOS

Billy Holmes from York was what was called 'an Empire Frontiersman', a veteran of the fighting in Britain's 19th century empire, in particular in South Africa against the Boers.

A small man with what was called then a 'tea-strainer moustache', he wore on festive occasions, brown riding boots complete with spurs, breeches, a blue tunic with metal epaulettes, all topped with a hat of the kind worn by Canadian 'Mounties'. When he walked he jingled.

Somehow Billy Holmes knew my great-uncle, also from York, who had been wounded with the King's Own Scottish Borderers at the Battle of Spion Kop (1900) and it is perhaps for that reason that these photos taken by Billy during and after the Boer War came into the possession of my family. By the looks of them they seem to depict life in the fortified villages which the British erected to keep out the Boers during their guerrilla warfare campaign and deprive them of supplies.

They are unique not because they were taken by an ordinary soldier, Billy Holmes, but they show an aspect of the Boer War campaign which has not really been recorded; ordinary 'squaddies' fraternising with the locals, black and white.

Charles Whiting

Acknowledgements

Dr. A. J. Peacock for his consuming passion for the history of all men and women of the Boer War period and his dedication in producing such a volume of work.

To David Crane for editing A. J. Peacock's original text.

To Charles Whiting for the use of the Billy Holmes photos and writing the descriptions of the main Boer War battles.

Paul Chapman, for the final chapter and proof reading.

Roland Richardson for photos and information on his uncle Frank Rhodes.

Mrs Carr, Wigginton, for photos and memorabilia on John Thomas Ward.

Sir George Wombwell for photos and much assistance on Stephen Wombwell.

Dora Bowman for photos and memorabilia on her father Mark Knowlson Brown.

Alma Nelson (née Dale) for photos of her uncle Walter Dale.

Tony Bolton for the George Hargreaves medals.

Kevin J Asplin, archive of the Imperial Yeomanry in the Boer War for The Relief of Middlepost by Thomas Cook.

Vryburg Town Council, South Africa

David Buckle for layout and his patience and all at G. H. Smith & Son for their professional efforts in producing this work.

YORKSHIRE FIGHTS BACK

Charles Whiting's latest book, *Yorkshire Fights Back*, is a thrilling, heart-warming account of Yorkshire folk in World War II. It tells the story of those dark days when Yorkshire was threatened by enemy invasion up the Humber or by enemy para drops on the Vale of York.

Whether male or female, old or young, soldier or civilian, the 'Tykes' fought back, at the front, abroad or at home. Many died. Six decades ago they gave us the freedom their grandchildren enjoy today.
They must never be forgotten.
Yorkshire Fights Back is a book which should be treasured in every honest 'Tykes' home as long as there is a Yorkshire.

To order Yorkshire Fights Back,
G H Smith and Son, The Advertiser Office, Market Place,
Easingwold, York YO61 3AB Telephone 01347 821329
email info@ghsmith.com www.ghsmith.com

Also available from all good bookshops ISBN 0 904775 63 1

OUT NOW